MONTREAL'S SQUARE MILE

The Making and Transformation of a Colonial Metropole

Montreal's Square Mile

The Making and Transformation of a Colonial Metropole

Edited by Dimitry Anastakis,
Elizabeth Kirkland, and Don Nerbas

UNIVERSITY OF TORONTO PRESS
Toronto Buffalo London

Toronto Buffalo London
utorontopress.com
Printed in the USA

ISBN 978-1-4875-0805-0 (cloth) ISBN 978-1-4875-3746-3 (EPUB)
ISBN 978-1-4875-2569-9 (paper) ISBN 978-1-4875-3745-6 (PDF)

Library and Archives Canada Cataloguing in Publication

Title: Montreal's Square Mile : the making and transformation of a colonial metropole / edited by Dimitry Anastakis, Elizabeth Kirkland, and Don Nerbas.
Other titles: Square Mile : the making and transformation of a colonial metropole
Names: Anastakis, Dimitry, 1970– editor. | Kirkland, Elizabeth, 1978– editor. | Nerbas, Don, 1980– editor.
Description: Includes bibliographical references and index.
Identifiers: Canadiana (print) 20230446892 | Canadiana (ebook) 20230446922 | ISBN 9781487525699 (paper) | ISBN 9781487508050 (cloth) | ISBN 9781487537463 (EPUB) | ISBN 9781487537456 (PDF)
Subjects: LCSH: Golden Square Mile (Montréal, Québec) – History. | LCSH: Neighborhoods – Québec (Province) – Montréal – History. | LCSH: Montréal (Québec) – History.
Classification: LCC FC2947.52 .M66 2024 | DDC 971.4/28—dc23

Cover design: EmDash
Cover image: Wm. Notman & Son. *Garden Party at Mr. Meighen's Residence, Montreal, QC, 1908*. 1908/07/31 VIEW-8764. McCord Stewart Museum.

We wish to acknowledge the land on which the University of Toronto Press operates. This land is the traditional territory of the Wendat, the Anishnaabeg, the Haudenosaunee, the Métis, and the Mississaugas of the Credit First Nation.

This book has been published with the help of a grant from the Federation for the Humanities and Social Sciences, through the Awards to Scholarly Publications Program, using funds provided by the Social Sciences and Humanities Research Council of Canada.

University of Toronto Press acknowledges the financial support of the Government of Canada, the Canada Council for the Arts, and the Ontario Arts Council, an agency of the Government of Ontario, for its publishing activities.

Canada Council for the Arts Conseil des Arts du Canada

ONTARIO ARTS COUNCIL
CONSEIL DES ARTS DE L'ONTARIO
an Ontario government agency
un organisme du gouvernement de l'Ontario

Funded by the Government of Canada Financé par le gouvernement du Canada Canada

Contents

Acknowledgments ix

INTRODUCTION 3
DIMITRY ANASTAKIS, ELIZABETH KIRKLAND, AND DON NERBAS

PART ONE: **FRAMEWORKS AND PERSPECTIVES**

The Square Mile: A Singular Topography 19
ALL OPENING VIGNETTES WRITTEN BY JULIA GERSOVITZ

1 The High Ground: Mansions, Mythology, and the Mountain 21
RODERICK MACLEOD

First Development: From Apple Orchards to Building Lots 53

2 Property and Power: Connecting the Dots 55
SHERRY OLSON

PART TWO: **CONSTRUCTING BUSINESS NETWORKS AND INSTITUTIONS**

Widening Influences 77

3 "Others of more enterprise": Thomas Morland and the Formation of Montreal Rolling Mills, 1858–1868 81
JEAN-PHILIP MATHIEU

McGill University 109

4 "Dear Richard ... send us a few buffalo tongues": Donald Smith's Fur Trade Contacts and Personal Credit Networks 111

MAX HAMON

PART THREE: **FAMILY, GENDER, AND PROPERTY**

Row and Terrace Housing 145

5 Marriage, Property, and the Law in a Square Mile Family: The Case of Annie Stevenson Anderson vs. David Morrice, 1884–1885 147

PETER GOSSAGE AND LISA MOORE

Hugh Allan and Ravenscrag 177

6 Searching for Intimacies beyond the Notman Photographs: The Case of Amy Redpath Roddick 181

ELIZABETH KIRKLAND AND MARY ANNE POUTANEN

The Creation of Mount Royal Park 217

7 Gender and Social Relations in the City above the Hill 219

ROBERT C.H. SWEENY

PART FOUR: **PROFESSIONAL AND BUSINESS WORLDS IN TRANSFORMATION**

Architects Unite 251

8 Max Aitken in Montreal: Financial Innovation and Creative Destruction in the Laurier Boom 253

GREGORY P. MARCHILDON

Houses of Worship 277

9 "Glad of your help": Scottish Architects in Montreal, 1860–1940 279

ANNMARIE ADAMS

The Stanley Street Presbyterian Church 313

10 The Changing of the Guard: Bartlett McLennan, Roy Wolvin, and the Leveraged Buyout of the Montreal Transportation Company, 1903–1921 315

M. STEPHEN SALMON

PART FIVE: **CRISIS AND DECLINE**

The Art Association, Phillips Square 351

11 Crossing Imperial Boundaries and Constructing Intimate Linkages: Reading Soldiers' First World War Letters 353
NICOLAS KENNY

A Consistent Material Palette 381

12 The Death of the Golden Square Mile? Understanding the Transformation of an Urban District, 1945–1985 383
HAROLD BÉRUBÉ

The 1920s: Beginning of the End 417

Afterword 421
BRIAN YOUNG

Contributors 427

Index 431

Acknowledgments

We must start by expressing our appreciation and admiration to the scholars who so enthusiastically agreed to share their time and expertise in this venture. In June 2019 we gathered in the heart of the Square Mile itself, at the Macdonald Engineering Building of McGill University, to begin the conversation that is now contained in the following pages. We thank the contributors for placing their confidence in the project and for the generosity they have continued to demonstrate through the entire process. We offer a special nod to Brian Young who, while unable to be present at the 2019 colloquium, bravely took on the task of writing the afterword. His observations on the conversation, in tandem with his reflections on a career working in and often on the Square Mile, brought a contemplative richness to the collection that we deeply appreciate, and that we expect readers will too.

We wish to thank Len Husband and the University of Toronto Press who quickly grasped the vision of this collection and provided the support needed to see it through to completion. *Montreal's Square Mile* benefitted from the careful reading and astute insights offered by the anonymous reviewers. We also wish to thank the institutions that gave permission to reproduce the more than 100 images that fill these pages, particularly the McCord Museum.

We are grateful for the crucial financial support that has made this volume possible, including support for the 2019 Square Mile colloquium. In particular, we would like to acknowledge the support of the Canadian Business History Association/l'association canadienne pour l'histoire des affaires, the L.R. Wilson and R.J. Currie Chair in Canadian Business History, the Macdonald Stewart Foundation, the

McGill Institute for the Study of Canada, and the St. Andrew's Society/McEuen Scholarship Foundation Chair in Canadian-Scottish Studies.

Finally, a word of gratitude to a colleague and friend, Jarrett Rudy. He helped locate the conversation, both physically and intellectually, in suggesting the brilliant space of the Macdonald Engineering Building for the colloquium and in spurring us to think deeper and wider in our understanding of history around the tables of the Montreal History Group, Thomson House, and at his beloved l'Amère à boire.

MONTREAL'S SQUARE MILE

Introduction

Dimitry Anastakis, Elizabeth Kirkland, and Don Nerbas

The Square Mile was a powerful symbol in Montreal's urban landscape at the end of the nineteenth century, an elite residential district that straddled the foot of Mount Royal, elevated above and apart from the city below. It existed as a discrete but roughly defined and porous physical space, extending northward from Dorchester Street (Boulevard René-Lévesque today) to the slopes of Mount Royal, and bounded by Park Avenue/Bleury Street in the east and Côte-des-Neiges/Guy Street in the west. Yet the Square Mile occupied a much larger space than its immediate urban form. It represented a dramatic new concentration of wealth in late nineteenth-century Canada that was developed from and mutually reinforced by interconnected spheres of activity. Social and cultural life and evolving family and professional networks; the articulation of identities, including the construction and negotiation of categories of gender and race; and capital investment and innovations in business life – these constitute elements of the Square Mile world explored in the chapters to follow.

This complex world has been obscured by mythologies of nationalist and popular historiography. As the quintessence of Montreal's commercial dominance, the Square Mile appeared as an inevitable outcome of historical and geographical forces in Donald Creighton's *The Empire of the St. Lawrence: A Study of Commerce and Politics*. Creighton's formulation of the "Laurentian thesis" in that work was itself an extension of Harold Innis's famous "staples thesis," which underlined the role of extracted commodities and their linkages – furs, timber, and wheat, and railways, banking and finance – in forging Montreal's central place within an east–west system of trade that prefigured the coming of the Canadian nation state.[1] In the early

1970s, popular historian Pierre Berton took on a subject that Innis had explored as a PhD student: the building of a transcontinental railway.[2] Berton's two-volume history of the Canadian Pacific Railway (CPR) cast business and political titans of the Square Mile – such as Donald Smith, George Stephen, Duncan McIntyre, J.J.C Abbott, and W.C. Van Horne – as the central actors in a nation-building drama.[3] Subsequent popular histories of the Square Mile built upon these themes in their celebratory depictions of the elite men of the Square Mile.[4]

Incorporating diverse approaches and historiographical influences, this volume offers the first scholarly collection devoted to the history of the Square Mile. It emerged out of a desire to explore what kinds of conversations would develop when scholars from different fields were brought together to examine a subject that, though a central edifice in different modes of Canadian historical writing, had rarely been subject to broad examination across subfields and disciplines. In other words, while countless works have examined various aspects of the Square Mile's history, few efforts have been made to bring these different approaches together to consider how it might deepen our overall understanding of the historical processes that made and shaped the Square Mile and its relationship to the imperial and colonial worlds in which it was situated.[5]

This volume examines the Square Mile as a complex intersection of multicausal processes of historical change, but one that is best pieced together through multiple narratives. In particular, as an elite suburb with a complex local history, and as an important node of the British world system and of a rapidly expanding Canadian political economy, the Square Mile requires investigation of the local alongside national, imperial, and global frames of analysis. By considering these frames together, it is possible to reconstruct how the Square Mile was made and unmade, how it was experienced by those who lived in it, and how its influence extended outward to shape the world around it.

At the centre of this story are the people of the Square Mile who constituted Canada's most important urban bourgeoisie before the Great War. While the Square Mile titans may have had expansive visions of national and transnational economies and businesses, these ventures were grounded in the intimate entanglements of familial relations, local municipal and property concerns, and the class-conscious and status-driven relations of the Square Mile itself, from its posh clubs to its churches to its physical space as "the city above the hill," removed from the hurly-burly of an industrializing city.[6] Conducting business in the Square Mile was as much about language, religion, race, ethnicity, and cultural capital as it was about limited liability corporations, financial innovation and competition, and real estate, trusts and wills. Contributing to an international literature on economic elites and bourgeois class formation during the long nineteenth century, this volume insists upon the importance of the broader social, cultural, and political contexts of the business and professional world.[7]

As with bourgeois cultures across the globe in the nineteenth and early twentieth centuries, family and gender powerfully shaped the operation of Square Mile society and its business and economic life. Historians of gender and empire have demonstrated that consciousness of class always takes a gendered form and must be observed in a transnational context, with careful attention paid to the experience and interpretation of race.[8] The circulation of ideas, people, and politics travelled across oceans and land masses so that empire was innately global yet always "played out in local spaces with thick and enduring histories."[9] Family relations performed a powerful, but often understated, role in the shaping of empire and the business opportunities associated with it.[10] In the Square Mile we see that family was "no mere private refuge, but a powerful corporation at the heart of public life."[11] The architectural historians and geographers in this collection remind us that family was at the centre of the built environments, where homes far outnumbered institutions or commercial spaces. Business historians highlight the ways that family acted as the sinew that laced business ventures with capital. Social and cultural historians reveal the ways family determined social obligations, forged emotional bonds, and served as moral referees. This approach allows one to consider the scions of Square Mile business not in separation from their roles as fathers, husbands, sons, and brothers, but as intimately embedded in their family networks. It also reveals to us what can be divined of the others in those households – the women, children, domestic workers, and travellers who never stayed long enough to fix their address within the Square Mile.

This volume, as the term *colonial metropole* in the subtitle suggests, addresses the structural roles of empire and settler colonialism in shaping the social and cultural history of the Square Mile and the multiple identities that Square Milers articulated. Unlike the imperial metropole, where social status was often anchored in generations of aristocratic tradition, Montreal had no such established aristocratic heritage and thus borrowed from British, French, and American traditions while responding to the specific challenges of Montreal and its position as a colonial hub.[12] The stories told in this collection reveal the ways that class formation in colonial society was dynamic and centred on the attainment of a "secure bourgeois status," which even at the highest echelons of the social order could be fragile.[13] Fur-trade families reached the apex of Square Mile society during Canada's industrial age. But for men such as Edward Clouston and Donald Smith, suggestion of Indigenous kin became a source of embarrassment in high-society circles.[14]

Before his full arrival as a Square Mile mogul, Donald Smith, as Max Hamon shows in his chapter, played an important role as a representative of the Canadian state during the Red River Resistance. The wealth of the Square Mile was indeed derived significantly from a dramatic acceleration of settler colonialism orchestrated by the Canadian state and the acquisition and exploitation of vast resource hinterlands across the continent during the late nineteenth century, from the forest and mineral resources of the Pacific Coast, to the wheat economy of the Prairies, to the coalfields of Nova Scotia.[15] As one of the wealthiest elite suburbs of the British Empire, the Square Mile and the social world that enveloped it represented at its height a grand, collective effort to establish home life and the domestic sphere as a fortress, but this impulse coexisted with cosmopolitan social networks and national and imperial commitments. Talbot Mercer Papineau, as Nicolas Kenny's chapter powerfully demonstrates, could find the Square Mile in London. He was also comforted by thoughts of home, Montebello, on the battlefields of Europe.

Montreal's Square Mile thus also contributes to our understanding of how capital investment and markets were made from historical processes, often deeply rooted in family networks and constituted by the state. The emphasis on Square Mile figures connected to railways, banking, and heavy industry that appeared not only in Canadian nationalist historiography but also in later studies influenced by "metropolitanism," dependency theory, and the priorities of the "new" social history of the 1970s and 1980s produced accounts of business enterprise and class formation that were mostly male-focused.[16] As the evidence presented by Robert C.H. Sweeny in this volume suggests, if we shift our focus to a different sector, real estate, the role of women in the economic life of the Square Mile becomes much more important. Moreover, as the research of T.W. Acheson demonstrated long ago, the Scots were particularly overrepresented within an "industrial elite" that was becoming increasingly interconnected with a wider corporate world at the commanding heights of the economy, also illustrated by Gilles Piédalue's important article.[17] The Scottish factor was itself a product of the transatlantic ties of the British Empire that uniquely shaped class formation in Montreal, and which, as Annmarie Adams's chapter demonstrates, resulted in Scottish dominance of important segments of the professional world of architecture.[18] On the other hand, consideration of landed wealth demonstrates an ethnic heterogeneity within the Square Mile bourgeoisie that can be underappreciated.

The structures of bourgeois economic life – embedded in family and carefully cultivated social relations – that had emerged from the Square Mile's nineteenth-century experience were in some ways challenged by exemplars of the new financial capitalism such as Max Aitken and Roy Wolvin, who arrived in Montreal during the early twentieth century. As the chapters by Gregory P. Marchildon and M. Stephen Salmon suggest, these outsiders engaged in episodes of "creative destruction" that helped to permanently alter Montreal's business and financial milieu. Nonetheless, they drew upon their own networks to execute their projects. Investment and the operation of financial markets thus remained deeply embedded in social networks and cultural performance and improvisation at a time when the ubiquity of corporations, stock valuations, and university-educated experts gave business life a new semblance of objectivity and impersonality.

By the 1930s, the Square Mile was coming to the end of a half-century of power and splendour, its patrician families humbled by the tragedy and death of the Great War, shifting economic fortunes, and the Great Depression. While much of the business of corporate Canada still operated out of the boardrooms of St. James Street, the Square Mile as a site of upper-class elitism, Victorian-age Britishness, and cozy, clubby exclusivity was fading.[19] But ultimately, as Harold Bérubé's detailed case study shows, capitalist activities that gave rise to the Square Mile a century before – the buying, selling, and subdivision of land – would contribute to its decline in the postwar period before heritage conservation groups emerged to defend a threatened built environment.

The contributors to the collection have been encouraged to stake their own perimeter of the Square Mile. We insist upon no one definition of its geographic space. The boundaries of the Square Mile were blurred across time and even within moments as those seeking upward social mobility negotiated their position by pushing against the geographical edges of the neighbourhood, looking for an entry point into Montreal's most elite circles. Yet the boundaries were fixed enough that those who lived in "the city below the hill" certainly understood their exclusion from the neighbourhood. The Square Mile was built and shaped to house Canada's emerging elite – their families, their institutions, their clubs, and their places of worship. While their business headquarters remained in the city core for most of this period, it was in the streets of the Square Mile where their lives were lived and individual and collective identities performed.

The chapters in *Montreal's Square Mile* are organized into five clusters, each with a distinctive yet overlapping theme that reflects the interdisciplinary nature of this collection. The volume is also organized in a roughly chronological fashion, and the chapters can be read in sequence as a series of intersecting narratives that contribute to a broad account of historical change.

Interspersed among the sections and chapters are a series of vignettes by architectural historian Julia Gersovitz. With expertise and a distinguished career in both architecture and restoration, Gersovitz invites readers on a neighbourhood walk, to view with a critical eye the buildings and landscapes of the Square Mile and its legacies. She points out for the readers the strategic placement of homes, institutions, and places of worship, the presence and disappearance of apple orchards, the planning of gardens and parks, the blending of international architectural styles, and the various materials that were shipped across the ocean or unearthed nearby, the literal bricks and mortar of the neighbourhood. These vignettes act as a visual album of the Square Mile's physical and built environment.

Part One, "Frameworks and Perspectives," provides two unique overviews of the Square Mile and its broader meaning within historical, geographic, and cultural contexts. In the opening chapter, Roderick MacLeod provides a broad-reaching introduction to the Square Mile. MacLeod's deep knowledge of the Square Mile and his extensive scholarly repertoire, dating back to his 1997 PhD dissertation, position him to range extensively across historical works and approaches to contextualize this space, which he sees as having a myriad of cultural, geographic, economic, religious, architectural, ethnic, and linguistic complexities. He argues that the space's romantic myth-making power was a consequence of its real-world concentration of influence and wealth, and its location atop Montreal's bustling cityscape, at the centre of a "transcontinental colonial project."

In chapter 2, the eminent historical geographer and historian of Montreal, Sherry Olson, endeavours to "interpret the myth" of the Square Mile by looking closely at owners, builders, residents, lenders, and designers to provide a heterodox, visually stunning, and multi-scalar analysis of the Square Mile's evolution as a complex ecosystem of intersecting relationships and networks. Utilizing a range of methods and data, from Kuznets cycles to city business directories to artwork, Olson provides snapshots from the 1840s, 1880s, and 1913 to tease out how networks of influence and wealth emerged and evolved over time.

Part Two, "Constructing Business Networks and Institutions," provides two biographical case studies that illustrate the operation of family, business, kinship, and ethnic networks in the making of important economic sectors and enterprises in the Square Mile. Jean-Philip Mathieu's chapter explores how Thomas Morland created new practices and corporate organizations to redefine the metals sector in the mid- to late nineteenth century with the formation of Montreal Rolling Mills. As Mathieu argues, Morland's innovations were realized through the mobilization of Square Mile networks and capital. As a consequence, the humble nail became tied to the joint stock corporation and the high-politics of the tariff, which all play overlapping roles in this engaging study of entrepreneurship and business change in nineteenth-century Montreal.

As Morland was reshaping the metals trade, Donald Smith and his Metis wife, Isabella Hardisty, were gravitating towards the economic and social networks of the Square Mile. Through examination of the enduring significance of Smith's fur-trade contacts, Max Hamon depicts a complicated story in chapter 4 about the making of Square Mile economic life. As Hamon argues, in shifting roles from a quintessential "HBC man" to a member of the Square Mile's financial and industrial elite, Smith "negotiated the transition by maintaining old ties and networks rather than forging a break with the past." Smith could not have successfully made this shift without Isabella Hardisty, the "daughter of an elite Metis family." Through "her family and personal relationships," Smith attained access to "a vast network of financial interests." Hamon's chapter thus reveals the "enduring capacity of Indigenous relations in settler spaces and economies," and the significance of fur-trade networks in the construction of the Square Mile's metropolitan business interests.

The importance of women in the Square Mile's story is further revealed in Part Three, "Family, Gender, and Property." Chapter 5 by Peter Gossage and Lisa Moore centres on the 1884 judicial separation of property case that Annie Stevenson Anderson brought against her husband, David Morrice. Morrice, a prominent wholesale merchant-turned-textile manufacturer, had emerged as one of Canada's "cotton lords" by the early 1880s. Overcapacity, however, created a sudden crisis in the industry in 1883–4 that hit Morrice particularly hard. Through this close case study, Gossage and Moore demonstrate the ability of moneyed couples to take advantage of a legal system that allowed them to protect their assets through the wife by providing a "legal smokescreen for an insolvent husband." Their analysis of the case allows for a deeper understanding of women's agency, the legal system, and the relationship between business and family life that formed the broader social context of Square Mile society.

Elizabeth Kirkland and Mary Anne Poutanen also use a biographical case study. In chapter 6, they explore gender, family, and sexuality through the life story of Amy Redpath Roddick. The Notman photographs serve as a central artefact in this analysis of a prominent Square Mile family marked by family tragedy, chronic illness, and premature death. Utilizing methodologies that incorporate the history of emotion with an intimate biographical approach, Kirkland and Poutanen probe beyond the staging of the photographs to explore how birth order, gender, sexuality, health, and death shaped life behind closed doors in one of Sherbrooke Street's iconic mansions. They argue that Amy, as default head of the household and like so many others in her social class, skilfully curated a trouble-free image to be projected to the "outside world," where public narratives and images were rewritten and restaged, while concealing the intensity of the family's emotions within the intimate space of the home. Elite identities, they argue, "were being carefully constructed and hidden: the public ones for the camera, the private ones when the camera was gone."

The theme of gender and female agency is further considered in chapter 7 by Robert C.H. Sweeny. As with so many of the chapters in this book, property holds a central place here. Utilizing geo-referenced databases constructed from a 1903 evaluation roll as well as the 1901 manuscript census, Sweeny pursues a sweeping yet meticulous reconstruction of property ownership patterns in the Square Mile and changing social relations. From his data- and map-intensive analysis, he shows that women were major property owners in the Square Mile, "the city above the hill." These "landed ladies," Sweeny concludes, emerged from "the complexity of gendered family interests in property," and they were active participants in "multigenerational strategies of accumulation." This important finding challenges traditional understandings of social structure, wealth, and family in Montreal in this period and suggests that women were engaged in Square Mile business enterprise on a scale that has yet to be adequately addressed in a historical literature that has traditionally emphasized male corporate heads. Like the other two chapters in this section, the reader is confronted with evidence of historical agency that demands reconsideration of old and untested assumptions.

Part Four, "Professional and Business Worlds in Transformation," consists of three chapters that examine historical change during the Square Mile's golden era of the early twentieth century. Canada's most famous financier, the transplanted New Brunswicker Max Aitken, is the subject of Gregory P. Marchildon's chapter. Aitken lived in Montreal for less than three years, from 1907 to 1910, before his departure for London, where he was made Lord Beaverbrook and embarked upon a public career that would bring him empire-wide fame. Nonetheless, his brief and mercurial presence in Montreal helped to usher in a revolution in Canadian finance, one that Aitken continued to influence from abroad long after he left Montreal. Aitken's impact upon securities trading, mergers and acquisitions, and financial services more generally disrupted the comparatively staid business culture of the Square Mile. Aitken – along with a small group he employed in Royal Securities, who came with him to Montreal from the Maritimes – had an enduring impact upon Montreal's financial community and beyond for decades to come.

Scottish architects left an equally indelible imprint upon Montreal, as architectural historian Annmarie Adams shows in chapter 9. From their scholarly perches at McGill University, Percy Nobbs and Ramsay Traquair helped to shape Montreal's architectural personality. Adams's methodological approach – the creation of an architectural family tree consisting of forty-one individuals with connections to

Scotland and Nobbs and Traquair – reveal the dense and overlapping networks of nationality, education, profession, and family that deeply influenced Montreal's built environment, illustrated in the images found in this chapter, but also in Gersovitz's rich architectural vignettes. Nobbs and Traquair participated in a "Scottish buddy system" that facilitated their careers at McGill and which, as Adams notes, incorporated "other Scottish-born architects in Montreal, many of whom designed buildings in and near Montreal's Square Mile."

In chapter 10, M. Stephen Salmon offers a detailed examination of the intricacies of the early-twentieth-century shipping industry and the financialization of the sector under the accumulation strategies of Roy Wolvin. The demand for ships caused by the Great War created an opportunity for Wolvin and his business associates connected to Canada Steamship Lines (CSL), as ships themselves became increasingly valuable commodities. In 1916, CSL pursued a leveraged buyout of an established shipping firm, the Montreal Transportation Company, connected with the McLennan family, with deep nineteenth-century roots in the Square Mile. Wolvin and his associates, as Salmon writes, "turned the venerable old firm into an ongoing play on shipping markets." The prioritization of short-term profits over "operational matters" would eventually lead to the near bankruptcy of CSL in 1921–2. Salmon thus provides a case study that, like the chapters of Mathieu and Marchildon, illustrates Montreal's and the Square Mile's place as a site for creative and sometimes ruthless business innovation.

In the loss and destruction of the Great War, the golden age of the Square Mile came to an end. Part Five, "Crisis and Decline," considers this phase of the Square Mile's evolution, following the horror and death of the Great War and the economic devastation of the Great Depression. Chapter 11 by Nicolas Kenny explores the wartime correspondence of Square Mile scion Talbot Mercer Papineau, a man who seemed destined for Canada's grandest stages, and that of working-class Englishman Willie Firth, posted to Canada for Royal Navy service. The two sets of letters examined by Kenny reveal the sprawling intimacy of a *fin de siècle* British Empire and all of its crumbling grandeur. The Great War struck deeply into the Square Mile's heart, with so many of its sons, brothers, and fathers lost. Kenny's chapter demonstrates how that event was experienced at a personal and intimate level, and how these experiences were powerfully mediated by class, gender, and national and imperial imaginings.

The Roaring Twenties in Canada could not reverse the Square Mile's relative decline. By the Great Depression of the 1930s, the area was quickly becoming a shadow of its former self. Harold Bérubé proposes a critical examination of the narrative of decline in the concluding chapter of *Montreal's Square Mile*. In Bérubé's contribution, we start at the symbolic end of the Square Mile – the infamous 1973 demolition of the Van Horne Mansion. But the chapter moves beyond the stately mansions of the precinct to examine the broader forces that reshaped the urban landscape of the Square Mile in the postwar period – forces that were influenced by the ideals of modernization and urban renewal. Through close analysis of the real-estate transactions involving the Sherbrooke-Burnside-McGill College-Victoria city block, Bérubé concludes that the Square Mile was, in part, "victim of the very forces that first allowed its growth and opulence in the nineteenth century." Residents and owners participated in the Square Mile's redevelopment in pursuit of commercial opportunities. "Thus, in many ways," Bérubé concludes, "the Square Mile died as it was born, through the lucrative activities of landowners, developers, and promoters."

Though its physical vestiges remained, in many ways the Square Mile world reconstructed in these pages had long disappeared by the 1960s and 1970s, when Brian Young arrived at McGill University. The collection ends with an afterword from Young, one of Montreal's, Quebec's, and Canada's most incisive and insightful historians. He provides a personal perspective of his own lifetime of interactions with the Square Mile, merging historical and human stories in a way that intertwines many of the subjects and themes of the collection – architecture, education, art, family, friendships, and networks – and situates the scholarship of the authors. Young also narrates his own fascinating scholarly trajectory as a consequence of these Square Mile connections, from business biographies and seminary studies to, eventually, social and cultural turns that shifted his enquiries, his methods, and his interests. He leaves the reader with a clarion call to avoid "the intellectual pitfalls of an unconsciously shared ethnic and colonial pride, of the blindness that may come from the osmosis of place, culture, and familiar memory, and of the potential intellectual contamination from tenure comfort in a university built on Square Mile wealth." Young reminds us that there are broader lessons to be learned in studying the history of the Square Mile, "an ideal case study in the meaning of Victorian civilization" whose contradictions persist into our times.

NOTES

1 Donald Grant Creighton, *The Empire of the St. Lawrence: A Study of Commerce and Politics* (Toronto: Macmillan, 1956). Originally published in 1937 as *The Commercial Empire of the St. Lawrence, 1760–1850*, the book was reissued in 1956 with its current title and has been republished since. On the continuing salience of the Laurentian thesis, see, for instance, John Ibbitson's probably premature eulogy, "The Collapse of the Laurentian Consensus: On the

Westward Shift of Canadian Power and Values," *Literary Review of Canada*, January–February 2012, https://reviewcanada.ca/magazine/2012/01/the-collapse-of-the-laurentian-consensus. This idea was further developed in Darrell Bricker and John Ibbitson, *The Big Shift: The Seismic Change in Canadian Politics, Business, and Culture and What It Means for Our Future* (Toronto: HarperCollins, 2013).

2 See Harold A. Innis, *A History of the Canadian Pacific Railway* (1923; repr., Toronto: University of Toronto Press, 1971).

3 Pierre Berton, *The National Dream: The Great Railway, 1871–1881* (Toronto: McClelland & Stewart, 1970); and *The Last Spike: The Great Railway, 1881–1885* (Toronto: McClelland & Steward, 1971). Both books have been subsequently republished.

4 See, for instance, Donald MacKay, *The Square Mile: Merchant Princes of Montreal* (Vancouver: Douglas & McIntyre, 1987). See also, in this volume, the historiographical discussions of Roderick MacLeod and Harold Bérubé in chapters 1 and 12, respectively.

5 See, for example, Paul-André Linteau, *Histoire de Montréal depuis la Confédération* (Montreal: Boréal, 1992); Michèle Dagenais, *Faire et fuir la ville: Espaces publics de culture et de loisirs à Montréal et Toronto aux XIXe et XXe siècles* (Quebec: Presses de l'Université de Laval, 2006); Bettina Bradbury, *Wife to Widow: Life, Laws, and Politics in Nineteenth-Century Montreal* (Vancouver: UBC Press, 2011); Elizabeth Kirkland, "Mothering Citizens: Elite Women in Montreal, 1890–1914" (PhD diss., McGill University, 2011); Sherry Olson and Patricia Thornton, *Peopling the North American City: Montreal, 1840–1900* (Montreal: McGill-Queen's University Press, 2011); Susan Wagg, *The Architecture of Andrew Thomas Taylor: Montreal's Square Mile and Beyond* (Montreal: McGill-Queen's University Press, 2013); Brian Young, *Patrician Families and the Making of Quebec: The Taschereaus and McCords* (Montreal: McGill-Queen's University Press, 2014); Robert C.H. Sweeny, *Why Did We Choose to Industrialize? Montreal, 1819–1849* (Montreal: McGill-Queen's University Press, 2015). See chapter 1 in this volume by Roderick MacLeod for an account of the evolution of historical writing on the Square Mile.

6 In his 1897 sociological survey of Montreal, Herbert Ames differentiated between what he called the "city above the hill," which included the Square Mile, and the "city below the hill," comprising the working-class neighbourhoods that were the focus of his study. Herbert Ames, *The City Below the Hill: A Sociological Study of a Portion of the City of Montreal, Canada* (Montreal: Bishop Engraving and Printing, 1897).

7 See, for instance, work on the American bourgeoisie: Sven Beckert, *The Monied Metropolis: New York City and the Consolidation of the American Bourgeoisie, 1850–1896* (Cambridge: Cambridge University Press, 2001); Steve Fraser and Gary Gerstle, eds., *Ruling America: A History of Wealth and Power in a Democracy* (Cambridge, MA: Harvard University Press, 2005); Sven Beckert and Julia B. Rosenbaum, eds., *The American Bourgeoisie: Distinction and Identity in the Nineteenth Century* (New York: Palgrave Macmillan, 2010); Noam Maggor, *Brahmin Capitalism: Frontiers of Wealth and Populism in America's First Gilded Age* (Cambridge, MA: Harvard University Press, 2017). See also David Motadel, Christof Dejung, and Jürgen Osterhammel, eds., *The Global Bourgeoisie: The Rise of the Middle Class in the Age of Empire* (Princeton, NJ: Princeton University Press, 2019); and Young, *Patrician Families.*

8 Catherine Hall and Leonore Davidoff, *Family Fortunes: Men and Women of the English Middle Class, 1780–1850* (London: Hutchinson Publishing, 1987); Antoinette Burton, *Moving Subjects: Gender, Mobility, and Intimacy in an Age of Global Empire* (Champagne: University of Illinois Press, 2008); Adele Perry, *Colonial Relations: The Douglas-Connolly Family and the Nineteenth-Century Imperial World* (Cambridge: Cambridge University Press, 2015); Antoinette Burton,

"AHR Roundtable: Toward Unsettling Histories of Domesticity," *American Historical Review* 124, no. 4 (2019): 1332–6.

9 Perry, *Colonial Relations*, 16. See also Kurt Korneski, *Race, Nation, and Reform Ideology in Winnipeg, 1880s–1920s* (Madison, NJ: Farleigh Dickinson University Press, 2015).

10 The high politics of Canadian business enterprise during this era and its imperial and transnational contexts have been explored in Andrew Smith, *British Businessmen and Canadian Confederation: Constitution Making in an Era of Anglo-Globalization* (Montreal: McGill-Queen's University Press, 2008); James Belich, *Replenishing the Earth: The Settler Revolution and the Rise of the Angloworld* (Oxford: Oxford University Press, 2009); John Darwin, *The Empire Project: The Rise and Fall of the British World-System* (Cambridge: Cambridge University Press, 2009); Phillip Buckner, "The Creation of the Dominion of Canada, 1860–1901," in *Canada and the British Empire*, ed. Philip Buckner (Oxford: Oxford University Press, 2010), 66–86; and Dimitry Anastakis and Andrew Smith, eds., *Smart Globalization: The Canadian Business and Economic History Experience* (Toronto: University of Toronto Press, 2014).

11 James Casey, *The History of the Family* (Oxford: Basil Blackwell, 1989), 6.

12 See, for example, Roderick MacLeod, "Salubrious Settings and Fortunate Families: The Making of Montreal's Golden Square Mile, 1840–1895" (PhD diss., McGill University, 1997); Brian Young, *Respectable Burial: Montreal's Mount Royal Cemetery* (Montreal: McGill-Queen's University Press, 2003); Gillian Poulter, *Becoming Native in a Foreign Land: Sport, Visual Culture, and Identity in Montreal, 1840–85* (Vancouver: UBC Press, 2010).

13 Perry, *Colonial Relations*, 9.

14 Kirkland, "Mothering Citizens," 30; Alexander Reford, "Smith, Donald Alexander, 1st Baron Strathcona and Mount Royal," in *Dictionary of Canadian Biography*, vol. 14, University of Toronto/Université Laval, 2003–, accessed 2 February 2023, http://www.biographi.ca/en/bio/smith_donald_alexander_14E.html. For more on the Clouston family, see Krista Barclay, "'Far asunder there are those to whom my name is music': Nineteenth-Century Hudson's Bay Company Families in the British Imperial World" (PhD diss., University of Manitoba, 2019).

15 For the CPR's relationship to settler colonialism in the Prairie West, see James W. Daschuk, *Clearing the Plains: Disease, Politics of Starvation, and the Loss of Aboriginal Life* (Regina: University of Regina Press, 2013), 99–158. For the metropolitan influence of the CPR and its role in shaping the nature of development and class formation in the West, see A.A. den Otter, *Civilizing the West: The Galts and the Development of Western Canada* (Edmonton: University of Alberta Press, 1982); John A. Eagle, *The Canadian Pacific Railway and the Development of Western Canada, 1896–1914* (Montreal: McGill-Queen's University Press, 1982); Robert A.J. McDonald, *Making Vancouver: Class, Status, and Social Boundaries, 1863–1913* (Vancouver: UBC Press, 1996), 149–74; and Jim Blanchard, *Winnipeg 1912* (Winnipeg: University of Manitoba Press, 2005). The growth of Montreal influence over Nova Scotia's coalfields is documented in James M. Cameron, *The Pictonian Colliers* (Halifax: Nova Scotia Museum, 1974), 34–73; David Frank, "The Cape Breton Coal Industry and the Rise and Fall of the British Empire Steel Corporation," *Acadiensis* 7, no. 1 (Autumn 1977): 3–34; and Ian McKay, "Industry, Work and Community in the Cumberland Coalfields, 1848–1927" (PhD diss., Dalhousie University, 1983), 65–179. The growing dominance of Square Mile business interests over the Maritime region's economic life in the late nineteenth and early twentieth centuries was documented by T.W. Acheson in his classic article, "The National Policy and the Industrialization of the Maritimes, 1880–1910," *Acadiensis* 1, no. 2 (Spring 1972): 22–7.

16 See, for instance, R.T. Naylor, *The History of Canadian Business, 1867–1914* (1975; repr., Montreal: McGill-Queen's University Press, 2006); Gerald Tulchinsky, *The River Barons:*

Montreal Businessmen and the Growth of Industry and Transportation, 1837–53 (Toronto: University of Toronto Press, 1977); Brian J. Young, *Promoters and Politicians: The North-Shore Railways in the History of Quebec, 1854–85* (Toronto: University of Toronto Press, 1978). Montreal's role in this dynamic was also implicit in the development of critical new approaches in sociology and in the new Canadian political economy, which was also largely male-focused. See, for example, Wallace Clement, *The Canadian Corporate Elite: An Analysis of Economic Power* (Ottawa: Carleton University Press, 1986); and John Porter, *The Vertical Mosaic: An Analysis of Social Class and Power in Canada* (Toronto: University of Toronto Press, 1965). Brian Young, it should be underlined, went on to explore a diverse variety of subjects connected, in various ways, to the history of the Square Mile, which included serious consideration of gender dynamics. See Young, *George-Etienne Cartier: Montreal Bourgeois* (Montreal: McGill-Queen's University Press, 1981); *The Politics of Codification: The Lower Canadian Civil Code of 1866* (Montreal: McGill-Queen's University Press, 1994); *Respectable Burial*; and *Patrician Families*. See also Young's afterword in this collection as well as the historiographical discussion in Sweeny, *Why Did We Choose to Industrialize?*

17 T.W. Acheson, "The Social Origins of the Canadian Industrial Elite, 1880–1885," in *Canadian Business History: Selected Studies, 1497–1971*, ed. David S. MacMillan (Toronto: McClelland & Stewart, 1972), 152–5; Gilles Piédalue, "Les groupes financiers au Canada, 1900–1930: Étude préliminaire," *Revue de l'histoire de l'Amérique française* 30, no. 1 (June 1976): 3–34.

18 T.W. Acheson, "Changing Social Origins of the Canadian Industrial Elite, 1880–1910," *Business History Review* 47, no. 2 (Summer 1973): 195–7, 203–4. The overrepresentation of Scots in the Square Mile bourgeoisie was representative of broader trends investigated by T.M. Devine in *To the Ends of the Earth: Scotland's Global Diaspora* (New York: Penguin, 2012). The articulation of Scottish ethnic identities in Square Mile society has received recent treatment in Florence Regimbald-Roy, "Elites and Scottishness in Montreal: Identity, Culture, and the Self in Portrait Photography, 1860–1900" (master's thesis, McGill University, 2021).

19 This decline was also reflected in political life. See Don Nerbas, *Dominion of Capital: The Politics of Big Business and the Crisis of the Canadian Bourgeoisie, 1914–1947* (Toronto: University of Toronto Press, 2013).

PART ONE
FRAMEWORKS AND PERSPECTIVES

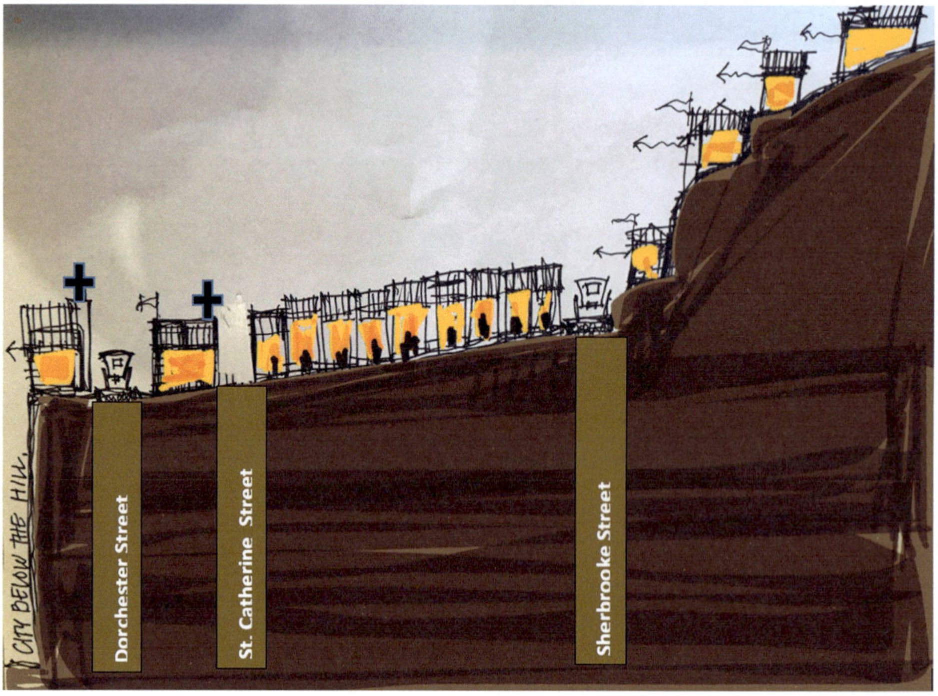

Figure V.1 The Square Mile: A singular topography.

The Square Mile: A Singular Topography

I scribbled this image (Figure V.1) to illustrate the singular topography of the Square Mile and to set the stage for the lecture I gave at the Square Mile colloquium in June 2019.

Starting in the 1840s, middle-class Montrealers began to discover the residential possibilities of the southern slope of Mount Royal. In contrast to the crowded conditions found in the old city, the air was salubrious, the views spectacular, and the possibilities for picturesque landscaping of personal "pleasure grounds" seemingly endless.

The topography set the development patterns of the district, which is traditionally bounded by Guy/Côte-des-Neiges Streets to the west, Pine Avenue to the north, University Street to the east, and Dorchester Street (now Boulevard René-Lévesque) to the south. The most desirable land was found on the slopes of the mountain, and it was there that the largest mansions were built within generous tracts of land. The major thoroughfares were already traceable on the James Cane map of 1846: the flattish plateaux became Sherbrooke, St. Catherine, and Dorchester Streets. More conventionally sized row houses, sheltered by canopies of majestic elms, lined the north–south streets.

Each of the major east–west streets developed a particular character, which was to remain intact until the gradual demise of the Square Mile after the First World War. Sherbrooke Street was lined with mansions and quickly earned the sobriquet of the "Fifth Avenue of Montreal." St. Catherine Street, at first residential and institutional, gradually began to yield space for the commercial needs of the Square Mile residents. Dorchester Street was residential and institutional. Its southern side overlooked the "city below the hill," as Herbert Ames defined certain working-class neighbourhoods in his 1890 cri de coeur. This bluff provided the residents of Dorchester Street with both exceptional views and a daily reminder, if they chose to look, of the intolerable living conditions within the poorer districts of Montreal.

CHAPTER ONE

The High Ground: Mansions, Mythology, and the Mountain

Roderick MacLeod

Above all, it is a place of romance.

For over two centuries we have been glamourizing Mount Royal and the well-heeled people who lived on its southern slopes to a degree that is out of proportion to the former's modest size and the latter's overall contribution to culture and social development. At the dawn of the British regime, artists such as Thomas Patten depicted Montreal as if it were on a South Sea island, the mountain's stark cliff rising into the clouds, dwarfing the town huddled at the water's edge (Figure 1.1). Subsequent visitors almost always noticed Mount Royal looming in the distance, and even that practical-minded Montrealer, the Reverend Newton Bosworth, referred to it as "a very conspicuous object."[1] The mountain has certainly been conspicuous in the city's evolving self-image. The residents of the elaborate mansions built on its flank have also been highly conspicuous in historical literature and the popular imagination – especially the male residents, who are typically depicted as captains, barons, princes, and gentlemen of substance.[2] This is the stuff of mythology.

Like all mythology, such depictions do contain a grain of truth, but in this case the task of separating truth from myth is hardly as interesting as exploring how the mythology itself works. Admittedly, there is much that bears demystifying behind the sober facades of both men and mansions, but this objective can be pursued even as one acknowledges the importance of mythology in understanding this infamous cohort. Indeed, the gentlemen who lived on the side of the mountain, and who figure so prominently in the city's, and Canada's, economic history, directly benefitted from this mythology, as did their families – and not just in hindsight. As we peruse the literature that romanticizes their lives, we learn that the people whose

Figure 1.1 Thomas Patten, *An East View of Montreal, in Canada,* 1762. McCord Museum, M19848.

names are associated with lavish mansions and whose faces adorn commemorative volumes were also historical players who worked to shape this mythology, which in turn helped forge their fortunes and cement their reputations. To dismiss this romanticization as "myth" and therefore unworthy of serious study, as social historians are perhaps inclined to do, is to overlook a critical aspect of social formation and mutual self-promotion. Elites do not merely germinate in well-turned socioeconomic soil; they also benefit from fertilizer.

Mythology can involve statistics. For example, historically, it was in this elite area that 70 per cent of Canada's wealth resided. This oft-repeated fact is possibly true, but its origins are very murky. I have yet to see it satisfactorily footnoted. Accurate or not, it serves as go-to information when referring to Montreal's elite, and it is rarely accompanied by further probing into questions such as how this elite came to live where it did, and what it says about Canada that 70 per cent of its wealth should be located in one small area. What is always achieved by quoting this statistic is to reinforce the glamour inevitably associated with the sort of wealth that can power a country – not abstractly, as a class, but directly, as a relatively small cohort with apparently superhuman abilities. Mythology can be enhanced by the rather casual recourse to an info-byte that has enjoyed a very long shelf life.

The mythology around this elite extends to the names we have given to its geographical location. In the popular imagination, the familiar term is the "Golden Square Mile," which conjures up visions of ornate mansions, elegant costumes, and sprawling gardens. This name is, of course, a relatively recent invention, as elderly residents (at any rate, those I encountered in the course of my doctoral work in the 1990s) would tell you. They preferred the less pretentious term "the Square Mile." The academic world does too, partly because that term has a longer pedigree and partly because it eschews, or appears to eschew, the romanticism inherent in "Golden." But this romanticism continues to resonate, today perhaps more than ever. Not so long ago, some advertising executive realized that reviving a vaguely historic-sounding name and applying it to an urban area long associated with wealth would make that area even more desirable. In real estate terms, the ensuing campaign was a matter of effectively gilding the lily – or in this case, goldening the Square Mile.

The cachet surrounding this part of town derives largely from our inexhaustible fascination for its great mansions, a few of which continue to dot the urban landscape. When the *Montreal Gazette* referred to "Golden Square Mile splendor" in a 2009 article about a renovated home, readers had a good sense of what was meant.[3] The commercial appropriation of the area's cachet has meant not only the addition of "Golden" to an older term but also the removal of "the." Advertisements refer to "Living in Golden Square Mile" as if it were an actual neighbourhood or borough. Even Google Maps clearly indicates "Golden Square Mile" as a district apparently on a par with "Downtown Montreal," labelled with the same font (Figure 1.2). There is even a "Golden Square Mile Tourism Development Society" whose mandate is "to promote the Golden Square Mile district, in downtown Montréal, as a unique destination with respect to eight pillars: architecture, art, business, education, fashion heritage, history, hospitality and nature."[4] The term clearly isn't going away anytime soon.

In my 1997 doctoral thesis on the area, I used "Golden Square Mile," and most frequently the acronym "GSM."[5] This was not laziness: my background in urban history convinced me that Montreal's wealthy nineteenth-century uptown neighbourhood needed to be demystified and depicted as generic. I saw parallels in other cities in which such elite spaces appeared: London's Mayfair, Edinburgh's New Town, New York's Upper East Side, Philadelphia's Society Hill, Boston's Beacon Hill, and Madrid's Barrio de Salamanca. These cities all had their own Golden Square Miles, as it were. A GSM, I suggested, should be a geographical term akin to CBD (central business district). That idea has not caught on, and it is very good that it hasn't, since I now think the idea of the Golden Square Mile is infinitely

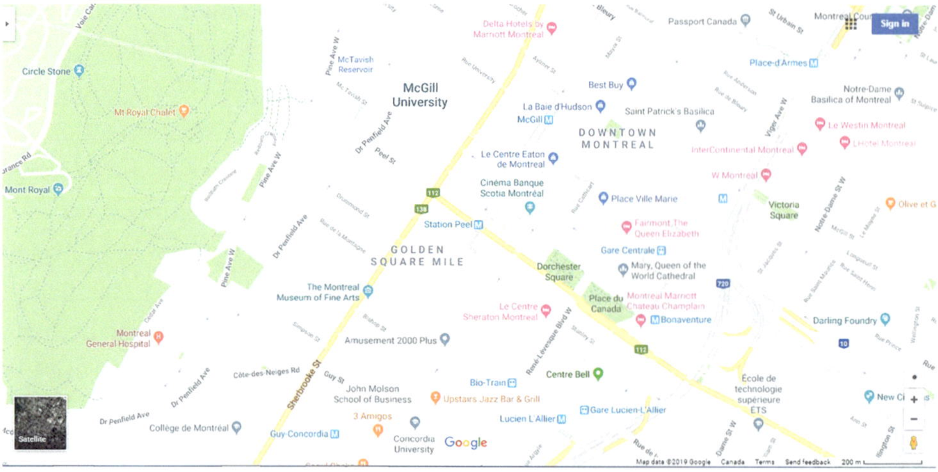

Figure 1.2 Central Montreal, Google Maps, June 2019.

more interesting as a specific cultural phenomenon than as a generic geographical reference.

My attitude towards this area on the side of Mount Royal is similar to my interpretation of the historical nature of Quebec society. I also think it is more interesting, and that it offers a deeper vein of historical gold (pun intended), to see Quebec as a distinct society rather than view it as *quelques arpents d'amérique*, a corner of North America that just happens to speak French.[6] It is quite reasonable to argue that the cultural differences between Quebec and the rest of the continent are sufficiently negligible as to permit historians to apply general models to an interpretation of the Quebec experience, and by extension to use the Quebec experience, even the Anglo-Quebec experience, as a case study for proving larger theories. That was essentially what I attempted with the GSM. But this approach overlooks a long history of religious and legal exceptionalism that will, at the very least, muddy attempts to generalize. By the same token, my thinking about the Golden Square Mile has evolved considerably since completing my thesis, notably in that now I doubt it can serve as a case study of anything. Instead, I see it as distinct from elite communities in other cities that it might resemble. It is distinct both because of the mountain on which it sits, with all its inherent romantic associations, and because it evolved within a society that is itself distinct within North America in terms of its particular combination of language, religion, and law. The Golden Square Mile was overwhelmingly English-speaking and Protestant, characteristics that must inevitably colour any discussion of class tensions, gender relations, and cultural expression.

Square Mile Literature

This ethno-cultural approach has not been a feature of most of the literature on this elite community any more than the commemorative coffee table books have paid attention to class tensions and gender relations. Considerable weight has been given to cultural expression, in that much of the literature has focused on architecture, especially the mansions. As examples of a wide array of styles, these buildings have intrigued architectural historians, and for good reason. Equally, the rate of destruction of these buildings at the hands of modern developers, including McGill University, has rightly preoccupied heritage activists.[7] Indeed, it was the demolition of the Van Horne Mansion in 1973 that galvanized the heritage community and ultimately transformed Montreal into a city that values its past (Figure 1.3). Many of the leading heritage activists of the 1970s were practising architects, including Michael Fish, Phyllis Lambert, Peter Lanken, and Julia Gersovitz. Such professionals combined private practice with very public advocacy of heritage preservation, articulating the case for conservation and often directly contributing to critical restoration projects.

Gersovitz was also a pioneer in the scholarly study of Square Mile architecture, writing a master's thesis on it (at Columbia, ironically) in 1980 and subsequent publications on the area's houses, both mansions and terraces.[8] Her work squarely ignored any reference to "Golden" and downplayed the area's romanticism, opting instead to identify a rich diversity of styles within this particular architectural ecosystem. Following her work was the volume by architectural historian François Rémillard and photographer Brian Merrett, published in French in 1986 as *Demeures bourgeoises de Montréal: Le Mille carré doré 1850–1930*.[9] Rémillard used what was by then a familiar term to francophone readers – "Mille carré doré" – for whom the shorter "mille carré" would have made little sense. Joshua Wolfe's 1987 English translation, *Mansions of the Golden Square Mile, 1850–1930*, retained the longer term, remembering that the heritage activists he had known in the 1970s added "Golden" out of reverence for the area's architectural importance.[10] He also felt that "mansions" resonated with English readers more than "demeures bourgeoises," which had a pejorative ring to it. One could also argue that "mansions" is a more accurate term for the subject of the book, since "demeures bourgeoises" ought by definition to include the equally bourgeois terraced houses. In any case, the book achieves its purpose with a subtle polemic when it comes to heritage. As both an inventory of demolished mansions and a series of profiles of mansions that have survived, it serves as a reminder that all such buildings are perpetually at risk.

Figure 1.3 Demolition of the Van Horne Mansion, *La Presse*, 10 September 1973. Archives La Presse.

Extolling the aesthetic virtues of Square Mile mansions has been a vital part of the larger effort to sensitize Montrealers to the importance of their historic built environment. Similarly, many successful restoration projects, particularly of houses now owned by McGill University, have shown that buildings once created as objects of conspicuous consumption can have a useful and productive second life. But the work of architectural historians and heritage-minded architects has also contributed indirectly to the romantic Golden Square Mile mythology by focusing on mansions. This emphasis was developed in glossy, popular treatments such as *The Square Mile: Merchant Princes of Montreal* (1987) by Donald MacKay, who opted not to use the term "Golden" because of its less impressive pedigree.[11] As MacKay's subtitle suggests, however, the book is a kind of corporate hagiography. Its focus is the residents, above all the men, who made this geographical entity where 70 per cent of Canada's wealth was concentrated. Given the widespread fascination for the "Lifestyles of the Rich and Famous," it is not surprising that popular treatments of the Square Mile have consistently underscored the area's wealth and glamour, trotting out the usual suspects by way of illustration (typically McGill, Molson, Allan, and Redpath) with little regard for their varied social origins, relationships to the local economy, or positions within the timeline of nineteenth-century history. The Lifestyles of the Rich and Famous narrative usually takes a heroic tone; "Merchant Princes" is certainly a pompous phrase. But the tone can also be one of melancholy, a *Gone with the Wind* sense of a vanished elegant but slightly corrupt civilization, as in Margaret Westley's frequently cited *Remembrance of Grandeur* (1990).[12] The mythology of the Golden Square Mile owes as much to its decline as it does to its rise. Nostalgia sells houses.

All who study this elite community rely on one invaluable primary source: the Square Mile's own photographer, William Notman. Although he never actually lived in the area, Notman became the community's biggest booster, providing the neighbourhood and its residents a vital service: he produced portraits of people and property that are both commemorative and status-confirming. Even the most sober and unprepossessing subjects are rendered in a romantic hue simply by virtue of the enviable status and leisure implied (Figure 1.4). This romance does cut across gender lines: even though it is the portraits of men that typically adorn the pages of popular histories, depictions of women are no less plentiful across the Notman oeuvre. Children, individually and in groups, are also well-represented, since parents were eager to celebrate how status and leisure impacted the next generation. Most often subjects were posed in Notman's lavishly decorated studio, but sometimes artfully crafted composite photos show entire families enjoying the comforts of their mansions and gardens. These portraits became a cottage industry to the Notman family, who benefitted from this intimate access to elite families as assuredly as these elite families benefitted from the clear yet comfortably unpenetrating gaze of Notman's lens. These often stunning black-and-white images have coloured our perception of Victorian society; in them, the Golden Square Mile all too often stands in for a much wider world, including countless places cameras never went.

Despite its anachronisms, "Golden Square Mile" is arguably a useful term, especially when we acknowledge that extravagance was an integral feature of the residents' public persona. They would have denied this claim, but that does not undermine its validity. The elderly residents I encountered who rejected the "Golden" modifier were echoing their predecessors' attitudes, irritably dismissing what struck them as pretentious and arriviste. The area's nineteenth-century elite carefully cultivated a facade of modesty. They did so in part because an absence of pride was integral to the core values of Protestantism, but also because an ingrained work ethic required that, ostensibly, money be used to move the economy rather than be spent on frills. This sense of becoming wealthy through hard work was reflected in the legends that families encouraged about their patriarchs' modest beginnings; John Redpath's legend has him arriving at the port in Quebec City from Scotland in 1816 and

Figure 1.4 William Notman, *John Redpath*, 1862. McCord Museum, I-3024.

walking barefoot to Montreal to save shoe leather.[13] Such claims could not easily be disproven, yet any impartial outside observer would have found the lifestyle of these families anything but modest.

Ostentation was, of course, the intended effect. To project flash while claiming simplicity was one of many paradoxes at the heart of Montreal's Anglo-Protestant social elite, and for that reason "Golden" seems to me to be an appropriate, if partly ironic, modifier to add to "Square Mile." "Golden Square Mile" captures the mystique of the place, as defined by the real estate hyperbole, the romance of mansions ("romansion" might be a catchy term to promote), the slick coffee table books, the Notman photos, and the notion that it was where 70 per cent of Canada's wealth lived. Such mythology has served this elite well, both locally and nationally. Rather than rejecting "Golden Square Mile" because it reinforces a popular and overly romanticized image of a community, we should embrace it for its acknowledgment of that image. Similarly, we should recast this community as a player in a drama – or rather (to continue the theatrical metaphor) as both a stage and a prop. The Golden Square Mile was not just a place where the elite lived but also a tool the elite used to become the elite. We need to explore the process whereby such people created the Golden Square Mile as a vehicle for social advancement.

"Square Mile," without the golden modifier, does not project the same level of romance, nor does it suggest the way this particular built environment was used to draw ambitious people into its environs and to signal their achievement of success once they were established there. Even so, "Square Mile" is a more authentic term than its gilded counterpart, albeit only to a degree; nobody referred to the area by either term in the nineteenth century. A further difficulty with "Square Mile" is that it can be confused with the more famous Square Mile of London, which is, curiously enough, that city's financial hub rather than its choicest residential neighbourhood: London's CBD rather than its GSM, as it were. In any event, as a name for the Montreal suburb, "Square Mile" is at least geographically accurate: the area measures roughly one square mile, if we define it (as I did in my thesis) as being the northern part of the old St. Antoine Faubourg, later the St. Antoine Ward. Using the ward boundary to demarcate my area of study was convenient, given that the archival material was identified by ward, but it also made sense historically and topographically. The upper part of the St. Antoine Ward was still farmland when the boundaries were drawn in 1840, while the lower part and the St. Lawrence Ward to the east were already fairly densely populated.[14] To the west, the vast domain of the Sulpicians constituted another natural boundary. By this reckoning, the Square Mile was defined by Guy Street and Côte-des-Neiges Road to the west, Alexander and City Councillors Streets to the east, La Gauchetière Street to the south, and the edge of Mount Royal Park to the north (Figure 1.5). Even so, urban

Figure 1.5 John Brophy, detail from *Plan of the City of Montreal with Its Present Boundaries and New Division of Wards*, 1889. Archives de la Ville de Montréal, CA M001 VM066-5-P036.

boundaries are fluid. To present a street as a boundary is to privilege political administration over the built environment. Some writers list slightly smaller boundaries for the Square Mile, citing, for example, Dorchester Street as the area's southern limit, but that is to ignore how a street like Dorchester was a united space, its buildings facing each other and implicitly making visual and social connections. But regardless of its fuzzy margins, the upper St. Antoine Ward had associations for nineteenth-century Montrealers long before anyone began to talk of square miles, golden or otherwise.

The other term for this area that was in use during the nineteenth century was "the New Town." This phrase began to be aggressively promoted for strategic reasons as of the 1840s, although its use dwindled over subsequent decades as the area became more settled and residents grew less keen to be thought of as "new." The pioneering study of this urban project, from which my own work drew extensively, was the 1977 master's thesis by David Hanna, "The New Town of Montreal."[15] Hanna, a geographer, wrote about land, and specifically about how subdividing land created residential suburbs. There was no "Square Mile" anywhere in the thesis, let alone a golden one. Instead, we got "the New Town," a term that denoted a vision of a particular built environment featuring terraced housing and a street grid. On a deeper level, the term "New Town" suggested a relationship to an Old Town, a relationship that was infinitely more complex than the mere addition of a residential suburb to a bustling city. The notion of the New Town implied a dynamic at play, a sense of contrast between new and old, and by extension a contrast between rich and poor. Hanna provided an image of this community as containing within it the idea of its opposite: the New Town was not just a place for the rich with their fabled 70 per cent of Canada's wealth, but a place that was distinct, deliberately distinct, from the world of the poor.

When discussing this elite community, "New Town" is the term to use if one wants to avoid anachronism at all costs. More to the point, the term actually comes out of the mid-century sales pitch that tempted Montrealers with visions of spacious and prestigious suburban frontiers. What the term does not convey, any more than any variations on "Square Mile," are the area's critical geographical, topographical, and environmental qualities. It does not suggest elevation. The New Town was marketed as urban space, but it was urban space located amid nature – specifically the agricultural and forested greenery that was Mount Royal. Advertisements emphasized the salubrious air at this elevation, and of course the marvellous views over the city and the river valley beyond.[16] Because the New Town was deliberately connected to the slopes of the mountain, I now find it more useful to avoid referring to square miles of any colour and simply describe this elite community as being located on "the mountainside." In fact, my preferred term for this location is "the High Ground," which, although not rooted in nineteenth-century usage, describes this community fairly well. The term denotes not only the physical heights from which residents could peer down on the rest of the city, but also the sense of moral superiority that they felt towards the lower orders – or at any rate a sense that they began to feel, or felt able to express, once they had reached the higher ground. To speak of this elite community without reference to the mountain, or to present the mountain essentially as part of the furniture (as it is in many Notman photos), is to miss the significance of the community's key building block.

Developing the Mountainside

The mountain, of course, has many aspects. Above all (again, pun intended), there is the summit, which until the 1880s was a rocky wilderness that visitors occasionally climbed up to, though not often, as it was private and dangerous. Henry David Thoreau, while visiting Montreal in September 1850, made a point of heading to the summit for the sensational views it afforded and was annoyed at having to pass “numerous signs threatening the severest penalties to trespassers.”[17] A quarter century later, Frederick Law Olmsted designed Mount Royal Park in such a way as to maximize the summit’s natural features, envisaging the open-air recreation usually associated with parks happening only on the gentler slopes of the mountain’s northern side, leaving the southern parts rocky and forested.[18] As Olmsted noted, one of the summit’s natural features is an especially steep cliff on its southeastern side, the side facing the city. Below this cliff there is still plenty of mountain, however. These lower slopes enjoy considerable elevation compared to the old city, as does the plateau that evens out somewhat at the level of today’s St. Catherine Street. At the southern end of this plateau lies the escarpment, which effectively represented the lower limit of the High Ground. Today, this escarpment is marked by the line of the Canadian Pacific Railway and the Ville-Marie Expressway, both of which serve to de-emphasize its visual impact. Nevertheless, the journey up from St. Antoine Street along any of the area’s north–south thoroughfares involves a distinct climb. When Herbert Ames wrote about the “city below the hill,” this was the hill he had in mind.[19] He was also taking a jab, of course, at the piously Protestant pretensions of those who might see themselves living on the biblical City on the Hill.

The mountainside has always been an attractive place to live. Long before there was talk of a New Town, large estates had been formed on the mountain, most of them strips of land only a couple of hundred metres wide but extending up from the escarpment right over the summit and part way down the other side (Figure 1.6). Early landowners cleared the lower slopes for orchards, their crops benefitting from the summit’s shelter and a southern exposure. The lower plateau was regularly used by early landowners as fields for grazing. By the late eighteenth century, most of these mountain estates had been acquired by retired merchants, notably fur traders, who retained the agricultural function of the estates and made use of the old farmhouses as summer homes. They also continued to exploit the forested summit for lumber and were not keen on others making free with this terrain – hence the aggressive signage that Thoreau encountered.

The lives of these mountain-dwelling fur traders always feature in the Square Mile literature; they tend to be presented as early versions of the captains and barons who would build the Victorian mansions, only without their morally restraining Anglo-Saxon respectability. Even so, the fur traders are an important element in the evolution of the High Ground. Apart from their role in the popular history of the Golden Square Mile, these fur traders contributed directly to the mythology that would help make the mountainside appealing to prospective residents in the nineteenth century. Let us consider two of them.

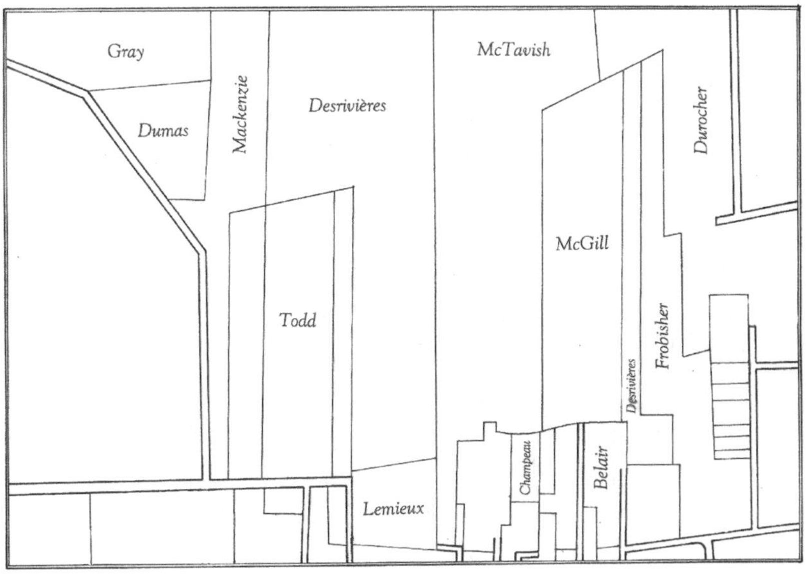

Figure 1.6 Landowners on the southern slope of Mount Royal, c. 1820. Artwork: Elena Cerrolaza.

First, inevitably, is Simon McTavish, a Scots Highlander straight out of legend who slashed his way across the North West and reigned like a lord over the North West Company. To be precise, he reigned like a "Marquis," which was, as the popular histories always remind us, his nom de guerre.[20] His forced entry into the local aristocracy was clinched by purchasing a mountain estate and starting to build a mansion there, by marrying a very young woman from an influential fur trading family, and by forging feudal links with old money back in Britain.[21] McTavish led an adventurous life – although, as things turned out, nothing in it became him like the leaving it. By dying suddenly in his prime, in 1804, McTavish left an intangible legacy of himself as a ghost and of his unfinished ruinous mansion as a haunted place. The mansion itself was tangible enough, of course, and appeared in several depictions of mountain scenery. It was often referred to as a "chateau," one step even further up the scale than a mansion. McTavish also left a very solid legacy in the form of his own tomb, situated high up in the rocks and trees of the lower mountain summit.

These sinister legacies contributed in their way to the mountainside's romantic cachet, even though the promoters of the New Town and its subsequent residents would distance themselves from the values McTavish represented. The respectable elite would effectively build over his traces. McTavish's ruined mansion was of no interest to land developers, and the person who bought the lot on which the

Figure 1.7 John Henry Walker, *The McTavish Monument*, c. 1850. McCord Museum, M751.

building sat promptly tore it down.[22] In the same spirit of reluctant embarrassment, the path up through Mount Royal Park in Olmsted's design largely bypassed the McTavish tomb (Figure 1.7), and does so even today despite ongoing fascination for the spot. Nineteenth-century Montrealers were prepared to revel in the mythical McTavish, but not to openly acknowledge his actual presence on the mountainside. Like good Victorians, they thrilled to the idea of McTavish's ghostly image, even as they secured their own respectability through sober New Town living.

James McGill, another fur trader and often McTavish's business partner, left a very different legacy. Most famously, his will, drawn up in 1811, left the estate on which the university named after him was built. This estate, located adjacent to McTavish's to the east, was also originally a farm, featuring apple orchards and grazing land. Like the other estates nearby, McGill's would be criss-crossed with streets and developed as the New Town at mid-century – save for the part that was transformed into a college campus. The campus would prove one of the most potent symbols of New Town respectability and, consequently, did sterling service attracting residents to adjacent streets. In order to project this level of respectability, McGill College (McGill University, after 1885) had to turn its back on James McGill the fur trader and slave owner, and promote James McGill the solid citizen, the benefactor, the "founder."[23] McGill himself had already taken pains during his lifetime to forge a sober reputation marked by responsible public service: in addition to bequeathing the means to launch the colony's first university, James McGill served in the assembly, in the militia, and as a commissioner supervising the dismantling of the eighteenth-century town walls at the turn of the century. He also strove to position himself as a loyal defender of the British Empire, which was a far cry from his early career as a Scots adventurer in the back country. Although, unlike McTavish, the Glasgow-born McGill was a Lowlander, and so implicitly more civilized, he glossed over even this aspect of his heritage; in his epitaph, McGill described himself as hailing from "North Britain," a place that exists only in the imagination of those desperate to avoid any association with Jacobite rebelliousness. The tomb on which this epitaph can still be read was moved to the university campus in 1875, as were McGill's mortal remains; like Simon McTavish, James McGill has a physical presence on the mountainside, adding in its way to the area's mystique.

McTavish, McGill, and other fur traders bought mountain land to reward themselves for their hard work running vast commercial networks linking the western hinterland to Europe via Montreal. These networks laid the foundation for later commercial empires, and their mountain estates laid the foundation for the High Ground. But the suburb that emerged in the 1840s was the product of modern capitalism. Mountain land would be sold as a commodity, its appeal lubricated by strategic advertising and its acquisition facilitated by a new municipal government keen on rational planning. The creation of this elite community can be attributed to the vision of a small number of men who were among the movers and shakers in the economic landscape of the first half of the century. Foremost were John Redpath and Thomas Phillips, and to a lesser extent John Bethune, who as principal of McGill in the early 1840s was ready to capitalize farmland as a way to fund the

Figure 1.8 James McGill's Tomb, McGill University, 2012.
Photo: Quebec Anglophone Heritage Network Collection / Rachel Garber.

fledgling college. Their social and economic vision was expressed aesthetically by surveyor and architect John Ostell.

Redpath and Phillips were stonemasons; they were trained to shape stone and so came to understand how to shape space. They were also very forceful personalities – Phillips even more than Redpath, although the latter proved more effective at getting his way through persistent negotiation and indirect intimidation. Both had worldly experience: Redpath's native Edinburgh and Phillips's adopted London had left impressions on them, influencing their urban vision of rectilinear streets and squares. In Redpath's case, the model was actually called the "New Town," and like its Montreal counterpart had ethno-cultural aspects: created in the wake of the suppression of Jacobitism, Edinburgh's New Town was anglicized, respectable space, turning its back on the dark, congested, medieval Old Town. Its streets were named for Hanoverian heroes (Frederick, George, Charlotte), unlike the old town's quaint Cowgate, Grassmarket, and Candlemaker Row. Montreal's New Town would honour British statesmen (Peel, Metcalfe, Stanley, Cathcart) unlike the old town's heavily French and Catholic nomenclature.

In 1840, Redpath and Phillips joined Montreal's new municipal council and came to dominate the City's powerful Roads and Improvements Committee, which determined the location of streets according to something resembling a master plan. This plan was conceived and largely surveyed by John Ostell, who had been appointed city surveyor thanks to the endorsement of Redpath and Phillips, although he was a natural choice given his rising fame, notably as the architect of the McGill College building. Because Ostell's time was largely taken up with survey work for the city, the task of drawing the plan fell to an underling, James Cane.[24] The result is a misleading document, as it shows numerous streets that had not yet been laid out by the time the map was published in 1846. Nevertheless, Cane's *Topographical and Pictorial Map of the City of Montreal* provides the best overall image we have of the Roads and Improvements Committee's vision of the New Town (Figure 1.9).

The master plan also shows, without drawing attention to it, Redpath's and Phillips's own plans for their own estates. Although the different landowners are not identified, the building lots are all indicated according to the individual estate plans. Most of these plans were also designed by Ostell, and the rest were drawn by surveyors working in full knowledge of Ostell's larger vision. The New Town was not merely a matter of urban aesthetics but a way to frame private real estate schemes and maximize the profit to be derived. Without the larger planned urban expansion, isolated mountain lots would have been difficult to sell – and impossible to sell at any great profit. For this reason, it was crucial to include all the individual estate subdivision plans on the master plan. Potential purchasers could easily see how their mountain lots would be connected by road to the commercial centre of Montreal, a convenience that the real estate advertisements always emphasized. The New Town had to be implanted in the mind before it could be constructed on the ground. Phillips died before the project got fully underway, but Redpath pursued his own real estate plans with the full force of the City behind him, writing municipal by-laws

Figure 1.9 James Cane, detail of *Topographical and Pictorial Map of the City of Montreal* (Montreal: Robert W.S. Mackay, 1846).

as suited his needs and sitting in judgment over cases brought against him by other landowners.[25] Today we would of course call this a conflict of interest.

One can perhaps get carried away when talking of "vision." These men, and these plans, were products of a particular social and economic environment. The actions of Redpath, Phillips, and Ostell were shaped by circumstances and the societies and economies they inhabited. They rode a tide of significant social, economic, and political change – namely, the transition from feudalism to capitalism, the rise of the middle class, the aftermath of the 1837–8 rebellions, and the creation of both the United Province of Canada and the municipal government of Montreal. The people who responded to their real estate schemes were the products of these same changes. By the 1830s, Lower Canada was seeing a growing number of prosperous families with some disposable income. That decade's political climate did not make for promising investment, however, and neither did the ongoing uncertainty over land tenure. But 1840 brought political stability, locally and nation-wide, along with the promise of an economic boom. Such confidence led to the widening of the

Lachine Canal, along which Canada's first industrial revolution would take root. Equally significant for Montreal was the long-awaited reform of land tenure, a critical step in the transition to industrial capitalism.

Changing notions of land tenure is crucial to an understanding of the emergence of the New Town. In Montreal today, we often begin public events by "acknowledging that the land on which we gather is the traditional and unceded territory of the Kanien'keha:ka (Mohawk), a place which has long served as a site of meeting and exchange amongst nations."[26] This statement is an important way to recognize the legally flawed foundations on which modern North American society is based, but it also underscores the irony surrounding the intense preoccupation Europeans have had with land tenure. The notion of "unceded land" would have made no sense to generations of White landowners and the notaries they employed to draw up deeds of land cession. In any event, blinkered to such ironies, nineteenth-century reformers implemented a new regime in landholding in Lower Canada, beginning with a trial run on the Island of Montreal in 1840. By the terms of the ordinance, people could free themselves and their properties from the complex burdens of feudal tenure with a single payment and then embrace modern British freehold tenure, which was infinitely simpler and potentially much more profitable.[27]

John Redpath engaged in land capitalization when embarking on his very lucrative career as a real estate developer in the 1840s. He commuted his mountainside estate, rendering the land highly desirable to ambitious people with cash. He then subdivided his estate, the plan indicating larger lots on the higher, orchard sections, presumably for detached houses, and smaller lots on the pasture lands for terraced housing. He also reserved a sizeable part of the orchard section for his own family's use and eventually rebuilt the estate's old farmhouse as a mansion, called Terrace Bank. In the early 1840s he sold dozens of building lots, each for considerably more than what the portion of the undivided estate would have been worth without the structure of a subdivision plan, the enticing advertising, and the general rhetoric of capitalist investment. Because of land tenure reform, and with the advantages derived from his position at City Hall, Redpath made a fortune. He would of course go on to enjoy a third career as a sugar manufacturer, but it was as a successful real estate developer that he was able to bankroll the building and equipping of the sugar refinery in the 1850s.[28]

Other landowners on the mountainside followed Redpath's lead with varying levels of success. Some of them launched their real estate schemes too late to make a profit in an economy that declined suddenly in the later 1840s, and they would not make significant money from real estate until the economy revived in the 1850s. In a striking number of cases, the work of later subdivision was carried out by women, complicating the hitherto very male world of mountain real estate. By the 1860s, several widows, armed with proof of marriage regimes and dower rights suitably waived, developed key sections of the mountainside.[29] Elisabeth Fisher Lockart, for instance, once the teenage bride of Attorney General James Smith, supported her long widowhood through lucrative sales of land on and off Peel Street.[30] Hannah Lyman, widow to "Martyr Mayor" John Easton Mills, escaped the public eye by subdividing her land located near what is now Place Ville Marie and retired to England, where her married daughters Ada and Alice had settled.[31] The last of the mountain estates was subdivided in the 1860s by an unmarried woman, Lydia Hoyle, who had clashed unsuccessfully with John Redpath a quarter century earlier over compensation for street expropriation and now made a profit on her own terms from valuable land west of Dominion Square.[32] These women built on the achievements of the original, male, developers of the New Town, but they took full advantage of their opportunities.

Because of the collapsing economy during the later 1840s, many of the people who purchased lots went bankrupt and were obliged to sell them in order to pay off debts. Others held onto their investments without venturing to build on the lots. We have no way of knowing the intentions of lot purchasers, of course, and can only make assumptions from their actions, but it is safe to say that the eagerness with which people bid at auctions and signed deeds during the early 1840s indicates the intention to build a house and move to the High Ground, or at the very least a confident desire to invest. In any event, by the end of the decade very few houses were actually built. Noting this absence of construction, David Hanna describes the 1840s launch of the New Town as a "faltering attempt at urban expansion," but he was thinking as a geographer, his bird's-eye perspective straining to see evidence of building.[33] On the ground, landowners made money, some people made sound investments, and the buzz throughout the decade was all about the New Town and its implications for social advancement.

In time, however, especially as of the 1850s, generous purchase terms attracted a number of speculative builders to these mountain lots. These builders put up the famous terraces (rows of attached units, often ten or more long), and in many cases they continued to live in one unit themselves with their families. Building this community provided lucrative opportunities for specialized craftspeople, many of them having apprenticed as masons, carpenters, and brickmakers. Henry Bulmer, for example, whose father operated a brickmaking business and whose father-in-law, Edward

Figure 1.10 John Henry Walker, *Terraced Houses on McGill College Avenue*, c. 1875. McCord Museum, M930.50.8.464.

Maxwell, was a master carpenter, made his own fortune building terraces on McGill College property, including one unit that he reserved for himself and his growing family. His biggest project was on the prestigious McGill College Avenue (Figure 1.10), a street that led majestically up to the campus gates and beyond, forming an uninterrupted vista right up to the college itself (later known as the Arts Building).[34]

The twelve units of Bulmer's elegant Mount Royal Terrace became one of the city's most desired urban addresses, welcoming such families as the Gaults, who would earn fame in life insurance and cotton manufacturing. Terraces become attractive places to live for middle-class families who were eager to join this emerging community as a mark of social advancement. Given the respectability and relative safety of the New Town, terraces proved attractive to female household heads, widows, and even some unmarried younger women. Terrace units also served as what we might call starter homes for families who were eventually able to move higher up the social scale (and typically higher up the mountain) into a mansion; the Gault siblings acquired or built themselves mansions (see Figure 1.11) but had their start in Mount Royal Terrace.

Figure 1.11 Wm. Notman & Son, *Mr. Gault's House, McTavish Street, Montreal*, c. 1890. McCord Museum, II-92918.

Landscapes of Respectability

Over the course of the 1850s, 1860s, and 1870s the mountainside acquired a distinct landscape, or rather a set of landscapes. The terrace landscape was the most urban in appeal, offering regularity and conformity. Interrupting the even lines of terraced streets, but contributing considerably to its aesthetics, were institutions. McGill College was already established, forming a beacon of Protestant values as well as a respectable swathe of urban greenery (which it remains to this day). Equally defining for this thickening residential and institutional space was Dominion Square, an elegant park whose walkways and landscaped foliage had been built over the old and by then unsightly St. Antoine burial ground; by the end of the century, the square had become a showcase for commemorative statuary celebrating political figures and imperial triumphs.[35] These public hubs, and the streets that opened around them, proved attractive to schools, museums, and above all churches. In the last case, congregations that had been rooted for generations in old town churches

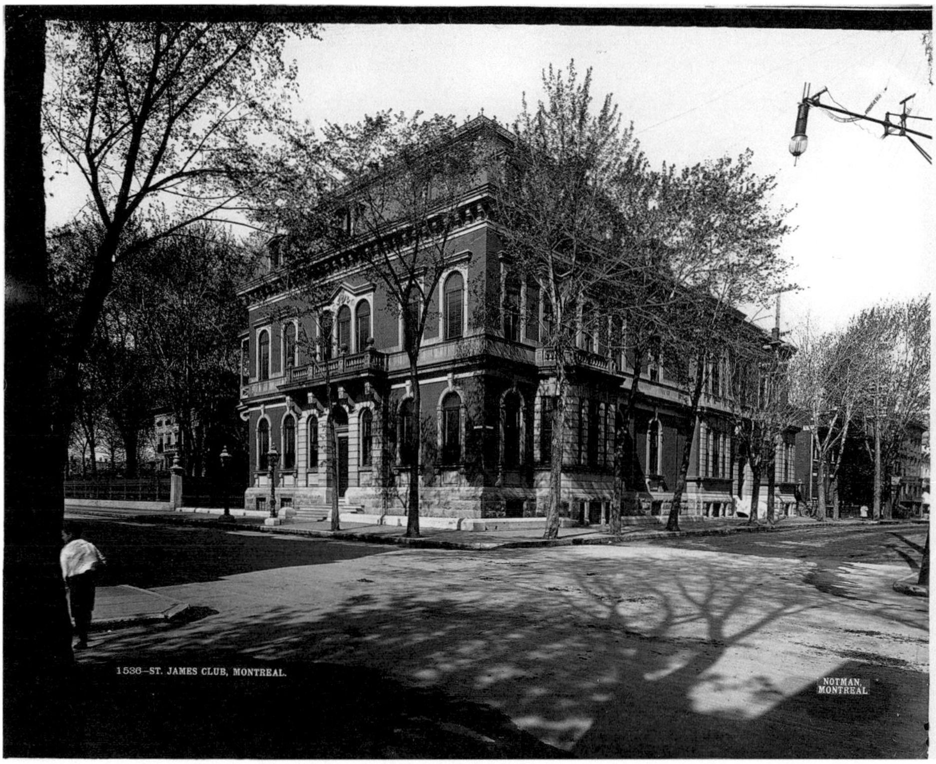

Figure 1.12 Wm. Notman & Son, *St. James Club, Dorchester Street*, c. 1895. McCord Museum, VIEW-1536.A.

often engaged in painful soul-searching before relocating to the higher ground, wrestling with the implications of recasting their places of worship as middle-class institutions and abandoning their poorer co-religionists to makeshift chapels in working-class areas.[36] As the appointed moral centres of families, women were especially engaged in the drive to relocate places of worship, even as the committees struck by each congregation to find new sites and oversee the building process were uniformly male.

When it came to relocating clubs, gyms, rinks, and other places of leisure, there was less soul-searching. Upper middle-class men did not mind travelling daily into the old town's financial heartland for work, but institutions that defined one socially had to be nearby, for convenience but also for show. For merchant Harrison Stephens, first president of the St. James's Club (Figure 1.12), whose sprawling mansion stood right next door on Dorchester Street, the club could not have been more convenient, but as an ornate architectural pile adorning this fashionable street its value was beyond measure.[37] Such institutions were male purviews, but promoters took pains to present the places of public exhibition and performance that they built on the High Ground as appropriate spaces for women. Be it the Art Association of Montreal, the Natural History Society Museum, the Fraser Institute, the Academy of Music, or even, briefly, the famed Crystal Palace, public institutions were far less gendered spaces than places of business. Propaganda for the 1860 Arts and Manufacturers exhibition in the Crystal Palace featured male and female symbolic figures sporting gender-appropriate attributes (a hammer and anvil for him, a canvas for her),[38] and the exhibition included a "Ladies Department," consisting of various suitable crafts from painting to writing to making "Quilts, Counterpanes, Curtains and Covers."[39] Descriptions of events held at the Crystal Palace, and later at the Academy of Music and the Art Association Gallery, clearly refer to "the fair ones of Montreal" in attendance.[40] Far away from the rough, uncultured streets of the old town, the New Town revelled in its refinement, best illustrated by the presence of ladies. Consequent to this refinement, the High Ground came to take on the role of Montreal's cultural centre, and the effect was to reinforce elite Anglo-Protestant cultural hegemony over the rest of the city and beyond.

The mansion landscape, much of it above Sherbrooke Street, was more romantic in appearance than the less ornate terrace landscape. Unlike terraced houses, mansions were set in gardens. Owners of mansions were often involved in the Montreal Horticultural Society and competed for prizes for best floral arrangements. According to the proceedings of the Society's first meeting, however, gardens had a higher purpose than "furnishing to the opulent amateur the honest gratification of displaying his treasures of fruit and flowers." Horticulture was an ennobling force, exerting as it did "an influence in refining our tastes and promoting our moral and intellectual improvement."[41] Gardeners became essential players in this noble objective and often lived on the estates, becoming mountain residents without having to buy or rent. The Redpaths' gardener, Henry Bauden, lived with his wife and daughter in the gatehouse at the foot of the road leading up to Terrace Bank; in the city directory and the census, Bauden is described variously as "labourer," "gardener," and even "farmer." But owners of mansions were not content with having prize-winning gardens; they wanted their entire estates landscaped. For this task, they might engage a professional surveyor, but more often the job was carried out by the resident gardener. Remarking on the home of the Greenshields family, located slightly west of Terrace Bank, one visitor praised their gardener, John Hele: "By raising the knolls here and there, the finest possible views are obtained, and most beautiful and comfortable ornamental seats brought from Scotland, are placed in the happiest positions. A carriage road is made to wind in perfect taste among trees and flower-beds … to a mansion of elegance and comfort."[42] A home's elegant grounds made a critical first impression, almost as much as its ornate architecture.

Urban landscapes have a dual role: as celebrations and affirmations of the achievement of wealth and status, and as examples to be emulated. To describe an urban landscape as "attractive" is to make assumptions about what was really a complex, chicken-and-egg process. Landscapes emerged, but they also influenced. Then as now, people were attracted to an area because it offered services such as churches and schools. But the key feature of mountainside landscapes as they formed in the later nineteenth century was the image they projected. Architectural styles, building materials, walls and fences, gardens and trees, along with the workforce required to keep it all shipshape – all this conveyed an image of wealth and privilege, safety and comfort, and above all respectability.

This landscape of respectability depended on many things, but it hinged on the image of the Victorian middle-class family, at the heart of which was the Victorian middle-class wife and mother. The New Town, with its comfortable homes and refined institutions, was a comparatively safe space for families, who did not have to venture into the congested old town to take part in cultural events or even to attend church. Mansions with manicured gardens were even safer. Notman photographs of ladies taking tea and children playing within the private boundaries of a landscaped estate are perhaps the ultimate expression of peaceful privilege (Figure 1.13), an image that has coloured the aspirations of lower middle-class families ever since. Although in many ways the High Ground would seem to make the old case for separate spheres, matters were not so clear cut. The domesticity enshrining mothers and children, as well as unmarried sisters and daughters, was the public face of respectability, a critical component of a larger image that included husbands, fathers, and providers whose work ethic and business savvy made the domestic comfort possible. As I have argued elsewhere, we need to think of this multifaceted projected image, with its distinct but interconnected gender roles, in terms of public space.[43] In effect, the intense and determined pursuit of privacy and distinction on the residents' parts was a major contributor to their public image, with all the romance and mythology that went with it.

The supporting players on this intricate public stage were of course the domestic servants (Figure 1.14). As cliché would have it, domestics were trained to be invisible in order to give the elite residents the illusion that rooms stayed spotless, food appeared on tables, and they themselves emerged from their boudoirs fully dressed, without any human agency. In other respects, however, servants were anything but invisible. To begin with, there were a great number of them: families living in terraced houses typically employed two or three, and in the larger mansions there could be a dozen or more if one included coach drivers and gardeners. These numbers make up a sizeable cohort, forcing the observation that this quintessentially

Figure 1.13 Anonymous, *Group in Garden at "Trafalgar," Côte-des-Neiges Road*, 1888. McCord Museum, MP-1975.233.1.

upper middle-class community included a substantial working-class population. Furthermore, since a great many servants were Catholic, even in Protestant households, it must be said that this overwhelmingly Protestant community had a minority Catholic resident population. Regardless of their religion, servants were items of conspicuous consumption as much as the houses' landscaped gardens, ornate exteriors, and gilded interiors; there can be no other explanation for the four unmarried Allan siblings in 1891 requiring a resident staff of sixteen.

Neighbours were conscious of each other's servants: how many, how efficient, and how well-behaved. For "invisible" people, domestic servants were among the most heavily scrutinized members of the community – which is one reason why, historically, they opted out of service whenever possible, especially women. Another reason was the back-breaking work and the interminable hours, to which even the infamous conditions of factory labour seemed preferable. Above all, domestic service put the bodies and reputations of women at greater risk than in most other occupations, forcing another observation that is never mentioned in the area's popular literature: that the Golden Square Mile was a place of considerable danger for many of its inhabitants.

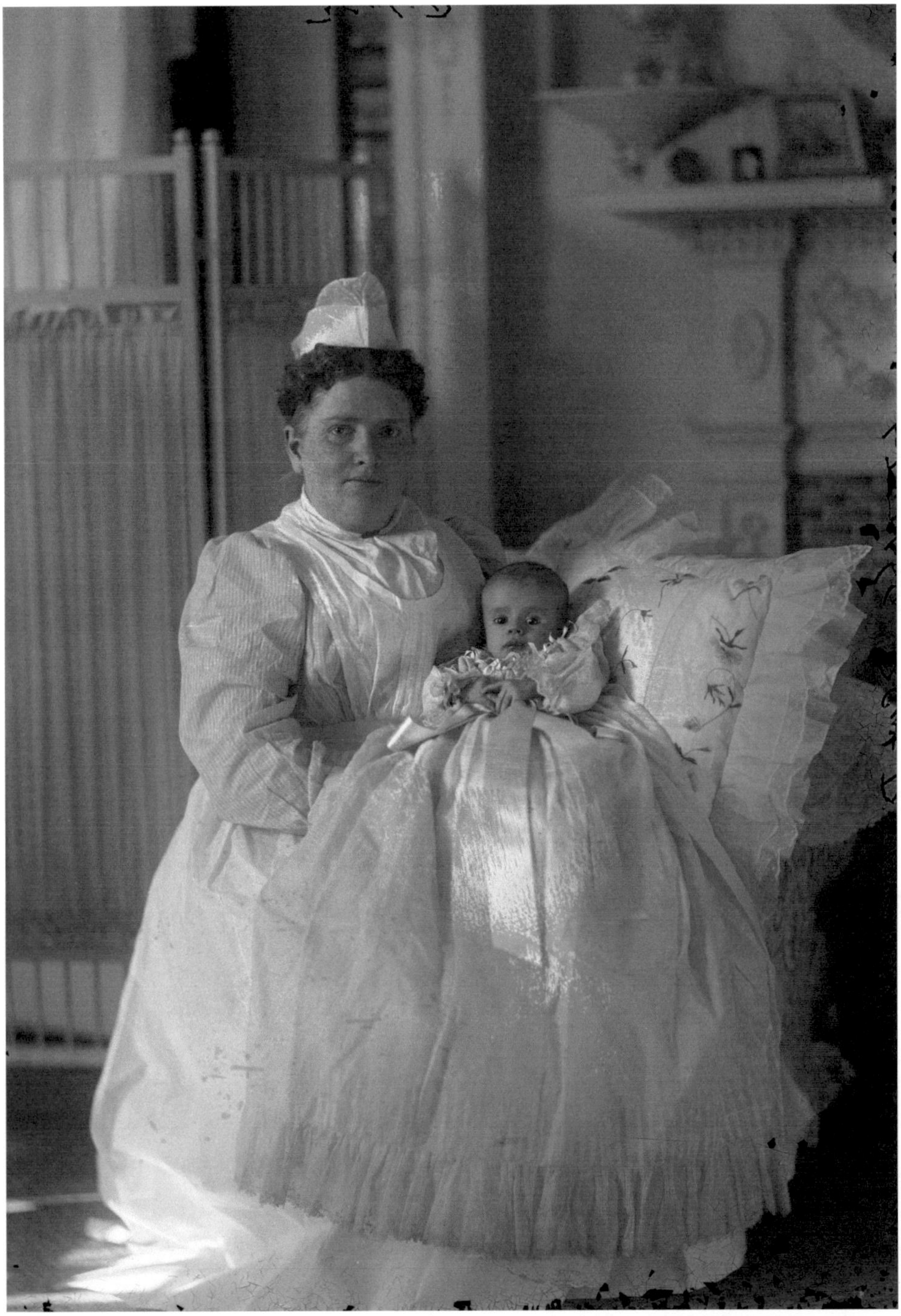

Figure 1.14 Wm. Notman & Son, *Mrs. Allan's Nurse and Baby*, 1898. McCord Museum, II-127160.

Figure 1.15 Alexander Henderson, *Christ Church Cathedral, St. Catherine Street*, 1869. McCord Museum, MP-0000.1452.16.

The projected image of respectability and safety did not extend to basements, back staircases, and other customary venues for sexual assault. It also did not extend to the many parts of town where the men of the High Ground could, and no doubt did, assert their privilege in brothels and other dens of vice.[44]

The mythology says otherwise. Through the careful cultivation of a sense of moral order, a good environment, and a solid work ethic, the residents of the mountainside could effectively claim the High Ground. The area was not only suffused with respectability but seemed to be a place where respectability could be acquired, or at any rate confirmed. On the High Ground, respectability was expressed in Anglo-Protestant terms. This expression reflected not only the demographic reality that the vast majority of the area's homeowners and their families were of British stock but also a more qualitative cultural impact. The relocation of dozens of congregations to the mountainside meant that the area became a showcase of Protestant church architecture; almost all of it adopted the Gothic style (Figure 1.15), which was seen as British in origins as opposed to the presumably Catholic baroque. It is true that, by the late nineteenth century, the city's Catholic (and emphatically baroque) cathedral came to be located on the High Ground, at the edge of Dominion Square, but it was seen by contemporaries as an anomaly and serves as an exception that proves the rule. Moreover, what had been the area's most noticeable

Catholic feature at mid-century, St. Antoine Cemetery, was closed and built over; the inept efforts to exhume some of the bodies had provoked widespread outrage, confirming Protestant determination to keep this unsavoury Catholic legacy out of sight. The new Mount Royal Cemetery on the far side of the mountain was a site for dignified burial, a place where Protestants could find respectability even in death.[45]

Conclusion

The tension between romance and reality, between the ostentatious and the invisible, informed every aspect of the evolution of this mountainside community. The mythic imagery involving ornate mansions, merchant princes, tea in landscaped gardens, Gothic churches, and selfless devotion to public service contrasts sharply with the reality of real estate development, political corruption, the appropriation of sacred space, the "invisibility" of servants, and the even greater invisibility of slaves. Yet, the carefully constructed and willingly perpetuated romance of the High Ground should not be seen merely as a layer to be stripped away to reveal positivist truth; rather, it should be valued as an integral part of this community's political and social success. Arguably, this is true for the formation of all elite communities. Perhaps in our attention to economic relations and impersonal dynamics we have too often overlooked the role of self-serving mythology in the implementation of modern capitalism.

Romance has certainly coloured Canada's heroic narrative of nation building, particularly when one considers the narrow and uncompromising agenda of the High Ground elite who have been so well served by this mythology. The people who controlled that infamous 70 per cent of Canada's wealth and occupied the high ground at the municipal, provincial, and national levels identified (to use a very anachronistic term) as Anglo-Protestant. They looked down at the people below the hill (many of whom, significantly, were also Protestant), but also at other cultural groups (notably Catholics and Jews) who nevertheless were admitted in limited numbers on limited terms (the Forgets and the Josephs will serve as examples). This attitude was part of the High Ground vision, from which perspective its leading residents surveyed the emerging nation. The transcontinental colonial project that took off in the second half of the century debated its strategies in Ottawa but controlled the strings from the slopes of Mount Royal. The much-touted national economic dominance of Montreal was essentially the dominance of the mountain. And the grand cultural project that accompanied this economic colonization was at its heart a mission of Anglo-Protestant hegemony, despite lip service to the mythology of the two founding peoples. This hegemony would outlive the residential community we call the New Town or the Square Mile or the Golden Square Mile. It would live on until Montreal at long last ceded its power to other cities and the elite that had formed the High Ground imploded in the wake of the Quiet Revolution.

NOTES

1 Newton Bosworth, *Hochelaga Depicta: The Early History of Montreal* (Montreal: William Grieg, 1839), 88.

2 See, for example, Richard Feltoe, *A Gentleman of Substance: The Life and Legacy of John Redpath, 1796–1869* (Toronto: Natural Heritage/Natural History, 2004).

3 Stephanie Whittaker, "Golden Square Mile Splendor," *Montreal Gazette*, 9 May 2009, F1.

4 "The Golden Square Mile Tourism Development Society," Bonjour Québec, accessed 7 February 2023, https://www.quebecoriginal.com/en/listing/tourist-information/local-tourism-promotion-agencies/golden-square-mile-tourism-development-society-387765744.

5 Roderick MacLeod, "Salubrious Settings and Fortunate Families: The Making of Montreal's Golden Square Mile, 1840–1895" (PhD diss., McGill University, 1997).

6 Gérard Bouchard, *Quelques arpents d'Amérique: Population, économie, famille au Saguenay, 1838–1971* (Montreal: Boréal, 1996).

7 Donna Gabeline, Dane Lanken, and Gordon Pape, *Montreal at the Crossroads* (Montreal: Harvest House, 1965), esp. chap. 2, "The Saga of the Van Horne House," and chap. 5, "What's the Matter with Old McGill?"

8 Julia Gersovitz, "The Square Mile, Montreal: 1860–1914" (master's thesis, Columbia University, 1980); "The Square Mile, Montreal: 1860–1914," *The Fifth Column* 1, no. 4 (1981): 8–13.

9 François Remillard and Brian Merrett, *Demeures bourgeoises de Montréal: Le Mille carré doré 1850–1930* (Montreal: Éditions du Méridien, 1986).

10 Joshua Wolfe, preface to *Mansions of the Golden Square Mile, 1850–1930*, by François Remillard and Brian Merrett, trans. Joshua Wolfe (Montreal: Meridian Press, 1987), 11

11 Donald MacKay, *The Square Mile: Merchant Princes of Montreal* (Vancouver: Douglas & McIntyre, 1987), 8.

12 Margaret W. Westley, *Remembrance of Grandeur: The Anglo-Protestant Elite of Montreal, 1900–1950* (Montreal: Éditions Libre Expression, 1990).

13 Richard Feltoe cites "later family stories" for this detail (Feltoe, *Gentleman of Substance*, 14).

14 Alan M. Stewart, "Settling an Eighteenth-Century Faubourg: Property and Family in the Saint-Laurent Suburb, 1735–1810" (master's thesis, McGill University, 1988).

15 David Hanna, "The New Town of Montreal: Creation of an Upper Middle Class Suburb on the Slope of Mount Royal in the Mid-Nineteenth Century" (master's thesis, University of Toronto, 1977).

16 See, for example, John Redpath's advertisements placed in the *Montreal Gazette* as of May 1840.

17 Henry D. Thoreau, *A Yankee in Canada* (Boston: Tickner and Fields, 1866), 90.

18 Frederick Law Olmsted, *Mount Royal, Montreal* (New York: G.P. Putnam's Sons, 1881), 45–8.

19 Herbert Brown Ames, *The City Below the Hill: A Sociological Study of a Portion of the City of Montreal, Canada* (Montreal: Bishop Engraving and Printing, 1997).

20 For example, MacKay, *Square Mile*, 14.

21 McGill Rare Books, MS431.3, Minutes and Resolves of the Executors of the Late Simon McTavish, 12 September 1804.

22 Bibliothèque et Archives nationales du Québec, Archive de notaires, James Stewart Hunter, 4082 and 4083, 16 November 1858.

23 For the sanitized view of James McGill, see Stanley Brice Frost, *McGill University: For the Advancement of Learning*. Vol. 1, *1901–1895* (Montreal: McGill-Queen's University Press, 1980); *James McGill of Montreal* (Montreal: McGill-Queen's University Press, 1995); Cyrus Macmillan, *McGill and Its Story, 1821–1921* (London: John Lane, 1921).

24 Archives de la Ville de Montréal, VM36, Committee on Roads and Improvements, Minute Books, 27 October 1843, 2 February 1844, 2 March 1844, 20 December 1844, 3 January 1845, 7 March 1845, and 25 April 1845.

25 See Roderick MacLeod, "The Road to Terrace Bank: Land Capitalization, Public Space, and the Redpath Family Home, 1837–1861," *Journal of the Canadian Historical Association* 14, no. 1 (2003): 165–92, https://doi.org/10.7202/010324ar. See also Archives de la Ville de Montréal, VM36, Committee on Roads and Improvements, Minute Books, 1841–3.

26 Canadian Association of University Teachers, *Guide to Acknowledging First Peoples and Traditional Territory* (Ottawa: Canadian Association of University Teachers, 2017), 9.

27 *Draught of an ordinance to incorporate the Ecclesiastics of the Seminary of St. Sulpice of Montreal, to confirm their title to the fief and seigniory of the Island of Montreal* [...] (Montreal: A.H. Armour and H. Ramsay, 1839).

28 MacLeod, "Road to Terrace Bank," 184.

29 For more on widows and property, see Bettina Bradbury, *Wife to Widow: Lives, Laws, and Politics in Nineteenth-Century Montreal* (Vancouver: UBC Press, 2011).

30 Bibliothèque et Archives nationales du Québec, Archive de notaires, Isaac Jones Gibb, 19179, 19 June 1861.

31 Bibliothèque et Archives nationales du Québec, Archive de notaires, James Stewart Hunter, 12820, 18 May 1867; and 14010, 23 July 1868. For details on the later life of Hannah Lyman, see Bradbury, *Wife to Widow*, 362.

32 Archives de la Ville de Montréal, VM36, Committee on Roads and Improvements, Reports, 24 June and 8 August 1842; Bibliothèque et Archives nationales du Québec, Archive de notaires, John Carr Griffon, 27458, 5 March 1867 (and many others).

33 Hanna, "New Town of Montreal," chap. 2.

34 McGill University Archives, R.G.4, c.3, Board of Governors Minute Book, 2 January and 19 March 1858; Bibliothèque et Archives nationales du Québec, Archive de notaires, Isaac Jones Gibb, 18300, December 1858 (and many subsequent deeds).

35 Alan Gordon, *Making Public Pasts: The Contested Terrain of Montreal's Public Memories, 1891–1930* (Montreal: McGill-Queen's University Press, 2001), 79–80.

36 Rosalyn Trigger, "God's Mobile Mansions: Protestant Church Relocation and Extension in Montreal, 1850–1914" (PhD diss., McGill University, 2004).

37 Edgar Andrew Collard, *The Saint James's Club* (Montreal: Gazette Printing Company, 1957), 5.

38 John Henry Walker, *Emblem of the Board of Arts and Manufacturers for Lower Canada*, McCord Museum, M930.50.1.484.

39 *Grand Exhibition of the Industrial Products of United Canada* [...] (Montreal: Owler and Stevenson, 1860), 5

40 *Illustrated London News*, vol. 37, 22 September 1860, 271.

41 Montreal Horticultural Society, *Proceedings Connected with the Formation of the Montreal Horticultural Society and its Constitution* (Montreal: J. Starke & Co., 1847), 6.

42 Quoted in J. Jay Smith, ed., "A Trip to Canada," *The Horticulturalist and Journal of Rural Art and Rural Taste*, n.s., 8 (1858): 397.

43 MacLeod, "Road to Terrace Bank," 186.

44 The clients who appear in the shadows of Mary Anne Poutanen's *Beyond Brutal Passions: Prostitution in Early Nineteenth-Century Montreal* (Montreal: McGill-Queen's University Press, 2015) are, not surprisingly, invisible.

45 Brian Young, *Respectable Burial: Montreal's Mount Royal Cemetery* (Montreal: McGill-Queen's University Press, 2003).

Figure V.2 Anonymous, *Harrison Stephens' House and Orchard, Dorchester Street, Montreal,* 1850–60. McCord Museum, VIEW-15338.0.

First Development: From Apple Orchards to Building Lots

When the French explorer Jacques Cartier arrived on the Island of Montreal in 1535, he encountered the Haudenosaunee village of Hochelaga several miles inland from the shore. He wrote admiringly of its location within the shelter of the mountain and surrounded by fertile cornfields cultivated by the local Indigenous population.

In 1832, another visitor, James McGregor, echoed Cartier's description of the verdant character of the mountain: "along its foot and particularly up its sides are thickly interspersed orchards, cornfields and villas; above which, to the very summit of the mountain, trees grow in luxuriant variety."[1]

By the 1840s, as the impact of the redevelopment of the area began to be explicitly visible, opposition began to mount, particularly in the popular French press. The following excerpt, from the 18 October 1845 edition of *La revue canadienne*, demonstrates both the very real pressure for change in the area and the consequent worries over the loss of the traditional rural existence:

> Le progrès de notre ville se dirigent plus vers l'ouest du côté de la montagne; les beaux domaines remplantés d'arbres fruitiers n'ont pas été respectés dans ces derniers temps, pars la fureur de bâtir. Un verger, aux yeux de propriétaire, n'est plus un verger – c'est des lots pour bâtir. Les familles les plus respectables, les plus anciennes ont abandonné et abandonnent, chaque année, le patrimoine de leurs pères ... aux envahissemens [*sic*] de progrès.[2]

> Our city is developing towards the west side of the mountain; the beautiful estates, planted with fruit trees are not preserved in recent years, in the frenzy of building. In the eyes of an owner, an orchard is not an orchard – it is just building lots. The most

> respectable and ancient families have abandoned, and continue abandoning every year, the patrimony of their fathers to the invasions of progress.[3]

However, the battle and the war were lost by the end of the decade, as the Square Mile became a residential suburb.

Harrison Stephens (1801–81) was an American-born businessman who settled in Montreal in the 1830s. According to his enigmatic entry in the *Dictionary of Canadian Biography*, he "made the most rapid fortune of any merchant in Canada."[4] Within twenty years of his immigrating, he was able to build a handsome Italianate house on a portion of his land holdings, facing Dorchester Street. This Notman photograph (Figure V.2), taken around 1859, is fascinating in part because it captures the Square Mile in its early period of transition, when apple orchards still coexisted with newly built villas.

NOTES

1 John McGregor, *British America*, vol. 2 (Edinburgh: W. Blackwood, 1932), 581.

2 "Histoire de la Semaine," *La revue canadienne*, 18 October 1845, 83.

3 Translation by Julia Gersovitz.

4 Gerald J.J. Tulchinsky, "Stephens, Harrison," in *Dictionary of Canadian Biography*, vol. 11, University of Toronto/Université Laval, 2003–, accessed 23 June 2020, http://www.biographi.ca/en/bio/stephens_harrison_11E.html.

CHAPTER TWO

Property and Power: Connecting the Dots

Sherry Olson

To interpret the myth of a "Square Mile," as described by Roderick MacLeod in chapter 1, we need to break out of the Square Mile to trace its claimants – owners, builders, residents, lenders, and designers – as they extended their grasp of resources. Traces they left in their immediate neighbourhood offer clues to their wider ambitions at the scale of confederation and at the scale of empire. In recent years, the spread of a submicroscopic particle has boosted awareness of our own dependence on both local and global connections. We've seen how a local accident disrupts routines worldwide, reveals the systemic, reroutes the flows, and rewrites histories. The flight of a drone over a silent city or an epidemiologist's dashboard has made us attentive to scale. As an experiment, I propose using the cartographic resources of the MAP project (https://map.cieq.ca) as a zoom lens for tracking the entrepreneurs who lived in the Square Mile.[1] The attempt to pin the actors to the map and connect the dots will trigger questions about the scale of their ventures. How far? How fast? How often? How big? How much? Over the span of 1840–1914, how did they redimension their enterprise?

One powerful rhythm of urban growth is displayed in Figure 2.1. In Montreal, as in the other cities of North America, construction surges every fifteen to twenty-five years. Known as the Kuznets cycle, the span approaches the turnover of a human generation (about thirty years).[2] Each upwelling matched a flow of fur, timber, grain, or oil on the St. Lawrence; the erection of taller buildings in the city centre; the widening of streets; and new factory layouts in the suburbs. A new slate of immigrants was hired and shunted, and architects and decorators in the Square Mile indulged new forms of elegance and hubris.

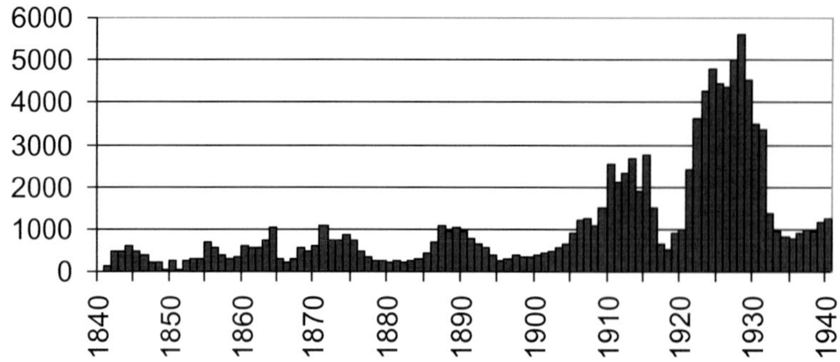

Figure 2.1 The rhythm of city-building, from construction permits issued by the City of Montreal, 1840–1940.

To examine such complexity, Figure 2.2 displays a now-common structure for system thinking. It was created by a team of ecologists who looked first at the physical complex and the biotic – rain, wind, soil, and seed – to argue for the inclusion of the social and engineering features of a city as part of a "humane ecosystem."[3] Most of the contributors to this book take their starting point in the social complex or the built complex. Business historians inquire into decisions made in the Square Mile to extend tracks and telegraph lines, lay cables, and deepen the channel. They address challenges of social organization, profit and non-profit, order and disorder, giving only a nod to the physical and biotic complexes of the larger system – the spaces paved, drained, or disrupted for appropriation of timbers, furs, and feathers.

Let me propose instead that we explore the ecosystem in terms of the scale of its components. As cartooned in Figure 2.3, each individual lodges in a home or workplace, embedded in the urban economy and nestled in a "big world."[4] Substituting these for Pickett's four boxes, we see in Figure 2.4 interactions at many levels. In a surge of urban growth, what happens in the subsystem? Day after day the individual factory worker or the horse in harness still requires about the same ration of calories to match the energy exerted, and the flea or the fly is replaced by another flea or fly of about the same size. The larger earth system, too, after fifteen or twenty years, shows only modest changes in its annual receipt of a spectrum of solar radiation. Typical interactions between the little critter and the big world persist: the young squirrels and worms cope with the freeze and thaw, storing what they can, each species distinct in its sensitivity to warmth and scent and vibration, in its appetites, and in its vulnerability to others. Over twenty years, the longer-lived maple sapling or the human child has grown and changed shape, but within the rigorous constraints of life on earth.

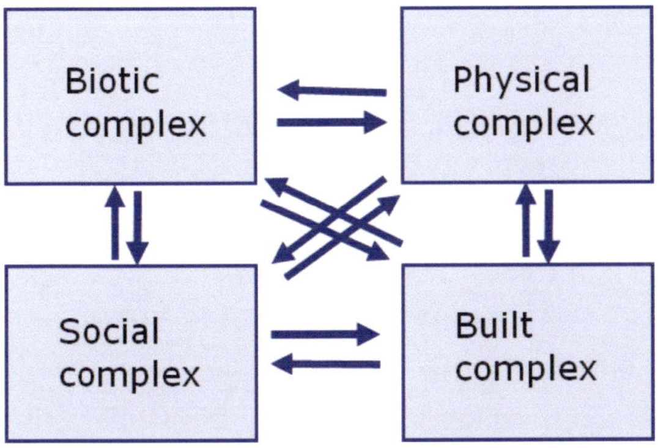

Figure 2.2 Ecological systems: A classic model.

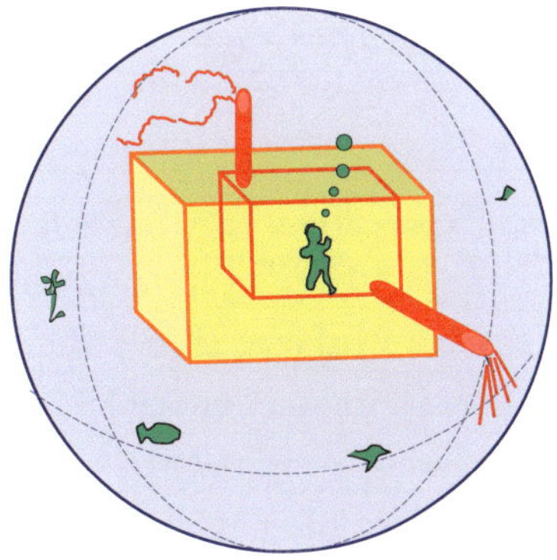

Figure 2.3 Nested subsystems.

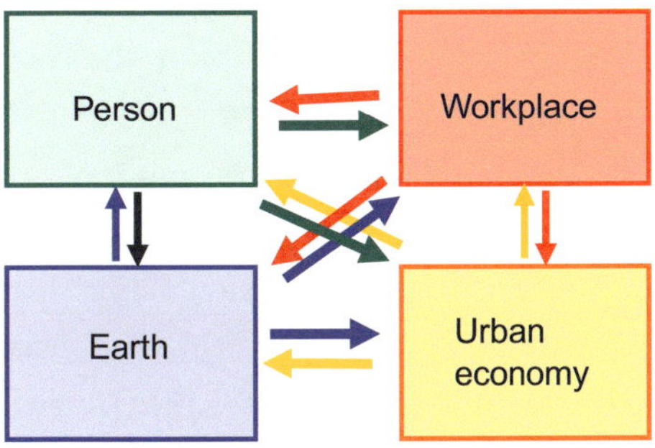

Figure 2.4 Ecological systems: An alternative model.

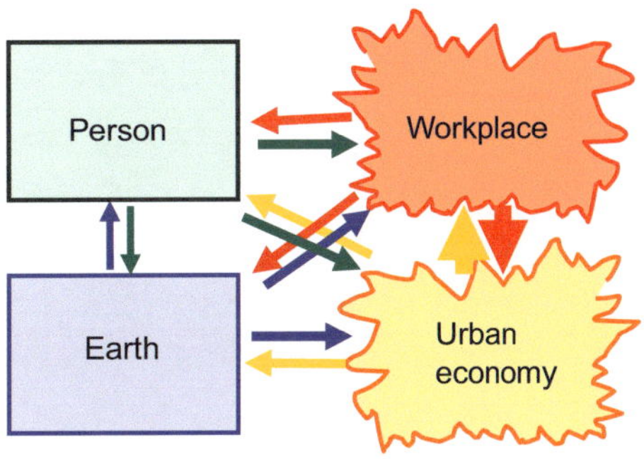

Figure 2.5 Growth trends in each subsystem.

Sources: The classic model (Figure 2.2) is drawn from Steward T.A. Pickett, Geoffrey L. Buckley, Sujay S. Kaushal, and Yvette Williams, "Social-Ecological Science in the Humane Metropolis," *Urban Ecosystems* 14, no. 3 (September 2011): 325. The alternative model (Figure 2.4) is taken from Sherry Olson, "An Ecology of Workplace Hazards," *Economic Geography* 55, no. 4 (October 1979): 30.

Some other parts of the system – the factory or the department store, the city or a particular neighbourhood – have meanwhile grown much faster, as suggested in Figure 2.5. In the 1840s, when so much of the Square Mile was garden or orchard, most of the city's workplaces operated at the scale of a household – storefront, bake oven, attic, or stable – and the tools most people handled were simple extensions of their own muscle power. Little by little, as more lots were occupied, Square Milers participated in more partnerships, and some of their corporate ventures grew ten- or twentyfold: a larger pool of capital, a larger workforce, heavier equipment, a bigger building. Consumption of energy in the workplaces multiplied, and traffic between them accelerated. What happened to the sound levels? To the circulation of wastes? The flow in the river? The schedules of work and play? The probabilities of encounter?

To situate the buildings of the Square Mile in relation to the rest of the city (ROC), we use a scaffolding of data from project MAP. The streets of the Square Mile, so sparse in 1846 (Figure 2.6), show a degree of isolation from the ROC,[5] while the denser web of streets in 1880 (Figure 2.7) carries heavier vehicles and more trips. For social interactions of all kinds, the street network is of formidable importance, connecting everybody to everybody else, just as the nervous system connects all the parts of the human body. In the "space syntax" proposed by Bill Hillier, "the fundamental correlate of the spatial configuration is movement."[6]

Networks of the 1840s

When Montreal was refounded and rechartered in 1840, the streets were the sole "public property" of the City, and their development was the raison d'être of the municipal corporation. The City invested in building streets to the limit of its authority, and private investments in toll roads extended supply lines into the countryside. Every spring for thirty years, Stanley Bagg, merchant and principal investor in the toll roads, sent his brother Abner to purchase flour, pork, and beef, each year a little further westward into the Great Lakes country. Much of the produce moved by canals, with high-risk transfers and processing in the mill towns of Ontario and New York State. Some of it was contracted to the British Army, some they forwarded to British ports, and some was destined for the public markets of Montreal.[7] In the decade of the 1840s, steam and the telegraph halved the time and cost of that traffic and increased the frequency and reliability of the news residents received from London, New York City, the war in Texas, and the goldfields of California and New South Wales. Closer to home, new forms of waste and debris accumulated, dumped in the harbour or a quarry.

Although the street grid was still sparse, social networks were already elaborate and fast evolving. Figure 2.8 illustrates a common routine for mutual support. At the semi-annual auction of stalls in the public markets, the butchers signed as guarantors for one another – sometimes a brother-in-law, often a neighbour renting the adjacent stall.

Using the same approach, I compiled from the city's business directory (1845–8) 115 little networks made up of the officers or directors of organizations such as the Bank of Montreal, the city council, masonic lodges, and the St. Andrew's Society. Included are some institutions that would come to flourish in the Square Mile: McGill College, half a dozen Presbyterian churches, the Natural History Society,

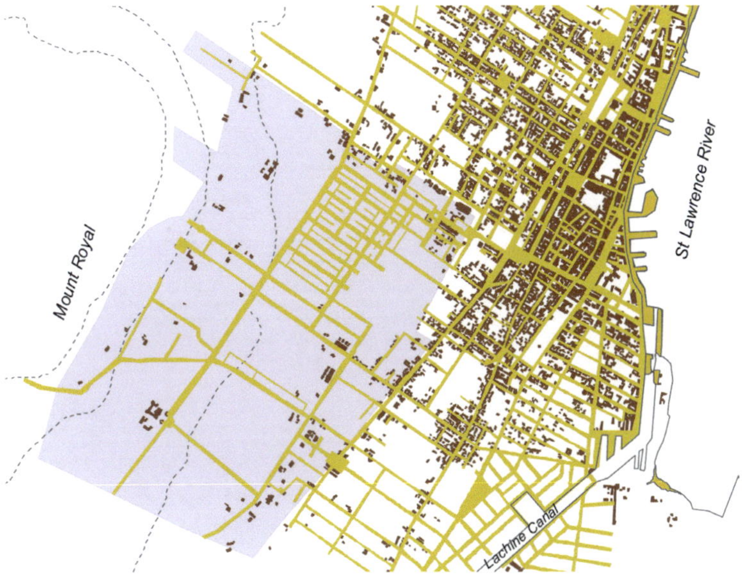

Figure 2.6 Street layout and building footprints in the Square Mile, 1846. The shaded Square Mile (MAP districts 12 and 10) is defined by the high rent levels. Its boundaries roughly match the topographic unit discussed in chapters 1 and 7 of this volume.

Sources: GeoBase MAP, redrawn from James Cane, *Topographical and Pictorial Map of the City of Montreal* (Montreal: Robert W.S. Mackay, 1846). For each street, the median value of household rents was calculated from the City of Montreal tax roll of June 1848.

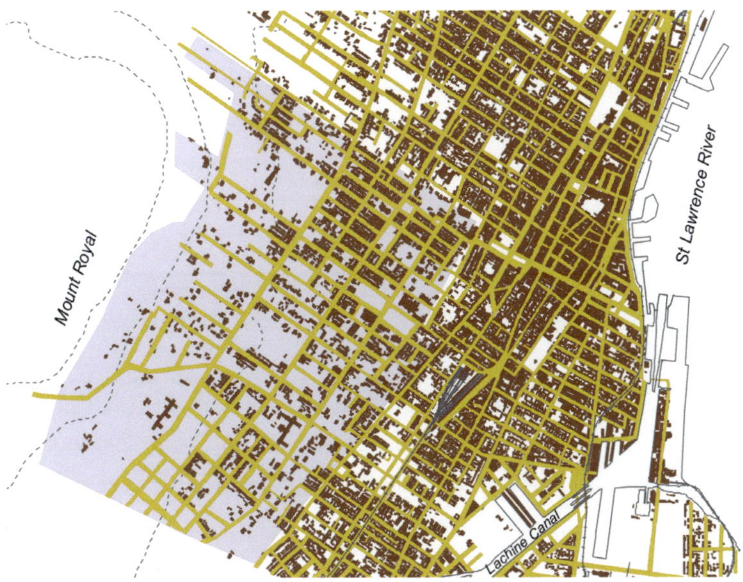

Figure 2.7 Street layout and building footprints in the Square Mile, 1881.

Sources: GeoBase MAP; Charles E. Goad, *Atlas of the City of Montreal* (Montreal: Charles E. Goad, 1881); City of Montreal tax roll of June 1880.

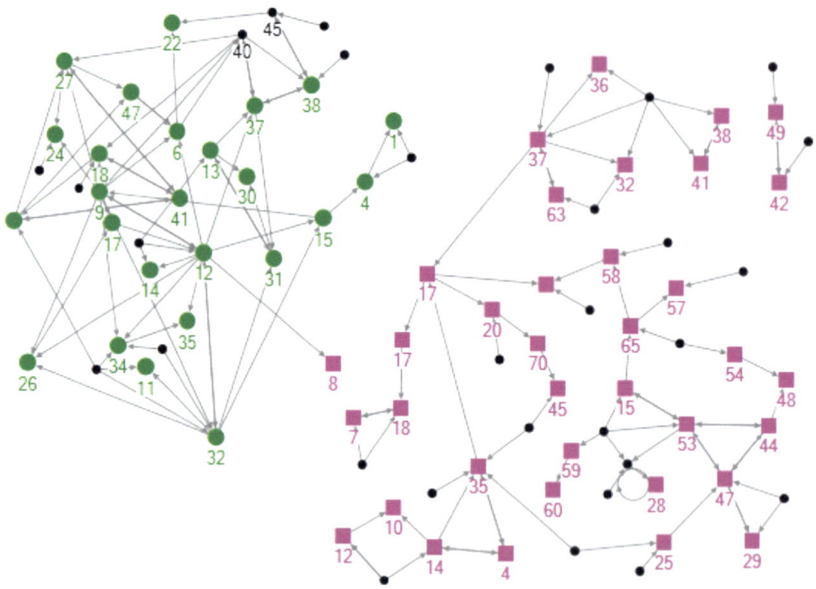

Figure 2.8 Butchers and their pledges, 1848, with stall numbers in St. Ann's Market (left, green dots) and Bonsecours Market (right, pink squares).

Sources: Compiled from BAnQ, Greffes de notaires, Repertory of William Ross, auctions of the leases of February and August 1848.

and the Art Association. There are many ways to lay out such a diagram, but every method shows the structural features apparent in Figure 2.9: a great rift between networks of Catholic and Protestant organizations and between French- and English-speaking societies, tight interlocks among board members of the several banks, and an especially dense cluster of proselytizing Protestant societies. A few distinctive bridging figures can be discerned, notably the Mechanics' Institute, the St. Patrick's Society, and the architect entrepreneur John Ostell, born in England, married into a Patriote family, and both a city surveyor and consultant to the Sulpician Seminary.[8]

Like the butchers, the bankers activated their connections as guarantors of financial responsibility. The Montreal Provident and Savings' Bank, for example, created in 1841 to promote thrift among small wage earners, was managed by twenty-two men whose credit was grounded in substantial ownership of real estate. Rumours started a run on the bank on 30 June 1848, and it closed on 14 July of that same year. Three years later, a legislative commission of inquiry reported the history of the bank's startling negligence. The manager and directors had allowed themselves,

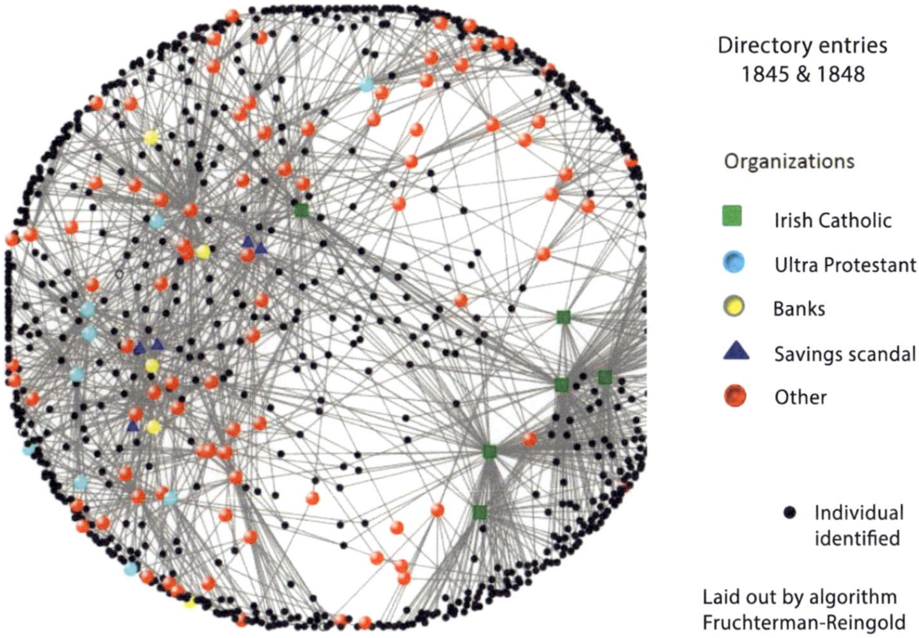

Figure 2.9 A network of social organizations in 1840s Montreal. Symbols in colour identify the 115 societies identified in city directories, with the black points identifying the 1,100 men named as their directors or executives. Only forty-two individuals were key players, ensuring multiple links among organizations. Those who appear in a single role are thrown to the periphery.

Sources: Data compiled from the front matter of R.S. Mackay, *The Montreal Business Directory* (Montreal: John Lovell, 1842–8), seven editions of which are accessible online from BAnQ; supplemented from R.D. Wadsworth, *The Family Christian Almanac* (Montreal, 1847–8); and *The Montreal Almanac; or, Lower Canada Register* (Montreal: James Starke and Company, 1845).

their relatives, their business partners, and their political allies to make deposits over the £300 limit authorized by the bank's own charter, to borrow without providing security for repayment, and to neglect daily entries in the ledger and annual balancing of accounts. The unsecured loans had financed real estate speculation on Beaver Hall Hill, construction of the (Protestant) High School of Montreal, and construction of numerous Protestant churches, several of them under the supervision of William Footner as architect. In the closing-out of accounts in July and August of 1848, the large depositors had been paid first, while delays imposed on small accounts had shifted the losses to the popular class for whom the institution was initially created.[9]

Those who benefitted directly from the manipulations included 40 of the city's 100 largest property owners. Among the directors of the bank were board members of the High School, whose loans were never repaid, board members of the Bank of British North America, where the savings were supposed to be deposited at the end of each day, and board members of the Montreal Fire Insurance Company, who in the next room sold the borrower a policy. Mayor James Ferrier was a director on all four boards as well as a major investor in the new railways and the New City Gas Company. He was a pillar of the Royal Institution for the Advancement of Learning (McGill College), the Methodist church, the Bible Society, and the Sabbath Observance Society.[10] In the violent election of March 1846, Ferrier was a candidate in St. Lawrence Ward, and in his role as mayor he commanded both the troops and the police.[11] The Savings' Bank scandal was smothered, but the relationships documented in the inquiry point to contributing factors in the structure of the social network: the isolation of three cultural communities, smaller cliques within each, the corporate interlocks, the strength of kinship ties, the power of property over the municipal corporation, and the uniquely powerful alliances of Ferrier.

About the time the Montreal Provident and Savings' Bank and the municipal corporation were founded, Proudhon had asked his famous question, "Qu'est-ce que la propriété?" (What is property?).[12] A house and lot in Montreal earned an income, of course, but rarely more than the legal interest rate. Property offered something more: stature, security, and voice – that is, the right to vote and hold office. (The qualification for city councillor was £500 and for mayor £1000.) Property could secure a construction loan or the purchase of additional properties; it grounded entry into a partnership, a marriage, or a corporate venture. *Urban* property had a further peculiar advantage: its value increased as the city grew. The municipal corporation, entirely dependent on the real estate tax to support its street-making operations, was as eager as the property owners to see the values rise. The large property owners; the bankers, speculators, and industrialists; and the mayor and city councillors were therefore collaborators in a "growth machine" that generated the unearned increment in each boom: "Il suffit d'attendre la marée" (Just wait for the tide to come in).[13] It generated, as well, a psychological increment: owning property engendered a sense of entitlement. The more you owned, and the more valuable it became, the more you were entitled to.

Networks of the 1880s

To keep the story within bounds, we now make a leap to 1880. The value of the largest personal fortunes had multiplied: Harrison Stephens, $400,000 in real estate within the city limits; Hugh Allan, $300,000; and on their heels William Dow, the Molsons, the Josephs, the Redpaths, and the Drummonds. Some, already wealthy in the 1840s, had enjoyed windfalls during the American Civil War (1861–5), Stephens by moving Confederate cotton; W.C. Macdonald by importing tobacco from Confederate and border states, processing it in Montreal, and then re-exporting it to the Union; and many others in the finance of blockade runners who loaded cargo in Montreal for transshipment in the Bahamas.[14] Keeping their offices close to the waterfront, those large capitalists were now among the 6 per cent of Montrealers who made their homes in the Square Mile and owned one-quarter of the property (by value) in the entire city. The same roster appears as the major stockholders in the chartered banks, and all of them were now sizable owners and directors of limited liability corporations. Their profit-oriented companies owned one in twenty properties in the city, and the large values recorded on the tax roll reflected large industrial plants such as the gas works and foundries, a ten-storey sugar refinery, and the curious appraisal of $755,000 for the tracks and yards of the Grand Trunk Railway.[15] Beyond the city limits, in Saint-Gabriel, were their railway shops, and in Saint-Henri and Hochelaga their cotton textile mills.[16] Local ownership gave little hint of the more distant assets – the western lands with which the railways were endowed, the mines and foundries that supplied them with coal and iron, and their spectacular stations, warehouses, chateau-style hotels, and the emerging clusters of summer resorts in Memphremagog, Cacouna, Banff, and St. Andrews.

The strategic importance of transport is evident in the local movements of striking ship labourers, as reported in the *Montreal Daily Star* on Monday, 27 June 1881: "The SS *Scotland* was looked upon as the great bone of contention, she having been unloaded with imported men and a strong armed force." By Saturday, 2 July 1881, "[t]hree of the Allan Line steamships, the *Sardinian*, *Grecian* and *Lucerne*, had arrived in port," and on 6 July, "[f]orty Union men [were] engaged in unloading the SS *Tintern Abbey*, although they were brutally beaten while on their way home." The next day it was reported that the strike was "weakening," but on 8 July, 1,000 labourers had assembled in Papineau Square, ready to "rush" the docks where ships were being unloaded: at the old Quebec Gate barracks, the SS *Viking* of the Ross Line and the SS *Cynthia* of the Donaldson Line, and at Victoria pier the SS *Lake Manitoba*. "Here fixed sword bayonets drove them from the pier towards the revetment wall." Moving west and south towards the Dominion sheds, they made a rush towards the SS *Teutonia* where "[p]olice fired with their new Colt revolvers."

At the Montreal hearings of the Royal Commission on Labour and Capital in February 1887, Square Milers were interrogated as large employers. The new scale of operations had changed the rhythm of the economy. Trains ran night and day; electric arc lights introduced in 1880 "enabled vessels to load by night." In the sugar refinery, workers were hired on a twelve-hour night shift and a ten-hour day shift, paid at the same hourly rate. In the shoe factories and manufactures of nails and bolts, the new machines set the pace of the worker. Testimony on waterfront labour shows how corporate bureaucracy distanced owners and financiers from operations on the ground. The Allan Line of steamships entered 20 per cent of tonnage to the port, but "independent" stevedoring firms selected the crews of labourers, wrote the contracts, and collected the obligatory fees for accident insurance, financed by another company in which Hugh Allan held controlling shares. The paymaster of the Allan Line claimed, "I have nothing to do with the wharf." When questioned on practices of withholding wages, he responded, "Our lawyer looks after the garnishees."[17]

The hearings made more visible the interlocks among corporations. Members of the Allan family were also large owners and strategists involved in the expansion of Canadian Rubber, Montreal Rolling Mills, the Williams Manufacturing Company, and Montreal Warehousing. David Morrice, who controlled thirty-five textile mills, was one of the first to install a home telephone, connecting him with the downtown offices and the shippers. The Royal Commission inquired into the more discreet agreements among corporations, such as the Dominion-wide pricing of sugar, but gave remarkably little attention to the FIRE sector – finance, insurance, and real estate – strategic in pyramids of control. Owners and managers of the FIRE firms were tightly interlocked and residentially concentrated in the Square Mile.

The telephone system, new in 1880, stimulated prompt creation of ambulance services, whose registers offer some cues for connecting the dots. Where did the accident happen? To whom? Where did the injured party live? Who paid the 80 cents a day for the hospital bed? The most frequent pickup points were the railway yards, the docks, the foundries, the rubber factory, the gas company, and the two sugar refineries.[18] In each of those giant-sized workplaces, "friends" paid the ambulance driver on the spot; fellow employees passed the hat annually for the Montreal General Hospital; and a contribution of the employer (lifetime governor at $5) entitled the victim to a bed. Hospitals began investing in aseptic procedure for amputations and surgical repairs. For the new Royal Victoria Hospital, Lords Strathcona (Donald Smith) and Mount Stephen (George Stephen) each gave $1 million. They were cousins and joint financiers of the Canadian Pacific Railway syndicate.

To Square Milers themselves, contagion was more worrying than accident. The insidious threat of sewer gas was dramatized in a map plotting the combined death rate from three infectious diseases: smallpox, diphtheria, and typhoid fever (Figure 2.10). Published in the *Montreal Daily Witness* at the initiative of two of the city's most distinguished scientists, the map drew attention to the "saturated

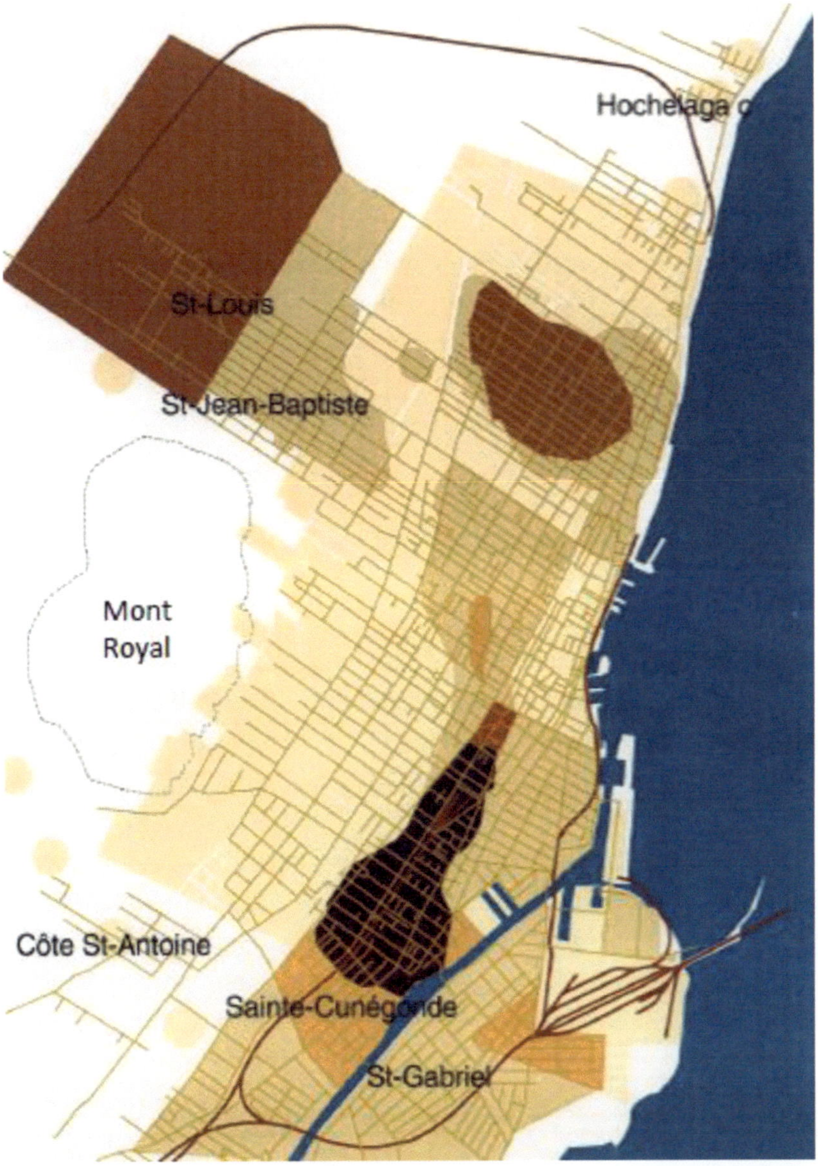

Figure 2.10 "Health Map," redrawn by the author from the *Montreal Daily Witness*, 22 November 1879, p. 3. Shading reflects the combined death rate, 1876–1878, from three diseases.

ground" bordering the Square Mile on the southeast. Since none of the three diseases was actually spread by sewer gas, the map was somewhat misleading.[19] Discussion of the plumber's trap and vent was a response to the new germ theory as well as to old anxieties of summer complaint, putrid smells, childhood vulnerability, and easily revived fears of the Other – the unwashed, the unvaccinated, or the unconverted.

Authorship of the map for the *Witness* invites a detour into the kinship network of the Square Mile. One of its two authors, J.W. Dawson, geologist and principal of McGill University, had just hired the other author, Henry Taylor Bovey, as the university's chair of Civil Engineering and Applied Mechanics. Bovey was about to marry Emily Jane, a daughter of John Redpath and aunt to John Dougall, editor of the *Witness*. Dawson, meanwhile, tempted by an offer from Princeton University, was influenced to stay at McGill by the offer of Peter Redpath (Emily Jane's older brother) to build and endow a museum of natural history.[20] The anecdote reminds us of the persistent power of the kinship network, in which many of Montreal's corporate initiatives were grounded. By pooling their capital and limiting their liability, Square Milers achieved a longer reach, faster circulation, and more rigorous assignment of "place" and priority.

Networks of 1913

The decade before the First World War was the heyday of the Square Mile.[21] At the time of the 1901 census, its households averaged twice as many rooms per person as the rest of the city and hired ten times as many live-in servants. The district housed twice as many accountants, bookkeepers, and travelling salesmen as we might expect as well as (in 1900) a high proportion of the city's volunteers for the War in South Africa, many of them inspired by the $1 million Lord Strathcona gave for a private cavalry unit and by the promotional work and $1-million pledge of Hugh Graham, publisher of the *Montreal Star*. The first-year membership of the Mount Royal Club (1899) shows the strong continuities of Square Mile wealth: Strathcona, Drummond and a son, Morrice, Baumgarten, Macdonald, Shaughnessy, Holt, two Molsons, and Angus with a son and two sons-in-law are all accounted for. The biography of each of these men shows a bright side in go-ahead and ingenuity and a dark side in the ruthlessness of the growth machine.

In 1904, Square Milers proposed drawing a red line around their turf. It would outline precisely the network of high-rent streets displayed in Figure 2.11. By excluding industry, the zoning proposal would protect their homes from the risks their own enterprises had created: the flammables, the germs, the clatter, the fumes, the alcohol, and the mobs of strikers. They did not, in fact, enact the proposed regulation for another decade, instead relying on the individualist strategy of exodus. The offspring of families who had moved onto the New Town and Redpath terraces in the 1850s and 1860s were now moving further west along the slopes of Mount Royal. Some leapfrogged beyond the city limit into a sphere

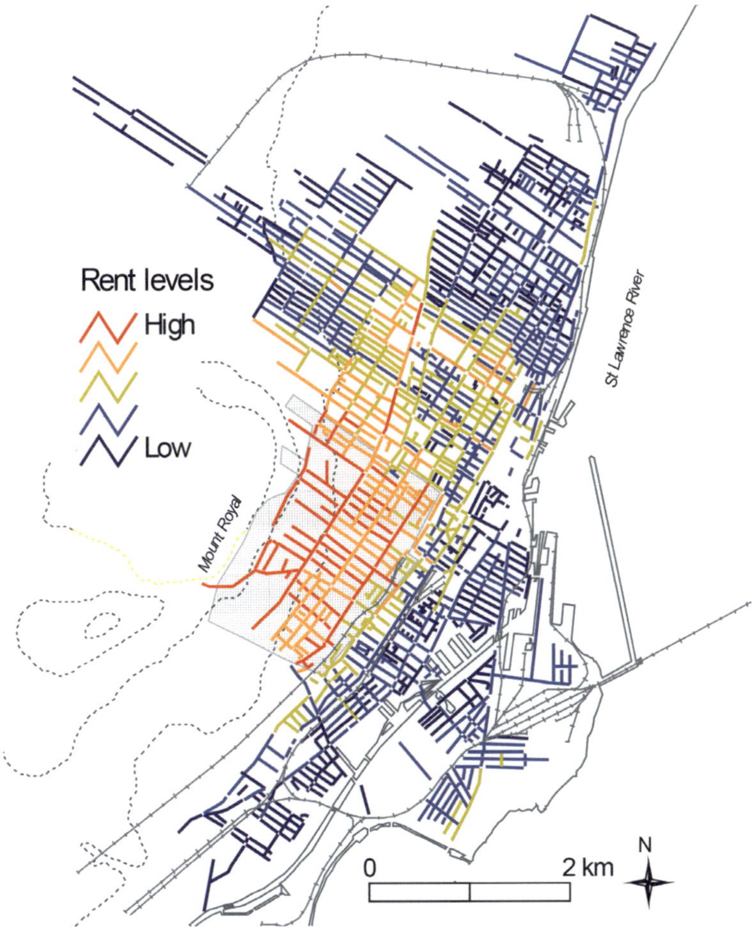

Figure 2.11 Rent levels in residential streets of central Montreal, 1904. The middling category (gold) results from the presence of both high- and low-rent occupants in higher-traffic streets. Such streets had professional offices and shops of various sizes, with upstairs dwellings for the owner, a clerk, or a caretaker.

Sources: GeoBase MAP, using rents reported in assessment roll of occupants, Ville de Montréal, June 1900. Street segments (twin block-faces) were classed for homogeneity by David Hanna and Robert Lewis.

of tighter control – Côte Saint-Antoine, the village renamed Westmount in 1895 and chartered as an independent city in 1908.[22] There was a perceptible trend to younger families moving, but in the Square Mile, too, new structures offered new lifestyles: elegant flats with elevator access and garage for the motorcar, for instance.[23]

In the seven fat years of a building boom, or in the transfer of power from one generation to the next, how did the entrepreneurial networks of Square Milers

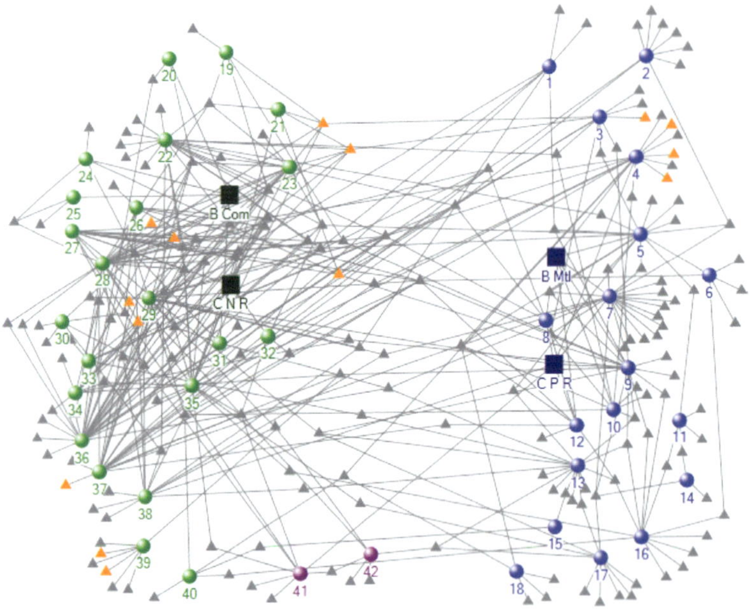

Figure 2.12 Interlocks among the directors of 204 of Canada's largest enterprises in 1913. Blue spheres (on the right) represent the capitalists based in Montreal, green (on the left) those in Toronto, violet those in Winnipeg. Individuals are identified by number in Table 2.1. Four large squares mark the flagship enterprises of the two groups: at left, the Bank of Commerce and the Canadian Northern Railway (Mackenzie and Mann); at right, the Bank of Montreal and the Canadian Pacific Railway. Their fourteen fast-growing ventures in the Caribbean and Central and South America are shown in orange. Grey triangles represent 173 other firms they directed or managed.

Source: *Grain Growers' Guide*, 25 June 1913, compiled from the published balance sheets of the 204 companies. Graphic by the author using NodeXL.

morph? Their connections can be traced through the architects they hired, the engineers, the law firms, or the firms of accountants.[24] The best-documented clues are the corporate directorships. Gilles Piédalue, in his analysis of the dynamics of the early twentieth century, drew links between corporations based on the number of board members and officers they shared.[25] In Figure 2.12, a rough snapshot for 1913, I have drawn the network to focus on the personalities based on counts published in the *Grain Growers' Guide*, whose editors asserted that forty-two men – "the aristocracy of wealth" – controlled one-third of the financial and industrial assets of Canada. Prominent in their estimate of $4.2 billion are members of the FIRE sector, which controlled the horizon of investment and the rail and navigation companies that controlled its geographic deployment.[26]

Table 2.1 Highest-status directors of Canadian corporations in 1913

Key	Toronto-based	Degree	Between	Key	Montreal-based	Degree	Between
19	Mann, D. Donald	5	263	1	Angus, R.B	7	697
20	Flavelle, J.W.	3	13	2	Curry, Nathaniel	9	1,419
21	Horne-Payne, R.M.	5	68	3	Allan, Hugh Montagu	11	1,151
22	Pellatt, Henry	21	2,518	4	Van Horne, William	16	2,431
23	Lash, Z.A.	15	797	5	Holt, Herbert S.	17	3,032
24	Walker, Edmund	5	380	6	Greenshields, E.B.	6	1,021
25	Jones, Lyman	3	235	7	MacKay, Robert	21	3,380
26	Jaffray, Robert	9	497	8	McGibbon, D. Lorne	5	217
27	Nicholls, Frederic	14	1,541	9	Hosmer, Charles R.	18	3,758
28	Wood, E.R.	23	1,540	10	Drummond, George E.	9	859
29	Matthews, Wilmot D.	18	2,301	11	Shaughnessy, Thos	5	602
30	Wilkie, D.R.	6	499	12	Strathcona (Smith)	8	738
31	Edwards, W.B.	5	398	13	Drummond, Thomas J.	15	2,294
32	Mulock, Cawthra	4	270	14	Gordon, Charles B.	3	416
33	Plummer, J.H.	8	518	15	McNicholl, D.	2	39
34	Morrow, George A.	10	629	16	Forget, Rodolphe	12	1,596
35	Hanna, D.B.	16	1,949	17	Ewing, S.H.	10	1,385
36	Cox, George A.	29	3,726	18	Ross, James	5	723
37	Mackenzie, William	29	3,134				
38	Osler, Edmund B.	13	1,385	**Key**	**Winnipeg-based**	**Degree**	**Between**
39	Moore, S.J.	7	1,371	41	Whyte, William	8	859
40	Meighen, Frank S.	5	629	42	Nanton, A.M.	6	651

Notes: Entries are ordered to match the nodes of Figure 2.12, Toronto associates on the left, Montreal associates on the right, numbered from top to bottom, with graph measures of degree and betweenness centrality. Degree is simply the number of seats the individual occupied as president, general manager, or corporate director.

Source: Data from *Grain Growers' Guide*, 25 June 1913. Graph measures calculated by the author using NodeXL.

The forty-two capitalists formed a connected network, "sympathetically allied," but which fell into two distinct groups, one based in Montreal, the other in Toronto. The former, according to the editors of *Grain Growers' Guide*, was older and stronger; its nineteen members lived in the Square Mile or its Westmount extension. The fifteen directors of the Canadian Pacific Railway were all directors of the Bank of Montreal, whose combined assets amounted to over $1 billion. Visible on Figure 2.12 are sunbursts of connectivity surrounding the richest and most powerful individuals, identified in Table 2.1. The same individuals – Hosmer, Mackay, Holt, Van Horne, and T. Drummond – also show highest "betweenness" (a measure of their strategic positions as links between clusters) with the Toronto group.[27]

Some kinships had persisted since the 1840s, others emerged as the "newly rich."[28] The attention of the *Grain Growers' Guide* reflects the surge of wheat exports in the Laurier years and farmers' resistance to what they termed "the triple alliance" of railway, banking, and manufacturing interests. Expansion of corporate assets coincided with the spectacular industrial mergers Max Aitken manoeuvred in Montreal: Canada Cement, Canadian Car and Foundry, and the Steel Company of Canada.[29] The corporations had reached unprecedented size, obtained control of new mineral resources, and created sizable beachheads offshore. They had also acquired the privileges of "a moral person," entitling them to the protections of freedom of action, privacy, speech, and silence.

Conclusion

The three moments selected (the 1846 hearings on the Savings' Bank scandal, the Royal Commission of 1887, and the 1913 estimates of the Grain Growers) illustrate the dramatic expansion of the limited liability corporation, that thick-walled cell whose mission is growth. Today, a smaller share of Canadian wealth is lodged in the Square Mile. The metropolitan road network, extended and costly, shows suburban curves and dramatically lighted multistoried interchanges. The kinship networks are less visible, and the personal connections to the corporate assets are largely anonymized. But the growth machine is unchecked. The scale of corporate assets surges. From the 1913 bases in FIRE, utilities, and goldmines, Canadians' offshore assets have expanded beyond measure. Concentration of personal wealth diminished in the 1930s and again in the 1950s but is today restored to 1913 levels.[30]

To understand a system – a wave of corporate mergers, transmission of a virus, or the heat exchange of ocean and atmosphere – the scientists of the 1850s taught us to observe the inputs and outputs to the mechanism hidden in the puzzling "black box." The engineer and fireman on Ferrier's 1842 locomotive tested and managed the relation between the shovel, the throttle, and the steam gauge. The baby experiments the same way with a crib toy: push, pull, shake, wiggle it, bite it, watch, and listen.[31] The responses of the engine or the toy provide cues to interpret its behaviour. From the historical behaviour we figure out how the system works.

According to the pre-eminent historian Lord Acton, at home in the operations of the Roman Empire as well as the British, "Power corrupts, and absolute power corrupts absolutely." Shall we infer that the Square Mile housed a unique concentration of corruption? Like Bovey and Dawson, the city's nineteenth-century doctors and preachers were preoccupied with the problem of corruption – corruption of the water supply, corruption of the funds, corruption of the body politic and of the human soul.[32] Their neighbours in the polished pews of the Square Mile were familiar with the words of the Pilgrim: "Sin and corruption, I said, would as naturally bubble out of my heart as water would bubble out of a fountain."[33] As historians, how shall we trace the percolation of so many streams of corruption, their periodic overflows, and the resurgence in our own generation?

NOTES

1 On the MAP: Montréal l'avenir du passé project more generally, see chapter 7 in this volume by Robert C.H. Sweeny. For additional interactive graphics, see https://mun.ca/mapm; and https://schemamontreal.uqam.ca/projets/montreal-en-1881.

2 Sherry Olson, "Downwind, Downstream, Downtown: The Environmental Legacy in Baltimore and Montreal," *Journal of Environmental History* 12, no. 4 (October 2007): 857, https://doi.org/10.1093/envhis/12.4.845.

3 Steward T.A. Pickett, Geoffrey L. Buckley, Sujay S. Kaushal, and Yvette Williams, "Social-Ecological Science in the Humane Metropolis," *Urban Ecosystems* 14, no. 3 (September 2011): 319–39, https://doi.org/10.1007/s11252-011-0166-7.

4 We could of course extend the nesting to yet smaller subsystems and larger ones.

5 In fact, James Cane's *Topographical and Pictorial Map of the City of Montreal* (1846) exaggerates the streeting of the Square Mile: some streets were not yet built.

6 Bill Hillier, *Space Is the Machine: A Configurational Theory of Architecture* (New York: Cambridge University Press, 1996).

7 The Bagg brothers lived outside the Square Mile, but their ledgers and correspondence in the McCord Museum provide remarkable detail of the pace of commerce experienced by other merchants such as Harrison Stephens and the Ogilvies.

8 On Ostell as an example of "the wearing of double hats, insider action and conflicts of interest," see Brian Young, *In Its Corporate Capacity: The Seminary of Montreal as a Business Institution, 1816–1876* (Montreal: McGill-Queen's University Press, 1986).

9 Report of 21 June 1851 of the Commissioners of Inquiry, *Journals of the Legislative Assembly of the Province of Canada*, vol. 10, 4th session (Quebec: R. Campbell, 1851), Appendix QQ. The sole newspaper that published the report was *The True Witness and Catholic Chronicle*, 22 and 29 April and 6 May 1853. The episode is glossed over in the biographies of those involved; only John Redpath assumed some responsibility for the subsequent decade of payments.

10 Gerald J.J. Tulchinsky, "Ferrier, James," in *Dictionary of Canadian Biography*, vol. 11, University of Toronto/Université Laval, 2003–, accessed 9 February 2023, http://www.biographi.ca/en/bio/ferrier_james_11E.html; Guillaume Sellier, "Itinéraire d'une collection Égyptienne: Le 'Grand Tour' de James Ferrier en Égypte (1859)," *Revue Histoire, Idées, Société* (2018), https://revuehis.uqam.ca/non-classe/itineraire-dune-collection-egyptienne-grand-tour-de-james-ferrier-egypte-1859.

11 Kinship ties prominent in the Savings' Bank affair were Ferrier's sons and his son-in-law; the Footners, father and son; and John Mathewson and his son. On the election violence, see Appendix EEE and Appendix AA to the fifth volume of appendices to the *Journals of the Legislative Assembly of the Province of Canada*, vol. 5, 2nd session (Montreal: R. Campbell, 1846); and Colin Grittner, "Of Bludgeons and Ballots: Political Violence, Municipal Enfranchisement, and Local Governance in Mid-Nineteenth-Century Montreal," in *Violence, Order, and Unrest: A History of British North America, 1749–1876*, ed. Elizabeth Mancke et al. (Toronto: University of Toronto Press, 2019), 327–50.

12 Pierre-Joseph Proudhon, *Qu'est-ce que la propriété?* (Paris: M. Augé-Laribé, 1840).
13 Maurice Halbwachs, *La population et les tracés de voies à Paris depuis cent ans* (Paris: Presses Universitaires de France, 1928), 10. Proudhon referred to it as *l'aubaine*, the great bargain. See also George Simmel, *The Philosophy of Money*, ed. David Frisby, 3rd ed. (London: Routledge, 2004), 217; Harvey Molotch, "The City as a Growth Machine: Toward a Political Economy of Place," *American Journal of Sociology* 82, no. 2 (1976): 309–32; Paul-André Linteau, *The Promoters' City: Building the Industrial Town of Maisonneuve 1883–1918* (Toronto: James Lorimer, 2000).
14 Barry Sheehy, *Montreal City of Secrets: Confederate Operations in Montreal during the American Civil War* (Montreal: Baraka Books, 2017).
15 See Robert C.H. Sweeny, *Why Did We Choose to Industrialize? Montreal, 1819–1849* (Montreal: McGill-Queen's University Press, 2015), 301; and chapter 7 in this volume.
16 Robert Lewis, *Manufacturing Montreal: The Making of an Industrial Landscape, 1850–1930* (Baltimore: Johns Hopkins University Press, 2000).
17 Royal Commission on the Relations of Labor and Capital, *Report of the Royal Commission on the Relations of Labor and Capital in Canada*. Vol. 5, Part 1, *Evidence, Quebec* (Ottawa: Queen's Printer, 1889).
18 For maps of telephones and ambulance pickups, see Sherry Olson, "Setting the Census Household into Its Urban Context: Visualizations from 19th-Century Montreal," *Demographic Research* 36 (2017): 1399–434, https://doi.org/10.4054/DemRes.2017.36.46.
19 Vaccination already offered full protection against smallpox; diphtheria is a droplet infection, antitoxin yet to come; control of typhoid outbreaks would require management of water and milk supplies. On the politics of sewer gas, see Nancy Tomes, "The Private Side of Public Health: Sanitary Science, Domestic Hygiene, and the Germ Theory, 1870–1900," *Bulletin of the History of Medicine* 64, no. 4 (Winter 1990): 509–39.
20 John Redpath's eldest daughter Elizabeth married John Dougall, founder of the *Montreal Daily Witness*, in 1840; the 1879 editor of the paper was their son George. The adjacent houses of the younger Dougall and Francis Redpath on Ontario Avenue were designed by A.T. Taylor. Francis was half-brother to Elizabeth and uncle to Amy Redpath (featured in chapter 6 of this volume by Elizabeth Kirkland and Mary Anne Poutanen). The Redpath Museum was inaugurated in 1882.
21 See chapter 12 in this volume by Harold Bérubé.
22 Pioneers in Côte Saint-Antoine included John Young, John Ogilvie, and Albert Furniss, as well as three figures central to the Savings' Bank affair: William Footner, John Eadie, and William Murray of the Beaver Line shipping company. Roy Wolvin (featured in chapter 10 of this volume by M. Stephen Salmon) was also important in the Westmount's prewar surge of growth.
23 For a single exclusive apartment house, The Chateau, on the northwest corner of Sherbrooke and Mountain Streets, see Ken Johnstone, "Montreal's Impeccable Home for the Well-To-Do," *Macleans*, 16 July 1960. In Toronto, Sherbourne Methodist Church was regarded as a comparable socio-cultural node; see Neil Semple, *The Lord's Dominion: The History of Canadian Methodism*, vol. 1 (Montreal: McGill-Queen's University Press, 1995), 337.
24 See Annmarie Adams, chapter 9 in this volume, as well as the vignettes by Julia Gersovitz; and Robert C.H. Sweeny, "Building for Power: The Maxwell Practice and the Montreal Business Community," in *The Architecture of Edward and W.S. Maxwell*, ed. Irena Murray, Daniella Rohan, and David McKnight (Montreal: Montreal Museum of Fine Arts, 1991), 35–9.
25 Gilles Piédalue, "Les groupes financiers au Canada, 1900–1930, une étude préliminaire," *Revue d'histoire de l'Amérique française* 30, no. 1 (June 1976): 3–34.

26 The estimates were based on paid-up stock. The silver dollar minted in 2013 for the centennial of the Canadian Arctic Expedition was worth about twenty-five of those 1913 dollars. Between 1842 and 1903, effects of inflation can be ignored; increase was modest in the decade 1903–13.

27 On betweenness centrality, see Jon Mackay, "Canadian Regional and National Business Elites in 1912: Who Was Connected, Who Wasn't and Why?," in *A History of Socially Responsible Business, c. 1600–1950*, ed. William A. Pettigrew and David C. Smith (Cham: Palgrave Macmillan, 2017), 189–212. Mackay's analysis, grounded in W.R. Houston's *Directory of Directors in Canada* (1912), bores deeper into local networks of the smaller cities. See also Claire Lemercier, "Formal Network Methods in History: Why and How?," in *Social Networks, Political Institutions, and Rural Societies*, ed. George Fertig (Turnhout: Brepols, 2015), 281–310; and Derek L. Hansen, Ben Schneiderman, and Marc A. Smith, *Analyzing Social Media Networks with NodeXL: Insights from a Connected World* (Burlington, MA: Morgan Kaufmann, 2011).

28 The Drummond fortune tallied in 1913 belonged to Thomas J. Drummond and his brother George E. Drummond, associate of J.T. McCall, suppliers of iron to Montreal foundries, rolling mills, car wheels, and nails. Robert Tremblay, "Drummond, George Edward," in *Dictionary of Canadian Biography*, vol. 14, University of Toronto/Université Laval, 2003–, accessed 9 February 2023, http://www.biographi.ca/en/bio/drummond_george_edward_14E.html.

29 See chapter 8 by Gregory P. Marchildon and chapter 10 by M. Stephen Salmon in this volume; Gregory P. Marchildon, *Profits and Politics: Beaverbrook and the Gilded Age of Canadian Finance* (Toronto: University of Toronto Press, 1996).

30 Alain Deneault, *Paradis fiscaux: La filière canadienne* (Montreal: Éditions Écosociété, 2014); Thomas Piketty, *Une brève histoire de l'égalité* (Paris: Éditions du Seuil, 2021); Sébastien Breau, "The Occupy Movement and the Top 1% in Canada," *Antipode* 46, no. 1 (2014): 13–33; Eric W. Sager, *Inequality in Canada: The History and Politics of an Idea* (Montreal: McGill-Queen's University Press, 2021). For the resurgence of Toronto and Montreal investors in gold mines, see Daviken Studnicki-Gizbert, *The Three Deaths of Cerro de San Pedro: Four Centuries of Extractivism in a Small Mexican Mining Town* (Chapel Hill: University of North Carolina, 2022), 178–93; and for Montreal participants in the network of oil and finance, see William K. Carroll, "Canada's Carbon-Capital Elite: A Tangled Web of Corporate Power," *Canadian Journal of Sociology* 42, no. 3 (2017): 247.

31 Omer Lavallée, "Dundee-Built Locomotives on Canada's First Railways," *Railroad History* 149 (Autumn 1983): 19–50; Alison Gopnik, Andrew N. Meltzoff, and Patricia K. Kuhl, *The Scientist in the Crib: What Early Learning Tells Us about the Mind* (New York: HarperCollins, 2000).

32 J.E.E. Dalberg, Lord Acton, Letter I, Cannes, 5 April 1887, in *Acton-Creighton Correspondence* (1887), https://oll.libertyfund.org/titles/2254.

33 John Bunyan, *Grace Abounding to the Chief of Sinners* (London: Religious Tract Society, 1905), 137. Avaliable online at https://www.gutenberg.org/files/654/654-h/654-h.htm.

PART TWO

CONSTRUCTING BUSINESS NETWORKS AND INSTITUTIONS

Figure V.3 Alexander Henderson, *The Lyman House, "Thornhill," McTavish Street, Montreal*, c. 1870. McCord Museum, II-273864.0.

Widening Influences

The first architects to practise in the Square Mile were immigrants from Britain, such as John Ostell, John W. Hopkins, and William Speir. Born in the first decades of the nineteenth century, they had arrived in Montreal as young men, eager to establish their reputations. Often, they supplemented their incomes with other professional practices, such as surveying. Their design sources were uniformly English – Palladian revival at first, and then enlarged to include Greek revival detailing.

The second wave were locally born men who apprenticed in architectural offices, often belonging to their fathers, or who had trained in construction and then improved their education through night courses at the Mechanics' Institute. They included William Tutin Thomas and his brother Cyrus Pole Thomas, Alexander Cowper Hutchison, John James Browne, and Victor Roy. Their sources of inspiration were more varied than the previous generation. Although they still looked to England, they were increasingly influenced by the American picturesque movement. A comparison of W.T. Thomas's design for the Lyman house on upper McTavish Street (Figure V.3) with a plate from A.J. Downing's influential book, *Cottage Residences* (Figure V.4) demonstrates striking similarities. The local architects were mastering new fashions.

The third wave of architects were born around the mid-century and arrived in Canada as experienced practitioners. Andrew T. Taylor was typical of this generation. Scots born and educated, he arrived in Montreal and quickly designed houses for his uncle George Drummond and his coterie of influential friends. Soon, he became the architect for the Bank of Montreal branches and was responsible for many of the pavilions that define the lower campus of McGill University. Again,

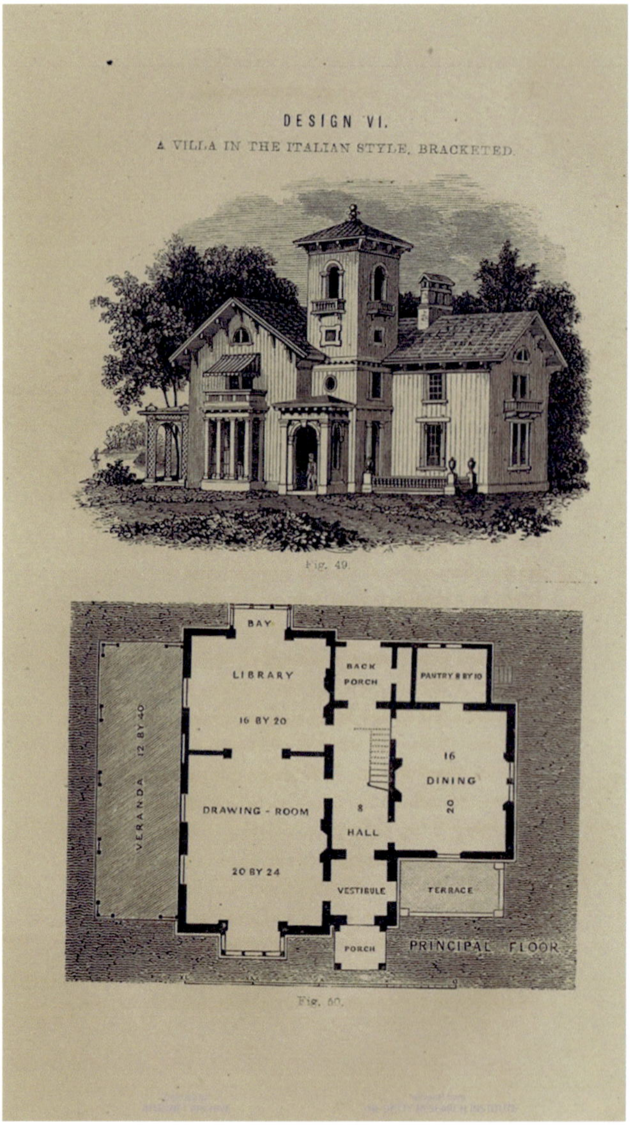

Figure V.4 "Villa in the Italian Style," from A.J. Downing, *Cottage Residences* (New York: John Wiley & Son, 1865).

Taylor was quick to assimilate new styles, including Richardsonian Romanesque, which he used to great acclaim in the design for George Drummond's house on Sherbrooke Street. By the end of his career in Canada, Taylor had brought the firm McKim, Mead & White to work in Montreal and was immersed in its classical language.

The last group of architects who built the Square Mile were university educated and usually Montrealers by birth. Edward Maxwell trained in Boston; his younger brother William Sutherland Maxwell graduated from the École des Beaux-Arts de Paris. Occasionally American architects arrived, but these men were not the interlopers who so enraged the local practitioners in the last decade of the nineteenth century but rather immigrants who had met Montrealers in American offices and decided to set up practice with them in the city. British architects, such as Percy Nobbs, also arrived in Montreal, often to take up teaching posts at McGill University and bringing with them an arts-and-crafts sensibility. By the end of the century, design sources were not limited; they were global.

- First Wave: William Footner (1799–1872); William Speir (1801–78); George Browne (1811–85); John Ostell (1813–92); John W. Hopkins (1825–1905).
- Second Wave: William T. Thomas (1828–92); Alexander C. Hutchison (1838–1922); John James Browne (1837–93); Victor Roy (1837–1902).
- Third Wave: Andrew T. Taylor (1850–1937); Robert Findlay (1859–1951).
- Fourth Wave: Edward Maxwell (1867–1922); William Sutherland Maxwell (1872–1951); Percy Nobbs (1875–1964).

CHAPTER THREE

"Others of more enterprise": Thomas Morland and the Formation of Montreal Rolling Mills, 1858–1868

Jean-Philip Mathieu

The formation of Montreal Rolling Mills in the spring of 1868 sent tremors through the city's hardware trade. Contemporaries immediately understood that the appearance of the new company was a significant event, and the fact that Thomas Morland, the hardware merchant who was the chief architect behind the firm's creation, found himself almost immediately at the centre of a controversy only exacerbated the feeling of trepidation over the new giant in their midst. As was often the case, the disagreement centred on the tariff. The minister of finance had just announced modifications to the schedule: henceforth, some semi-finished metal commodities were to be subject to duties. The hardware merchant William Darling, in the name of a "[c]ommittee appointed by the Hardware Trade," sent a telegram to Thomas Workman, member of Parliament for Montreal Centre: "Are we to understand that all the articles used in the factories of Messrs. Morland, Rose & Watson are to be exempt from duty – namely, puddled bars, white and red lead, steel in bars, and sheets cut into shapes, and pig lead – while bar iron, boiler plate and nail plate are subject to duty?" Workman simply replied, "Yes."[1]

The disagreement over the new tariff schedule reflected a perceived "disturbance to the existing relations and arrangements of manufacturers and merchants."[2] And the firm that Thomas Morland built was nothing if not a major disturbance. Unhappy with the prices he was receiving from his suppliers, Morland formed a company that consolidated both the manufacturing and wholesaling aspects of his enterprise. The form that the enterprise would take was an unusual one in the world of Montreal's hardware trade. Wholesalers like Darling and manufacturers like John Pillow were almost all in business either on their own or, more commonly, in private partnerships. But Morland chose to form a joint-stock corporation. Why did he go this route? This chapter will argue that the joint-stock corporation gave Morland political and economic power that would not have been available to him otherwise, power that radiated out from Montreal's Square Mile. The businessmen recruited to form Montreal Rolling Mills were centred there, and the neighbourhood would be Morland's power base. It was what allowed him to form his company as an early version of a multidivisional firm, which would be a crucial steppingstone towards a more resolutely modern enterprise in the following decades. More importantly, the joint-stock corporation served to both protect and consolidate wealth, and those capitalists like Morland with the resources and foresight to adopt it would have a dominant edge in the decades to come.

Few historians have looked at Montreal Rolling Mills, and fewer still have interrogated the person of Thomas Morland. Existing studies are mainly interested in the company's place in the eventual advent of The Steel Company of Canada (Stelco) and have, for the most part, missed the radical shift that Montreal Rolling Mills itself represented.[3] More generally, the connection between the rise of the joint-stock corporation and the consolidation of bourgeois capital and power has not enjoyed the scrutiny I believe it deserves. Much of the literature on the joint-stock corporation is focused on explaining how it became the dominant form of business organization by the end of the nineteenth century but has frustratingly little to say about the wider impact this new form had on politics and society, let alone class structures.[4] One notable exception is Sven Beckert, who in his monumental study of the New York bourgeoisie briefly mentions that "[t]he explosive growth of joint-stock companies effectively brought together investors from places large and small, east and west, and linked them to single economic undertakings."[5] However, the thrust of Beckert's argument about class consolidation centres on sociocultural institutions such as "clubs, debutante balls, voluntary associations and museums, and, in exceptional circumstances, even in political mobilizations."[6] But the bourgeoisie was a group that principally understood itself in terms of property and wealth, and the business forms that they created should be at the forefront.

This chapter will begin by recounting Thomas Morland's rise in Square Mile society along with the expansion of his business interests before looking at the broader context of the 1860s. I will then analyse the development of the joint-stock corporation in the Province of Canada before turning to the actual formation of Montreal Rolling Mills in 1867–8. Finally, I will circle back to the tariff controversy in the spring of 1868 that centred on Morland and his company. But first let us begin with the commodity at the centre of this story. For those in the hardware trade, the key product they were selling, and the generator of their wealth, was the manufactured nail.

A Brief Interlude on the Humble Nail

In all our homes, under layers of spackle and paint, rest thousands of nails. We live our lives surrounded by these ubiquitous metal shards. The manufactured cut nail is perhaps the blandest product of the first Industrial Revolution. After all, what could be more boring than a simple spike of iron used for joining pieces of wood? But the invention of the manufactured nail caused a seismic transformation in the ability of people to house themselves. Nails were nothing new, of course. The Romans made nails. But for millennia homebuilders were faced with a dilemma: nails are very efficient at binding wood together, but they had to be individually forged by blacksmiths, and buying enough of them to build even a small cottage was beyond the means of most people. Indeed, nails were so valuable that people burned their houses down to collect them from the ashes.[7] The other option was the ancient art of joining, the back-breaking work of whittling wooden beams so that they slot into each other. Nails were efficient but expensive; joining was cheap but labour intensive.

In the late eighteenth century major advances were made in nail production. Much of this innovation came from New England, as labour shortages made the production of hand-forged nails impractical. By contrast, in Europe, labour surpluses and resistance to mechanization by skilled artisans meant that well into the nineteenth century hand-forged nails continued to be produced. But, as was the case with so many traditional crafts, artisans could only resist the pressures of industrialization for so long. By the late nineteenth century, an English nailer using traditional methods could make 112 pounds of nails per day, while a North American labourer operating machines could produce 5,400 pounds in the same amount of time.[8]

Producing manufactured nails required several steps (Figure 3.1). First, wrought iron was heated and then worked into flat sheets. This was traditionally accomplished with water or hand-powered hammers, until in 1784 an English patent was issued for using grooved rollers. This much more efficient method involved passing heated wrought iron between two heavy rollers until it was flattened into a sheet called nail plate or nail rod. The nail plate or rod was then put into a cutting machine that sheared the iron into a spike shape (the nail blank). In early factories, workers collected the blanks and then hammered on a head by hand, but by the early nineteenth century machines were invented that could both cut and then head a nail.[9]

The manufactured nail was a revolutionary invention that bound together more than just beams of wood. The nail bound together iron miners in England with

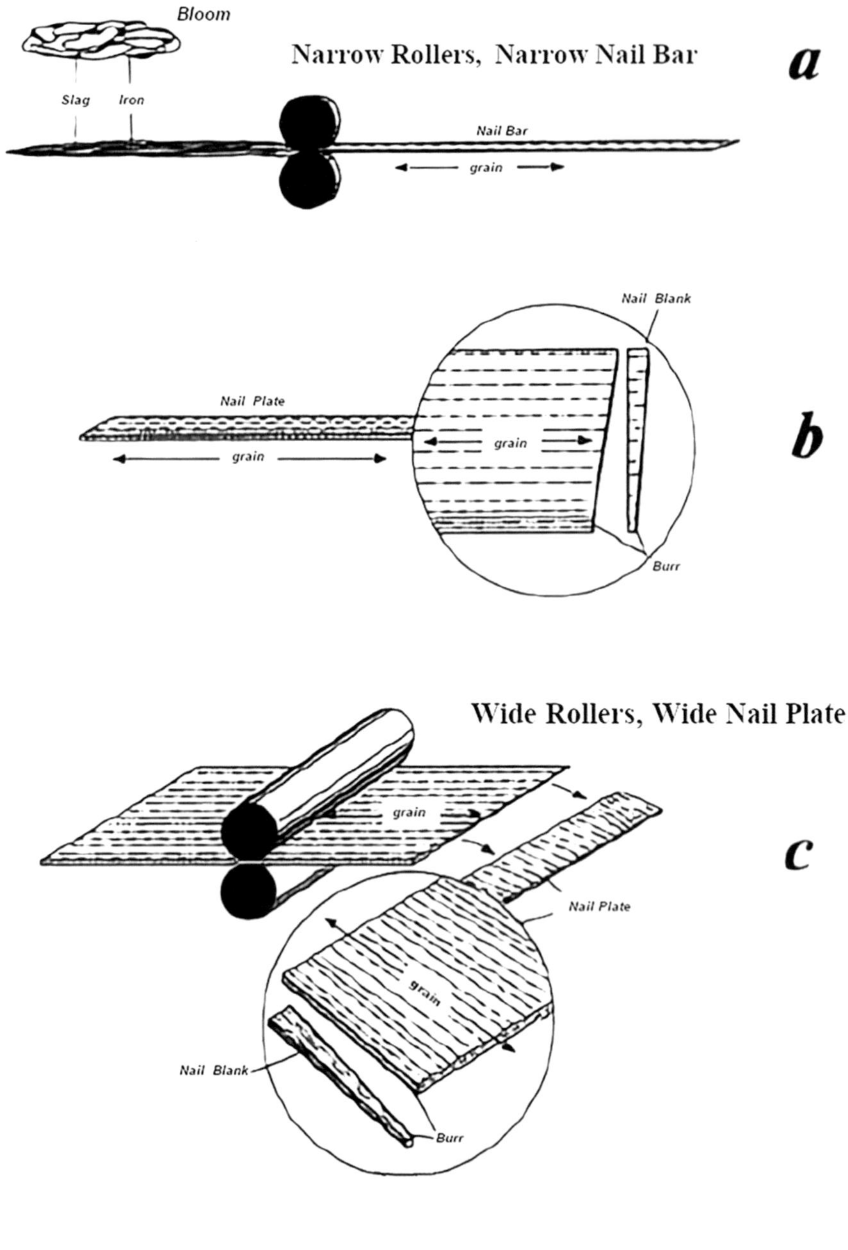

Figure 3.1 Methods of making nail rods and plate: "*a*, slag in the bloom is drawn out with the iron, narrow rollers form the narrow nail plate with the grain running the length of the bar, nails cut from narrow nail plates are cross-grained; *b*, narrow rollers form the narrow nail plate with the grain running the length of the bar, nails cut from narrow nail plates are cross-grained; *c*, wide rollers produce sheets, which are then sheared across the grain to produce nail plates, nails made from such plates are in-line-grained."

Source: Tom Wells, "Nail Chronology: The Use of Technologically Derived Features," *Historical Archaeology* 32, no. 2 (1998): 88.

rolling mill operators in Canada. It bound together poor cutting and heading machine operators on the Lachine Canal with wealthy investors in their Square Mile mansions. It bound together hardware wholesalers with shipping magnates and former artisan nailers turned industrialists. The nail can be seen as a microcosm of how manufactured commodities created contact zones that bound individuals together during the epochal transformations of industrialization. And at the centre of this particular microcosm was Thomas Morland.

Thomas Morland

Morland (Figure 3.2) was born in Wigtownshire, Scotland, in 1826, and very little is known about him before he moved to the Province of Canada in the late 1840s.[10] He entered into a partnership with William Darling around 1848 as a traveller for his hardware firm, quickly becoming a full partner with the firm renamed Morland & Darling. Business was clearly booming, as in 1853 he became an early resident of the Square Mile, in what his credit report describes as "the finest place in Town" – Bellevue Terrace on Dorchester Street.[11] By this time, Darling's firm had dissolved, and Morland went into business on his own while simultaneously becoming involved in every facet of Montreal bourgeois society; he was commissioned as a lieutenant in the militia and became chairman of the Great Western Insurance Company, governor of the Montreal General Hospital, and possibly of greatest significance for his status, president of the Ball Committee to welcome the Prince of Wales in 1860.[12]

In Victorian Montreal, social and familial networks could not be disentangled from business, something that Morland's credit reports clearly underline. In 1853, Morland married Jane Graham, a woman of some means according to the report of Dun, Wiman & Co., a windfall that certainly improved his financial standing among his peers. Meanwhile, the prestigious social positions he held doubtlessly translated into business opportunities; he "associates chiefly with officers and people of fashion."[13] In 1856, Morland was widowed, his credit report noting tragically that he was not left with any of Jane's money, something compounded by significant losses in the Panic of 1857. Nevertheless, by the early 1860s, Thomas Morland had righted himself and was the very definition of a successful Square Mile bourgeois.[14]

There is no indication that Morland actively sought to dominate Montreal's hardware trade. Indeed, the first step towards the integration of his firm seems to have come quite accidentally. In 1860, his main saw supplier was in difficulty. S.S. Campbell had been bought out, leaving his partners Edward Jones and George Hinton on their own, and unfortunately they were hovering near failure. After a lawsuit, the hardware dealer James Hutton purchased the business, but he ran into a problem

Figure 3.2 William Notman, *Thomas Morland, Montreal*, 1869–1870. McCord Museum, I-42177.

when the owner of the building, Ira Gould, made a claim on the machinery. Hutton approached Morland and convinced him to cover Gould's claims and then purchase the machinery from him. Morland came up with the money, buying out both Gould and Hutton, and became the direct owner of his main saw supplier, hiring the former owners, Jones and Hinton, as salaried managers.[15]

In early 1861, Morland entered into a partnership with Charles Watson, a recent arrival from Great Britain with good connections in London, and James Rose, Morland's clerk, conveniently the brother of John Rose, then the solicitor general for

Canada East. The new firm, Morland, Watson & Co., was capitalized at roughly $80,000.[16] In the 1860s, Morland continued his involvement in bourgeois business and society, becoming president of the Victoria Skating Club, the first president of the Montreal City Passenger Railway Company, and auditor to the Grand Trunk Railway, the largest and most powerful company in the Province of Canada.[17] In 1863, Morland married Helen Elizabeth Servante, the daughter of Colonel Henry Servante, commander of the Royal Engineers in Canada.[18] This alliance doubtlessly served to solidify his prestigious connections to the British Empire within Square Mile society and underlines the importance of imperial networks for bourgeois Montrealers in this period.

Around 1863, Morland was approached by the nail manufacturer John Mansfield Holland about investing in the construction of a rolling mill. Holland was one of many New Englanders who had come to Montreal in the first half of the nineteenth century bringing state-of-the-art nail manufacturing technologies to the fledgling industrial metropolis. His nail factory on the south side of the Lower Lachine Rapids had been in operation since the early 1850s, and in March 1859, with the financial backing of the retired paper maker Thomas F. Miller, he built the first rolling mill in Canada. Miller, however, was disappointed by the enterprise and forced Holland out a year later.[19] Holland's proposal to Morland was for the latter to put up the capital to build a new mill and, once complete, for Holland to supply Morland, Watson & Co. with finished nails.[20] But the context had changed between the 1850s when Morland was building his enterprise and when Holland completed the construction of the rolling mill in 1867. The intervening years saw a series of crucial developments that opened an even greater world of opportunities as the Canadian economic and political system shifted gears in response to a major downturn.

Crash Politics

In the fall of 1857, the capitalist world was shaken by another of its regular economic crises. A decade of manic railway speculation left hundreds of corporations and the governments that had chartered them swimming in debt, while Russia's re-entry into the global grain market following the Crimean War caused a decline in the high wheat prices that these railroads needed to be profitable – or at the very least avoid bankruptcy.[21] In this teetering economy, drunk off the excesses of the great boom of the 1850s, came a series of shocks that brought everything crashing down. The most important of these was the failure of the Ohio Life Insurance and Trust Company. It had lent immense sums to new railroad companies in Michigan, Ohio, and Illinois, and tried to call in its loans in the summer of 1857, quickly learning that the railroads did not have the liquidity to pay. In August, more than a dozen railroads suspended payment on their loans, and with seemingly solid investments going bust, investors rushed to offload their bonds.[22] The Panic of 1857 had begun.

In the Province of Canada, no more isolated then than now from convulsions of its southern neighbour, the economic crisis that followed the Panic ravaged provincial finances, forcing the government to adopt new tariffs to raise desperately needed revenue, mainly to service the immense debts it had accumulated in its own fit of railway over-building that it could not afford. As the depression deepened in the winter of 1857–8, protectionists in the province's major cities began to mobilize to push the Legislative Assembly to use these tariffs to go beyond raising money and encourage Canadian industry. In Montreal, the Tariff Reform Association was formed in 1858, which sent delegates to a major meeting in Toronto that drew up recommendations for the government, some of which influenced the new tariff schedules put into place that year. The Cayley-Galt (1858) and Galt (1859) tariffs, named after the provincial Inspector Generals (Finance Ministers) William Cayley and Alexander Tilloch Galt, were ostensibly designed as revenue tariffs, and any protection was "incidental." Historians have long debated whether the tariffs were incidental or effective, that is to say designed to be protective. In a now classic study, D.F. Barnett persuasively suggests that Galt had a very clear understanding of effective protection.[23] Michael Piva, however, argues that "Ministers of Finance design policies to solve problems: Galt faced a fiscal crisis, not a trade crisis." But he concedes that "what made Galt unique was his consideration of both the trade and revenue implications of his tariff proposals."[24] In a more recent study, Ben Forster also takes a nuanced position: "[r]evenue was [Galt's] chief concern in 1859; protection, in his mind, was an important, though secondary, and most particularly a temporary, consideration." For Forster, "Galt was a committed opportunist, and quite possibly a free trader."[25]

Whether or not Galt saw protection under the 1858–9 tariffs to be incidental and secondary, much of Montreal's business community quickly came to view it as a matter of life and death. It is remarkable how clearly these businessmen articulated their support for protection in an era so dominated by the ideology of free trade. Notably, in 1866 when Galt reduced the general tariff rate from 20 to 15 per cent, Montreal businessmen organized again, forming the Tariff Reform and Industrial Association.[26] Among such important individuals as Mayor Henry Starnes, his future successor William Workman, J.B. Rolland, A.W. Ogilvie, and John Redpath, was Thomas Morland. Starnes argued that "the tariff of 1859, which gave incidental protection, was all they wanted. It was remarkable what under that tariff Montreal and Canada had become." Workman added that "the Customs Tariff adopted in

1858, at a time of general depression, imparted fresh vigor to every branch of trade and industry."[27] The association demanded that the government make the 1859 protective tariff permanent to reassure capitalists, because "nothing was more cowardly than capital," while seventy-six businessmen signed on as a provisional committee to draft a constitution.[28]

The shift from an economic system centred on free trade to one where protection was accepted as essential, whether it was incidental or not, is a clear example of what Scott Reynolds Nelson termed "crash politics."[29] The process of trying to solve the financial problems laid bare by the Panic of 1857 eventually led to the splitting up of the Province of Canada and the reorganization of much of British North America into a new federal union. Beneath it all was a desire to reassure nervous British investors, as Canada's economic fortunes both before and after Confederation were dependent on the continued import of British capital. And one of the keys to keeping the money coming was convincing British investors that Canada was not becoming too democratic and that their capital would be safe from the mob.[30] This was part of a larger effort in the 1850s–1860s to de-democratize Canadian society to protect wealth from the lower orders who were seen as dangerous and having too much political power stemming from an enlarged franchise.[31] Connected to this was the transformation of the province's laws regarding joint-stock corporations, making it possible to incorporate a company without interference from the people's representatives.

A Safe Space for Capital

Mansfield Holland's company would be purchased by a new venture, a joint-stock corporation by the name of The Montreal Rolling Mills Company. Before the 1840s there was nothing inherently entrepreneurial about the corporation as an organization, having developed as a subordinate form of government created to meet the needs of feudal societies. It was a method of political sanction by monarchies for social organizations such as municipalities, religious orders, hospitals, and universities. The corporation gave its members certain rights, notably independent decision-making powers, continuity beyond the participation of specific individuals, transferability of things like stocks without threatening that continuity, the creation of a judicial personhood allowing the corporation to sue and be sued without affecting its members, and in most cases limited liability for those members. By the eighteenth century, European monarchies began to charter increasing numbers of profit-seeking corporations to fill their coffers, the privileges and monopolies granted attracting numerous speculators. In Britain this all came to a head when the South Sea Company collapsed in 1720, dragging much of the economy down with it. Parliament responded forcefully by severely limiting the formation of new joint-stock corporations.[32]

One of the British Parliament's main concerns was the perceived irresponsibility that came with limited liability. The risk of losing one's fortune was considered to be a necessary deterrent against fraud, and while the United States and continental Europe moved in the direction of expanded limited liability, "Britain moralistically resisted it."[33] While debates raged in the metropole, in Canada the argument was more subdued, and most incorporation charters included limited liability protections. The 1849 Interpretation Act went further, making limited liability the norm unless an exception was made. In both Canada and Britain, the arguments against expanded limited liability protection were the same: "debts should be paid," it would lead "to monopoly," and it "gave a corporation an unfair advantage over an individual businessman."[34] Also, and crucially, it struck at the core of how capitalists justified their wealth. The bourgeoisie "had been able to justify its inequalities with the thought that they were not only more diligent and resourceful, but also more daring than the workers, and consequently more vulnerable."[35] Critics pointed out that limited liability allowed them to maintain this inequality while also reducing their vulnerability.[36] But businessmen did not seem overly bothered by the contradiction of painting themselves as heroic entrepreneurs while sealing off their riches from the consequences of their actions. Wealth had to be protected, even at the cost of consistency.

Traditionally, the process of incorporation required Parliament to pass a law granting a charter – it was a political act. Individuals would present a petition to the Legislative Assembly that would be debated in first and second readings and then voted upon by legislators before becoming law. This was a long and laborious process, with no guarantee of success, and charters were only granted at the end of a parliamentary session. Legislators needed to weigh the public good and the balancing of interests before approving a charter, or at least appear to do so. There were any number of reasons that petitions for incorporation could be denied. Elsbeth Heaman notes, for example, that in the late 1830s "there were almost no municipal charters in British North America because authorities distrusted local public opinion,"[37] while Peter Bischoff argues that the Legislative Assembly refused to incorporate associations for trades like ship carpentry because "[l]es députés craignent en effet que les corporations de métier se muent en syndicats et en viennent à faire obstacle à la libre entreprise."[38] The process of obtaining an act of incorporation was thus politicized and arbitrary.

Table 3.1 underlines the problem. Once a petition was presented in the Legislative Assembly, there was a very good chance of a charter being granted. However,

Table 3.1 Number of requests made compared to charters granted by the Legislative Assembly, 1857–1866

Year	No. of requests	No. of requests considered	No. of charters granted	Per cent (%) of requested charters granted
1857	43	28	23	53.5
1858	37	19	9	24.3
1859	31	20	13	41.9
1860	22	16	12	54.5
1861	25	17	12	48.0
1862	26	15	8	30.8
1863	39	23	21	53.8
1864	58	46	40	69.0
1865	37	23	14	37.8
1866	54	21	20	37.0

Note: This table was compiled by comparing the notices of individual requests for incorporation in the *Canada Gazette* with individual charters considered and granted by the Legislative Assembly of the Province of Canada. This is not an exact science. Requests for individual charters were never uniform and often so vague it is impossible to say conclusively what the petitioners intended the corporation to do. I have attempted to pick out all requests for profit-seeking businesses and not associations, societies, towns, or villages. However, the lack of precision and clarity in the requests makes it impossible to make a comprehensive list. Collating requests with acts considered and passed is similarly imprecise as some requests were renamed when they were introduced in the Legislative Assembly. Nonetheless, most charters granted could be traced back to the original requests, and therefore this table serves as a very good approximation of the wide gulf that existed between petitions and successful incorporations.

Sources: *Canada Gazette*, 1856–66; *Journals of the Legislative Assembly of the Province of Canada*, 1856–66.

perhaps owing to time constraints, disinterest, or even hostility, a significant number of petitions were never even considered by the legislature. For a petition to be presented to Parliament, the petitioner was required to first publish a notice in the official governmental publication, the *Canada Gazette*, although that rule could be suspended by the legislature. In the decade before Confederation, at most around half of the requests published in the *Canada Gazette* were eventually granted charters. Even those companies that had their requests granted often had to make multiple attempts before they were successful. For example, the Clifton Suspension Bridge Company tried four times before finally being incorporated in 1868. Businessmen were thus at the mercy of elected officials, and it should come as no surprise that when presented with the opportunity to circumvent the Legislative Assembly, they did so in droves.

Starting in the 1830s, the process of obtaining a charter was gradually liberalized with the advent of general incorporation statutes. These were laws that laid out a process whereby a group of individuals could create a joint-stock corporation without a specific act of Parliament. This typically involved writing an application for a charter of incorporation that included the names and residences of the applicants (usually the future shareholders and directors), the proposed name of the company, the location where the company would operate, the purpose of the company, the amount of nominal capital of the company, and the number and value of shares initially issued. Some of these acts required the application to be sent to the provincial secretary for approval, but more commonly it had to be published in the *Canada Gazette* and in at least one major newspaper in the municipality where the company would operate, after which a charter of incorporation could be issued.[39] This went a long way towards depoliticizing the incorporation of joint-stock business corporations, as charters could now be granted without being debated by legislators. In British North America, the move towards general statutes began in 1836, starting with building societies and infrastructure projects, such as roads and bridges, before extending to railroads and banks. Mining and manufacturing companies received the right to incorporate without an act of Parliament in 1850, with two other acts in 1860 and 1864 making significant modifications to the process.[40]

In a landmark study, Jean-Marie Fecteau argues that the rise of the general incorporation statute for profit-seeking companies in the mid-nineteenth century was often spoken of in terms of the triumph of liberalism over bureaucracy and the state, but he points out that the corporation exposed many of the contradictions of the liberal order. After all, what could be more antithetical to the liberal ethos of individualism than the common ownership of capital? And what of the administrative hierarchy of the corporation, based on stock ownership or elected positions – did that not infringe on the individual businessman's equality in a world of private enterprise? And was that most fundamental liberal principle, that individuals are responsible for their own actions, not challenged by the granting of limited liability? The business corporation allowed individuals to renounce their liberty (and reduce their risk) in the pursuit of collective profits for them and their associates.[41]

For Fecteau, the devolution of power from the state to individuals with regards to the creation of joint-stock corporations was an example of democratization. Individuals seeking to form a corporation no longer needed to make a specific request to the state but simply had to conform to established norms. State oversight was thus severely restrained, limited to instances of fraud or other abuses of a corporation's charter.[42] This may have been true in the 1840s, but as we have seen, by the time the primary general incorporation statutes were coming into force in the 1860s, the problem capitalists sought to overcome was not the lack of democracy but rather the perceived threat of too much democracy. The devolution of authority

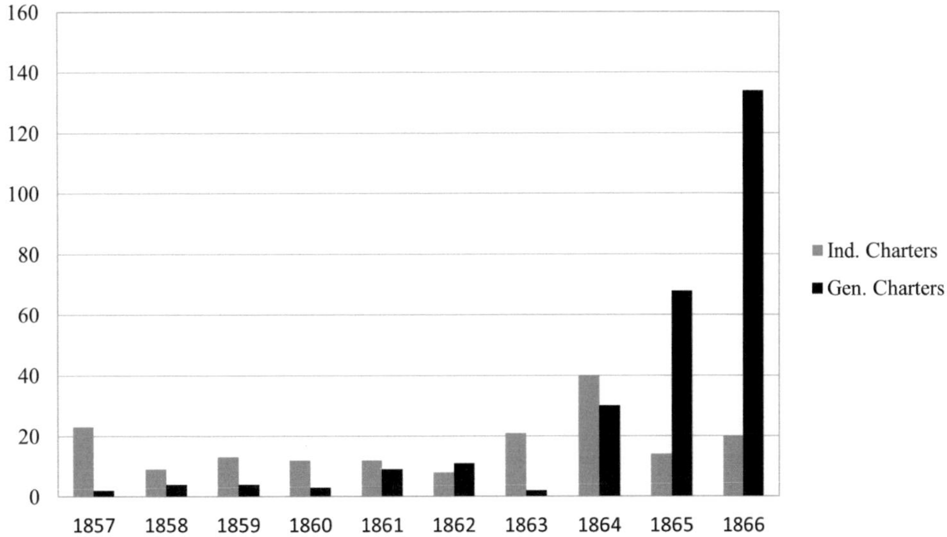

Figure 3.3 Comparison of requests for individual charters and requests for general charters, 1857–1866.
Source: Data derived from the *Canada Gazette*, 1857–1866.

to form corporations from the state to individuals can thus be seen as part of a wider defence against the perceived threat of popular opposition.

The 1864 act proved to be the watershed moment. Before its passing, very few businesses were incorporated via general statutes, but as Figure 3.3 shows, as soon as the 1864 act was made law the number of requests increased dramatically. The 1860 and 1864 acts were superficially similar but contained several important differences. Most notably, in 1860 the awarding of a charter was not automatic but rather was subject to investigation by the Superior Court, and it included a provision that any person, including the solicitor general, could object to the company's incorporation. The 1864 act did away with this, offering no real mechanism for refusing incorporation to a company that completed all the requirements of the request. If defects were detected, the applicant had an opportunity to send a corrected version. In the 1860s, roughly half of the requests made were found to have defects, and half of those were satisfactorily corrected, meaning two-thirds of requests for general incorporation charters were granted.[43] This was a significantly higher success rate than for those that petitioned for individual charters from the Legislative Assembly. Furthermore, the number of companies requesting individual acts remained fairly steady, suggesting that it was not so much a question of businessmen switching from requesting individual statutes to general ones but rather that many dozens of companies perhaps did not bother to request a charter from Parliament before

1864. The other major advantage of general incorporation was that company rules and regulations were held internally and could be modified at any time by directors, while corporations created through individual statutes were forced to petition elected officials for amendments to what were, after all, Canadian laws.

Thus, the 1860s saw the culmination of a process of removing the joint-stock company from democratic oversight, as businessmen seeking the benefits of corporate rights, notably limited liability, were no longer subject to the scrutiny of the Legislative Assembly. Also gone was the fluidity and imprecision of the earlier system, replaced by a rational framework. The political process was hereafter excised from oversight of corporate formation among those capitalists who had the resources to take advantage of the new legal structure. But this is still insufficient to explain why Morland built Montreal Rolling Mills the way he did. Mansfield Holland's firm was valued for purchase at $75,000, which is the exact amount Morland, Watson, and Rose invested in the enterprise. Further, Dun, Wiman & Co. reported in 1866 that their company was worth more than $100,000.[44] This suggests that Morland had the capital to buy Montreal Rolling Mills without fifteen other investors, which of course was precisely what he had done with the Jones and Hinton saw factory in 1860. But the joint-stock corporation not only consolidated wealth, it consolidated the wealthy. Therefore, an important part of the answer to why he went the direction he did lies with the specific people he recruited to invest in Montreal Rolling Mills.

Recruiting the Elite

The company's list of initial shareholders reads like a veritable "who's who" of Canada's business elite. Among them was the great shipping magnate Hugh Allan, one of the wealthiest men in the British Empire, Charles John Brydges, the general manager of the Grand Trunk Railway, the largest company in the Dominion, and Edwin Henry King, the general manager of the Bank of Montreal, the Dominion's largest financial institution. Also included was Peter Redpath, whose sugar refinery was one of Montreal's largest industrial establishments, William Markland Molson, who together with his brothers represented one of Montreal's great economic dynasties, Edward Hopkins, an agent for the venerable Hudson's Bay Company, Thomas Reynolds, the former administrator of the Ottawa and Prescott Railway, and the powerful merchants George Stephen and J. Gordon Mackenzie.[45]

Alongside these representatives of the *haute bourgeoisie*, Morland appears to have also recruited people who could bring a certain expertise to the firm. Notably, shareholders included George Hinton, manager of Morland's saw factory since

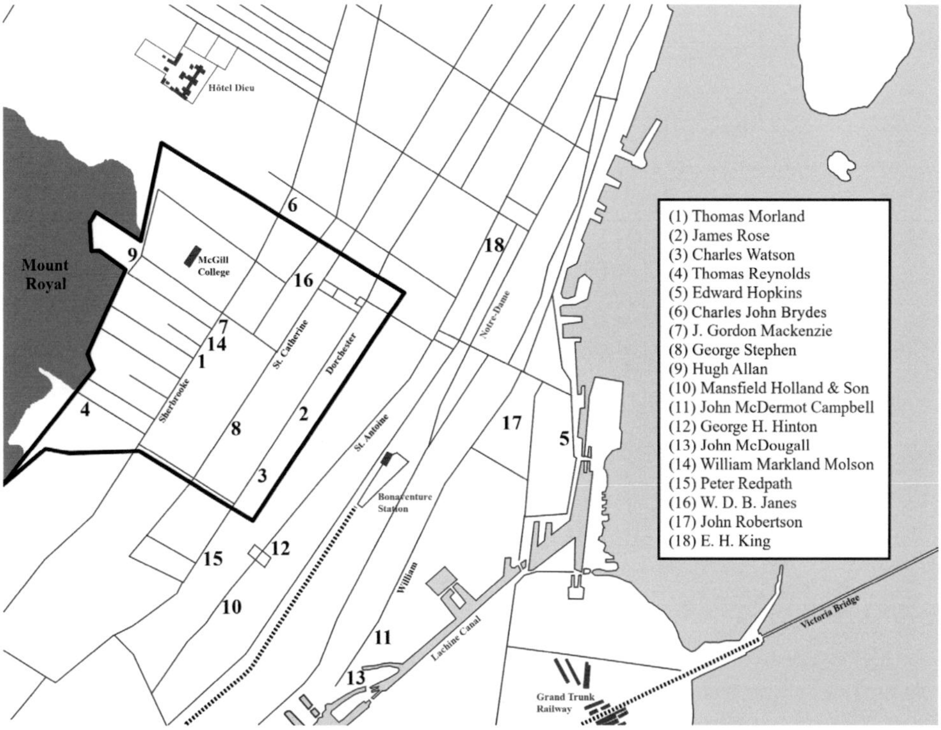

Figure 3.4 Residences of initial shareholders of Montreal Rolling Mills, 1867–1868. Locations were found using *Mackay's Montreal Directory* for 1867–8, with the exception of John Robertson who does not appear in that issue, so the 1868–9 directory was used for him. The inner frame indicates the traditional borders of the Golden Square Mile.

Source: Adapted from *Contoured plan of Montreal and its environs, Quebec, triangulated in 1865 and surveyed in 1868–9 under the direction of Lieut. H. S. Sitwell, R. E. and under the superintendence of Lieut. Col. Wm. F. Drummond Jervois* (Southampton: Ordnance Survey Office, 1870).

he purchased it in 1860, W.D.B. Janes, a coal merchant, John McDougall, a millwright and machinist, John Robertson, an engineer at Canada Lead Works, and John McDermott Campbell, a bookkeeper. Upon Montreal Rolling Mills' official incorporation in May 1868, Robertson was hired as salaried manager of the lead works, and Campbell as manager of the rolling mills proper. Rounding out the initial shareholders were Thomas Morland, Charles Watson, and James Rose, who collectively owned 75 of the 152 shares initially issued by the company. The final shareholder was Mansfield Holland, whose business was purchased.[46]

It was the Square Mile that would provide Morland with his power base. Eleven of the eighteen businessmen lived in the neighbourhood or immediately adjacent to it (see Figure 3.4). With the exception of Edwin King, who lived in the Bank

Figure 3.5 James Inglis, *Prince of Wales Terrace, Sherbrooke St., Montreal*, 1860. McCord Museum, MP-1974.82. The Prince of Wales Terrace is on the north side of Sherbrooke Street. McTavish Street is to the right of the image, and the terrace ends at Peel Street on the left. From right to left, the residents of the terrace in 1867–8 were John Molson, Colonel C.E. Ford, F.B. Archer, Andrew Allan, J. Gordon Mackenzie and the three other Mackenzies that formed his company, William Molson, Thomas Workman, Colonel John Dyde, and finally Thomas Morland.

of Montreal building, and Edward Hopkins, who remained in the old downtown core, those outside the Square Mile represented the engineers, millwrights, and smaller industrialists whom Morland brought into the enterprise. Although these men were important for the company's success, it was the concentration of Square Mile capital and the power it wielded that would give Montreal Rolling Mill a decisive edge over its competitors.

By 1867, Morland had moved into the prestigious Prince of Wales Terrace on Sherbrooke (Figure 3.5), a residence that "served to enhance the image of the row house from a standard comfortable middle-class dwelling to a veritable mansion distinguishable from most grand villas merely by the fact that it formed a united whole with its immediate neighbours."[47] The power concentrated in this newly

NOTICE is hereby given that Hugh Allan, Edward M. Hopkins, Charles John Brydges, George Stephen, Thomas Reynolds, Gordon Mackenzie and Thomas Morland, all of Montreal, will apply to His Excellency the Lieutenant Governor of the Province of Quebec, in Council, after the expiration of one month from the publication of this notice, for a charter to incorporate a company under an Act of the Parliament of the late Province of Canada, intituled, "An Act to authorize the granting of Charters of Incorporation to Manufacturing, Mining and other Companies," to be called "The Montreal Rolling Mills Company," for the manufacture, purchase and sale of Iron and other metals, nails, spikes and other articles of hardware, at the city and in the parish of Montreal, Province of Quebec, where the operations of the company are to be carried on. The amount of the capital stock of the Company is to be $200,000 in 200 shares of $1000 each. The amount subscribed is $150,000, and $10,000 is to be paid in before the charter is granted.

Montreal, 31st January, 1868. 458-5

Figure 3.6 Notice of application for a charter of incorporation for Montreal Rolling Mills. *Canada Gazette*, 15 January 1868, p. 377.

constructed residence cannot be overstated. Among Morland's neighbours were his new partners J. Gordon Mackenzie and William Monkland Molson, along with Molson's brother John; Hugh Allan's brother and partner in the Allan Line, Andrew; and Thomas Workman, member of Parliament for Montreal Centre, part of the powerful hardware firm Frothingham and Workman, and brother of the newly elected mayor, William Workman. Also residing in the Prince of Wales Terrace were reminders of the neighbourhood's links to the Biritish Empire: Colonel John Dyde, commandant of the active volunteer force; F.B. Archer, commissariat general and comptroller of army expenditure; and Colonel Charles Erskine Ford, commander of the Royal Engineers in Canada.[48] This single block of row houses between McTavish and Peel on the north side of Sherbrooke was a microcosm of the incredible concentration of wealth and power in the Square Mile.

The organizational technology of the joint-stock corporation was what allowed Morland to take advantage of this concentration, something the application published in the *Canada Gazette* illustrates (Figure 3.6). The names listed were, in order, Allan, Hopkins, Brydges, Stephen, Reynolds, Mackenzie, and Morland. Besides

Morland, none of these men were major shareholders. Indeed, Charles Watson and James Rose, who were not listed, together had as many shares (thirty) as the first six names in the notice of incorporation combined. Hugh Allan was listed first not because he was an important shareholder but because he was Hugh Allan. Montreal Rolling Mills served to pull the elite into Morland's social and economic orbit. Square Mile capitalists like Allan and Brydges provided Montreal Rolling Mills with power and prestige, something noted by contemporaries, the credit reporting agency Dun, Wiman & Co. writing excitedly, for example, that "the company is composed of Brydges King Hopkins + others influential [*sic*]."[49]

Montreal Rolling Mills was also a very conspicuous display of wealth. Publishing the notices of incorporation in major newspapers served the concrete purpose of informing the public, but it also widely broadcasted the unity and power of Montreal's ascendant bourgeoisie. Morland advertised himself to everyone as allied with the most powerful men in the Dominion and wielding incredible wealth. As James Taylor notes, "show and display were necessary for the success of the joint-stock company because it was by these means that it won the trust and confidence of the public."[50] Extravagant displays of power and wealth such as imposing corporate headquarters or, in our case, advertising that some of the most powerful men in the Dominion were directors (even when they in fact did not take up directorships) were a way of showing investors that the company was not a fly-by-night operation but rather a permanent and stable enterprise, and that their investments would be safe. Having Hugh Allan and Peter Redpath as shareholders was as good a credit rating as anyone could get.

Some of the advantages of the team Morland put together could perhaps be more tangible. None of his papers are known to have survived, and the only documents from Montreal Rolling Mills covering this period are the company minute books, which were public documents and thus contain no information about the kind of secret arrangements or insider contracts that Morland might have set up with his partners. However, letter books from the 1880s offer clues as to how the company's more informal networks operated. Both in the 1860s and 1880s the puddled iron bars that the rolling mill needed to produce nail plate came from England and were generally shipped from Liverpool on the Allan Line. After arriving in Montreal, the bar was rolled into plate, cut into nails, and then sold by Morland, Watson & Co. to customers in the city or shipped on the Grand Trunk Railway to customers in Quebec City, Toronto, Guelph, and Hamilton. Among the most intriguing letters is one from 1887, wherein Charles Watson, Morland's successor, apologized to Andrew Allan for importing bar on a non-Allan Line ship and reassured Allan that he would always have "preference."[51]

Figure 3.7 Montreal Rolling Mills in 1868. The view is from the north side of the works looking south, with the Lachine Canal at the back of the image. This engraving was widely reproduced in different publications, but the original was printed in a circular advertising the prospective company, a copy of which is pasted in the company's first minute book.

Source: Stelco, vol. 101, file 1, "Minute Book 20 April 1868–6 February 1889."

Although Morland consolidated his enterprise, this was still not quite what Alfred Chandler considered a "modern" corporation, defined as a multidivisional organization with salaried middle-managers.[52] The main components of Morland's business were separate companies, not units (see Figure 3.7). Morland, Watson & Co., a private partnership made of up Thomas Morland, Charles Watson, and James Rose, was a hardware wholesaler. As a firm it had majority control over Montreal Rolling Mills, which was a hardware manufacturer managed by an elected board of directors, and whose president was initially Thomas Morland. That company had two units, the rolling mill and nail and tack works, and the lead works, both which had salaried managers, John McDermott Campbell and John Robertson, respectively, both of whom were minor shareholders in the company. Morland, Watson & Co. also directly owned the saw and axe manufacturer Montreal Saw Works, which Morland had purchased in 1860 and which had its own manager, George Hinton, who was also incidentally a minor shareholder in Montreal Rolling Mills. This was thus not quite the rationalized and efficient Chandlerian corporation; indeed, Montreal Rolling Mills would not transition into a more modern form until the late 1880s, when William McMaster became the company's first salaried general manager. However, the company in 1868 was a crucial steppingstone towards a more modern, integrated corporation, fulfilling many of the same functions and combining sales and production, the latter units run by salaried managers. It was a large, consolidated firm built using the organizational forms available to Morland at the time.

Joint-stock corporations like Montreal Rolling Mills consolidated wealth and, more importantly, consolidated the wealthy. The capitalists who purchased shares in the company obviously had a vested interest in its success, and they deployed their political and social power in the company's service. It is this, more than anything else, that explains why Morland created Montreal Rolling Mills, and why its appearance caused such an immense controversy in the spring of 1868.

Thomas Morland Upsets the Hardware Trade

When the minister of finance, John Rose, adjusted the tariff schedule, Morland and his new company were in a uniquely advantageous position. Montreal Rolling Mills could produce from raw materials most if not all of the products that Morland sold, while most of his competitors needed to import semi-finished materials and sell finished commodities to wholesalers. Nail plate was the biggest issue. Producing nail plate required a rolling mill, of which there were only three in Montreal at the time, including the one Montreal Rolling Mills had just purchased. The new schedule imposed a 5 per cent duty on imported nail plate, but placed imported raw iron on the free list, putting any manufacturer that did not have access to a rolling mill at a huge disadvantage, compounded by the fact that Montreal Rolling Mills did not need to sell to a wholesaler as Morland himself was the wholesaler. Added to this was the belief that Morland had exploited his political connections to convince Rose to create a tariff schedule that benefited Montreal Rolling Mills. This was why the ire of the hardware trade was concentrated on Thomas Morland – neither John Pillow nor Thomas Peck, owners of the other two rolling mills in Montreal, were ever mentioned by name. As William Darling put it in his letter to *The Gazette*,

> M. Morland presented a petition and asked that – five articles … used in the factories of himself and colleagues, should be admitted free. … The [hardware] committee were quite aware of the efforts Mr. Rose made, when member for Montreal Centre, to benefit those gentlemen by legislation and Messrs. Morland, Rose, and Watson have now the pleasure of being able to say that they got everything they asked for in their petition.[53]

In response to Darling's letter, an anonymous party calling themselves "PROGRESS," who claimed to not know much about the hardware business but was in fact suspiciously well informed, responded that

> [t]he Montreal Rolling Mills appears to be the *Bête noir* of … the signers of the telegram [which included Darling]. … The personal bitterness of … the signers of the noted telegram, inclines me to think that it is not the 5 per cent on imported iron that galls them, but that others of more enterprise have successfully established important works, while this little clique is left out in the cold.[54]

Both supporters and opponents of Rose's adjustments to the tariff dug up petitions in support of their positions, both claiming to represent the majority of the hardware trade. The first, from 3 March, signed by fifty-one businessmen and firms including Morland and Montreal's other two rolling mill operators, requested a small protective duty on nail plate. The second, from 4 April, signed by fifty-three businessmen and firms including William Darling, suggested that all hardware should either be on the free list or have the same duty. It is notable that the two petitions were very similar, neither questioning the logic of protection. In fact, the two positions were similar enough that fully twenty-five businessmen and firms signed both petitions.[55] Furthermore, the petitions were several weeks old by the time they were brought up. This once again suggests that the debate that took over the front page of *The Gazette* for the whole month of May 1868 was more about Montreal Rolling Mills' political and economic power than about a minor modification to the tariff schedule.

It should be noted that Darling perhaps even understated Montreal Rolling Mills' political clout. After all, Morland's partner James Rose was the minister of finance's brother. But political influence was always more than family ties. Darling would not have known that Morland's other partners Brydges, Allan, and Stephen had donated a significant amount to Rose's election campaign only a few months before. Brydges had commented to Rose in a private letter, "I presume you will not be embarrassed by the possession of so much money!"[56] There is no way to be sure if John Rose was influenced by family relations or favours owed, or if as a prominent Montreal business lawyer who had firm ties with the city's economic elite he simply considered their interests when making policy, but Morland was capable of taking advantage of any of these factors.[57] And even in the event that Darling's accusations were wrong and it was all a coincidence, Morland's company with its consolidation of manufacturing and wholesaling was uniquely capable of profiting from Rose's changes. There was thus good reason for the hardware trade to be concerned in the spring of 1868. Morland was now positioned to dominate.

Conclusion

Thomas Morland found himself widowed again when his second wife, Helen, died in childbirth in June 1869, his fourth child with her surviving. The next spring, he visited Thomas Reynolds in Ottawa, and on 25 May 1870 he went to Government House, residence of the governor general, and was seen to be in good health. That night, Reynolds awoke to "pneumatic groans" and found Morland collapsed on his hands and knees. Reynolds immediately sent for Charles Watson and Morland's doctor, J. Sutherland, to come to Ottawa, but by the time they arrived Morland had died.[58] He was only forty-three. His four orphaned children were sent back to Great Britain to live with their grandparents, Henry Servante having by now been promoted to general,[59] while the firm that carried his name would continue for another decade under Watson before being dissolved as Montreal Rolling Mills became his primary focus. After Morland's death, a number of his friends set up a fund in his honour and had a wing of the Montreal General Hospital named after him, one of the few testaments to his importance to the Square Mile bourgeoisie.[60] He was, however, survived by Montreal Rolling Mills, a company that, by the twentieth century, was one of the largest in the country.

Montreal Rolling Mills was a creature of the Square Mile. The immense concentration of wealth and power in that neighbourhood allowed the individuals who lived there to take advantage of new organizational forms in a way that most people could not. A Square Mile bourgeois like Thomas Morland had the opportunity to create a company that was cutting-edge, using newly relaxed regulations for joint-stock corporations as well as an early form of the multidivisional firm. As Gregory P. Marchildon explores in chapter 8 of this volume, the Square Mile would continue to be the site of business innovation, as it was from here that Max Aitken would deploy advances in finance to transform the landscape of Canada's economy, including his merger of Montreal Rolling Mills with four other firms to form The Steel Company of Canada in 1910. Furthermore, it was Square Mile capitalists and their enterprises that provided the crucial link between the British Empire and Canada's rapidly growing national economy. As Canada's principal port, it was in Montreal that British goods made landfall. Some of these commodities were consumed locally, while others were transferred onto smaller ships to continue their journey westward or were transformed by Montreal's rapidly expanding industrial sector before being shipped to customers throughout the Dominion. In linking manufacturers of puddled bars in Britain with homebuilders in Canada, Montreal Rolling Mills underlines the transatlantic connections that were central to the development of the Canadian economy in the nineteenth century.

Finally, Montreal Rolling Mills contributed to and reflected a growing class consciousness among the bourgeoisie, as they consolidated their power and pushed back against the rapidly expanding working class in one of the first colonial cities to experience industrialization. Companies like the one Morland put together provided a means of protecting wealth from an electorate that was increasingly seen as too democratic. Joint-stock corporations were repositories of wealth, permanent and stable, legally functioning as artificial citizens that could buy and sell, sue and be sued, but more powerful than any flesh-and-blood person, and unless wound up by their shareholders, immortal. The Square Mile bourgeoisie, British North America's richest group of people, was particularly concerned about perceived threats to their property from the lower class, and fear of the mob and of the "mobocracy" led to ever increasing wealth-based restrictions on the franchise in the mid-nineteenth century.[61] The rise of the joint-stock corporation was thus part of a socio-political process in a period when Montreal's bourgeoisie came to accept the logic of a class conflict – and became determined to be its winners.

NOTES

1 *The Gazette* (Montreal), 30 April 1868, 1.

2 *The Gazette*, 4 April 1868, 1.

3 The most notable of these is obviously William Kilbourn's book written as part of Stelco's fiftieth anniversary celebration, *The Elements Combined: A History of the Steel Company of Canada* (Toronto: Clark, Irwin & Company, 1960), which devotes its second chapter to Montreal Rolling Mills. Gregory P. Marchildon, for his part, wrote in *Profits and Politics: Beaverbrook and the Gilded Age of Canadian Finance* (Toronto: University of Toronto Press, 1996) about the demise of the company as it was integrated by Max Aitken into one of his famous mergers.

4 The UK has a very robust literature on the subject, much of it centred on the question of how England moved from an absolute disdain for joint-stock corporations with limited liability after the failure of the South Sea Company to embracing it by the 1840s–1850s. See Boyd Hilton, *The Age of Atonement: The Influence of Evangelicalism on Social and Economic Thought, 1785–1865* (Oxford: Clarendon Press, 1986); Ron Harris, *Industrializing English Law: Entrepreneurship and Business Organization, 1720–1844* (Cambridge: Cambridge University Press, 2000); and James Taylor, *Creating Capitalism: Joint-Stock Enterprise in British Politics and Culture, 1800–1870* (London: Royal Historical Society, 2006). In Canada there has been considerably less interest in the joint-stock corporation, although a few key studies have been produced. In English Canada the landmark study remains R.C.B. Risk, "The Nineteenth-Century Foundations of the Business Corporation in Ontario," *The University of Toronto Law Journal* 23, no. 3 (Summer 1973): 270–306, https://doi.org/10.2307/825061, while in Quebec it is Jean-Marie Fecteau, "Les 'petites républiques': Les compagnies et la mise en place du droit corporatif moderne au Québec au milieu du 19e siècle," *Histoire sociale/Social History* 25, no. 49 (May 1992): 35–56.

5 Sven Beckert, *The Monied Metropolis: New York City and the Consolidation of the American Bourgeoisie, 1850–1896* (Cambridge: Cambridge University Press, 2001), 240.

6 Beckert, *Monied Metropolis*, 264.

7 Kilbourn, *Elements Combined*, 4–5.

8 Tom Wells, "Nail Chronology: The Use of Technologically Derived Features," *Historical Archaeology* 32, no. 2 (1998): 88. Much of the research on the history of nails and nail technology has come from historical archaeologists because nails are a very effective way of dating buildings. See also Maureen L. Phillips, "'Mechanic Geniuses and Duckies': A Revision of New England's Cut Nail Chronology before 1820," *APT Bulletin: The Journal of Preservation Technology* 25, no. 3/4 (1993): 4–16, https://doi.org/10.2307/1504461; and William Hampton Adams, "Machine Cut Nails and Wire Nails: American Production and Use for Dating 19th-Century and Early-20th-Century Sites," *Historical Archaeology* 36, no. 4 (2002): 66–88, https://doi.org/10.1007/BF03374370.

9 Wells, "Nail Chronology," 79–84.

10 His birth year is indicated on his gravestone in Mount Royal Cemetery, the traditional resting place of his class. There is no entry for Thomas Morland in *Census of the Canadas, 1851–52*, but there is one with the correct birth year in the contemporary English and Welsh census, indicating that he lived in Warwickshire, near Birmingham. It is entirely likely that Morland kept a home in England, especially as he had until recently been a traveller for Darling. This English census entry indicates that he was born in Wigtownshire, where there is a gravestone for Thomas Morland Sr., who died in 1879 at eighty-five years old, mentioning his son Thomas who died in Montreal.

11 R.G. Dun & Co. credit report volumes, Canada, vol. 8, Baker Library, Harvard Business School [hereafter Dun & Co.], entries for 28 September 1852 and 31 May 1856, p. 196. His credit report indicates that he was a traveller "for a number of years," but the municipal directory for 1849 makes it clear that he was in full partnership with Darling.

12 "Appointments, &c," *Montreal Herald*, 31 January 1856, 2; "Great Western Insurance Comp'y," *Montreal Herald*, 13 May 1859, 2; "Montreal General Hospital," *Montreal Herald*, 14 May 1859, 2; "The Visit of the Prince: Continuation of the Festivities on Tuesday," *Montreal Herald*, 27 August 1860, 6.

13 Dun & Co., entry for 12 October 1857, 196.

14 Dun & Co., entries for 14 September 1854, 27 December 1856, and 12 October 1857, 196.

15 Dun & Co., entry for 16 March 1861, 196.

16 Dun & Co., entry for 29 June 1861, 93.

17 "Grand Trunk Railway Company of Canada," *Montreal Herald*, 20 July 1861, 2; *Montreal Herald*, 7 November 1861, 2; "Victoria Skating Club," *Montreal Herald*, 29 November 1866, 2.

18 *The Quebec Directory for 1862–63, Containing a Complete List of All the Inhabitants of the City, with Full Description of Their Businesses and Professions*, ed. G.H. Cherrier (Quebec: John Lovell, 1862); *Census of the Canadas, 1860–61*, vol. 1, *Personal Census* (Quebec: Board of Registration and Statistics, 1863).

19 Larry McNally, "Technical Advance and Stagnation: The Case of Nail Production in Nineteenth-Century Montreal," *Material History Review* 26 (Fall 1992): 39.

20 Dun & Co., entry for 29 October 1860, 125; Library and Archives Canada, The Steel Company of Canada (Stelco) Fonds, R15513 [hereafter Stelco], "Pillow-Hersey Manufacturing Company" series, vol. 125, file 6, "Extract from Autobiography Randolph Hersey, Montreal, 1913."

21 James L. Huston, *The Panic of 1857 and the Coming of the Civil War* (Baton Rouge: Louisiana State University Press, 1987), 5–6.

22 Scott Reynolds Nelson, *A Nation of Deadbeats: An Uncommon History of America's Financial Disasters* (New York: Vintage Books, 2012), 164–5.

23 D.F. Barnett, "The Galt Tariff: Incidental or Effective Protection?," *The Canadian Journal of Economics/Revue canadienne d'Économique* 9, no. 3 (August 1976): 391.

24 Michael Piva, *The Borrowing Process: Public Finance in the Province of Canada, 1840–1867* (Ottawa: University of Ottawa Press, 1992), 151.

25 Ben Forster, "Common Knowledge: Theory, Concept, and the Prosaic in Making the Tariff of 1859," in *Essays in Honour of Michael Bliss: Figuring the Social*, ed. E.A. Heaman, Alison Li, and Shelley McKellar (Toronto: University of Toronto Press, 2008), 137–8.

26 Forster, "Common Knowledge," 135–6; "Tariff Reform Association," *The Gazette*, 27 October 1866, 2.

27 "Meeting Last Night to Organize an Industrial Association," *True Witness*, 27 October 1866, 2.

28 "Meeting Last Night," 2; "Tariff Reform Association," *The Gazette*, 27 October 1866, 2.

29 Nelson, *Nation of Deadbeats*, 20.

30 Andrew Smith, *British Businessmen and Canadian Confederation: Constitution Making in an Era of Anglo-Globalisation* (Montreal: McGill-Queen's University Press, 2008), 4.

31 See Colin Grittner, "Of Bludgeons and Ballots: Political Violence, Municipal Enfranchisement, and Local Governance in Mid-Nineteenth-Century Montreal," in *Violence, Order, and Unrest: A History of British America, 1749–1876*, ed. Elizabeth Mancke et al. (Toronto: University of Toronto Press, 2019), 336.

32 Fecteau, "Les 'petites républiques,'" 36–9.

33 Hilton, *Age of Atonement*, 257.

34 Risk, "Nineteenth-Century Foundations," 298.

35 Hilton, *Age of Atonement*, 267.

36 Hilton, *Age of Atonement*, 267.

37 E.A. Heaman, *Tax, Order, and Good Government: A New Political History of Canada, 1867–1917* (Montreal: McGill-Queen's University Press, 2017), 30.

38 Peter Bischoff, *Les débardeurs au port de Québec: Tableau des luttes syndicales, 1831–1902* (Montreal: Huturbise, 2009), 76–7. Bischoff suggests that this should be seen in the context of the political elite's fear of secret societies following the Rebellions of 1837–8. See Jean-Marie Fecteau, "Les dangers du secret: Note sur l'État canadien et les sociétés secrètes au milieu du 19e siècle," *Canadian Journal of Law and Society/La Revue Canadienne Droit et Société* 6 (1991): 91–111.

39 In Canada East (and later in Quebec) the application would have to be published in both a French and an English newspaper.

40 An Act to Provide for the Formation of Incorporated Joint Stock Companies, for Manufacturing, Mining, Mechanical or Chemical Purposes, 1850, 13 & 14 Vic. c. 28; An Act Respecting the Judicial Incorporation of Joint Stock Companies for Certain Purposes, 1860, 23 Vic. c. 31; An Act to Authorize the Granting of Charters of Incorporation to Manufacturing, Mining, and other Companies, 1864, 27 & 28 Vic. c. 23. See also Risk, "Nineteenth-Century Foundations," 273–6.

41 Fecteau, "Les 'petites républiques,'" 45–6.

42 Fecteau, "Les 'petites républiques,'" 44–5.

43 Risk, "Nineteenth-Century Foundations," 277n40.

44 The firm's "pecuniary worth" was listed as "1½" in *The Mercantile Agency Reference Book for the British Provinces*, vol. 3 (Montreal: Dun, Wiman & Co., 1866), 255, corresponding to $100,000–$250,000.

45 Stelco, vol. 101, file 1, "Minute Book 20 April 1868–6 February 1889."

46 Stelco, vol. 101, file 1, "Minute Book 20 April 1868–6 February 1889." Occupational details were compiled from *The Quebec Directory for 1867–68, Containing a Complete List of All*

the Inhabitants of the City, with Full Description of Their Businesses and Professions, ed. G.H. Cherrier (Quebec: John Lovell, 1867), with the exception of John Robertson who is not listed in that year, appearing instead in the directory for 1868–9.

47 Roderick Macleod, "Salubrious Settings and Fortunate Families: The Making of Montreal's Golden Square Mile, 1840–1895" (PhD diss., McGill University, 1997), 135.

48 *Quebec Directory for 1867–68.*

49 Dun & Co., 94.

50 Taylor, *Creating Capitalism*, 35.

51 Letter from Watson to Allan, 28 September 1887, Stelco, vol. 28, file 1, "Correspondence, May 1879–1894."

52 Alfred D. Chandler Jr., *The Visible Hand: The Managerial Revolution in American Business* (Cambridge, MA: Harvard University Press, 1977), 1–2.

53 "To the Editor of the Gazette," *The Gazette*, 2 May 1868, 1.

54 "Hardware and the Tariff: To the Editor of the Gazette," *The Gazette*, 6 May 1868, 1.

55 "The Hardware Trade: To the Editor of the Gazette," *The Gazette*, 1 May 1868, 1.

56 Letter from Charles Brydges to John Rose, n.d., McGill University Archives, MS 397/5, "Rose, Correspondence, 1867."

57 David M.L. Farr, "Rose, Sir John," *Dictionary of Canadian Biography*, vol. 11, *1881–1890* (Toronto: University of Toronto Press, 1982).

58 "The Late Mr. Thomas Morland," *Montreal Herald*, 27 May 1870, 1.

59 Morland's eldest son Thomas is far better known than his father, having served as a corps commander in the Great War. However, his biography contains several factual errors about his father, notably that he was a "manufacturing engineer," when in fact he was a wholesaler, and that he "played an important part in the construction of the Canadian Pacific Railway," which of course is impossible since he died a decade before it was started. J.M. Bourne, "Morland, Sir Thomas Lethbridge Napierlocked (1865–1925)," in *Oxford Dictionary of National Biography* (Oxford: Oxford University Press, 2004), https://doi.org/10.1093/ref:odnb/35109.

60 *The Globe* (Toronto), 30 June 1870, 1. This donation is mentioned in the most recent history of the hospital, but nothing is said of Morland himself beyond the name of the wing, misspelled "Moreland." See Joseph Hanaway and John H. Burgess, *The General: A History of the Montreal General Hospital* (Montreal: McGill-Queen's University Press, 2016), 37.

61 Grittner, "Of Bludgeons and Ballots," 336.

Figure V.5 Wm. Notman & Son, *McGill College Campus, Montreal*, 1865.
McCord Museum, VIEW-25069.0.

McGill University

The history of the Square Mile and McGill University are inextricably connected. The bequest of James McGill is well known. The northern portion of his farm, Burnside Place, became the grounds of the main campus, and courses were held from as early as 1829 in the farmhouse. The sale and consequent subdivision of the southern portion of the estate in the 1840s spurred the development of the south-eastern section of the Square Mile.

Sir John William Dawson, who was principal from 1855 to 1893, is credited with creating the "Harvard of the North." His first impressions of the campus were "two blocks of unfinished and partly ruinous buildings, standing amid a wilderness of … rubbish, overgrown with weeds and bushes."[1] While this photograph (Figure V.5), taken about ten years after he arrived, shows the buildings to advantage, the goat in the foreground hints at the continuing unkempt landscape of the campus. This situation was not acceptable to Dawson, who devoted his academic career to building McGill's reputation. According to Stephen Leacock, the humourist and McGill professor, it was Dawson who personally designed the layout of the lower campus as it still is today.

Throughout Dawson's tenure, the monies that would fund professorships, buildings, laboratories, and libraries came primarily from Square Mile families. Sir William Macdonald, McGill's greatest benefactor, lived in relatively modest circumstances in the Prince of Wales Terrace (see Figure V.6). Faculty also chose to live nearby, often in the row houses that lined the north–south streets of the sector, and of the present McGill Ghetto to the east.

NOTE

1 Quoted in “Canadian Celebrities: No. VI – Sir William Dawson,” in *The Canadian Magazine*, vol. 13 (Toronto: Ontario Publishing Company, 1899), 344.

CHAPTER FOUR

"Dear Richard … send us a few buffalo tongues": Donald Smith's Fur Trade Contacts and Personal Credit Networks

Max Hamon

On April 1867, from Montreal, Isabella Hardisty-Smith wrote to her brother Richard in the Northwest:

> Mamma got letters from you, William and Thomas on the 23rd [of March] and it afforded her much pleasure to hear that you were all well at the date of your letters. Mother sent you last summer by Bishop Taché a mourning ring with poor Papa's hair in it and also a necktie and collar. He was to leave it with Mr. William Mactavish, as you say nothing about it, in your letter she is afraid … Mr. Smith has often said that he would like to hear from you. Could you not send us a few buffalo tongues? You could either send them to the Hudson's Bay House London, or by way of St. Paul's addressed of course to D.A. Smith.[1]

The archival imprint of Hardisty-Smith,[2] as is frequently the case for women married to "famous" men, is not extensive. Her claim to fame has been her relationship to her husband, Donald Smith, Lord Strathcona, one of the Square Mile's most powerful businessmen and financiers. This chapter inverts that perception to examine *her* contribution to the personal credit of her husband. It argues that fur trade contacts were foundational to the transcontinental relationships that sustained the personal credit networks of Lord Strathcona. The accumulation of wealth in the Square Mile is often explained as a product of a transition to industrial capitalism, but this chapter suggests that Smith's ties to women and Indigenous networks are an important and overlooked aspect of this story.

The above letter, sent in 1867 from the Hardisty family home in Lachine, highlights the day-to-day intimate relationships that have often passed unnoticed next to the formal and political relations on which historians of the business elite have focused. Isabella, the daughter of a Hudson's Bay Company (HBC) chief trader and a Metis woman, was ordering buffalo tongues from Carleton House (in present-day Saskatchewan) to be sent via London or St. Paul's, Minnesota, to her husband who would bring them to Montreal. Isabella's grasp of the complex trade routes connecting the Northwest to Montreal and the rest of the world is a metaphorical fissure in the archive that invites historical consideration.

Like other women of her background, Isabella maintained ties to the fur trade and "mixed-race" communities of the Northwest. The interlocking movement of goods, people, and information was second nature to the Hardisty family and their relations. That buffalo meat, that iconic resource that fostered the emergence of the Metis nation, remained a treasured element of Isabella and her family's life is significant. More than merely a culinary curiosity, it represents the role that Indigenous resources and relationships continued to play in the imperial careers of men like Smith,[3] which in turn draws our attention to the enduring capacity of Indigenous relations in settler spaces and economies.

Isabella inherited the Lachine home on her father's death. Her father, Richard Hardisty, a former HBC Factor, died in November 1865. The house remained a significant node in a network of former fur traders. Isabella's mother, Margaret Hardisty, continued to reside there, and her brothers regularly visited. Lachine itself was an important hub of fur-trade relationships. Isabella's letters, often written from Lachine, contain references to numerous old HBC employees and their wives, illustrating how the community in Lachine remained well connected with the Northwest. The house remained in her name, and is further evidence of a tactic, identified by Peter Gossage and Lisa Moore in this volume, of elite families protecting their wealth from the grasp of creditors.

Isabella, and her husband, profited from this social milieu, yet, in the summer of 1869, Donald Smith and Isabella Hardisty moved to a new house built on Mansfield Street between St. Catherine Street and Burnside Place. It was at the heart of the Square Mile. The move to the house on Mansfield reflects the shifting economic and social aspirations of the time. City directories reveal that their new neighbours included the residences of business clerks and lawyers, a private boys high school, and Mrs. Simpson's Ladies School. Consequently, the couple's move to the Square Mile has been interpreted as "a declaration that they were not intending to establish themselves among the mixed-blood HBC population which still clustered around the old headquarters [in Lachine]."[4] And yet, those tender ties, as Sylvia Van Kirk might call them, continued to powerfully link the Smith-Hardisty family to Lachine and to the Northwest.[5]

This chapter suggests that the Square Mile was entangled in a web of transcontinental and transnational financial and family network relationships. Further, it demonstrates how the history of the Metis and "Half-breed"[6] communities that emerged in the Northwest is relevant to the Square Mile. Reconstructing this history through intimate ties, this chapter connects the residents of Montreal's Square Mile to a rich literature on the personal and family networks that sustained the fur trade and the Metis.[7] Understanding that intimacy sheds new light on the political and economic history of the Square Mile.[8] As others have shown, biographical study reveals surprising colonial relationships,[9] and letters between family members can provide a rich vein to link the local and the global dynamics of settler colonialism.[10]

Study of the networks that sustained the Square Mile offers insight into the negotiation of imperial power.[11] My interest in this story is inspired by recent transnational and imperial history that considers the overlap between intimacy and governance. As one study has noted, "family and empire were entangled in a wide variety of ways."[12] In the Square Mile, just as in the "frontier," networks interacted with culture to reduce risk, generate trust, and facilitate efficient communication.[13] Richard White points out that networks produced knowledge valuable to nineteenth-century business.[14] However, while networks bridge gaps between people, they do not erase difference. While acknowledging that a network concentrates power in certain people and places, this chapter suggests that the study of family relations can incorporate histories and perspectives not always heard, particularly those of women.[15]

This chapter also contributes to the history of the shift from mercantile social relations to the industrial era of what is called the "Gilded Age." Often described as the replacement of a business culture oriented around older, family-oriented relationships with impersonal, legal, and corporate relations,[16] this shift would be better seen as layered with connections forged between the old and the new.[17] Historians have argued that old wealth transported to new urban centres played an important role in structuring society.[18] And, as Pamela Walker Laird argues, revealing these connections challenges the liberal individualist myth of a post-industrial era characterized by individual achievement that is constituted by equality of opportunity and high social mobility.[19] As theorists have argued, networking creates social capital.[20] The social privileges of the Smith-Hardisty family, formed in older economic systems, were maintained as they transitioned into a new urban space.

Finally, by linking diverse biographies across far-flung territories and recovering the "contact zone" of the Square Mile within the diaspora of the fur trade,[21] this chapter implicitly shows how "forgetting" history has also constituted this urban space.[22] The erasure of Indigenous, and especially female Indigenous, identities in the Square Mile was part of constructing and buttressing the racial order of the British Empire. Settler colonialism intended to define this space as one apart from Indigenous stories. By contrast, the history of the Smith-Hardisty family reveals what Edward Said would call "other ways of telling" the history of this place.[23]

Settling into Montreal

Lord Strathcona is best known for his role as a railroad investor and philanthropist. He is most famous for his investment – with his cousin George Stephen, later Lord Mount Stephen – in the Canadian Pacific Railway (CPR). The image of Smith driving "the last spike" at Craigellachie in 1885 is iconic and one of the best known in Canadian history (Figure 4.1). He became the land commissioner, governor, and principal shareholder of the HBC. He served as president of the Bank of Montreal. He founded numerous Canadian companies, including the Canada Rolling Stock Company, the Commercial Bank of Manitoba, the Central Telegraph Company, and the Manitoba Insurance Company. He also served as member of Parliament for Selkirk and Montreal in the Canadian House of Commons. He owned numerous properties, one of which was the sumptuous Strathcona mansion at 1157 Dorchester Street. Later dubbed Strathcona House, it once hosted King George and Queen Mary.[24] He was also instrumental in the support of iconic Square Mile institutions including McGill University and the Royal Victoria Hospital. From the Square Mile he became a staunch empire builder. He was chairman of the Anglo-Persian Oil Company. Later, he was Canada's High Commissioner to England and, most flamboyantly, paid for equipping a military division called "Strathcona's Horse" in the South African War. He also served as chancellor of McGill University and the University of Aberdeen.[25]

Donald Smith was born in Forres, on the Moray Coast in Scotland. He started his career with the Hudson's Bay Company working in Labrador in 1838. His first job was in Lachine working as an apprentice clerk, but he quickly ascended the company ladder. From the beginning, he was mentored and vetted by George Simpson, the HBC governor, who gave him responsibility for the Mingan trade, a region extending from Tadoussac to Labrador (Figure 4.2). He modernized the company through the effective use of steamships. In Labrador, he married Isabella, the daughter of Richard Hardisty and Margaret Sutherland. The marriage cemented his ties to the fur trade and transformed him into a member of the local colonial elite.[26] His in-laws catapulted Smith into a dense network of multi-generational HBC families and aided his ascension of the company hierarchy. Smith moved from

C-003693

Figure 4.1 Photograph of Donald A. Smith "driving the last spike" at Craigellachie in 1885. Library and Archives Canada / C-003693. This image has been symbolic of the completion of the CPR and of Canadian Confederation itself. Donald Smith is in the centre. The two men over his left shoulder are William Cornelius Van Horne and Sandford Fleming. John Henry McTavish can be seen over his right shoulder, and James Ross is visible in profile just to the right (with the dark beard).

clerk to trading factor, to chief factor, to representative of land sales, and, finally, to governor of the company.

The "Company of Adventurers," with harrowing adventures, drinking, manliness, and hardscrabble spirits, has attracted its fair share of romantic history. But that history is not always rigorous. Closer attention reveals a far more interesting history of how older economic relations exerted profound influence on new financial arrangements. Smith's networks show how wealth accumulated from the fur trade would drive the financial synergies of Montreal's Square Mile.

In the 1860s, the Square Mile was emerging as a residential space for Canada's wealthy. It is less well known that this space was partly built with capital accumulated from the fur trade. While many traders retired or resettled their families in

Figure 4.2 William Hind, *Donald Smith (Lord Strathcona) at North West River*, c. 1860. Library and Archives Canada, Acc. No. 1988-245-1. This is the only image of Donald A. Smith depicting him at work in the fur trade at this time.

Red River and various towns in Ontario, others, as noted in chapter 1 by Roderick MacLeod, such as Edward Clouston, William Connolly, Dugald MacTavish, and Richard Hardisty, came to Montreal.[27] Prince of Wales Terrace, one of the most sumptuous multi-unit residences in the Square Mile, was erected at the corner of Sherbrooke and MacTavish Streets by former HBC Governor George Simpson. When the head office of the HBC moved from Lachine to Montreal, administrators like Edward Hopkins, the chief factor, took up residence there.

Donald Smith was appointed chief factor of the HBC when Hopkins retired in 1868. However, already in 1866, while still officially posted to Labrador, the Smith-Hardistys were planning to move. Donna McDonald argues that in 1867

Donald Smith was already purchasing crystal and china in London that could only have suited an urban household, not a trading post.[28] Donald Smith's Square Mile residence put him in proximity to powerful financial circles in Montreal. These financial circles would be the beating heart of financial investment in the new Dominion, particularly the Bank of Montreal and the Canadian Pacific Railway. Social associations encouraged financial arrangements. Smith's regular trips to the head office of the HBC in the Toupin Building on the Places d'Armes were part of this. The building was also occupied by the City Passenger Railway Company, the London Assurance Company, the Scottish Provincial Assurance Company, as well as an assortment of notary offices and the St. Patrick's Literary Association. The Place d'Armes itself was the site for the City Bank, the Bank of Montreal, and a host of other important business institutions.[29] According to Donna McDonald, Smith attended an 1866 meeting in Montreal with George Stephen, Hugh Allan, and Edward King. He formed the Canada Rolling Stock Company with these men and Robert Reekie in 1869.[30] These are the classic associations we might expect of businessmen in the coming industrial age, however the key to Smith's power was located in the associations that were formed through his marriage.

Donald Smith's career and success is inexplicable without incorporating the influence of his wife Isabella Sophia Hardisty (Figure 4.3). The daughter of an elite Metis family, her family and personal relationships enabled Donald Smith and the various corporations and associations he represented to access a vast network of financial interests. Her extensive transcontinental personal correspondence seems trivial, but it shows that her knowledge of the way goods and information moved through a vast trade network was second nature to the Hardisty family.

Who was Isabella? She met Donald Smith in Labrador, but she was born in the Northwest and went to school in Red River. She had moved with her father, Richard Hardisty, to Labrador when he was appointed chief factor for the Esquimaux Bay district. The northern waterways of the HBC's territory provided the means of their travel. In Labrador, she married a Red River Metis man, James Grant, but within months had separated from him. They had been married *à la façon du pays* (according to the custom of the country), so the separation was also an informal affair. Shortly afterwards she married Smith, also *à la façon du pays*. This caused controversy for Donald, but especially for Isabella.[31] The controversy of marital arrangements situated outside of the norms of legality and morality of the metropolitan and Christian state illustrates the hardening of racial sensibilities in Canada and the British Empire more broadly. The court case over the inheritance of William Connolly, another Square Mile resident, made this abundantly clear in the 1860s.

Figure 4.3 Photograph of Isabella Hardisty-Smith, c. 1870–1880. Provincial Archives of Manitoba, 1979/53/52, N646.

The children from Connolly's second wife unsuccessfully contested the inheritance claims of the children from the first wife.[32]

Isabella Hardisty's identity is one of the more difficult components of this story to unravel. The Metis nation self-consciously emerged in the Northwest in response to a particular history. Although Isabella had ancestors and family members who were Metis, she did not associate with the "New Nation" that emerged as a result of the buffalo hunting kin networks that historians now see as essential to Metis nationhood.[33] She did, however, socialize with other elite Metis families in Red River and in the Northwest, and later in life, Isabella's racial Otherness was the basis for racist attacks on her character: one observer privately described her as a "hoddy-doddy squaw."[34] It is not entirely clear, however, if Isabella was embarrassed by her racial Otherness. Scrip claims indicate that the Hardisty family recognized their "Half-breed" heritage.[35] The fact that Donald Smith attempted to obfuscate her Indigenous parentage in the biographies he authorized suggests that he saw it as slander, but conversely it also reveals that he understood the truth of her Indigeneity. Racial boundaries inflected networking differently in different social contexts.[36] In light of the absence of her own declaration, I have, unsatisfactorily, concluded that she had Indigenous heritage but did not wish to be identified as Metis.

Isabella Hardisty's letters – in which we see that her handwriting was far superior to Donald Smith's – reflect the quality of her education, her strong personality, and her ability to carefully manage the affairs of an extended family. Isabella provided reports on her father's business to her brother. She also encouraged her other siblings in their work and empathetically lamented their misfortunes.[37] She took charge of visitors, placed children of family friends in boarding schools, and managed multiple households. She paid careful attention to the welfare of her siblings' children.

Her private correspondence gives us an image of a dynamic and thoughtful woman who made her own decisions, but who also felt a strong sense of responsibility to her family. The correspondence that does survive is evidence of the regularity of her travels across the continent and the globe. It is worth emphasizing that the motivation for this movement was often intimate and personal: that a grandmother might see her grandchildren, or a chance to visit a sister. One letter records the satisfaction of Margaret Hardisty, Isabella's mother, with the arrival of family: "the youngsters kick up a great noise in the house ... so I have no fear of being lonesome."[38] Frequently, Isabella mediated the migration of Northwest families into Montreal and its environs. In 1866, Isabella brought Mr. Connolly's daughters (likely from his second marriage) with her and found places for them in the Lachine convent.[39] In October 1867, she and her younger brother Thomas "brought down" the children of another brother, William, to their mother's house.[40] While not directly visible in the archive, such correspondence reveals that mothers and grandmothers managed family networks, and therefore social capital, across multiple households.

The way that affective ties motivated travel and selection of home clearly impacted the Smith-Hardisty family's move to Montreal's Square Mile. The move would have also had an impact on other familial and social obligations. Isabella, a woman with Metis heritage, now residing in the Square Mile, tied Donald to an extensive network. And the benefits between relations were mutual, as Donald Smith could guarantee that the extended Hardisty family would continue to have access to capital markets in Montreal and London; Richard Charles Hardisty, for example, was recognized as the richest man in the Northwest by the 1880s.[41]

Continued Ties to the Northwest

Perhaps most significantly, Smith's marriage into this Metis family was integral to his role in the Confederation of Manitoba during the Red River Resistance led by Louis Riel and the Metis. In the summer of 1869, three of Richard Hardisty's sons, Tom, William, and Richard Charles, as well as their brother-in-law Joseph McPherson (married to Mary Hardisty) were in Lachine. Isabella was likely there, as was their mother. It is uncertain whether the Smith-Hardisty family children, James and Maggie, were also there – they spent much of their time in England for their education. The family, worried about the growing agitation of the French Metis, would have discussed the impending sale of the HBC territories in the Northwest to the new Canadian Dominion and the worries of the HBC wintering partners with respect to the sale.

That same summer, opposition to Canada was being organized in Red River. A group of largely francophone Metis, under the guidance of Louis Riel, formed a National Council, and an armed group occupied Fort Garry in the fall of 1869. They blockaded the roads and confronted William MacDougall, the Canadian-appointed governor. Lacking the authority and the force to enter the settlement, MacDougall returned to Canada humiliated. The Metis proceeded to form a provisional government and arrested their opponents. Fearing American opportunism, the Canadian Prime Minister John A. Macdonald took emergency measures, and Donald Smith, in his capacity as chief factor for the HBC, was appointed as special commissioner for the Canadian government. In late December 1869, Smith arrived in Red River Settlement in the company of his brother-in-law Richard Charles Hardisty. Educated at the Red River Academy and apprentice post-master for the Red River district, Richard Charles was well connected to the community.

In the official report sent to the government, Smith obscured how his success was highly contingent upon his personal connections and his willingness to concede to local interests. As William Morton pointed out, the report was carefully crafted to suit political interests.[42] By unpacking his family links, we can complicate Smith's efforts to cast his success in negotiation as the result of rhetorical persuasion of Canadian goodwill.

Upon arrival in Red River, Smith was viewed with suspicion, and it was only due to his careful building of alliances, along kinship networks, that he was even allowed to address the Red River public. Once he had taken up residence (under the watchful eye of French Metis) in Fort Garry, Smith announced that he had official papers from the Canadian government that would clarify their intentions with respect to the future of the Northwest territory. However, the papers were in Pembina for safe keeping. Louis Riel and Smith made an agreement to send Richard Charles Hardisty and Modeste Lagimodière (Riel's cousin) to fetch the papers.

Meanwhile, working behind Riel's back, Smith recruited more "loyalists," and a second party set out to intercept Hardisty and the papers. When he heard what had happened, Riel was furious and personally rode out to confront the conspirators and, following a chase on horseback, declared that he would only allow them to pass over his dead body. Events escalated when one of Smith's allies, Pierre Léveillé, pointed his pistol at the head of the Metis chief. Fortunately, cooler heads prevailed, and, following negotiation, the entire party retired to Fort Garry where a public meeting was announced for 19 January.[43]

The public meeting at Fort Garry held on 19–20 January 1870 was the turning point of the Resistance. Upwards of 1,000 people attended to listen to Riel and Smith together on a platform. Smith read the papers and Riel translated.[44] Generally, Smith restrained himself to merely reading the documents from the government, the governor general, and from the HBC officers. But, after presenting all of these credentials, he added a personal comment:

> Though personally unknown to you, I am as much interested in the welfare of this country as others. On both sides I have a number of relations in this land (*cheers*) – not merely Scotch cousins, but blood relations. Besides that, my wife and her children are natives of Rupert's Land. (*cheers*) Hence, though I am myself a Scotchman, people generally will not be surprised that I should feel a deep interest in this great country and its inhabitants. (*cheers*) I am here to day [*sic*] in the interests of Canada, but only in so far as they are in accordance with the interests of this country. (*hear, hear and cheers*)[45]

Donald Smith did not bow to presumption easily and chose his words carefully. He recognized that, in Red River's public sphere, personal relations were vital to political legitimacy.[46] Here, public trust and intimacy overlapped.

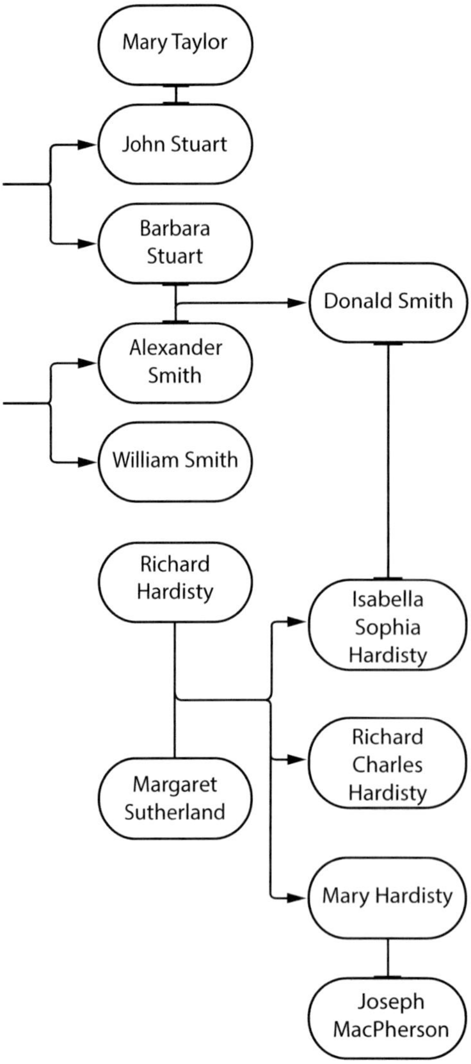

Figure 4.4 Direct relations of Donald Smith and Isabella Sophia Hardisty. The Smith-Hardisty marriage was part of a network of family connections in the Red River Settlement.

A few historians have speculated about the nature of these relations to the people of the Northwest.[47] They are worth careful consideration. Most conspicuous is Smith's marriage to Isabella Hardisty. As I have argued elsewhere, relationships with local women lent legitimacy and credibility to non-Indigenous men in Indigenous public spheres.[48] As the husband of a Red River woman, Smith could count on support derived from his in-laws in the Red River public sphere.

Family genealogy provides evidence of these "relations" – "not merely Scotch cousins" on his mother's side (Figure 4.4). Donald Smith's maternal uncle was John Stuart, one of the first European fur traders to enter the Pacific Northwest. Stuart was extensively involved with the North West Company (NWC) and, after the union, with the HBC. Alexander Ross, a Red River historian and social commentator, was one of Stuart's closest companions. Alexander Ross's son James was the most prominent representative of the English "Half-breed" community.[49] Stuart also married a Red River woman, Mary Taylor, according to the custom of the country, but there is no record of children.[50] She followed Stuart to Scotland, but when he refused to marry her under Scottish law she returned to North America. The separation may have strained the ties between the Taylor and Smith family networks, but they remained in contact. In 1867, Isabella wrote to her brother, Richard Charles Hardisty, to say that Mary was living in Lachine with a daughter.[51] Mary's older brother and sister continued to reside in Red River in the parish of St. Andrew.[52] Donald Smith, the new HBC factor, would also have been recognized by Stuart's extended family in Red River. Mary's nephew, George Taylor, and his wife had a home and family in St. Andrew's Parish in Red River. Mary's older sister Margaret had married Amable Hogue in 1831, and they had a house in St. Charles Parish.[53] Both families were likely at the meeting in 1870.

Furthermore, Smith claimed, "On both sides I have a number of relations." The incompleteness of the archival record is an obstacle, but there is some evidence that his father had relations in the country. Edward Mortimer, his father's cousin, had been a NWC clerk and former chief factor in the Athabasca and Mackenzie River districts. Edward Smith, a fur trader posted to Norway House, may also have been a relative of Smith's father.[54] We can take Donald Smith's claim of "relations in this land" at face value.

Certainly, Smith used the term "Scotch cousin" with a some irony.[55] In other words, he expected his relations would prove to be more than "scotch." Yet, the phrase may also have intentionally referred to ancient ideas of Scottish clan ties. Many Northwest traders came from the Strathspey valley in Scotland, the traditional territory of the Grant clan (Figure 4.5).[56] Smith's mother was a Grant. According to both Rosemary Omner and Maureen Molloy, clan ties had little social force by the mid-nineteenth century in Scotland, but as an idea the *clann* still manifested itself in real social ways.[57]

Indeed, the Grant clan has been recognized as a force in Red River.[58] In 2012, the Grant clan honoured Cuthbert Grant at an event in Winnipeg.[59] Cuthbert Grant (son of Cuthbert, son of David) led the NWC against the HBC in the Victory of Frog Plain (otherwise known as the Battle of Seven Oaks) in 1816. Cuthbert Grant was appointed "warden of the plains" and considered a representative of the Metis and "Half-breed" community: he was Roman Catholic, bilingual, and a respected captain of the buffalo hunt.[60] His mother was a Metis woman,[61] and his siblings,

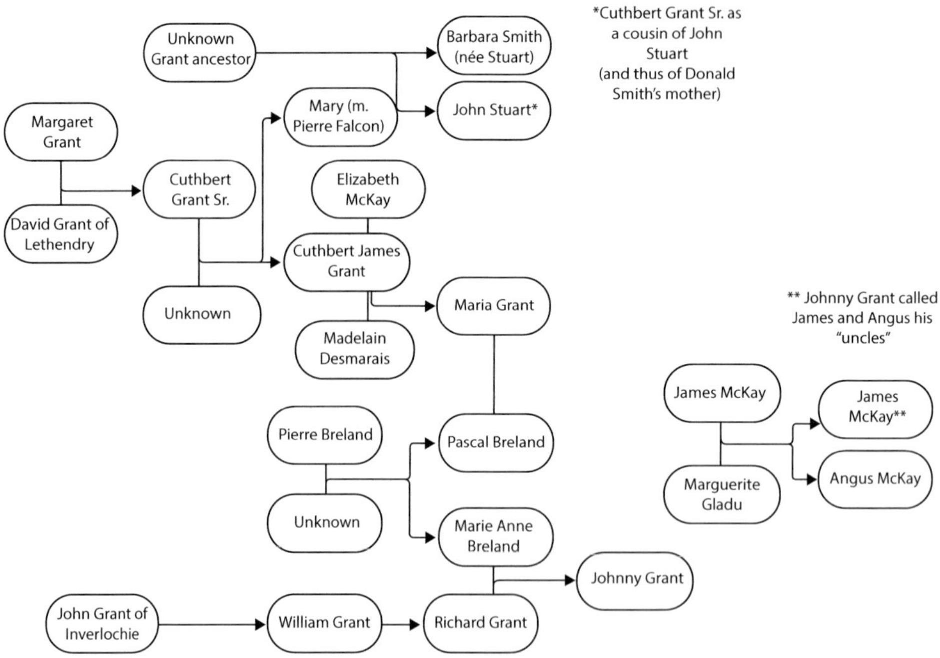

Figure 4.5 Sketch of extended Grant clan relations at the time of the Red River Resistance. Donald Smith's ties to the Grant families in the Red River Settlement were significant for his diplomatic position in the settlement.

educated in Montreal and Scotland, were the basis for an extended assemblage of links between the Northwest, Montreal, and Scotland. Interestingly, a will from 1822 states that Grant Senior was the cousin of the NWC explorer John Stuart (the uncle of Donald Smith).[62]

Ties within the Red River Grant "clan" become significant when we consider the background of Smith's allies. The men sent to guard Smith's papers were Johnny Grant, Angus McKay, and Pierre Léveillé. All can be linked to the Grant clan of Red River. Johnny Grant was a descendant of the Grant Clan of Inverlochie.[63] Angus McKay was Johnny Grant's uncle. Cuthbert Grant had also married Elizabeth McKay, although her relation to Angus is not clear. Even Pierre Léveillé, the man who threatened Riel with a pistol, was related to the Grants through the marriage of his son to Pascal Breland's daughter.[64] Breland, who had married Grant's daughter, Mary, was widely considered Cuthbert's heir.

Relations, Scotch or not, were important for Smith's diplomacy during the Metis resistance. Historians have argued that the Scottish diaspora within the British Empire was underpinned by ideas of kinship.[65] Notwithstanding the importance of the Scottish diaspora, imperial understandings of family were situated alongside Indigenous cultural practices. In Red River, it seems that Scottish and Metis ideas of relations or, to use the Cree term, *wakhootowin*, overlapped in a kind of middle ground of kinship discourse that generated legitimacy for Smith. Nicole St-Onge, Brenda Macdougall, and others argue that kinship was central to Metis understandings of community. Moreover, kinship provided a framework for governance and gave Metis buffalo hunting brigades political consciousness.[66] This overlap, or "creative misunderstanding," to use the expression of Richard White, was crucial to Smith's political legitimacy.[67]

The force of family ties, often dubbed loyalty, can easily be criticized as "corruption," particularly when they are coupled with economic relationships. However, this interpretation of what is essentially social and economic capital operating in the political realm misrepresents how these ties operated in the socio-political economies of Red River. There is evidence that kinship ties were reinforced by economic motivations or relations. Pascal Breland, Cuthbert Grant's heir, was reportedly absent from the settlement in the fall of 1869 – it was rumoured that he wanted to avoid being tied to the political agitation.[68] Yet, in a letter dated 9 February 1870, just after the public meeting, William MacTavish outlined a list of goods to be shipped to Breland's address in St. Paul for the coming spring.[69] Apparently, his credit rating with the company was still good, if not improved, following Donald Smith's visit. In 1869, Smith had been given a sum by Macdonald to deal with his expenses on behalf of the Canadian government. In early 1875, the Canadian government paid out rewards to the "loyal French," including $250 to Grant, McKay, and Léveillé.[70] The social capital stored in kinship networks was reinforced with monetary relationships. Johnny Grant recounts that he forgave the debts of customers at his store and bought votes for Smith's election in 1871 at $5–10 a vote.[71]

For the wintering partners and the extended family of fur traders, crude bribery was not necessary. Credits could be had at the HBC store, while positions as tripmen and carters, as well as personal loans and mortgages, were at Smith's fingertips.[72] More importantly, letters and other documents reveal that for the old wintering partners, Smith's access to markets in the east was far more significant. In 1869, Donald Smith took over the responsibility for the personal investment accounts.[73] This was a practice started by George Simpson in 1841. Invariably it mixed family and financial interests. For instance, in 1871, Smith wrote to his brother-in-law, Richard Hardisty, complaining about the temerity of free traders who used liquor, the establishment of a new Board of Health, and the news about the 1872 Outfit,[74] and he concluded by relating that Hardisty's mother was laid up with a bad leg, that his sister (Donald Smith's wife) had been in Winnipeg with the children James and

Maggie, and that they had returned to Montreal.[75] He also informed Richard about the returns on his investments in the Canada Rolling Stock Company. During his career, Smith fulfilled a wide range of personal requests for many HBC employees and members of his extended family network.[76] HBC correspondence to and from Smith contains numerous powers of attorney and orders to purchase stock in the Bank of Montreal, the Canada Rolling Stock Company, and other ventures on behalf of the inhabitants of Red River.

The overlap between family relations and financial relationships is significant, but, in fairness, this was not just a family affair. On 12 March 1871, Smith forwarded notes of exchange from the Lord Bishop McRae, detailing a payment on the government committee's account to former HBC employee and manager of the Winnipeg branch of the Merchant's Bank of Canada, Duncan MacArthur. He also asked MacArthur to open new private cash accounts for Robert Tait and Bishop Antonin-Alexandre Taché, and he agreed to make a payment on the account of Mrs. James McKay.[77]

On 26 July 1870, Smith had received the following requisition from widow McKay:

> Referring to the power of attorney to dispose of the Canadian [funds? stocks?] … under the estate of my late husband. I am anxious that you should exercise your discretion with regard to the sale of them with a view to take advantage of any opportunity that may seem to afford the best result to the estate. I think it proper to state as much, although I am conscious that your friendly interest would have anticipated my wish in this respect.[78]

The expression "your friendly interest" is suggestive of the personal stake involved in arranging these affairs. Long-term trust was built on the basis of such personal ties. In 1871, Donald Smith purchased Rowand House from John Henry McTavish, an English "Half-breed" and the HBC accountant in 1869, for £905. McTavish had once been rumoured to sympathize with Louis Riel's Metis but would become closely tied to Donald Smith. He would become a founder of the Winnipeg Board of Trade and the Commercial Bank of Manitoba and, finally, the CPR's land commissioner.[79] In 1871, with the lieutenant governor renting the HBC buildings at Fort Garry, Donald Smith moved the HBC office to the old Rowand House, now renamed Silver Heights.[80] Family, company, and government interests intertwined in these exchanges.

Smith was seen as a Scotsman and a representative of foreign and imperial institutions, but he was also the husband of a Red River woman. At later public appearances, Smith consistently framed his intentions in the community as family interests. Smith's speech at a banquet held in his honour at the Winnipeg Opera House in February 1872 is a good example.[81] Smith responded to the toasts by once again underlining his personal connections:

> [My] relatives and friends were among the originators of the North-West Company which subsequently amalgamated with the Hudson Bay Company. It is a somewhat singular coincidence that I should see the last of the old regime of the Hudson Bay Company; and have been empowered by that company to aid it in taking up a new lease of prosperity (*cheers*) – a prosperity in which all present and future inhabitants of this land are closely concerned.[82]

Transforming Fur Trade Connections

The removal of the Smith-Hardistys from Lachine to the Square Mile can be seen as symbolic of the broader socio-economic transformation of this period. The "old regime" was being displaced by new corporate and less personal socio-economic relationships, often formalized with legal charters. Social capital took on a different hue in the liberal economy. Donald Smith's involvement in the new financial arrangements of the Dominion and the British Empire illustrate his leadership in the new corporate environment. And yet, he defended and strengthened old relations, particularly the interests of the wintering partners who he referred to in public as friends and relatives.

The capitalization of the HBC's massive land claims was a prime opportunity for company reform. All shareholders, in London and in the Northwest, financers, and wintering partners admitted that the administration of the territory had grown too costly. The HBC accepted the offer of purchase from the Canadian government to avoid responsibility for "Indian claims" and for carrying out land surveys.[83] Furthermore, the Canadian government became responsible for security, criminal justice, and other social affairs. The sale of the land would certainly benefit shareholders, but whether the wintering partners were eligible to receive a share of this payment was highly contested.

In 1865, the wintering partners had been excluded from profits derived from the sale of the HBC's Oregon territory to the United States, and it took a court case for the board of directors to agree to share the profits from the sale of the HBC's London office buildings on Fenchurch Street. In 1869, faced with once again missing out on this windfall, company men across the continent united, and in 1870, a legal challenge was mounted by A.K. Isbister against the HBC shareholders. Subsequent to this movement, Donald Smith was appointed to represent the interests of the wintering partners at an extraordinary meeting in Norway House. His report to the director's council forced the shareholders to agree to pay the wintering partners.[84] As William MacTavish (in Fort Garry) wrote to Richard Charles Hardisty in August 1871, "One thing I can assure you of, Mr. Smith is doing all that man can do and he is backed up by the Directors, but what can they do against a pack of rapacious proprietors who are now trying to screw the last penny out of the concern."[85]

Another downside of the new administration was that a new government meant a new tax arrangement that would cut into the profits of wintering partners. Previously, the HBC imposed a paltry 4 per cent tariff on imports. With Confederation, Canada intended to raise the tariff to 20 per cent. London saw reduced costs, but the wintering partners saw reduced profit. HBC correspondence from the Northwest communicated widespread concern about the future of the trade under Confederation. In May 1869, William MacTavish forwarded to the London office a copy of a letter from an American agent to Joseph Howe regarding the excitement over the land returns, the new tariffs, and reciprocity. In November, he noted, "any change in the Indian tariff will certainly be met with considerable opposition on the part of the Natives."[86]

Consequently, taxation was prominent during the negotiations of the List of Rights sent to Ottawa by the Convention of Forty at Red River, an indication of the relative strength of the wintering partners in public opinion. From the list adopted on 3 February 1870, the first two points demanded that taxes stay low:

> Article 1. That in view of the present exceptional position of the North-West, *duties upon goods imported into the country shall continue as at present (except in the case of spirituous liquors) for three years*, and for such further time as may elapse until there be uninterrupted railroad communication between Red River Settlement and Lake Superior.
>
> Article 2. That during this period, there shall be *no direct taxation* except such as may be imposed by the local legislature for municipal or other local purposes.[87]

These conditions were included directly following Smith's intervention in January 1870. Riel and his party likely accommodated themselves to these articles because it strengthened their bargaining position with Canada. It may have also been part of a deal in which the wintering partners recognized Riel's authority, gave the Metis party a loan, and promised to recirculate company bills.[88]

Smith's mobility between the Northwest, Montreal, and London were critical to bringing the Northwest partners' interests to the attention of the policymakers in Ottawa. The revolt against Canada's new taxes was carried over into the Manitoba Act.[89] Article 27 stated: "The Customs duties now by Law chargeable in Rupert's Land, shall be continued *without increase for the period of three years*."[90] Later, in 1876, Smith sided with the Liberal government to argue that there was no need for taxation in this weakly administered territory.[91] For taking the side of the company men, Smith was publicly derided as a corrupt representative of the company interests rather than that of his constituents.

Smith also brought these concerns of lowered profits to the attention of the London HBC board and shareholders. He successfully negotiated a new profit-sharing agreement. The "Deed Poll," as it was called, had originally been signed in 1821.[92] It gave the traders some decision-making powers and was an important tool for protecting the HBC monopoly. The Deed Poll not only meant greater stability in terms of income, but it also allowed the HBC traders to aggressively compete with smaller independent traders (driving them out of business by offering to purchase furs at higher prices). The effects were remarkable: stockholders received dividends of 10 per cent between 1825 and 1863, sometimes as high as 15 per cent. Chief factors earned on average £720 per year, and chief traders £360 as their share of profits between 1821 and 1872.[93]

This agreement could not survive the declining harvests of furs, nor the increased competition by free traders and European settlement, and on 1 June 1869, the governor and committee announced that they were not intending to extend the agreement.[94] During conversations at the Hardisty home in the summer of 1869, and that winter in the Red River Settlement, Smith heard the views of the Northwest wintering partners. In the spring of 1871, Donald Smith travelled to Washington to report to Lord Northcote and draft a new profit-sharing agreement.[95] In August 1871, Smith advised the London committee that the fur traders had agreed to revoke the old Deed Poll and would consider a new deal.[96] Impressed by his influence with wintering partners, the London board charged Smith with collecting the signatures of the partners on the new Deed Poll – a deal that took away their decision-making powers. Figure 4.6 is a photograph taken in William Notman's studio in Montreal after these men had signed the agreement. It is a graphic illustration of the transcontinental links connecting Montreal, and the Square Mile, to the Northwest. From left to right, they are Lawrence Clark, Donald Smith, James Bissett (below, lying on the animal skin), Peter Warren Bell, George MacTavish, an unidentified man, and Colin Rankin.[97] MacTavish was one of the sons or adopted sons of Dugald MacTavish and Maria Louisa Simpson of Red River. Colin Rankin was an HBC

Figure 4.6 William Notman, *James Bissett and Friends, Hudson's Bay Company Factors, Montreal,* 1871. McCord Museum, I-66968.1. At a meeting of HBC factors in Montreal, these men signed the new profit-sharing agreement for wintering partners.

officer mostly working in Northern Ontario, north of Ottawa, in the Temiskaming district. Peter Bell at this time worked in Moose Factory. Donald Smith and James Bissett, Smith's secretary, both lived in the Square Mile. (Bissett lived on St. Antoine between Dominion and Fulford, now Boulevard Georges-Vanier.) Over the next few months Smith received letters from Roderick Findlayson, James Stewart Clouston, Mr. Lockhart, and numerous others giving their consent.[98]

Smith informed London on 18 and 24 August 1871 that these men, as well as Alexander Macdonald, Joseph Hardisty, and Bernard Ross, had signed the agreement.[99] On 4 December, Donald Smith informed the wintering partners that he had "an agreement in my hands"[100] providing them with £170 per share on the profits from the land sale and a new Deed Poll. A memorandum titled "1872 Deed Poll" in the Inward Correspondence from HBC commissioners lists the traders and factors in each district.[101]

Through careful positioning via their Square Mile connection, the wintering partners sought to secure their position.[102] In 1878, a group of traders, the "Fur

Trade Party," led by Chief Factor John Henry McTavish, demanded a permanent salary from the HBC board. However, the HBC Chief Commissioner James Grahame refused to broach the matter with the board. Shortly after, McTavish approached Donald Smith, who, in February 1879, travelled to London to negotiate a minimum annual salary of £150. This incensed Grahame. He wrote a letter to John McTavish raging against the formation of this so-called Fur Trade Party: "How is it that you, an Officer in so high a position and in an instant personal communication with myself should have been in any way mixed up in a combined movement?"[103] Grahame was mistaken to think he was dealing with nascent unionist action. The Fur Trade Party was drawing upon social credit that was invested in their personal relationship with Donald Smith. It was more like family loyalty.

Donald Smith's treatment of the HBC partners has drawn outrage and praise from historians. For Peter C. Newman, Smith "reduced [his former colleagues] from patriarchs of the forests to supervised employees."[104] By contrast, Donna McDonald interprets Smith's actions as altruistic.[105] Both perspectives ignore the agency of the fur traders themselves and the shifting economic context. Regular wages and access to credit allowed old fur traders to invest their earnings in the Bank of Montreal and other stocks. Together, John McTavish, Joseph James Hargrave, and Donald Smith founded the Commercial Bank of Manitoba and the Manitoba Insurance Company. These traders were not starry-eyed dupes of a wily Strathcona.

Smith became a key figure linking the economic and social capital contained in the older fur-trade networks to the new industrial economic order. As the HBC's land commissioner and financier of the Canadian Pacific Railway, he was in an ideal situation. The decline in fur-trade profits coupled with the rise of European settlement on the northwest plains were symptoms of a massive economic reorganization. Donald Smith was an instrument of these changes, and his move to the Square Mile was emblematic of that reorganization. Yet, at the same time, he balanced these changes carefully with his old relationships. In chapter 8 of this volume, Greg Marchildon points to the process of "creative destruction" through which Max Aitken and Edward Clouston radically transformed the Canadian investment environment. Edward Clouston's father, James Stewart Clouston, was one of the wintering partners, and his mother was Miles Margaret, a "Half-breed" from Moose River. It is useful to contrast the father and the son. James Stewart Clouston, like Donald Smith, was more entangled in the older economies and social capital. For some, fur-trade marriages had a lingering influence in the Square Mile.

Conclusion

Even after his death, Lord Strathcona's fortunes were tied to the Northwest interests by the old network. His will stipulated a payment to "Retired Chief Factor Roderick MacFarlane and other retired Factors of the Hudson's Bay Company, who now receive a reduced allowance."[106] A memorandum in the Strathcona papers reinforces his intentions:

> For about *140 years the undersigned and his wife have by virtue of blood relationship, and by marriage*, been connected with the Old North West Company of Montreal, and with the amalgamated Hudson's Bay Company of Canada and England, while the herein relative names have nearly all been born by Partners of the former, and by commissioned Officers, or "Wintering Partners" of the latter.[107]

The longevity of Smith's family and financial networks within Montreal's Square Mile and beyond to the Northwest reinforces the argument that these ties generated significant financial and social capital. To understand this urban space, we need to see it as entangled in the threads of an invisible web of family and personal ties spread across the continent.

The networks that supported and entangled Donald Smith are one example of how intimate and official spheres overlapped among the Square Mile financial elite. Isabella brought Smith into the Hardisty family network, but kin ties alone do not determine political affiliations, and more work still needs to be done on the influence of Scottish ideas of family, or "clan," in Red River.[108] It is clear, however, that the relationships formed in the Northwest fur trade played a key role in social and financial networks of the Square Mile. Understanding the role that women of Indigenous parentage played in maintaining family and economic networks, even while moving into Montreal, needs greater attention. By detailing these connections, this chapter sheds light on the role that women might have played in forging social networks and, in this case as well as that of William Connolly and James S. Clouston, offers a surprising instance of how Indigenous connections might be relevant to understanding what has been considered a settler urban space. Indigenous perspectives and agency matter in the negotiation and forging of empire – even at its heart. Seeking out those connections and contributions will provide a richer and more complex history of social capital, and of men like Donald Smith and the Square Mile.

A long historiographical tradition argues that "family compacts" corrupted Canadian governance.[109] This chapter, following in the steps of Adele Perry and others, suggests that our understanding of the role of family in Canadian governance needs to be revisited. These relationships structured state building and the funding of empire. To put it another way, the groups that, according to Elsbeth Heaman, sought to "prop up structures of power and authority throughout society" in the second half of the nineteenth century were constituted by family relationships.[110] They helped shape a consensus that, despite a predominant liberalism, remained an important constituent of the capitalist empires of the late nineteenth and early twentieth centuries. In other words, "Canada-as-Empire" was held together not only by its liberal or loyalist orders but by family matters.[111]

When Donald and Isabella Smith moved from Lachine into the Square Mile it was more than symbolic; it reflected fundamental shifts in Canadian economic life. Following Confederation, the "project of empire" in British North America shifted away from the mercantilist fur trade to industrial-settler capitalism. The railroads were a key part of this shift, and Smith's role in that national project is well recognized. As a celebrated member of the Scottish diaspora, Smith helped make Canada's industrial order. However, in some respects, the old ties to the fur trade formed by relationships between European men and Indigenous women continued. Smith's role in the economic and social transformation was singular, but he also represented a particular constellation of networks that formed a bridge with the past.

NOTES

I thank Don Nerbas, Elizabeth Kirkland, Dimitry Anastakis, and all the participants of the Annual Colloquium of the St. Andrew's Society/McEuen Scholarship Foundation Chair in Canadian-Scottish Studies as well as the Canadian Business History Association Colloquium for their help and comments.

1 Isabella Smith to Richard Charles Hardisty, 4 April 1867, Glenbow Museum Archives, Richard Hardisty Fonds, Series 23–2, M 5908–1487.

2 The family was only referred to as "Smith," however in an effort to emphasize the role of Smith's wife and her family ties, I have chosen to use this admittedly anachronistic label. The politics of family ties and of hidden identities is at the heart of this chapter, and I suggest that drawing our attention to these links matters.

3 Laura Ishiguro argues that epistolary discussions of food sustain a broader politics of everyday knowledge of a family's sense of home. Ishiguro, "'A Dreadful Little Glutton Always Telling You about Food': The Epistolary Everyday and the Making of Settler Colonial British Columbia," *Canadian Historical Review* 99, no. 2 (June 1999): 258–83, https://doi.org/10.3138/chr.99.2.04v.

4 Donna McDonald, *Lord Strathcona: A Biography of Donald Smith* (Toronto: Dundurn Press, 1996), 135.

5 Sylvia Van Kirk, *Many Tender Ties: Women in Fur-Trade Society in Western Canada, 1670–1870* (Winnipeg: Watson & Dwyer, 1980). See the discussion of Van Kirk's influence in Valerie Korinek and Robin Jarvis Brownlee, eds., *Finding a Way to the Heart: Feminist Writings on Aboriginal and Women's History in Canada* (Winnipeg: University of Manitoba Press, 2012).

6 The term "Half-breed" is used here only because it was a prescriptive and preformed label of English "mixed-race" peoples from the Northwest. I recognize that it reflects a faulty racial logic and discriminatory attitudes that obscure the identity and experience of these people. Quotation marks highlight its contingent nature. If we redefined the term according to current critiques of racism, it might be appropriate to call Isabella Hardisty Metis. She was slandered as a "Half-breed," and her brothers applied for scrip. However, state categories and the practice of Othering are never good standards for determining identity. Hardisty left that community behind, and the care with which her husband attempted to edit her Indigenous heritage out of his biography suggests a concerted effort to insulate her from association with "Indians." For some of the best considerations of the issue, see Chris Andersen, *Métis: Race, Recognition, and the Struggle for Indigenous Peoplehood* (Vancouver: UBC Press, 2014); Brenda Macdougall, "The Myth of Metis Cultural Ambivalence," in *Contours of a People: Metis Family, Mobility, and History*, ed. Nicole St-Onge, Carolyn Podruchny, and Brenda Macdougall (Vancouver: UBC Press, 2010), 422–59; and Nicole St-Onge, "Familial Foes? French-Sioux Families and Plains Métis Brigades in the Nineteenth Century," *The American Indian Quarterly* 39, no. 3 (Summer 2015): 302–37. See also Adele Perry, *Colonial Relations: Douglas-Connolly Family and the Nineteenth-Century Imperial World* (Cambridge: Cambridge University Press, 2015), 73, 151–5.

7 The literature here is considerable. Some key titles are Van Kirk, *Many Tender Ties*; Jennifer Brown, *Strangers in Blood: Fur Trade Company Families in Indian Country* (Vancouver: UBC Press, 1980); Carolyn Podruchny, *Making the Voyageur World: Travellers and Traders in the North American Fur Trade* (Toronto: University of Toronto Press, 2006); Brenda MacDougall, *One in the Family: Metis Culture in Nineteenth-Century Northwestern Saskatchewan* (Vancouver: UBC Press, 2010); Jean Barman, *French Canadians, Furs and Indigenous Women in the Making of the Pacific Northwest* (Vancouver: UBC Press, 2014).

8 As Adele Perry writes, connecting the personal with the political "not only alerts us to the politics of everyday life but to the familial, intimate and gendered character of the high politics that form the stuff of conventional historical scholarship." Perry, "Historiography That Breaks Your Heart: Van Kirk and the Writing of Feminist History," in *Finding a Way to the Heart: Feminist Writings on Aboriginal and Women's History in Canada*, ed. Valerie Korinek and Robin Jarvis Brownlee (Winnipeg: University of Manitoba Press, 2012), 92.

9 David Lambert and Alan Lester, eds., *Colonial Lives across the British Empire: Imperial Careering in the Long Nineteenth Century* (Cambridge: Cambridge University Press, 2006); Perry, *Colonial Relations*; Cecilia Morgan, *Travellers through Empire: Indigenous Voyages from Early Canada* (Montreal: McGill-Queen's University Press, 2017); Jean Barman, *Iroquois in the West* (Montreal: McGill-Queen's University Press, 2019).

10 Laura Ishiguro, *Nothing to Write Home About: British Family Correspondence and the Settler Colonial Everyday in British Columbia* (Vancouver: UBC Press, 2019).

11 Elizabeth Mancke, "Negotiating an Empire: Britain and Its Overseas Peripheries, c. 1150–1780," in *Negotiated Empires: Centers and Peripheries in the Americas, 1500–1820*, ed. Christine Daniels and Michael V. Kennedy (New York: Routledge, 2002), 235–65. See also Manke, *A Company of Businessmen: The Hudson's Bay Company and Long-Distance Trade, 1670–1730* (Winnipeg: Rupert's Land Research Centre, 1988); Aisling MacQuarrie, "Running the Rivers: The North West Company and the Creation of a Global Enterprise: 1778–1821" (PhD diss., University of Aberdeen, 2014). On the relationship between culture and power in business history more broadly, see Craig Muldrew, *The Economy of Obligation: The Culture of Credit and Social Relations in Early Modern England* (New York: St. Martin's Press, 1998); Robert Lee, "Commerce and Culture: A Critical Assessment of the Role of Cultural Factors in Commerce and Trade from 1750

to the Early Twentieth Century," in *Commerce and Culture: Nineteenth-Century Business Elites*, ed. Robert Lee (Burlington, VT: Ashgate, 2011), 1–36; Tony Ballantyne, "The Changing Shape of the Modern British Empire and Its Historiography," *The Historical Journal* 53, no. 2 (2010): 429–51.

12 Esme Cleall, Laura Ishiguro, and Emily J. Manktelow, "Imperial Relations: Histories of Family in the British Empire," *Journal of Colonialism and Colonial History* 14, no. 1 (Spring 2013), https://doi.org/10.1353/cch.2013.0006.

13 For an overview of networking in Canadian business, see Michael Bliss, *Northern Enterprise: Five Centuries of Canadian Business* (Toronto: McClelland & Stewart, 1987), 111. Robin Pearson and David Richardson stress reduction of risk in their article "Business Networking in the Industrial Revolution," *The Economic History Review* 54, no. 4 (2001): 657–79.

14 Richard White, "Information, Markets, and Corruption: Transcontinental Railroads in the Gilded Age," *Journal of American History* 90, no. 1 (2003): 19–43, https://doi.org/10.2307/3659790.

15 As Helen Doe notes, for instance, "Women loaned money through informal arrangements that are not always traceable despite the fact that they were 'important locations of power within the wider family network.'" Doe, *Enterprising Women and Shipping in the Nineteenth Century* (Woodbridge: Boydell Press, 2009), 111.

16 Muldrew, *Economy of Obligation*, 1–8.

17 In his study of the term *corruption*, White argues that "the gilded age did not replace local, face-to-face markets with an international market dealing with security issues in the tens or hundreds of millions of dollars; rather it layered those markets and forged connections between them." White, "Information," 24.

18 Robert A.J. McDonald, "'Vancouver's Four Hundred': The Quest for Wealth and Status in Canada's Urban West, 1886–1914," *Journal of Canadian Studies* 25, no. 3 (1990): 55–73. See also Don Nerbas, "Wealth and Privilege: An Analysis of Winnipeg's Early Business Elite," *Manitoba History* 47 (Spring/Summer 2004), https://www.mhs.mb.ca/docs/mb_history/47/winnipeg businesselite.shtml.

19 Pamela Walker Laird, *Pull: Networking and Success since Benjamin Franklin* (Cambridge, MA: Harvard University Press, 2007), 1–7.

20 Pierre Bourdieu draws our attention to the way in which power is transferred over generations, creating enduring inequality. Bourdieu, "Strategies de reproduction et modes de domination," *Actes de la recherche en science sociales* 105 (December 1994): 3–12, https://doi.org/10.3406/arss.1994.3118. See also Bourdieu, *The State of Nobility: Elite Schools and the Field of Power* (Stanford, CA: Stanford University Press, 1998).

21 For an excellent application of Mary Louisa Pratt's phrase "contact zone" to Montreal, see Bettina Bradbury, *Wife to Widow: Lives Laws, and Politics in Nineteenth-Century Montreal* (Vancouver: UBC Press, 2011), 29.

22 The history of forgetting Indigenous presence in urban spaces is increasingly the subject of exciting research. For one excellent example, see Coll Thrush, *Native Seattle: Histories from the Crossing-Over Place* (Seattle: University of Washington Press, 2018). See also Evelyn Peters and Chris Andersen, *Indigenous in the City: Contemporary Identities and Cultural Innovation* (Vancouver: UBC Press, 2014).

23 Edward W. Said, "Representing the Colonized: Anthropology's Interlocutors," *Critical Inquiry* 15, no. 2 (Winter 1989): 225, https://doi.org/10.1086/448481.

24 McDonald, *Lord Strathcona*, 350.

25 See Alexander Reford's excellent entry, "Smith, Donald Alexander," in *Dictionary of Canadian Biography*, vol. 14, University of Toronto/Université Laval, 2003–, accessed 14 May 2020, http://www.biographi.ca/en/bio/smith_donald_alexander_14E.html.

26 Perry, *Colonial Relations*, 37.

27 Silvia Van Kirk identified Archibald Macdonald, George Barnston, as well as Colin Robertson, William MacTavish, Peter Warren Dease, and Allan McDonnell as bringing their families to Montreal. Van Kirk, "The Role of Women in the Fur Trade 1700–1850" (PhD diss., Queen Mary College, 1975), 315.

28 McDonald, *Lord Strathcona*, 125.

29 "Street Directory, 1865–66," in *Collection d'annuaires Lovell de Montréal et sa région, 1842–2010* (Montreal: Bibliothèque et Archives nationales du Québec, 2019–), https://numerique.banq.qc.ca/patrimoine/details/52327/3652493.

30 McDonald, *Lord Strathcona*, 125.

31 In 1896, the couple was "re-married" in a private ceremony. Some biographers argue that it was a matter of social respectability. McDonald argues that Smith was more worried about potential challengers to his will. See McDonald, *Lord Strathcona*, 401.

32 Connolly married an Indigenous woman, Suzanne, but repudiated her to marry Julia Woolrich. Suzanne eventually moved back to Red River to live with her family, while Julia and Connolly took up residence at the western edge of the Square Mile on Côte-Sainte-Catherine. The children of his first family successfully defended their inheritance against a court case by the Woolrich family in a Lower Canadian Court. Incidentally, William directly preceded Donald Smith's tenure at Minigan. See the discussion of this case in Perry, *Colonial Relations*, 102–6. See also Constance Backhouse, *Petticoats and Prejudice: Women and Law in Nineteenth-Century Canada* (Toronto: University of Toronto Press, 1991).

33 See Jean Teillet, *The Northwest Is Our Mother: The Story of Louis Riel's People and the Métis Nation* (Toronto: Harper Collins, 2019); Gerhard J. Ens and Joe Sawchuk, *From New Peoples to New Nations: Aspects of Metis History and Identity from the Eighteenth to Twenty-First Centuries* (Toronto: University of Toronto Press, 2016).

34 Reford, "Smith"; McDonald, *Lord Strathcona*, 405.

35 There is no record of Isabella's application for scrip, but claims exist for her brother Richard Charles. See scrip claims for the Hardisty family in Library and Archives Canada, C-14939 (http://central.bac-lac.gc.ca/.redirect?app=fonandcol&id=1497903&lang=eng). Also of note is the application by Isabella's sister-in-law, Mary Thomas (wife of William Lucas Hardisty), on behalf of her son Richard Thomas Hardisty, who died at Batoche in 1885 fighting for the Canadian Army. See Library and Archives Canada, C-15006 (http://central.bac-lac.gc.ca/.redirect?app=fonandcol&id=1515358&lang=eng). Doris MacKinnon argues that such scrip claims should be understood as claims to identity rather than monetary interest; see MacKinnon, *Metis Pioneers: Marie Rose Delorme Smith and Isabella Clark Hardisty Lougheed* (Edmonton: University of Alberta Press, 2018), 166.

36 Morgan, *Travellers through Empire*, 148. Historians generally agree that Isabella was subject to social exclusion as a result of her racial Otherness (see Reford, "Smith"), yet that does not accord with her continued presence at public events. Consider that entrepreneur James Lougheed owed much of his later success to his marriage to Isabella Clark Hardisty, also a "Half-breed." Like Lougheed, Donald Smith's wealth was stimulated through forming linkages to the wealth of the Northwest. David J. Hall and Donald B. Smith, "Lougheed, Sir James Alexander," in *Dictionary of Canadian Biography*, vol. 15, University of Toronto/Université Laval, 2003–, accessed 14 May 2020, http://www.biographi.ca/en/bio/lougheed_james_alexander_15E.html. See also MacKinnon, *Metis Pioneers*, xxiii–xxv; Sylvia Van Kirk, "From 'Marrying-In' to 'Marrying-Out': Changing Patterns of Aboriginal/Non-Aboriginal Marriage in Colonial Canada," *Frontiers: A Journal of Women Studies* 23, no. 3 (2002): 1–11; Perry, *Colonial Relations*, 79–108.

37 Glenbow Museum Archives, Richard Hardisty Fonds, Series 23–1, nos. 1442–85.

38 Margaret Hardisty to Richard Charles Hardisty, 9 October 1867, Glenbow Museum Archives, Richard Hardisty Fonds, Series 23–2, nos. 5908–1489.

39 Richard Isabella Smith to Charles Hardisty, 14 April 1867, Glenbow Museum Archives, Richard Hardisty Fonds, Series 23–2, nos. 5908–1487.

40 Margaret Hardisty to Richard Hardisty, 7 September 1867, Glenbow Museum Archives, Richard Hardisty Fonds, Series 23–2, nos. 5908–1489. The letter is filed in September, but a postscript within the letter indicates it was mailed on 9 October.

41 MacKinnon, *Metis Pioneers*, 79–80.

42 Smith to Howe, Confidential, 12 January 1870, Secretary of State of the Province. Reprinted in W.L. Morton, *Manitoba: The Birth of a Province* (Winnipeg: Manitoba Record Society, 1965), 25–45. Joseph Howe edited the first draft of the report to remove any implication that the French-speaking delegates had hindered the work of Donald Smith; see Morton, *Manitoba*, 25

43 The first confrontation took place at Rivière-Salée during a wedding feast, and the party swelled in size as it proceeded to Red River. See Alexander Begg, *A History of the Red River Troubles* (Toronto, 1871), 220–2; John Francis Grant, *A Son of the Fur Trade: The Memoirs of Johnny Grant*, ed. Gerhard Ens (Edmonton: University of Alberta Press, 2008), 214–20.

44 For a description of this event, see *New Nation*, 21 January 1870, 2, http://hdl.handle.net/10719/2743887. See also Grant, *Son of the Fur Trade*; and Pierre Léveillé's response to Donald Smith in *New Nation*, 27 May 1870, 3, http://hdl.handle.net/10719/2743867. The first letter, dated 10 December 1869, was from Joseph Howe, the secretary of state for the Dominion of Canada, and described his commission on behalf of the Canadian government. The second, from the governor general of Canada to Donald Smith, asked Smith to communicate the wishes of the Queen to the settlement. The third was an official proclamation by the governor general to the Canadian Commissioner that described the Crown's intent with respect to the territories and people of the settlement. Smith proceeded to read more letters on the second day, one from the governor general to William MacTavish, and another from Joseph Howe to Mr. MacDougall. Riel translated each of the letters into French for the crowd.

45 Donald Smith quoted in *New Nation*, 21 January 1870, 2, http://hdl.handle.net/10719/2743887.

46 Riel himself used the rhetoric of family loyalties as justification for unity. For instance, when confronted by James Ross at the first convention on the source of his authority, Riel stated, "Voyez ce que dit Monsieur McTavish. Il dit que de cette assemblée et des décisions de cette assemblée peut venir un bien incalculable. Unissons-nous: le mal qu'il redoute n'aura pas lieu. Voyez comme il parle. Est-ce étonnant, ses enfants sont des Métis comme nous?" (You see what Mister McTavish says. He says that an incalculable good may come from this assembly and its decisions. Let us unite. The evil that worried him has not occurred. Look at what he says. Is it astonishing, his children are Metis like us?). Riel, "Compte rendu incomplet de la convention de novembre-décembre 1869," Societé Historique Saint-Boniface, MG3 D1–628.

47 As early as 1939, Wallace wondered if "the fact that [Smith] was related by blood to some of the metis [*sic*] in the Canadian West, as well as the fact that his wife herself had Indian blood in her veins, may not have had an important influence on the course of events." W.S. Wallace, "Strathspey in the Canadian Fur-Trade," in *Essays in Canadian History Presented to George MacKinnon Wrong for His Eightieth Birthday*, ed. Ralph Flenley (Toronto, 1939), 278–95.

48 Max Hamon, "Recognize Us as a People and Not as Buffalos: Louis Riel and the Gendering of the Red River Public Sphere," in *Violence, Order, and Unrest: A History of British North America, 1749–1876*, ed. Elizabeth Manke, Jerry Bannister, Denis B. McKim, and Scott W. See (Toronto: University of Toronto, 2019), 264–91.

49 James married a Scottish woman by the name of Smith while living in Toronto, however I was unable to trace her background. Nor is there any evidence that Donald Smith and James Ross were ever in communication with each other. The historical record is surprisingly silent on this relationship. Sylvia Van Kirk, "'What if Mama is an Indian?' The Cultural Ambivalence of the Alexander Ross Family," in *The New Peoples: Being and Becoming Métis in North America*, ed. Jacqueline Peterson and Jennifer Brown (Winnipeg: University of Manitoba Press, 1985), 195–206.

50 John Stuart, Biographical Sheet, HBC Archives, Provincial Archives of Manitoba (PAM), accessed 21 February 2023, https://www.gov.mb.ca/chc/archives/_docs/hbca/biographical/s/stuart_john.pdf.

51 Isabella Smith to Richard Hardisty, 14 April 1867, Glenbow Museum Archives, Richard Hardisty Fonds, Series 23–2, nos. 5908–1487.

52 George Taylor Jr. entered the HBC service in 1819, first as a clerk and then as a sloop master in York Factory before he was appointed to Fort Garry in 1827. He married Jane Prince in 1811. He was responsible for making the first map of the Red River Settlement that was the basis for the land grants from the HBC. For more information, see Jackie Corrigan, "The Taylor Family," *As Canadian as Can Be: My Hogue Ancestors* (blog), 18 June 2014, https://hoguegirardin.wordpress.com/2014/06/18/the-taylor-family.

53 Hogue died in 1854, Margaret in 1885. "Amable Hogue (1796–1858), Margaret Taylor (1805–1885)," Red River Ancestry, last updated 16 December 2015, https://www.redriverancestry.ca/HOGUE-AMABLE-1796.php. Marriages of his children connected him to the Bremner, Morrisette, Turcotte, Robillard, McMillan, Brown, and Welsh families.

54 Mortimer was married to Donald's aunt. McDonald, *Strathcona*, 540. Mortimer eventually sold his house to Edward Smith. Smith bequeathed it to Joseph MacPherson who married Isabella Hardisty's sister Mary. The same house later came into Donald Smith's possession when his brother-in-law, Joseph MacPherson, died and the mortgage on it could not be paid off. John Brannen, "A Look Back at the Mortimer House's 200-Year History," *NGNews*, 11 January 2013, https://www.ngnews.ca/news/local/a-look-back-at-mortimer-houses-200-year-history-76599. See also Susan Buggey, "Mortimer, Edward," in *Dictionary of Canadian Biography*, vol. 5, University of Toronto/Université Laval, 2003–, accessed 14 May 2020, http://www.biographi.ca/en/bio/mortimer_edward_5E.html.

55 According to the *Oxford English Dictionary*, the term *Scotch cousin* is "an allusion to the practice of many Scots tracing clan lineage back to remote degrees."

56 Wallace, "Strathspey."

57 Rosemary Omner, "Highland Scot Migration to Southwestern Newfoundland: A Study of Kinship," in *The Peopling of Newfoundland*, ed. John Mannion (St. John: Memorial University Press, 1977), 212–33; Maureen Molloy, "'No Inclination to Mix with Strangers': Marriage Patterns among Highland Scots Migrants to Cape Breton and New Zealand, 1800–1916," *Journal of Family History* 11, no. 3 (1986): 221–43, https://doi.org/10.1177/036319908601100302.

58 Cuthbert Grant, a North West Company fur trader, was sent by Peter Pond to the Athabasca River district. Cuthbert was the son of David Grant. Hartwell Bowsfield, "Grant, Cuthbert (d. 1799)," in *Dictionary of Canadian Biography*, vol. 4, University of Toronto/Université Laval, 2003–, accessed 14 May 2020, http://www.biographi.ca/en/bio/grant_cuthbert_1799_4E.html.

59 Matt Preprost, "Scottish Clan Chief's Visit Unites Grant Descendants," *Winnipeg Free Press*, 15 July 2012, https://www.winnipegfreepress.com/local/scottish-clan-chiefs-visit-unites-grant-descendants-162502666.html.

60 Although raised as a Protestant and baptized in the St. Gabriel Street Presbyterian Church in Montreal, he later converted to Roman Catholicism to marry a Metis woman. See

Margaret MacLeod, *Cuthbert Grant of Grantown* (Montreal: McGill-Queen's University Press, 1963), 3.

61 Cuthbert Grant (senior) married twice, first to Elizabeth McKay, and later to Metis woman, Madelaine Desmarais.

62 Wallace, "Strathspey," 278–95.

63 Grant, *Son of the Fur Trade*, 362.

64 Pierre's sister married a grandson of Cuthbert Grant's (a Falcon), and he lived in St. Francois Xavier Parish, the home of Cuthbert Grant. Lawrence J. Barkwell, "Léveillé, Pierre II," Gabriel Dumont Institute, 8 April 2020, http://www.metismuseum.ca/resource.php/12142.

65 John M. MacKenzie has suggested that the Empire did not create an overarching British identity but "enabled the sub-nationalisms of the United Kingdom to survive and flourish." MacKenzie, "Empire and National Identities: The Case of Scotland," *Transactions of the Royal Historical Society* 8 (1998): 230, https://doi.org/10.2307/3679295. See also James Kennedy, "Responding to Empire: Liberal Nationalism and Imperial Decline in Scotland and Québec," *Journal of Historical Sociology* 19, no. 3 (September 2006): 284–306, https://doi.org/10.1111/j.1467-6443.2006.00283.x.

66 Brenda Macdougall and Nicole St-Onge, "Rooted in Mobility: Metis Buffalo Hunting Brigades," *Manitoba History* 71 (Winter 2013), https://www.mhs.mb.ca/docs/mb_history/71/metisbrigades.shtml; Nicole St-Onge and Carolyn Podruchny, "Scuttling along a Spider's Web: Mobility and Kinship in Metis Ethnogenesis," in *Contours of a People: Metis Family, Mobility, and History*, ed. Nicole St-Onge, Carolyn Podruchny, and Brenda Macdougall (Vancouver: UBC Press, 2010), 59–92; Adam Gaudry, "Kaa-Tipeyimishoyaahk – 'We Are Those Who Own Ourselves': A Political History of Métis Self-Determination in the North-West, 1830–1870" (PhD diss., University of Victoria, 2014).

67 Richard White, *Middle Ground: Indians, Empires, and Republics in the Great Lakes Region, 1650–1815* (Cambridge: Cambridge University Press, 1991).

68 Lynne Champagne, "Breland, Pascal," in *Dictionary of Canadian Biography*, vol. 12, University of Toronto/Université Laval, 2003–, accessed 14 May 2020, http://www.biographi.ca/en/bio/breland_pascal_12E.html.

69 William MacTavish to Kittson, 9 February 1870, PAM, D11.1.

70 Hector Langevin wrote to Alexander Morris at the beginning of 1875 that $2,500 was to be paid to "loyal French." See McDonald, *Lord Strathcona*, 242.

71 Gerhard Ens, introduction to *Son of the Fur Trade*, xxiv.

72 Peter C. Newman speculated, "When persuasion failed, Smith had at his disposal several thousand dollars to bribe wavering Métis, credits to hand out at HBC stores for winter supplies, and jobs as tripmen for next summer's canoe and cart brigades." Newman, *A History of the Hudson's Bay Company: Merchant Princes*, vol. 3 (Toronto: Penguin Canada, 1991), 48. Indeed, there is little archival evidence for this, but Smith's personal letters for later periods provide evidence of parents looking for employment for their sons.

73 McDonald, *Lord Strathcona*, 134.

74 An Outfit is a period of time around which the HBC fur trade was structured. Employee contracts and accounts began and ended on an annual cycle from the summer of one year to the spring of the next.

75 Donald Smith to Richard Hardisty, 9 March 1871, PAM, Donald Smith Outward Correspondence, M131.

76 It was common practice for company officials. See E.E. Rich, *The History of the Hudson's Bay Company, 1670–1870*, vol. 3 (London: Hudson's Bay Record Society, 1960).

77 Donald Smith to Duncan MacArthur, 12 March 1871, PAM, Donald Smith Outward Correspondence Outward, M131.
78 D. Mactavish to Donald Smith, 26 July 1870, PAM, Donald Smith Inward Correspondence, D12.1.
79 Gordon Goldsborough, "John Henry McTavish (1837–1888)," *Memorable Manitobans*, Manitoba Historical Society, accessed 19 May 2020, http://www.mhs.mb.ca/docs/people/mctavish_jh.shtml. McTavish was a Catholic and married to Maria Rowland, a Metis woman. He spoke French and had been educated in Montreal in the 1850s.
80 McDonald, *Lord Strathcona*, 199.
81 *Manitoban and Northwest Herald*, 26 February 1872, 2, http://hdl.handle.net/10719/2691896.
82 Donald Smith quoted in *Manitoban and Northwest Herald*, 26 February 1872, 2, http://hdl.handle.net/10719/2691896.
83 Rich, *Hudson's Bay Company*.
84 See Glenbow Museum Archives, Richard Hardisty Fonds, Series 23–2, Personal and Business Papers 1867–1875, nos. 1494 and 1495; Rich, *Hudson's Bay Company*, 893; McDonald, *Lord Strathcona*, 188–9.
85 William MacTavish to Richard Charles Hardisty, Fort Garry, 5 August 1871, Glenbow Museum Archives, Richard Hardisty Fonds, Series 23–2, Personal and Business Papers 1867–1875, no. 1501.
86 See MacTavish to W.G. Smith, 24 July 1869, 2 November 1869, and 19 May 1870, PAM, Inward Correspondence from North American Governors, A12/45.
87 "Convention at Fort Garry, English and French Delegates in Council. Mr. Smith's Commission, Bill of Rights," *New Nation*, 4 February 1870, 1–2, http://hdl.handle.net/10719/2743741; PAM, E.9/1, 6–8; emphasis added. Earlier versions of the Bill of Rights, designed by Riel and the Metis, emphasized political interests. Thomas Flanagan, "Political Theory of the Red River Resistance," *Canadian Journal of Political Science* 11, no. 1 (March 1978): 153–64; Darren O'Toole, "Thomas Flanagan on the Stand: Revisiting Métis Land Claims and the Lists of Rights in Manitoba," *International Journal of Canadian Studies* 4, no 1 (2010): 137–47.
88 Louis Riel, Lettre à William Mactavish, 28 March 1870, doc. no. 47, in *The Collected Writings of Louis Riel*, vol. 1, ed. George F.G. Stanley and Raymond Huel (Edmonton: University of Alberta Press, 1985), 68; *New Nation*, 8 April 1870, 2, https://digitalcollections.lib.umanitoba.ca/islandora/object/uofm:2743776.
89 On tax revolts in Canada, see Elsbeth Heaman, *Tax, Order and Good Government: A New Political History of Canada* (Montreal: McGill-Queen's University Press, 2017); Shirley Tillotsen, *Give and Take: The Citizen Taxpayer and the Rise of Canadian Democracy* (Vancouver: UBC Press, 2017).
90 Government of Canada, *An Act to amend and continue the Act 32 and 33 Victoria, chapter 3; and to establish and provide for the Government of the Province of Manitoba*, S.C. 18770, c. 3, https://www.sac-isc.gc.ca/eng/1100100010208/1618941272137; emphasis added.
91 Government of Canada, *Debates of the House of Commons of the Dominion of Canada*, Third Session, Third Parliament. 22 February 1876, https://www.canadiana.ca/view/oocihm.9_07185_2.
92 The Deed Poll was a deal struck between the NWC and the HBC in the amalgamation of the two companies. Rich, *Hudson's Bay Company*, 402–8; John S. Galbraith, *The Hudson's Bay Company as an Imperial Factor, 1821–1869* (Toronto: University of Toronto, 1957).
93 Rich, *Hudson's Bay Company*, 499.
94 The agreement was £550 for a chief factor and £275 for a chief trader. However, the London board calculated the minimum on the average of five years, while the traders expected that the minimum be calculated on an annual basis. McDonald, *Strathcona*, 188–9.
95 McDonald, *Strathcona*, 188.
96 Smith to Armit, 24 August 1871, PAM, HBC Inward Correspondence from Commissioners (1871–1873), A11.129. Microfilm 730.

97 An annotated copy identifies the men. See BAC-LAC, Jean Murray Cole Collection, MIKAN 3202350.

98 James Clouston, Moose Factory to Donald Smith, 19 September 1871, PAM, Inward Correspondence to Governor, Chief Factors, and Chief Traders (1870–1879), D.12.

99 Donald Smith to William Armit, 18 August 1871, PAM, Inward Correspondence from Commissioners, A.12.14. Microfilm 740.

100 Donald Smith to unidentified, 4 December 1871, PAM, Donald Smith Outward Correspondence (1871–1873), D11.2. Microfilm 131.

101 PAM, Inward Correspondence from Commissioners, A12.14. Microfilm 740. See also McDonald, *Lord Strathcona*, 191–3.

102 The Hardisty papers detail the position, rejection, negotiation, and finally the acceptance of HBC terms between December 1878 and April 1879. Glenbow Museum Archives, Richard Hardisty Fonds, Series 23–4.

103 Grahame to John McTavish, 20 November 1878, HBC Archives, D. 16/1, quoted in McDonald, *Lord Strathcona*, 250.

104 The quote in full reads, "Reduced from patriarchs of the forests to supervised employees, the winterers at last realized how the colleague they had so fervently hoped would champion their cause had betrayed them." Newman, *History*, 97.

105 McDonald writes, "It was apparent from correspondence and conversations that he genuinely cared about their [the winterers] well being." McDonald, *Lord Strathcona*, 246. According to McDonald, Smith argued that the "Fur Trade Party represented unfinished business from 1871 when the Governor and Committee had refused to comply with a request for a guaranteed minimum." *Lord Strathcona*, 249.

106 BAC-LAC, Lord Strathcona Fonds, Miscellaneous, MG 29, A 5, vol. 13. There was nevertheless a scandal, as the will did not include traders. Roderick MacFarlane was sure this was a slip of the pen. The solicitors thought otherwise, but I have found no record of the outcome.

107 BAC-LAC, Memorandum, Miscellaneous, MG 29, A 5, vol. 13; emphasis added.

108 A social geography, such as Rosemary Omner has done for the settlement of Newfoundland, would be possible and fruitful in Red River. For instance, looking at family names and genealogy, geographic settlement, and religious affiliation would be quite interesting for the population with Scottish heritage. See Omner, "Highland Scot."

109 The Family Compact as a historical concept is notoriously difficult to define. Denis McKim, "Upper Canadian Thermidor: The Family Compact and the Counter-Revolutionary Atlantic," *Ontario History* 106, no. 2 (Fall 2014): 235–62. S.F. Wise provided the best-known article on the topic, "Upper Canada and the Conservative Tradition," in *God's Peculiar Peoples: Essays on Political Culture in Nineteenth-Century Canada*, ed. A.B. McKillop and Paul Romney (Ottawa: Carleton University Press, 1993), 169–84.

110 Elsbeth A. Heaman, "Rights Talk and the Liberal Order Framework," in *Liberalism and Hegemony: Debating the Canadian Liberal Revolution*, ed. Jean-François Constant and Michel Ducharme (Toronto: University of Toronto Press, 2009), 154–5.

111 Ian McKay, "The Liberal Order Framework: A Prospectus for a Reconnaissance of Canadian History," *Canadian Historical Review* 81, no. 4 (2000): 617–45. See also the essays discussing this article in Jean-Francois Constant and Michel Ducharme, eds., *Liberalism and Hegemony: Debating the Canadian Liberal Revolution* (Toronto: University of Toronto Press, 2009); and Jerry Bannister and Liam Riordan, *The Loyal Atlantic: Remaking the British Atlantic in the Revolutionary Era* (Toronto: University of Toronto Press, 2014).

PART THREE
FAMILY, GENDER, AND PROPERTY

Figure V.6 James Inglis, *Prince of Wales Terrace, Sherbrooke St., Montreal*, 1860. McCord Museum, MP-1974.82.

Figure V.7 James Inglis, *Montreal from "Ravenscrag" Showing McTavish Street and the Reservoir*, 1869. McCord Museum, MP-0000.194.6.

Row and Terrace Housing

The grey stone pavilion, set in lush gardens and with commanding views, remains the defining image of the Square Mile. However, as the area developed from about the middle of the nineteenth century to the 1920s, the most prolific housing types were the row and terrace houses. (A row house is one that shares party walls with its neighbours. A terrace house is also a row house, but it is part of single construction, whereby the individual units contribute to an imposing, unified composition.)

The typology of the terrace house was popular in Britain and Canada from 1770 to 1860 as a form of middle-class housing. In Montreal, the first one is said to date to 1844, a time when the managerial, professional, and merchant classes were growing. But the popularity of the imported typology did not last long in Montreal; by 1874 it was supplanted by the individual row house, designed to reflect the personal taste of its owner. The most celebrated example in the Square Mile was the Prince of Wales Terrace, built in 1859 on Sherbrooke Street for George Simpson, governor of the Hudson's Bay Company (Figure V.6). It was demolished by McGill University in 1971.

Figure V.7 captures the area in 1869. The McTavish reservoir is in the immediate foreground, with McTavish Street descending the hill to the far right. The rear facades of the Prince of Wales Terrace can be seen to the right (west) of the intersection of McTavish and Sherbrooke Streets. Just above the Prince of Wales is Prince Rupert Place, built as a speculative venture in 1862. Originally named Annonay Place, its developer, Edward Martin Hopkins, changed its name shortly after construction to one that resonated with the history of the Hudson's Bay Company, with which he was associated. It may be that the name change was made for marketing purposes, since its royal title competed more favourably with its neighbour, the Prince of Wales Terrace. Three of its original eight units are still standing and are owned by McGill University.

CHAPTER FIVE

Marriage, Property, and the Law in a Square Mile Family: The Case of Annie Stevenson Anderson vs. David Morrice, 1884–1885

Peter Gossage and Lisa Moore

This chapter focuses on a civil suit launched in November 1884 by Annie Stevenson Anderson against her husband of twenty-five years, the Scottish-born textile magnate and prominent Square Miler David Morrice. By all accounts, Morrice was one of the richest and most successful businessmen in Montreal – perhaps in Canada. In the early 1880s, however, he had been "unfortunate in his business affairs" in ways and for reasons we will describe more fully in the following pages.[1] For now, suffice it to say that by November 1884, David's financial embarrassment had reached the point where his wife would seek the remedy of a judicial separation of property, as was permitted under Article 1311 of the Civil Code of Lower Canada, which reads as follows: "Separation of property can only be obtained judicially, before the court of the domicile, when the interests of the wife are imperiled and the disordered state of the husband's affairs gives reason to fear that his property will not be sufficient to satisfy what the wife has a right to receive or to get back. All voluntary separations are null."[2]

Anderson vs. Morrice is part of a collection of over 1,800 civil and criminal cases from the Quebec judicial archives that we have assembled, as members of a SSHRC-funded team project called Familles, droit et justice au Québec, 1840–1920 (FDJQ). From 2013 to 2018, in collaboration with Donald Fyson, Thierry Nootens, and Eric H. Reiter, we explored the archives of three judicial districts (Montreal, Quebec, and Trois-Rivières) in search of cases that could shed light on family and gender dynamics in the province. These included criminal prosecutions for bigamy and domestic assault, civil suits for seduction or breach of promise of marriage, a number of child-custody cases, as well as numerous disputes related to inheritance, marital obligations, and family honour.[3] Within that wider collection, we identified 167 cases (about 9 per cent of the total) in which married women applied to the court for a judicial separation of property, or a *séparation de biens par voie judiciaire*. These are interesting proceedings in which married women sued their husbands in Superior Court over ownership and control of their combined assets. We continue to work with that larger set of judicial separations, which we have discussed in another, closely related essay that we are currently revising for publication.[4]

Anderson vs. Morrice, however, merits special attention and raises some interesting questions for this volume of essays about the boundaries and linkages that characterized Montreal's Square Mile in its heyday. The case stands out for a number of reasons, including the fact the Morrice family was so prominent and left such a rich trail of archival sources, both upstream and downstream from the 1884 court case. Another reason is the apparent contradiction between Annie's appeal to the courts for protection against her husband's insolvency and the fact that she and David remained very wealthy and continued to live in the lap of Square Mile luxury throughout their lives. By looking at this one case in detail, then, we propose to explore the themes of married women's agency and property rights in a context of legal pluralism, with specific attention to the way privileged families – within and beyond the Square Mile – used certain provisions of the Civil Code to their advantage. We also hope to say something useful about connections and boundaries in the world of well-heeled Square Mile families like the Morrices, especially those organized around some key social vectors such as wealth, social class, gender, kinship, and the civil law.

To explain the workings of a judicial separation of property, we should begin by reminding readers that community of property was the default matrimonial regime in Quebec under the civil law traditions inherited from the Custom of Paris and codified in the Lower Canada Civil Code of 1866. Community of property meant that the entirety of a couple's property of whatever nature, real or moveable, present and future, was to be jointly owned by the couple in equal parts and placed under the exclusive management of the husband. The only exclusions were for *biens propres*, or lineage property, generally meaning inherited assets (especially real estate), which were excluded from the community and deemed to remain within each spouse's line of descent. This regime was part of a resolutely patriarchal system that subsumed a married woman's legal and civil identity within that of her husband. It applied to all Quebec marriages with the exception of those where the parties had signed a notarized ante-nuptial contract stipulating that the married woman would continue to own and, with her husband's authorization, manage her own separate property. Most privileged, propertied couples took advantage of this provision, as

Thierry Nootens shows in his recent study of gender, patrimony, and civil law in the period 1900–30.[5] For the majority of women, those who married under community of property, the recourse to a judicial separation of property was also available, but only under specific conditions, to be discussed more fully below. Such a proceeding, if successful, would ultimately have the same effect as a notarized marriage contract stipulating the *séparation de biens* régime, dissolving the community and authorizing the wife to hold property separately from her husband.

We hasten to add that judicial separations of property were *not* the suits for separation of bed and board (*séparation de corps*) that historians have used to study marital breakdown in a province where divorce was next to impossible prior to the 1960s.[6] A separation of bed and board could be obtained by wives or (more rarely) husbands on a variety of serious grounds, including infidelity and domestic violence. While not dissolving the marriage or freeing either party to remarry, it did authorize a legally separated woman to live apart from her husband. And assuming the couple had married under the community of property regime, it necessarily entailed a separation of property under the civil law. But the reverse was not the case, meaning that civil suits for separation of property, such as the 167 cases in the FDJQ database, do not necessarily reveal situations where a marriage had failed. The women who initiated these proceedings, rather, were using the courts and the particular provisions of Lower Canadian civil law to protect themselves and their children from their husband's creditors and to recover a degree of the legal and financial autonomy they had surrendered when they married under the community of property regime.

Few historians have examined the circumstances in which women in Quebec used judicial separations to dissolve their marital communities and establish the legal right to hold property in their own names.[7] In a broader sense, however, married women's legal and property rights have been attracting significant scholarly attention for some time. There is an especially interesting debate in the literature about whether certain provisions of the French civil law tradition actually provided married women in Quebec with more protections and greater autonomy than were available to women in common law jurisdictions, at least prior to the adoption of the Married Women's Property Acts in the second half of the nineteenth century.[8] Bettina Bradbury has offered the concept of "companionate patriarchy" to add a compelling note of dissonance to this discussion, pointing out that in the early nineteenth century, "the spread of romantic sensibilities and the idea of companionate marriage associated with them was uneven and class specific, and its effects were heavily gendered."[9] For his part, Thierry Nootens has argued that notwithstanding the protections offered by the civil law tradition, the economic and judicial autonomy enjoyed by Quebec women (even the most privileged ones) was singularly fragile, and that any relative advantage they enjoyed over women in places like Ontario had been dramatically reversed by the turn of the twentieth century.[10] These are the sorts of perspectives we believe to be the most useful, with their emphasis on married women's agency and their struggle to exert some legal and financial autonomy, but within a legal, economic, and social system that was deeply patriarchal, in a province, as we know, where resistance to gender equality and women's citizenship rights remained strong until the 1960s.

Even more relevant for present purposes is a recent study by Jean-Philippe Garneau that focuses specifically on civil suits for separation of property in Lower Canada.[11] Garneau's essay examines 250 civil suits for *séparation de biens* heard in the judicial district of Montreal in the period from 1795 to 1829, the better part of a century before the period we are examining. His conclusions about the motivation of these 250 Lower Canadian women who chose to initiate what he calls the costly legal "brouhaha" of a judicial separation of property and about the outcome of these proceedings are worth quoting at length, not least because they help us in framing some of the key questions for our study:

> Au terme d'une procédure coûteuse, l'épouse n'obtenait donc souvent que la seule capacité juridique sur les biens qu'elle pourrait acquérir ultérieurement. Pour celles qui faisaient commerce ou qui exerçaient déjà un métier, l'avantage n'était sans doute pas négligeable. L'acquisition d'une personnalité juridique permettait pour bon nombre d'obtenir du crédit. Dès le jugement, les cordons de la bourse des parents et amis se déliaient sans risquer de voir ce nouvel apport être dilapidé par le mari ou englouti par sa faillite. Nul doute que cette embellie ne profitait pas qu'à l'épouse. Mais pour celles qui ne pouvaient plus compter sur leur mari, obtenir du crédit s'avérait essentiel. La séparation de biens avait également pour effet d'empêcher que le mari absent, une fois de retour à la maison, fasse main basse sur le fruit du travail et des économies de son épouse industrieuse.[12]

For Garneau, moreover, it is abundantly clear that "pour bon nombre de femmes séparées de biens, la nouvelle personnalité juridique ainsi acquise constituait surtout un paravent légal pour l'époux insolvable."[13] Nancy Christie and Michael Gauvreau, studying the same period as Garneau, have described these proceedings similarly as "a strategy frequently employed by both husbands and wives to protect the marital property against creditors."[14] And Nootens, discussing the early twentieth century, points out that most husbands made no defence against these suits. "Ils ont tout intérêt, en principe," he writes, "à ce que le tribunal réponde favorablement à la poursuite; une partie du patrimoine familial serait dès lors à l'abri des réclamations de tiers."[15]

Why, then, did Annie Stevenson Anderson sue her wealthy and powerful husband, David Morrice, for separation of property before Montreal's Superior Court in November 1884? What use did she plan to make of the new legal identity and financial autonomy to which a successful suit would lead? Was she trying to protect herself and her children from a husband whose apparent (if outwardly implausible) insolvency was part of a broader pattern of neglect or abandonment? Or was this lawsuit part of a strategy in which David Morrice was fully complicit, designed to use the provisions of the civil law to place certain assets out of the reach of his creditors? To answer these questions, we propose to begin by taking a narrative approach: by telling the story of Annie, David, their family life on Redpath Street, and the reversal of David's business fortunes that precipitated legal action by his wife in November 1884. With that story in place, we will assume a more analytical voice in an attempt to tease out some of the broader meanings of this Square Mile story, especially as it touches on issues of married women's agency and property rights in a context of legal and cultural pluralism, and with special attention to the many layers of boundaries and linkages it helps to reveal.

Family, Property, and Privilege

David Morrice was born in St. Martins, Perthshire, Scotland, on 11 August 1829 to a family of modest means.[16] After completing his schooling in Scotland, Morrice spent time in Manchester and Liverpool, where he first developed an interest in the textile industry. Enticed by the prospect of economic prosperity in British North America, Morrice emigrated in 1855 and settled in Toronto, where he became a salesman for a textile manufacturing company.[17] Shortly after his arrival, Morrice joined the Presbyterian Church on Gould Street in St. James Ward, an institution that served the city's Scottish community.[18] Through his involvement in the congregation, Morrice developed a network of business contacts and established important social connections. In June 1860 he married Annie Stevenson Anderson, the nineteen-year-old daughter of fellow parishioners James Anderson and Isabella Mathers, who had married in Roxburghshire, Scotland, twenty years previous.[19] Annie had emigrated to British North America with her parents and settled in Toronto, where in the spring of 1861 she was living with her new husband in a three-storey brick house on Church Street in St. James Ward.[20]

Dissatisfied, it seems, with his work as a textile salesman and seeking more challenging business opportunities, Morrice moved with his young family to Montreal

Figure 5.1 Notman & Sandham, *Mrs. David Morrice, Montreal,* 1880. McCord Museum, II-54963.1.

Figure 5.2 Notman & Sandham, *David Morrice, Montreal,* 1880. McCord Museum, II-57433.1.

in 1863. As Canada's flourishing commercial metropolis, Montreal was the ideal place for Morrice to establish his company, D. Morrice & Co., which specialized in the wholesale trade of textiles. Morrice's relocation to Montreal could not have come at a more opportune moment: the completion of the Victoria Bridge in 1859 had facilitated trade across the St. Lawrence River while the Civil War had resulted in the closure of several mills in the northern states, eliminating much of the Canadian textile industry's American competition.[21] Acutely aware of the wider domestic market these circumstances created, Morrice seized on the opportunity to expand his business within Canada. As his company prospered, Morrice sought to solidify his position within Montreal's business elite.

The city directories show the Morrice family living first on Metcalfe Street in 1863 and then on Aylmer Street in 1864, both in St. Antoine Ward, before taking up residence at Gibraltar Cottage in 1865, which was situated in Côte-des-Neiges village on the western outskirts of the city.[22] By 1867, they had four children – William, David, James, and Robert – and were quickly outgrowing Gibraltar Cottage. The

Figure 5.3 Anonymous, *David Morrice Sr. House, 10 Redpath St., Montreal,* c. 1909. McCord Museum, MP-0000.2345.9.

home was also situated at a considerable distance from Morrice's office on Bleury Street and, more importantly, from the city's business leaders, who largely resided in the affluent Square Mile neighbourhood. Seeking to confirm his place among these prominent men, he hired the architect John James Browne in 1870 to design a stately home for his wife and young children at 10 Redpath Street, in the heart of the Square Mile.[23] By the late 1860s, Browne had become well-respected among the Square Mile community thanks to his involvement in the construction of the Molson Bank Building (1864–6) and the Merchants' Exchange Building (1866), both in Montreal's financial district.[24] Since demolished, the Morrice mansion was a prime example of Square Mile opulence (Figure 5.3). Its completion was announced in the *Montreal Herald*, which described the house as a villa "similar in design to the one on Sherbrooke Street by Mr. Joseph McKay, from the designs and under the superintendence of John James Browne," consisting of "extensive outbuildings, handsome entrance gates, and railings."[25] In 1881, when the census was taken, the couple was living there with six children, aged three to fifteen, and six domestic servants to keep the place running.[26]

Even before commissioning the construction of the Redpath Street mansion, Morrice had integrated himself into Square Mile society through his affiliation with various institutions, associations, and clubs that catered to Montreal's elite.

Described by his contemporaries as a devout Christian, it is no surprise that Morrice joined the Crescent Street Presbyterian Church not long after settling in Montreal.[27] He oversaw the Church's Sunday school for thirty-seven years (a role he seems to have also held at the Gould Street Presbyterian Church in Toronto) and was appointed an elder of the congregation in 1899.[28] Morrice was also closely involved with the Presbyterian College of Montreal, becoming a member of the board in 1871 and serving as its chairman in 1877. He made a substantial donation to the college in 1882, a philanthropic gesture that garnered him much praise but that also caused him significant financial strain, something we discuss in further detail later in the chapter. Morrice also held memberships in the Mount Royal Club, the St. James Club, the Forest & Stream Club, and the Montreal Hunt Club, all highly exclusive and prestigious organizations where the city's English-speaking elite gathered to conduct business and to engage in social activities. It is likely that one of these establishments was the venue for Morrice's first encounter with railway industrialist and fellow Square Miler Sir William Van Horne. The driving force behind the construction of the Canadian Pacific Railway, Van Horne was also a prominent art collector who inspired his neighbour and friend David Morrice to become a patron of the arts.[29] Through his connection with Van Horne, Morrice joined the board of directors of the Art Association of Montreal (now the Montreal Museum of Fine Arts) and regularly loaned works from his private collection for its gallery exhibitions. What these various social and philanthropic activities make clear is that over the years, Morrice's position in Square Mile society came to reflect his increasing wealth and reputation in the Canadian textile industry.

By the early 1880s, in fact, David Morrice's firm had established itself as the exclusive selling agent for more than thirty-five textile mills in Quebec, Ontario, New Brunswick, and Nova Scotia.[30] In addition to monopolizing the distribution and sale of cotton textiles, Morrice was by this time a major shareholder in several textile manufacturing companies across the four provinces.[31] His success was bolstered by the implementation of the National Policy tariffs in 1879, which had all but eliminated British and American competition in the industry. New domestic markets also opened up as the federal government's plans to settle Western Canada were realized, creating further opportunities for the expansion of his wholesale activities.[32] In 1882, the Toronto *Globe* described David Morrice and other leading textile manufacturers such as Andrew F. Gault and Victor Hudon as the "cotton lords" of Canada.[33] One biographer of his son, the painter James Wilson Morrice, describes him as "the father of Canada's cotton industry, and it was reckoned that he knew more about the cotton business than anyone else in the land."[34]

A Reversal of Fortunes

The National Policy tariffs had generated a significant period of growth for the cotton textile industry, with more than a dozen mills founded in the late 1870s and early 1880s.[35] Around 1883, however, the industry experienced serious difficulties. Textile manufacturers were producing cotton goods at a rate that far exceeded the demands of the Dominion, which led to a dramatic decrease in prices.[36] David Morrice was particularly hard hit by the crisis that gripped the industry in 1883 and 1884. According to R.T. Naylor, "The Montreal banks who heavily backed the activities of the Montreal commercial community in their cotton escapade had made large loans to Morrice on the basis simply of consignments from the mills, instead of *bona fide* sales. As long as Morrice got advances from the banks – whose directorates were intimately linked with those of the cotton companies – the accumulation of unsold goods went on."[37] As the price of cotton textiles plummeted and the market for them dried up, Morrice was unable to sell his goods at their original cost, accruing a substantial debt that he owed to his creditors at the banks. He was also burdened financially by the $80,000 donation he had promised to the Presbyterian College of Montreal for the construction of a building that would greatly expand the college's facilities.[38] Dedicated as Morrice Hall in November 1882, the building was later integrated into the McGill University campus (Figure 5.4). In the early months of 1883, however, it represented a major financial sacrifice for a struggling David Morrice, whose commitment to the Presbyterian Church and to a philanthropic life made it impossible for him to withdraw his support.[39]

In important ways, the strategies used by David Morrice to maintain his wealth and prestige in the wake of the textile crisis of 1883–4 are at the heart of this chapter. It should be noted that there was no federal bankruptcy legislation in effect during the 1880s, following the repeal of the 1869 and 1875 Insolvent Acts in 1880.[40] Would Morrice have filed for bankruptcy under a federal Insolvent Act had such a law been in force? There is no way of knowing. We do know that Morrice obtained a measure of protection from his creditors by signing a deed of assignment before the notary John Fair on 14 May 1884.[41] "Assignments," as Robert Sweeny explains,

> were a Scottish notarial practice introduced after the Conquest to deal with firms in financial difficulty where there was no bankruptcy legislation. … The firm's creditors drew up the assignment. It assigned to trustees for the creditors the assets of the firm and generally set out a payment schedule for the creditors. By signing the deed, the creditors agreed to act as a group, so not only would they not take further action individually against the firm, but they would oppose individual or collective attempts by other creditors, who had not signed the agreement, to modify the payment schedule or to seize the assets of the firm.[42]

Figure 5.4 Wm. Notman & Son, *Morrice Hall, Presbyterian College, Montreal,* c. 1887. McCord Museum, VIEW-1597.1.

In Morrice's assignment, three bankers – Edward S. Clouston, James H. Plummer, and William John Ingram – and two textile manufacturers – Andrew F. Gault and William J. Whitehead – were named as the trustees to whom his assets were assigned. As Sweeny has also explained, "Clouston was the manager of the Montreal branch of the Bank of Montreal, while Plummer was the Montreal manager of the Allan controlled Merchants Bank, i.e. the two largest banking operations in the city. Gault and Whitehead would both have long involvements in the textile industries."[43] These were major figures in the city's financial and industrial circles, and they played a key role in Morrice's effort to survive his reversal of fortunes.

The Morrice deed of assignment, dated 14 May 1884, can be considered as consisting of three parts.[44] First, it refers explicitly to a detailed agreement signed on 19 October 1883 between Morrice and his creditors, described rather cryptically in the document as "several banks" and "several merchants and manufacturers." By

Figure 5.5 Wm. Norton & Son, *Edward S. Clouston, Montreal*, 1891. McCord Museum, II-94702.1.

Figure 5.6 Notman & Sandham, *Andrew F. Gault, Montreal*, 1882. McCord Museum, II-66236.1.

the terms of this October agreement (reproduced as an appendix to the notarized deed), Morrice had placed all his property in trust with Clouston and the others for the purpose of satisfying his creditors. He had also agreed to a repayment schedule, whereby his debts were to be repaid by the trustees in four equal installments, three, six, nine, and twelve months after their dates of maturity.[45]

Second, the assignment gave legal effect to the promised transfer of all Morrice's assets to the trustees and included an itemized list for that purpose. These assets, in a word, were considerable. They included over $300,000 worth of shares in joint-stock companies including the Montreal Cotton Company (428 paid-up shares worth $100 each), the Victor Hudon Cotton Mills Company (980 shares worth $100 each), and various textile, knitted-goods, and other firms. There were also promissory notes valued at $10,000 each from the sale of his interest in the North Shore Railway Company and the Stillwater Coal Company, both to industrialist and financier John McDougall.[46] With respect to real estate there were nine separate lots or portions of lots in the St. Antoine and St. Ann Wards of Montreal, including two contiguous lots on St. Joseph Street "with two large cut stone stores or warehouses thereon erected," which he had owned since 1880, as well as the residential property at 10 Redpath Street "with a villa residence, coach house and stables, and other buildings thereon erected." The furnishings of both the St. Joseph Street warehouse and the Square Mile villa were also mentioned specifically, although not described in any detail; still, "all and every of the articles of household furniture and effects in the residence number ten Redpath Street in Montreal" were explicitly conveyed to Clouston and the other trustees (with no hint, by the way, that they might have been jointly owned by Annie Stevenson Anderson).

Third, the deed of assignment enjoined the five trustees, with a majority authorized to act on behalf of the whole, to "sell and dispose of all property moveable and immoveable" assigned and transferred to them "either by public sale or by private contract," and out of the proceeds to pay the claims of Morrice's creditors "according to their rank and priority," beginning with those (not mentioned by name) who held "privileged or hypothecary claims." Once all the creditors' claims had been satisfied, the trustees agreed to transfer back to Morrice all the property they had been assigned, "or such portion thereof as may not have been disposed of in fulfillment of the trusts of this present deed."

David Morrice's financial embarrassment in 1883–4 was profound, and he marshalled a wide range of strategies to dig himself out of it. The deed of assignment signed before notary John Fair in May 1884 was certainly the central piece in his plan. There was also a flurry of activity that we can trace through the notarial archives around this time. In some cases, Morrice seems to have been simply calling in debts, as with a transaction completed in June 1884, one month after the deed of assignment, which transferred to Morrice $15,000 in outstanding real estate debts from a Massachusetts-based textile manufacturer named Joseph Couture.[47] He was also, it would appear, selling off assets, surely in order to pay his creditors under the terms of the deed of assignment; he sold three lots in St. Ann's Ward to the Dominion Transport Company for $21,000, for instance, in November of 1886.[48]

But some of this activity looks very much like an attempt to protect assets from his creditors by transferring them to members of his family. We know, for instance, that Morrice made a transfer to his eldest son and employee, William James Morrice, just two weeks after the deed of assignment was signed.[49] We also know that Morrice had dissolved his partnership with Montreal clothing manufacturer John W. MacKedie on 29 November 1883,[50] and that three months later, in February 1884, he transferred three insurance policies with a total value of $15,000 – policies that he had held on the life of his former business partner – over to MacKedie himself. MacKedie then turned around the very same day and transferred those policies

Figure 5.7 Wm. Notman & Son, *Mrs. David Morrice's Library, Montreal*, 1899. McCord Museum, II-128255.

Figure 5.8 Wm. Notman & Son, *Mrs. David Morrice's Bedroom, Montreal*, 1899. McCord Museum, II-128254.

to Morrice's wife, Annie Anderson. As we shall see, this would raise the question of whether Annie was legally entitled to hold property separately from her husband – the very question at the heart of any judicial separation of property.[51] But especially given section 1265 of the Civil Code, which expressly forbade husbands and wives from making *inter vivos* gifts or donations to each other except under the terms of a marriage contract, this does begin to look like a strategy to shelter some of Morrice's assets by transferring them to his wife.[52]

When Annie Anderson sued David Morrice for separation of property on 20 November 1884, then, it was almost certainly a strategic move to shield certain assets from Morrice's creditors. In the writ and declaration submitted by her attorney A.W. Atwater, Anderson confirmed that her husband's business dealings were in disarray. "Of late years," she declared, "said Defendant has been unfortunate in his business affairs and has lost large sums of money & contracted obligations and debts far in excess of his means to pay and he is at the present time insolvent." The couple's son, William (who, as just mentioned, received a transfer from his father six months earlier), testified that Morrice had "been unable to meet his liabilities in full as they matured and his property and estate is now held by the Bank of Montreal in trust for the payment of his creditors."[53] This was corroborated by accountant James Welsh, who dated Morrice's difficulties back one year to October 1883, at which time the debt repayment scheme, later formalized in the deed of assignment, was signed. For her part, Annie Anderson also claimed to have in the course of their marriage "contributed, loaned, paid and advanced and given to her said husband a large sum of money and she now finds the whole of said sum lost and spent without much hope of recovery."[54] To protect herself from further losses, Anderson argued, she should be granted "the management and administration of her affairs and of her property."[55] Morrice gave no response to the declarations made by his wife, son, and accountant; a certificate of default in the file indicates that he never even appeared in court to participate in the proceedings.

Morrice's recent business reversals, the fact that his property had been assigned to a group of trustees linked to the Bank of Montreal, and the absence of any opposition on his part to his wife's submission were judged sufficient grounds for a judicial separation of property by Superior Court Judge Louis-Amable Jetté, who delivered his decision for the plaintiff on 6 February 1885. Following the judgment, Anderson renounced her share of the assets and liabilities of the former community on 24 February 1885, that renunciation being made on the formulaic grounds "that the acceptance of said community would be more onerous than profitable" for her.[56] Notary William de Montmollin Marler filed his detailed report as the *praticien* (practitioner) on 2 March 1885, in which he stated that Anderson "had

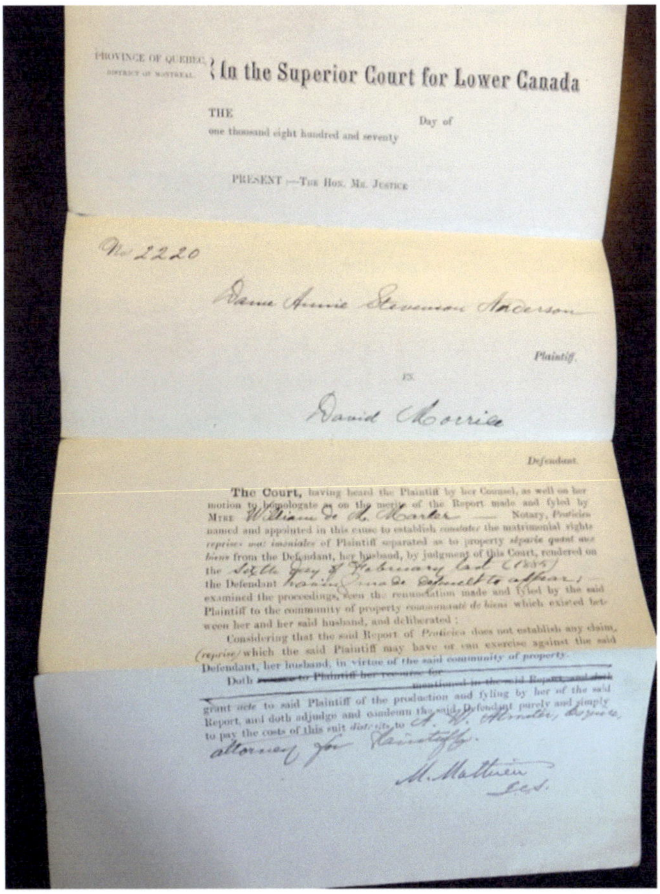

PROVINCE OF QUEBEC, DISTRICT OF MONTREAL. } In the Superior Court for Lower Canada

THE Day of one thousand eight hundred and seventy

PRESENT :—THE HON. MR. JUSTICE

No 2220

Dame Annie Stevenson Anderson

Plaintiff.

vs

David Morrice

Defendant.

The Court, having heard the Plaintiff by her Counsel, as well on her motion to homologate as on the merits of the Report made and fyled by MTRE William de M. Marler — Notary, *Praticien* named and appointed in this cause to establish *constater* the matrimonial rights *reprises matrimoniales* of Plaintiff separated as to property *séparée quant aux biens* from the Defendant, her husband, by judgment of this Court, rendered on the sixth day of February last (1885) the Defendant having made default to appear, examined the proceedings, seen the renunciation made and fyled by the said Plaintiff to the community of property *communauté de biens* which existed between her and her said husband, and deliberated :

Considering that the said Report of *Praticien* does not establish any claim, (*reprise*) which the said Plaintiff may have or can exercise against the said Defendant, her husband, in virtue of the said community of property.

Doth ~~reserve to Plaintiff her recourse for ... mentioned in the said Report, and doth~~ grant *acte* to said Plaintiff of the production and fyling by her of the said Report, and doth adjudge and condemn the said Defendant purely and simply to pay the costs of this suit *distraits* to ... attorney for Plaintiff.

M. Mathieu J.C.S.

Figure 5.9 A page from the judicial dossier in Anderson vs. Morrice (1884–1885). This is a draft of the judgment on the practitioner's report, delivered in Montreal Superior Court, 14 March 1885.

Source: BAnQ-CVM, TP11, S2, SS2, SSS1, 1987-05-007 \ 3144, 1884, no. 2220, Anderson vs. Morrice, "Draft of Judgment upon Report of Praticien," 14 March 1885.

no immoveable property at the time of her marriage or any other property which did not fall into the community; and that she acquired no property during the existence of the community." Marler therefore concluded that "the said Plaintiff has no matrimonial rights to exercise against the said community of property."[57] This was the basis for the judgment on the practitioner's report delivered by the Hon. Justice Michel Mathieu on 14 March 1885 using a printed form (Figure 5.9), which stated: "Considering that the said Report of *Praticien* does not establish any claim (*reprise*) which the said Plaintiff may have or can exercise against the said Defendant, her husband, in virtue of the said community of property … doth adjudge and condemn the said Defendant purely and simply to pay the costs of this suit to A.W. Atwater, Esquire, attorney for the plaintiff."[58]

Connections and Boundaries

What, then, do we make of all this? What does the case of Anderson vs. Morrice tell us about married women's agency and property rights in a context of legal pluralism? In what ways did privileged families use provisions of the Quebec Civil Code to their advantage? And what have we learned through this study about *connections* and *boundaries* in the world of prominent Square Milers like Annie Anderson and David Morrice?

In the paper we presented in 2018 at the Canadian Historical Association's conference in Regina, we examined a selection of judicial separations from the 167 in the FDJQ database and proceeded to group them into one of two categories using a simplified grid we called *women's agency* versus *marital collusion*.[59] Which married women, we asked, were using these proceedings for their own purposes, through their individual *agency*, to protect their interests and those of their children against a failed provider and his creditors? And, conversely, in which cases do we find evidence for *collusion* between the husband and wife? That is, evidence of a coordinated effort to protect assets (and in one reading at least, to defraud creditors) led perhaps by a financially embarrassed husband and his legal advisors, and notwithstanding the admonition in the relevant article of the Civil Code that "all voluntary separations are null." In that paper, we placed Anderson vs. Morrice squarely on the "collusion" side of this ledger, for reasons that may be obvious by now. Annie Anderson did not criticize David Morrice for his recent reversal of fortune, nor did she seem to be seeking greater control over her one-half share of the couple's joint property. This is in contrast to other married women who, as plaintiffs in this collection of judicial separations, publicly blamed their husbands for mismanagement, poor judgment, and sometimes for other failings. Élise Roberge, for instance, called her husband out in open court as a drunk and a wastrel whose failure in the quarry business was the result of his own bad decisions; Vitaline Émard and Anna Renaud both sued their husbands to protect their own assets and especially, it seems, their earning power from imprudent or intemperate husbands who had made foolish investments in their respective grocery and butcher shops.[60]

While the proposed dichotomy between "agency" and "collusion" can be helpful in the analysis of judicial separations, we are inclined to reconsider it for present purposes. To deny any agency to married women who acted to support their husbands in legal manoeuvres designed to avoid financial ruin seems unfair and inaccurate, notwithstanding Thierry Nootens's observation – supported by court records – that propertied women very often left such matters entirely to their husbands' discretion.[61] Meanwhile, the term "collusion" seems rather strong – with its connotations of fraud, deceit, and trickery – for the kind of spousal solidarity and collaboration demonstrated by couples who worked together through the legal system to protect a family's assets from creditors.[62] Surely it is the creditors' aggrieved perspective that is privileged by this sort of language, which also occludes the potential here to observe Bradbury's "companionate patriarchy" in action. Still, there is a clear distinction to be made between two categories of women as plaintiffs in these cases: those who used the proceedings to cope as individuals (and very often as mothers) with their husbands' incompetence, intemperance, extravagance, or wastefulness; and those who considered their husbands as having been simply *unfortunate* in their business dealings, and who were therefore willing to participate in whatever legal proceedings might be deemed necessary to avoid financial ruin and restore the level of wealth, status, and security to which they were accustomed.[63]

In the end, it seems clear to us that Annie Anderson belongs to this second group. In suing her husband for separation of property, she was indeed cooperating with him and his legal advisors in a strategy designed to protect the Morrice family fortune and maintain their privileged status into the next generation. Or perhaps the word *tactic* is more appropriate here, since David Morrice's overall *strategy* for weathering the financial crisis of 1883–4 involved many different manoeuvres – every trick in the book, one might say. It also generated piles of notarized documents and drew on a range of legal traditions – including Scottish notarial practice with the deed of assignment and Lower Canadian Civil Law with the judicial separation. Even though she was his adversary in these proceedings, Annie Anderson's role in the overall strategy was as Morrice's companion and ally. Whether she played a significant role in devising the overall strategy or, more to the point, the place of a judicial separation within it remains a matter of speculation. But the tactic could not have worked without her active participation. There would have been no separation of property, in short, without her willingness to stand as her husband's opponent in Superior Court proceedings, to bring the extent of his financial embarrassment under scrutiny, and to argue – convincingly, in the end – that her "interests were imperiled" (as they surely were) by "the disordered state of her husband's affairs," to return to the language of Article 1311 in the Civil Code.

If there was a degree of *collusion* here to protect assets from David Morrice's legitimate creditors, we might further suggest that the network of co-conspirators extended beyond this prominent Square Mile couple to include other actors in the courtroom drama. John W. MacKedie was David Morrice's friend and former business partner who owned a prosperous clothing manufacturing company in Montreal. William Marler was not just any notary but a professor of real estate law at McGill whose son, also a notary, would become a prominent diplomat. Marler seems to have been a key Morrice advisor here; his role as *praticien* with respect to the dissolution of Annie and David's community of property has been noted, but he also prepared most of the relevant deeds we have located, beginning early in 1884. Albert William Atwater was still a young lawyer in 1884, but a decade later he would become a city councillor, a Conservative MLA, and briefly provincial treasurer. So, if *linkages* is one of the major themes for this volume, then the Morrice family's excellent connections at the highest levels of not only Montreal's commercial and financial spheres but its legal and political networks as well are worth remembering.

We have just gestured towards legal pluralism, but there is a related thread here that needs to be picked up. It seems to us that when David transferred those three life insurance policies to Annie, through the intercession of his former business partner, John MacKedie, in February 1884, the couple may have been genuinely confused about the matrimonial regime that governed the legal and property dimensions of their union. In her initial filing before the Superior Court, in fact, Annie expressed surprise at the idea that her marriage to David might be subject to the community of property provisions of the Quebec Civil Code. Because of their Toronto marriage, with no marriage settlement or other ante-nuptial agreement, she declared, "grave doubts exist as to the Plaintiff being separate as to property and she has latterly been treated and considered common as to property *commune en biens* with her said husband the Defendant according to the Law of the Province of Quebec."[64] One theory about this is that the couple may have been blissfully ignorant of the legal provisions that governed their union. This seems out of character, however, so another possibility, since their Toronto marriage dates to 1860, is that they believed that their union was subject to the provisions of Upper Canada's Married Women's Property Act of 1859, which, according to legal historian Lori Chambers, "shield[ed] some family property from seizure by creditors" and "made all inherited property the statutory separate estate of the wife."[65] From this perspective, Annie's suit for separation might begin to look more like a genuine attempt to recover a degree of protection and control over assets she may have acquired from her own parents or other relatives (about whom we know rather little). This would be consistent with her claim in court to have "contributed, loaned, paid and advanced and given to her said husband a large sum of money" over the course of their marriage, and notwithstanding Marler's opinion in his role as the ostensibly neutral *praticien*, and based on a different set of legal assumptions, that Annie "had no immoveable property at the time of her marriage or any other property which did not fall into the community." The *boundary* between Upper and Lower Canada, Ontario and Quebec, and common and civil legal traditions played an important role here, as did the Victorian ideology of separate spheres, which reified gender as one of the most significant social, legal, and cultural boundaries of all.

Conclusion

David Morrice and Annie Stevenson Anderson emerged very well indeed from their insolvency crisis and the resulting judicial separation of property in the early 1880s. Morrice remained a prominent industrialist and financier. Together with Andrew F. Gault, he spearheaded the 1890 merger of seven mills into Dominion Cottons as well as the 1892 merger of yet another seven mills into Canada Coloured Cotton.[66] He also played a key role in the 1905 establishment of the Dominion Textile Company, which became the most prominent textile manufacturing company in Canada during the first half of the twentieth century.[67] As Mark Sholdice revealed during the conference that led to this anthology, Morrice was still one of the forty-eight most well-connected corporate directors in Canada in 1909.[68] A 1913 biographical dictionary called *Canadian History Makers* describes him as one of the founding members of the Montreal Board of Trade; as president of Canadian Cottons, Montreal Freehold Investment Company, and Penmans; and as a director of the Bank of Montreal.[69] Morrice was also keeping up his philanthropic activities. In 1900, for instance, he served on the committees of the Montreal General Hospital, the Montreal Foundling and Baby Hospital, the McKay Institute for Protestant Deaf Mutes and the Blind, the Hervey Institute, the Protestant House of Industry and Refuge, and the Canadian Society for the Prevention of Cruelty to Animals.[70] According to an exhibition brochure from 1909, Morrice also remained involved with the Art Association of Montreal as a member of its patronage committee, which would mean he played a role in planning its 1912 relocation to Sherbrooke Street near Redpath, just steps from where he lived.[71]

On the home front, and unlike some other cases in our collection, there was no hint at all of any conflict here that was "properly interpersonal" (to use Thierry Nootens's phrase) or which might have led to marital breakdown. We can tell from the census records and other sources that Annie and David remained together long after she sued him for separation of property in 1884. In December 1899, they called on their trusted notary William Marler to draw up their last wills and testaments. In David's will (Figure 5.10), he bequeathed to "his dear wife Annie" the "use, usufruct, and enjoyment during her natural lifetime of *my* House, No. 10

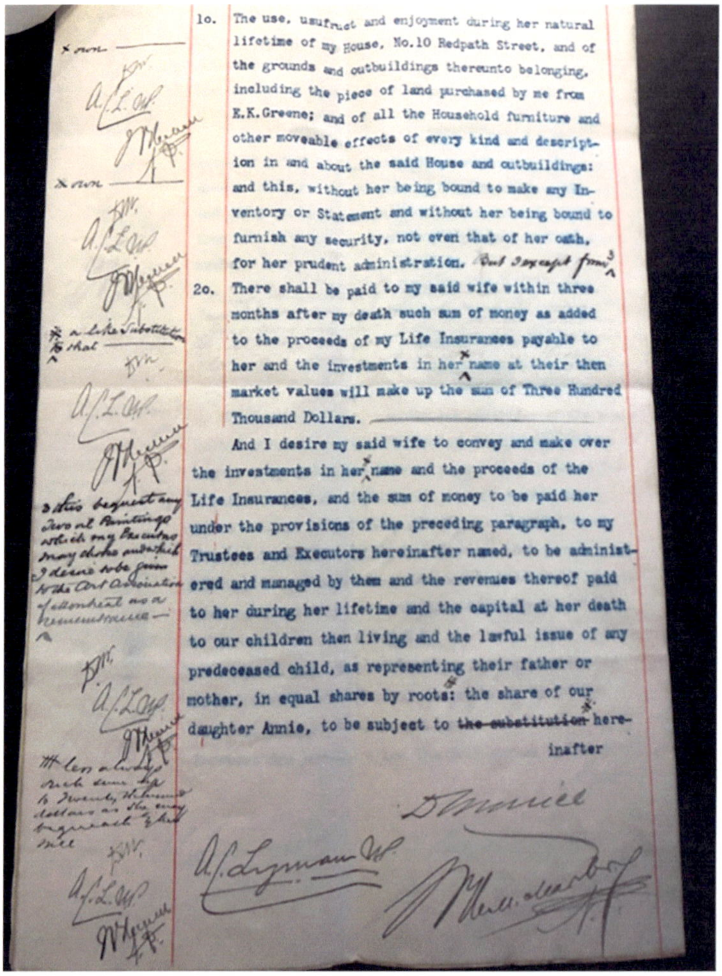

1o. The use, usufruct and enjoyment during her natural lifetime of my House, No.10 Redpath Street, and of the grounds and outbuildings thereunto belonging, including the piece of land purchased by me from E.K.Greene; and of all the Household furniture and other moveable effects of every kind and description in and about the said House and outbuildings: and this, without her being bound to make any Inventory or Statement and without her being bound to furnish any security, not even that of her oath, for her prudent administration. But I except from 3

2o. There shall be paid to my said wife within three months after my death such sum of money as added to the proceeds of my Life Insurances payable to her and the investments in her name at their then market values will make up the sum of Three Hundred Thousand Dollars.

And I desire my said wife to convey and make over the investments in her name and the proceeds of the Life Insurances, and the sum of money to be paid her under the provisions of the preceding paragraph, to my Trustees and Executors hereinafter named, to be administered and managed by them and the revenues thereof paid to her during her lifetime and the capital at her death to our children then living and the lawful issue of any predeceased child, as representing their father or mother, in equal shares by roots: the share of our daughter Annie, to be subject to ~~the substitution~~ hereinafter

D Morrice

Figure 5.10 A page from David Morrice's last will and testament, describing his bequests to his wife, Annie Stevenson Anderson, signed before notary William de Montmollin Marler in December 1899.

Source: BAnQ-CVM, CN601, S577, 2008-01-001 \ 255: Greffe of William de Montmollin Marler, minute no. 24187, Last Will and Testament of David Morrice, 19 December 1899.

Redpath St."[72] and virtually all of its elaborate furnishings, with the exception of two paintings to be selected from his collection by the Art Association of Montreal. Annie would also enjoy the annual revenues on the impressive sum of $300,000, to be made up of life insurance payments, investments in her name, and whatever amount of cash was needed to make up the difference, with the capital to revert to his residual heirs, the Morrice children, upon her death.[73] A decade after preparing these wills, in June 1910, Annie and David celebrated their fiftieth wedding anniversary, and their son the painter, James Wilson Morrice, made a special trip home from Paris to celebrate the occasion.[74] In the end, Annie and David died within three weeks of each other in December 1914 and are buried together at the Mount Royal Cemetery.

Pillars of the Square Mile and of Montreal's largely English-speaking "haute-bourgeoisie," the Morrice family were not old-stock "patricians" in the mould of the McCords and Taschereaus studied recently to great effect by Brian Young.[75] David Morrice, rather, was a wholesale merchant turned industrial capitalist, a "self-made man" who built his great wealth on investments in the cotton textile industry, with help from his fellow Conservatives in the federal Parliament and their policy, after 1879, of protecting domestic manufacturing with high import tariffs. A Scottish emigrant to Upper Canada, he found his way to Montreal in the early 1860s, accompanied by his wife Annie Stevenson Anderson, a fellow Scot about ten years his junior whom he had met and married in Toronto. Twenty years later, Annie sued her husband in the Superior Court of the District of Montreal, pleading successfully for the right to hold property separately from her husband, the defendant in this action. She did so in the context of her husband's attempts to weather a financial storm of epic proportions, just a few months after he had placed all his wealth in trust with a group that included the most powerful bankers in the city, for the purpose of satisfying his many impatient creditors. Annie Anderson's refusal in this moment, articulated by her lawyer A.W. Atwater, to accept that her marriage might be governed by the customary provisions of the Civil Code and its community of property regime is the central event around which this chapter revolves. That she sued her husband in order to obtain the legal right to hold, receive, and manage assets independently from him is clear; and that this action was designed to shield those assets from her husband's creditors is consistent with the evidence and with what other scholars have written about these kinds of proceedings.

Beyond this it is difficult to go much further, at least along a path that would allow us to disentangle Annie Anderson's interests and agency in these proceedings from those of her rich and powerful, but momentarily embarrassed, husband. Our ongoing work with a significant collection of similar cases should provide more insights here. In that work, we must be attentive to the range of circumstances – legal, material, and emotional – in which the couples we are studying (very few of them as privileged as the Morrices) lived their intimate lives. "Law, contracts, and individual personalities," writes Bradbury, "produced marriages with diverse sets of authority relations and wives with different legal identities and property claims, without ever toppling husbands' broadest powers."[76] Where did Annie and David fit on this spectrum? In suing David for separation of property, Annie was certainly asserting her legal right to protect herself and her children from imminent financial ruin by establishing for herself a separate legal identity and hence the ability to own and receive assets in her own name, without fear of claims by her husband's creditors. At the same time, she may have been following her husband's advice and deferring to his view that the vast property holdings (as well as the debts) he had accrued since 1860 were his and his alone, notwithstanding any provisions of the Quebec Civil Code, including those around community of property, which the couple seems to have been genuinely surprised to see applied to their Toronto marriage.[77]

While it remains difficult to say much more about the emotional landscape or the balance of authority within the Morrice-Anderson marriage, the present case drawn from the judicial archives has much to teach us about the boundaries and connections – whether legal, gendered, financial, cultural, spatial, or otherwise – that structured life in the Square Mile. It also reminds us of what a rich and valuable source legal records can be for the study of private life in former times and, indeed, of the many questions that still remain to be explored, with these sources and others, about marriage, the family, and domestic life in nineteenth-century Quebec.

NOTES

1 Bibliothèque et Archives nationales du Québec [hereafter BAnQ], Centre du Vieux-Montréal [hereafter CVM], Fonds of the Superior Court for the District of Montreal, Greffe de Montréal, Matières civiles en général [hereafter designated by its reference number, TP11, S2, SS2, SSS1], 1987-05-007 \ 3144, 1884, no. 2220, Anderson vs. Morrice.

2 *Civil Code of Lower Canada: From the Amended Roll Deposited in the Office of the Clerk of the Legislative Council as Directed by the Act 29 Vict. Chap. 41, 1865* (Ottawa: Malcolm Cameron, Law Printer to the Queen's Most Excellent Majesty, 1866), Article 1311, p. 361.

3 Broadly speaking, there are 1,836 cases in the FDJQ database, drawn from the judicial districts of Montreal (948 cases), Trois-Rivières (359 cases), and Quebec City (529 cases) between 1840 and 1920. This collection was assembled using SSHRC funding within the broader research program of the Centre interuniversitaire d'études québécoises (CIÉQ) with the help of an exceptional team of research assistants including Marie-Laurence B. Beaumier, Marilyne Caouette, Myriam Cyr, Giselle Giral, Aude Maltais-Landry, Frédéric Mercier, Lisa Moore, Anne-Frédérique Morin, Mathieu Morin, Nathalie Ricard, Marie-Hélène Vanier, and Meagan Wierda. There is no published overview of the project, but we have presented its broad lines at several academic gatherings. See, for instance, Peter Gossage, "Familles, droit et justice au Québec, 1840–1920: Aperçu d'un projet en cours" (paper presented at Canada's Legal Past: Future Directions in Canadian Legal History/Passé juridique du Canada: Les orientations futures de l'histoire juridique canadienne, Calgary, 18 July 2017); and Peter Gossage, "Familles, droit et justice au Québec, 1840–1920" (roundtable presentation with Donald Fyson, Thierry Nootens, and Eric H. Reiter at Séminaires du Centre d'histoire des régulations sociales, Montreal, 9 November 2018). The participating scholars have also drawn on the FDJQ database for their recent publications, including Eric H. Reiter, "Family Defamation in the Quebec Civil Courts:

The View from the Archives," in *Canada's Legal Pasts: Looking Forward, Looking Back*, ed. Lyndsay Campbell, Ted McCoy, and Mélanie Méthot (Calgary: University of Calgary Press, 2020), 11–29. We will continue to do so, while at the same time working to make these data more widely accessible to interested scholars.

4 Lisa Moore and Peter Gossage, "Married Women's Property on Trial: Séparations de biens in Montreal's Superior Court, 1850–1920" (paper presented at Canadian Historical Association, Regina, 28 May 2018).

5 Thierry Nootens, *Genre, patrimoine et droit civil: Les femmes mariées de la bourgeoisie québécoise en procès, 1900–1930* (Montreal: McGill-Queen's University Press, 2018). See also Bettina Bradbury, Peter Gossage, Evelyn Kolish, and Alan Stewart, "Property and Marriage: The Law and the Practice in Early Nineteenth-Century Montreal," *Histoire sociale/Social History* 26, no. 51 (1993): 9–39.

6 Among the existing studies, see in particular Sylvie Savoie, "Les couples séparés: Les demandes de séparation aux 17e et 18e siècles," in *Les marginaux, les exclus et l'autre au Canada aux 17e et 18e siècles*, ed. André Lachance (Saint-Laurent: Fides, 1996): 245–82; Marie-Aimée Cliche, "Les procès en séparation de corps dans la région de Montréal, 1795–1879," *Revue d'histoire de l'Amérique française* 49, no. 1 (1995): 3–33, https://doi.org/10.7202/305398ar; Cliche, "Les séparations de corps dans le district judiciaire de Montréal de 1900 à 1930," *Revue canadienne droit et société* 12, no. 1 (1977): 71–100, https://doi.org/10.1017/S0829320100005214; and Catherine Gélinas, "La violence conjugale dans le district judiciaire de St-François entre 1866 et 1893 d'après les procès en séparation de corps" (master's thesis, Université de Sherbrooke, 2000). There are about 180 suits for separation of bed and board in the FDJQ database, and they will be the object of a separate analysis.

7 As far as we can tell, only Jean-Philippe Garneau has approached the topic directly, while others have dealt with it in passing. See the references in note 11 below.

8 For important contributions, see Nootens, *Genre, patrimoine et droit civil*; Bettina Bradbury, *Wife to Widow: Lives, Laws, and Politics in Nineteenth-Century Montreal* (Vancouver: UBC Press, 2011); Bradbury et al., "Property and Marriage"; Jan Noel, *Along a River: The First French-Canadian Women* (Toronto: University of Toronto Press, 2013); and Nancy Christie and Michael Gauvreau, "Marital Conflict, Ethnicity, and Legal Hybridity in Postconquest Quebec," *Journal of Family History* 41, no. 4 (2016): 430–50, https://doi.org/10.1177/0363199016665432. On married women's property in the common law jurisdictions of Canada, see Lori Chambers, *Married Women and Property Law in Victorian Ontario* (Toronto: University of Toronto Press, 1997); and Peter Baskerville, *A Silent Revolution? Gender and Wealth in English Canada, 1860–1930* (Montreal: McGill-Queen's University Press, 2008).

9 Bradbury, *Wife to Widow*, 62. Bradbury's typology of marital arrangements in Lower Canada (described as customary, collaborative, liberal, and conservative patriarchies, respectively) is clearly articulated to the specific provisions spelled out in the marriage contracts she has studied from the 1820s and 1840s (or in the absence of such a contract, in the "customary" provisions of the civil law), with particular attention to the greater or lesser level of autonomous rights thereby afforded to these married women. Bradbury, *Wife to Widow*, 63–86.

10 "[L]e sort des épouses s'est considérablement amélioré dans les juridictions de *common law* canadiennes à partir de la seconde moitié du 19e siècle," writes Nootens, "alors que les Québécoises ne bénéficièrent de progress équivalents" (Beginning in the second half of the nineteenth century, the position of married women in Canada's common law jurisdictions improved considerably, while at the same time Québécoises did not benefit from similar advances). Nootens, *Genre, patrimoine et droit civil*, 19–20; our translation. See also Thierry

Nootens, "'Des privations ne peuvent pas constituer une fortune': Les droits financiers des femmes mariées de la bourgeoisie québécoise face au marché, 1900–1930," *Revue d'histoire de l'Amérique française* 65, no. 1 (2011): 59–96.

11 Jean-Philippe Garneau, "Poursuivre son mari en justice: Femmes mariées et coutume de Paris devant la cour du Banc du roi de Montréal (1795–1830)," in *Canada's Legal Past: Looking Forward, Looking Back*, ed. Lyndsay Campbell, Ted McCoy, and Mélanie Méthot (Calgary: University of Calgary Press, 2020), 149–77. This is the only study we know of that focuses primarily on judicial separations of property. The procedure is discussed in passing, however, in several other places, including Nootens, "'Des privations'"; Nootens, *Genre, patrimoine et droit civil*; Bradbury, *Wife to Widow*; and Christie and Gauvreau, "Marital Conflict." For an interesting study of separation proceedings in France, albeit for a much earlier period, see Julie Hardwick, "Seeking Separations: Gender, Marriages, and Household Economies in Early Modern France," *French Historical Studies* 21, no. 1 (1998), 157–80, https://doi.org/10.2307/286931.

12 "At the end of a costly procedure, then, the wife might obtain little more than her legal capacity over property to be acquired in the future. For those already engaged in commerce or a trade, this was not an insignificant advantage. For many, acquiring a legal identity meant access to credit. Once the judgment was pronounced, friends and family could untie their purse strings without fear of having these new contributions squandered by the husband or absorbed in his bankruptcy. Surely this was an improvement that allowed others, besides these wives, to profit. But for those who could no longer count on their husbands, the ability to borrow proved essential. Another benefit was that a judicial separation of property prevented wandering husbands, once they returned home, from getting their hands on the fruits of a hardworking wife's labour and savings." Garneau, "Poursuivre son mari en justice," 166; our translation.

13 "For many women seeking judicial separations of property, the new legal identity served essentially as a legal smokescreen for an insolvent husband." Garneau, "Poursuivre son mari en justice," 166; our translation.

14 Christie and Gauvreau, "Marital Conflict," 433.

15 "They had every interest, in principle, in the court responding favourably to these proceedings, which would serve to shelter a portion of the family fortune from third-party claims." Nootens, *Genre, patrimoine et droit civil*, 65; our translation.

16 Many biographical details were found using the online databases of Ancestry.ca. For David's birth information, see "Scotland, Select Births and Baptisms, 1564–1950" (online database), https://www.ancestry.ca/search/collections/60143.

17 Wayne Larsen, *James Wilson Morrice: Painter of Light and Shadow* (Toronto: Dundurn Press, 2008), 127.

18 Larsen, *James Wilson Morrice*, 10.

19 For the Morrice-Anderson wedding in 1860, see "Ontario, Canada, County Marriage Registers, 1858–1869" (online database), https://www.ancestry.ca/search/collections/8510. For Annie's parents' wedding in 1840, see "Scotland, Select Marriages, 1561–1910" (online database), https://www.ancestry.ca/search/collections/60144..

20 See "Census Returns for 1861" (online database), https://www.ancestry.ca/search/collections/1570.

21 R.T. Naylor, *The History of Canadian Business, 1867–1914* (Montreal: McGill-Queen's University Press, 2006), 48.

22 *Lovell's Montreal Directory for 1863–64: containing an alphabetical directory of citizens, a street directory, an advertisers' business directory, and a miscellaneous directory* (Montreal: Lovell, 1864); *Lovell's Montreal Directory for 1864–65: containing an alphabetical directory of citizens, a street directory, an advertisers' business directory, and a miscellaneous directory* (Montreal: Lovell,

1865); *Lovell's Montreal Directory for 1866–67: containing an alphabetical directory of citizens, a street directory, an advertisers' business directory, and a miscellaneous directory* (Montreal: Lovell, 1867).

23 G. Blair Laing, *Morrice: A Great Canadian Artist Rediscovered* (Toronto: McClelland & Stewart, 1984), 32.

24 John James Browne was hired in 1870 by dry goods merchant John Foulds to build his "Rockmount" residence on Summerhill Avenue, and by John James Redpath to design the Redpath Mansion. For more on John James Browne's work in the Square Mile, see Julia Gersovitz, "The Square Mile, 1860–1914" (master's thesis, Columbia University, 1980).

25 "New Buildings in 1870," *Montreal Herald*, 29 November 1870, 1. Like the house of businessman and philanthropist Joseph McKay, named Kildonan after his place of birth in Scotland, the Morrice mansion was described as "Presbyterian Gothic" in style by a local journalist in 1870. It was so admired by Morrice's associates, writes the same reporter, that Andrew F. Gault, a major textile manufacturer, hired Browne to design his house on Sherbrooke Street in the same style.

26 Laing, *Morrice*, 32, 34. The servants listed in the 1881 census were all women aged twenty-seven to forty, except for Henry Burns, their twenty-seven-year-old Irish Presbyterian coachman. See "1881 Census of Canada, Roll" (online database), https://www.ancestry.ca/search/collections/1577.

27 "The Munificence of Mr. Morrice," *Montreal Herald and Daily Commercial Gazette*, 29 November 1882, 4.

28 John Stirling, *A Short Sketch of the History of Crescent Street Church, Montreal* (Montreal: Morton, Phillips, 1899); Larsen, *James Wilson Morrice*, 10.

29 Larsen, *James Wilson Morrice*, 15. Van Horne may even have convinced Morrice of the artistic talent of his son, James Wilson Morrice, who went on to become a celebrated painter whose work is now displayed at the Montreal Museum of Fine Arts and the National Gallery of Canada.

30 Gail Cuthbert Brandt, *Through the Mill: Girls and Women in the Quebec Cotton Industry, 1881–1951* (Montreal: Baraka Books, 2018), 31.

31 Naylor, *History of Canadian Business*, 51.

32 Cuthbert Brandt, *Through the Mill*, 26.

33 See the series of articles by Thomas Phillips Thompson on the growth of Canada's textile industry in the *Globe*, May and June 1882, quoted in Michael Hinton, "Gault, Andrew Frederick," in *Dictionary of Canadian Biography*, vol. 13, University of Toronto/Université Laval, 2003–, accessed 24 March 2023, http://www.biographi.ca/en/bio/gault_andrew_frederick_13F.html.

34 Laing, *Morrice*, 38.

35 Cuthbert Brandt, *Through the Mill*, 26.

36 Cuthbert Brandt, *Through the Mill*, 31.

37 Naylor, *History of Canadian Business*, 51.

38 See "Morrice Hall (Formerly Presbyterian College)," Virtual McGill, accessed 12 June 2020, http://cac.mcgill.ca/campus/buildings/Morrice_Hall.html; "If Walls Could Speak: The History of Morrice Hall," McGill Library, last updated 4 July 2018, https://www.mcgill.ca/library/channels/event/exhibition-if-walls-could-speak-history-morrice-hall-284345.

39 Laing, *Morrice*, 36.

40 Thomas G.W. Telfer, *Ruin and Redemption: The Struggle for a Canadian Bankruptcy Law, 1867–1919* (Toronto: Published for the Osgoode Society for Canadian Legal History by University of Toronto Press, 2014), 3.

41 On Morrice's assignment, see also Naylor, *History of Canadian Business*, 51.

42 Robert C.H. Sweeny, *Why Did We Choose to Industrialize? Montreal, 1819–1849* (Montreal: McGill-Queen's University Press, 2015), 46, 345n26.
43 Robert C.H. Sweeny, personal communication, 7 June 2019.
44 BAnQ-CVM, Fonds of the Superior Court for the District of Montreal, Greffes de notaires, John Fair (CN601, S179), 2009-08-002 \ 681, 1884, "Transfer and Assignment from David Morrice to Edward S. Clouston et al. Trustees," no. 156, 14 May 1884. Before locating this deed of assignment in the archives, we found detailed references to it in several other documents, including a transfer of some Square Mile real estate to the Morrices' next-door neighbour, Ada Maria Mills, the widow of John James Redpath, in August 1884. BAnQ-CVM, Fonds of the Superior Court for the District of Montreal, Greffes de notaires, William de Montmollin Marler (CN601, S577), 2008-01-001 \ 256, "Sale by Edward S. Clouston et al. Trustees and David Morrice to Dame Ada Maria Mills, Widow of John James Redpath," no. 10539, 14 August 1884.
45 The absence of a detailed list of Morrice's creditors and the amounts they were owed is mildly frustrating, but one assumes they were numerous, if only based on the fact that the October 1883 agreement was printed, presumably for fairly wide distribution.
46 McDougall (1825–92) was a fellow Scot and a significant figure in the iron and steel industry. See Maurice Milot, "McDougall, John," in *Dictionary of Canadian Biography*, vol. 12, University of Toronto/Université Laval, 2003–, accessed 21 February 2023, http://www.biographi.ca/en/bio/mcdougall_john_1892_12E.html.
47 BAnQ-CVM, Fonds of the Superior Court of Montreal, Greffes de notaires, William de Montmollin Marler (CN601, S577), 2008-01-001 \ 256, "Transfer, Joseph Couture to David Morrice," no. 10451, 27 June 1884.
48 These properties were among those assigned to the five trustees two years previous; they were later transferred to Edward Clouston in Trust for the Bank of Montreal in October 1884, but they were explicitly "reconveyed" from the bank to Morrice for the purpose of this sale. BAnQ-CVM, Fonds of the Superior Court of Montreal, Greffes de notaires, William de Montmollin Marler (CN601, S577), 2008-01-001 \ 266, "Sale by David Morrice to the Dominion Transport Company Limited," no. 12498, 2 November 1886.
49 BAnQ-CVM, Fonds of the Superior Court for the District of Montreal, Greffes de notaires, John Helder Isaacson (CN601, S469), "Transfer from David Morrice to William J. Morrice," no. 26733, 31 May 1884.
50 BAnQ-CVM, Fonds of the Superior Court for the District of Montreal, Greffes de notaires, Theodore Doucet (CN601, S549), 1971-00-000 \ 617, "Dissolution of Partnership between David Morrice and John W. MacKedie," no. 21182, 29 November 1883.
51 These two transactions are minute numbers 10148 and 10149 in Marler's greffe, both dated 22 February 1884. BAnQ-CVM, Fonds of the Superior Court of Montreal, Greffes de notaires, William de Montmollin Marler (CN601, S577), 2008-01-001 \ 255, "Transfer by David Morrice and Dame Annie S. Anderson to John W. MacKedie," no. 10148, 22 February 1884; BAnQ-CVM, Fonds of the Superior Court of Montreal, Greffes de notaires, William de Montmollin Marler (CN601, S577), 2008-01-001 \ 255, "Donation by John W. MacKedie to Dame Annie S. Anderson, Wife of David Morrice," no. 10149, 22 February 1884.
52 The text of section 1265 is as follows: "After marriage, the marriage covenants contained in the contract cannot be altered [even by the mutual donation of usufruct, which is abolished]; nor can the consorts in any other manner confer benefits *inter vivos* upon each other, except in conformity with the provisions of the act 29th Vict., ch. 7, under which a husband may, subject to the restrictions and conditions herein mentioned, insure his life for the benefit of his wife and children." See also Nootens, *Genre, patrimoine et droit civil.*

53 BAnQ-CVM, TP11, S2, SS2, SSS1, 1987-05-007 \ 3144, 1884, no. 2220, Anderson vs. Morrice, "Deposition of W.J. Morrice for Plaintiff," 28 January 1885.

54 BAnQ-CVM, TP11, S2, SS2, SSS1, 1987-05-007 \ 3144, 1884, no. 2220, Anderson vs. Morrice, "Writ & Declaration," 20 November 1884.

55 BAnQ-CVM, TP11, S2, SS2, SSS1, 1987-05-007 \ 3144, "Writ & Declaration," 1884.

56 BAnQ-CVM, Fonds of the Superior Court of Montreal, Greffes de notaires, William de Montmollin Marler (CN601, S577), 2008-01-001 \ 258, "Renunciation by Dame Annie S. Anderson wife of David Morrice of the Community of Property which Subsisted between Them," no. 10964, 24 February 1885.

57 BAnQ-CVM, TP11, S2, SS2, SSS1, 1987-05-007 \ 3144, 1884, no. 2220, Anderson vs. Morrice, "Rule Naming Praticien," 2 March 1885.

58 BAnQ-CVM, TP11, S2, SS2, SSS1, 1987-05-007 \ 3144, 1884, no. 2220, Anderson vs. Morrice, "Draft of Judgment upon Report of Praticien," 14 March 1885.

59 Moore and Gossage, "Married Women's Property."

60 BAnQ-CVM, TP11, S2, SS2, SSS1, 1987-05-007 \ 2303, 1890, no. 1920, Roberge vs. Limoges; BAnQ-CVM, TP11, S2, SS2, 1987-05-007 \ 2308, 1895, no. 1940, Émard vs. Pitre; BAnQ-CVM, TP11, S2, SS2, 1987-05-007 \ 2016, 1900, no. 1000, Renaud vs. Reinhardt.

61 Throughout his book, Nootens emphasizes the limits of women's knowledge in the areas of finances and civil law: "Ce savoir sociojuridique s'arrêtait bien précisément à l'univers domestique, au coût du maintien des enfants, aux charges de la maisonnée et aux obligations masculines 'naturelles' en milieu bourgeois, telle la responsabilité faite au chef de ménage d'entretenir son épouse selon son rang. Il s'agit là d'une manifestation non équivoque, et lourde de conséquences, de l'existence d'une sphère féminine à l'aube du 20e siècle" (This social and legal knowledge was strictly limited to the domestic realm, to the cost of raising children, to household expenses, and to the "natural" duties of middle-class men, including a husband's responsibility, as household head, to maintain his wife at a level consistent with her rank or status. This was an unequivocal and deeply meaningful manifestation of the existence of a distinct women's sphere at the dawn of the twentieth century). Nootens, *Genre, patrimoine et droit civil*, 204; our translation.

62 The *Oxford English Dictionary* defines *collusion* as a "secret agreement or understanding for purposes of trickery or fraud; underhand scheming or working with another; deceit, fraud, trickery." We borrowed this term from Jean-Philippe Garneau, who writes as follows about the Montreal cases he studied, dating from the period 1795–1829: "Clairement, les femmes n'ont pas toujours agi de leur propre initiative. La collusion entre les conjoints était manifeste, peut-être plus fréquente à Montréal qu'ailleurs" (Clearly, these women did not always act on their own initiative. The collusion between husbands and wives was obvious and perhaps more frequent in Montreal than elsewhere). Garneau, "Poursuivre son mari en justice," 159–60; our translation.

63 In our ongoing work with judicial separations of property, then, we plan to apply another, more salient dichotomy to the analysis of these cases, borrowed once again from Nootens's detailed study of civil suits involving privileged and propertied married women in Quebec between 1900 and 1930 in *Genre, patrimoine et droit civil.* Nootens divides his monograph into two parts, looking first at "le sort des femmes mariées de l'élite lorsque leur statut financier et leur aisance étaient menacés par la poursuite d'un créancier du ménage ou par les transactions de leur mari" (the fate of married women when their financial status and their affluence were threatened by the legal action of a household creditor or by their husband's transactions) in what the author would call the public sphere; and second, at situations in which "l'échec proprement interpersonnel du mariage" (the properly interpersonal failure of a marriage), characterized

by "des tensions conjugales [qui] se soldent par des abandons ou des séparations" (conjugal tensions culminating in abandonment or separation), could lead to "de graves conséquences patrimoniales et financières" (grave financial and patrimonial consequences). Nootens, *Genre, patrimoine et droit civil*, 4, 19, 91; our translation. There is a need, in other words, to account for both *external* and *internal* pressures on bourgeois marriages, their property, and their prestige, and that might be a better way to classify the 167 couples in the FDJQ collection.

64 BAnQ-CVM, TP11, S2, SS2, SSS1, 1987-05-007 \ 3144, Anderson vs. Morrice, "Writ & Declaration," 1884.

65 Chambers, *Married Women and Property Law*, 71.

66 Naylor, *History of Canadian Business*, 170.

67 Cuthbert Brandt, *Through the Mill*, 37–8.

68 Mark Sholdice, "Towards a Taxonomy of Financial-Industrial Networks in Canada, 1867–1914" (paper presented at *Crossing Boundaries and Constructing Linkages: The History of Montreal's Square Mile in National and International Context*, Montreal, 19 June 2019).

69 *Canadian History Makers: A Volume Containing Accurate and Concise Sketches of Men Who Have Done Things in the Dominion of Canada Past and Present Together with Photogravures Made from Their Latest Photographs* (Montreal: Canadian Publication Society, 1913), 149.

70 *Lovell's Montreal Directory for 1900–1901: containing an alphabetical directory of citizens, a street directory, an advertisers' business directory, and a miscellaneous directory* (Montreal: Lovell, 1901).

71 Art Association of Montreal, *Exposition d'Art Français* (Paris: Imprimerie Henri Guiton, 1909).

72 Emphasis added.

73 BAnQ-CVM, Fonds of the Superior Court of Montreal, Greffes de notaires, William de Montmollin Marler (CN601, S577), 2008-01-001 \ 255: Greffe of William de Montmollin Marler, minute no. 24187, Last Will and Testament of David Morrice, 19 December 1899; minute no. 24188, Last Will and Testament of Dame Annie S. Anderson, wife of David Morrice, 19 December 1899.

74 This is according to Nicole Cloutier, who also writes this about the younger Morrice: "The best description of Morrice comes from Matisse: 'As a man, he was a true gentleman, a good friend with plenty of wit and humour. He had, as everyone knows, an unfortunate craving for whisky … He was a Canadian of Scottish descent, from a rich family, very rich himself, but he did not show it. He was always over hill and dale, a little like a migrating bird but without any fixed landing place.'" Nicole Cloutier, "Morrice, James Wilson," in *Dictionary of Canadian Biography*, vol. 15, University of Toronto/Université Laval, 2003, accessed 15 June 2020, http://www.biographi.ca/en/bio/morrice_james_wilson_15E.html.

75 Brian Young, *Patrician Families and the Making of Quebec: The Taschereaus and McCords* (Montreal: McGill-Queen's University Press, 2014).

76 Bradbury, *Wife to Widow*, 63.

77 "Englishmen," writes Bradbury, "were particularly prone to assume that the peculiar powers that the common law offered them as husbands were rights that should accompany them wherever they moved and settled." Bradbury, *Wife to Widow*, 66. We might guess that this was the case for certain Scots as well.

Figure V.8 William Notman, *Sir Hugh Allan, Montreal*, 1871. McCord Museum, I-63541.1.

Hugh Allan and Ravenscrag

The first non-agricultural residents of the Square Mile were Scots who had made fortunes in fur trading. Washington Irving, writing about 1830, reminisced about the "commercial aristocracy of … hyperborean nabobs" who ran the North West Company, and their riotous feasting and general revelry.[1] By the 1860s a new social order was in place: still Scottish, still new money, but now gaining power from the infrastructure that was being built as the country of Canada began to take shape.

The exemplar of this next generation of Square Milers was Hugh Allan (1810–82) (Figure V.8). His story is not strictly a rags-to-riches one. His father, who had established the Allan Shipping Line in his native Scotland, sent his sixteen-year-old son to Montreal to establish connections. Over the course of a decade, Allan moved from clerical tasks to a partnership in a local shipping company. By the mid-1850s, he was well-positioned to become a political influencer and financier. The construction of his palatial mansion Ravenscrag (Figure V.9), nestled high on the slopes of Mount Royal, reflected his social status and financial power.

How Ravenscrag came to be designed remains a mystery. The Prince of Wales came to Montreal in 1859 and stayed in the Square Mile at Rosemount, the residence of the Honorable John Rose. It can be conjectured that Allan, who lived in a large house on St. Catherine Street near City Councillors Street, would have been outside of the enchanted orbit of the prince. This perceived exclusion may have been the genesis of Allan's decision a year later to relocate to the most prominent property in the Square Mile.

Instead of turning to one of the established architects in the city, such as J.W. Hopkins (1825–1905), Allan launched a competition c. 1860 and selected the design of a

Figure V.9 Wm. Notman & Son, *"Ravenscrag," Residence of Hugh Montagu Allan, Montreal*, 1901. McCord Museum, VIEW-4867.

Figure V.10 Anonymous, *View of Montreal, Looking South from Hugh Allan's House*, c. 1870. McCord Museum, MP-1983.14.20.1–2.

young draughtsman, Victor Roy (1837–1902). Roy was working in the architectural office of William Speir (1801–78), who is credited with being the supervising architect for the project. Such a complex arrangement of different roles and responsibilities was not standard practice at the time.

By every measure, Ravenscrag eclipsed all other residences in the city, if not the country. The residence was enormous, with over 800 square metres of space on each floor. The ballroom, for example, as Allan himself noted in a letter to Abbé Labelle, was built to accommodate as many as 500 guests. Outbuildings included a gatehouse, stables, an orangerie, and conservatories for both vegetable and flower production. Ravenscrag became the unofficial residence for visiting royalty; Lord Dufferin stayed in 1872. Allan no longer ceded social place to anyone. He was the de facto leader of Square Mile society.

The severity of the neo-classical architecture, consistent with the Italianate style, was softened by the picturesque massing and the verdant landscaping. The estate was designed to be viewed by passers-by and was early the subject of engravings in the popular press. At the same time, the house had features that permitted the residents to survey the city that lay before them. The design included an imposing 23-metre tower from which Allan could see his steamships in the harbour and the Green Mountains of Vermont in the far distance. The stereoscopic view (Figure V.10) provides a glimpse of this vista. The property was a manifestation in built form of power, and even today in its diminished condition the estate resonates with it.

In 1940, Allan's son and daughter-in-law donated the property to the Royal Victoria Hospital. Known today as the Allan Memorial Institute, it has another, more recent association with the unethical psychiatric experiments of Dr. Ewan Cameron.

NOTE

1 Washington Irving, *Astoria; or, Anecdotes of an Enterprise beyond the Rocky Mountains* (London: Richard Bentley, 1839), 9.

Figure 6.1 Wm. Notman & Son, *Lady Roddick in Her Livingroom, Montreal*, 1930. McCord Museum, II-297449.

CHAPTER SIX

Searching for Intimacies beyond the Notman Photographs: The Case of Amy Redpath Roddick

Elizabeth Kirkland and Mary Anne Poutanen

Introduction

Lady Amy Redpath Roddick is shown in this William Notman photograph (Figure 6.1) alone in her sitting room at 1065 Sherbrooke Street West.[1] She appears pensive, assertive, grand, and sophisticated. Middle age has not robbed her sense of style, and the camera records a scene that is altogether one of quiet strength and poise. While the photograph provides us with a glimpse into the intimate world of her home, Amy keeps her face turned just far enough away that we are unable to read what it may have to tell us about the life she has lived.

Renowned photographers William Notman and William McFarland Notman, of Wm. Notman & Sons, produced a vast visual record of life in the Square Mile. Their beautiful photographs, which serve as documentation throughout this volume, offer an important window into the past, not only for what is shown in the pictures in terms of built environments and the people who inhabited them but also, we argue, for questioning the perspectives that were behind the staging of the captured scenes. Image construction was key to maintaining and shaping Montreal's elite society and was performed repeatedly through ritual, dress, social activities, consumption, building, and, as a case in point, photography.[2] Those who hired Wm. Notman & Son were investing in a public staging of the affluence and prestige that undergirded their status as elites and would last into perpetuity. Roderick MacLeod's introductory piece at the beginning of this volume describes the way contemporary coffee table books continue to present these idealized images as a way of capturing the essence of a "Golden" Square Mile.[3] But for all the beauty portrayed by Wm. Notman & Son, we assert that life in the Square Mile was far more complex than the images that were so carefully fashioned and presented to the public. Those who lived in the Square Mile lived intimate lives that subjected them to the joys, the anxieties, the surprises, the sorrows, and the calamities of everyday life. Buffered by their wealth and healthy living conditions, residents of the Square Mile were never immune from the anguishes of life, despite what the photographs might present. This study is not intended to analyse the photographs themselves but rather to explore the lived experiences of the subjects when the camera was not focused on them. What were the stories that were happening behind the photographs that remain for our observation?

This chapter, therefore, offers an intimate biography of one of Notman's frequent subjects: Amy Redpath Roddick. Using an intimate biographical approach such as this, we can uncover deep layers of a life that may otherwise be missed in larger studies of the Square Mile. Amy's life at 1065 Sherbrooke Street was both decadent and full of turmoil. She lived in one of the Square Mile's beautiful mansions yet navigated the complicated daily struggles that resulted from her father's early death, her mother's failing health, and the eventual murder-suicide of her mother and youngest brother at her home in 1901. Because Amy left a rich trove of historical sources – diaries, poetry, plays, photographs, and a public persona – we can delve into a study of emotions, intimacies, and relationships. Yet these sources are not without their own silences and gaps, which in turn serve as another form of testimony to the past in and of themselves. By adopting a case study approach to Amy Redpath Roddick, we consider how birth order, gender, sexuality, health, and death shaped life for one of the Square Mile's central families and argue that Amy employed deliberate strategies to project a trouble-free image to the "outside world" (that might be glimpsed in a Notman photograph, for example) while confining the intensity of the family's emotions within the intimate home space, thereby protecting the family from exposure. Containment was both about keeping out and keeping in. And Amy was far from alone in this process. She was deeply embedded in a community that was constructing an elite social identity, an ongoing process that encouraged families to present sanitized public images while keeping other intimate details hidden. Like all case studies, Amy's story is both unique in its details and yet common enough to reveal what life might have been like behind the doors of the Square Mile mansions, when the public camera was not fixed upon its subjects.

This study revisits previous research associated with understanding the intimate and political lives of elite women in Montreal conducted by Elizabeth Kirkland in her dissertation "Mothering Citizens: Elite Women in Montreal, 1893–1914," which included Amy Redpath Roddick as one of the twenty women studied in the collective biography. It also revisits the research conducted for the Redpath Mansion Mystery project launched in 2008 on the Great Unsolved Mysteries in Canadian History website.[4] Our chapter situates itself in the histories of gender, family, and sexuality upon which these two aforementioned projects were built. We also position this case study in the history of emotions that has emerged from the historian's quest to understand the performance and experience of emotions across time and space. The field borrows from well-trodden terrain in anthropology, psychology, and neuroscience, among other interrelated disciplines.[5] Like the study by Nicolas Kenny on the letters of two soldiers in the First World War (letters that were being written contemporarily to those of Amy Redpath Roddick), we utilize the methodologies of the history of emotions to push more tenaciously against the boundaries between private and public, the personal and the collective.

We begin with a short history of the Redpath family to situate Amy's place in it with regard to her childhood, her father's death, her mother's illness, and the responsibilities with which she was burdened. Next, we discuss the circumstances and responses to the violent deaths of Amy's mother, Ada, and her youngest brother, Clifford. Finally, we conclude with Amy's efforts to rebuild her life following her marriage to Thomas Roddick and her attempts to reconstruct Ada and Clifford's deaths as natural.

The Redpath Family

The Redpath family requires little introduction, though one can easily get lost in the web of prolific offspring emerging from John Redpath's two marriages. Figure 6.2 demonstrates Amy's place in that family web of the first marriage between John Redpath and Janet McPhee. She was the eldest child of John James Redpath and Ada Maria Mills, born in Montreal in 1868, exactly nine months after their marriage.[6] Amy was just briefly acquainted with her grandfather, patriarch John Redpath, before his death in 1869.[7]

John James, or "Jack," as he was known, was the youngest son of John Redpath's first marriage to Janet McPhee, making him their seventh child (Figure 6.3). He followed in his brother Peter's footsteps by showing an early interest in the family sugar company, yet by the time of Amy's birth, Jack had moved out of the inner workings of the sugar business and had little to do with any of the Redpath companies.[8] His energies seemed more focused on engagement with the Victoria Rifles (which he helped found) and travelling with his young family, a privilege afforded by the massive wealth being passed on to this second generation of entrepreneurial families.

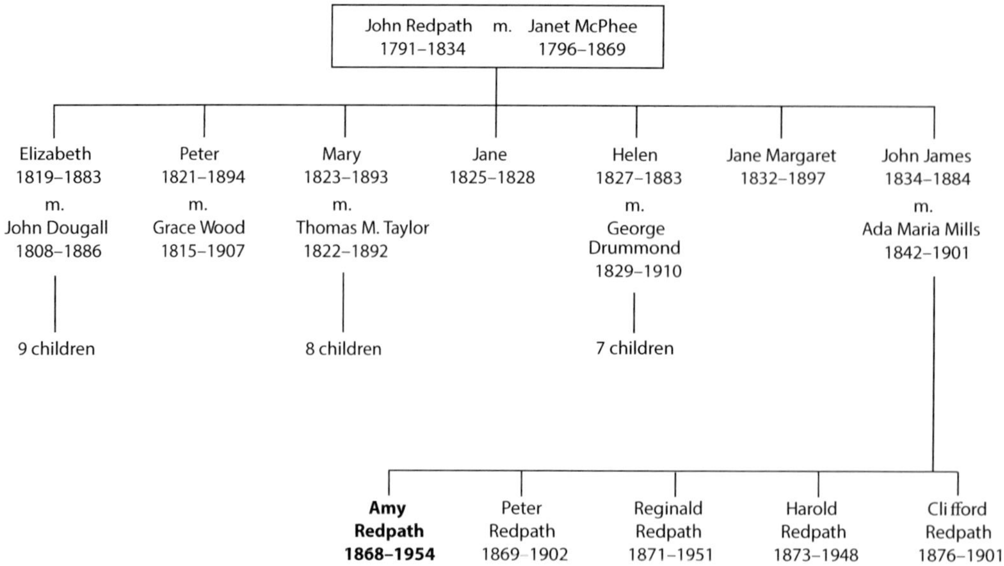

Figure 6.2 Amy Redpath's partial family tree, created by Roderick MacLeod, 18 June 2019. This family tree is limited to her grandfather John Redpath's first marriage to Janet McPhee and does not include his second marriage to Jane Drummond or their ten children.

Ada Maria Mills (Figure 6.4) was born in Montreal in 1840. Her father was a successful merchant and one-time mayor of Montreal, while her mother, Hannah Lyman, was one of the daughters of the well-established pharmaceutical Lyman family. Ada brought significant wealth into her marriage to Jack, which she secured through a marriage contract.[9] It was Ada who bought and paid for their house at 1065 Sherbrooke Street West.[10]

From Ada's diary, we get a glimpse of the very happy ambiance into which Amy was born. In the months following her birth, Ada and Jack set up house in Putney, England, surrounded by Ada's widowed mother and her sisters and their families. There the young family could visit with Jack Redpath's family, Uncle Peter Redpath and Aunt Grace Wood at Chislehurst, creating a tight family network that mirrored their home neighbourhood of the Square Mile, and also access the Continent for short trips away.[11]

Amy's arrival ushered Ada into motherhood, a role she assumed with great delight while in good health. Although she had the help of a nurse and eager aunties, Ada kept Amy close by her. She took great pleasure in observing Amy's early growth and development: "Sometime in March we went with Maggie and Alice to Westman Ho. where we spent a very happy six weeks. There darling Amy learned

Figure 6.3 William Notman, *John J. Redpath, Montreal*, 1864. McCord Museum, I-12692.1.

Figure 6.4 William Notman, *Miss Ada Mills, Montreal*, 1862. McCord Museum, I-2480.1.

Figure 6.5 William Notman, *Mrs. John J. Redpath and Child, Montreal,* 1871. McCord Museum, I-64488.1.

to creep & I first learned to sew for her. I made her some print dresses."[12] Ada also seemed very happy in her relationship with Jack. As a present for Ada's twenty-seventh birthday, Jack arranged for the two of them to have a couple days in London, "the first time in many months that we have been alone together."[13] This short lovers' escape was made possible by the fact that Ada had been employing a wet nurse for Amy.[14] Jack also doted on Amy, and the small family was nearly always together in that first year. The following July, Ada gave birth to Peter Whiteford, Amy's first brother. These happy early years did little to foreshadow the grief and tragedy that would follow.

Figure 6.6 Wm. Notman & Son, *Mrs. John Redpath's House, Sherbrooke Street, Montreal*, 1899. McCord Museum, II-129781.

In 1870, Jack, Ada, and the two children returned to Montreal and settled into their home on Sherbrooke Street where three more brothers – John Reginald "Reg," Harold Mills, and Jocelyn Clifford "Cliff" – joined them over the next five years.[15] The children were raised among their extended family of cousins, aunts and uncles, and close friends. While the young family continued to travel extensively, spending long periods of Amy's childhood in Europe, primarily in England and France, home was decidedly established for Amy as the mansion on Sherbrooke Street. As a young woman, this entrenched her position near the centre of the Square Mile's elite networks of family and fortune. Later in life, she reflected on these years as very happy times.[16]

William Notman photographed the children together in 1881. The full-group photographs place Amy at the centre, surrounded by her brothers, with the family dog comfortably stationed at their feet (Figure 6.7). Amy clearly held a central

Figure 6.7 Notman & Sandham, *Mrs. John J. Redpath's Group, Montreal*, 1881. McCord Museum, II-59824.1.

Figure 6.8 Notman & Sandham, *Master and Missie Redpath, Montreal*, 1881. McCord Museum, II-59826.1.

role in the family as the only daughter and as the eldest. This was characterized by a particularly close relationship with her mother, yet already at the time of this photograph we know that Ada was beginning to experience poor health. It would only continue to deteriorate in the years to come and shape much of what happened in the household.[17] Leonore Davidoff, in her study of nineteenth-century English families, explores the ways gender, birth order, and class created hierarchical relationships among siblings.[18] Davidoff reminds us that "[w]ithin all kinship systems, gender assignment, however rigid or flexible, becomes a building block on which the edifice rests. … Since sibling position is also often aligned with age and birth order, here too, power relations are played out."[19] Amy would have been expected to provide oversight for her younger siblings as well as assume the household management tasks that Ada was becoming increasingly unable to fulfil. In spite of her gender and young age, Amy, as the eldest child, stepped into a variety of surrogate roles as the proxy head of household.

William Notman photographed Amy on her own twice in the following years, first at the age of fourteen (Figure 6.9) and then four years later as a young woman of eighteen years (Figure 6.10). These photographs record the passage into adulthood but give little sense of how perilous this time was for Amy. When she was sixteen, her father died. His funeral was a very public affair, with the Victoria Rifles accompanying the long parade of mourners from 1065 Sherbrooke Street up to Mount Royal Cemetery beginning at 8 p.m. on Saturday, 7 June 1884.[20] Amy conserved no writings from this time in her life, and so we have little insight into her emotional response to the death of her father. We can imagine that she felt his absence keenly, for he had been very present in her day-to-day life. What we can be sure of is that this marked a turning point in her life. Jack's death coincided with a pronounced decline in Ada's health, leaving Amy to assume many of the duties of "matriarch" of the family including that of guardian of the family image.

In the years following the death of Jack, and in the face of Ada's deteriorating health, Amy's attention turned increasingly towards keeping the family intact. Access to a bevy of domestic help eased many of these responsibilities and allowed Amy to pursue diverse activities outside the home like others of her age and social class. She filled her days attending lectures, shopping, visiting friends and kin, putting on plays, walking and riding on the mountain, and travelling, all of which brought her some degree of happiness. She also took up the mantle of social convenor, establishing a rigorous routine of calling and receiving, celebrating birthdays (though her own was often missed over the years), attending weddings and balls, writing condolence letters, and feting the New Year with her neighbours and relations so that public social obligations were being met. Amy maintained close friendships

Figure 6.9 Notman & Sandham, *Missie Redpath, Montreal*, 1882. McCord Museum, II-65585.1.

Figure 6.10 Wm. Notman & Son, *Miss Redpath, Montreal*, 1886. McCord Museum, II-79609.1.

with several relatives and neighbours, most notably cousins Maud Redpath and Lily Dougall (who each lived two blocks away from Amy), and the Misses Marguerite and Emma Roddick (who lived a twenty-minute walk east of the Redpath home). These latter two friends lived with their older brother, Dr. Thomas George Roddick, himself a recent widower, who was a frequent visitor to the Redpath house for both professional and social reasons.[21]

Amy was also responsible for any type of self-education she wished to pursue. It is unclear why she never registered at Royal Victoria College, which began offering

Figure 6.11 William Notman, *Dr. Thomas G. Roddick and His Sisters, Montreal*, 1876. McCord Museum, II-40842.1.

courses to women in 1885, but likely it was related to her familial obligations. She replaced an institutional education with an extensive schedule of educational activities, attending weekly lectures on world architecture and art given by the Montreal Art Association, frequenting student parties at her Aunt Emily Redpath and Uncle Henry Bovey's house, and listening to papers on Ruskin and Ibsen (among others) at weekly literary meetings at her Uncle George and Julia Parker Drummond's house. Like many other elite Square Mile women, she was tutored in both French and German as a young woman. Relatively fluent in French at a young age, Amy pursued perfecting her German throughout adulthood. She made weekly visits to her German tutors, the Gebhardts, and spent hours translating poems, plays, and novels into German, including Henrik Ibsen's *A Doll's House*.[22]

For some time, she could count on the oldest of her brothers to accompany her in these duties and activities. But as they pursued their own adult lives and moved out of 1065 Sherbrooke, Amy was again left with the bulk of the household and family responsibilities. Peter suffered from poor health and frequently travelled to health spas in Europe, the United States, and across Canada seeking treatment for sciatica and a cure for tuberculosis. Amy experienced perpetual anxiety about Peter's condition and missed him desperately when he was away. On 14 August 1899, Amy confided in her diary, "Peter leaves tomorrow for another winter in Colorado. We shall be a lonely little party again this winter. Only Mama, Cliff and I."[23]

Reginald left Montreal in 1889 to establish a cattle ranch in Pincher's Creek, Alberta, and although Reginald's relationship with Amy seems to have been somewhat more distant, Amy kept up regular correspondence with him and hosted his Albertan friends and neighbours when they were in Montreal. Amy was particularly anxious when Reginald joined the Canadian Mounted Regiment in December 1899 to fight in the South African War. She scoured the newspapers every day for details about the fighting, hoping to find some small assurances that Reginald and his troop were safe. She studied a large table map of South Africa that she received as a gift in order to better understand the geography and topography of the country as she followed the war through her brother's letters.[24] Reginald's safe return to Canada early in 1901 brought Amy significant comfort and relief, though she continued to see very little of him as his life remained fixed in Western Canada.

Harold married Alice Watson in 1897 and settled in nearby Westmount. It seems that Harold, a sportsman, never had a career, choosing to live off his inheritance. Amy called on Harold and Alice regularly at their home on Olivier Street, increasing these visits following the birth of their daughter Elizabeth Grace (Betty) in April 1898. Amy was not particularly kind toward Betty immediately following her birth, as this unflattering description in her diary indicates: "Harold was in this P.M. I

Figure 6.12 Wm. Notman & Son, *Mr. J.C. Redpath, Law Graduate, Montreal*, 1900. McCord Museum, II-133577.

asked him if the baby was as ugly as they usually are & he said that it was much worse. Nothing would induce him to touch it. He was horribly disappointed that it was not a boy. I suppose he wanted someone to play football with. I am glad it is a girl."[25] Three days later, Amy recounted her introduction to "ugly" Betty: "I daresay she is all right as babies go; but I don't admire her & hope she will improve. She seems very tiny. I never saw so young a baby before."[26] Over time, however, Amy became especially fond of her niece, recording in her diary each time she saw her in Westmount and at family celebrations of Betty's milestones such as the christening and birthdays. Amy was likely drawn to her niece given the birth order and gender they shared. Three more children followed Betty – all boys – mimicking Amy's own family configuration of eldest daughter with four younger brothers and reinforcing her identification with Betty. Typical of wealthy households in Montreal, Harold and the family summered in Georgetown at "Bonnie Brae," a farm he purchased

Figure 6.13 Anonymous, *J. Clifford Redpath with Dog*, date unknown. Redpath Sugar Museum.

in 1901. They left Montreal for British Columbia in the 1920s, where eventually his marriage to Alice fell apart and ended in divorce. Harold subsequently married Marie-Adèle Prendeville in 1938, later dying in 1948 at Saanich, British Columbia.

Clifford, who was pursuing a law degree at McGill University, remained the only sibling with Amy in the family home by 1897. He gradually assumed many of the duties associated with an elite household and, once Clifford was of age, was encumbered with the added responsibility of administering the family fortune – although with some guidance from his eldest brother Peter and likely a few uncles. While this gendered distribution of duties left the official burden of managing finances on Clifford's shoulders as the only son at home, Amy's diaries provide glimpses of her stepping into this role as well: "… Had to sign papers transferring the executorship of Papa's estate from Uncle George & Dunbar Taylor to Peter & Harold."[27] Clifford and Amy developed a supportive and cooperative rhythm in these responsibilities. Cliff accompanied Amy to soirees and dances; they went to church, entertained, and roamed the mountain for hours together. Theirs was a very close sibling relationship.

Yet none of the household duties seemed as arduous as overseeing their mother's health needs and meeting her numerous demands, positioning Ada at the centre of the household albeit with few responsibilities. In the years before her untimely death, Ada could still entertain occasionally, accompany her daughter on rides around the mountain, on shopping trips, and to visit family members. Amy noted at the beginning of 1898 that her mother had been confined to bed since the new year and that "[s]he does not seem even as well as usual this winter & suffers so that life is really a burden to her."[28] By 1900, Ada seldom left her bedroom and was unable to even attend family functions and celebrations. Letters and diary passages reveal just how much Ada was physically and emotionally dependent upon Amy and Clifford, who took turns sitting with Ada, calling for doctors, and doing their best to ease her pain. It was exhausting. While Amy's writing reveals a strong devotion to her ailing mother, there are hints of tensions and of ambivalence. In August 1898, for example, she wrote in her diary about a scene at the train station: "At ten went to the station to see Mama & Peter off – M. clung to me, feeling too ill to be left so there & then I made up my mind to go with her. I don't think any one [*sic*] ever went to Saratoga with so few impediments before, not even a pair of gloves."[29] Even though Ada was travelling with Peter to Dr. Strong's Sanitarium in upstate New York and was to meet Clifford there, her insistence that Amy accompany her must have been very trying. Although her diary excerpt is cloaked in loyalty, Amy had not planned to go and may have been looking forward to some time to herself, leaving her mother's taxing health needs in someone else's hands. Notwithstanding Clifford's anticipated arrival, and having both Amy and Peter at her side, Ada then wrote a letter to Clifford the following day reiterating her expectations of him: "Oh, how I miss you! I have come so dependent on you that I am lost without you. Nothing seems worthwhile without you."[30] In the years leading up to the tragedy, the atmosphere in the Redpath household appears heavily laden with sickness, worry, stress, and perhaps unspoken frustration and anger. When crisis hit 1065 Sherbrooke Street, Amy's role of containing the household was put to its greatest test.

The Tragedy

It is a challenge to be certain from historical sources what actually took place on 13 June 1901 at the Redpath mansion on Sherbrooke Street regarding the violent deaths of Ada and Cliff. This tragedy became one of the subjects of the Great Unsolved Mysteries in Canadian History project precisely because the details of what happened remain so murky. The police were never called, newspaper articles provide contradictory information, Amy did not write about this moment of violence in her diary, and any letters of condolence that may have contained details about Clifford or Ada's state of mind or even what had happened behind closed doors have been expunged. A few months after the tragedy, Amy admitted in a letter to sister-in-law Alice Watson Redpath that she had sorted and destroyed old letters while on holiday with Peter at Sainte-Agathe-des-Monts.[31] The Redpaths made every effort to limit information pertaining to Ada and Clifford's demise and thus to manage their public image. The *Quebec Daily Mercury* reported: "The family have issued a statement, but from it nothing can be learned as to the details of the tragedy beyond the fact that the two people are dead. The family have refused all applications for details and every effort is being made to have as little public attention as possible drawn to the tragedy."[32] What do we know happened that day?

According to testimony given by Peter, who was presumably the only other family member at home at the time, Clifford returned to the house at 6:00 p.m. appearing tired and unwell, went immediately upstairs to Ada's bedroom, and seconds later three gunshots were heard. After breaking down the door to the locked room, Peter discovered his mother and brother lying on the floor, both having suffered gunshot wounds to the head. The two maids who were present in the house at the time ran to a neighbour's house to obtain the services of a physician.[33] We have no idea where Amy was that day or even if Peter's retelling of the events was accurate.[34] Local newspapers reported that Ada was pronounced dead at the scene and that Clifford was transferred to the Royal Victoria Hospital where he died in the early hours of the morning.[35]

A coroner's inquest was held the following day, 14 June 1901. Thirteen city elites heard witnesses Peter Redpath, housemaid Mary Rose Shallow, and businessman and relative Charles Fleet testify as to what had taken place the day before.[36] Dr. Thomas Roddick, the family's personal physician, also testified, suggesting that twenty-four-year-old Clifford, labouring under an epileptic seizure, "must have killed his mother and then shot himself afterward."[37] Much was made of his epileptic seizure, even though there is no other evidence that Clifford ever suffered from this malady. It was, however, a means to explain such an unpredictable, violent act by a young respectable bourgeois man. At the coroner's inquest, Roddick's assessment was accepted, and it was determined that fifty-nine-year-old Ada had died from a gunshot wound to the back of the head inflicted by her son Clifford, who then turned the gun on himself. Three days later, Ada and Clifford were laid to rest in the family plot at Mount Royal Cemetery following a private high Anglican funeral at St. John the Evangelist Church.[38] The Redpath pedigree coupled with the priest's sanction allowed Amy to arrange such a service, even though it was against Anglican practice to pay holy tribute to someone who committed a homicide or died by suicide.

The sensationalism of this tragedy tore away the carefully constructed veil that maintained a respectable separation of the public and private lives of the Redpath family. The public eagerly followed every detail of the scandal, and the story was copied in newspapers across the country and beyond. Amy undoubtedly felt very exposed. The Redpaths suddenly found themselves in what Annmarie Adams, Valerie Minnett, Mary Anne Poutanen, and David Theodore have argued was a paradoxical imperative.[39] They had to perform intimate and private matters in public rituals while choreographing the public event to make it private, reshaping the deaths within the customs of bourgeois respectability. Despite shock and raw grief, Amy did this by controlling access to information, invoking silence, and treating the deaths as natural rather than violent.

In the months leading up to this tragedy, Amy had suddenly stopped writing in her diary, the pages left blank. Were there growing tensions with Cliff or with Ada or the two of them together that remain hidden in the silences? The empty pages of Amy's diary continued in the weeks and months that followed the murder-suicide. We have little knowledge about what Amy was thinking or experiencing. The traces that are left come through letters written to her during these months. From her Aunt Grace Redpath:

> What a tragedy! Mother, and son, both gone, what has happened – the dear Mother has suffered so long, that all must have been prepared, for her loss, that is, if we are ever prepared to part – with our loved ones … I read your cable, to try, and believe there must be some mistake that Clifford was also taken from you, from us, for that dear boy won my heart, and I think the hearts of all who met him.[40]

We know that Amy found solace in particular relationships and places. Amy and Peter travelled to the Redpath Manor House (Figure 6.14) in Chislehurst, England, to recuperate; it protected Amy from prying eyes and rumourmongers as she mourned the deaths and planned for the future. Within her elite social milieu,

Figure 6.14 Anonymous, *Chislehurst, England*, date unknown. Redpath Sugar Museum.

friends and relatives rallied around Amy, empathizing with the situation she faced and buttressing her normalization of Clifford's death; and like Amy, they described in letters of condolence their admiration for his beautiful and innocent nature, his heroic stature, and his final achievement of peace in death surely at odds with the events of 13 June. Ellen Plimsoll wrote that she had chosen lilies to symbolize the "purity of his life and character. A sweeter smile than his I never saw – very, very few young men have had so high an ideal in life and I think, if I had been asked for a perfect type of life, I should have thought of him as a model."[41] Anna Harrington penned a short note to Amy about "his strong courage & his college work which with the devotion to his home, made him the truest of heros [*sic*]."[42] In another sympathy letter, Aunt Alice E. Redpath reassured Amy that Clifford was "entering on a new & fuller life, with all his faculties unimpaired," implying that they had indeed been impaired on 13 June.[43] Some of the letters of condolence were contradictory. For Amy's cousin Helen Redpath, Ada was no longer in pain, and as for Clifford, "how happy we know he is now," insinuating that he had not been happy prior to his death.[44] George Plimsoll wrote that Clifford was cheerful, joking, and hopeful about his bar exams, his future, and travelling with him part way to Muskoka: "I had never seen him more happy & gay as he called out 'au revoir' from his front door, dear dear Clifford!"[45] Perhaps he had made a decision to end his life and found relief in doing so, but it was only Jane C. Cooper who offered a reason for Clifford's act:

> I was by no means blind to his beautiful character. How could I be when I had seen his unusual devotion to your invalid mother and to yourself. For years I have been full of reverence & admiration for him knowing how brave & self-controlled he was. And Amy dear, the marvel to me is that he did not collapse long, long ago – for however noble the air in life the … spirit in the air is but set in the fragile frame of humanity with its physical limits.[46]

Amy herself rarely articulated her feelings in public about the tragedy, and even her diary remained silent during these periods of deep grief. Yet we know she would have been devastated by these sudden and violent losses, especially that of her brother Clifford with whom she had been especially close. She did eventually find expression in poetry. In a poem dedicated to J.C.R. (Jocelyn Clifford Redpath) she wrote candidly of her grief:

Must I dwell alone the many, dismal morrows,
Far from blissful hope together spanned,
Hope of service through assuaging dearth and sorrows,
Hope of golden deeds together planned?

No, the heavy, mourning weeds I tear asunder,
Struggle from the clouds that blacken round,
Close my ears to their unholy, woesome thunder
Rise anew to life from grief unbound.[47]

Amy and Peter had no intention of forsaking the family home on Sherbrooke Street, and they returned there from Chislehurst by summer's end. Since winter in neither England nor Montreal was suitable for Peter's ailing health, they, along with housemaid Rose and dog Neptune, left for Redlands, California, where they would again escape the gossip and scandal circulating in Montreal.[48] Throughout the winter, Peter's condition worsened to the point that Amy beckoned her brother Reginald to come. She recorded in her diary on 18 May 1902 that she had written to her sister-in-law Alice saying that Peter was very unwell. Peter died that day. Once again, Amy had to pick up the pieces to make a long journey home, this time across the continent – a second period of mourning for a second brother she had dearly loved.

But for Amy, life did begin to rise anew … from grief unbound. Following Peter's death, she once again returned to the safety of Chislehurst, accompanied by Reg. There she permitted Aunt Grace and her cousin Agnes to take care of her as she grieved: "Two weeks yesterday since we arrived. Feel much better for the change though the lonely moments do come. … We generally go for a walk in the mornings & a long drive in the afternoon. The drives are beautiful & so numerous. I don't think we have repeated a drive yet."[49] In the midst of this respite, a new quality of an old relationship began to emerge: "Left by 8 p.m. train for England via New York accompanied by Reg & Dr. Roddick. The latter going over to see Lord Strathcona on faculty business."[50] That Roddick's business interests aligned so well with Amy's travel plans was likely not a coincidence. "Dr. R" had been a frequent visitor at the Redpath house for many years. Until this period in her diary, there had been little indication that it was anything but professional and friendly visiting. One might speculate in looking back in time that, in fact, a quiet courtship had been unfolding over the better part of a decade. What is clear is that in the period following Peter's death, Amy writes with increasing intimacy about her relationship with Dr. Roddick: "One day Dr. Roddick came to lunch. I met him at the Beckley Station. … We had a very pleasant visit and luckily it cleared up so that I could show the Doctor the Garden with its pretty walks & nooks. Had a nice talk."[51]

Amy spent the next couple years travelling in Europe, Mexico, and Cuba, away from Montreal and the painful memories there; yet the correspondence between Amy Redpath and Thomas Roddick persisted. The first mention of her marriage to Thomas Roddick she recorded in her diary on 17 July 1906: "Roddick and I signed our marriage contract today."[52] This was followed by a fast getaway to England, where Amy set about the business of "express speed [trousseau] getting" in London and visiting her family there, including her beloved Aunt Grace who was entering the final stages of life.[53] While there were many congratulations offered to and received by the couple, there is no indication that this wedding took anyone by surprise.

Amy and Thomas married in a small parish church in Chislehurst on 3 September 1906. Amy recorded the event in great detail and joy: "My wedding day! … When I reached the chancel Agnes in a tailor made dress of white Canadian homespun & a pink hat carrying pink flowers, Betty, a little fairy in white with a wreath of ivy & luten carrying a basket of sweetpeas and daisies walked from their pews & stood behind me. Harold gave me away. Alice, Rose & John were in the front pew. … A heavenly day!"[54] The couple left later that night to begin their honeymoon. Upon their return to Montreal, Thomas Roddick moved into the Redpath family home.

Figure 6.15 *Amy's Marriage to Dr. Roddick at Chislehurst*, 1906. Redpath Family Papers, Rare Books and Special Collections, McGill University Library.

The marriage seems to have been a happy and comfortable one, with much travel and friendship between them: "We celebrated our wedding day by taking a beautiful two hours' drive in the Forest with three happy years to look back upon."[55] Whether there was passion or sexual zeal underlying the relationship is harder to ascertain. Amy wrote in her diary in obscure ways about the relationship. The night before her wedding she confided that she and Roddick had had a lovers' talk under "the Judas tree" where she records that they also had a "good-bye one … a lovely moonlight night and !!!!!"[56] That the two were sexually intimate before their marriage seems likely considering the opaque comments in her diary, the tracking of her menstrual cycle, and the length of the courtship itself.[57]

Her marriage to Roddick also seems to have brought an emotional stability that provided a space for Amy to pursue writing as more than a hobby. She became a prolific, if not acclaimed, author, publishing thirteen collections of poetry and plays beginning in 1918 with *The Flag and Other Poems*. Perhaps better suited to the Victorian age of her childhood, these publications nevertheless became the platform that established Amy as an author in her own right. Unlike the writing in her diaries, her published voice was highly romanticized and emotional. She wrote with an unguarded sentimentality, giving her imagination free rein to recount the past in tender, thrilling, and fervid narratives. The Kanien'kehá:ka of Kahnawake (or the Mohawk of Caughnawaga, as Amy would have known them) were a recurring inspiration for these dreamy reimaginations, serving as the main characters in many of her works including *The Seekers: An Indian Mystery Play*, *The Birth of Montreal and Other Poems*, *The Tomahawk: A Playlet*, and *The Iroquois Enjoy a Perfect Day*. But so too were the personal tragedies that she had held so privately in the past. From the distance that time allowed and, we contend, in the context of the security that married life provided, Amy allowed herself to grieve publicly the losses of Clifford and Peter through poetry. It was Peter she was mourning in her poem entitled "Because He Lived":

Though laughter lurked in his blue eyes,
Their sweetness linked the soul with God.
A spirit walked in earthly guise,
And sacred where his feet have trod.

No broken pillar marks his grave –
The shortest songs beguile the heart –
A splendrous youth was what he gave,
The morn's fulfilment was his part.

Because he lived this earth seems good
Enshrining such dear memory,
Though young, he suffered, understood;
Because he lived I hold Life's key.[58]

Another close relationship undergirded the security of this time in Amy's life. Amy first met Mary Rose Shallow, called Rose, when she joined the Redpath household as a housemaid in early 1901, arriving from Newfoundland just prior to the deaths of Cliff and Ada. Rose entered the Redpath family during a very dark and chaotic moment yet quickly found herself devoted to their well-being, and to Amy in particular. She would have been an enormous help to Amy in the immediate

Figure 6.16 *Rose Shallow and Amy Redpath Roddick in Wheeled Chair*, date unknown. Redpath Family Papers, Rare Books and Special Collections, McGill University Library.

Figure 6.17 G. Georgoulas, *Rose Shallow and Amy Roddick in Egypt*, date unknown. Archive of Amy Linda Redpath.

aftermath of the tragedy, ensuring that the household continued to function and proving her steadfastness by staying on as a domestic when many others might have looked for a way out. Rose, who was just two years younger than Amy, helped Amy maintain the family's privacy and thus moved beyond a loyal housemaid to a friend and confidante. As co-witnesses to this trauma, they became profoundly bonded to each other, creating a trust that continued to deepen and grow over the years, with Rose spending the rest of her life working and living at the Sherbrooke Street house.

From this historical distance, it is difficult to get a full understanding of the nature of the relationship between the two women. It is clear that it went beyond simply employer–employee; Rose and Amy shared a deep and intimate friendship. Whether it was a physically sexual relationship, as theatre historian Kym Bird has claimed, cannot be confirmed by the extant evidence. It certainly remains a possibility.[59] Rose travelled with Amy on all of her voyages, including her wedding trip and subsequent honeymoon. Following Roddick's death in 1923, the two women maintained an extraordinarily close relationship and travelled even more extensively, including a much-anticipated trip to Egypt in their later years (Figure 6.17).[60] Amy left Rose a sizeable annual allowance of £1,200 as well as all of her "wearing apparel" in her will.[61] After Rose's death in 1943, Amy had her body exhumed the following year from the Roman Catholic cemetery Notre-Dame-des-Neiges and reinterred in the Redpath family plot at Mount Royal Cemetery. The headstone commemorates Rose as the "beloved companion of Lady Roddick."[62]

But also buried in the family plot and commemorated as "Housekeeper and Friend" on the same headstone is Maggie Shallow Coleman. Sixteen years older than her sister Rose, Maggie had immigrated to Montreal from Newfoundland in 1895 and soon after married John Coleman. Her move into the Redpath household occurred some years before Coleman died in 1914, suggesting that Maggie's arrival coincided with a marital separation. These circumstances would have created a very different dynamic between Amy and Maggie than the relationship that had been forged earlier between Amy and Rose. And yet, the evidence suggests that Amy also deeply valued her relationship with Maggie. In her will, she bequeathed £600 per annum to Maggie and reserved a burial spot for her in the family plot, despite the fact that Maggie's husband was buried in Notre-Dame-des-Neiges Cemetery.[63] For Amy, who had no sisters of her own, it must have been a gift to be included in this sisterhood. Like most sisterhoods, each of the individual relationships would have had their own dynamic, playing out as interests and compatibility designed, a situation that would have been further complicated by the fact that Amy was also their employer. Yet in the years following the tragedy and again after the death of Roddick, these two sisters were a source of friendship, solidarity, and support for Amy. This long period in Amy's life could have been filled with loneliness but for the Shallow sisters who became her trustworthy companions and friends.

Rose died in 1943 and Maggie four years later in 1947. Amy maintained her home on Sherbrooke Street with the help of another "family" of domestic workers: Joe and Mary Hornyak employed as "houseman" and "cook," respectively, and Catherine Gunnel as a domestic. At her death in 1954, Amy left $40,000 to Joe Hornyak and $5,000 each to Mary Hornyak and Catherine Gunnel. She also designated $75,000 to McGill University for the Peter W. Redpath and Jocelyn Clifford Redpath Memorial Fund; $25,000 to McGill University for the Sir Thomas and Lady Roddick Library Fund; and $10,000 and a painting of Roddick by Robert Harris to the Montreal General Hospital. The remainder of her estate, estimated to be worth $2,000,0000, was to be divided between her four nephews and niece.[64]

Conclusion

We have taken a broad look at Amy Redpath Roddick's life from birth to death in order to identify the joys and heartaches that spanned her lifetime. We have also sought to parse the boundaries that Amy created between public and private,

Figure 6.18 Wm. Notman & Son, *Lady Roddick in Her Livingroom, Montreal,* 1930. McCord Museum, II-297450.

controlling what the observer sees. This final photograph (Figure 6.18) – with a focus on the room in which she is sitting, the furnishings, and the act of reading that amplify her bourgeois life while obscuring her emotions – reminds us once again of the tactics she employed to contain these private intimacies. The peacefulness that exudes from this photograph of Amy was hard won.

As we have recounted here, Amy's life story exposes the intentionality that went into both containing emotion and constructing public manifestations of this emotion later. In the aftermath of the 1901 tragedy, for example, she maintained her privacy by refusing to speak to the press and then strategically distanced herself by leaving the city. She destroyed letters that would have exposed her private horror and her diary remained untouched, keeping the most intimate of emotions safeguarded from even the imagined community of future readers. From the deep privacy of her mourning, it appears that Amy was already planning public displays of grief that would certainly be sanitized and constructed for public consumption.

Married life and middle age ushered in a period of peace and stability that Amy had likely not experienced since the death of her father, and it was from that place that she began the process of making public her sorrow. She expressed her grief for Clifford and Peter through significant donations to McGill University in their honour: both money and memorial bookplates to the Redpath Library bear their names. In her published poetry and plays, she explored emotions through the voices of others. She wrote extensively about idealized feelings associated with a sentimentality more at home in the Victorian period but distanced from an array of emotions she experienced in the everyday: anger, jealousy, vanity, and sadness in addition to love, joy, and friendship. Her poem, "Perfect in thy Promise," describes Clifford as "a bud unfolding," "pure and good," and a "perfect spirit," erasing any association of murder to him.[65] Following Roddick's death, she expressed her grief through the erection of the iconic Roddick Gates on Sherbrooke Street, impacting the landscape of downtown Montreal for generations to come in his memory.

The mother–daughter relationship was clearly much more complicated for Amy to navigate. No extant evidence of Amy's private or public sorrow for her mother Ada exists. As far as we know, she commissioned no portraits, gave no donations, and erected no monuments in Ada's memory. In fact, Ada is commemorated on her gravestone merely as the "Wife of John James Redpath."[66] There are no favourable adjectives, no nod to her identity as a mother, and indeed no emotion expressed at all. In contrast to the public manifestations of grief constructed for other family members, the absence here speaks volumes about the ambivalence and complexity that surrounded Ada's death for her children.

Although Amy suffered much loss and sadness, she also found joy and companionship throughout her life. In her early years, she was surrounded by cousins and brothers who filled her days with outings and adventure. In the devastating years following the deaths of her brothers and parents, Amy realized intimate friendship and sisterhood with Rose and Maggie Shallow. She also discovered companionship and peace in her marriage with Roddick. She travelled and explored places with the people she loved most. She enjoyed keeping up with her niece and nephews.

Amy strove to reinforce, display, and etch her representation of the family's legacy onto the city's landscape as an antidote to the violence associated with Ada and Clifford's deaths, but also as a public form of her grief for those she lost in the aftermath. In her final days, she maintained her desire to control how the public would remember her loved ones with her generous bequests to McGill University in the names of Peter W. Redpath, Jocelyn Clifford Redpath, and Sir Thomas George Roddick once again.

Inside every Montreal home, families experienced many of these same things – illness and early death, romance and solitude, petty aggressions and even violence, and secrets and accomplishments. The commonality of these shared emotions reduces some of the distance between the bourgeoisie and the working class, yet at the same time highlights the way class and social position afforded Amy and others in the Square Mile the privilege of rewriting the public narrative and restaging a public image. Elite identities were being carefully constructed and hidden: the public ones for the camera, and the private ones when the camera was gone.

NOTES

1 The house on Sherbrooke Street went through various numberings. When the Redpath family first occupied the house, it was 1065 Sherbrooke Street. By the time of Amy Redpath Roddick's death, it was 1459 Sherbrooke Street West.

2 Catherine Hall, *Civilising Subjects: Metropole and Colony in the British Imagination, 1830–1867* (Chicago: University of Chicago Press, 2002); Roderick MacLeod, "Salubrious Settings and Fortunate Families: The Making of Montreal's Golden Square Mile, 1840–1895" (PhD diss., McGill University, 1997); Amanda Vickery, *The Gentleman's Daughter: Women's Lives in Georgian England* (New Haven, CT: Yale University Press, 2003); Brian Young, *Patrician Families and the Making of Quebec: The Taschereaus and the McCords* (Montreal: McGill-Queen's University Press, 2014); Brian Young and Geoffrey James, *Respectable Burial: Montreal's Mount Royal Cemetery* (Montreal: McGill-Queen's University Press, 2003); and Brian Young, *The Making and Unmaking of a University Museum: The McCord, 1921–1996* (Montreal: McGill-Queen's University Press, 2000).

3 Consider, for example, Doug Bellevue, *Montreal's Golden Square Mile: A Neighbourhood* (self-pub., 2017); Maxime Catellier, *Golden Square Mile* (Montreal: L'Oie de Cravan, 2015); François Rémillard, *Demeures Bourgeoises de Montréal* (Montreal: Éditions de Méridien, 1997); Donald MacKay, *The Square Mile: Merchant Princes of Montreal* (Vancouver: Douglas & McIntyre, 1990); and Margaret W. Westley, *Remembrance of Grandeur: The Anglo-Protestant Elite of Montreal, 1900–1950* (Montreal: Libre expression, 1990).

4 Elizabeth Kirkland, "Mothering Citizens: Elite Women in Montreal, 1893–1914" (PhD diss., McGill University, 2011); Redpath Mansion Mystery, Great Unsolved Mysteries in Canadian History, accessed 24 March 2023, https://www.canadianmysteries.ca/sites/redpath/home/indexen.html.

5 For a good overview of the emergence of the history of emotions as a field of study, see Nicole Eustace, Eugenia Lean, Julie Livingston, Jan Plamper, William M. Reddy, and Barbara H. Rosenwein, "AHR Conversation: The Historical Study of Emotions," *American Historical Review* 117, no. 5 (2012): 1486–1531, https://doi.org/10.1093/ahr/117.5.1487. A more recent overview of the field can be found in Rob Boddice, *The History of Emotions* (Manchester: Manchester University Press, 2018).

6 Richard Feltoe, *A Gentleman of Substance: The Life and Legacy of John Redpath, 1796–1869* (Toronto: Natural History, 2004), 112.

7 Feltoe, *Gentleman of Substance*, 112.

8 Feltoe, *Gentleman of Substance*, 112.

9 In the small world that was Montreal's elite society, it was typical that families intermarried extensively. This union between John James Redpath and Ada Maria Mills was no exception. Just prior to their marriage, John James's half-brother, George Drummond Redpath, had married Ada's sister, Alice Stiles Mills. George D. Redpath, as curate, performed the marriage of his half-brother and his sister-in-law at Putney, England, just three months after his own wedding in 1867. Feltoe, *Gentleman of Substance*, 110.

10 Annmarie Adams, Valerie Minnett, Mary Anne Poutanen, and David Theodore, "'She must not stir out of a darkened room': The Redpath Mansion Mystery," *Material Culture Review* 72 (Fall 2010): 15, https://id.erudit.org/iderudit/mcr72art01. For more discussion of marriage contracts in Quebec, see chapter 5 in this volume by Peter Gossage and Lisa Moore.

11 This time in England and Europe is recorded in Ada Mills Redpath's diary, which begins with an entry from 1 January 1869: "In Rome … with Mama, Mary, Minnie, Jack and Baby Amy." Rare Books and Special Collections, McGill University, MSS 659, Diary of Ada Mills Redpath, January 1869.

12 Rare Books and Special Collections, McGill University, MSS 659, Diary of Ada Mills Redpath, March 1869.

13 Rare Books and Special Collections, McGill University, MSS 659, Diary of Ada Mills Redpath, April 1869.

14 "In the middle of May, Amy was weaned and her wet nurse returned to Canada." Rare Books and Special Collections, McGill University, MSS 659, Diary of Ada Mills Redpath, May 1869.

15 The Redpath children's birthdays are as follows: Amy Redpath was born in Montreal on 16 May 1868, Peter Whiteford Redpath was born in England on 17 July 1869, John Reginald Redpath was born in Montreal on 16 January 1871, Harold Mills Redpath was born in Montreal on 9 November 1873, and Jocelyn Clifford Redpath was born in Montreal on 17 November 1876.

16 Rare Books and Special Collections, McGill University, MSS 659, Diary of Amy Redpath, 7 August 1902.

17 Rare Books and Special Collections, McGill University, Box MS 818 c.2, Redpath Family, File 2.11, Redpath Family Correspondence, Ada Mills Redpath, Letter to children from Ada, 12 February 1880; Letter to Peter from Ada, 13 February 1880; and Letter to Reginald from Ada, 25 July 1880. See also Rare Books and Special Collections, McGill University, MS 659 Sir Thomas Roddick, Amy Redpath, Diary No, 4, 1898, Amy Redpath Roddick, 5 January 1898.

18 Leonore Davidoff, "Kinship as a Categorical Concept: A Case Study of Nineteenth Century English Siblings," *Journal of Social History* 39, no. 2 (2005): 411–28, https://doi.org/10.1353/jsh.2005.0132.

19 Davidoff, "Kinship," 413.

20 "John James Redpath – Obituary," *Montreal Daily Star*, 6 June 1884, 4.

21 Lily Dougall's family lived at 294 Drummond Street while the Roddicks lived at 80 Union Avenue. Maud was the daughter of Alice Mills and George Drummond Redpath and grew up primarily in England. As a young woman, she spent time in Montreal as well, likely staying with her step-grandmother at Terrace Bank and other relatives around the Square Mile.

22 On this exercise, Amy commented: "I find [it] very good exercise. It is every day [*sic*] language. The more I study this play, the more it charms me. Ibsen's insight into female nature is wonderful." Rare Books and Special Collections, McGill University, MSS 659, Diary of Amy Redpath Roddick, 6 February 1897.

23 Rare Books and Special Collections, McGill University, MSS 659, Diary of Amy Redpath Roddick, 14 August 1899.

24 Rare Books and Special Collections, McGill University, MSS 659, Diary of Amy Redpath Roddick, 16 March 1900.
25 Rare Books and Special Collections, McGill University, MSS 659, Diary of Amy Redpath Roddick, 3 April 1898.
26 Rare Books and Special Collections, McGill University, MSS 659, Diary of Amy Redpath Roddick, 6 April 1898.
27 Rare Books and Special Collections, McGill University, MSS 659, Diary of Amy Redpath Roddick, 11 March 1898.
28 Rare Books and Special Collections, McGill University, MS 659 Diary of Amy Redpath Roddick, 5 January 1898.
29 Rare Books and Special Collections, McGill University, MS 659 Diary of Amy Redpath Roddick, 11 August 1898.
30 Private Archives of Amy Linda Redpath [hereafter PAALR], Letter from Ida Mills Redpath to Jocelyn Clifford Redpath, 12 August 1898.
31 PAALR, Letter to Alice from Amy Redpath, 24 August 1901.
32 "Redpath Tragedy in Montreal," *Quebec Daily Mercury*, 14 June 1901, 2.
33 Bibliothèque et Archives nationales du Québec à Montreal [hereafter BAnQ-M], Cour du Coroner, Ada Maria Mills Redpath, 14 June 1901; BAnQ-M, Cour du Coroner, Jocelyn Clifford Redpath, 14 June 1901.
34 Adams et al., "Redpath Mansion Mystery," 14.
35 See, for example, "A Sad Affair," *The Gazette* (Montreal), 14 June 1901, 3.
36 The jury for the inquest was comprised of those who would have known the Redpath family well, including next-door neighbour William Morrice. Other jurors who lived within a stone's throw of the Redpath house were Charles Esdaile, George Hyde, Lansing Lewis, Bartlett and Francis McLennan, John Savage, Herbert Wallis, and W.W. Watson. These were the close neighbours, friends, and associates of the Redpath family. The remaining jurors included John Dunds Jr., H. Browning, E.C.B Featherstonhaugh, and John Walker. BAnQ-M, Cour du Coroner, Ada Maria Mills Redpath, 14 June 1901; BAnQ-M, Cour du Coroner, Jocelyn Clifford Redpath, 14 June 1901.
37 BAnQ-M, Cour du Coroner, Ada Maria Mills Redpath, 14 June 1901; BAnQ-M, Cour du Coroner, Jocelyn Clifford Redpath, 14 June 1901.
38 "Sad Occurrence," *Montreal Daily Star*," 14 June 1901, 2.
39 Adams et al., "Redpath Murder Mystery," 12–13.
40 McGill University Archives [hereafter MUA], MS 818 c.1 Redpath Family, 1.1 Redpath Family Collection, Sympathy Letters concerning June 13 1901 from Family Friends, letter to Amy and Peter Whiteford Redpath from Grace Wood Redpath, 14 June 1901.
41 MUA, MS 818 c.1 Redpath Family, 1.1 Redpath Family Collection, Sympathy Letters concerning 13 June 1901 from Family Friends, letter from Ellen Plimsoll to Amy Redpath, undated. Ellen and George Plimsoll were the cousins of Amy's cousins through marriage.
42 MUA, MS 818 c.1 Redpath Family, 1.1 Redpath Family Collection, Sympathy Letters concerning 13 June 1901 from Family Friends, letter from Anna L. Harrington to Amy Redpath, 29 June 1901. Anna was the daughter of McGill University Principal William Dawson.
43 MUA, MS 818 c.1 Redpath Family, 1.1 Redpath Family Collection, Sympathy Letters concerning 13 June 1901 from Family Friends, letter from Alice E. Redpath to Amy Redpath, 23 June 1901.
44 MUA, MS 818 c.1 Redpath Family, 1.1 Redpath Family Collection, Sympathy Letters concerning 13 June 1901 from Family Friends, letter from Helen Redpath to Amy Redpath, 26 June 1901.

45 MUA, MS 818 c.1 Redpath Family, 1.1 Redpath Family Collection, Sympathy Letters concerning 13 June 1901 from Family Friends, letter from G. Plimsoll to Amy Redpath, 15 June 1901.
46 MUA, MS 818 c.1 Redpath Family, 1.1 Redpath Family Collection, Sympathy Letters concerning 13 June 1901 from Family Friends, Letter from Jane C. Cooper to Amy Redpath, 17 June 1901.
47 Amy Redpath Roddick, "Perfect in thy Promise – To J.C.R.," Redpath Mansion Mystery, Great Unsolved Mysteries in Canadian History, accessed 24 March 2023, https://www.canadianmysteries.ca/sites/redpath/archives/poetry/5322en.html.
48 Rare Books and Special Collections, McGill University, MSS 659, Diary of Amy Redpath Roddick, 21 October 1901.
49 Rare Books and Special Collections, McGill University, MSS 659, Diary of Amy Redpath Roddick, 30 July 1902.
50 Rare Books and Special Collections, McGill University, MSS 659, Diary of Amy Redpath Roddick, 4 July 1902.
51 Rare Books and Special Collections, McGill University, MSS 659, Diary of Amy Redpath Roddick, 30 July 1902.
52 Rare Books and Special Collections, McGill University, MSS 659, Diary of Amy Redpath Roddick, 17 July 1906.
53 Rare Books and Special Collections, McGill University, MSS 659, Diary of Amy Redpath Roddick, 7 August 1906.
54 Rare Books and Special Collections, McGill University, MSS 659, Diary of Amy Redpath Roddick, 3 September 1909.
55 Rare Books and Special Collections, McGill University, MSS 659, Diary of Amy Redpath Roddick, 3 September 1909.
56 Rare Books and Special Collections, McGill University, MSS 659, Diary of Amy Redpath Roddick, 3 September 1909.
57 Amy's first diary entry as a married woman suggests that their honeymoon was a time of sexual activity: "Slept all afternoon making up for two absolutely sleepless nights." Rare Books and Special Collections, McGill University, MSS 659, Diary of Amy Redpath Roddick, 4 September 1909.
58 Rare Books and Special Collections, McGill University, MSS 659, Amy Redpath Roddick, "Because He Lived – To P.W.R.," undated.
59 Kym Bird, "Money, Matricide, and a 'Boston Marriage': A Contextual Interpretation of Amy Redpath Roddick's Italian Closet Drama *An Old Bologna Tale*" (paper presented at the Canadian Association for Theatre Research, Vancouver, June 2008).
60 Amy confided that she was looking forward to the trip, which included various stops around the Mediterranean, but would only take it if Rose recovered from an unknown illness in time: "… have now to settle down & make a new will & then if Rose makes progress, prepare for our trip." Rare Books and Special Collections, McGill University, MSS 659, Diary of Amy Redpath Roddick, 2 March 1926.
61 Rare Books and Special Collections, McGill University, MS 818 c.3, Amy Redpath Roddick, "Last Will and Testament of Amy Redpath Roddick," 29 January 1925.
62 Brenton Nader, "Inscription on Rose Shallow's Gravesite," Redpath Mansion Mystery, Great Unsolved Mysteries in Canadian History, accessed 24 March 2023, https://www.canadianmysteries.ca/sites/redpath/archives/photographorpainting/indexen.html.
63 Rare Books and Special Collections, McGill University, MS 818 c.3, Amy Redpath Roddick, "Last Will and Testament of Amy Redpath Roddick," 29 January 1925.

64 "An Act Respecting the Will and Codicil of the Late Lady Amy Redpath Roddick," 3–4 Elizabeth II c.180 (16 December 1954): 905–10.

65 Amy Redpath Roddick, "Perfect in thy Promise," Redpath Mansion Mystery, Great Unsolved Mysteries in Canadian History, accessed 24 March 2023, https://www.canadianmysteries.ca/sites/redpath/archives/poetry/5322en.html.

66 Brenton Nader, "Inscription on Ada Maria Mills Redpath's Gravesite," Redpath Mansion Mystery, Great Unsolved Mysteries in Canadian History, accessed 24 March 2023, https://www.canadianmysteries.ca/sites/redpath/archives/photographorpainting/indexen.html.

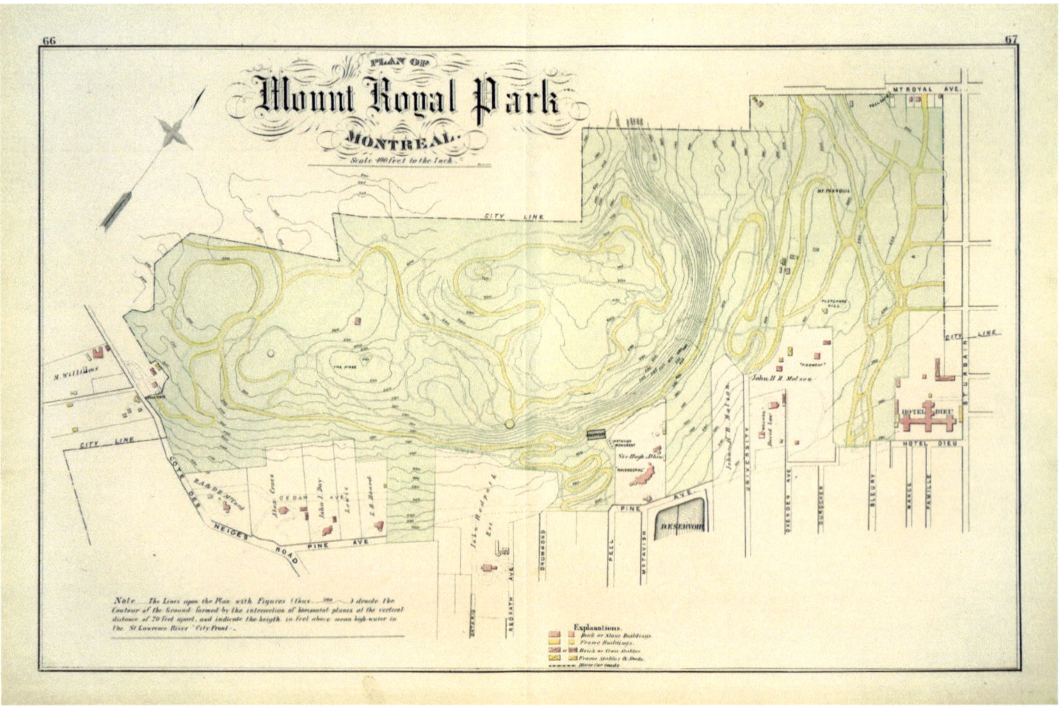

Figure V.11 Plan of Mount Royal Park, Montreal, c. 1880. McCord Museum, M992.22.2.

The Creation of Mount Royal Park

Today, the creation of Mount Royal Park by the city commissioners in the 1870s is well known. What may be more obscure is the reluctance of Frederick Law Olmsted, the celebrated American landscape architect, to take the project on, and the resistance some of the Square Milers had to it.

In his book entitled *Mount Royal, Montreal*, Olmsted wrote of how he declined the project several times, until "I was finally induced to accept it by information and assurances which, given in good faith, were misleading."[1] Olmsted's initial hesitation stemmed from his disquiet about designing without deeply knowing the site. However, he continued to be unhappy about ease of access to the park. Olmsted wanted the commissioners to "[e]ncourage the use of the mountain by all classes of people, even your poorest workingman, to come here by families, once or twice a week, late in the day, during the hot season, to take their evening meal."[2] Economical and egalitarian access from the south was critical to his vision, which no doubt collided with the privileged opinions of the Square Milers.

The 1890 map of Mount Royal Park (Figure V.11), with sizable gaps in its southern boundary as the park skirted several large estates,[3] demonstrates the fundamental power that these citizens could exert against the park project. In 1872, when a small portion of Sir Hugh Allan's property was expropriated, he sued, claiming that his compensation was worth ten times what he was paid. The lawsuit outlived Allan, winding its way up to the Supreme Court of Canada. It was dismissed with costs in 1894.

The opening of the park enhanced the value of land in the Square Mile in a number of ways. First, of course, by taking hundreds of acres of potential real estate off the market, it increased the worth of the remaining land that could be developed. Second, it added value to the area, which now boasted a natural and protected park as its own playground and backdrop. The mountain became an extension of the Square Mile, where the wealthy could retreat from their increasingly urban environment to picnic, stroll, and ride their horses.

NOTES

1 Frederick Law Olmsted, *Mount Royal, Montreal* (New York, 1881), 8.

2 Olmsted, *Mount Royal, Montreal*, 55–6.

3 See Charles E. Goad, *Atlas of the City of Montreal* (Montreal: Charles E. Goad, 1890).

CHAPTER SEVEN

Gender and Social Relations in the City above the Hill

Robert C.H. Sweeny

In November 1896, Herbert Brown Ames hired "experienced men from the district" to conduct a house-to-house canvass of a one-square-mile area south of Lagauchetière and west of McGill Street. He called it "the city below the hill." They interviewed members of 7,671 households, asking all manner of intrusive questions: from how many rooms people got for the rent they paid, to where they shat. Through their canvassing, they identified 1,442 workplaces. Ames then aggregated all this information into thirty subdistricts, not only compiling statistics on personal and familial data but also establishing how many men, women, and children were employed in each subdistrict compared to the number of people who actually lived there. The results showed many people commuting to work in the area, so Ames had his investigators stand at shift change on key intersections linking this "nether city" with the rest of Montreal and its suburbs to estimate the scale of working away from home. In April of 1897, informed by his preliminary analysis, Ames sent his people back to the area to interrogate half the households he had classified as poor.[1] Although often misrepresented,[2] Ames's "sociological study of a portion of the City of Montreal" is a disturbingly revealing and often surprisingly detailed examination of the living conditions of turn-of-the-century Montreal's working class.

We possess no such examination for the "city above the hill ... home of the classes ... the exclusive habitat of the rich and the well-to-do." Of course, "the captains of industry, the owners of real estate and those who labour with brain rather than hand"[3] would never have deigned to permit, let alone answer, the type of intrusive and dehumanizing questions that constituted the essence of Ames's study. There is, therefore, a certain poetic justice in my belated turning a sociological gaze not towards the square mile Ames studied, and where by 1903 he owned $64,000 in rental units that generated for him $3,770 in rent annually,[4] but the square mile where he actually lived. To do so, I rely primarily on two early twentieth-century sources: a 1903 evaluation roll listing the owners of Montreal and the 1901 manuscript census. Both, however, have been completely transformed using twenty-first century technologies so that they are now geo-referenced databases integrated into MAP: Montréal, l'avenir du passé's research infrastructure.[5]

Heir to a fortune accumulated in the manufacture of shoes, in 1901, Ames was a thirty-seven-year-old Presbyterian and city alderman. He resided at 26 Ontario Avenue, now rue du Musée, in a sixteen-room house, assessed at $20,000, owned by his thirty-year-old wife, Louisa Marion Kennedy, a Baptist. Henry Alymer, a twenty-four-year-old Anglican student born in rural Quebec, lived with Herbert and Louisa, who was no doubt ably assisted in her "tending" for this household of three, by Margaret Boyle, a thirty-five-year-old Irish Catholic tablemaid who was born in urban Quebec; Katherine Price, a twenty-six-year-old English-Catholic housemaid only recently arrived from India; and Jessie Gillies, a forty-three-year-old Presbyterian cook born in rural Quebec.

In his assessment of "work units" per household, Ames had calculated a woman as being worth one-half, and a child one-quarter, the value of a man. In real life, he was considerably more miserly than that, for altogether these three women earned that year $488 in wages – $144 for each maid and $200 for the cook – while Frederick Greening, the thirty-six-year-old Anglican groom who had emigrated from England in 1887, was paid $500. For his part, Ames declared an income of $10,000, almost eighteen times the average annual income for an entire household below the hill.[6]

Defining the "Square Mile"

As Montrealers chose to industrialize in the mid-nineteenth century, a geological feature came to mark a social divide. An escarpment, running parallel to and just south of Dorchester Street and east to Beaver Hall Hill, then veering northwards to just below Sherbrooke Street at Bleury Street, and then on to the Côte à Barron and the Côte de la Visitation, came to split the city into two quite unequal parts. Largely popular-class, industrial neighbourhoods on either side of the old city and port lay below the escarpment, while petty-bourgeois and bourgeois neighbourhoods set the tone above.[7] By the 1880s, this enduring social divide had been deepened by unprecedented levels of linguistic, ethnic, and religious segregation.[8] In 1906, the city would formally sanction this more recent sundering of the urban

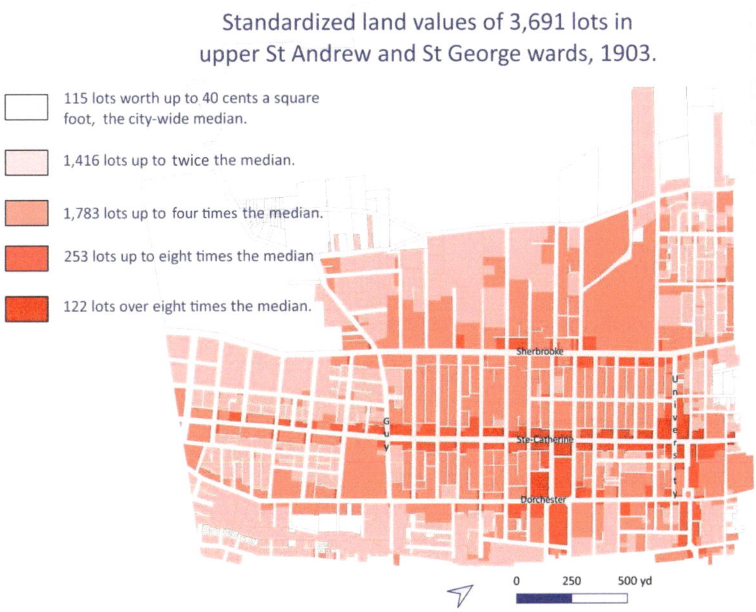

Figure 7.1 Land values in 1903.

Source: MAP's Geo-referenced Evaluation Roll of 1903.

core by dividing all streets running parallel to the river into east or west at St. Lawrence Boulevard.[9] For most of the twentieth century, it was this division between an English-speaking west-end and a French-speaking east-end that defined the Montreal imaginary.[10] In the late 1930s, just as the defining neighbourhood of the former was losing its lustre, it began to be called the "Square Mile." Then, in the 1970s, after it had been thoroughly eclipsed, it was posthumously raised to the "Golden Square Mile."

Faced with more than a century of overlapping and often contradictory imaginaries, it is a salutary antidote to renew with the terminology of Ames. To talk of cities above and below the hill conveys so much more effectively the degrees of historical distance and social separation than a present-day stroll up Beaver Hall Hill ever could. It reminds us that we need to take considerable care in defining not just our terms but also the very object of our inquiry.

Urban property evaluations are notoriously controversial and to minimize the number of appeals, the city developed in the early twentieth century a standardized approach to assessing land. Values ranged from a low of 2 cents a square foot in parts of Hochelaga Ward to $18 on Greater St. James Street in the financial district of the old city. The median for the city as a whole was 40 cents a square foot. As is clear from Figure 7.1, very little of the city above the hill in the west had so low an evaluation. Mount Royal Park had been assessed at 15 cents a square foot and this probably explains why so many of the adjacent properties were evaluated below the city-wide median, but it should be noted that these included the land upon which stood the city's greatest mansion, Sir Hugh Allan's Ravenscrag, the Sulpician's Grand Séminaire, and the city's most prestigious classical college, the Sulpician's Collège de Montréal. Elsewhere, properties at or below the median were only to be found on the slopes of the escarpment to the west and in two small clusters of properties east of University Street.

Five coherent clusters of relatively low-valued properties are clearly discernible in Figure 7.1: a band of properties running along the escarpment below Dorchester; the area now known as Shaughnessy Village on either side of Tupper between Dorchester and St. Catherine in the west; the properties on either side of Lincoln west of Guy, below Sherbrooke; Milton-Park to the east of University above Sherbrooke; and finally properties along parts of Aylmer, City Councillor, and St. Alexandre Streets below Sherbrooke and east of University. A much smaller band, along Cathcart Street below St. Catherine, had similar values. Many of these properties were valued at 65 to 75 cents a square foot, so almost double the city-wide median, but still well below the $1.00 to a $1.60 a square foot that characterized so much of the rest of the area.

Moderate to high values were accorded to almost all the properties lying between Sherbrooke and Dorchester, from Guy to University, and they provide our clearest delineation of a potential core for the "Square Mile." High-value strips are clearly visible on the major east-west thoroughfares of Sherbrooke, St. Catherine, and Dorchester. In particular, St. Catherine from Guy to University stands out, as well it might, for, along with the west side of Phillips Square and the west and north sides of Dominion Square, these were the only properties in the city to rival the land values of Greater St. James Street and Place d'Armes in the old city. An axis formed by Beaver Hall Hill, the century-old link between the old city and estates above the escarpment and University was the only really high-valued, north-south running corridor.

Sherbrooke had some higher-valued residential properties running west of this core, but clearly not the number or extent that Dorchester did. Over the previous generation, St. Catherine Street had become the city's bourgeois shopping precinct and it is clear from these evaluations that, by 1903, this largely commercial corridor extended as far west as Atwater Avenue. Values, however, dropped precipitously west of Guy. From $4.00 a square foot for the property on the north-west corner of Guy and St. Catherine, where the Toronto Dominion Bank now stands, values were halved to a maximum of $2.00 for all properties west to Atwater.

Standardized prices for land constitute an important, socially constructed indicator of value, but as Ravenscrag and adjacent mansions clearly demonstrated, they are not a sufficient basis to spatially define affluence. So, I turned to the Lovell's Street Directory for 1903, available online from the Bibliothèque et Archives nationales du Québec (BAnQ).[11] It provides occupational information for the principal residents at each address on the street. I examined each of the streets surrounding the core as described above and eliminated from consideration any outlying street, or blocks of a street, where bourgeois and professional occupations were not in a clear majority. Unquestionably, this excludes some wealthy residents from inclusion in the "city above the hill" with which they may well have identified; indeed, in some cases, perhaps considered themselves to be charter members. But, I think, when dealing with imagined categories, in particular retrospectively invented ones such as the "Square Mile," one is best to err on the side of caution. This exercise reduced the number of privately owned properties under consideration from 3,683 to 2,039. It also created a recognizable square, albeit one with extensions running out along Dorchester, down Beaver Hall Hill, and to a lesser extent on Sherbrooke Street and Pine and Cedar Avenues.

When people think of the "Square Mile" they do not think of land values, and if they think of it as the "Golden Square Mile," they are undoubtedly thinking of the built environment. But not just any old building, rather great homes, like the Van Horne mansion demolished on the orders of David Azrieli under the cover of darkness in the early morning hours of 8 September 1973.[12] So, does my new delimitation of the city above the hill capture some of that grandeur? By comparing the value of buildings on each lot to the median value of buildings on the lots in the rest of the city, as I do in Figure 7.2, we can begin to see how exceptional this city above the hill really was.

The differences were even more marked than Figure 7.2 might first suggest. Residential housing in turn-of-the-century Montreal consisted of three types in roughly equal numbers: single-family dwellings, duplexes, and triplexes. Single-family dwellings could be stand-alone, semi-detached, or row houses, but in all three styles there was one housing unit per lot. Duplexes had at least two units or flats, generally consisting of four and a half[13] rooms each, but often enough two attached duplexes were built on the same lot, so there could be four housing units on a single lot. Triplexes generally had three five-and-a-half-room flats, but by 1900, it was not uncommon to see the third floor divided into two smaller apartments, and occasionally both the second and third floors were so divided, so a triplex normally consisted of three units but could house four and sometimes five families on

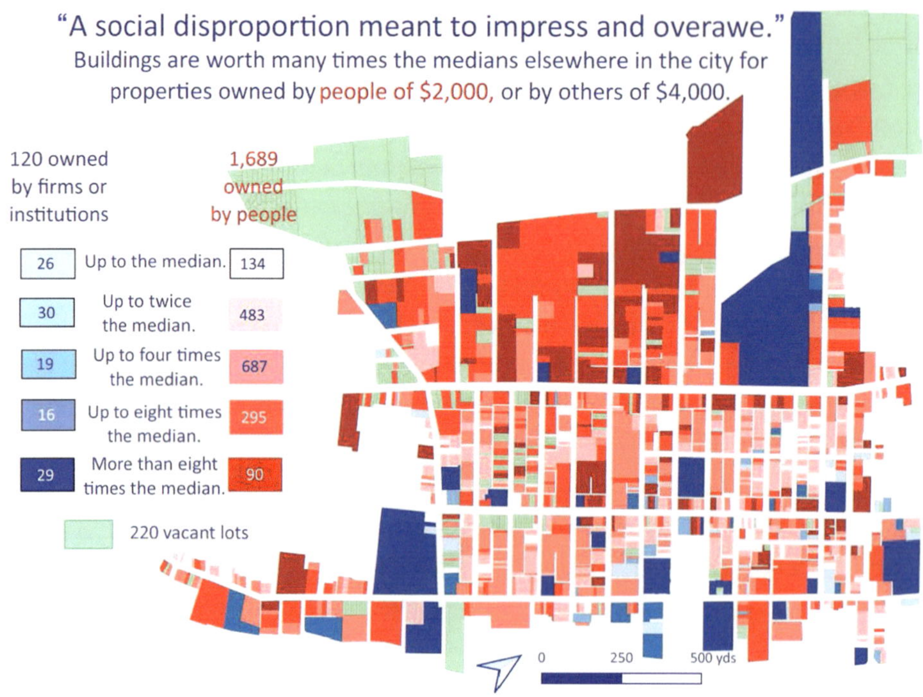

Figure 7.2 Building values in 1903.

Source: MAP's Geo-referenced Evaluation Roll of 1903.

a single lot each in their own home. The sharing of a unit by two or more families was quite exceptional,[14] although mews were not.[15]

This variety would not matter in understanding Figure 7.2 if these differing housing types had been equally distributed throughout the city, but they were not. Properties in the city above the hill, owned by people and, therefore, most likely residential, had only half the housing units per lot as properties owned by people elsewhere in the city.[16]

In 1903, the median value for buildings *outside* the city above the hill was $2,000 for lots owned by people and $4,000 for lots owned by firms or institutions. *Inside*, the buildings on one in five lots owned by a firm or institution were worth so little, but only one in twelve lots owned by a person. Most Montrealers would have compared these homes to the flats where the vast majority of them actually lived. So, it mattered then, and it should to us now, that buildings on three-fifths of the lots owned by people were worth more than five times the median value of a housing unit elsewhere in the city. A quarter were worth twenty or more times. To translate these values into present-day terms,[17] the median value of buildings on a lot in the city above the hill was more than $2.1 million, while on one in four lots the median value of buildings exceeded $7.6 million.

Raymond Williams in his classic analysis of town/country relations in literature asked us to reflect on the generations of accumulated labour represented by any of the great homes that so conspicuously mark the English countryside. He pointedly commented that all too often authors, and here he singled out Jane Austen, had enjoyed, indeed preferred, the privileged view looking out from these estates.[18] I might venture the same could be said for the relationship between historians and the mansions of the city above the hill. Williams argued that it is only by viewing these great homes in their context, looking at them from the outside-in as it were, that we can appreciate the unprecedented scale of accumulation they represented. Williams's penetrating analysis provided the title for Figure 7.2.

Unlike standardized land values, building values are both a reflection and an important component of the accumulated wealth of their owners. The exceptional values on Figure 7.2 are all the more remarkable when one realizes in how short a time this wealth had been accumulated. Two generations, and at the most three, are all the pedigree these bourgeois could claim, many not even that. Fortunes founded on the "ghost acres" created by the unequal numbered treaties' mass expropriation of Indigenous land in Western Canada and subsequent construction of the Canadian Pacific Railway (CPR) do figure prominently.[19] They account for five of the top fifteen mansions by built value: R.B. Angus (third), Lord Strathcona and Mount Royal (sixth), James Ross (seventh), Sir William Van Horne (thirteenth), and Robert Meighen, Lord Mount Stephen's brother-in-law and by 1903 owner of his Drummond Street mansion (fifteenth). However, the fiftieth rank for CPR president Sir Thomas Shaughnessy's mansion, now the centre piece for the Canadian Centre for Architecture, does serve to remind us that most of the great fortunes represented by this built environment were not the direct product of this the most prominent Montreal-based corporation. Many, however, were the beneficiaries of that other plank of Macdonald's National Policy: high-protective tariffs. Still others were based on the extensive property market that had developed in the city since the 1840s of which this city above the hill was itself one of its earliest products.

Mansions of quite another sort account for the highest valued privately owned built properties. Along St. Catherine Street, palaces of consumption led by Henry Morgan's department store, assessed at a total value of $450,000, and Henry Birks's jewellery store, worth $300,000, underscored the importance as consumers of the approximately 2,000 bourgeois and petty-bourgeois families inhabiting the city above the hill. This new shopping precinct, dating from the 1880s, involved both the move of well-established companies from the central business district, such as

Morgan's, to the city above the hill and the creation of a new, more diversified and specialized retail sector. Similar spatial reorganizations of consumption marked most major urban centres in the North Atlantic world, and everywhere it was linked to the regendering of the central business districts as primarily male spaces and its corollary of a feminized shopping district that bourgeois and petty-bourgeois young women could frequent unchaperoned.[20]

Interestingly, family-owned stores remained quite literally that. Companies only owned twelve properties the entire length of St. Catherine from Guy to St. Alexandre: three by banks, five by land companies, and four others by individual firms. One of these land companies owned a new type of property: the Bellevue apartment building. It was one of only three such buildings in the city above the hill. The other two, owned by Roswell Corse Fisher, were on Stanley and Sherbrooke Streets.[21]

It is difficult for us to fully appreciate the scale and significance of the institutional presence in the city above the hill. After all, this is now downtown Montreal, but in 1903, the city's central business district was a considerable distance away, well below the escarpment in what is now known as Vieux Montreal. Certainly, most of the male heads of bourgeois households as well as the professionals in law, accounting, engineering, and brokerage, but not those in medicine, would be required to make a daily commute through congested streets to the old city. With his groom Frederick Greening at the reins, Herbert Brown Ames's commute to his office on Greater St. James Street was probably typical. It would have taken approximately forty minutes to travel the mile and a half (2.5 kilometres) from their residence.

McGill University is the only institutional presence on Figure 7.2 that predates the development of the city above the hill.[22] All of the other major institutional investments in the built environment represent late-19th-century choices by powerful forces in religion, education, and health to privilege and, in an important sense, to sanction this "new town."

In 1852, the centrally located Catholic Cathedral at the corner of St. Catherine and St. Denis was destroyed by fire. Archbishop Ignace Bourget then authorized the construction of a new Cathedral and Bishop's Palace on the east side of Dominion Square, a major new public space that had just been created by moving the Protestant Burial Ground to the mountain.[23] His decision to build the largest church in Quebec on this site was political. A mile from the nearest predominately Catholic community of Griffintown, which was already well served by two national parishes, St. Patrick's and St. Anne's, it certainly was not a practical decision. By so asserting the sovereignty of his See, Bourget encouraged his compatriots to take back their city and communicated to English Protestant communities that they ignored Catholic French Canada at their peril.[24] Difficulties related to the ongoing conflict with the Sulpicians delayed his plans, and construction did not really get underway until 1875 at the end of his episcopacy. The building was completed in 1896. In 1903, the Cathedral of St. James, as it was then known, and the Bishop's Palace complex were assessed at $680,000.

Meanwhile, the various Protestant denominations moved their churches *en masse* from the town centre to the city above the hill, to be closer to the wealthiest members of their congregations.[25] Constitutive of this new Jerusalem were the Anglicans' Christ Church Cathedral and palace complex ($460,000), St. Georges ($112,000), and St. James the Apostle ($100,000); the Methodists' St. James Street ($200,000) and Dominion Square ($68,000); the Presbyterians' Erskine ($120,000), St. Paul's ($98,000), Crescent Street ($90,000), American ($80,000), St Andrew's ($75,000), Knox ($60,000), St Gabriel's ($40,000), and Stanley Street ($20,000); and the Baptists' First ($58,000) and Olivet ($48,700). The Unitarians, already at the bottom of Beaver Hall Hill, were the only ones who chose not to move. Meanwhile, in the face of sustained Jewish immigration from Eastern Europe, the "uptown Jews" built Temple Emmanuel ($130,900), the synagogue of German and Polish Jews ($25,000), and the Spanish and Portuguese Synagogue ($20,000) two miles west of this rapidly developing immigrant community in St. Louis Ward.

The story was the same in the field of education. McGill University ($2,028,000) was the principal presence of Protestant pedagogy, with its affiliated Diocesan Theological College ($71,000), Presbyterian College ($100,000), and Wesleyan Methodist Theological College ($35,000), while Lord Strathcona personally owned the affiliated Victoria College for Women ($170,000). The High School of Montreal ($250,000), the Sacred Heart Convent ($235,000), the Young Men's Christian Association ($103,000), the Trafalgar Institute ($90,000), the Jesuits' Loyola College ($75,000), the Young Women's Christian Association ($40,000), the Art Association of Montreal ($35,000), the Congregational College ($28,000), the Hervey Institute & Home and School of Industry ($25,000), the Fraser Institute ($20,000), the Natural History Society ($14,000), and Queen's College ($8,000) all worked at improving minds and souls above the hill. Because they are just outside my boundaries, the following were not on this imposing list: the Grand Séminaire and Collège de Montréal ($900,000) of the Sulpicians to the west and the Jesuits' Collège Ste. Marie ($376,000) to the south-east.

The newest health care facility in the city was the Royal Victoria Hospital ($425,000) at the top of University Street. Its placement reflected the growing concern for clean air, sunlight, and proper ventilation in hospital settings, considerations that had influenced the moves of both the Grey Nuns and the Hôtel Dieu out of the old city in the 1870s. The Western Hospital ($18,000), bordering on the west side of the city above the hill, was the area's first hospital, while right in the centre on McGill College was the Montreal Homeopathic Association ($13,000) with its live-in staff of eight nurses. These moves and new constructions left only three lay hospitals to service the rest of the city: the fledgling Montreal Maternity Hospital ($8,000) in Chinatown, the Montreal General ($190,000) just east of Chinatown, and the Notre Dame ($35,000) in the east ward of the old city.

Health care in the city above the hill, however, was not yet primarily institutional. Physicians had long practised their profession out of offices in their homes, and in the 1850s and early 1860s these professionals were among the first to move from the old city to townhouses on Beaver Hall Hill and Belmont. By 1903, numerous private clinics with small live-in nursing staffs were to be found on most of the adjacent streets. Working as private duty nurses in the homes of their patients was how most nurses earned their living, so in the census returns of those who could afford this service, it was not unusual to find a live-in nurse. Most nurses, however, lived with kin or sought accommodation in local boarding houses. An alternative was offered by the twenty-three-room Nurses Home at 15 University Street, between the Fraser Institute and the McGill Gymnasium, opposite the St. James Club. Run by Alice M. Sullivan, a thirty-eight-year-old nurse who declared an annual income of $480, assisted by her older sister Mary and Melina Beaudouin, a servant paid a mere $72 a year, it was home to twenty-four female lodgers: two retired women, two stenographers, Jessie McGregor, a forty-eight-year-old Scottish-trained public nurse who earned $750, and nineteen nurses between the ages of twenty-four and thirty-three, each earning $300 a year.

In what may well have been the most affluent neighbourhood in the British Empire, it is surprising to see a significant institutional presence of charitable organizations serving the needy. It is very difficult to assess the impact on the neighbourhood that the largest of these organizations, indeed the largest institution in the city above the hill, had. In the 1870s, the Grey Nuns had moved their mother house from Pointe à Callière to a purpose-built complex at the corner of Guy and Dorchester that in 1903 was assessed at $800,000. The census enumerator in 1901 listed 926 occupants: a mother superior, three assistants, a mistress, 116 nuns, 90 novitiates, 95 lay sisters, and 20 "help" caring for 75 "poor men," 145 "poor women," 31 "poor girls," 45 infant "foundlings," 165 "orphan boys," 84 "orphan girls," and 36 "foundlings" now children, while 19 elderly female "lodgers" took presumably paying rooms in the nunnery.

The next largest Catholic institution dedicated to the needy was Les petites soeurs des pauvres ($40,000) on Seigneurs Street, which ran a long-term care facility for the elderly with 162 "inmates," according to the 1901 census, while St. Patrick's

Orphan Asylum ($20,000) had a staff of thirty-five, caring for 115 "inmates." The thirty-room Protestant Orphan Asylum ($55,000) on Summerhill Street had a staff of seven to care for an unknown number of children. Opposite the Grey Nuns on Guy, the Church Home ($20,000), with a head and three domestics, cared for seventeen mostly elderly "boarders," while further up the street, the Protestant Infant's Home ($16,500) had five nurses, eight domestics, and eight new mothers who cared for fifty-eight "inmates" under the age of six. Like the Protestant Industrial Rooms ($10,000) on Metcalfe, these Protestant charities were all a distance only money can measure away from the host communities of the people they served. They were, however, conveniently located for the women who volunteered as visitors and board members.

This remarkably diverse institutional presence, combined with the almost complete absence of a corporate presence, cannot be explained by the limited number of great mansions. Indeed, I am tempted to say their differing presence matters in spite of the mansions, for it speaks to the significance of the other residents whose interests and activities defined so much of the character of the city above the hill. These families ranged from middling to wealthy, but were not plutocrats. These were the bourgeois and the petty-bourgeois who sat in the pews, purchased from the stores, sent their children to the schools and colleges, worked in the city centre, helped out in charitable causes, and ran complex households. Overwhelmingly, these families did not live in the mansions of the Golden Square Mile imaginary. They lived in affluent circumstances to be sure, but they read rather than appeared in the society pages of the newspapers. Nevertheless, a clear majority of these families were not just assisted, but literally empowered to conduct all these activities by a small army of domestic servants.

Naturally enough, in looking at Figure 7.3, our eye is caught by the remarkable concentrations of domestic labour in the great homes on the slopes of Mount Royal west of McGill. Equally noticeable, and perhaps a bit more surprising, is the unquestionably elite character of Sherbrooke along both sides of its entire length. We can also easily discern clusters of households on Dorchester enjoying qualitatively different levels of service than the majority of their neighbours, while the paucity of live-in domestics on St. Catherine Street, which it will be recalled had the highest standardized land values and the most expensive buildings, underscores its largely commercial, as opposed to residential, nature.

In the city above the hill, there was a clear relationship between the size of homes and the number of domestic servants. Even after deducting for the sleeping quarters of the domestic servants, there was a marked progression in the number of rooms per household. Households without a live-in domestic in 1901 had a median

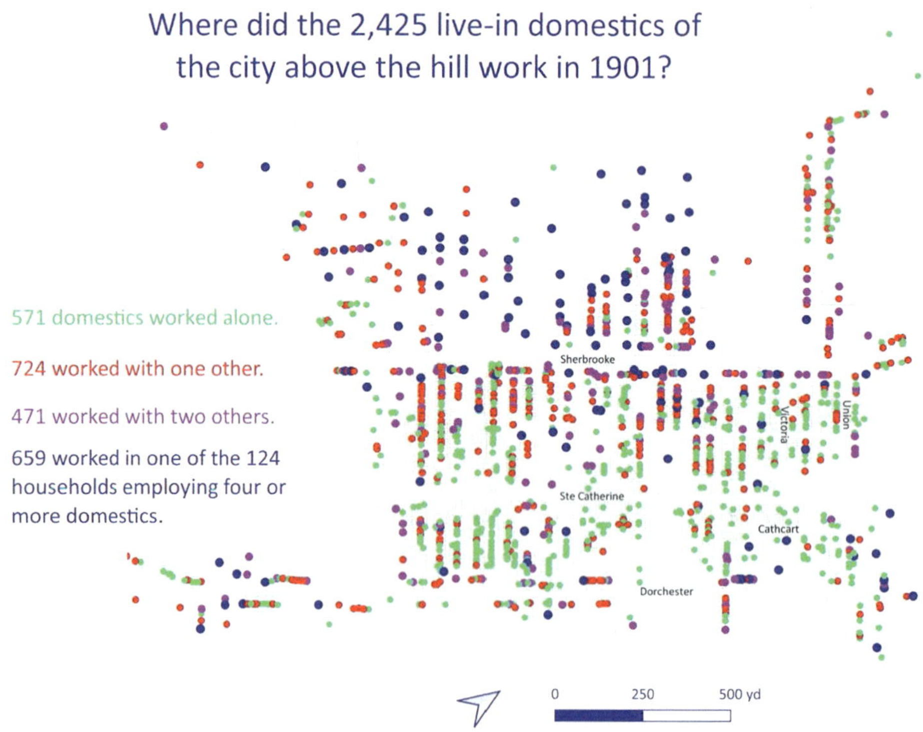

Figure 7.3 Live-in domestics in 1901.

Source: MAP's Geo-referenced Index of Household Heads, 1901 Census, linked to MAP's Geo-referenced Evaluation Roll of 1903.

size of 8 rooms; those with one domestic, a median of 11 rooms; with two domestics, 13 rooms; with three domestics, 15 rooms; and with four or more domestics, 17 rooms. "Tending" a dwelling with turn-of-the-century technology was a labour-intensive enterprise. What is historically significant is not that the more spacious lifestyle of the truly wealthy relied more heavily on extensive domestic labour but just how ubiquitous paid domestic labour was in this city above the hill. Six out of ten households (59 per cent) employed at least one servant, while a third had two or more live-in domestic workers servicing their needs. This contrasts sharply with the situation elsewhere in the city where fewer than one in twelve households (6.7 per cent) had a live-in domestic servant, and only one in eighty-five (1.2 per cent) of these 45,471 households employed two or more.

What was a woman's role was the subject of considerable debate throughout the North Atlantic world in the early twentieth century. The independence and self-reliance shown by nurses might be thought of as representing one option, while the choice by 326 women to live and work in the nunnery at Guy and Dorchester, another, although both involved caring for others. What there was little debate about, either at the time or in the subsequent historiography, was that "home" was conceived as a pre-eminently domestic female space. Now, I think this regendering was a recent construction in the wake of a rupture of the millennial-old relationship that tied men's work to their homes. In Montreal, this gendered sundering of the household economy occurred in the second quarter of the nineteenth century and, I have argued, was a prerequisite for industrialization at mid-century.[26] Be that as it may, what these statistics on domestic service show is that here the majority of bourgeois and petty-bourgeois women were employers, actively managing the labour of their servants. Indeed, given the rapid development of salaried positions in management and the professions, a significantly greater number of married women were employers of labour than their husbands would have been in their world of work.

We can better understand the centrality of these highly gendered social relations to the functioning of these complex households by examining the silences in the record. Who in the city above the hill did not have a live-in domestic? In all, 878 private households had no live-in domestic listed in the 1901 census. There are whole streets where most households did without: Victoria (61 per cent), Guy (63 per cent), St. Catherine (74 per cent), Union (77 per cent), and Cathcart (83 per cent). Although these streets are still well below the proportion doing without elsewhere in the city (93 per cent), it is clear that households on these streets are of a qualitatively different kind. The institutional nature of Guy and the commercial nature of St. Catherine have already been noted, and in the latter case most of the households employing a live-in domestic would have been located above a store, whereas on Union, Victoria, and Cathcart, it is a quite different type of servicing of the community.

Historically, the wealthy tend to have larger households, because it takes time to accumulate wealth and so younger families are under-represented. We can see this quite clearly in the distribution of households on the right-hand side of Figure 7.4. After excluding live-in domestics, both in the city above the hill and elsewhere, households employing servants are considerably larger than those who do not employ any. Households are twice as likely to have only one to four people if they do not employ servants. A strange anomaly appears, however, when we look at the distribution in terms of the number of people in each household category, shown on the left-hand side of Figure 7.4. Above the hill, many more people without servants live in larger households than one would expect. While employers of domestics lived in considerably smaller households than their counterparts elsewhere in

Figure 7.4 The relative size of households.

Source: MAP's Geo-referenced head of household file, 1901 Census.

the city. As we have already seen, above the hill, the houses where domestics worked were considerably larger, and now we know that the households occupying those larger homes were significantly smaller.

Why are these patterns and this anomaly above the hill important? They speak to the increasing social complexity of this neighbourhood as it matured. Large households that did not employ live-in domestic servants were heavily concentrated in the older parts of the city above the hill, in particular along Victoria, Cathcart, and Union Streets.[27] As Figure 7.5 shows, these were relatively large brick or stone row houses, terraces to use the language of the day, dating from at least the 1870s. These were once-fine homes, but if they had remained all there was to the city above the hill, there would have been no imagined Golden Square Mile. By 1903, many of these older buildings were no longer just homes, they were also businesses offering accommodation to lodgers. Running these boarding houses took very considerable labour. Without live-in domestics, male-headed households would have relied on the unpaid labour of their wives and other female relatives to make these businesses work. On these streets, however, women headed half of the larger households, and so like Alice Sullivan, they too would have had to rely on the unpaid domestic labour of female relatives.

Figure 7.5 highlights another important aspect of the city above the hill. So much of it was new, built in the previous two decades. This was, of course, true for mansions financed by fortunes accumulated through the National Policy, which only came into effect in 1879, but it was even more the case for the core streets of

Figure 7.5 Age of buildings and large households without servants.

Sources: MAP's Geo-referenced head of household file, 1901 Census; and MAP's Goad of 1880.

affluence, Crescent, Mountain, and Drummond between Sherbrooke and Dorchester east of Guy, which were just lots awaiting development in 1880.

The presence of over a thousand lodgers in what frequently must have been cramped quarters in the oldest part of the city above the hill combined with the evident newness of construction in the affluent core brings us full circle to that major concern of Herbert Brown Ames: overcrowding. Ames argued that unlike many other major cities, overcrowding in Montreal's working-class districts was the exception rather than the rule. It was mostly to be found in quite restricted pockets, particularly where the city had allowed construction of mews in the back courtyards. Overall, Ames established the average to be one room per person, a finding confirmed by the 1901 census.[28]

How different was it in the city above the hill? One in eight households had it worse off than this average, while one in four enjoyed at least three and half rooms per person. The prize, fittingly enough, goes to Jane Redpath, the eighty-five-year-old sister of the principal promoter of the city above the hill: John Redpath. She lived by herself, in a thirty-two-room mansion on Sherbrooke, attended to, in ascending value of their annual wages, by two housemaids, ($168 each), a lady's maid ($180), a housekeeper ($200), and a cook ($240). So, for $956 a year these five workers "tended" not only a prominent elderly person but also added value to this $250,000 property owned by John Redpath's estate.

The city above the hill was neither the "Golden Square Mile" nor even the "Square Mile" of our imaginaries. It was never simply a site for the display of great wealth accumulated elsewhere. It was itself home to varied forms of value creation and appropriation and as the women and men in the city above the hill made their life choices, they created new and greater inequalities. Homes were key sites for these complex processes and both gender and social relations mattered. The lives of men have so dominated our historical narratives of this city above the hill that few realize how partial and misleading, indeed I think impoverished, these stories we have so long told ourselves really are.

Landed Ladies of the City above the Hill

By 1903, women owned a third of the properties owned by individuals in the city above the hill and a further 761 properties elsewhere in the city. Women also controlled eight institutions owning eleven properties above the hill and a further 105 properties elsewhere in the city. As Figure 7.6 shows, women owned properties in all parts of the city above the hill. A gendered segregation of property ownership had yet to develop. So, I start with two related phenomena: the importance of family, and the relative absence of a corporate presence at this the heart of the most spectacular creation of late-nineteenth-century Canadian capitalism. I will then discuss the question of control, before assessing the significance of the spatial distribution of these landed ladies' properties elsewhere in the city. I conclude with a reflection on what this all might mean for how we think of the social structure of turn-of-the-century Montreal.

I think the most fruitful point of entry to make sense of the remarkable number of women owning property is to recognize the centrality of family. Family mattered for both men and women, but because the avowed aim of the city in publishing a list of proprietors was to encourage speculation, it provided details on marital status only for the women. Of the 445 individual women who owned property in the city above the hill, 55 were unmarried, 220 were married, 157 were widowed, and 13 appear as estates. Both legally and socially, these distinct stages in the life cycle

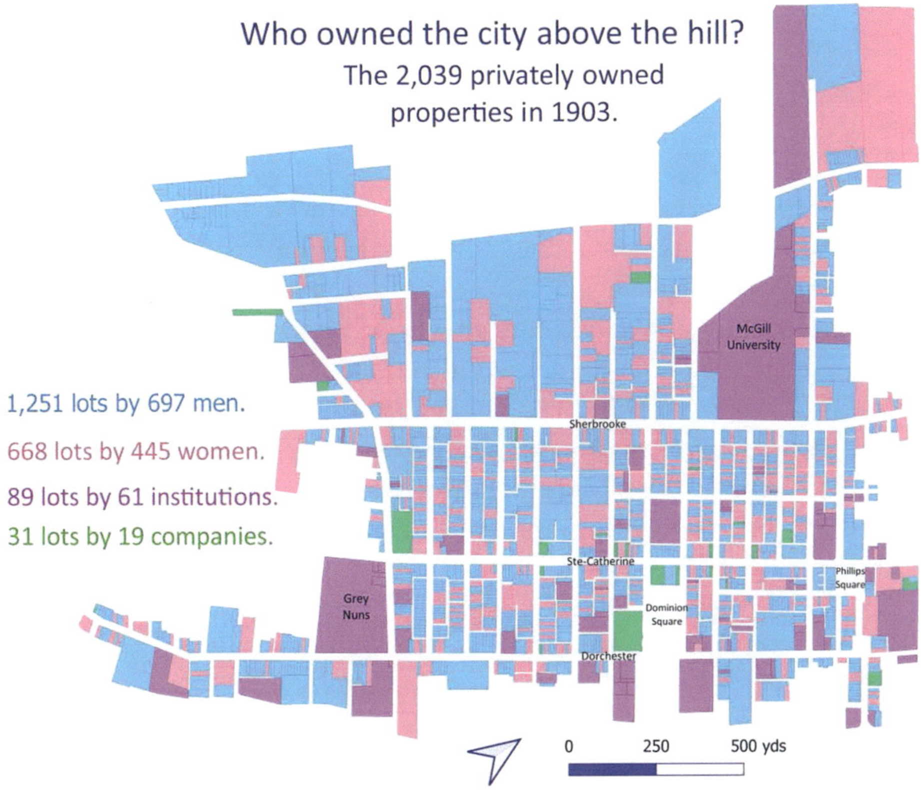

Figure 7.6 Ownership of the Square Mile in 1903.

Source: MAP's Geo-referenced Evaluation Roll of 1903.

mattered, as the marked differences in their respective mean nominal income from rents testify: $1,303, $1,149, $1,551, and $1,860.

Women faced serious constraints that their fathers, brothers, and husbands did not.[29] The most severe restrictions were those placed on married women, but there could be considerable variation in their nature. The age of majority was twenty-one, and minors were subject to the rule of their fathers if they remained unmarried, and to their husbands if they married. At majority, they enjoyed the free exercise of their civil rights which, however, were highly gendered in Quebec until the third quarter of the twentieth century. The default marriage regime was a community of property administered by the husband with the wife exercising a veto only over the sale of real property. In this largely Protestant and propertied part of the city, however, most couples by 1900 would have opted for a marriage contract.[30] Upon entering widowhood, a woman gradually regained her limited legal rights that had been lost during her marriage. Estates prolonged the legal personage of a deceased person beyond the grave and, therefore, offer the best place to start our examination of familial dynamics, gender, and property.

By defying mortality, estates structured the lives of future generations. In the city above the hill, 100 estates owned 236 properties assessed at $3.2 million. Elsewhere in the city, these estates owned a further 467 properties assessed at $4.2 million. Executors named by the deceased in his/her will administered the estate, but this could be subject to review by a family council.[31] In a time when women could not sit on juries and had only very limited and partial exercise of the franchise, these court-appointed tribunals were one of the few venues where women could exercise rights comparable to their male relatives. So, while it does matter that eighty-seven of the estates were for deceased men, as it speaks to the patriarchal origins of most rentier fortunes, this should not blind us to the role women potentially played in managing these family trusts, nor to their share of the $372,300 in rents these estates generated in 1903.

The Masson family provides a good example of a successful use of estates to achieve long-term familial strategies.[32] Joseph Masson, a pot-ash dealer and junior partner in the modest-sized export firm of Robertson & Masson, began investing in land in the early 1820s. Joseph died in 1847, leaving an estate that included twenty-eight city properties worth $11,478, including several on Beaver Hall Hill.[33] By 1903, his estate had grown to sixty-one city properties worth $599,690, while the estate of Sophie Raymond, his wife, member of a long-established rentier family, owned twelve properties worth $88,250. Three of their off-spring also survived into 1903 as estates with nine properties worth $73,050. These estates co-operated, for example by 1903 they shared ownership of the west side of Beaver Hall Hill. In all, they generated $46,340 in rents to be shared by the heirs.

One hundred and fifty-seven widows owned 258 properties above the hill worth $3.47 million and a further 284 properties worth $1.89 million elsewhere in the city. As we can see in Figure 7.7, they invested everywhere in the city above the hill. Inheritance played a part in these portfolios, but not necessarily from their deceased husbands. Widowhood meant regaining control of any property they may have brought into the marriage or any property they may subsequently have inherited from their own family. Furthermore, strict limitations on the exercise of dower, what a widow had the legal right to take away from a marriage, restricted the number of properties they could expect to inherit from their husbands. Customary dower in Quebec was limited to 50 per cent of the real property of the deceased husband if a lien had been duly registered. As the date of registration established the priority of the lien, long-standing creditors of the deceased husband would have

Figure 7.7 Female proprietors' marital status.

Source: MAP's Geo-referenced Evaluation Roll of 1903.

a prior claim on any recently acquired properties. Many, perhaps most, Protestant couples chose to opt out of customary dower, by fixing a set sum decided on in the marriage contract to be settled on the widow upon the death of her husband. Concretely, this meant that any improvements in family fortunes that occurred during the marriage, to which she had in all likelihood contributed, did not accrue to the wife, but remained with the husband's estate.[34] Testamentory freedom meant husbands could, should they so wish, will a greater amount to their surviving spouses, but they were under no legal obligation to do so, nor would the rise in misogynistic practices more widely have so encouraged them.[35]

Two hundred and twenty married women owned 291 properties above the hill, worth $3.5 million, and a further 243 properties worth $1.26 million elsewhere in the city. They, too, were widely dispersed, accounting for a clear majority of female-owned properties above Sherbrooke and on the affluent residential streets of Crescent, Mountain, Drummond, and Dorchester. Married women were legally expected to live with their husbands and, if he owned the family home, she would have to own another property above the hill to appear here as a landed lady. We will explore these cases shortly, but a woman whose husband owned property above the hill could also own property in her own right elsewhere in the city. In all, a further sixty married women were just such landed ladies *from* above the hill, owning 205 properties in the city below.

The city published details on the marital status of female proprietors, so we can establish how frequently the husbands of our landed ladies themselves owned property. A mere sixteen husbands and twelve deceased husbands of property-owning women owned property above the hill. Another fifty-six owned properties elsewhere in the city, generally the business premises of a family-owned firm. Three-quarters of the 392 husbands identified by the city owned no property at all.[36] Thus, properties owned by a married woman would not normally have been managed as part of her husband's real estate portfolio, because he did not have one.

Fifty-five unmarried women owned eighty-four properties above the hill worth $1 million, and a further 109 properties worth $574,100 elsewhere in the city. Twenty-seven women were identified with the title of "Miss." The location of their properties in the older part of the neighbourhood suggests they might have inherited them from grandparents or other older kin. The properties were not on the three streets with the most lodgers. The remaining women I classified as "unmarried" because no husband, living or dead, was identified by the city. Nine women appear as the head of a household employing domestic servants in the 1901 census. Seven of their other properties also housed servants, however the male head of households in these properties had no apparent kinship ties with the proprietors. The remaining properties, all without servants in 1901, were split evenly between male and female heads of household, which means they must have chosen to privilege female tenants. On Cathcart, Union, and Victoria Streets, twenty-seven properties owned by women had households of eight or more in 1901. Only three were owned by unmarried women, none by our "Misses," again suggesting the importance of unpaid domestic labour for the success of these businesses.

This presence of women as proprietors above the hill is truly remarkable. Women owned a third of all privately held properties. Where in the world today do women own such a major economic asset? Family is central to understanding this historic presence. People owned property as a part of larger, familial investment strategies, which is why property ownership characterized every stage of these women's life cycles. Inheritance provided a start for many women while still quite young, while still others would have brought property from their parents or other kin into the marriage. The management of property by widows was not, therefore, a new activity stemming from the death of their husband but a continuation of a set of practices many had been familiar with for their entire adult lives. The limited number of female estates does speak to the secondary role that female property owners most frequently played within these larger family strategies, but clearly in these cases women did possess sufficiently coherent portfolios that it was judged best not to break them up. Otherwise, there would have been no need to establish an estate.

The active management of extensive property assets has long been a hallmark of rentier families who succeed by controlling space through time.[37] This meant for young rentiers and young rentières the discipline of a restricted marriage market favoured alliances with those who already possessed property.[38] By 1903, local rentier families dominated the ownership of residential housing in all the popular-class neighbourhoods of the city.[39] They did not, however, dominate the city above the hill. Clearly, certain families, most notably the Redpaths and Phillips, had greatly benefited from the capital gains associated with this most successful of real estate developments, but a handful of dominant families did not control the neighbourhood. Instead, many families owned multiple properties. No fewer than thirty-nine families owned at least ten properties each in the city above the hill, while two-thirds of the "Misses" were from yet other families, suggesting a dispersal of property ownership among many affluent families.

We have already seen that companies were conspicuous by their absence on St. Catherine Street, and their presence was no greater anywhere else above the hill. It is the complexity of gendered family interests in property that explains this extraordinarily weak presence of corporate proprietors. When we recognize that multigenerational strategies of accumulation require the active participation of women at all stages of their life cycles in order to succeed, we better understand how this multiplicity of reciprocal social and familial relations impeded the development of a "free" market in real estate. Property was not merely an investment, it was a primary means of ensuring the long-term well-being of family members, and its successful handling was key to the co-operation between both siblings and generations that a coherent family-based accumulation strategy required. Eventually, forms of corporate governance would develop that permitted through share ownership and family trusts the achievement of something like the stability that bourgeois families craved, but that would take us well into the twentieth century. For now, the family business and the family's property were still that: familial and, therefore, subordinate to family interests.

We have, of course, failed to see all this because our focus in this city above the hill has been on the "captains of industry," treating them as free agents without a familial constraint in the world. When the "Napoleon of St. François-Xavier Street," Louis Joseph Forget, returned to his mansion on Sherbrooke St., it was to a home owned by his wife, Marie Raymond. We can be sure he never forgot this, and it behooves us to do the same.

Marie Raymond and Louisa Kennedy, as noted in this chapter, as well as Amy Redpath, as noted in chapter 6 in this volume, might be thought of as examples of women owning assets that they did not control. This interpretation of the evidence is based on the wide-spread bourgeois practice of placing the family home in the name of the wife so that it would be protected from the creditors of the husband should he face legal action. There clearly are instances where this might have been the case, but before presenting that evidence, let us first review the argument.

Marriage is an economic agreement between two people and, during this period, two families for a lifetime. In Quebec, the rules governing that agreement were determined by the provisions of the civil code and the marriage contract. The guarantee that the wife would be well taken care of in the case of her husband's premature death was a major preoccupation of both families and the law. It was also a major concern for liberal theorists who worked hard to do away with the encumbrances that buttressed socially defined rights to property such as dower.[40] As we have seen, they were largely successful and, by the turn of the century, not only was dower not a guarantee of very much at all, but the forms adopted to replace it worked against the long-term economic interest of the wife. So, when a family home was placed in the name of the wife it was not simply a way of pulling one over on the creditors – although no doubt they saw it that way – it provided economic security for the wife that the law no longer did. It also, and in the early twenty-first century this needs to be said, was a social and economic commitment to the marriage as a binding relationship "til death do they part."

One hundred twenty-six married women owned a single property that was located in the city above the hill (see Figure 7.8). I verified if these properties were their family homes in the Lovell's City Directory, using the husbands' personal information. In 102 cases, the women lived at these properties. In sixteen cases, however, Lovell's listed the wife or her husband as living elsewhere. In these cases, I think it is safe to assume that these properties were an investment, generating rent for the owners. In a further eight cases, there was no confirmation that the women lived at these addresses. I double checked these cases against the heads of household file from the 1901 census and was unable to find either the husband or the wife listed as living at any of these dwellings. I think these, too, are quite likely to be premises that were rented out; certainly Lovell's, and sometimes the 1901 census, always had someone else living at these locations.

Residential properties owned by women in Montreal more generally were managed quite differently than those owned by men in two important respects. First,

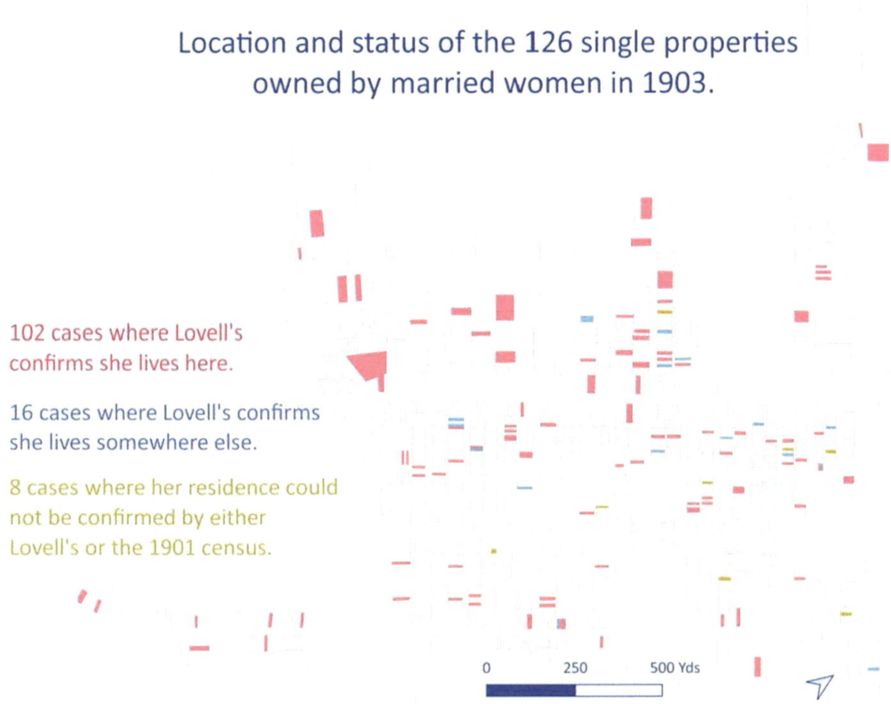

Figure 7.8 Married females owning a single property in 1903.

Sources: MAP's Geo-referenced Evaluation Role of 1903; MAP's Head of Household File, 1901; BAnQ's online Annuaire Municipale Lovelle's, 1903.

there was an almost complete absence of situations of overcrowding on properties owned by women. Overcrowding was also absent from the properties owned by most men, but if you found a slum landlord, it was a landlord, not a landlady. Second, in a city where the lines of segregation along language, religion, ethnicity, and race were very clearly drawn, landladies enforced the conventions of segregation with very considerably less vigour than did the landlords. I used all households headed by immigrants for this test case. The remarkably even distribution of Chinese laundries throughout the city was the most telling result of these qualitatively different leasing practices. After all, everyone would have had dirty laundry, even if that seemed not to have occurred to most landlords.[41]

MAP's recently completed, and highly successful, linkage of household heads to the evaluation roll lots permits an enriching of this earlier analysis.[42] In 1901, female-headed households within the city above the hill were twice as common as elsewhere: 24 per cent versus 12 per cent. Above the hill, almost half of these female-headed households, 244 of 509, employed a live-in domestic servant. Clearly, independence for women was easier if they had money. Even more significantly, female heads of households lived disproportionately on properties owned by women. Above the hill, where women owned a third of the properties, 42 per cent of female heads of households lived on a property owned by a woman.[43] Elsewhere in the city, where women owned a fifth of all properties, one-third of female heads of household lived on a property owned by a woman. Whether it was landladies seeking out female tenants, or female heads of household preferring a landlady to a landlord, it is too early to tell. In all likelihood, it was a great deal more complicated than this simple dichotomy might suggest. So, too, was the question of control.

Turn-of-the-century Montreal was profoundly riven by complex gender and social divisions of labour. The management of property would not have proved an exception. Posing the question of control as an individual matter effectively denies this complexity, by imposing an explanatory framework rooted in mythical ideas of male entrepreneurship. In most cases, control was familial, not individual. Landed ladies managed their properties within the context of multi-generational strategies and they would have played important roles in the elaboration and application of those strategies. I would argue the same could and should be said about landlords. What these marked differences in the leasing practices of landladies as opposed to landlords demonstrate, beyond any reasonable doubt, however, is that female property ownership mattered to the women of Montréal.

The landed ladies of the city above the hill owned more properties elsewhere in the city than they did in the neighbourhood where they lived. There is, however, a remarkable spatial concentration to their investments, one that does not characterize the portfolios of landed gentlemen. They invested in petty-bourgeois neighbourhoods adjacent to the city above the hill, in St Laurent ward west of Bleury,[44] and in the old city. They chose not to invest in most of the city below the hill, the one exception being directly below the escarpment as far as the Grand Trunk mainline and even this limited engagement may well have been a relic of earlier times.[45] Their absence from the primarily Protestant working-class neighbourhoods within Pointe St. Charles and St. Anne is remarkable. Only two major familial strategies took some of these ladies east of "the Main." The Boyer women participated actively in a major play along Christophe Colombe in the St. Jean Baptiste Ward just to the north of Lafontaine Park, while the Pilkington sisters extended the play initiated by some of their in-laws, the Molsons, along Fullum in the St. Marie Ward and Frontenac in the Hochelaga Ward. With these exceptions to prove the rule, the landed ladies of the city above the hill chose to keep their distances from the working class.

Their investments both within and without the city above the hill were nevertheless highly remunerative. If we make the generous allowance that all of the living landed ladies, save our "Misses," owned the home they lived in and we further assume it was worth what the homes of 102 verified single-family-dwelling landed ladies were assessed for their homes, then the gross income from their rental properties was $496,295, for an average of $1,464 a year. Clearly not the income of a Herbert Brown Ames, but more than twice the annual income of a family below the hill.

The remarkably uneven spatial distribution suggests a qualitatively different social structure within the English Protestant community than that which characterized either of the city's major Catholic communities. French Canadian and Irish rentier families interacted regularly with working-class tenants. This presence of both bourgeois women and men fashioned important aspects of neighbourhood life elsewhere in the city. The landed ladies of the city above the hill, by contrast, inhabit a much more polarized and segregated space, one where their only interactions with working people would have been highly gendered and spatially restricted: with the domestics in their homes and with the sales clerks in the shops along St. Catherine Street.

What are we to make of all this? Clearly gender and social relations are intimately related; we cannot understand the one without the other. Furthermore, the scale of the reliance on both paid and unpaid domestic labour qualitatively challenges facile dichotomies between a public sphere of social production gendered male and a private sphere of reproduction gendered female. Through both their investments and their social relations, the landed ladies above the hill created a privileged bourgeois space for themselves and their families. It was different than the one inhabited daily by their husbands, brothers and sons, but it too was characterized by inequality. The differing scale and scope of these inequalities matter. Landed ladies faced daily constraints their male kin never would. The evidence suggests that when they could, they acted differently, and in so doing contributed to making a space of such affluence that its legendary status in our imaginary has hidden from view both the nature and the importance of their choices.

NOTES

During the years between the conference and the deadline for submissions, considerable progress was made on the databases upon which both the original paper and this chapter are based. This allowed for a more extended discussion of the issues raised by my original paper "Landed

Ladies," which is still available from my academia.edu page. I would like to thank Elizabeth-Anne Malischewski for her astute criticisms and wonderful suggestions as this chapter was written. Once completed, Tony Chadwick, Gilles Lauzon, Sherry Olson, and Brian Young all made valuable suggestions on needed improvements.

1 All passages in quotations are from Herbert Brown Ames, *"The City Below the Hill": A Sociological Study of a Portion of the City of Montreal* (Montreal: The Bishop Engraving and Printing Company, 1897).

2 One of the most important findings of Ames's study was that poverty was, relatively speaking limited; he classified as poor only 888 families and called them the "submerged tenth" (*City Below the Hill,* 23, 50–6). Furthermore, despite an extended discussion of density and overcrowding, he made the bold claim that there were no "real 'slum districts'" (18). And yet the best-known analysis of Ames's work by Terry Copp is entitled *Anatomy of Poverty: The Condition of the Working Class in Montreal, 1897–1929* (Toronto: Oxford, 1974), while the republication of Ames's pamphlet by the University of Toronto Press in 1975 changed the subtitle to *The Slums of Montreal, 1897.*

3 The quotations are from Ames, *City Below the Hill*, 3–4.

4 *Geo-referenced Evaluation Roll of 1903* (Montreal: MAP, 2018–20), http:\\www.mun.ca\mapm.

5 MAP's historical GIS consists of five "layers" anchored to four period maps (1825, 1846, 1880, 1912) and a 1903 map of our own confection that has been reshaped to the same coordinates, so one can "drill down" to see changes over time. We then "people" these maps by linking a diverse array of period sources: tax rolls, city directories, census returns, commutation records, pew rentals, wage books, notarial deeds, and so on. In chapter 2, Sherry Olson draws on two of our earlier layers. Our project website provides an overview and two downloadable QGIS applications relevant to this study: *Who Owned Montreal in 1903?* and *Residential Landlord/Tenant Relations in 1901*, www.mun.ca/mapm. Online queries of some of our databases are possible through two websites: https://schemamontreal.uqam.ca/projets/montreal-en-1881 and www.map.cieq.ca.

6 Tending a house was the rather endearing way Ames described those working-age adults who were not engaged in waged or salaried employment outside the home. The assessment comes from MAP's *Geo-referenced Evaluation Roll of 1903*, while the entry for Ames's household in the 1901 manuscript census is St. Antoine A47, page 4, starting at line 49: https://central.bac-lac.gc.ca/.item/?app=Census1901&op=img&id=z000155139.

7 An important exception were the bourgeois streets of St. Denis and St. Hubert linking the nineteenth-century residential east ward of the old city to the Côte à Barron. Anchored by the Montreal campus of Laval University, this French-Canadian corridor retained its bourgeois prestige well into the twentieth century, much longer than its western counterpart of Beaver Hall Hill.

8 Robert C.H. Sweeny, *Why Did We Choose to Industrialize? Montréal 1819–1849* (Montreal: McGill-Queen's University Press, 2015).

9 Robert C.H. Sweeny, "Divvying Up Space: Housing Segregation and National Identity in Early Twentieth-Century Montréal," in *Sharing Spaces: Essays in Honour of Sherry Olson*, ed. Robert Sweeny (Ottawa: Canadian Museum of History and University of Ottawa Press, 2020), 111–28.

10 In my family, the boundary was drawn much further west. I had a great aunt, who in her eighty plus years as a Montrealer never went east of Bleury Street. As an elementary school student in the early 1960s, I was allowed free rein anywhere downtown, up to but not past the System Theatre, just east of Morgan's, kitty-corner to Phillips Square on St. Catherine Street. When, in

Grade 5, Billy Clennett and I rode our bikes from the Notre-Dame-de-Grâce neighbourhood east to "the Main" to taste a "steamie," I was grounded for a week. Crossing imaginary boundaries can have real consequences.

11 Bibliothèque et Archives nationales du Québec, "Collection d'annuaires Lovell de Montréal et sa region, 1842–2010," accessed 3 February 2023, http://numerique.banq.qc.ca/ressources/details/lovell.

12 This particular act of cultural vandalism has obtained mythic status, credited with launching the city's heritage movement, as if the tenants of Faubourg à m'lasse's 1962 struggle against the demolition of their neighbourhood to make way for Radio Canada's office tower and the Notre Dame expressway, or the Goose Village resident's 1964 resistance to the Drapeau administration's demolition of Victoriatown – the city's only majority owner-occupied working-class community – to make a parking lot for the six months of Expo 67, or the multi-year struggle starting in 1968 by the Milton-Park Citizen's Committee to halt Cité Concordia, and so many other community-based actions to defend popular-class communities are not to be considered part of our heritage.

13 In Montreal parlance, the half refers to the water closet or indoor toilet.

14 The exemplary research of Gilles Lauzon should have laid to rest this particular misrepresentation of popular-class life years ago, but unfortunately it lives on. Robert C.H. Sweeny, "Lessons from the Database Debates" (paper presented at the Social Science History Association, Montreal, November 2017).

15 Mews, or housing in the rear of a property, were scattered throughout popular-class neighbourhoods and were often of very substandard condition. It was against this particular form of housing that Ames marshalled his harshest criticisms.

16 The 1,689 built lots owned by people averaged 1.27 known civic numbers per lot, while elsewhere in the city it was 2.42 per lot. MAP's *Geo-referenced Evaluation Roll of 1903*.

17 Using the 2015 median value of a dwelling in Montreal from Community Profiles, 2016 Census, Statistics Canada: https://www12.statcan.gc.ca/census-recensement/2016.

18 Raymond Williams, *The Country and the City* (New York: Oxford University Press, 1973), 105–19.

19 "Ghost acres" is a concept developed by environmental historians to categorize often unseen areas of the world whose radical transformation financed highly visible concentrations of wealth. For a fine example, see Jim Clifford, "London's Soap Industry and the Development of Global Ghost Acres in the Nineteenth Century," *Environment and History* 27, no. 3 (2021): 471–97.

20 In the case of Montreal, the old city was regendered as an almost exclusively male space for more than a generation. See Robert C.H. Sweeny, "Property and Gender: Lessons from a 19th-Century Town," *London Journal of Canadian Studies* 22 (2006/2007): 9–34.

21 None has survived, although a fourth just outside my boundaries on Milton has.

22 Indeed, its corporate body, the Royal Institution for the Advancement of Learning, was a key player in creating the neighbourhood by subdividing the lower half of James McGill's estate. It should be noted that the Sulpician domain, just to the west of the city above the hill, dates from the seventeenth century.

23 Brian Young, *Respectable Burial: Montreal's Mount Royal Cemetery* (Montreal: McGill-Queen's University Press, 2003).

24 Roberto Perin, *Ignace de Montréal: Artisan d'une identité nationale* (Montreal: Boréal, 2008).

25 For the debates this transformation engendered in the Presbyterian congregations, see Rosalyn Trigger, "Protestant Restructuring in the Canadian City: Church and Mission in the Industrial

Working-Class District of Griffintown," *Urban History Review* 31, no. 1 (2002): 5–18. On a somewhat lighter note, it was the resulting plethora of Protestant churches that prompted Mark Twain to observe at a banquet in his honour at the Windsor Hotel: "This is the first time I was ever in a city where you couldn't throw a brick without breaking a church window. Yet I was told that you were going to build one more. I said the scheme is good, but where are you going to find room? They said, we will build it on top of another church and use an elevator." *New York Times*, 10 December 1881.

26 Sweeny, *Why Did We Choose to Industrialize?* In particular chaps. 7 and 9.

27 It was my mother, a Trafalgar-Institute "old girl," who set the boundaries of my youth, and the System Theatre was on the north-east corner of Union and St. Catherine, so her sense of urban geography may well have been more historically rooted than I ever gave her credit for.

28 The 207,845 people living in private households that did not employ a live-in domestic lived in 212,171 rooms. MAP's *Geo-referenced Index of Household Heads, 1901 Census* (Montreal: MAP, 2018–20), http://www.mun.ca/mapm.

29 Marie Gérin-Lajoie, *Traité de droit usuel* (Monteal: C.O. Beauchemin et Fils, 1902).

30 Only valid if negotiated before a Notary Public prior to the marriage, contracts could run the gamut from imposing the English Common Law's eradication of the wife's legal personage to establishing an equitable basis for a companionate marriage with each being completely separate as to property. An excellent introduction to these options is Bettina Bradbury, *Wife to Widow: Lives, Laws and Politics in Nineteenth-Century Montreal* (Vancouver: UBC Press, 2011), 65–70.

31 Executors could be of either sex, but if a woman was married, she required a court order before assuming the role. The court appointed the seven members of a family council, drawn from both sides of the family. Only the widow or ascendant female relatives were eligible to be members.

32 For an examination of the difficulties they encountered, see Thierry Nootens, "Je crains fort que mon pauvre Henri ne fasse pas grand chose...": Les heritiers "manqués" et les querelles de la succession Masson, 1850–1930, *Revue d'histoire de l'Amerique française* 59, no. 3 (2006): 223–57.

33 MAP's *Municipal Evaluation Roll File, 1848* (Montreal: MAP, 2018–20).

34 This was a contributing factor to the marked difference, 212 per cent more, in the nominal value of rents accruing to men's estates over those of women by 1903. The experience of Bessy Pentland, who married Herbert Molson in 1899, provides an object lesson in how this might work. When Herbert died in 1937, an annuity amounting to a mere 0.114 of 1 per cent of the value of his estate was settled on Bessy. Robert C.H. Sweeny, "Herbert Molson," *Dictionary of Canadian Biography*, University of Toronto /Université Laval (forthcoming).

35 An integral part of the profoundly conservative turn that characterized North Atlantic cultures in the last half of the nineteenth century, in Canada these practices were book-ended by the disenfranchisement of female voters in 1848 and the legalization of rape in marriage in 1896.

36 Fortunately for them, the law considered property owned by the wife as enfranchising the husband where, as in the city of Montreal, the vote was restricted to property owners.

37 Robert C.H. Sweeny, "Spatial and Social Dynamics of Rentier Capital in an Industrializing Town: The Case of 19th Century Montreal" (paper presented at the Economic History Association, Austin, Texas, 6 September 2007).

38 This was most in evidence among rentier families with rental incomes in excess of $20,000, where more than a third of rentier marriages and a quarter of rentière marriages involved another rentier family. Robert C.H. Sweeny, "Going Together Like a Horse and Carriage: Rentier Marriages and Property Accumulation in Montréal, 1825–1903," *Histoire Sociale/Social History* 54, no. 112 (2021): 481–90.

39 Robert C.H. Sweeny, "Property, Gender and Popular Class Housing in Turn of the Century Montréal" (paper presented at the Social Science History Association, Toronto, November 2014).

40 For an extended discussion of how this worked itself out in Montreal, see chap. 8 in Sweeny, *Why Did We Choose to Industrialize?*

41 Robert C.H. Sweeny, "Gender, Discrimination and Housing in Turn-of-the-Century Montréal. What Mapping the Census Returns of Immigrants Can Tell Us," *Frontiers in Digital Humanities* 3, no. 8 (2016): 1–18.

42 MAP's *Residential Landlord/Tenant Relations* places 99.97 per cent of all households on a lot within their proper census subdivision.

43 The proportion was lowered by the one in six properties lived in by a married couple, but owned by the wife shown in Figure 7.8. As one might expect, there were very few female-headed households living on these properties: only three households lived in the 102 properties. Whereas, nine female headed households lived in the twenty-four properties that did not appear to be owner-occupied.

44 So perhaps my great-great aunt was not alone in her understanding of urban boundaries.

45 With the construction of the CPR mainline along the edge of the escarpment in the early 1880s, an additional social and visual boundary was created. This increased the liminal nature of the area lying below Dorchester down to the Grand Trunk tracks. Investments by landed ladies in this area may well have predated this change in status.

PART FOUR

PROFESSIONAL AND BUSINESS WORLDS IN TRANSFORMATION

Figure V.12 Reproduction of group photograph of Montreal members of the Province of Quebec Association of Architects presented to the Quebec members, October 1894. From *Canadian Architect and Builder* 8, no. 1 (January 1895).

Architects Unite

The Notman Studios did a brisk business in composite photographs, a sort of precursor to Photoshop. The photographers would take individual portraits and then assemble them against an appropriate backdrop, which they would rephotograph to create a single image. Outdoor sporting groups might be set against a woodland landscape of snow-laden trees and the occasional moose. Here, the Montreal members of the Province of Quebec Association of Architects are posed as if they have convened their annual meeting within the staterooms of a Renaissance palazzo (Figure V.12).

The impetus for forming the association in 1890 was partially protectionist. By the last decade of the nineteenth century local architects were alarmed by the number of commissions that were going to their American counterparts. The pill was hardest to swallow when the commissions were snatched from local drafting boards. In 1890, the Montreal architect who was working on the James Ross residence on Upper Peel Street was dismissed and the mandate was given to the New York architect Bruce Price. Price had just completed the prestigious commission of Windsor Station for the Canadian Pacific Railway, and Ross was one of its executive officers. The situation prompted one critic to write: "I cannot understand how it is when Canadians have any money to spend, they always avoid local men and prefer to employ alien architects." The Ross mansion, deliberately sited so as to overlook the city, must have been a gallingly visible reminder of foreign interference for Montreal's architects, and particularly to the anonymous one who had been fired.[1]

NOTE

1 *Canadian Architect and Builder* 3, no. 7 (July 1890), 78.

CHAPTER EIGHT

Max Aitken in Montreal: Financial Innovation and Creative Destruction in the Laurier Boom

Gregory P. Marchildon

Introduction

William Maxwell (Max) Aitken lived in Montreal for less than three years between 1907 and 1910. He then moved to England where he would become Lord Beaverbrook, the prominent press baron, political fixer, and cabinet minister in Churchill's wartime government.[1] Yet, in this short time, he had an indelible impact on the business and financial titans who dominated Montreal's Square Mile. When he shifted his own enterprises and their centre of gravity from Halifax to Montreal, this created a chain reaction that resulted in other talented Maritimers moving to Montreal. Some of these individuals, most notably Izaak Walton Killam and Arthur J. Nesbitt, would themselves emerge as establishment figures in the financial community in the Square Mile from the 1920s until the 1950s, orchestrating investment banking in Canada from their headquarters in Montreal.

The type of capitalism practised by Max Aitken reflected a version that the great twentieth-century economist Joseph Schumpeter famously labelled "creative destruction." According to Schumpeter, the "gale of creative destruction" is the innovation that destroys the economic status quo by replacing it with new and more effective institutions and processes.[2] Aitken was that gale in Montreal, destroying existing ways of doing financial business and replacing well-worn institutions and the people who ran them with a younger generation of investment bankers.

But Aitken was a dangerous man to get close to, one who could be as damaging to his erstwhile allies, friends, and employees as his enemies. Indeed, you could forgive some of Aitken's partners and allies for wondering at times whether they were treated worse than his enemies. Some figures who supported Aitken – most prominent among whom was Sir Edward Clouston, Canada's leading banker and Montreal's leading merchant prince – saw how their association with Aitken could stall or destroy their careers and diminish their lofty reputations. To say that he made enemies during his time in Montreal would be an understatement. He went out of his way to outmanoeuvre rivals and dominate his partners and left a trail of human devastation behind him in his short time in the city.

Unfortunately for the old Square Mile guard, Aitken ran his Montreal businesses and directed his young associates for years after he departed the scene. These individuals, under Aitken's direction and subsequently in their own right, came to dominate the financial scene in Montreal, a legacy that shaped Montreal as the financial capital of Canada until it began to lose that position to Toronto in the 1970s. This was Aitken's long-standing legacy in Montreal, and it left a footprint far deeper than any single individual could leave, whether they lived in a city for three years or for a lifetime.

Aitken's Circuitous Road to Montreal

Born in 1879, Max Aitken grew up in Newcastle (now Miramichi), New Brunswick. To his parents' consternation and embarrassment – his father was a straight-laced Presbyterian clergyman who had emigrated from Scotland – Aitken was born a mischief-maker.[3] He was also a natural entrepreneur, a pint-sized peddler who convinced his customers to return the soap wrappers to him so that he could get a free bike through the soap company's promotion, and his own newspaper, which he called the *Leader*, he produced free of charge using the town newspaper's equipment.[4]

These ventures were relative successes compared to the failures Aitken suffered in the first years after he left home. As an apprentice lawyer, he was fired because of his inattention to the work. His dreams of profit by providing meat to railway work camps in Western Canada were dashed by unforeseen delays and spoiled product. With accumulating debt, he moved back east to Saint John, New Brunswick, where he sold insurance to make his payments.[5]

When he turned twenty-one, Aitken's luck began to improve as he shifted into the business of selling stocks and bonds. As a small wholesaler of existing securities in the Maritimes, he got to know the Halifax businessmen who were pulling the strings. These included William B. Ross, Charles Cahan, and most notably John F. Stairs, perhaps the most prominent merchant and financier at the time.[6] Aitken cosied up to Stairs and became his personal secretary. At the time, Stairs and his associates were investing in street railways in the Caribbean. Aitken's first job for Stairs was to help sell the bonds of the Trinidad Electric Company.[7]

Aitken's big break came in 1903 when Stairs and his Halifax friends set up the Royal Securities Corporation. As president, Stairs made Aitken the secretary of the new enterprise. The only other firm of its type – the Dominion Securities Corporation – had been set up in Toronto three years earlier. When Stairs fell ill and died unexpectedly a few months later from a failing heart, Aitken assumed the position of general manager, a role he had already been playing to a large extent as secretary. With Stairs no longer around to support him, Aitken worked like a madman to prove himself to the men who bankrolled Royal Securities for street railways in the Caribbean along with industrial finance and bank mergers in the Maritimes. Unfortunately for Aitken, the more successful he became, the more he seemed to generate resentment among Stairs's old business partners, almost all of whom were a generation older than Aitken. He was the powerhouse behind the success of Royal Securities, yet they insisted on treating him as Stairs's lowly executive assistant.[8]

Aitken had choices. Some of his underwriting syndicates in his utility companies were major bankers and industrialists from central Canada. In his mind, the two most impressive were Sir William Van Horne of Canadian Pacific Railway fame[9] and Edward Clouston, the general manager of the Bank of Montreal who had recently been made vice-president of the bank and a director on the bank's board as well as president of the Canadian Bankers Association.[10] Both Van Horne and Clouston became major investors in Aitken's newest utility in British Guiana, the Demerara Electric Company, after observing Aitken's success in making the Trinidad Electric Company a profitable enterprise.[11] Aitken in turn looked up to these Montrealers as the epitome of Canadian finance, a position that he very much coveted for himself.

To accomplish this, Aitken could not remain in Halifax. Although that city was a very important regional economic centre for the Maritimes, its national importance was declining. In 1901, Halifax, with a population of almost 41,000, was the seventh largest city in the country, a position that would drop to eighth place by 1911 even though its population had increased to almost 47,000. This size paled in comparison to Montreal that had solidified its position as the largest city in Canada, with a population that grew from roughly 268,000 in 1901 to almost half a million people in 1911, a spectacular increase that made the city the principal beneficiary of the pre–First World War economic boom in Canada.[12]

More importantly, however, Montreal was the financial capital of Canada. This meant it was the centre of investment banking, which is, at its essence, the business of issuing new stocks and bonds in order to raise money in order to create

Figure 8.1 Wm. Notman & Son, *Max Aitken, later Lord Beaverbrook, Montreal*, 1905. McCord Museum, II-1565371.

new enterprises as well as expand and reconfigure existing firms. In addition, Montreal was home to the largest secondary market in securities – the Montreal Stock Exchange.[13] Even as late as 1910, the trading volume on the Montreal Stock Exchange was well over double the volume of the Toronto Stock Exchange, a dominant position that would not be relinquished until the Great Depression of the 1930s.[14]

In order to grow his investment business, Aitken was propelled to extend his operations in Montreal. Already travelling to Montreal from Halifax on a periodic basis – a rail journey of roughly twenty-eight hours[15] – Aitken had to get boots on the ground in the city. In December of 1905, he established a branch of Royal Securities at 244 St. James Street, surrounded by other financial service firms, insurance companies, and banks, including Clouston's Bank of Montreal office at 119 St. James Street.[16] Aitken sent one of his newest men, Arthur J. Nesbitt, to run the

Figure 8.2 Montreal Stock Exchange, St. François Xavier Street, Montreal, c. 1905. McCord Museum, VIEW-8728.

branch office of Royal Securities.[17] A fellow New Brunswicker from Saint John, Nesbitt was twenty-five years of age, one year younger than Aitken.

Montreal Trust and Montreal Engineering: Aitken's Foothold in Montreal

In 1907, Aitken moved to Montreal. He purchased a large house at 3489 Drummond Street high up the mountain in the Square Mile. Built in 1898, it was the home of a succession of wealthy families and once hosted Bram Stoker, the Irish author of *Dracula* who stayed at the house for a period during the interwar years. Today, it is the elegant home of the Consulate General of Italy.[18] It is unclear exactly when Aitken purchased the house and when his wife Gladys joined him in Montreal. He was located just over two blocks from Rodolphe Forget's house at 3685 Du Musée Street. The birth record of Janet Gladys (Bodie) Aitken, the first born in the family, indicates that she was born in Halifax on 9 July 1908;[19] however, John William Maxwell (Max) Aitken was born in Montreal on 15 February 1910.[20]

The move was perhaps inevitable given the young financier's trajectory, but the proximate cause was his takeover of the Montreal Trust and Deposit Company and his establishment of the Montreal Engineering Company. The Montreal Trust story began in 1905 when Aitken established the Commercial Trust Company in Halifax. Creating a new bank under Canadian law was (and remains) extremely difficult, but a trust company – which could take deposits and loan money just like a bank – was very easy in comparison. The trust company offered Aitken the opportunity to use the deposits as the basis upon which to offer call loans to the investors and stockbrokers who were underwriting or selling his new issues of securities. Within months, Commercial Trust was acquiring funds in the United States as well as Canada and then relending the money as call loans to brokers in Montreal and New York. However, Commercial Trust was hampered by its lack of a base in Montreal, so Aitken asked Nesbitt to scout out some buildings on St. James Street to set up a branch of the Commercial Trust. One of the reasons that Aitken was keen to have a trust company in Montreal was that a sizeable secondary market for a street railway and other utility securities had been established and many more of these were trading on the Montreal Stock Exchange rather than the Toronto Stock Exchange.

However, Aitken also knew he needed a larger capitalization and the easiest way to achieve this was to merge with an existing trust company. At the time, the three largest trust companies operating in Montreal were the Royal Trust Company, controlled by the Bank of Montreal; the National Trust Company, aligned with the Toronto-based Canadian Bank of Commerce; and the Montreal Trust and Deposit Company, one of the first trust companies established in Canada and

Figure 8.3 House owned by Max Aitken at 3489 Drummond Street, Montreal. Currently the home of the Italian Consulate in Montreal. Photograph taken in 2019 by Sarah Boumedda.

which remained independent of the chartered banks. The smallest of the three and in part because of its lack of affiliation with a bank, Montreal Trust had been declining in vitality. When his offer was rebuffed, Aitken bribed Richard Wilson-Smith, the previous mayor of Montreal and current president of Montreal Trust, with a guaranteed $5,000 profit if he would support the merger.

The bribe was accepted and the details of the merger were finalized in May 1907. Aitken would move immediately to Montreal and take over as managing director while William B. Ross would become vice-president as soon as he changed his domicile from Halifax to Montreal. Two other prominent Haligonians – Aitken's utility lawyers Charles H. Cahan and Almon Lovett – left Halifax in order to establish their own law firms in Montreal. The main client of both law firms was Max Aitken and his numerous enterprises. An experienced utility lawyer, Cahan took over as legal counsel for Royal Securities and Montreal Engineering while Lovett became corporate counsel for Montreal Trust.[21] The move made the front page of the *Halifax Herald*, the paper lamenting the loss of these "Good Halifax Men."[22]

As the general manager of Royal Securities, Aitken ran his new empire in the heart of Montreal's financial district. His routine was quickly set. In the early morning hours before the banks opened, he worked alongside Nesbitt in the Royal Securities' office on St. James Street. After two to three hours of focused attention on the securities business, he walked across the street into Place d'Armes where he spent the rest of the day managing Montreal Trust. The only question in his mind was why he had wasted so much time "trying to do business from Halifax."[23] Aitken rejoiced in the fact that he was at the centre of finance in Canada. He told one of his young associates that he had found "more of interest in Montreal in a few days than in many weeks of Halifax life."[24]

The Royal Securities' branch office on St. James Street was soon shared by another Aitken tenant, the Montreal Engineering Company, the new in-house purchasing, consulting, and accounting arm of the utility enterprises financed by Royal Securities. The first of its type in North America, Montreal Engineering was a brilliant innovation on Aitken's part. The company was configured in a way that it could provide a core of engineering expertise while also purchasing high-quality utility equipment at the lowest possible prices. Montreal Engineering also provided expert accounting advice and services to its family of utilities so that problems could be detected and the investment in new practices could be assessed in a timely way. As a holding company, the new firm was well ahead of the curve of what other utility consortiums were doing in the United States and Canada.[25] From its creation in 1907 until the early 1950s, Royal Securities held a controlling block of shares in Montreal Engineering and the company was never publicly listed.[26]

Although Aitken had originally considered New York City as a desirable site for the head office, he changed his mind for two key reasons. One was that he wanted as close collaboration as possible between Royal Securities and Montreal Engineering. The second reason was that, from the perspective of purchasing electrical equipment, Montreal was almost as good a location as New York in that two key American companies – the White Company and the Fairbanks Company – had set up branch plants in Montreal where they could observe their operations. In addition, Montreal Engineering would not be far from Canadian General Electric in Hamilton and Canadian Westinghouse in Toronto. As discussed further below, this integrated system would pay dividends for decades to come in terms of the efficiency of the utilities serviced by Montreal Engineering and their profitability.[27]

Transforming Royal Securities and Promoting Industrial Mergers

Although Aitken continued to look for new street railway and hydroelectric opportunities in the Caribbean and Latin America, he began to focus more heavily on utility and industrial opportunities in Canada after the short-lived financial panic of 1907.[28] Although some Canadian financiers were caught flat footed by the sudden collapse in the securities market, Aitken weathered the storm in large part because of his diversified financial operations and, especially, Montreal Engineering and Montreal Trust, both of which made a great deal of money even while Royal Securities had to endure some major losses. These losses led to considerable grumbling by Aitken's old associates in Halifax. To cover the losses, Aitken recommended a complicated scheme whereby Montreal Trust and Royal Securities would have overlapping share ownership. He no longer had time, he argued, to run Royal Securities from a base in Halifax given his many interests in Montreal. If the investors refused, he warned, he would be forced to walk away from Royal Securities.

Convinced that Aitken would soon hollow out the Halifax operation, the main shareholders of Royal Securities refused. No longer willing to be their managing director, Aitken said that the shareholders would have to wind up Royal Securities, and having no one to take his place, they did just that. Although the name was purchased by Royal Securities' sales manager, the assets of Royal Securities were sold, and the cash was distributed to the Halifax investors and to Aitken as a minority shareholder. Aitken promptly set up the Utilities Securities Company, with shares limited to loyalists who agreed with his plans to centralize the securities business in Montreal. A few months later, however, he purchased back the Royal Securities name, and purchased a majority share of stock through the Utilities Securities Corporation and Montreal Trust, the two organizations he controlled.

Aitken then invited new shareholders, handpicked Montrealers, to purchase the remaining stock in Royal Securities. Among the first he sought out were Sir Edward Clouston and Arthur Doble, Clouston's executive assistant at the Bank of Montreal. He then included loyal transplants to Montreal such as Cahan and Lovett. Unlike Aitken's lawyers, however, Clouston and Doble had to keep their affiliation with Aitken hidden because of the Bank of Montreal's close affiliation with the Royal Trust Company. They could not be seen supporting a competing trust company such as Montreal Trust.

The reconfiguration of Montreal Trust and the establishment of Montreal Engineering would turn Aitken from a follower into a major leader and innovator in Canadian business. The new interloper from the sticks of New Brunswick quickly became known to the Montreal establishment. No one was neutral to Aitken. While he was liked by Clouston and his most inner circle, he was distrusted or hated by others for his disruptive business practices and what many viewed as his hubris. These views would become increasingly polarized as Aitken moved into the merger business and became a millionaire almost overnight.

Merger Promoter

By the end of 1908, Aitken was running out of new security issues. The downturn caused by the financial panic of 1907 had run its short course and a full-fledge bull market was gaining momentum as the price of shares and the volume of transactions began to climb in the Montreal, Toronto, New York, and London stock exchanges. Aitken especially wanted to tap the much larger British investment market through the City of London, which he visited in the last two months of 1908. He concluded that his Caribbean utility companies were not large enough to attract the kind of attention he needed in order to pique the interest of most British investors, but they would be willing to buy bonds and shares in very large industrial enterprises.[29]

As soon as he returned from London, Aitken began to scout out opportunities. Infused with new capital and a network of companies he controlled, he began to examine the opportunities presented by merging existing companies under a more progressive management team prepared to employ new industrial techniques and centralize manufacturing in order to gain economies of scale and scope. He looked at numerous companies but was most interested in cement and steel enterprises, industrial products that were the two most critical inputs of the building and manufacturing boom in the years immediately preceding the First World War.

Aitken started with the cement industry, judging that the producers in the country looked ripe for the picking. The manufacture of cement had recently been revolutionized by scientific and industrial improvements that required significant new investments in powerful rotating kilns and a much scaled-up manufacturing process. By combining some of the newest and most efficient plants with some of the older companies with name and product recognition, Aitken could create a company capable of manufacturing most of the cement in the country and perhaps, eventually, set prices in a market notorious for cyclical swings. To get added leverage in negotiating options to purchase with the targeted companies, Aitken struck a deal with (the recently knighted) Sir Edward Clouston for the Bank of Montreal to act as the cement merger's banker.[30]

While Clouston insisted on a deal that was low risk (yet high profit) for the bank, he personally signed up for $333,000 of the merger's underwriting. He was joined by his assistant Arthur Doble and by William E. Stavert, the superintendent of the Bank of Montreal's Maritime branches, each of whom underwrote $100,000. Rodolphe Forget, the prominent French-Canadian financier whose mansion[31] was a

Figure 8.4 Wm. Notman & Son, *Edward S. Clouston, Montreal,* 1899. McCord Museum, II-130516.1.

couple of blocks from Aitken's own house, took a whopping $500,000 of the underwriting, an amount that slightly exceeded Aitken's own share. A long-time Aitken ally, Forget was a millionaire with deep pockets and was chair of the Montreal Stock Exchange from 1907 until 1909.[32] This meant that close to three-quarters of the $2 million cement underwriting was held by the Bank of Montreal men, Forget and Aitken, a real made-in-Montreal merger even if the industrial plants were spread throughout the country.[33]

With the Bank of Montreal as the proposed merger's banker, prospective cement company owners for the merger were in powerful financial hands. After Aitken

Figure 8.5 Edward S. Clouston's Montreal residence, Upper Peel Street, Montreal, c. 1890. McCord Museum, MP-0000.2345.8.

explained all the benefits that would flow from the merger to the chief shareholders, Charles Cahan swooped in to do the dirty work of negotiating as low a price as possible for the purchase price of the individual companies. Twelve companies were brought into the merger by the summer of 1909. Ambitiously styled *the* Canada Cement Company, the merger was among the first and largest of the consolidations of the great Canadian merger wave of 1909–13. To raise new money for the company, $29 million worth of face-value stock was issued to new investors who were eager to buy the shares.

The underwriting – a guarantee to repurchase if investors were not forthcoming – turned out to be a fantastic money maker for the small group of underwriters. With the successful flotation of the merger's securities, Aitken was hailed as the financial wizard of St. James Street. A short time after the merger, the *Busy Man's Magazine* (soon to be renamed *Maclean's*) described him as a financial Napoleon, "courageous, confident, insistent, and yet a man of impulse."[34] If it had stopped there, everything would have been fine, but lingering unhappiness from a few of the cement owners persisted and would become a major headache for both Clouston and Aitken later in 1910.

In the meantime, Aitken negotiated and launched two new consolidations in Canada: Canadian Car and Foundry and the Steel Company of Canada (Stelco). Aitken had originally intended to establish one enormous integrated steel company by combining the iron and steel manufacturers of Nova Scotia with the secondary steel manufacturers in Montreal and southern Ontario. However, his old associates in Halifax, still resentful about Aitken's shift of his operations and men to Montreal, thwarted his ambitions. Instead, Aitken focused on two somewhat smaller mergers. He started with the railway car manufacturers, the equivalent of today's aircraft industry.

Between 1904 and 1910, the production of steel rails in Canada grew tenfold, from 40,000 short tons to 410,000 tons while track mileage was expanded by roughly 20 per cent.[35] Naturally, the demand for rolling stock grew apace. In 1904, the Canadian Pacific Railway's Angus car plant began operating in Montreal, the same year that a group of American investors set up their own car factory – the Canada Car Company – in Montreal. This was followed in 1906 by a third car manufacturing plant in the city, the Dominion Car and Foundry Company. Aitken put Canada Car and Dominion Car and Foundry together with Rhodes Curry, a rolling stock manufacturer in Amherst, Nova Scotia, that he had refinanced just months before. The flotation of the shares of the new company went even smoother than Canada Cement and, once again, Aitken made buckets of money for himself and fellow financiers. The new securities were in such demand by investors that he was able to sell the bonds of the Canadian Car and Foundry merger at 2.5 per cent above par value.[36]

Although Aitken's dream of a Canadian steel monopoly headquartered in Montreal had been dashed, he quickly accepted a less ambitious but profitable approach. He readily accepted an invitation by Sir Edward Clouston to meet with William McMaster, the largest shareholder in, and managing director of, the Montreal Rolling Mills.[37] Clouston was the figurehead president as Montreal Rolling Mills had been a long-time client of the Bank of Montreal. An old man, McMaster wanted to sell out at a high price through a steel merger. Aitken then assembled options on the companies he thought would best fit within an integrated steel company, including the Dominion Wire Manufacturing Company of Montreal and three steel product manufacturers in southern Ontario. The result was the Steel Company of Canada (Stelco). This would turn out to be an even more lucrative merger than the previous two, although the Toronto syndicate representing the Ontario interests felt that Aitken and his fellow St. James Street financiers had got the better of the deal.[38]

Grumbling about the profits made in such mergers among the underwriters and the largest shareholders of the companies being merged was par for the course. However, the "internal" discord concerning the Canada Cement merger went well beyond the usual. Admittedly, Aitken played hardball in his initial assessment of the value of the plants coming into the merger. Since he was in a rush to get the new securities sold before the market became saturated with other mergers, Aitken agreed that the final amount would only be determined after a formal appraisal, sometime after the merger. To the dismay of the cement owners, these adjustments almost always ended up in Aitken's favour. However, in one case, Aitken refused to provide an option on one of the major enterprises in the country, Western Canada Cement, ultimately forcing the company into bankruptcy. The assets were then snapped up by Canada Cement at fire-sale prices.

The owners of Canada Cement felt that they had been misled by Aitken and Cahan who had promised to purchase the company. However, they had no intention of doing so. A close financial inspection had revealed that the company had hidden the true state of its indebtedness and would only weaken the merger. Playing for time, Aitken purposely let the company think its problems would soon be solved by the merger only to be left in the cold. As weeks turned into months, and still no option, Sir Sandford Fleming, Western Canada Cement's chief shareholder, launched a public attack. First, Sir Sandford attacked Aitken and the merger. Rather than serving to embarrass Aitken into bringing Western Canada Cement into the merger, the tactic produced the opposite reaction.

Irritated, Aitken worked with Clouston to bring Sir Sandford's company to the ground. Heavily indebted to the Bank of Montreal, Western Canada Cement was called on its loans. Of course, as both Aitken and Clouston were aware, the company was unable to pay. Royal Trust then began proceedings in the Supreme Court of Alberta to get consent to sell Western Canada Cement's assets. In February 1911, Canada Cement acquired the assets. Sir Sandford then shifted his attack to the Bank of Montreal, which, by this time, realized it had a very embarrassing problem on its hands.[39] When the Bank of Montreal's board of directors discovered that three of its senior officers, including the man who had been groomed to be president, had been working hand-in-hand with Aitken potentially against the interests of the Bank of Montreal, the matter was quietly settled. Clouston resigned for health reasons while Arthur Doble left the bank to become the new manager for the Royal Securities' Montreal office as Aitken departed for England. William E. Stavert left to join Charles Cahan's newly established investment bank, Corporation Agencies.[40]

Keeping the Canada Cement affair secret was essential to protecting the reputation and position of the Bank of Montreal. Clouston's name was never publicly associated with the scandal. Nor were Doble and Stavert publicly implicated. Indeed, a couple of decades later, Stavert was able to return to the Bank of Montreal in a senior role.[41] Aitken was not so lucky. He was publicly roasted in the newspapers, particularly in the agrarian press in Western Canada where he was seen as a Central Canadian plutocrat and monopolist who was responsible for fixing prices in the industry, even though the retail price of cement continued to drop throughout the period.[42]

In comparison to Aitken who would later delight in the image of himself as a scoundrel, Sir Edward Clouston's fall from grace was quietly tragic. He had been judged unworthy by the members of his own bank board, a veritable who's who of the Montreal establishment.[43] Even if the bank did everything it could to avoid causing Clouston personal embarrassment when he announced his resignation in November 1911 – the bank gave him a retainer and allowed him to remain on the board of directors – Clouston had to continue living with the shame of it all. The bank had also stated that his departure was necessitated by health, an excuse perhaps not believed at the time given Clouston's good physical condition, but there may have been something more to it.[44] On 23 November 1912, Clouston went to visit Arthur Doble at the Royal Securities' office on St. James Street. Part-way through the conversation, Clouston suddenly collapsed and died from what was then called "apoplexy," a term at the time commonly used for either a cerebral haemorrhage or a stroke.[45] He was only sixty-three years of age.

Although Aitken had to take most of the heat in the Canada Cement scandal, he could deal with it at a safe distance from Canada. When he and Gladys had departed for Britain after he completed the Steel Company of Canada merger in the summer of 1910, they thought they were going for an extended vacation. The bombs from the Canada Cement scandal had not yet exploded when he boarded the steamer in New York City headed for Britain in August 1910. However, the rumours about Aitken's arrogance and sharp practices had been circulating in the Square Mile for many months before he left. The gossip only accelerated as those who felt bested by Aitken in his mergers had the opening to launch their own attacks.

By the time he was headed to England, Aitken was feeling rejected by Montreal society. Just months before, his application for membership in the Mount Royal Club had been turned down. The most prestigious gentleman's club in Canada, the Mount Royal Club was described by Lord Birkenhead as "one of the best clubs I know in the New World, with the indefinable atmosphere about it of a good London club."[46] From its founding in 1899, it had become the place to be among the city's business elite. Understandably, Aitken wanted to be able to rub shoulders and dine with the mighty, especially the powerful individuals who sat on the boards of the Canadian Pacific Railway and the Bank of Montreal, the two most august institutions in the country.[47] It is hardly surprising that Aitken had been blackballed given the way he had upset the establishment applecart in Montreal.[48]

Little wonder that Aitken's vacation turned into a permanent move. In fact, there was no real vacation. Almost as soon as he arrived, Aitken established a branch of Royal Securities in the City of London and bought a mansion in the countryside, all courtesy of his merger profits. In fact, his life was about to change dramatically. In addition to the securities business, he began to invest in British firms such as Rolls Royce, buy newspapers, and enter politics. Although he was now across the ocean, Aitken's associates in Montreal continued to upset the once predictable world of Montreal finance. Through his enterprises and his young transplants from New Brunswick and Nova Scotia, the financial world of the Square Mile would continue to face the gale of creative destruction originally generated by Aitken.

Aitken's Continuing Legacy: Creative Destruction in the Square Mile

Although Aitken would continue to run Royal Securities from his base in London, he had to leave the day-to-day business to his manager in Montreal. This task remained in the hands of Arthur Doble who was named president of Royal Securities in 1912. However, Doble's overall direction of Royal Securities was being supervised in London by Aitken and, increasingly in Canada, by Izaak Walton Killam

(1885–1955). In the interwar years, this "mystery man of Canadian finance" became one of the most powerful investment bankers in Canada. From his perch on St. James Street, Killam would become one of the wealthiest men in Canada. After his death, the Government of Canada honoured his request to use his inheritance taxes to establish the Canada Council for the Arts. Money from his estate also financed the Killam Trusts to fund academic research and activities, the Izaak Walton Killam Hospital for Children in Halifax, and the Montreal Neurological Institute, now part of the McGill University Health Centre network.[49]

Originally hailing from Yarmouth, Nova Scotia, Killam started out as a salesman in the Halifax and Saint John offices.[50] In 1909, at twenty-four years of age, Killam established and managed the Royal Securities' branch office in Quebec City. By the end of 1910, he was managing – side-by-side with Aitken – the Royal Securities' office in London, England. In 1914, Killam was sent to Montreal to figure out what was wrong with the head office. Aitken felt that Arthur Doble and his people had become too complacent. Ward C. Pitfield, an ambitious salesman from Saint John, New Brunswick, who had been recently hired by Aitken, accompanied Killam in the review of the Montreal head office.[51]

The visit caught Arthur Doble by surprise. He had received kudos from Aitken for successfully steering Royal Securities through the sharp market downturn in 1913. Dismay turned to shock when Killam and Pitfield began to take over the day-to-day management, cutting overhead and pushing more sales. Doble complained to Aitken that the place was beginning to be "run like a pawn shop instead of a respectable business," but the last statement of Doble's plea convinced Aitken that his Montreal manager had, in fact, become like many of the staid bankers, insurance men, and financiers that he had fought so hard to displace in Montreal: "After all our past successes I do not see why we should not keep up some degree of appearance and preserve our self-respect."[52]

To Aitken, this statement simply meant that Doble was more concerned with appearance than reality, and he encouraged Killam and Pitfield to continue to take a wrecking ball to Doble's operations and replace it with an efficient operation focused on getting immediate results. By the end of 1914, Doble resigned. Killam took over as general manager with Pitfield as a second-in-command.[53]

With the First World War came further changes. Early in 1915, Aitken engineered his own appointment as eyewitness for the Canadian Expeditionary Force in Europe, in charge of recording the war through paintings and managing the information flow between the front line and Ottawa.[54] To make himself as free as possible for wartime work, he turned over the presidency of the Royal Securities Corporation, though he would not sell his ownership shares to Killam until after the war. Effectively, however, Killam became the sole manager of Royal Securities from 1915 until his death. He forged an even tighter relationship with Montreal Engineering and acquired more utility enterprises throughout the Americas.[55] By the early 1920s, Royal Securities and Montreal Engineering had acquired and converted hydroelectric and street railway operations in Bolivia, Venezuela, El Salvador, Mexico, Cuba, Puerto Rico, and Newfoundland.[56]

In 1926, Killam established the International Power Company. Working hand in glove with Montreal Engineering and Royal Securities, this innovative holding company provided technical-engineering, construction, financial, management, and accounting services and consulting advice to the family of utility enterprises. International Power and its family of companies were so successful that they managed to weather the 1929 stock market crash better than the two other major utility holding companies in Canada – Brazilian Traction and Mexico Tramways.[57]

Although Killam most directly carried on Aitken's legacy on St. James Street, other transplanted Maritimers who had trained under Aitken would play major roles in the city's financial scene but through their own businesses. Of these, Arthur J. Nesbitt was the most notable.[58] After leaving Royal Securities in 1909, Nesbitt set up his own securities house, the Investment Trust Company, to become a merger promoter in his own right. His mergers included Canadian Cereal and Milling (1910), Canadian Steel Foundries (1911), and the International Milling Company of Canada (1911). He sold many of his securities in the British market through Investment Trust's branch office in London.

Towards the end of 1911, Nesbitt dropped Investment Trust in favour of forming a new financial vehicle with his friend and partner, Peter Thomson. Styled Nesbitt, Thomson and Company, the new investment firm had a head office on St. James Street and a branch office in Hamilton. The firm initially specialized in mining and natural resource industries, including new electric power generating companies. Nesbitt used his experience of merger promotion to make Nesbitt Thomson one of the leading merger promoters in Canada during the merger wave in the second half of the 1920s.[59]

Nesbitt was the brains behind the establishment of the Power Corporation of Canada, a holding company for hydroelectric utilities financed by Nesbitt Thomson. Beginning operations in 1925, Nesbitt served as Power Corporation's first president. Two years later, Nesbitt purchased the Ogilvy department store in downtown Montreal, which his eldest son, James Aird Nesbitt, would manage for the next half century.[60] Nesbitt's family lived in Westmount in a large house he purchased in 1910. Nesbitt's second son, A. Deane Nesbitt, would take his father's position in

Nesbitt Thomson and the presidency of Power Corporation.[61] A. Deane Nesbitt would go on to organize the financing of the TransCanada pipeline in the 1950s, the largest natural gas pipeline in the world at the time.[62]

Conclusion

In a book about the Square Mile in Montreal, it may seem strange to have a chapter on an individual who only lived in the city for three years. In this context, Max Aitken may seem an anomaly. However, the financial changes wrought by Aitken and his fellow Maritimers would leave a permanent mark in Montreal and Canada. The financial enterprises they spawned – Royal Securities, Montreal Trust, Montreal Engineering, Nesbitt Thomson and Power Corporation – would be major edifices in the landscape of the Square Mile in the twentieth century.

Behind these enterprises and individuals was Max Aitken. He was the originator of this gale of creative destruction in the financial world of Montreal and through Montreal to the rest of Canada. He could say, as Julius Caesar did in a letter to the Roman Senate reporting on a recent victory, "I came, I saw, I conquered" (*Veni, vidi, vici*). Although he departed the Square Mile in 1910 with a tarnished reputation, his legacy would continue for decades.

NOTES

1 There are many biographies of Lord Beaverbrook but the most balanced account (though focused on his life in Britain) was written by Anne Chisholm and Michael Davie, *Beaverbrook: A Life* (London: Hutchison, 1992). Although heavily biased in his favour, A.J.P. Taylor's *Beaverbrook* (New York: Simon & Schuster, 1972) is comprehensive. The most recent and salaciously revealing volume by Charles Williams, *Max Beaverbrook: Not Quite a Gentleman* (London: Biteback Publishing, 2019), briefly summarizes Aitken's Canadian years, including his time in Montreal.

2 Joseph Schumpeter, *Capitalism, Socialism and Democracy* (1942; repr., London: Routledge, 1994), 82–3.

3 Aitken's failures and his subsequent successes are amusingly covered by New Brunswick novelist David Adams Richards in *Extraordinary Canadians: Lord Beaverbrook* (Toronto: Penguin Canada, 2011).

4 Gregory P. Marchildon, *Profits and Politics: Beaverbrook and the Gilded Age of Canadian Finance* (Toronto: University of Toronto Press, 1996), 19.

5 For an entertaining account of these and other ventures, see Richards's *Lord Beaverbrook.*

6 James D. Frost, *Merchant Princes: Halifax's First Family of Finance, Ships and Steel* (Toronto: Lorimer, 2003); J.B. Cahill, "Stairs, John Fitzwilliam," in *Dictionary of Canadian Biography*, vol. 13, *1901–1910* (Toronto: University of Toronto Press, 1994), 978–82.

7 Gregory P. Marchildon, "John F. Stairs, Max Aitken and the Scotia Group: Finance Capitalism and Industrial Decline in the Maritimes, 1890–1914," in *Farm, Factory and Fortune: New Studies in the Economic History of the Maritime Provinces*, ed. Kris Inwood (Fredericton, NB: Acadiensis Press, 1993), 197–218.

8 Marchildon, *Profits and Politics*, 72–129.

9 W.L. Grant and Gregory P. Marchildon, "Horne, Sir William Cornelius Van (1843–1915): Railway Builder and Financier in Canada," in *Oxford Dictionary of National Biography* (Oxford: Oxford University Press, 2004); Theodore D. Regehr, "Van Horne, Sir William Cornelius," in *Dictionary of Canadian Biography* vol. 14, *1911–1920* (Toronto: University of Toronto Press, 1998), 1030–6. More recent biographies include Valerie Knowles, *William C. Van Horne: Railway Titan* (Toronto: Dundurn Press, 2010). The Van Horne Mansion was located at the corner of Sherbrooke Street and Stanley Street, once a landmark in the heart of Montreal's Square Mile. It was demolished in 1973.

10 Carman Miller, "Clouston, Sir Edward Seaborne," in *Dictionary of Canadian Biography*, vol. 14, *1911–1920* (Toronto: University of Toronto Press, 1998), 219–22.

11 Marchildon, *Profits and Politics*, 47.

12 Montreal's population in 1901 (268,826) and 1911 (470,480) was well above Toronto's population in 1901 (208,040) and 1911 (381,383). See Peter G. Goheen, "Some Aspects of Canadian Urbanization from 1850 to 1921," *Urban History Review/Revue d'histoire urbaine*, suppl. issue (1980), 78.

13 J.S. Johnson, "History and Organization of the Montreal Stock Exchange" (master's thesis, McGill University, 1934); Ranald C. Michie, "The Canadian Securities Market, 1850–1914," *Business History Review* 62, no. 1 (1988): 35–73. On the pre-history of the Montreal Stock Exchange, see David McKeagan, "Development of a Mature Securities Market in Montreal from 1817 to 1874," *Business History* 51, no. 1 (2009): 59–76.

14 Joe Martin and Darren Karn, *How Toronto Became the Financial Capital of Canada: The Stock Market Crash of 1929* (Toronto: University of Toronto, Rotman School of Management Case Study, 2012).

15 This estimate was based on the Intercolonial Railway's *Maritime Express* train between Halifax and Montreal from 1900 and 1912. See "*Maritime Express*," Wikipedia, accessed 24 February 2023, https://en.wikipedia.org/wiki/Maritime_Express.

16 Aitken in a letter to Lovett, quoted in Marchildon, *Profits and Policies*, 111. On the names of businesses on St. James Street, see "Saint Jacques Street," Wikipedia, accessed 24 February 2023, https://en.wikipedia.org/wiki/Saint_Jacques_Street.

17 Marchildon, *Profits and Politics*, 67.

18 Sarah Boumedda, "An Architectural Gem," *The City Magazine: Concordia University's Department of Journalism*, 2019, accessed 24 February 2023, http://thecitymag.concordia.ca/Archive/The_City_2019/italian-consulate-is-an-architectural-gem (site no longer active).

19 "Janet Gladys 'Bodie' Aitken Kidd," Find a Grave, accessed 24 February 2023, https://www.findagrave.com/memorial/11317176/janet-gladys-kidd.

20 "CPT John William Maxwell 'Max' Aitken," Find a Grave, accessed 24 February 2023, https://www.findagrave.com/memorial/169186748/john-william_maxwell-aitken.

21 On Cahan and Lovett, see Gregory P. Marchildon, "The Role of Lawyers in Corporate Promotion and Management: Case Study and Theoretical Speculations," *Business and Economic History* 19 (1990): 193–202.

22 "Montreal Gains Three Good Halifax Men," *Halifax Herald*, 14 May 1907, 1.

23 Aitken in a letter to Lovett, 20 March 1907, quoted in Marchildon, *Profits and Politics*, 112.

24 Aitken in a letter to Lovett, 22 April 1907, quoted in Marchildon, *Profits and Politics*, 112.

25 Gregory P. Marchildon, "The Montreal Engineering Company and International Power: Overcoming the Limitations of the Free-Standing Utility," in *The Free-Standing Company in the World Economy, 1830–1996*, ed. Mira Wilkins and Harm Schröter (New York: Oxford University Press, 1998), 391–418.

26 J. Sexton, *Monenco: The First 75 Years* (n.p., 1982).

27 Marchildon, *Profits and Politics*, 85.

28 On the US origins of the 1907 Financial Panic, see Gregory P. Marchildon, "A Financial Panic Results from a Run on the Knickerbocker Trust," in *Great Events in History II: Business and Commerce* (Pasadena, CA: Salem Press, 1994), 134–9.

29 Gregory P. Marchildon, "'Hands across the Water': Canadian Industrial Financiers in the City of London, 1905–20," *Business History* 34, no. 3 (1992): 69–95.

30 Marchildon, *Profits and Politics*, 151–67.

31 For a picture of this still-standing house at 3685 Du Musée Street, see "Fichier:Rodolphe Forget House, Montreal 01.jpg," Wikipedia, accessed 24 February 2023, https://fr.wikipedia.org/wiki/Fichier:Rodolphe_Forget_House,_Montreal_01.jpg. Also see Victor Swoboda, "Forget Mansion Stands Proudly," *Montreal Gazette*, 29 May 2013, https://montrealgazette.com/homes/forget-mansion-stands-proudly.

32 Jack Jedwab, "Forget, Sir Rodolphe," in *Dictionary of Canadian Biography*, vol. 14, *1911–1920* (Toronto: University of Toronto Press, 1998), 366–71.

33 E.R. Wood and the Dominion Securities Corporation of Toronto held the last 25 per cent of the underwriting. Marchildon, *Profits and Politics*, 164–5.

34 W.R. McCurdy, "A Young Canadian with a Genius for Organization," *Busy Man's Magazine* [*Maclean's*], January 1910, 24. McCurdy was Aitken's journalist friend from Halifax; see Marchildon, *Profits and Politics*, 303.

35 M.C. Urquhart and K.A.H. Buckley, eds, *Historical Statistics of Canada* (Cambridge, UK: Cambridge University Press, 1965), series Q282, Q286, S24, S78, and S85.

36 Marchildon, *Profits and Politics*, 183–6. The plants were eventually purchased by Bombardier. On the post-merger history of Canadian Car and Foundry, see "Canadian Car and Foundry," Wikipedia, accessed 24 February 2023, https://en.wikipedia.org/wiki/Canadian_Car_and_Foundry.

37 On Montreal Rolling Mills, see Larry McNally, "Technical Advance and Stagnation: The Case of Nail Production in Nineteenth-Century Montreal," *Material History Review* 36 (1992): 38–48. Also see Desmond Bliek and Pierre Gauthier, "Understanding the Built Form of Industrialization along the Lachine Canal in Montreal," *Urban History Review / Revue d'histoire urbaine* 35, no. 1 (2006): 3–17.

38 Marchildon, *Profits and Politics*, 198–201.

39 Laurence B. Mussio, *Whom Fortune Favours: The Bank of Montreal and the Rise of North American Finance*, vol. 1, *A Dominion of Capital, 1817–1945* (Montreal: McGill-Queen's University Press, 2020), 168–9.

40 Marchildon, *Profits and Politics*, 178; Mussio, *Whom Fortune Favours*, 249.

41 In addition, Charles Cahan would become a director on the board of the Bank of Montreal. See Mussio, *Whom Fortune Favours*, 249.

42 Annual data (1900–14) on price per barrel of Portland cement from A. Ernest Epp, "Cooperation among Capitalists: The Canadian Merger Movement, 1909–13 (PhD diss., Johns Hopkins University, 1973), 459, 462, and reproduced in Marchildon, *Profits and Politics*, 159.

43 Clouston was on the board from 1905 until 1912. At the time of his death, the other board members were E.B. Greenshields (1886–1917); Sir William Macdonald of McDonald's Tobacco

(1887–1917); R.B. Angus of the Bank of Montreal and CPR (1891–1922); James Ross (1899–1913); David Morrice of Dominion Textile (1907–14); Thomas G. Shaunghnessy, president of the CPR from 1899 to 1918 (1907–23); Charles R. Hosmer of the CPR and founder of the Ritz-Carlton Hotel in Montreal (1908–17); A. Baumgarten, owner of the St. Lawrence Sugar Refining Company (1909–17); and Sir Vincent Meredith of the Bank of Montreal and Clouston's successor as general manager (1910–29). D. Forbes Angus (1912–43), H.R. Drummond (1912–57), and Sir Charles Gordon (1912–39) joined the board in 1912. See Merrill Denison, *Canada's First Bank: A History of the Bank of Montreal*, vol. 2 (Toronto: McClelland & Stewart, 1967), 422.

44 Miller, "Clouston," 221.

45 Marchildon, *Profits and Politics*, 230.

46 Frederick Edwin Smith Birkenhead, *My American Visit* (1918; repr., New York: Arno Press, 1974), 214. On the history of the Mount Royal Club, see Donald Mackay, *The Square Mile: Merchant Princes of Montreal* (Vancouver: Douglas & McIntyre, 1987).

47 Lord Strathcona was the first president of the Mount Royal Club. See Kathryn J. Banham, "The Architecture and Painting Collection of the Mount Royal Club, Montreal, 1899–1920" (MA thesis, Concordia University, 2006), who correctly observed that the small membership (sixty-five at its founding) "represented the wealth and power in the city" (7).

48 Marchildon, *Profits and Politics*, 152.

49 Douglas How, *Canada's Mystery Man of High Finance* (Hantsport, NS: Lancelot Press, 1986).

50 Marchildon, *Profits and Politics*, 67–8.

51 How, *Canada's Mystery Man*, 86. Born in Saint John, New Brunswick, W.C. (Ward Chipman) Pitfield would go on to establish his own firm – Pitfield, MacKay, Ross. His son, Ward C. Pitfield Jr., would go on to lead the investment firm in the Square Mile until 1984, when it was merged with the Toronto-based Dominion Securities Corporation (Ian Austen and Lenny Glynn, "Big Merger on Bay Street" *Maclean's Magazine*, 7 May 1984), 48–9, which, in turn four years later, was acquired by the Royal Bank of Canada. See Duncan McDowall, *Quick to the Frontier: Canada's Royal Bank* (Toronto: McClelland & Stewart, 1993), 429, and Don Nerbas, "Adapting to Decline: The Changing Business World of the Bourgeoisie in Saint John, NB, in the 1920s," *Canadian Historical Review* 89, no. 2 (2008): 151–87. His grandson, Michael Pitfield, was Clerk of the Privy Council and Secretary to the Cabinet under Prime Minister Pierre Trudeau from 1975 until 1982. See Peter Bregg, "Pierre Trudeau Ally Michael Pitfield was Canada's Top Bureaucrat," *Globe and Mail*, 20 October 2017, https://www.theglobeandmail.com/news/national/trudeau-ally-michael-pitfield-was-canadas-top-bureaucrat/article36680434/.

52 Aitken in a letter to Doble, 15 June 1914, quoted in Marchildon, *Profits and Politics*, 234.

53 Marchildon, *Profits and Politics*, 234.

54 See Maria Tippett, *Art at the Service of War: Canada, Art and the Great War* (Toronto: University of Toronto Press, 1984).

55 Sexton, *Monenco*.

56 Marchildon, "Montreal Engineering Company," 398–9; How, *Canada's Mystery Man*, 58.

57 Marchildon, "Montreal Engineering Company," 398–414. The histories of the other two companies are covered in Duncan McDowall, *The Light: Brazilian Traction, Light and Power Company Limited, 1899–1945* (Toronto: University of Toronto Press, 1988); and Christopher Armstrong and H.V. Nelles, *Southern Exposure: Canadian Promoters in Latin America and the Caribbean, 1896–1930* (Toronto: University of Toronto Press, 1988).

58 A.R. Deane Nesbitt, *Dry Goods and Pickles: The Story of Nesbitt, Thomson* (Toronto: Nesbitt, Thomson, 1989).

59 Marchildon, *Profits and Politics*, 145–9.
60 "Arthur James Nesbitt," Wikipedia, accessed 24 February 2023, https://en.wikipedia.org/wiki/Arthur_James_Nesbitt.
61 "Arthur Deane Nesbitt Norman Hillmer," Wikipedia, accessed 24 February 2023, https://en.wikipedia.org/wiki/Arthur_Deane_Nesbitt Norman Hillmer; and Norman Hillmer, "Arthur Deane Nesbitt," *The Canadian Encyclopedia*, last updated 16 December 2013, https://www.thecanadianencyclopedia.ca/en/article/arthur-deane-nesbitt.
62 William Kilbourn, *Pipeline: Transcanada and the Great Debate: A History of Business and Politics* (Toronto: Clarke Irwin, 1970).

Figure V.13 Wm. Notman & Son, *The Shaar Hashomayim Synagogue, McGill College Avenue,* c. 1910–11. McCord Museum, VIEW 10763.

Houses of Worship

According to the 1901 census, 76 per cent of the Montreal population of 375,000 identified as Roman Catholics, 19 per cent as Protestants, and 2 per cent as Jews. It would be expected that the Square Mile, with about 25,000 residents, would present a similar demographic portrait. However, by the last decade of the nineteenth century, there were eleven Protestant churches, two synagogues, and only the Roman Catholic cathedral that were located either within or bordering on the Square Mile. Another four Protestant churches were located within close walking distance.

These Christian denominations established their houses of worship in free-standing buildings on prominent sites, usually fronting on either Dorchester or St. Catherine Streets. In contrast, the synagogues occupied secondary locations on north–south streets. The Shaar Hashomayim synagogue opened in 1886 on McGill College Avenue, and the Spanish and Portuguese synagogue opened in 1890 on Stanley Street. In contrast to the churches, which were almost all neo-Gothic in style, the synagogues were decidedly outré – the Spanish and Portuguese synagogue was in an Egyptian revival idiom and the Shaar Hashomayim incorporated elements of the Moorish Revival. They made a striking contrast to the adjacent row houses.

CHAPTER NINE

"Glad of your help": Scottish Architects in Montreal, 1860–1940

Annmarie Adams

Introduction

Scottish-born architects Percy Nobbs (1875–1964) and Ramsay Traquair (1874–1952) figure largely in the history of Montreal architecture. Nobbs designed many institutional buildings, especially at McGill University, that established an urban vernacular style we now associate with the city, but mostly outside the Square Mile. In John Bland's eulogy for his colleague, Nobbs, on 15 November 1964, the influential architectural educator linked Nobbs's architecture to his character: "[A] series of beautiful buildings established for all to see and enjoy, his remarkable humanity, unerring taste, scholarship and love for tradition."[1] Residences by Nobbs, such as the red-brick, Westmount house he designed for himself in 1913, marked the importation of Scottish arts-and-crafts ideals to Canada. Like its British counterpart, Scottish arts-and-crafts architecture was explicitly understated. It drew on rural and nature-based imagery, and even a handmade aesthetic, to showcase craftsmanship. It also professed a certain moral high ground, markedly different than the relatively ostentatious residential architecture that characterized much of Montreal's Square Mile, whose mansions often drew on classical and Beaux-Arts precedents.

Despite the fact that Traquair built nothing in Canada, he too was a cultural tastemaker. His main influence was through his magnum opus, *The Old Architecture of Quebec*, published in 1947, described at the time of his death five years later as "the standard authority on the subject."[2] The 324-page book comprises exquisite measured drawings and photographs of buildings of New France, many measured by McGill School of Architecture students and today conserved by the John Bland

Figure 9.1 John Colin Forbes, *Portrait of Ramsay Traquair*, n.d. McGill University Visual Arts Collection, 1973–263.

Canadian Architecture Collection.[3] Another indication of Traquair's cultural capital is that John Colin Forbes (1846–1925), a prominent Toronto-born, London-educated artist, painted his portrait. Forbes also painted Canadian Prime Ministers John A. Macdonald and Wilfrid Laurier, British Prime Minister William Gladstone, and King Edward VII and his Queen-empress Alexandra.[4] Both Traquair and Nobbs were influential educators of generations of Canadian architects, including those, like Bland, who went on to shape twentieth-century modernism. "Traquair taught many brilliant pupils and must have influenced them greatly," said McGill University

Figure 9.2 Harry Mayerovitch, *Portrait of Percy Nobbs*, n.d. John Bland Canadian Architecture Collection, McGill University, 2022–002.

registrar T.H. Matthews in 1952.[5] Bland called out Nobbs's unmatched skill as a teacher in the same eulogy: "[F]or those who were fortunate to be his students, we can say that he was the most gifted and admirable teacher we have known."[6]

Nobbs and Traquair were roughly the same age. They had known each other in Scotland, through arts-and-crafts architect Robert Lorimer, and became particularly close during their twenty-six overlapping years in Montreal, a relationship likely amplified by their shared Scottish heritage. Their career trajectories were also somewhat similar, although Nobbs was much more involved in practice and professional architectural associations. Architecture librarian and scholar Irena Murray, who collected much of this material for the John Bland Canadian Architecture Collection, says their trajectories were "opposite."[7] Nonetheless, Nobbs helped Traquair get hired at McGill and settle in Montreal. Traquair succeeded Nobbs as director of the School of Architecture and as Macdonald chair. Before accepting the job in Montreal, Traquair wrote to Nobbs: "[Y]ou and I know each other well enough to work together," he said, "and I should be glad of your help in every way that you care to give it."[8] Today, their framed portraits – Nobbs was painted by Montreal architect Harry Mayerovitch posthumously – sit happily together in the faculty meeting room of the School of Architecture they both directed. How did Nobbs and Traquair interact? Were other Scottish-born architects in Montreal "glad of help" from each other? How did their educations and earlier life experiences in Scotland shape their life stories in Canada? What do the ways Scottish architects interacted tell us about the architectural profession in Montreal and/or in Canada in the twentieth century?

Nearly twenty-five years ago, architectural historian Isabelle Gournay suggested that Scottish architects were particularly "adaptable to other cultures" as a way of explaining the massive diaspora of architects from Scotland in the nineteenth and twentieth centuries.[9] "[T]he contribution of Scots to empire was far in excess of their population size proportionate to the United Kingdom as a whole,'" claims architectural historian G.A. Bremner. "Whether as merchants, planters, soldiers, settlers, doctors, scientists, teachers, administrators, engineers, or even architects, they were to be found everywhere."[10] I propose adding the power of Scottish networking to Gournay's "chameleon effect" theory. My research shows that influential figures such as Percy Nobbs and Ramsay Traquair did not act very chameleon-like, but rather used their Scots backgrounds to stand out among Montreal's architects. Their Scottish backgrounds equipped them to articulate a Canadian architecture, based in local cultures, materials, and traditions. Even the ample evidence of how Nobbs and Traquair alone boosted each other's careers illuminates a Scottish buddy system that today would trump Canadian egalitarian values. This chapter begins to untangle the multilayered personal and professional relationships among Nobbs, Traquair, and other Scottish-born architects in Montreal, many of whom designed buildings in and near Montreal's Square Mile.[11]

Methodology and List of Architects

To understand the nature of this network of Scottish support among Montreal-based architects, I have employed a multilayered methodology. Biographical data can be effusive, and this approach was engaged in order to isolate a group of Scottish architects, almost like producing a group portrait over a long period. Firstly, I derived a list of Scottish-born Montreal architects from Robert G. Hill, a Toronto architect who has been amassing an enormous database, *Biographical Dictionary of Architects in Canada*, since the 1970s. Hill's material rendered a list of names across a long expanse of time, 1800–1950. This list was then supplemented by names of architects included in the *Dictionary of Scottish Architects* database, as having practised in Montreal or in Canada, for a total of forty-one architects.[12] Standard biographical sources – entries in reference works, obituaries, research papers, biographies and monographs, unpublished theses – were then mined for additional information on these architects' life stories. Where were they born and where did they die? Where were they educated? When did they arrive in Montreal? When available, where did they work? Who did they know and when? Sufficient biographical information was found on these forty-one architects to show how birthplace, education, professional networks, and mobility shaped their life stories and architectural culture in Montreal (see Table 9.1).

Birthplace

Did birthplace matter? Traquair and Nobbs were born one year and sixteen miles apart. Traquair was born in Edinburgh and Nobbs was born in nearby Haddington. This pattern of close colleagues sharing a birthplace (or close enough) was not exclusive to the academy. Inverness is a case in point.[13] Three architects of the list of forty-one were born in Inverness in the Scottish Highlands: John Archibald, Robert Findlay, and James Rhind. All three were prominent in Montreal, but especially Archibald and Findlay, who went on to design some of the city's signature buildings. Findlay, for example, designed Westmount City Hall and several fine dwellings in the Square Mile; Archibald, who arrived in Montreal in 1893 and entered into partnership with Charles Jewett Saxe in 1897, was responsible for hotels and school buildings. John Bland referred to him as a "culminating figure."[14] Not surprisingly, the careers of these Inverness-born architects overlapped considerably. Rhind and Findlay had both apprenticed with John Rhind, the older brother of James, in Scotland. In the case of Inverness, we can conclude that birthplace mattered.

Although Archibald designed only a few houses in the Square Mile, he was responsible for important buildings along its edges. The most spectacular was Montreal's 1930 Masonic Memorial Temple, on Sherbrooke Street at the corner of St. Marc Street. A monumental, neoclassical building of Queenston limestone, it was described at the time in *Construction* (1930) as akin to the Lincoln Memorial

Table 9.1 Biographical chart of forty-one Scottish architects who practised in Montreal

ARCHITECT	BORN	DIED	EDUCATION	ACTIVITY IN MONTREAL
Eric Mann	Edinburgh, 1848	Montreal, 1929	Apprentice, Sir David Bryce	Practised independently (from 1873); founding member of the PQAA (1890)
Andrew Edwin Martin	Glasgow, 1879	Unknown	Glasgow School of Art; Glasgow & West of Scotland Technical College	Hutchinson & Wood (1901–4); Brown & Vallance (1904–after 1912)
Thomas Mclaren	Perth, 1879	Montreal, 1967	Apprentice, George Penrose Kennedy Young (1894–8); Glasgow School of Art	Andrew Thomas Taylor (1902–c.1904); Bank of Montreal, under Frank Peden (1905); Peden & McLaren (1906–17)
David James Moir	Perth, 1885	Montreal, 1957	Apprentice, Maclaren & Mackay (1903–7); Glasgow School of Art	Nobbs & Hyde (1912–after 1945); taught occasionally at McGill School of Architecture
Percy Erskine Nobbs	Haddington, 1875	Montreal, 1964	School of Design, St. Petersburg; Edinburgh Collegiate School; Rowland Anderson's School of Applied Art, University of Edinburgh; apprentice, Robert Lorimer (1896–1901)	Macdonald Chair of Architecture (1904–9); Nobbs & Hyde (1910–44); Nobbs & Valentine (1944–50); Nobbs & Nobbs (1950–60); president of the PQAA (1924)
John Wilson Orrock	Edinburgh, 1870	Montreal, 196S	Trained with E. Calvert, Edinburgh Surveyor	Canadian Pacific Railway (1891–1937); Chief Draughtsman (1904), Engineer of Buildings (1924)
Arthur Prideaux	Cornwall, England, 1891 (moved to Edinburgh before 1907)	Montreal, 1937	Apprentice, J.N. Scott & A. Lorne Campbell (1907–11); Edinburgh College of Art	Nobbs & Hyde (1913–38)
James Robert Rhind	Inverness, 1853	Inverness, 1918	Apprentice, John Rhind (c. 1868–before 1880)	Supervising architect for Saxon Snell, RVH (1890–3)
James Seath-Smith	Cupar, 1864 (moved to Canada as a child)	Westmount, QC, 1947	Apprentice, John James Browne of Montreal	Fitzjames E. Browne (1893–before 1898); member of the PQAA (from 1898)

Andrew Sharp	Glasgow, c. 1876	California, c. 1986	Apprentice, John Hutchinson (1891–6); Glasgow School of Art	Robert Findlay (1900–2)
David Shennan	Dumfries, 1880	Montreal, 1968	Apprentice, John A. MacGregor (1896–9)	Saxe & Archibald (1906–15); John S. Archibald (c. 1919–33)
John Roxburgh Smith	Greenock, 1881	Montreal, 1975	Glasgow School of Art	E. & W.S. Maxwell (1904–14); James Cecil McDougall (1917–20); Maxwell Atelier, École des Beaux-Arts; Fetherstonhaugh & McDougall (1916–23); McDougall, Fleming & Smith (1946–after 1951); elected president of the PQAA (1941)
George M. Stewart	Glasgow, 1884	Montreal, 1951	Apprentice, Stewart & Paterson (1901–6); Glasgow School of Architecture	Member of the PQAA (from 1921); practised independently (from c. 1923)
Andrew Thomas Taylor	Edinburgh, 1850	London, England, 1937	Apprentice, Pilkington & Bell (1864–9); Royal Academy Schools; University College London	Practised independently (1883–1904); founding member and president of the PQAA (1890)
Francis Orr Templeton	Glasgow, 1904	Montreal, 1972	Apprentice, Sir John J. Burnet (c. 1922–before 1927); Glasgow School of Architecture	John S. Archibald (1929–32); Archibald & Illsley (after Second World War)
Alexander Cameron Todd	Unknown, 1879	Unknown	Apprentice, Steele & Balfour (1894–9); Glasgow School of Art	Robert Findlay (1906–7); A.H. Lapierre (1907–8); Brown & Vallance (1908–after 1912)
John Turnbull	Ayr, 1888	1968	Glasgow School of Art; Glasgow & West Technical College	E. & W.S. Maxwell (1912–20); James Cecil McDougall (1920–3, 1929–after 1930); Philip John Turner (1923–6); member of the PQAA (from 1931)

(*Continued*)

Table 9.1 (*Continued*)

ARCHITECT	BORN	DIED	EDUCATION	ACTIVITY IN MONTREAL
Ramsay Traquair	Edinburgh, 1876	Guysboro, NS, 1952	Edinburgh College of Art; apprentice, S.H. Capper (c. 1892–7)	Director of the School of Architecture, McGill (1913–38)
Hugh Allan Inglis Valentine	Dundee, 1904 (moved to Canada as a child)	Port Hope, ON, 1978	McGill University	Ross & MacDonald (1920–8); David R. Brown (1928–31); Bell Telephone (1935–44); Nobbs & Valentine (1944–50); chief architect (1950–70); president of the PQAA (1957)
John Wilson Wood	Kilmarnock, 1885	Unknown, 1964	Kilmarnock School of Art; apprentice, Andrew & Newlands (1900–5); Glasgow School of Art; Glasgow & West of Scotland Technical College; Maxwell Atelier, École des Beaux-Arts	Canadian Pacific Railway (1908–11); Hugh Griffith Jones (1911–33); Canadian National Railway (late 1930s)
James Wright	Glasgow, 1833	Montreal, 1911	Apprenticed to carpenter trade in 1848	Robert Findlay (1888); William S. Wright (1889 onward)

Design by Emily Cline based on earlier versions by Valentina Davila.

in Washington, DC, and the J.P. Morgan Library in New York City, both iconic American landmarks.[15] All three structures are relatively windowless and serve as memorials. Archibald excelled in the design of hospitals and hotels (many outside Montreal); he also designed several key buildings for working-class Montrealers. The antithesis of the Square Mile mansions in many ways, these buildings were nevertheless splendid and dignified. These would include the Montreal Technical School on University Street, just east of McGill University, and Baron Byng High School, on St. Urbain Street, where children of Jewish immigrant families were educated.

It is tempting to speculate on how Archibald's Scottishness may have brought him this wide range of jobs and clients. Bremner suggests that many Scots businesspeople were relatively ambitious:

> [I]t has been suggested by some that the Scottish presence throughout the empire tempered British imperialism in certain ways, giving it (in places, and at times) a particular Scottish character. Here colonial business and trade might be pointed to in particular, where an overrepresentation of Scots was evident. The reasons for this are varied, ranging from fewer opportunities in Scotland, to the relative inability of Scots to penetrate elite English business circles. This not only gave Scots reason to seek new prospects in the wider colonial world, but also the occasion to shape that world in their own image and interests.[16]

Archibald's small-town roots, for example, may have made him practical and wary of financial risk. Apparently, Archibald turned down jobs that might make his clients lose money. Also, he was known as the "business and construction" partner, complementing Saxe's more artistic leanings in his partnership with Charles J. Saxe. In certain instances, he appears to have used his personal network in order to get work. For example, he was a Freemason, which may have led to his commission for the Masonic Temple. The best example of an insider advantage may be Archibald's design for the Craig Street Terminal following his joining the Tramways Commission. Relatedly, Archibald may have hired Scottish brethren because of their Scottish roots, but not necessarily because of the particular town where they were born. The following architects from the list of forty-one architects worked at some time for Saxe & Archibald: James Bisset Crockart (born in Stirling, 1885), Thomas Morgan Forrest (born in Perth, 1879), and David Shennan (born in Dumfries, 1880).

Although the Inverness connections are intriguing, the two most common birthplaces for Montreal-Scottish architects were Glasgow and Edinburgh, the country's largest cities (see Figure 9.3). Of our forty-one architects, nine were born in Glasgow,

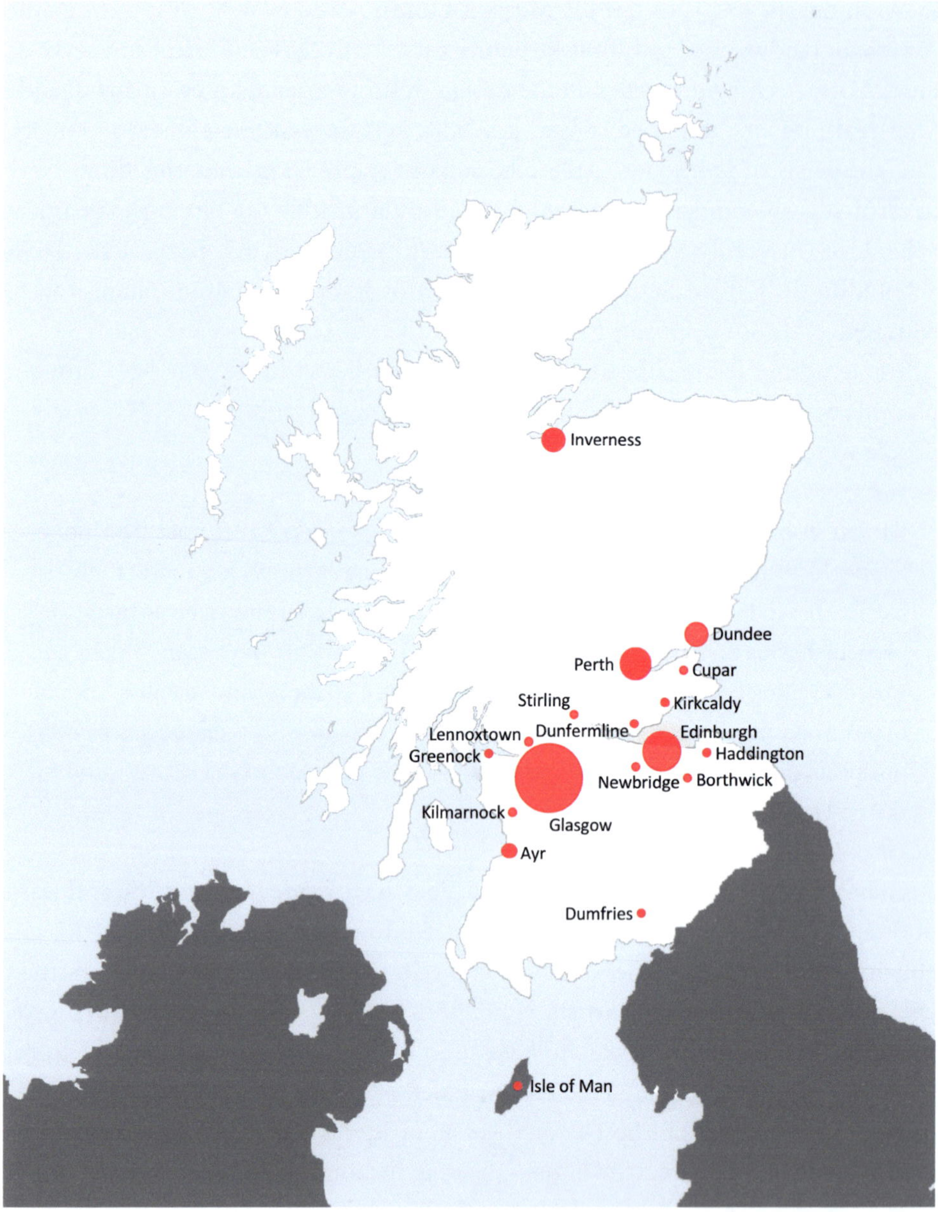

Figure 9.3 Map of Scottish-Canadian architects' birthplaces, showing most common locations, especially Glasgow. Design by Emily Cline based on earlier versions by Valentina Davila.

almost twice the number from Edinburgh (five). Particularly notable among those from Glasgow was James Wright, who eventually became a partner of Inverness-born Findlay. In terms of architectural production, Wright altered the house of the Honourable George Alexander Drummond in 1906, which had been designed by Edinburgh-born Andrew Taylor (see just below).[17] Andrew Francis Orr Templeton worked for Montreal-born Ian T. Archibald, the son of Inverness-born John Archibald in the post–Second World War period, when he partnered with Hugh Percival Illsley (who had joined the office of J. Archibald in 1922). The complex links among these architects through the Burnet office in Glasgow has been well studied in a PhD dissertation by Holly Kinnear.[18] Needless to say, it is not obvious that architects from Glasgow always worked for each other once in Montreal.

Examples of architects from multiple birthplaces working together in Montreal abound. Andrew Taylor, one of the best-known architects on the list of forty-one and the subject of a book-length biography, designed many buildings at McGill University and in the Square Mile. Originally from Edinburgh (as mentioned), Taylor employed Perth-born and Glasgow-educated Thomas McLaren. Between 1902 and 1904, McLaren assisted in the design of several Canadian bank buildings before taking a position at the Bank of Montreal's architectural department in 1905.[19]

Taylor designed significant mansions in the Square Mile with his London-based partner George Gordon.[20] Biographer Susan Wagg says: "[I]t was in this sector [the Square Mile] that Taylor was most active."[21] As explained above with regards to James Wright, a particularly significant house (see Figure 9.4) was for George Alexander Drummond in 1888–9, at the corner of Sherbrooke West and Metcalfe Streets.[22] Edinburgh-born Drummond, a wealthy businessman, was connected to Taylor through the Redpath family.[23] Wagg describes this house as "one of the city's grandest," noting the influence of American architect H.H. Richardson.[24] Taylor also added to one of the Square Mile's largest and most luxurious houses, Ravenscrag, extending the east wing in 1889 and enlarging the stables in 1898.[25] As Wagg has noted, Taylor was related by marriage to McGill University principal William Dawson. In 1891, Taylor married Mary Elliot, Dawson's daughter-in-law's sister, who was eighteen years his junior. Mary's sister Florence had married William Bell Dawson, son of the university administrator, "reinforc[ing] Taylor's ties to the university."[26]

Taylor's work spanned educational, residential, and business establishments, including branches of corporations run by powerful Square Mile men. His designs for banks are particularly distinctive in his oeuvre. As Wagg has noted, Taylor designed Bank of Montreal branches across Canada. In Montreal itself, however, the most significant works are his remodelling of the Bank of Montreal headquarters

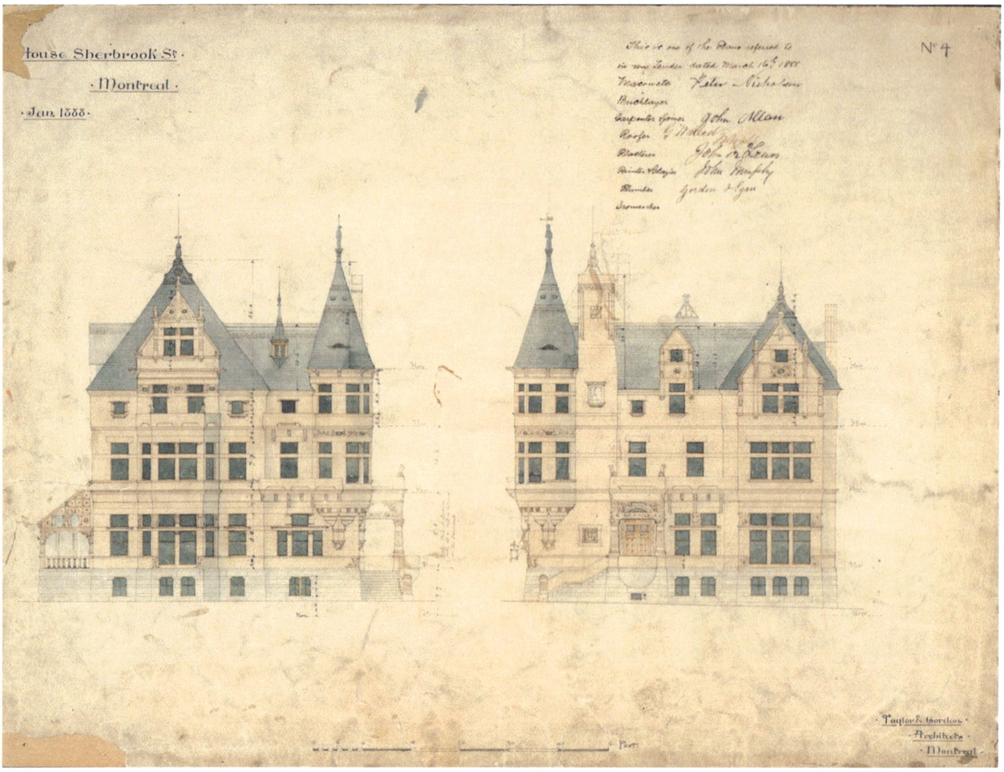

Figure 9.4 George Alexander Drummond's house, Montreal. Metcalfe Street elevation, 1888. Attributed to Andrew Taylor. Taylor and Gordon Fonds, John Bland Canadian Architecture Collection, McGill University Library.

on Place d'Armes; the Bank of Montreal branch at the corner of St. Catherine and Mansfield Streets, not far from the residence of George Drummond; and branches on Notre-Dame Street and in Pointe St. Charles, on the corner of Wellington and Madeleine Streets.

There are many examples like the connection between Taylor and McLaren through the banks that point to Scottish connections, as well as partnerships like Taylor and Gordon's, where one partner is born somewhere else. Percy Nobbs's partner after 1910, George Hyde, for example, was born in Montreal. Interestingly, Hyde worked for a time in the office of Taylor and Gordon. Another partner of Nobbs was Hugh Allen Inglis Valentine, who became partner upon the death of Hyde and is on the list of Scottish-born architects who were born in Dundee. It is worth noting that at least three of these architects – Archibald, Nobbs, and Wright – practised with their Montreal-born sons: Ian T. Archibald (1903–71), Francis John

Nobbs (1912–2000), and William S. Wright (1868–1939). Also notable is the fact that some of the forty-one architects got architectural training in Montreal rather than in Scotland. William George De Belle became an architect at age fifty, graduating from the École des Beaux-Arts de Montréal in 1928. Hugh Allen Inglis Valentine graduated from McGill University in 1927.

Significantly, at least five Scottish-born architects trained or worked in the Montreal office and/or atelier of Edward and William Maxwell, who may have self-identified as Scottish but were born in Montreal and trained in Boston and Paris, respectively. This includes John Archibald, John Roxburgh Smith, John Turnbull, and William Haldane. William Maxwell had attended the atelier Pascal in Paris, associated with the École des Beaux-Arts, and later set up the atelier Maxwell "adjoining his own office" on that model in Montreal.[27] John Roxburgh Smith, who was working for the Maxwells' architectural office, "helped establish the Maxwell Atelier at the École des Beaux-Arts in Montreal."[28] John Wilson Wood emigrated to Montreal, "where he attended the Maxwell Atelier, an informal studio based on the École des Beaux-Arts model."[29] Material produced by the Canadian Architecture Collection suggests an American link: "For a time W.S. Maxwell conducted a teaching atelier in Montreal in connection with the New York Beaux-Arts Institute of Design."[30] In an obituary for William Maxwell in the *Journal of the Royal Architectural Institute of Canada*, John Roxburgh Smith says, "His great interest in the 'Atelier Maxwell,' connected with the Beaux-Arts Institute of Design in New York, of which he was the guiding spirit, should be recorded among his professional efforts."[31] The Maxwells were responsible for some of the most significant houses in the Square Mile, including the J.K.L. Ross house.

A second, significant office in which Scottish architects seem to have gathered, even though the principals were born other places, was Ross & MacFarlane (later Ross & MacDonald). From our list of forty-one architects, Arthur Robert Doggart, Donald MacPherson Gordon, Joseph Browne Dick Gorman, Robert William Gall Heughan, and Hugh Allen Inglis Valentine all worked there. The firm was responsible for some of Canada's most iconic buildings, such as the Royal York Hotel and Union Station in Toronto, the Chateau Laurier in Ottawa, and Montreal's Eaton's and Holt Renfrew stores, as well as significant apartment buildings. Ross and MacFarlane were born in Montreal; MacDonald came from Australia. All this to say that for *some*, birthplace mattered.

Education and Professional Networks

Many of the links between and among Scottish-born architects in Montreal were established through two schools: Edinburgh University and the Glasgow School of

Figure 9.5 Diagram of networks of Scottish architects in Montreal, showing place of education, the frequency of connections, and the significance of Percy Nobbs. Design by Emily Cline based on earlier versions by Valentina Davila and Peter Grabitz.

Note: Nodes represent architects, edges represent connections between them. Node size is proportionate to the number of connections. Node colour represents the school with which the architect is affiliated.

Art. It is important to keep in mind that throughout the late-nineteenth and early-twentieth centuries, many architects apprenticed in offices and did not attend architecture schools. In order to assess the school connections among Scottish-born architects in Montreal, I employed the open-source software called R for statistical computing and graphics to sort out the complex networks at play.[32] Note that the diagram shown in Figure 9.5 does not include about a dozen architects who surfaced in the meantime and who are included in Table 9.1.[33] So, in the analysis of twenty-nine architects, as this diagram shows, Glasgow dominated the academic scene, but there are roughly the same number of Montreal architects trained in Edinburgh and Glasgow who were practising in the city (six trained at Edinburgh and eight at Glasgow).

A key finding is that the Edinburgh-Glasgow divide appears to have dissolved in Canada over time. In other words, Scottish architects supported architects from other schools, with school-based connections mattering less over time. Of course, there are architects born in Edinburgh and trained in Glasgow, and vice versa, so it is impossible to tease out these factors with certainty.

Unsurprisingly, Percy Nobbs appears to be the most "connected" of all the Scottish émigré architects, touching many of the other architects directly. Figure 9.5 illustrates the nature of relationships emanating from Nobbs with twenty-nine of the Scottish-born Montreal architects, the size of the bubble indicating the degree of connectedness. An architect excluded from our list because he was born in England, but very connected for this group, is William Careless or Carless. His connections come from having worked in Dundee for some years, and Careless was personally invited by Nobbs to move to Montreal in 1912.[34] Note that three architects on the list were born in Dundee. New digital technologies allow us to reconstruct a personal network for someone like Nobbs, inspiring us to think about architectural history as an open-system network, or a series of relationship-based activities that produces the built environment.

Overlaying a network of Scottish-born clients on our diagram of connected architects might produce a web that is too interconnected to understand. But before that we might note the extra-curricular activities and institutions that brought and bound Scottish architects together, such as the St. Andrew's Society and the Caledonian Club, as noted by Kinnear.[35] Many Scottish-born architects excelled in sports. By this I do not mean in recreational sports, but rather they excelled as the best in Canada or even the best in the world. Percy Nobbs, for example, represented Canada in fencing at the 1908 Olympics.[36] John Smith Archibald loved hunting and fishing and participated in a variety of social outdoor activities.[37] Interestingly, he combined his interests in sports and architecture as designer of the Montreal Forum (1924) for hockey; the Delorimier Downs Stadium (1927) for baseball; and the pool and gymnasium at Queen's University in Kingston, Ontario.[38]

Mobility

What is also interesting, with regards to mobility, is the number of Scottish-born architects who moved back and forth between Montreal and other Canadian and American cities during their lives. Examples of this mobility from the list would include David Colville (Vancouver), Francis Orr Templeton (Ottawa), George M. Stewart (Toronto), John Turnbull (New York), and James Adam (Philadelphia, Ottawa). Valentine, described above in connection with his partnership with

Nobbs, worked in Wilmington, Delaware, for a time. Further study might reveal, for example, that Montreal served as a hub or almost a supply centre for firms in other cities. In addition to Taylor, two other Scottish-born architects returned to England or Scotland after practising in Montreal. David Morton Brown came to Montreal in 1905, and stayed only a year. Inverness-born James Robert Rhind returned from Montreal to his birthplace after seven years, where he died in 1918.

Nobbs and Traquair

With regards to Gournay's chameleon theory, it is worth noting the cultural conservatism of many Scottish architects in Montreal. The photo in Figure 9.6 shows Ramsay Traquair with a bayonet, attacking a stool with a potato sack placed on the top of the stool, possibly stuffed with straw, and a counterweight placed between the legs of the stool, all meant to simulate the height and mass of an enemy soldier (happily this is no longer part of Canadian architectural education). Known affectionately as "The Laird" to his close friends, Traquair retired to Guysborough, Nova Scotia, in 1939, where he fished, drank tea, and wore a kilt every day.[39]

Traquair's cultural conservatism also meant actively excluding women from the architectural profession. As elucidated in a co-authored book on Canadian women architects, women were part of the apparatus of modern architectural practice, and so it is perhaps not surprising as a staunch anti-modernist that Traquair wanted nothing to do with women.[40] In two articles published in the 1920s in *Atlantic Monthly*, Traquair surveys what he sees as women's negligible contributions to the fine arts, science, philosophy, and religion, and then blames the influence of mothers and women teachers for what he describes as the inevitable "intellectual death" of contemporary society.[41] "Woman takes but she never gives back, for, as we have seen, what woman takes becomes womanly and therefore forbidden to men," he warned in 1929.[42] One of many photos of Traquair in the university's yearbooks, *Old McGill*, shows him surrounded by male students, seated as a patriarch (see Figure 9.7). The first woman was admitted to the School of Architecture only in 1939, just as Traquair retired. When in 1929 the Montreal Women's Club demanded the admission of women to architectural studies, Traquair refused on financial grounds, saying that the admission of women would require additional supervision of the drafting studio, as the genders could mix there until as late as 10 p.m., "put[ting] the School to extra expense for which it has no funds."[43]

Traquair was openly racist, discriminating against Blacks, Jews, and Asians.[44] Throughout his years in Montreal he had a soft spot for francophone Quebecers, and a long and committed relationship with Antoine Gordon Neilson, who

Figure 9.6 Photograph of Ramsay Traquair, n.d., which appears in the personal diary of J. Campbell Merrett / McGill, 1926–1931, p. 38. Private collection.

provided assistance in photography and French. Traquair described French Canadians as virile and "pure." Did his near obsession with New France help him fit into Quebec? Was it a chameleon-like gesture? It gained him an honorary degree from the Université de Montréal in 1948. Certainly, with so few architecture schools in Canada in the first half of the twentieth century – there were six, depending on how one counts: University of Toronto (1890), McGill University (1896), Université de Montréal (1907), University of Manitoba (1919), Beaux-Arts in Quebec City

ARCHITECTURE

Nobbs Macdonald Romans Prof. Traquair Jones Dixon

THE ARCHITECTURAL SOCIETY

Hon. Pres.	Prof. Ramsay Traquair	President	Gordon S. Macdonald
Vice-Pres.	H. Kingsford Jones	Secretary	Michael G. Dixon
Treasurer	Henry M. Romans	Librarian	Francis J. Nobbs

As in previous years, meetings were held during which invited speakers addressed the members on subjects pertaining to Architecture. On Thursday evening, December 6th, 1934, Mr. P. R. Wilson of the faculty staff spoke on Water Colouring and Rendering. The speaker outlined the various schools of water colouring, explaining the technique and advantages of each. The talk was illustrated with many examples of prominent water-colourists' work as well as with examples of the speaker's own work. This talk proved very interesting and instructive, especially to the newer members.

This term saw the members of the Society participate in several branches of sport. The Society entered a hockey team in the Inter-faculty and the Inter-class Leagues. The team was managed by dapper Ken Gowans (Architecture's "Bobby Bell"—hats and all) and put up many interesting and closely contested games. Architecture was also represented in Rugby, English Rugby, B.W. & F., and track events.

The Society is especially proud of the fact that a fellow member, Francis J. Nobbs, was elected McGill Track Captain and are hoping that more members will follow his example in representing our Alma Mater on the field of sport.

OLD McGILL VOLUME 38 » A.D. 1935 95

Figure 9.7 Group portrait and annual report, The Architectural Society, School of Architecture, McGill University, Montreal, showing Ramsay Traquair with librarian and students. From *Old McGill* (1935), p. 135.

(1923–39), and University of Alberta (1920–39)[45] – Traquair's attitudes kept the profession very white, Christian, and male.

As discussed, Traquair is best known for his magnum opus, *The Old Architecture of Quebec,* published in 1947. The massive 324-page tome features measured drawings of early churches and houses done by McGill School of Architecture students under Traquair's guidance over thirteen years (1924–39) – he only got interested in Quebec architecture at age fifty, perhaps about the time of the Forbes portrait – and the book earned him a reputation as an explicator of Quebec architecture and material culture. According to Nicola Spasoff's 2002 dissertation on Nobbs and Traquair, the two men had known each other in Edinburgh, having worked in the office of Robert Lorimer and with many colleagues in common, including Patrick Geddes and Stewart Henbest Capper, the founding director of the McGill School of Architecture. Spasoff notes that Traquair's mother, accomplished arts-and-crafts artist Phoebe Anna [Moss] Traquair, corresponded with Nobbs for two decades and that the two pen pals highly valued each other's opinions on a range of artistic matters.[46]

Given Traquair's negative attitudes towards women, it is somewhat unexpected and paradoxical that his mother played such a pivotal role in both his move to Montreal and his significant relationship with Percy Nobbs. Historical studies of Phoebe Traquair, such as Elizabeth Cumming's 1986 dissertation, "Phoebe Anna Traquair HRSA (1852–1936) and her Contribution to Arts and Crafts in Edinburgh," highlight the significance of Nobbs's friendship with the older woman, quite apart from his relationship with her eldest son. Cumming cites correspondence between Phoebe Traquair and Percy Nobbs, between 1900 and 1920 (and in a private collection), as one of two of the most important archives on her life.[47] According to Cumming, Nobbs (or "Nobby," as Lorimer called him) sought Phoebe Traquair's advice on decorative aspects of his buildings, "sending her coloured drawings for comment … Her replies were highly valued and retained in typescript."[48] There is some evidence that what began as a mentoring relationship about design evolved into a friendlier camaraderie that included confiding in one another and the communication of family events.

The death of Traquair's father may also have affected the architect's decision to move to Montreal. Palaeontologist Ramsay Heatley Traquair Sr. died at home on 22 November 1912, just six days before his son applied for the McGill position. R.H. Traquair was an expert in fish fossils, especially for their classification.[49] Architect Ramsay Traquair wrote to his mother's friend Percy Nobbs on 28 November 1912. He commented on the death of his father, "we were fully prepared," and expressed his strong preference to defer to Stewart Henbest Capper should he want the job.

He also wrote, "My mother has given me your letter," a reference which points to the importance of the Phoebe Traquair-Nobbs correspondence in the early days of their friendship.[50] Capper had left Canada in 1903, after seven years at McGill University, but clearly Traquair believed he may want to return.

Nobbs, too, acknowledged the important role of Traquair's parents in his friend's life. In an article in the *Journal of the Royal Architectural Institute of Canada* about architect Ramsay Traquair's retirement, he describes Phoebe and Ramsay H. Traquair. "An Irishwoman and an artist, in whom the authentic spirit of the thirteenth century was manifested," he says of Phoebe. "There is something in him of both his parents," Nobbs admits as a way of characterizing Ramsay Traquair. In the same article, Nobbs recalls spending time with Ramsay Traquair, the architect, in Italy in 1900, about the time his correspondence with his mother began, according to Cumming.[51]

As outlined, while Nobbs left a substantial built legacy, Traquair built next to nothing in Canada, focusing instead on measuring existing buildings. However, Nobbs and Traquair both left massive archives, including correspondence, photographs, drawings, lecture notes, and personal artefacts. Drawing heavily on their outsider positions, both men advocated a national architectural style in Canada. Juxtaposing their archives illustrates the high cultural status of Scottish architects in Canada and allows us to unravel their remarkable professional and familial interrelationships. We know from dozens of documents, such as this letter in Figure 9.8 held in the John Bland Canadian Architecture Collection at McGill University, that Traquair's move to Canada was at Nobbs's suggestion and that the decision to leave Scotland was unsettling for him, but for some reason imperative.[52] On 24 April 1913 Traquair wrote to Nobbs in Montreal: "I am tearing up my roots here gradually. It is astonishing how deep they go. But up they have to come."[53] In another letter, dated 3 June 1913, he wrote: "It is a terrible job getting clear of ones' [*sic*] native place and it gets worse every day."[54] We can derive significant information from Traquair's eloquent correspondence to Nobbs: he may have known one other Scottish architect in Montreal before his emigration. On 5 June 1914 he wrote to Nobbs, "I hope you got your things all right which I gave to Drummond." This is likely the Glaswegian architect George Fairly Drummond, who had just arrived in Montreal in 1913. Also, the letters show that Nobbs sent Traquair money, in this instance $180.[55] Perhaps most importantly, Traquair understood that Nobbs had helped him get the coveted Macdonald Chair at McGill University, named for one of McGill's most generous benefactors, tobacco baron William Macdonald: "I must thank you for your efforts on my behalf." As mentioned, he had confided early on in the process that should Stewart Henbest Capper be applying, he would defer to the older Scot.[56] Traquair even stayed with Nobbs when he arrived in August 1913, until he arranged for his own lodgings.[57]

Like Traquair's "uprooting" in 1913, Nobbs's move ten years earlier had been enabled by significant connections but with slightly less mobile Scots. Gerard Baldwin Brown, a professor of fine arts and pioneering preservationist at the University of Edinburgh, had proposed Nobbs to McGill's principal William Peterson, who originally hailed from Edinburgh.[58] In 1895, Stewart Henbest Capper, Nobbs's predecessor, had also been recommended by Baldwin Brown, who was a close friend of Peterson, perhaps from their overlapping years at the University of Edinburgh. Capper's assistant on the Ramsay Gardens project in Edinburgh (often considered his most important work) was Ramsay Traquair! It is curious today to think that two of the McGill School of Architecture's early leaders were picked by an art historian in Scotland who had no real connection to Montreal or to the profession, except through his friendship with the Montreal-based principal.

Scottish Architecture in Montreal

It is important to note that Scottish architects conveyed significant architectural concepts, expertise, and spatial experiences to Canada, including but not limited to the strong imagery of the Scottish castle. James Rhind is a good example. Rhind was the local architect in charge of the construction of the Royal Victoria Hospital erected in 1893 (Figure 9.9), which was modelled on the Royal Infirmary in Edinburgh designed by architect David Bryce. The massive stone architecture and expansive pavilion plan of the Montreal hospital, by British hospital specialist Henry Saxon Snell, is often described as Scottish baronial.[59] Snell included an aerial view of the Edinburgh hospital in his co-authored book, *Hospital Construction and Management*, of 1883 (Figure 9.10). It is tempting to speculate that Rhind was hired because of this "authentic" connection to Scotland. Another early connection to Bryce is Eric Mann, who had apprenticed with Bryce before he moved to Montreal in 1873. According to my research, Mann was the third Scottish architect to arrive in the city (see Figure 9.12). He designed an extraordinary number of buildings, especially Montreal's characteristic greystone triplexes and two notable synagogues.[60] With George Alexander Drummond and two others, Mann co-founded the Royal Montreal Golf Club.[61]

Kinnear points out that Findlay gained significant experience in John Rhind's office, especially on sumptuous residences.[62] Good examples of Findlay's residential work in the Square Mile include the Mortimer B. Davis house (1906) and the Alice Graham Hallward House (1912), both owned for many years by McGill University

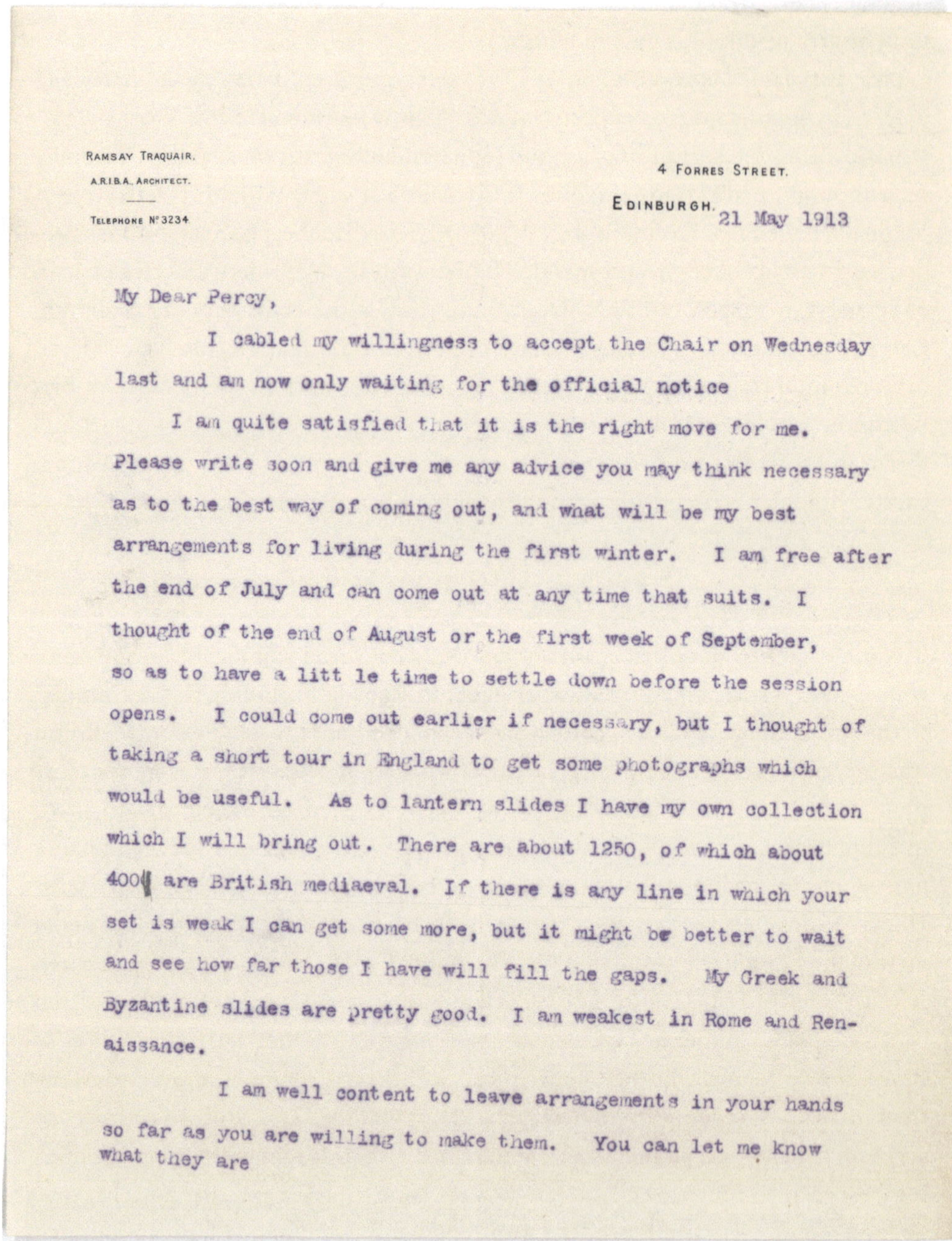

RAMSAY TRAQUAIR.
A.R.I.B.A. ARCHITECT.

TELEPHONE Nº 3234

4 FORRES STREET.

EDINBURGH. 21 May 1913

My Dear Percy,

I cabled my willingness to accept the Chair on Wednesday last and am now only waiting for the official notice

I am quite satisfied that it is the right move for me. Please write soon and give me any advice you may think necessary as to the best way of coming out, and what will be my best arrangements for living during the first winter. I am free after the end of July and can come out at any time that suits. I thought of the end of August or the first week of September, so as to have a litt le time to settle down before the session opens. I could come out earlier if necessary, but I thought of taking a short tour in England to get some photographs which would be useful. As to lantern slides I have my own collection which I will bring out. There are about 1250, of which about 400 are British mediaeval. If there is any line in which your set is weak I can get some more, but it might be better to wait and see how far those I have will fill the gaps. My Greek and Byzantine slides are pretty good. I am weakest in Rome and Renaissance.

I am well content to leave arrangements in your hands so far as you are willing to make them. You can let me know what they are

Figure 9.8 Letter from Traquair to Nobbs, regarding his acceptance of the position as chair at the School of Architecture and noting that he is "tearing up his roots," 21 May 1913. Percy Erskine Nobbs Fonds, John Bland Canadian Architectural Collection, McGill University.

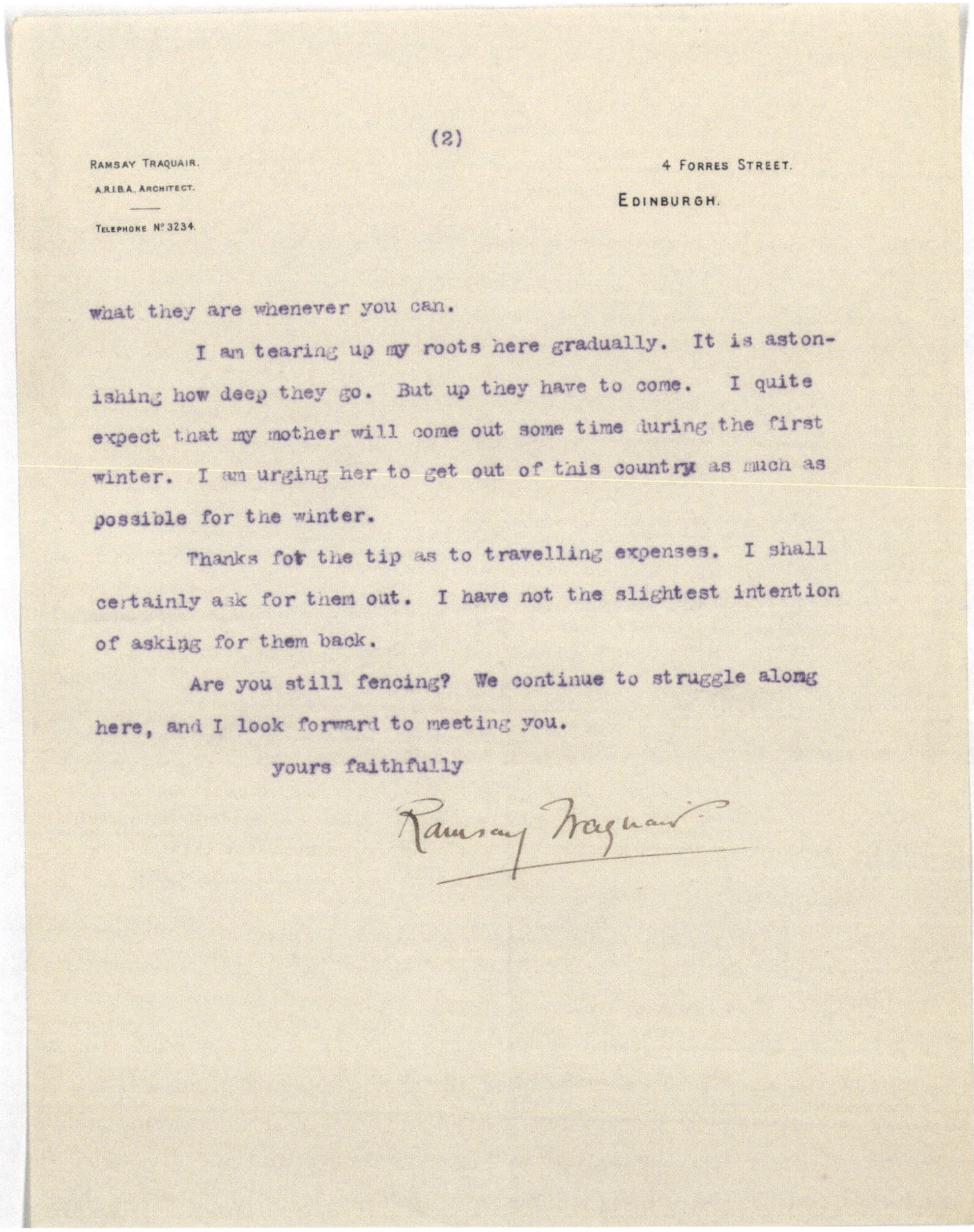

(2)

RAMSAY TRAQUAIR.
A.R.I.B.A. ARCHITECT.
TELEPHONE Nº 3234.

4 FORRES STREET.
EDINBURGH.

what they are whenever you can.

I am tearing up my roots here gradually. It is astonishing how deep they go. But up they have to come. I quite expect that my mother will come out some time during the first winter. I am urging her to get out of this country as much as possible for the winter.

Thanks fot the tip as to travelling expenses. I shall certainly ask for them out. I have not the slightest intention of asking for them back.

Are you still fencing? We continue to struggle along here, and I look forward to meeting you.

yours faithfully

Ramsay Traquair

Figure 9.8 (*Continued*)

Figure 9.9 Photograph of the Royal Victoria Hospital, Montreal, c. 1894, reprinted in 1940, designed by architect Henry Saxon Snell. McCord Museum, VIEW-2553.0.

and occupied by the Faculty of Medicine and Health Sciences. The two houses reveal Findlay's wide range of styles and clients.

Davis was a prominent Jewish industrialist, founder of the Imperial Tobacco Company. He was also a generous philanthropist, endowing Montreal's Jewish General Hospital in 1928. Occupying a prominent corner at the intersection of Pine Avenue and Peel Street, the house is a "chaste, symmetrical, classical cube" with a flat roof, constructed of Indiana limestone. Its design is distinguished by classical detailing, especially its five-bay elevational composition facing Pine Avenue.[63] The main floor, characteristically raised from the ground level as a *piano nobile*, boasts monumental arched windows. The elegant masonry cladding camouflaged a modern structure of steel framing and concrete floors, highly unusual in residential design. On the east side, facing Peel Street, was a prominent conservatory for plants. The relationship of interior and exterior were further linked through an elaborate, terraced landscape, including a somewhat mysterious tunnel that

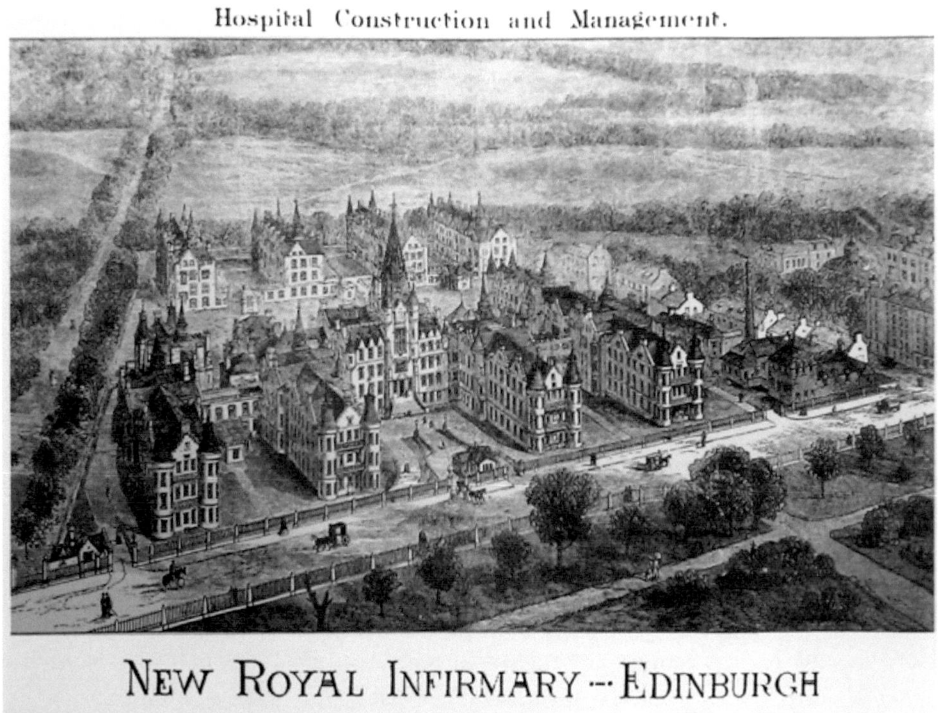

Figure 9.10 James Akerman, *Aerial Perspective of the Royal Infirmary, Edinburgh*, n.d. From Frederic J. Mouat and H. Saxon Snell, *Hospital Construction and Management*, 2nd ed. (London: J. & A. Churchill & Co, 1889), p. 33.

Figure 9.11 Photograph of the Mortimer B. Davis residence, Montreal, c. 1910, designed by Robert Findlay. McCord Museum, MP-0000.831.8.

links the basement to the sidewalk on Peel. The Alice Graham Hallward House (1925), however, has second-generation Scottish connections and is characteristic of Findlay's non-classical, more romantic aesthetic interests. It is more in line, for example, with Findlay's design for Westmount City Hall, which is "reminiscent of Scottish castles."[64] Kinnear notes that John Rhind's firm, where Findlay had worked in Scotland, specialized in Scottish baronial design.[65] Alice Hallward's grandfather, Robert Walker Graham, hailed from Mildlothian, a historic county bordering the City of Edinburgh.[66] Her father Hugh Graham owned the *Montreal Star* newspaper and retained strong links to Scotland throughout his life in Canada,[67] including receiving an honorary degree from the University of Glasgow in 1909.[68] Hallward's parents commissioned the house for their daughter and her husband, Bernard M. Hallward, as a wedding gift.[69] The house was purchased by McGill University in 1966.

Empire

How was the British Empire extended and reinforced by these networks of architects? What is the historical significance of Scottish architects in the cultural rendering of Montreal, and the Square Mile in particular, and how did this reinforce what was happening across the empire? Scottish-born architects extended and reinforced the British Empire in many major cities, not just Montreal. Architectural historians have uncovered similar networks in India and Australia, for example. Stuart King describes the contributions of Scottish architects in Tasmania, Australia, as "multi-textured," operating as an "interplay between empire, region, identity, and building."[70] In India, Scots John Begg and George Wittet contributed to architectural culture in ways eerily similar to Nobbs and Archibald: through the design and construction of nationally significant buildings, leadership in shaping the profession, and architectural education. "Scottish architects and their role in the shaping of imperial cities around the world have remained largely absent from much of the rich history of Scotland and empire," says architectural historian Sarah Longair.[71]

There is little evidence that Scottish architecture in Montreal was perceived by Montrealers as a link to other imperial cities, such as Melbourne and Mumbai. I would argue, instead, that the cultural work of Scottish architects in Montreal did quite the opposite. It pushed the articulation of a distinctive Canadian style, as a vital contribution to the empire.[72] As leaders in the profession and principals in some of the country's most prolific firms, Scottish-born architects were well-placed to articulate what differentiated Canadian buildings from other places, particularly Britain. Nobbs wrote frequently about what constituted a Canadian style; Traquair illuminated, for an English-speaking audience, the rich, unique architectural legacy of New France; others designed iconic buildings that are sometimes still understood as our "national" style, such as the famous railway hotels.[73]

Kelly Crossman, in *Architecture in Transition*, credits Nobbs with the establishment of a Canadian style, drawing a line from Gerald Baldwin Brown's influential teaching in Edinburgh, through Stewart Henbest Capper, to McGill principal William Peterson (born Edinburgh). Crossman argues that Brown's insistence on the proximity of art and society had a profound impact on his Montreal-bound students. Throughout his six decades in Montreal, Nobbs insisted that Canadian architecture would arise from local culture, materials, and climate, in direct opposition to the Beaux-Arts theory of architecture, which proposed more universalizing solutions to buildings across the world. Nobbs saw Beaux-Arts architecture, and its associated atelier system of education, as evidence of the Americanization of Canada (and presumably the empire).[74] Still, Nobbs never lost sight of Canada's membership in the empire. In "British Art and the Empire," a letter from 1912, he talks about "the problem ... of providing for the departments of architecture and sculpture in our museums throughout the Empire." In his mind, Canadian architects had created a powerful Canadian architecture up until about 1825, when they somehow had lost sight of local traditions. "Nobbs was the first to suggest that these vernacular forms might form the basis for a new national architecture," says Crossman.[75]

Conclusion

When was the golden age for Scottish architects in Montreal? The timeline illustrated in Figure 9.12 shows the wave of Scottish arrivals by date, and the peak of Scottishness in the Montreal architectural scene roughly between the years 1912 and 1940. This is during the final decades of the construction of the Square Mile, a generation after the appearance of institutions such the Royal Victoria Hospital, and notably, nearly a century after the establishment of McGill University. We cannot say with any certainty, then, that the work and the prosperity associated with these urban projects brought Scottish architects to Montreal. If so, it took them some time to arrive. We can perhaps say that the success and prosperity that the earlier generation had obtained might have enticed a further cohort to emigrate. Also, we might speculate that the Scottish network in Montreal architecture circles had to reach a certain scale before it could efficiently accommodate more newcomers.

In conclusion, biographical data on these forty-one architects does show four important points. Birthplace mattered, but not that much. School-based networks mattered for the initial invitation or decision to move to Canada, and then became

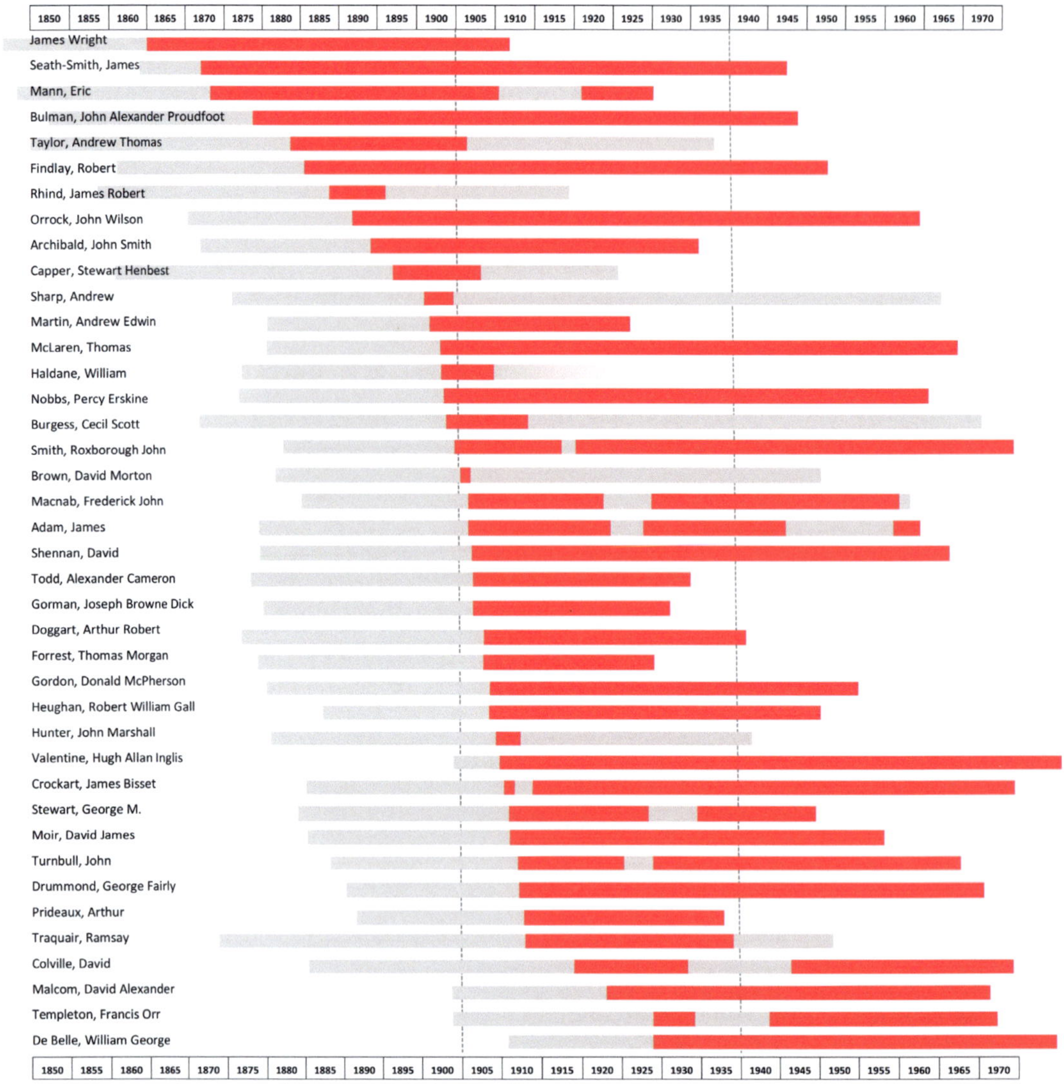

Figure 9.12 Timeline showing the lifespan, arrival, and residency dates of Scottish architects, showcasing the period between 1912–40 as the peak era of contributions. Design by Emily Cline based on earlier versions by Valentina Davila.

less important with time. Personal networking was the way many Scottish architects got established in Montreal. This included direct invitations, references for promotions, offers of employment, a guest bedroom when needed, and even cash in the mail. The most important insight from this comparative method is that it might bring us closer to how architectural practice in the twentieth century actually operated: through a series of networked economic and personal relationships, in this case Montreal with the country of origin as a key factor. The next step, for example, might be to study Scottish-born architectural clients. Did Scottish architects actively seek out support from one another? Montreal-Scottish architects were tactical in this regard. I believe that being Scottish allowed them to succeed as Montreal architects, or made them think they would succeed.

Finally, the use of new tools in our midst, such as software that allows us to study networking, should push us to think about architecture and architectural history differently: for example, to see buildings as the outcomes of networked activities and economic relationships. The case of the Scottish diaspora is a good illustration of its power.

NOTES

This chapter was presented as a paper at the Society of Architectural Historians annual meeting in Glasgow, Scotland, 2017. I am grateful to Emily Cline who helped to transform it from a conference paper to a book chapter. I am also thankful to Valentina Davila, Katrin Zavgorodny-Freedman, Jennifer Phan, Robert Hill, Peter Grabitz, Julia Gersovitz, Peter Gossage, and Brian Merrett for assistance and inspiration. Thanks to McGill University colleagues Jennifer Garland, Greg Houston, and Gwendolyn Owens for the images.

1 John Bland, "In Memoriam: Percy Erskine Nobbs, St. Mary's Church, Como, November 15th, 1964," Canadian Architecture Collection (CAC), McGill University Archives (MUA), 2.
2 T.H. Matthews, "Tribute to Ramsay Traquair," *RAIC Journal* 29, no. 11 (1952), 344.
3 Ramsay Traquair, *The Old Architecture of Quebec: A Study of the Buildings Erected in New France from the Earliest Explorers to the Middle of the Nineteenth Century* (Toronto: The MacMillan Co. of Canada Ltd., 1947).
4 Royal Collection Trust, "Explore the Collection: Queen Alexandra (1844–1925)," https://www.rct.uk/collection/406683/queen-alexandra-1844-1925.
5 Matthews, "Tribute," 344.
6 Bland, "Memoriam," 3.
7 Irena Murray, "A Scout of the Past: Ramsay Traquair and the Legacy of the National Art Survey of Scotland in Quebec," in *Kingdom of the Mind: How the Scots Helped Make Canada*, ed. Peter E. Rider and Heather McNabb (Montreal: McGill-Queen's University Press, 2006), 202.
8 Traquair to Nobbs, 24 April 1913, John Bland Canadian Architecture Collection (CAC), McGill University Archives (MUA).
9 Isabelle Gournay, "The First Leaders of McGill's School of Architecture: Stewart Henbest Capper, Percy Nobbs, and Ramsay Traquair," *SSAC Bulletin* 21, no. 3 (1996): 63.

10 G.A. Bremner, "The Expansion of England? Rethinking Scotland's Place in the Architectural History of the Wider British World," *Journal of Art Historiography*, no. 18 (2018): 5.
11 On the architecture of Montreal's Square Mile, see Donald MacKay, *The Square Mile: Merchant Princes of Montreal* (Vancouver: Douglas & McIntyre, 1987); Julia Gersovitz, "The Square Mile, Montreal, 1860–1914" (MSc thesis, Columbia University, 1980).
12 "Sources Consulted," *Dictionary of Scottish Architects, 1660–1980,* last updated 17 August 2008, http://www.scottisharchitects.org.uk/.
13 Murray notes the importance of Inverness. Murray, "Scout," 202.
14 Irena Murray, ed., *John S. Archibald and His Associates: A Guide to the Archive* (Montreal: Canadian Architecture Collection, McGill University, 1990), 4.
15 "Masonic Memorial Temple, Montreal," *Construction*, no. 23 (1930): 386, 387–91.
16 Bremner, "Expansion," 6.
17 On George A. Drummond, see Michèle Brassard and Jean Hamelin, "Drummond, Sir George Alexander," in *Dictionary of Canadian Biography*, vol. 13, Université Laval/University of Toronto, 2003–, accessed 2 February 2023, http://www.biographi.ca/en/bio/drummond_george_alexander_13E.html.
18 Holly E.B. Kinnear, "Building a Scottish Canada?: Five Architects in Montreal 1883–1914" (PhD diss., University of Edinburgh, 2006), 133–5.
19 "McLaren, Thomas," in *Biographical Dictionary of Architects in Canada, 1800–1950,* ed. Robert G. Hill, accessed 2 February 2023, http://www.dictionaryofarchitectsincanada.org/node/2239. The entry reads: "He emigrated to Canada in July 1902 and joined the office of Sir Andrew T. Taylor in Montreal, and while there, he gained extensive experience in the design of bank buildings in Canada. When Taylor left Canada and returned to London, England in January 1904, McLaren decided to take time to travel in Europe, then returned to Montreal in 1905 where he joined the architectural department of the Bank of Montreal." Note that the *Dictionary of Scottish Architects* says he was employed by (Sir) Andrew Thomas Taylor from 1902 to approximately 1905, accessed 2 February 2023, http://www.scottisharchitects.org.uk/architect_full.php?id=202495.
20 "Gordon, George William Hamilton," in *Biographical Dictionary of Architects in Canada, 1800–1950,* ed. Robert G. Hill, accessed 2 February 2023, http://www.dictionaryofarchitectsincanada.org/node/1938.
21 Susan Wagg, *The Architecture of Andrew Thomas Taylor: Montreal's Square Mile and Beyond* (Montreal: McGill-Queen's University Press, 2013), 4.
22 See *The Builder* 51 (6 November 1886): 662; *The Canadian Architect and Builder* 2, no. 11 (November 1889): 125; *The Canadian Architect and Builder* 3, no. 4 (April 1890): 44; and François Rémillard and Brian Merrett, *Mansions of the Golden Square Mile, Montreal, 1850–1930* (Montreal: Meridian Press, 1987), 51–2.
23 See Wagg, *Taylor*, 27–8, 31, where she writes: "[Taylor's] mother's sister, Jane Drummond (1815–1907), became in 1835 the second wife of John Redpath (1796–1869), who established the family's wealth and influence. John had trained in Edinburgh as a stonemason under George Drummond, Taylor's builder grandfather, and left Scotland in 1816, seeking a better life"; "In 1853, while visiting Edinburgh, [Redpath] engaged as its manager his brother-in-law George Alexander Drummond (1829–1910). The young man was studying at Edinburgh University and arrived in Montreal in 1854 with vital technical expertise. He married Helen Redpath, a daughter of John and his first wife, Janet McPhee"; and "Taylor's first domestic commissions in Montreal included a terrace of five rental houses for his mother's wealthy and powerful brother George Alexander Drummond on Mansfield Street new McGill University."
24 Wagg, *Taylor*, 46.

25 See *Répertoire d'architecture traditionnelle sur le territoire de la Communauté urbaine de Montréal. Architecture domestique I. Les résidences* (Montreal: Communauté urbaine de Montréal, 1987), 18–25.
26 *Répertoire d'architecture*, 170.
27 John Bland, "William Sutherland Maxwell Biography," in Maxwell Architectural Archive CAC, McGill University, accessed 2 February 2023, http://cac.mcgill.ca/maxwells/willbio2.htm.
28 "Smith, John Roxborough," in *Biographical Dictionary of Architects in Canada, 1800–1950*, ed. Robert G. Hill, accessed 2 February 2023, http://www.dictionaryofarchitectsincanada.org/node/466.
29 "Basic Biographical Details: John Wilson Wood," *Dictionary of Scottish Architects, 1660–1980*, accessed 2 February 2023, http://www.scottisharchitects.org.uk/architect_full.php?id=206670.
30 John Bland, "Edward Maxwell Biography," in Maxwell Architectural Archive, Canadian Architecture Collection (CAC), McGill University, accessed 2 February 2023, http://cac.mcgill.ca/maxwells/edbio2.htm.
31 John Roxburgh Smith, "Obituary: William Sutherland Maxwell," *RAIC Journal* 29, vol. 10 (1952): 311.
32 Peter Grabitz introduced me to the software R. I am grateful for his invaluable help.
33 The first version of this chapter assessed thirty-three architects, four of whom were later found to not meet the guidelines; due to COVID-19, detailed archival research was not possible for the architects uncovered after March 2020. Nonetheless, the links among two-thirds of the architects are still interesting.
34 "Basic Biographical Details: William Edward Careless (or Carless)," *Dictionary of Scottish Architects, 1660–1980,* accessed 2 February 2023, http://www.scottisharchitects.org.uk/architect_full.php?id=200519.
35 Kinnear, "Building a Scottish Canada," 121–2, 172.
36 Annmarie Adams, "The Place of Manliness: Architecture, Domesticity, and Men's Clubs," in *Making Men, Making History: Canadian Masculinities across Time and Place*, ed. Peter Gossage and Robert Rutherdale (Vancouver: UBC Press, 2018), 126 and note 34: "He started fencing in 1901 and was a member of the Canadian Olympic fencing team in 1908. Although it is often written that Nobbs won a silver medal, there is no evidence that he got an Olympic medal during the 1908 London games." A note explains, "This story is reported in various and ambiguous ways. In Nobbs's eulogy, however, Bland clearly states, 'When he was 33 he won a silver medal for fencing in the Olympic games of 1908' … Official documents from the 1908 Olympics show that he competed in the first round of the épée event, coming sixth and therefore not advancing. The confusion stems from the fact that Nobbs participated in a foil fencing display, for which he perhaps received an award."
37 "John Smith Archibald, F.R.S.A.," in *The Storied Province of Quebec, Past and Present*, ed. William Wood and William Henry Atherton, vol. 4 (Toronto: The Dominion Publishing Co., Ltd., 1931), 494–5.
38 Annmarie Adams, "John Smith Archibald," in *Dictionary of Canadian Biography*, vol. 16, University of Toronto/Université Laval, 2003–, accessed 2 February 2023, www.biographi.ca/en/bio/archibald_john_smith_16E.html.
39 Matthews, "Tribute," 344: "Although Traquair was a bachelor he was what Max Beerbohm calls a 'hostish' person and, to appreciate his full flavour and see him at his best, you had to be his guest in his summer home – a lovely place – in Guysborough. There he was in complete harmony with his setting, cultivating his beautiful garden, fishing the local rivers, drinking tea at all hours on his verandah and talking to his friends. Within his own grounds he normally wore a kilt and was always 'The Laird' to his close friends."
40 Annmarie Adams and Peta Tancred, *Designing Women: Gender and the Architectural Profession* (Toronto: University of Toronto Press, 2000).

41 Ramsay Traquair, "Women and Civilization," *Atlantic* 132 (1923), 296.
42 Ramsay Traquair, "A Regiment of Women: A Plea for Equal Treatment," *Atlantic* 143 (1929), 350.
43 Quote is from "Extracts from Minutes of October 2, 1929, regarding 'Admission of Women to Architecture,'" MUA. See Annmarie Adams, "'Archi-ettes in Training: The Admission of Women to McGill's School of Architecture," *Society for the Study of Architecture in Canada Bulletin* 21, no. 3 (1996), 71.
44 Annmarie Adams, "Picturing *The Old Architecture of Quebec*: Ramsay Traquair and Cultural Conservatism, 1913–39," in *Photogenic Montreal*, ed., Martha Langford and Johanne Sloan (Montreal: McGill-Queen's University Press, 2021), 151–73.
45 Marco Polo, "Architectural Education," *The Canadian Encyclopedia*, 18 January 2010, last edited 16 December 2013, accessed 2 February 2023, https://www.thecanadianencyclopedia.ca/en/article/architectural-education.
46 Nicola Spasoff, "Building on Social Power: Percy Erskine Nobbs, Ramsay Traquair, and the Project of Constructing a Canadian National Culture in the Early Decades of the Twentieth Century" (PhD diss., Queens University, 2002), 47.
47 Elizabeth Cumming, "Phoebe Anna Traquair HRSA (1852–1936) and Her Contribution to Arts and Crafts in Edinburgh" (PhD diss., University of Edinburgh, 1986), 12. See also Elizabeth Cumming, *Phoebe Anna Traquair 1852–1936* (Edinburgh: National Galleries of Scotland, 2005).
48 Cumming, "Phoebe Anna Traquair," 201.
49 See "Ramsay H. Traquair, M.D., LL.D., F.R.S. L. & E., F.G.S." *Geological Magazine* 10, no. 1 (1913): 47–8, https://geologyglasgow.org.uk/wp-content/uploads/2019/04/017_070__traquair_1484824606.pdf.
50 Traquair to Nobbs, 28 November 1912, 3, CAC.
51 Percy E. Nobbs, "Ramsay Traquair, Hon. M.A. (McGill) F.R.I.B.A.: On His Retirement from the Macdonald Chair in Architecture at McGill University," *RAIC Journal* 16, no. 6 (1939): 147.
52 Traquair to Nobbs, 28 November 1912, 3, CAC: "If my application would have a fair chance of success I will send it in. The ties I have here are very slight now and the struggle against family interests here is very heavy. Things are slack & tho' I know that it only means time yet I would be quite prepared to leave."
53 Traquair to Nobbs, 24 April 1913, CAC.
54 Traquair to Nobbs, 3 June 1913, CAC.
55 Traquair to Nobbs, 5 June 1914, CAC.
56 Traquair to Nobbs, 28 November 1912, 2, CAC.
57 Traquair to Nobbs, 1 July 1913, 2, CAC: "Many thanks for your invitation to come to you for a while. I think it would probably be best for me to take a couple of rooms & if your old landlady is able to take me I should be very glad."
58 Spasoff, "Building on Social Power," 50n16.
59 Neville Terry, *Royal Vic: The Story of Montreal's Royal Victoria Hospital, 1894–1994* (Montreal: McGill-Queen's University Press, 1994), 21.
60 See "The Corner-Stone of New Synagogue," *The Gazette* (Montreal), 2 August 1902, 9; obituary in *RAIC Journal* 6, no. 10 (1929): xxxii; and "Eric Mann," in *Montreal Board of Trade Souvenir* (1938), 160.
61 "Eric Mann Dead in His 82nd Year," *The Gazette* (Montreal), 27 September 1929.
62 Kinnear, "Building a Scottish Canada," 104.
63 Gersovitz, "Square Mile," 90.

64 "Westmount City Hall," Wikipedia: The Free Encyclopedia, last modified 31 July 2022, https://en.wikipedia.org/wiki/Westmount_City_Hall.

65 Kinnear, "Building a Scottish Canada," 104.

66 ScotlandsPeople, "Church Registers – Old Parish Registers Births and Baptisms – Search Results," National Records of Scotland, Crown Copyright, accessed 22 June 2020, https://www.scotlandspeople.gov.uk/guides/church-registers.

67 "Peer of the Press: Lord Atholstan, The Crusading Baron of the Fourth Estate," reprinted from the *Huntingdon Gleaner* (Huntingdon, QC), 2 April 1930, 1.

68 "Peer of the Press," 7: "On November 9th, 1908, the honor of knighthood came to him from His Majesty King Edward VII, through Earl Grey, Governor-General of Canada, in recognition of his services in many public and philanthropic enterprises, and particularly in recognition of his services of an Imperial character.

"On February 12th, 1917, the crowning honor of his life came to him – his elevation by King George V, through the Duke of Devonshire, to the Peerage of the United Kingdom as Baron Atholstan of Huntingdon, in the Province of Quebec, and of the City of Edinburgh, Scotland … He was a delegate to the Imperial Press Conference held in London in 1909, and was selected to reply to Lord Rosebery's great speech at the memorable banquet. While in Great Britain he received the honorary degree of Doctor of Laws from the Scottish University of Glasgow."

69 Darryl Lundy, "Hon. Alice Hamilton Graham," *The Peerage*, last modified 16 November 2003, http://www.thepeerage.com/p4270.htm#i42692.

70 Stuart King, "Scottish Networks and their Buildings in Van Diemen's Land and Tasmania," in "Building the Scottish Diaspora," ed. G.A. Bremner, Harriet Edquist, and Stuart King, special issue, *ABE Journal: Architecture beyond Europe* 14–15 (2019): 35, 37, https://doi.org/10.4000/abe.5887.

71 Sarah Longair, "Scottish Architects, Imperial Identities and India's Built Environment in the Early Twentieth Century: The Careers of John Begg and George Wittet," in "Building the Scottish Diaspora," ed. G.A. Bremner, Harriet Edquist, and Stuart King, special issue, *ABE Journal: Architecture beyond Europe* 14–15 (2019): 2, https://doi.org/10.4000/abe.5767.

72 This is consistent with a broad view in social-political history, perhaps first articulated by Berger, which frames English Canadian nationalism as having a form (and not in contradiction to) of British Imperialism. Nascent Canadians embraced the cold climate and, to some extent, Indigenous and French-Canadian culture (canoes, snowshoes, toboggans, etc.) and celebrated these unique features and their connection to the greatest Empire of the era. Poulter says the same, with specific reference to sport and visual culture. See Carl Berger, *The Sense of Power: Studies in the Ideas of Canadian Imperialism, 1867–1914* (1970; repr., Toronto: University of Toronto Press, 2013), 49–77; and Gillian Poulter, *Becoming Native in a Foreign Land: Sport, Visual Culture and Identity in Montreal, 1840–85* (Vancouver: UBC Press, 2009). I am grateful to historian Peter Gossage for these insights.

73 Harold Kalman understands the chateau-style hotels as a national style in his two-volume survey of Canadian architecture. Bremner, "Expansion," 16; Harold Kalman, *A History of Canadian Architecture*, 2 vols. (Toronto: Oxford University Press, 1994).

74 Kelly Crossman, "Percy Nobbs and a National Theory," in *Architecture in Transition: From Art to Practice, 1885–1906* (Montreal: McGill-Queen's University Press, 2014), 122–35.

75 Crossman, "Percy Nobbs," 130.

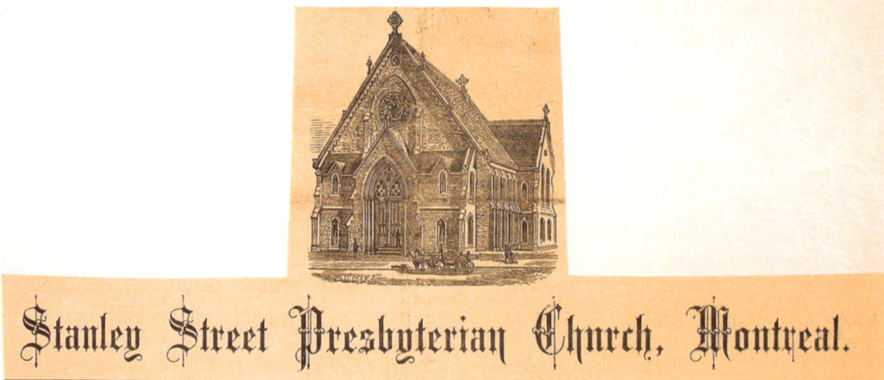

Figure V.14 Stanley Street Presbyterian Church, Montreal. McCord Museum, M993X.5.322.

The Stanley Street Presbyterian Church

At the beginning of the 1870s, the Montreal Presbyterian community splintered over the role of music within its religious services. Sir William Dawson, at that time the principal of McGill University, left the Erskine Presbyterian Church on Dorchester Street with similar like-minded fundamentalists within the congregation. To modern sensibilities, it is almost impossible to imagine that there could be such passionate disagreement over religious practices, or that a man of science such as Dawson could be so deeply implicated in the battle.

In 1874, a new Presbyterian church opened on Stanley Street. This secondary location, on a north–south street, was an anomaly for a Christian house of worship in the Square Mile, perhaps due to the speed with which the split happened. Its architect is unknown. A.C. Hutchison and William T. Thomas were two Montreal architects who designed many Presbyterian churches, but the authorship of the Stanley Street church did not belong to either of them. Perhaps its controversial raison d'être rendered it untouchable for mainstream architects.

Early images show it to be a neo-Gothic structure, with unadorned stonework and a compressed nave. The foreshortening of the plan may have been due to the constrained dimensions of the lot, or because there was a desire to have an amphitheatre form of seating, which was just coming into vogue among certain Protestant denominations.

The building served its congregation until just before the First World War, when Hutchison, Wood and Miller was commissioned to design a new church in Westmount, with an organ incorporated into the design of the sanctuary. The name remained the Stanley Street Presbyterian until 1926, when it was simplified to the Stanley Presbyterian Church. In 1972, the Westmount property was sold to the Seventh Day Adventist Church and the congregation ceased to exist in 1986.

CHAPTER TEN

The Changing of the Guard: Bartlett McLennan, Roy Wolvin, and the Leveraged Buyout of the Montreal Transportation Company, 1903–1921

M. Stephen Salmon

Introduction

The sound was not deafening on that day in August 1918. German artillery fire had been rather desultory for most of the morning but, late in the afternoon, Lieutenant-Colonel Bartlett McLennan and his party reconnoitering enemy positions outside of Amiens found themselves in the wrong place at the wrong time. McLennan, the commander of the 42nd Battalion of the Canadian Expeditionary Force, was killed when the group took a direct hit.[1]

McLennan's death was mourned by all in the Canadian Corps. His loss was keenly felt at home in Montreal where his family presented a stained-glass window to the Church of Saint Andrew and Saint Paul in his memory. On St. James Street, the former president of the Montreal Transportation Company's (MTC) sacrifice at the Front evoked respectful comment.[2] But, in the boardroom of his old firm, it was business as usual. Indeed, at the time of McLennan's death, his successor, the expatriate American Roy Wolvin, was negotiating a deal that could have earned the company a profit of more than $500,000. McLennan had inherited from his father a conservatively managed company that did not borrow money and that consistently turned a profit. After McLennan had left for France in the service of his King and Empire, Wolvin and his associates saw an opportunity. It was a risk enabled by the Allies' insatiable demand for ships. Starting in the fall of 1916, Wolvin and his partner J.W. Norcoss, the managing director of Canada Steamship Lines (CSL), and other members of the CSL maritime private equity network (the Network) mounted a successful takeover of the MTC. With the company under their control, they turned the venerable old firm into an ongoing play on shipping markets. Wolvin realized that ships themselves were commodities. He was in fact acting as a traditional Greek shipowner, buying low and selling high. The deal was an early example of a leveraged buyout (LBO) with financial considerations taking priority over operational matters. The profit maximization that derived from the LBO enriched the members of the Network.[3] However, in the end, it would be a significant factor in CSL's near bankruptcy in the winter of 1921–2.

The historiography of LBOs primarily focuses on the growth of the financial engineering method in the United States from the late 1970s. In the financial history literature a nod is given to the first merger wave in American markets between 1897 and 1904 with J.P. Morgan's US Steel merger being leveraged at 61 per cent. However, the "bootstrap" operations of George Ohrstrom and others in the 1950s, followed by Jerome Kohlberg's acquisition of Stern Metals in 1965 are normally taken as the historical antecedents of the modern LBO. The takeover of Lake of the Woods Milling Company by David Russell and James Greenshields in 1902 can be considered an early Canadian LBO.[4] Maritime historians lay claim to another of Morgan's mergers, International Mercantile Marine in 1902, as being a prototypical LBO. Fifty years later Malcolm McLean's takeover of Waterman Steamship Co. has also been heralded as the first LBO.[5] Indeed, shipowning, an industry where the productive assets are themselves commodities with their own markets, is particularly vulnerable to financial engineering.

The First World War is remembered as a great disaster. The world was never the same after the slaughter in the trenches and the collapse of three European empires. For Great Britain and France, the cost of Armageddon made the defeat of the Central Powers a pyrrhic victory. Only the United States could be considered a real victor. However, the war can be viewed in a different light. For many businessmen the Great War was an opportunity. In Canada, the Laurier boom had ground to a halt in the winter of 1912–13 with the faltering of world money markets. Canadian gross national product (GNP), which peaked in November 1912, had collapsed by the summer of 1914. Manufacturing was particularly hard hit with a decline of greater than 13 per cent. And with the two new transcontinental railways facing bankruptcy, the Dominion was in trouble.[6] Thus, the outbreak of war was seen as a lever to kick start the economy.

The previous decade and a half had seen growth in Canada on an unprecedented scale. Between 1896 and 1913 the Dominion's GNP had almost quadrupled. This spectacular takeoff was fuelled by the settlement of the Prairies and the concurrent construction of two new transcontinental railroads.[7] The boom was symbolized in 1905 with the establishment of the new provinces of Saskatchewan

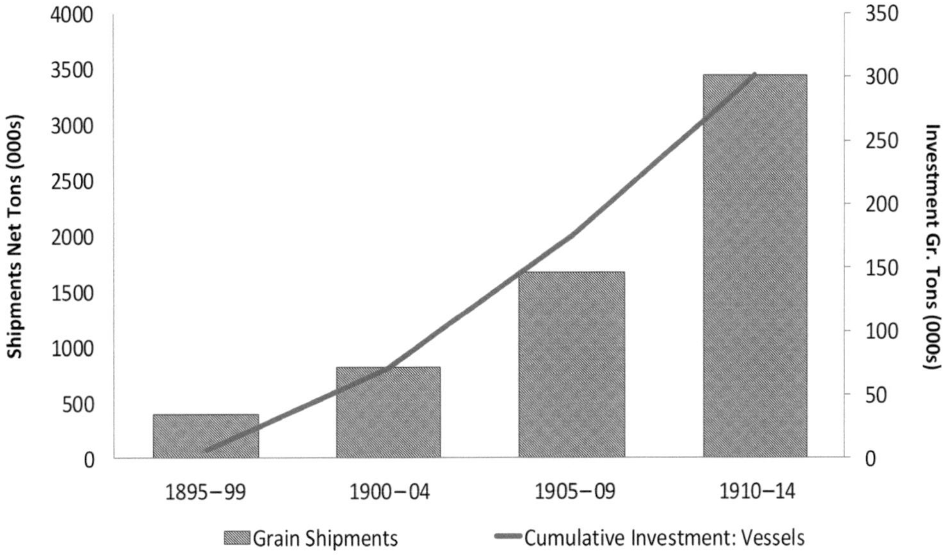

Figure 10.1 Estimated Thunder Bay grain shipment/cumulative investment Canadian vessels, quinquennial averages, 1895–1914.

Source: Canada, *Sessional Papers*, 1896–1915, and Salmon, "A Prosperous Season."

and Alberta. In practical terms, the Laurier boom was best exemplified by the growth of the Western grain trade. Grain shipments increased from the twin Lake Superior ports of Fort William and Port Arthur, Ontario, from an estimated 393,000 tons in 1896 to 5,465,000 tons in 1913.[8] Investment in Canadian shipping on the Great Lakes grew in step with the flow of grain. Between 1895 and 1914, 114 vessels of 300,000 gross tons were acquired by Canadian Great Lakes shipowners (Figure 10.1). Almost all of this investment was made in freighters. Only five major passenger vessels were added to the Canadian Upper Lakes fleet during this period. Shipowners bought two sizes of vessels. Ships too long to pass through the canal system between Lake Erie and Montreal were known as lakers. The Welland Canal (from 1887) and the St. Lawrence River canals (from 1902) that connected Montreal with Lake Erie could only accommodate vessels shorter than 260 feet in length. These vessels became known as canallers. Thus, cargoes shipped through the complete system either had to be carried only in canallers or, for downbound grain cargoes, had to be transhipped from lakers at Port Colborne, Ontario, the southern entrance to the Welland Canal, to canallers. Modern canallers in 1914 had a capacity at canal draft of 70,000 bushels of wheat while the largest lakers could load more than 400,000 bushels.[9]

By 1914 the shipping industry had adapted to the use of formal corporate structures. On the Canadian side of the Great Lakes practically all vessels were owned by companies that issued shares and occasionally bonds. Several were listed on the Montreal and Toronto Stock Exchanges. However, the key to understanding how the shipping industry worked lay not in the formal corporate organizations but in the networks of linkages that tied together the shipowners, their bankers, and their users.[10] In the Canadian Great Lakes trades the most significant consumers of tonnage were grain dealers, millers, steel producers, and coal companies. These entrepreneurs developed networks that informally tied their enterprises together. Canadian shipowners had prospered during the Laurier boom in keeping with their ties to the expanding wheat economy.[11]

The Montreal Transportation Company: A Successful Second-Generation Firm

The MTC was the oldest Canadian bulk-freight shipping company operating on the Great Lakes. Its origins stem from a partnership between the brothers John and Hugh McLennan in 1853. In 1868 the business was expanded and formally incorporated as the Montreal Transportation Company. Utilizing its fleet of river barges, the MTC specialized in forwarding grain from Kingston, Ontario, at the lower end of Lake Ontario, to Montreal. By the early 1880s the firm had a virtual monopoly on this traffic.[12] The completion of the third Welland Canal allowed the MTC to expand its field of operations to the Upper Lakes. After the death of Hugh McLennan, the surviving brother from the original partnership, the MTC was reorganized in 1903 under the leadership of his son Bartlett McLennan (1868–1918). The younger McLennan had studied engineering at the Royal Military College in Kingston and had an interest in the evolving technologies of the second industrial revolution. While there was no doubt that McLennan was a competent businessman, he was better known for his interest in outdoor sports, particularly polo and horse racing, and for his involvement in that bastion of colonial nationalism, the militia.[13] Ownership of the MTC was spread among three groups of shareholders: descendants of the original 1868 incorporators, descendants of other long-term shareholders, and consumers of the company's services. This latter group included grain dealers, millers, and coal merchants. In 1902 the combined McLennan, Ogilvie, Kinghorn, and Allan families controlled more than 75 per cent of the MTC's shares. Another 9 per cent of the shares were held by other major users of the company's services. By 1910, the last year for which shareholder lists are available, control had shifted a step further from the descendants of founders and long-term consumers to trust companies and estates. Indeed, trust companies and estates

Table 10.1 Montreal Transportation Company: Floating assets, 1903–1916

Year	Canallers (Steel)	Canallers (Wooden)	Tugs	Barges	Book Value ($ 000s)
1903	1		5	30	373.3
1904	3	1	6	28	688.3
1905	3	2	6	25	696.3
1906	3	2	7	38	648.8
1907	5	3	8	36	772.0
1908	6	3	9	36	1,074.0
1909	6	3	9	36	1,247.2
1910	6	3	7	36	1,244 0
1911	6	2	7	35	1,236.0
1912	6	2	7	33	1,201.0
1913	6	2	7	34	1,184.9
1914	7	2	7	32	1,288.0
1915	7	4	7	30	1,287.8
1916	4	4	7	30	937.5

Note: Vessels owned by the MTC at the beginning of the navigation season (April–May) for 1903–14, and 1 January for 1915–1916. Two new canallers were delivered to MTC in June 1903.

Source: QUA, CSL fonds, boxes 116 and 117, MTC minute books.

controlled more MTC shares than the firm's customers. McLennan was fully aware that a significant percentage of the company's stock was held by (or for) female and minor descendants of deceased shareholders.[14] The most prominent among the firm's consumers were two grain dealers (James Carruthers and A.G. Thomson) and two coal dealers (Abner Kingman and Farquhar Robertson). Together, the four dealers controlled 16 per cent of the company's shares. After the death of the last original partner, George Kinghorn in 1906, the only significant tie to the MTC's original management was Bartlett McLennan. The survival of the company would depend on his continued interest in maintaining it as an independent entity.[15]

Under the younger McLennan's leadership, the MTC remained a sound, conservatively managed firm. Between 1903 and 1914, the company increased its capital from $300,000 to $913,000 while the size of the fleet more than tripled (see Table 10.1 and Table 10.2). Almost without exception this expansion was not financed with debt. Instead, new assets were paid for by issuing more stock, all of which was fully paid up. Bartlett McLennan's conservative financial strategy was combined with an aggressive acquisition policy that saw the MTC swallow up three competitors between 1903 and the start of the Great War. Originally, the company's canallers carried grain from ports on the Upper Lakes, particularly Thunder Bay and Chicago to Kingston, where the cargoes were transhipped to the company's barges for

Table 10.2 Montreal Transportation Company: Profit/loss, 1903–1916

Year	Capital ($ 000s)	Assets ($ 000s)	Earnings ($ 000s)	Profit ($ 000s)	Dividend %
1903	300.0	1,004.5	251.0	83.9	10
1904	400.0	1,012.1	156.6	22.0	4
1905	400.0	988.2	290.1	122.1	16
1906	500.0	1,134.2	417.8	156.2	15
1907	600.0	1,443.0	619.2	286.4	20
1908	700.0	1,601.9	397.3	113.8	10
1909	700.0	1,594.4	362.9	107.9	10
1910	800.0	1,610.6	375.7	48.8	7
1911	800.0	1,582.1	402.9	108.4	10
1912	800.0	1,605.7	491.0	158.9	14
1913	800.0	1,590.9	556.6	185.9	17
1914	890.0	1,709.5	378.8	62.1	6
1915	913.4	1,818.9	403.3	144.3	11
1916	913.4	2,440.4	555.1	183.4	5

Note: Assets are listed at book values.

Source: QUA, CSL fonds, boxes 116 and 117, MTC minute books.

carriage to Montreal. Initially, the transfer from lake vessel to barge had been done by the company's floating elevators, but in 1899, it built a shore-side elevator with a storage capacity of 800,000 bushels. This capital investment was followed in 1903 by the purchase of the bankrupt Prescott Elevator Company's one-million-bushel elevator.[16] This traditional strategy was continued in 1906 when the MTC bought out its remaining rival in the St. Lawrence River forwarding trade, the Kingston and Montreal Forwarding Company. The smaller firm's thirteen barges and real estate in Portsmouth, Ontario, cost the MTC $53,100.[17]

Before the war, the MTC could not be accused of financial engineering; however, it did not entirely resist innovation. Operationally, it was in the forefront of development in marine propulsion systems. Beginning in 1911, the MTC ordered two canallers from British shipyards: one with a diesel engine, and the second with a diesel-electric engine. Their trials were not successful. Both vessels were rejected because the engines were not sufficiently powerful to navigate the St. Lawrence River.[18] Now short of tonnage, the MTC found partial relief by acquiring in 1913 a modern canaller and two wooden barges from the Calvin family of Garden Island, Ontario, for $144,000 worth of MTC shares. For the transaction, the MTC valued its shares at $160, not the $100 listed on the company's books. Significantly, this evaluation was done in the 1913 market, before the war-induced demand for ships raised the price of tonnage. In 1914 the MTC purchased Calvin's two remaining freighters, both smaller wooden canallers, for 234 MTC shares again valued at $160 each. Thus, at the start of the war the company valued itself at $1,460,000 and not the $913,000 listed on its balance sheet. Given that the MTC had a healthy reserve fund, this was a reasonable evaluation of the company's net worth.[19]

However, the MTC's familiar way of doing business was beginning to change. Increasingly, the ships went the entire distance through the newly enlarged St. Lawrence River canals to Montreal with their cargoes. While grain shipments still provided the MTC with the majority of its freight before the Great War, other commodities became significant as well. Most notably, the company began shipping steel rails from Sydney, Nova Scotia, to Thunder Bay, Ontario, and other Great Lakes–St. Lawrence River ports. After a successful trial in 1904, the MTC signed a long-term contract with Dominion Iron and Steel Co. (DISCO). Two canallers were built specifically for this trade.[20] In January 1908, in the aftermath of the financial panic, DISCO's president J.H. Plummer made an offer to the MTC to acquire the stock of the company for $275 a share. This was a 20 per cent premium on the MTC's book value (Table 10.2). Plummer and his associates were given an option while they tried to raise the money on the London market. This they were unable to do within the allotted time. Then in July they made another attempt, with a mixed offer of $750,000 in cash and $1 million in 5 per cent bonds. McLennan tried to negotiate an increase in the bond rate but the deal fell through. He and the MTC's other second-generation shareholders were willing to sell out if the price was right. The significance of the failed takeover was not that it was unconsummated, but rather that outside interests considered the MTC a worthwhile investment even at a premium.[21]

In the decade before the start of the war, the MTC performed well, its profits matching the growth of the Canadian grain trade. By the start of the war, the MTC owned seven modern steel-hulled canallers, four older wooden canallers, four lake barges, seven tugs, as well as thirty river barges with a book value of $1,287,000 (Table 10.1). This was a sevenfold increase in modern steel canallers from the opening of the 1903 navigation season. While the numbers of barges and tugs did not see such a numerical increase, qualitatively this tonnage was improved with the addition of composite and steel-hulled barges, and the retirement of many of the older wooden river barges.[22] Despite this growth, the MTC was no longer the largest Canadian bulk carrier operating in the Great Lakes–St. Lawrence system. Even before the formation of Canada Steamship Lines (CSL) in 1913, other bulk shippers had surpassed the MTC.[23]

The war caused significant changes in the MTC's plans and operations. Its modern canallers were chartered for coastal and overseas employment at great profit but increased risk. Beginning in May 1915, five canallers were chartered for service between North American East Coast ports and the Caribbean at $6,500 a month to American interests. A second charter was also arranged with the Dominion Coal Co. for the other two canallers and a lake barge. Taking on these charters was a profitable strategy for the MTC, with monthly earnings from these contracts totalling $32,250. What made these contracts attractive for the company was that they came during the spring and summer months when the grain trade was traditionally slow. But with opportunity came the greater risk of sailing in unfamiliar waters. A canaller was lost by grounding in the Bahamas in August, and in October a second was sold. Both the insurance settlement and the sale were profitable for the company. However, the removal of two canallers from the company's books, and the withdrawal of much of the MTC's tonnage from its Great Lakes trade, made it difficult for the company to fulfil its commitments to its traditional customers. To help meet some of these demands the MTC decided to order its first laker: the 550-foot ship, designed to carry 385,000 bushels of wheat, was built by Collingwood Shipbuilding for $465,000.[24]

In the meantime, five remaining canallers were chartered for the winter months at rates ranging from $7,000 to $8,000 a month. This profitable arrangement was interrupted when another canaller was lost off the Virginia coast in December 1915. Notwithstanding the greater risks associated with operating ships designed for the Great Lakes in deep sea trades, the MTC showed a profit after depreciation of $197,300. Almost half of this amount came from the insurance settlements for the two lost canallers and the profit from the sale of the canaller *Westmount*. The company declared an 11 per cent dividend for 1915 (Table 10.2). Still, the company was so flush with cash that it issued a call loan to the National Trust Co. for $200,000 at 5.5 per cent. Then it purchased $75,000 of Anglo-French war bonds.[25] Yet 1915 had not been a complete success for the MTC. Significantly, its losses included more than three of its ships. The MTC's president, Bartlett McLennan volunteered for service in the Canadian Expeditionary Force and by the summer he was in France.[26] With his departure, active control of the company passed to the vice-president, Farquhar Robertson, and the managing director, Lawrence L. Henderson.

Although deep sea and coastal operations were more profitable than inland service, they also imposed greater costs. Particularly onerous was the need to meet higher insurance standards. Yet despite these elevated expenditures, the MTC remained a profitable business (Table 10.2). With a monthly income of $31,000 from four ships operating outside of its core business and almost $300,000 available in liquid assets on its balance sheet, the MTC became a takeover target. The company's prospects were enhanced when, in February 1916, the Dominion Coal Co. chartered three canallers at $16,000 a month each. Initially, the contract was meant to last six months. Later the geographical limits of the contract were expanded to include the West Indies for an additional $3,000 per month per vessel.[27]

In April 1916 the MTC was approached by A.B. Mackay, a shipowner and broker based in Hamilton, Ontario, with an offer to purchase the company. He represented an unnamed group of investors, who were ready to purchase 75 per cent of the MTC's shares. His "associates" were never identified, although press speculation mentioned interests connected with the Nova Scotia Steel & Coal Co. or J.S. Norris, the Chicago grain merchant, as possible candidates. A more likely scenario was that Mackay was acting as the front man for James Playfair. Mackay and Playfair had worked together on the merger that led to the formation of Inland Lines Ltd. in 1910.[28] After haggling over terms, an amount of $225 a share was agreed upon; however, the MTC's board would only accept payment in cash. When Mackay was unable to come up with the money, the deal fell apart.[29] In June the MTC lost one more asset when yet another canaller went ashore on the Nova Scotia coast. Charter rates remained high but the tonnage to earn this income was disappearing. By the fall of 1916 the company's only substantial assets were a laker under construction, three steel canallers, two steel-hulled tugs, and its goodwill (Table 10.1).[30] Still, the MTC was a valuable firm not only because of its reputation but also because the market knew that the company's board would accept the right offer.

The CSL Network at Work

By comparison, the CSL Network was not merely larger than its older competitor; it was much more a product of the merger mania that developed in the closing days of the Laurier boom.[31] CSL was the result of a prolonged gestation that took five years to come to fruition, from 1910 to 1914. It brought together seven major steamship firms (and numerous small companies). Collectively, the Network operated in the Great Lakes freight and passenger trades, the eastern North American coastal waters, and the Caribbean. Great Lakes shipowners, grain dealers, and Canadian financiers joined the British shipping mogul Sir Christopher Furness and the industrial conglomerate Vickers Ltd. in creating the largest shipping enterprise on the Canadian side of the Great Lakes.[32] The most aggressive members of this disparate group eventually formed a prototype of a private equity network (see Table 10.3). For these men, finance was more important than operational matters. During its first decade, CSL was the centrepiece of a maritime network that included more than

Table 10.3 CSL Network, 1913–1920

1913	1917	1920
C.A. Barnard	C.A. Barnard	C.A. Barnard
	Henry Black	Henry Black
Edmund Bristol	Edmund Bristol	Edmund Bristol
	H.W. Brown	H.W. Brown
James Carruthers	James Carruthers	
Sir Trevor Dawson	Sir Trevor Dawson	Sir Trevor Dawson
Sir Stephen Furness		
M.J. Haney	M.J. Haney	M.J. Haney
W. Grant Morden	W. Grant Morden	W. Grant Morden
J.W. Norcross	J.W. Norcross	J.W. Norcross
H.B. Smith	H.B. Smith	H.B. Smith
J.P. Steedman	J.P. Steedman	J.P. Steedman
J.F.M. Stewart	J.F.M. Stewart	J.F.M. Stewart
	James Whalen	James Whalen
Roy Wolvin	Roy Wolvin	Roy Wolvin

Note: Not every member of the Network was active in all phases of its operations. James Walen's involvement with the Network began with the acquisition of the Canadian North West Steamship Co. in 1915. H.W. Brown did not participate in its Great Lakes activities. Sir Stephen Furness succeeded his uncle, Lord Christopher Furness, after the latter's death in December 1912.

Sources: QUA, CSL fonds, box 117, MTC Bond and Shareholder Lists, Correspondence, minute book, 1917–1921; MMK, CSL fonds, 996.39.7, CSL minute books, 1913–1921; and Salmon, *This Unsatisfactory Condition*.

twenty separate firms operating in the Great Lakes–St. Lawrence system's shipping and related sectors (Figure 10.2). This Network was run to benefit the active members of the group as individuals. The legally separate corporations controlled by the Network were all ostensibly operated to turn a profit. However, as the wartime shipping boom gave way to the postwar depression in shipping rates, the only publicly traded firm in the group, CSL, became a repository of last resort for the Network's more problematical investments.

These transactions demonstrated the insider Network's abilities at many forms of short-term asset value enhancement, including leveraged buyouts, stock manipulation, and fraudulent evaluations. Moreover, CSL's governance structure had from the firm's inception been designed to facilitate the Network's aggrandizement. By the time CSL became operational in the spring of 1914, several Network members had been marginalized. However, twelve members of the original syndicate remained (Table 10.3). Network members' influence grew or declined in tandem with the company's fortunes. As the maritime opportunities presented by the Great War increased, the more aggressive members of the Network took full control, and the more conservative members either left or were forced out.[33]

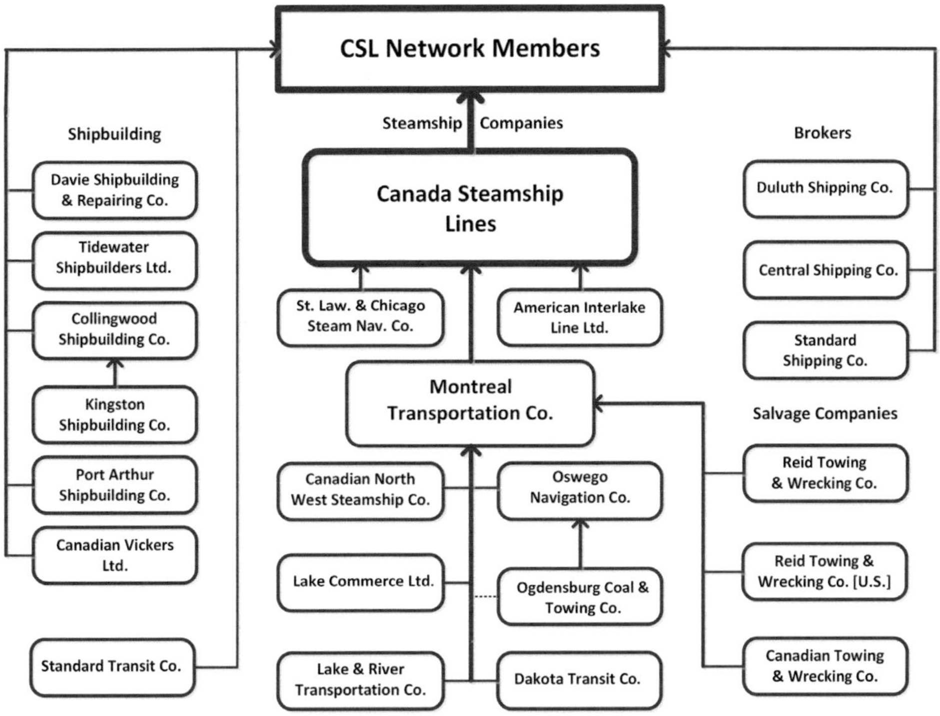

Figure 10.2 Canada Steamship Lines' Great Lakes Network, 1913–1920.

Sources: QUA, CSL fonds, boxes 116 and 117, MTC minute books; MMK, CSL fonds, 1996.19.7, CSL minute books; and *Duluth News-Tribune,* 1910–20.

After W. Grant Morden left for England in 1913, Roy M. Wolvin (1880–1945) gradually became the driving force behind the Network's activities on the Great Lakes–St. Lawrence system. He was intent on making his own fortune with a drive and a financial acumen that far eclipsed the competent second-generation businessman Bartlett McLennan. Wolvin, a young expatriate American, had begun his career in his cousin's Duluth, Minnesota, shipping office while still a teenager. By the age of twenty-two he was made manager of the Great Lakes and St. Lawrence Transportation Co. that operated canallers from US Upper Lake ports to Quebec and Montreal. In 1910 Wolvin emigrated to Canada, where in partnership with J.W. Norcross he had established the Mutual Steamship Co. in 1907. This was followed by the incorporation of the Winnipeg-based shipping agency Standard Shipping in 1909. A year later Wolvin's entrepreneurial talents fully blossomed with the formation of the Canadian Interlake Line Ltd. Canadian Interlake became an integral piece in the series of mergers that led ultimately to the creation of CSL.[34] After the outbreak of the war, Wolvin was to develop a strategy based on his connections to

Great Lakes shipping, shipbuilding, and North American grain markets that made him the natural leader of the Network's Canadian activities.

That CSL was moulded in the interests of the Network that created it was evident in the company's by-laws. By virtue of the by-laws, the president, the vice-presidents, and the managing director all became members of the company's board of directors. A quorum of directors was only five members. Thus, all significant corporate power was placed in the hands of CSL's senior officers. Because the Network controlled the information presented to the board, the board became little more than a rubber stamp for the actions of the company's management. Its few outside directors had little opportunity to provide independent oversight of the firm's management. Further to this, board members acting in their capacity as CSL board members were allowed to enter into contracts with themselves as individuals. Taken together, CSL's by-laws were no more than an invitation for the Network to follow its own opportunistic instincts at the expense of the company.[35]

After a difficult start in 1914, CSL appeared to have had a good war. High freight rates both on the high seas and the Great Lakes would seem to have made sure that the conflict was profitable for the company. Yet even before the postwar decline in freight rates set in, CSL's financial weakness was evident. These difficulties were the result of its weak corporate governance structure that was designed to put all power in the hands of the Network. So while the war was profitable for CSL, the Network members on the steamship company's board were able to control the direction of its activities. This led CSL to invest in areas that profited Network members first, and only secondarily the company. Eventually, in the winter of 1921–2, CSL's finances reached the point of near bankruptcy after the company was unable to float a bond issue in Montreal. The company then had to go to New York markets for assistance. As part of a bailout package, the consulting firm of Coverdale and Colpitts was called in by the investment bankers Kissell, Kinnicutt & Co. to do a thorough study of CSL finances. As a result of the report written for the bank, the consulting firm's senior partner William Coverdale became president of CSL. His subsequent reforms dismantled the original maritime Network and turned CSL into a modern corporation with strong corporate governance structures.[36]

While the corporate entity that was CSL went from boom to bust, the remaining members of the CSL Network profited handsomely. The Network's good fortune was based on the Allies overwhelming demand for shipping of all types. The Network was not merely opportunistic; it created openings for itself. The first evidence of the Network's members operating outside of CSL's formal corporate structure came in the fall of 1914. They revived a minor component of the original CSL merger, Lake Commerce Ltd. Originally a single ship company whose only asset became part of CSL, its principals included Haney, Wolvin, Norcross, and Stewart.

In the fall of 1914, they purchased a second-hand American laker. This was followed in 1915 by the acquisition of a small obsolescent canaller. Lake Commerce was capitalized for a mere $74,600 with laker *Valcartier* carrying a $90,000 mortgage. While this investment was certainly insignificant when compared to CSL, it did demonstrate that the Network members' loyalty belonged to a larger more informal organization. CSL and Lake Commerce, although quantitatively different, were merely part of a single expanding Network (Figure 10.2).[37]

Before the end of 1915 the Network members acquired a further addition to their holdings, the Canadian North West Steamship Co. This firm, which had been controlled by the Marks and Wiley families of Thunder Bay, came on the market after the death of its two founders. Canadian North West was not a major vessel owner but it did own four older lakers (all of the vessels were built before 1900) for a total of 10,700 tons. Six members of the Network took part in this transaction with Norcross, Wolvin, Haney, and Stewart each holding a sixth of the shares while Dawson and Morden between them had another 16.6 per cent interest, with the remaining sixth being held by James Whalen.[38]

The growing wartime demand for tonnage made it profitable to scavenge for vessels of any description. None realized this more than the Network members, as demonstrated by their formation of the Lake and River Transportation Co. With a capital of $50,000 this recently incorporated firm's only assets were two thirty-two-year-old wooden package freight canallers. Control of Lake and River rested firmly with the Network, but in this case Wolvin and Norcross held one-third of the shares, while the remaining shares were held by CSL managers or employees of Wolvin's Standard Shipping.[39] Simultaneous with the creation of Lake and River, Wolvin and Norcross organized a major offensive that demonstrated the Network's ability for financial innovation as well as its fiscal strength.

The Network's targets were the St. Lawrence and Chicago Steam Navigation Co. (SLCN) and the MTC. At first sight, CSL's takeover of SLCN in 1916 appears to have been a straightforward friendly acquisition of a firm already partly within the Network's orbit. But there was a twist. At the start of the war, SLCN was a profitable grain carrier owning five vessels, four lakers, and a canaller. It had paid a 12 per cent dividend in 1915 while maintaining a surplus account of $390,000, all with a paid up capital of only $966,000.[40] As a publicly traded company, it was susceptible to a hostile takeover bid. In the spring of 1916 with SLCN's shares trading at $115, the company became the subject of such an acquisition attempt by the former Network member and now rival Great Lakes shipowner, James Playfair. Realizing that it could not let SLCN's lakers fall into Playfair's hands, as such an acquisition would have doubled his laker tonnage, CSL entered the bidding as a friendly suitor. But after the trustees for CSL's debentures objected to the attempted acquisition, individual Network members formed a syndicate and on 20 April purchased all of SLCN's stock for $187.75 a share, for a total of $1,814,415. After fully disclosing their conflict of interest, the syndicate sold SLCN to CSL on 11 July. Some of the financing for the purchase came from the Home Bank of Canada. Wolvin and Stewart borrowed $100,000 from the bank at rates ranging from 6 to 8 per cent using Canadian North West Steamship and Canadian Locomotive shares as collateral. The syndicate made a profit of $187,000 for an annualized rate of return of 45 per cent. The price was steep, but CSL had acquired a valuable set of assets.[41]

The Network performed well for itself and in the longer term well for CSL with its handling of the SLCN takeover. However, its acquisition of the MTC in the fall of 1916 was a more complex affair with a rather muddied outcome. The Network employed a number of financial innovations that can be seen as an exaggerated sequel to the formation of CSL. These included a leveraged buyout, asset stripping, and fraudulent evaluations, leading to the creation of an entirely new Montreal Transportation Co. The result was highly profitable for Network members. Wolvin and Norcross offered $225 a share for 75 per cent of the MTC's stock on 22 September 1916. Their offer was subsequently modified to include all the company's 9,134 shares for a total of $2,055,150. The offer involved a down payment of $50,000 plus $60 dollars a share (minus the down payment), due ten days after shareholders representing 75 per cent of the company's stock had accepted the offer, and 6 per cent promissory notes due in January and February 1917 for the remainder (Figure 10.3).[42] The deal was a leveraged buyout from the start, with the offer being contingent on the purchasers being allowed to sell off MTC assets to pay the notes: "[T]he offer ... will contain amongst other provisions an arrangement for our [the purchasers] obtaining the effective control of the Board of Directors in such a manner that we will be able to make sales of the property providing the collateral held by you to our notes is fully protected."[43]

The company's shareholders' rights were given greater protection by having its managing director, Lawrence L. Henderson, serve as interim president until the deal was finalized. The first order of business after the Network had taken control of the MTC's board of directors was to authorize the interim president to sell the company's remaining steel-hulled canallers. They were sold for a net of $1,217,000 or four times their book value. These proceeds, together with the insurance settlement on the ship lost in June 1916, paid off the Network's debts. The venerable firm had cost the Network $550,000 cash. That was only 40 per cent of the MTC's pre-war evaluation and a mere 27 per cent of the total price. By playing the wartime shipping market, the Network had been able to profitably leverage its acquisition of the MTC while satisfying the company's original shareholders (Figure 10.4).[44]

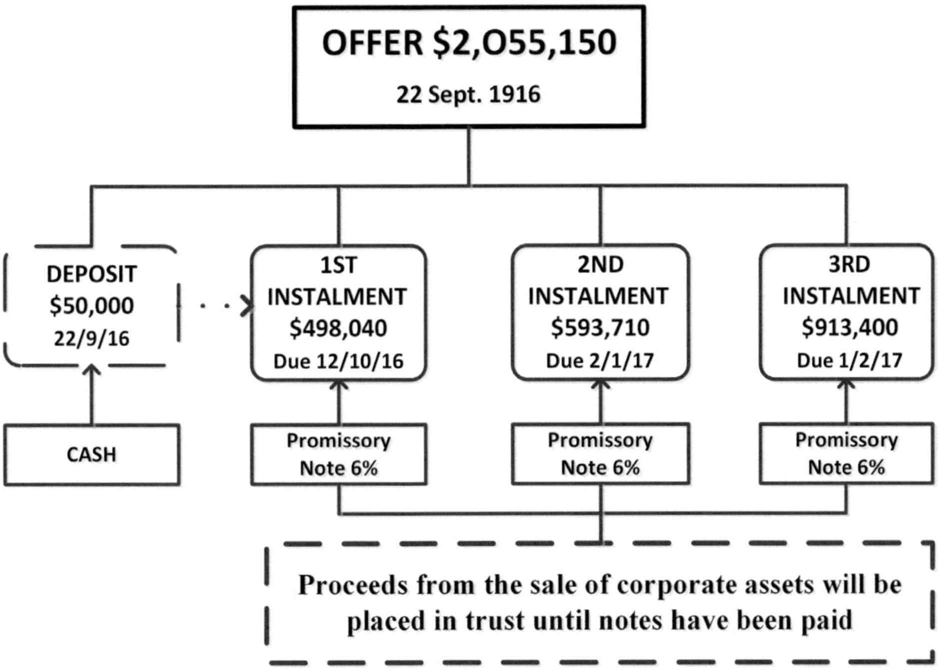

Figure 10.3 CSL Network offer for the Montreal Transportation Company, 1916.

Source: QUA, CSL fonds, box 116, MTC minute book.

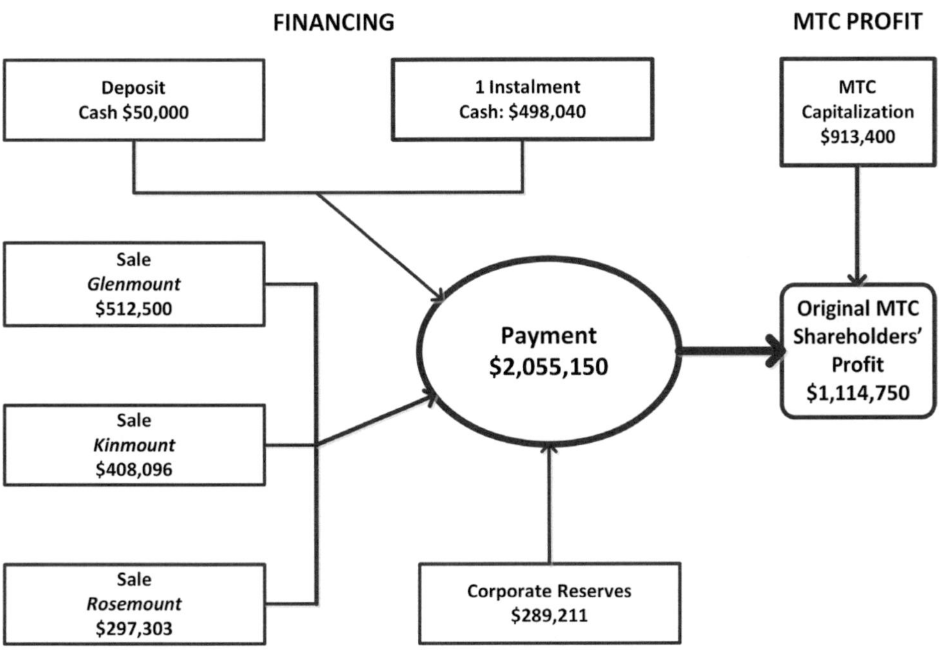

Figure 10.4 Montreal Transportation Company, leveraged buyout financing, 1916–1917.

Source: QUA, CSL fonds, boxes 116 and 117, MTC minute book.

The New Montreal Transportation Company

The stripped down MTC was to be used as a vehicle for the Network's further expansion outside of the constraints of CSL. The first acquisition was the small thirty-year-old composite-hulled laker *Omega* that cost $75,000.[45] However, before more assets were added, the old firm was to undergo a complete financial face lift. A new Montreal Transportation Company (MTC17) was incorporated in March 1917 with an authorized capital of $4,000,000. Wolvin became president of the new firm with Stewart as its vice-president. The MTC17 purchased the MTC's assets which "friendly" marine surveyor Henry Black had revalued for $2,557,000 (Table 10.4). This was 58 per cent more than the value shown on the old company's books, which was justified by wartime demand for tonnage and the lack of available shipbuilding berths. The MTC17 bought the old company (now controlled by the Network) for $400,000 cash, 14,411 shares, and $715,900 in ten-year 6 per cent serial bonds. The $400,000 cash was merely a bookkeeping entry because the old firm used the payment to purchase 4,000 shares of the MTC17.[46]

The Network now consolidated all its non-CSL Canadian Great Lakes floating assets in the new company (Figure 10.5). Canadian North West Steamship's four old lakers were acquired for $212,700 in bonds and 5,473 shares; Lake Commerce received $23,800 in bonds and 612 shares for its old canaller; and River and Lake Transportation got $47,600 worth of bonds and 1,224 shares for its two elderly canallers. Thus, the new firm's entire $1 million issue of bonds was distributed to the Network members.[47] The real capital in the MTC17 was represented by its bonds while the shares were mostly water. In fact, the bonds represented a fair evaluation of its most significant asset, the new laker *Westmount*, which entered service in the spring of 1917. The MTC17 had only two first-class assets: the *Westmount* and the steel-hulled tug *Emerson*.[48]

Although it is not possible to determine how all of the individual members of the Network financed their share of the MTC scheme, estimates can be made for three contributors: Haney, Stewart, and Barnard. This subgroup of the Network borrowed their share of the MTC takeover from the Home Bank of Canada. For 25 per cent of the profits of the 27 per cent interest held by Haney, Stewart, and Barnard in the MTC deal, the bank loaned the three Network members $179,000. This was initially done through Haney's Miller Cartage Co. The debt was later transferred to Stewart's account. The bank's profit from the deal was $135,000 for a return of 75 per cent. Depending on when the subgroup took their profits, their individual returns could have been as high as 300 per cent (before dividends).[49]

Table 10.4 Montreal Transportation Company (1917), floating asset revaluation, 1917

Vessel Type	Book Value Dec. 1916 ($ 000s)	Book Value Apr. 1917 ($ 000s)	Increase (1917/1916)
Montreal Transportation Co.			
Lakers	540	1,000	85%
Canallers	59	141	138%
Tugs	128	355	177%
Barges	307	718	133%
Sub-Total	1,034	2,214	114%
Canadian North West Steamship Co.			
Lakers	[170]	630	[270%]
Lake Barge	[40]	130	[225%]
Sub-Total	[210]	760	[261%]
Lake Commerce Ltd.			
Canallers	[38]	85	[123%]
Lake and River Transportation Co.			
Canallers	[50]	170	[240%]
Grand Total	[1,339]	3,229	[141%]

Note: MTC laker valuation for 1916 includes the contract price for the vessel under construction and the cost of the *Omega* (purchased from American owners, November 1916).

Source: QUA, CSL fonds, boxes 116 and 117, MTC minute books.

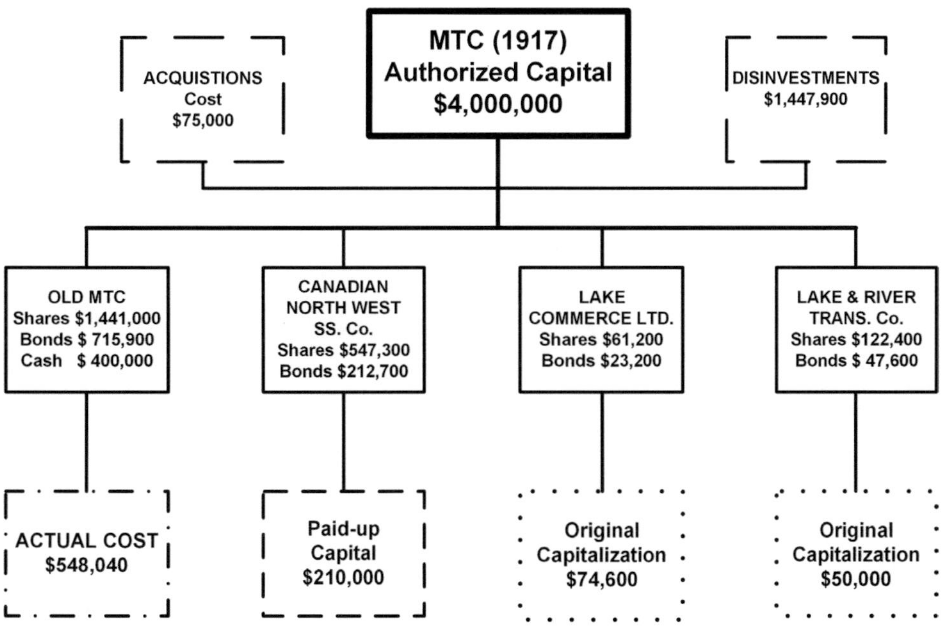

Figure 10.5 Montreal Transportation Company (1917): Formation

Source: QUA, CSL fonds, boxes 116 and 117, MTC minute books.

For the remainder of its existence, the MTC17 was run more like an asset play than a Great Lakes bulk carrier firm. This meant treating ships not merely as assets but as commodities to be bought and sold as if they were any other commodity. Acquired vessels were still supposed to make a profit on their operations but if they could be sold at a profit themselves then they were.[50] This strategy depended on the opportunities provided by the war. The key to this strategy was information management, in particular Wolvin's knowledge of shipping and grain markets. His understanding of future trends came not just from a knowledge of wartime shipping markets but also from access to North American crop reports through the three shipping agencies he controlled. These firms – Standard Shipping (Winnipeg), Central Shipping (Chicago), and Duluth Shipping – provided direct access to grain dealers, elevator operators, and Great Lakes shipowners.[51] The increased demand for North American grain could be taken as a given as long as the war continued, for two reasons: first, the closure of the Dardanelles embargoed Black Sea grain exports, and second, the success of Germany's U-boat campaign made the cost of Australian and Argentinian grain imports increasingly expensive in ton-mile terms.[52] Wolvin used this knowledge of the grain trade, Great Lakes shipping, world freight markets, and the Allied demand for foodstuffs to plan his market moves.

In the MTC17's initial year of operation only two assets were sold, the tug *Emerson* and the barge *Ungava*. Both were modern steel vessels. Reflecting the wartime demand for tonnage they were sold for $400,000 or a profit of 33 per cent on their MTC17 book value in April 1917. This was a 350 per cent windfall over their value on the MTC's books in December 1916.[53] In contrast to these meagre sales, Wolvin mounted significant acquisition offensives on two separate fronts. First, in May 1917 the MTC17 gained control of the Reid family's transborder salvage and towing business based in Sarnia, Ontario, and Port Huron, Michigan. This was done through two newly formed companies. The new Canadian firm had a Dominion charter while its American counterpart was incorporated in West Virginia. This was followed in December by the acquisition of James Whalen's Canadian Towing and Wrecking Co., based in Thunder Bay. Whalen, through his original holdings of the Canadian North West's stock, was a shareholder in the MTC17. The financing was complex with the cost including cash and stock totalling $315,000. Consequently, by the end of 1917, Wolvin and his associates controlled the most important Canadian salvage firms on the upper Great Lakes along with a significant interest in the American side of the business. This allowed the Network to have direct control over a substantial portion of the Great Lakes salvaged tonnage.[54]

Wolvin's second move was an attempt to acquire tonnage to serve Montreal's market for coal. The city's coal was supplied from two sources: coalfields in either the Maritime provinces or in Pennsylvania. Much of the tonnage required to move coal from Eastern Canada had been requisitioned for wartime service, while many of the canallers that carried coal from American ports on Lakes Erie and Ontario to Montreal had also been enticed by high freights to take part in North Atlantic trades. The Network's opportunity came with the death of John Hannan, owner of the Ogdensburg Coal & Towing Co. in April 1916. In partnership with Hannan's surviving family members, the Network incorporated a Canadian-based firm of the same name while the old company was wound up.[55] Among the firm's assets were three old wooden canallers and two wooden barges. The average age of these vessels was thirty-five years. An offer of $153,000 was made by the MTC17 for the Ogdensburg Coal & Towing's fleet but the sale was held up by the United States Shipping Board. Permission was granted to transfer to the Canadian registry only one of the canallers. The cost was $60,000. A separate corporation, the Oswego Navigation Co., was set up to run the remaining four vessels (Figure 10.6).[56]

By the end of 1917, MTC17 purchases only amounted to two old canallers and a wooden barge at a total cost of $190,000. While only two vessels were lost in 1917, one of them was a former Canadian North West laker wrecked near Manitoulin Island. It represented 10 per cent of the MTC17's Upper Lakes carrying capacity. The vessel had been valued at $210,000. Despite this mishap, the MTC17 had a profitable year. Earnings after depreciation totalled $470,000. Given the leverage built into the company's capital structure, the MTC17's estimated rate of return for Network members was 32 per cent. The maximum amount Network members had invested in the original four firms that made up the MTC17 was $882,640 (Figure 10.5). Similarly, while the company's official dividend was 6 per cent, in real terms for Network investors it was closer to 18 per cent (Table 10.5 and Table 10.6).[57]

The year 1918 was a much more active year for vessel sales and acquisitions. The demand for tonnage, whether on the high seas or the Great Lakes, had reached the point where vessels no matter their age or condition could find a buyer. In the MTC17's case this included a thirty-six-year-old composite-hulled barge that was reconstructed into a steamer. In May the company acquired four small tugs for $56,000.[58] Then the MTC17 chartered the four former Ogdensburg Coal & Towing vessels from the Oswego Navigation Co. The contract was for the carriage of coal from Lake Erie and Lake Ontario ports to St. Lawrence River ports, and for grain from Port Colborne to Montreal. The handling of this charter marked a shift in the MTC17's investment strategy. While it would still trade in ships when it saw the opportunity for a profit, it now began to take heed of the Network's postwar requirements for its Great Lakes operations. This new dual-track strategy was signalled when the company paid more than $41,700 for rebuilding the

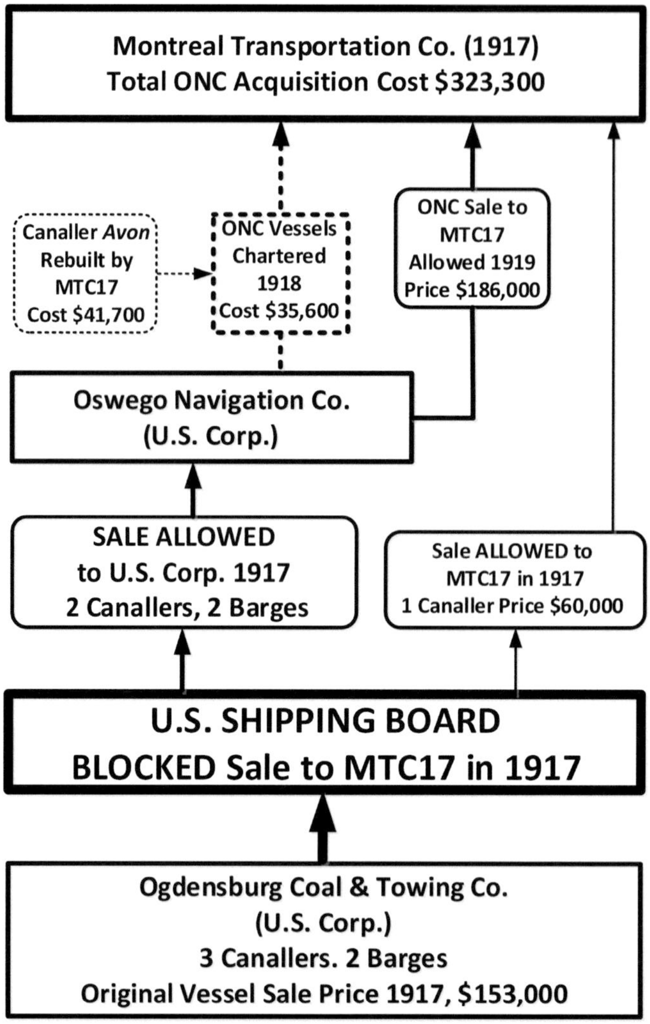

Figure 10.6 Acquisition of Ogdensburg Coal & Towing Co. fleet, 1917–1919.

Source: QUA, CSL fonds, boxes 116 and 117, MTC minute books.

Table 10.5 Montreal Transportation Company (1917): Estimated profit/loss, 1917–1919

Year	Capital	Earnings	Net Operational Profit	Asset Sales Profit	Net Profit
	($ 000s)	($ 000s)	($ 000s)	($ 000s)	($ 000s)
1917	2,667.5	774.6	186.3	100	286.3
1918	2,667.5	313.8	193.4	482.9	676.3
1919	2,667.5	1,695.4	180.4	[230.0]	[410.4]

Source: QUA, CSL fonds, box 117, MTC Minute Book, "Directors' Reports."

Table 10.6 Montreal Transportation Company (1917): Estimated Network Rate of Return

Year	Dividend	Estimated Network Dividend	Estimated Network Rate of Return
	%	%	%
1917	6	18	32.2
1918	7	21	76.6
1919	14	42	46.4

Note: The Estimated Network Dividend and the Estimated Network Rate of Return are based on the maximum possible investment made by Network members in acquisition of the MTC and the three smaller companies that became part of the MTC17 upon its formation in 1917.

Source: QUA, CSL fonds, box 117, MTC minute book.

badly damaged *Avon* while the canaller was still owned by Oswego Navigation (Figure 10.6).[59]

Of more immediate significance for the MTC17 were the negotiations begun by Wolvin in August 1918 to sell much of the firm's tonnage. This was the continuation of the asset-stripping strategy that had begun with the original takeover. In September contracts were signed with a Cuban shipbroker, whose clients included a Belgian shipowner, for the sale of the three remaining former Canadian North West lakers and three old canallers, for a total of $1,435,000 (Figure 10.7). This was $800,000 more than their book value. Such was the demand for tonnage that each of the remaining Canadian North West lakers sold for more than the Network had paid for the entire company in 1915. The three lakers were to be cut in half and taken through the canal system to Montreal before being rebuilt for ocean service. Under normal conditions such vessels could not have been profitably operated on the high seas but the wartime demand for tonnage made it worthwhile to bring these old timers out of the Great Lakes. The sudden end of the war in November 1918 did not immediately cause a decline in ocean freight rates but the demand for rebuilt lakers did fall. The deal started to unravel. First, the purchaser of one laker and two of the old wooden canallers defaulted and forfeited the deposit of $135,000 on the purchase. A new contract for the laker of $290,000 (with a deposit of $50,000) was drawn up. The sale of the other two lakers and the old iron-hulled canaller was completed, from which the MTC17 made a profit of $477,400.[60] Wolvin, the financial entrepreneur, had crafted a deal that put immediate profit ahead of steady growth. Six weeks after Bartlett McLennan's death on the Western Front, the last vestiges of his sustained growth strategy were sold to the highest bidder.

Profits from vessel operations declined in 1918, only totalling $231,600, due in part to the continued collapse in the grain trade. However, the MTC17's surplus

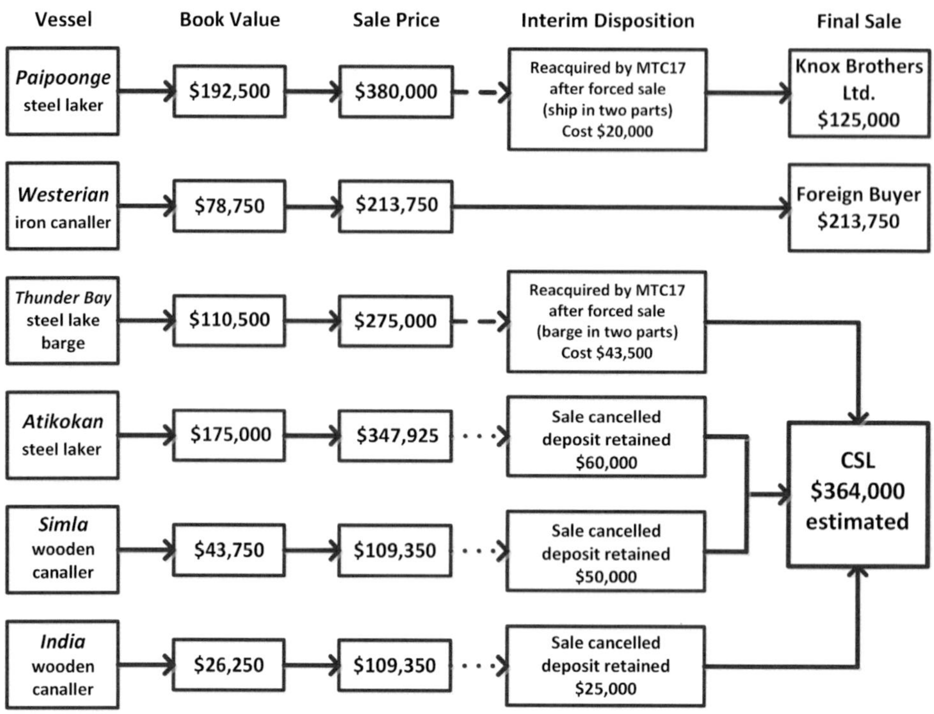

Figure 10.7 Montreal Transportation Company (1917) vessel sales, September 1918.

Source: QUA, CSL fonds, boxes 116 and 117, MTC minute books.

account was fattened by the revenues from ship sales. After setting aside more than 10 per cent for depreciation, shareholders were rewarded with a 7 per cent dividend. When the MTC17's leveraged capital structure is taken into account, the dividend rate was closer to 21 per cent and its real rate of return was more than 76 per cent (Table 10.5 and Table 10.6).[61] Wolvin's aggressive asset-stripping strategy appeared to be paying off.

For Wolvin and the MTC17 peace meant a continuation of the dual-track strategy. Saleable (and obsolete) assets would be sold off while efforts to find replenishment tonnage for CSL's wartime canaller losses was pushed. In January 1919 the MTC17 sold ten old wooden barges to the Sincennes-McNaughton Line Ltd. for $75,000.[62] This was followed up in February with the purchase of the Oswego Navigation's two wooden canallers (including the rebuilt *Avon*) and two barges for $186,000. The Network members who had invested in Oswego Navigation made a profit of at least $100,000 on the deal (Table 10.6).[63] The spring saw a further decline in the value of old lakers suitable for conversion to ocean service. The purchaser of the *Paipoonge* and the *Thunder Bay* abandoned the vessels when he defaulted on their shipyard and towage bills. The Network reacquired the *Paipoonge* at a sheriff's sale as it lay at Port Huron in two halves for a mere $20,000. Its cost was split between the MTC17 and the Collingwood Shipbuilding Co. It was then resold to Knox Brothers Ltd., Montreal lumber exporters, for $125,000.[64] After a more complex series of transactions, the two pieces of the lake barge *Thunder Bay* ended up being owned by the shipbuilding company and the MTC17 (Figure 10.7).[65]

Operational profits from shipping operations totalled $180,000 in 1919. From this, shareholders received only a 1.5 per cent cash dividend. However, with the surplus account now standing at more than $600,000, Wolvin decided to capitalize a portion of these funds by giving shareholders a 12.5 per cent dividend in company shares. Shareholders, the majority of whom were Network members, had the added bonus of not paying income tax on the shares received. The total estimated dividend to Network members was 42 per cent (Table 10.5 and Table 10.6).[66]

Late in December at the close of the shipping season, the MTC17 gave another nod to its replenishment strategy when it purchased a small laker from its subsidiary, the Canadian Towing and Wrecking Co., for two barges and $120,000 in cash. This was followed early in 1920 by the acquisition of the laker *Valcartier* for $363,000. Finally, the MTC17 provided one last service to the Network. In February 1920, it acquired the stern half of an old laker from the now near-bankrupt Barnard. This arrangement not only helped his finances, it provided work for Davie Shipbuilding as the MTC17 gave it the contract to construct a new bow section.[67]

The MTC17's asset decisions since the start of 1919 were clearly based on acquiring a postwar fleet. The old tonnage acquired from Oswego Navigation can be seen as a stopgap measure until more modern vessels were available. On the other hand, the shutting down of the MTC17's grain elevators at Kingston and Prescott, when combined with the sale of ten barges to Sincennes-McNaughton, also signalled an intention to leave behind the old ways of forwarding grain to Montreal. These changes were reinforced by the resignation of L.L. Henderson as managing director of the MTC17 in June 1919. He was the last survivor the old MTC regime. Henderson was replaced as managing director by T.R. Enderby. An engineer by training, he had impressed Wolvin while working for the Network's British Columbia based affiliate, Canada West Coast Navigation Co.[68]

From the time Wolvin and Norcross had taken over the original MTC in the fall of 1916, the company had acted in the interests of the larger CSL Network. While CSL proper had continued to operate its lakers profitably in the bulk trades during the war, it focused more and more attention on developing trans-Atlantic trades.[69] Squeezed in the middle was CSL's canaller operations. This essential link between Lake Erie and Montreal was drained of tonnage as a large number of steel-hulled canallers went overseas. To some extent the MTC17's old wooden canallers and barges filled this gap. But as the war came to a close, the more aggressive members of the Network had greater dreams. The Allied demand for tonnage created a shipbuilding boom in Canada. The Network participated in the Allied and Canadian programs through their control of six Great Lakes–St. Lawrence River shipyards (Figure 10.2). From the time of the incorporation of Halifax Shipyards in 1918, members of the Network began to conceive of a plan to set up an integrated steel, shipbuilding, and shipping conglomerate based on the existing steel industry in Nova Scotia. The prime movers of this dream were W. Grant Morden and Roy Wolvin. Their conception would eventually bear fruit as the British Empire Steel Corporation.[70]

By the fall of 1919 Wolvin had little time to run a second-class shipping company. His intention to sell the MTC17 to CSL was signalled in the bonus share dividend issued in January 1920. Then on 20 April, Wolvin resigned as president of the company, claiming that because of "onerous other work ... it would be impossible for him to devote the time necessary for the performance of his duties."[71] His resignation signalled a complete change in the Network's strategy. On the same day, CSL established a committee to consider the acquisition of the MTC17. On the surface, those members of the Network who were both members of CSL's board of directors and shareholders of the MTC17 followed all the norms of ethical corporate governance. They claimed conflict of interest and did not vote on the purchase. However, none of the members of the CSL committee that reported favourably on the acquisition had practical experience as shipowners. Furthermore, they had used a survey of the MTC17's floating property done by Network member Henry Black, who was a shareholder of the MTC17. Then Barnard, as CSL's legal counsel (and a MTC17 bond and shareholder), recommended that a special general meeting of CSL shareholders be held to approve the board's decision. Before the meeting was held on 20 June 1920, CSL reached an agreement with the MTC17 to purchase all of the smaller company's shares. The terms were $3,000,000, one-third in cash and the remainder in CSL's notes. Four days later, Enderby at the behest of Wolvin made an offer to purchase all of the MTC17's shares. At the same time the MTC17 sold six vessels to CSL for $650,000. CSL shareholders ratified the agreement the same day. This action confirmed Wolvin's plan to consolidate all the Network's floating assets in CSL. Non-Network MTC17 shareholders were shut out of the incipient British Empire Steel merger.[72]

However, the final details of the buyout of the MTC17 were not completed for another year because of CSL's financial difficulties. The $1 million in cash had been paid in June 1920. For the rest, the MTC17's shareholders used their leverage to force CSL to convert its notes into $1,075,000 in 7 per cent bonds and $975,000 in cash. CSL also assumed all of the MTC17's liabilities that totalled $430,000. The MTC17's real estate and other assorted investments were valued at $1,220,000. The implied value of the floating assets was $2,210,000. The acquisition of the MTC17 was an expensive bargain for CSL. In fact, what CSL received were twenty-eight vessels of which only one, the laker *Westmount*, was a fully modern ship. Almost all of these assets were overvalued compared to their MTC17 book values.[73] CSL then spent more than $679,000 on improvements to four vessels. These investments can be considered reasonable expenditures as the four vessels continued in company service long enough to be laid up in the early years of the Great Depression. The remaining twenty-three vessels were wooden- or composite-hulled and were disposed at a loss by 1926.[74] CSL had effectively spent $3,338,000 for one modern laker and miscellaneous pieces of real estate.

Coverdale in his 1922 report damned the acquisition with faint praise:

> The purchase ... represented a transaction in which [CSL] directors were interested and presumably profited [in] ... A fleet of vessels which barely contributed a fair return in the way of net earnings ... We are of the opinion that the transaction can be justified on a basis of assets and income, but barely so; and that the danger of adverse possession was slight.[75]

He went on to claim that the vessels had not been a "burden," ignoring the fact that they had cost a cash-strapped CSL funds that could have been used elsewhere during the difficult winter of 1921–2.

Conclusion

Had Bartlett McLennan survived the Great War, it is doubtful that he would have recognized what had happened to his old firm. McLennan, the gentleman capitalist, who looked after the affairs of the widows and orphans among the MTC's shareholders while he directed its sustained growth during the Laurier boom, saw the way forward as providing a service to the company's main customers. The old MTC was organized to operate transportation facilities for the grain dealers, flour millers, steel producers, and coal importers who were its clients. Some of these men sat on the firm's board. Together they formed a network whose chief purpose was to supply their businesses with needed transportation facilities. The MTC's steady profits were an essential part of the arrangement. Profitability was a necessary condition for the company's survival, for without a balance sheet in the black, the MTC could not have continued to exist. The old network members may have been in it for their own separate businesses, but what they wanted was continuity. They needed the MTC services this year, next year, and five years hence. The war changed all that. Gradually, they were faced with a new unpredictable situation. Greater profits and unknowable risks were now the norm. The easiest way forward was to take money offered by the CSL Network.

For the Network, the Great War was an opportunity. Led by Roy Wolvin, its members grasped it with a flourish. Their leveraged buyout and reconstruction of the MTC was, after the formation of CSL itself, the pinnacle of their achievement. A company with dissipating assets became, in the space of a few short months, worth $2.6 million. The leveraged buyout appeared to have created all this wealth. But in actuality, it was merely a financial tool that allowed the Network to capitalize on the demand for shipping created by the war. Wolvin's asset-stripping strategy succeeded in the short term only because the war had inflated prices for vessels of all sorts from modern tugs to old obsolete lakers. When the conflict suddenly ended in November 1918, the market for old Great Lakes vessels began a steep decline. However, by then the members of the Network had profited handsomely. Their return on the Network's investment in the four firms that made up the MTC17 in cash dividends alone was 43.5 per cent (if the share dividend is added then the dividends totalled was more than 80 per cent, Table 10.6). The Network members estimated the real rate of return on their initial investment was at least 360 per cent (including dividends). This rate compares favourably with other businesses during the Great War.[76]

Wolvin's creation of a new Montreal Transportation Co. in 1917 demonstrated his ability as a financial entrepreneur. Whereas the old MTC's strategy put a premium on sustained growth to supply a service for its customers, the new company's focus was all about short-term profits. By the time the MTC17 had run out of marketable assets, Wolvin and the more aggressive members of the Network had set their sights on a larger dream, the British Empire Steel Corporation. They used their insider status with CSL to foist the MTC17, with its one first-class asset, on the larger firm. In the end, the Network's incestuous dealings with the new company that carried the venerable name was one of the prime reasons why Canada Steamship Lines faced bankruptcy in the opening months of 1922.

NOTES

1 Canadian Expeditionary Force, "The 42nd Infantry Battalion War Diary (1915–1919)," Internet Archive, accessed 21 February 2023, https://archive.org/details/42ndInfantryBattalionWarDiary1915-1919; and C. Bereford Topp, *The 42nd Battalion, C.E.F., Royal Highlanders of Canada, in the Great War* (Montreal, 1931), 204–5.

2 University of British Columbia Library Rare Books and Special Collections (UBC), McLennan family fonds, box 1, file 2, Hugh McLennan file, J.S. McLennan, *Hugh McLennan 1825–1899* (n.p., n.d.), 63; and "Lt.-Col. McLennan Killed in France, Widely Mourned," *Montreal Gazette*, 6 August 1918.

3 For private equity networks see, Eileen Appelbaum and Rosemary Batt, *Private Equity at Work: When Wall Street Manages Main Street* (New York: Russell Sage Foundation, 2014), 41–91. The development of Greek shipping can be followed in Gelina Harlaftis, *A History of Greek-Owned Shipping: The Making of an International Tramp Fleet, 1830 to the Present Day* (London: Routledge, 1996), 277–83.

4 Allen Kaufman and Ernest J. Englander, "Kohlberg Kravis Roberts & Co. and the Restructuring of American Capitalism," *Business History Review* 67, no. 1 (1993): 66–97; George P. Baker and George David Smith, *The New Financial Capitalists: Kohlberg Kravis Roberts and the Creation of Corporate Value* (New York: Cambridge University Press, 1998), 50–4; and Alexander Reford, "Robert Meighen," in *Dictionary of Canadian Biography*, vol. 14, University of Toronto/Université Laval, 2003–, accessed 20 February 2023, http://www.biographi.ca/en/bio/meighen_robert_14E.html.

5 Thomas R. Navin and Marian V. Sears, "A Study in Merger: Formation of the International Mercantile Marine Company," *Business History Review* 28, no. 4 (1954): 291–328; René De La Pedraja Tomán, *The Rise and Decline of U.S. Merchant Shipping in the Twentieth Century* (New York: MacMillan, 1992), 4–8, 197–202; and Marc Levinson, *The Box: How the Shipping Container Made the World Smaller and the World Economy Bigger* (Princeton, NJ: Princeton University Press, 2010), 44–7.

6 Byron Lew and Marvin McInnis, "Guns *and* Butter: World War I and the Canadian Economy," Research Gate, accessed 24 February 2020, https://www.researchgate.net/profile/Byron_Lew/publication/228434035_Guns_and_Butter_World_War_I_and_the_Canadian_Economy/links/53dfee510cf27a7b830833bb.pdf; Kenneth H. Norrie, Douglas Owram, and J.C. Herbert Emery, *A History of the Canadian Economy*, 4th ed. (Toronto: Thomson Nelson, 2008), 261–79; John Herd Thompson, *The Harvest of War: The Prairie West, 1914–1918* (Toronto: McClelland & Stewart, 1978), 47–8; and M.C. Urquhart, *Gross National Product, Canada, 1870–1926: The Derivation of the Estimates* (Montreal: McGill-Queen's University Press, 1993), 13–14, table 1.1.

7 In 1896 Canada's GNP was estimated at $638,418,000, by 1913 it had grown to $2,649,621,000. See Urquhart, *Gross National Product*, 13–14, table. 1.1. The population of the Canadian Prairies grew from 400,000 in 1901 to 1.3 million in 1911; see Series A2–14 in M.C. Urquhart and K.A.H. Buckley, *Historical Statistics of Canada* (Toronto: Macmillan, 1965), 14. Railway track across the Prairies increased from 4,100 miles in 1901 to 11,600 miles in 1911. Richard Pomfret, *The Economic Development of Canada*, 2nd ed. (Scarborough, ON: Nelson Thomson Learning, 1993), 66. For an overview of the wheat economy during this period, see Norrie, Owram, and Emery, *History of the Canadian Economy*, 193–208.

8 M. Stephen Salmon, "A Prosperous Season: Investment in Canadian Great Lakes Shipping, 1900–1914," in "*A Fully Accredited Ocean*": *Essays on the Great Lakes*, ed. Victoria Brehm (Ann Arbor: University of Michigan Press, 1998), 107–54. Fort William and Port Arthur were amalgamated into one municipality in 1970. In this chapter, they will be referred to collectively by their current name, Thunder Bay.

9 Salmon, "Prosperous Season," 134–5. For canallers see, James Gilmore, "The St. Lawrence River Canals Vessel," *Transactions of the Society of Naval Architects and Marine Engineers* 61 (1956): 111–61. The development of lakers can be followed in Richard J. Wright, *Freshwater*

Whales: A History of the American Shipbuilding Company and Its Predecessors (Kent, OH: Kent State University Press, 1969).

10 For a discussion of shipping networks, see Gordon Boyce, *Information, Mediation, and Institutional Development: The Rise of Large-Scale Enterprise in British Shipping, 1870–1919* (Manchester: Manchester University Press, 1995); Harlaftis, *History of Greek-Owned Shipping;* and Michael B. Miller, *Europe and the Maritime World: A Twentieth-Century History* (Cambridge: Cambridge University Press, 2012).

11 Salmon, "Prosperous Season," 119–27.

12 M. Stephen Salmon, "Competition and Monopoly: The Structure of the St. Lawrence River Forwarding Trade 1860–1895" (paper presented to the Congress of the International Commission for Maritime History, Montreal, Quebec, August 1995).

13 UBC, McLennan family fonds, box 1, file 2, Hugh McLennan file, J.S. McLennan, *Hugh McLennan 1825–1899* (n.p., n.d.), 63–4.

14 The MTC's 1910 shareholders' list contains seventeen women and eight names that are identifiable as children. Only four females held more than 100 shares each, of which two were Bartlett McLennan's sisters. There were eight estates and ten trusts (some for female descendants) represented among the shareholders. The majority of the trusts were administered by the Royal Trust Co. Bartlett McLennan was a director of Royal Trust. Queen's University Archives (QUA), Canada Steamship Lines fonds (CSL), Montreal Transportation Company (MTC), box 116, minute book, "Rights Paid for by B. McLennan, in Trust," [1908], "Rights Allotted to Shareholders by B. McLennan, in Trust," [1908], and [Shareholders' List], [January 1910].

15 QUA, CSL, MTC, box 116, minute book, "List of Shareholders," [June 1903] and [Shareholders' List], [January 1910]; Salmon, "Prosperous Season," 136–41.

16 "The Prescott Elevator," *The American Elevator and Grain Trade* 17, no. 6 (15 December 1898), 233–4; "Grain Elevator Notes," *Railway and Shipping World* (November 1903);and QUA, CSL, box 116, MTC minute book, "Directors Statement," 31 December 1903.

17 QUA, CSL, box 116, MTC minute book, 10 April 1906.

18 For the negotiations concerning the diesel powered *Toiler*, see QUA, CSL, box 116, MTC minute book, 20 January 1911, 1 September 1911, and 13 November 1911. The prolonged problems with the diesel-electric powered *Tynemount* can be followed in QUA, CSL, MTC, minute book, box 116, MTC minute book, 29 May 1912 through 11 June 1914.

19 QUA, CSL, box 116, MTC minute book, 19 February 1912 to 3 July 1914, box 116.

20 QUA, CSL, box 116, MTC minute book, 25 July 1906 and 10 October 1906.

21 QUA, CSL, box 116, MTC minute book, 6 January 1908 passim, and Library and Archives Canada (LAC), Sir William Van Horne fonds, MG 29 A 60, vol. 67, Business Correspondence file P, J.H. Plummer to Sir William Van Horne, 22 January 1908.

22 QUA, CSL, box 116, MTC minute book, 3 July 1914 and 16 July 1914, and "1914 Directors Report," 19 January 1915, and John Duerkop, "Montreal Transportation Co., 1868–1921," Maritime History of the Great Lakes, accessed 28 March 2020, http://images.maritimehistoryofthegreatlakes.ca/114718/data?n=2.

23 Salmon, "Prosperous Season," 120–1.

24 QUA, CSL, box 116, MTC minute book, 18 February 1915 to 15 December 1915.

25 QUA, CSL, box 116, MTC minute book, 20 January 1916, and "1915 Directors Report," 20 January 1916.

26 LAC, Records of the Department of Militia and Defence, RG 9, vol. 183, Bartlett McLennan Personnel file. McLennan did not actually resign his position as president of the MTC until November 1916, see QUA, CSL, box 116, MTC minute book, 14 November 1916.

27 QUA, CSL, box 116, MTC minute book, "1915 Directors Report," 20 January 1916, and 16 February 1916.

28 "Rumored Sale of Montreal Transportation Co's Business," *Canadian Railway and Marine World* [hereafter *CRMW*] (June 1916); M. Stephen Salmon, "This Unsatisfactory Condition: The Formation and Financing of Canada Steamship Lines, 1910–1915," *International Journal of Maritime History* 12, no. 1 (2000): 151–2; M. Stephen Salmon, "This Remarkable Growth: Investment in Canadian Great Lakes Shipping, 1900–1959," *The Northern Mariner/Le marin du nord* 15 no. 3 (2005): 9–15.

29 QUA, CSL, box 116, MTC minute book, 17 April 1916 to 26 May 1916.

30 QUA, box 116, MTC minute book, "1916 Directors Report," 25 January 1917.

31 For the Laurier boom merger wave, see the appendix to Gregory P. Marchildon, *Profits and Politics: Beaverbrook and the Gilded Age of Canadian Finance* (Toronto: University of Toronto Press, 1996), 244–59. The appendix is entitled "The First Canadian Merger Wave in International Perspective."

32 The creation of CSL can be followed in Gordon Boyce, *The Growth and Dissolution of a Large-Scale Enterprise: The Furness Interest* (St. John's, NL: 2012), 195–201; and Salmon, "This Unsatisfactory Condition," 145–76. CSL also had an American subsidiary, the American Interlake Line Ltd.; see Marine Museum of the Great Lakes at Kingston (MMK), CSL, 996.39.7, minute books, 1913–1921. The American Interlake Line's relationship with its parent firm will not be discussed in this chapter.

33 M. Stephen Salmon, "'Lying ... Partly Submerged': Corporate Governance and Insider Networks at Canada Steamship Lines, 1913–1926" (paper presented at the Association of Business Historians Annual Meeting, Wolverhampton, England, June 2007). For the original members of the Network see, Salmon, "This Unsatisfactory Condition." Two additional members were later added: James Whalen, a lumberman and president of the Port Arthur Shipbuilding Co., and H.W. Brown who first managed the Network's Canada's West Coast Navigation Co., and then its Steam Navigation Company of Canada. For Whalen see, Wright, *Freshwater Whales*, 170, 177–8. Brown's role in the Network is discussed in M. Stephen Salmon, "'... she cannot earn anything in Europe': The Marine Investments and the Failure of the Home Bank of Canada, 1916–1923"(paper presented to the Business History Conference, Annual Meeting, Frankfurt, Germany, 2014).

34 "Boats for New Route," *Cleveland Leader*, 7 February 1902; "A Young Man's Success," *Port Huron Daily Times*, 28 February 1902; and Salmon, "This Unsatisfactory Condition," 165–9. The Standard Shipping Co. was incorporated in Manitoba in 1909. It received a Dominion charter in 1918. LAC, Corporations Branch, RG 95, vol. 945, Standard Shipping Co. file., [Note to file], n.d. and "Annual Summary," 23 June 1922.

35 MMK, CSL, 1996.39.46, Coverdale & Colpitts, "Preliminary Report on Canada Steamship Lines, Limited," 10 March 1922, 1996.39.14, "By-Laws" Canada Transportation Lines, Limited, [1913], and 1996.39. 6, Canada Transportation Lines/CSL minute book, 1 June 1913.

36 MMK, CSL, 1996.39.46, "Preliminary Report," 1996.39.7; and Salmon, "This Remarkable Growth," 13–15. For a traditional defence of Coverdale's reforms, see Maurice D. Smith, "CSL – Manuscript History 2013" (unpublished manuscript). I would like to thank the author for access to chapter 3, "The Coverdale Years: 1922 to 1949." The definition of what is a "modern" corporation is disputed by some scholars, note Niels P. Petersson, "Shipping as a Knowledge Industry: Research and Strategic Planning at Ocean Group," in *Shipping and Globalization in the Post-War Era: Contexts, Companies and Connections*, ed. Niels Petersson, Stig Tenold, and Nicholas J. White (New York: Palgrave Macmillan, 2019), 157–82.

37 Haney, Wolvin, Norcross, and Stewart each held 21 per cent of Lake Commerce's stock while three CSL senior managers – H.W. Cowan (operating superintendent Toronto), F.S. Isard (comptroller), and W. E. Burke (assistant manager) – held a total of 14 per cent of the company's shares. Archives of Ontario (AO), Records of the Corporation Branch, RG 55–5, Lake Commerce Limited file, Summary of the State of Affairs 31 December 1915, 11 May 1916; "Ontario and the Great Lakes," *CRMW* (October 1914); "Ontario and the Great Lakes," *CRMW* (May 1915); and Salmon, "This Unsatisfactory Condition," 165–7.

38 QUA, CSL, box 117, Montreal Transportation Company file, "Canadian North West Trans. [*sic*] Co., Distribution of Bonds," [1917]; LAC, RG 95, vol. 1251, Canadian North West Steamship Company, Draft Form of Letters Patent, 17 June 1903; Annual Return, 3 September 1918; and AO, RG 55–5, Canadian North West Steamship Company, Summary of the State of Affairs 31 December 1915, 13 April 1917. Whalen would join with other Network members in forming the Canada West Coast Navigation Co. that operated motorized schooners in the Australian timber trade, see LAC, RG 95, vol. 2689, Canada West Coast Navigation Company file, Letters Patent, 28 June 1916; "Canada West Coast Navigation Co. Limited," *CRMW* (September 1916); "Wooden Shipbuilding in British Columbia," *CRMW* (February 1917); and "Auxiliary Schooner Building in British Columbia," *CRMW* (August 1917).

39 QUA, CSL, box 117, "Lake and River Transportation Co. Ltd., Distribution of Bonds," [1917?]; LAC, RG 95, vol. 2731, Lake and River Transportation Company file, "Application for Incorporation," 25 March 1916.

40 Carruthers had been a SLCN shareholder since at least 1901, and he was listed as a director from January 1910. Carruthers remained as a director of SLCN after he became the president of CSL in November 1913. QUA, CSL, box 152, St. Lawrence and Chicago Steam Navigation Co. minute book, 11 January 1902, and 5 January 1910; and "St. Lawrence and Chicago Steam Navigation Company's Annual Report," *CRMW*, (February, 1916).

41 MMK, CSL, 996.39.6, CSL minute book, 4 April 1916, 1 June 1916, 11 July 1916, 27 July 1916; London Advisory Committee minutes, 3 April 191[6] [this entry is erroneously dated 1918], 3 November 1916; 996.39.46, "Preliminary Report"; "St. Lawrence and Chicago Steam Navigation Company's Annual Report," *CRMW* (February 1916); "Absorption of St. Lawrence and Chicago Steam Navigation Co. Ltd.," *CRMW* (May 1916); and Salmon, "This Remarkable Growth," 15–16. Haney had been made a director of the bank in December 1915 followed by Barnard in January 1916. Haney had effective control of the bank from the time he was made vice-president in March 1916, see LAC, Home Bank of Canada fonds (HB), MG 28 II 11, vol. 335, minute book, 29 December 1915, and 27 March 1916. For the Home Bank financing, see LAC, HB, MG 28 II 11, vol. 134, Agenda Book A, "[Canadian North West Steamship Co.] Application for Credit," 17 April 1916, and "[J.F.M. Stewart] Application for Credit," 17 April 1916, vol. 335, minute book, 17 April 1916; and Salmon, "'... she cannot earn anything in Europe.'"

42 QUA, CSL, box 116, MTC minute book, 26 September 1916, and "Agreement between Lawrence L. Henderson, and Roy M. Wolvin and Joseph W. Norcross date 12 October 1916 [with Royal Trust Deposit Agreement]," 23 October 1916, and enclosed correspondence, R.M. Wolvin and J.W. Norcross to L. Henderson, Managing Director Montreal Transportation Company, 22 September 1916 (2 letters), Wolvin and Norcross to Henderson, 26 September 1916, Henderson to Wolvin and Norcoss, 2 October 1916, and Wolvin and Norcross to Henderson, 2 October 1916.

43 QUA, CSL, box 116, MTC minute book, R.M. Wolvin and J.W. Norcross to L. Henderson, Managing Director, Montreal Transportation Company, 22 September 1916.

44 QUA, CSL, box 116, MTC minute book, 29 December 1916, and 18 January 1917.

45 QUA, CSL, box 116, MTC minute book, 14 November 1916. After the sale of the canaller *Glenmount* in December 1916, the *Omega* was renamed the *Glenmount*.

46 QUA, CSL, boxes 117, MTC minute book, 12 April 1917, "Memorandum of Agreement between Montreal Transportation Company Limited (1903) and Montreal Transportation Company Limited (1917)," 14 April 1917, 29 May 1917, and "1917 Directors Report," 12 February 1918. The MTC's floating property and real estate was valued (minus the canallers *Kinmount* and *Rosemount* sold in January 1917 and with the addition of the new laker *Westmount* and the second-hand laker *Glenmount*) at $1,347,000 on 31 December 1916, MTC minute book, box 116, "1916 Directors Report," 25 January 1917. Henry Black was later described as "our friend" by Hubert W. Brown, managing director, Steam Navigation Company of Canada to Roy M. Wolvin, QUA, CSL, box 151, Bishop Navigation Company correspondence, 9 September 1919.

47 QUA, CSL, box 117, MTC minute book, 3 April 1917, and "Distribution of Bonds," n.d. Canadian North West Steamship had sold its only canaller for overseas service in 1915, "Great Lakes Vessels in Ocean or Coasting Trade," *CRMW* (March 1916). Lake Commerce had sold its laker, the *Valcartier*, to the Sault Shipping Company in December 1916 for $295,000. Sault Ste. Marie Public Library, Sault Ste. Marie, ON, Sault Shipping Company fonds, Sault Shipping Company, Journal no. 1.

48 First class assets are defined as powered steel-hulled vessels less than twenty-one years old. Composite- and wooden-hulled ships, tugs, and barges are best considered second-class assets. The steel-hulled tug *Bartlett* was sold to French interests in March 1917 before the sale of the MTC to the MTC17 was finalized; see, QUA, CSL, box 116, MTC minute book, 28 March 1917.

49 LAC, HB, MG 28 II 11, vol. 131, J.F.M. Stewart: Account Historical, "Historical [Memorandum]," n. d., vol. 153, Speculative Profits: Court Evidence, "Speculative profits made in the fiscal years 1917 to 1920 inclusive," n. d, and QUA, CSL, box 117, MTC correspondence, "Montreal Transportation Company Limited, Distribution of Bonds," n.d.

50 Although using vessels as an asset play is generally considered a specialty of Greek shipowners it has been practised by maritime investors from many different countries. See Helge W. Nordvik, "Entrepreneurship and Risk-Taking in the Norwegian Shipping industry in the Early Part of the Twentieth Century: The Case of Lauritz Kloster," in *From Wheel House to Counting House: Essasys in Maritime History in Honour of Professor Peter Neville Davies*, ed. Lewis R. Fischer, 323–48 (St. John's, NL, 1992); and Stig Tenold, "Risks and Rewards: The Business of Norwegian Shipping," in *The World's Key Industry: History and Economics of International Shipping*, ed. Gelina Harlaftis, Stig Tenold, and Jesús M. Valdaliso, 220–34 (London, 2012).

51 The Duluth Shipping Company was incorporated in Minnesota, see *Duluth News-Tribune* 12 July 1910 and 6 August 1910, while the Central Shipping Company was incorporated in Illinois, *The Chicago Daily News*, 29 May 1914. For Wolvin's control of these firm's note, *Cleveland Plain-Dealer*, 6 November 1916.

52 See E.A.V. Angier, *Fifty Years' Freights, 1869–1919* (London: "Fairplay," 1920), 140–54; and C. Ernest Fayle, *The War and the Shipping Industry* (Oxford: Oxford University Press, 1927), 44, 193–7.

53 QUA, CSL, vol. 116, MTC minute book, "Director's Report [to the Annual General Meeting]," 25 January 1916, and box 117, MTC minute book, "Schedule A: Montreal Transportation Company Limited, Description of property and valuation," 14 April 1917.

54 QUA, CSL, vol. 116, MTC minute book, 1 June, 1917, and 11 December 1917.

55 For John Hannan's obituary, see *The Ogdensburg Journal*, 8 April 1916. QUA, CSL, vol. 116 and vol. 117, MTC minute books, "Director's Report [to the Annual General Meeting]," 25 January 1916 and "Schedule A: Montreal Transportation Company Limited, Description of property

and valuation," 3 April 1917. LAC, RG 95, vol. 1755, Ogdensburg Coal & Towing Co. file, C.A. Barnard to [Thomas] Mulvey, Under Secretary of State, 29 October 1917.

56 QUA, CSL, vol. 117, MTC minute book, 9 October 1917, and 11 December 1917. While the evidence is not completely clear, it appears that Wolvin controlled the Oswego Navigation Co. See *Departmental Reports of the State of Ohio*, vol. 7 (Columbus, OH: Department Reports Publishing Company, 1918), 191, and "Frank S. Masten, Marine Lawyer, Dies Suddenly at Toronto," *Cleveland Plain Dealer*, 5 January 1918. Masten died in the Toronto law office of Rowell, Reid, Wood and Wright. S. Casey Wood was a lawyer used by Wolvin and other members of the Network. Masten handled the incorporation of the Oswego Navigation Co. in Ohio shortly before his death.

57 The "1917" Directors' Report" gives a surplus of $180,000 from the sale of assets. The accounts presented with the report do not support this assertion. Profits from the sale of vessels were $100,000 while vessels purchased cost $150,000 cash and $40,000 worth of shares, see QUA, CSL, box 117, MTC minute book, "Schedule A: Montreal Transportation Company Limited, Description of property and valuation," 14 April 1917, 10 July 1917, 2 August, 1917, 9 October 1917, and "1917 Directors' Report," 12 February 1918.

58 The barge *Cataract* had been built as the steamship *Myles* in 1882. QUA, CSL, box 117, MTC minute book, 5 March 1918 and 14 May 1918, and box 117, Henry Black, "Valuation Report of the Montreal Transportation Company Fleet," 1 July 1917.

59 QUA, CSL, box 117, MTC minute book, and 11 June 1918; "Montreal Transportation Company Balance Sheet, 31 December 1918." For the salvage of the *Avon*, see Walter Lewis and Rick Neilson, *The River Palace* (Toronto: Dundurn Press, 2008), 196.

60 QUA, CSL, box 117, MTC minute book, 10 August 1918, 10 September 1918, 8 October 1918, 10 December 1918, "Montreal Transportation Company [Valuation]," [20 January 1919], "1918 Directors' Report" [20 January 1919].

61 QUA, CSL, box 117, MTC minute book, "1918 Directors' Report," [20 January 1919]. For the fall off in the grain trade see, *Annual Report of the Lake Carriers' Association 1928* (Cleveland, OH: Lake Carriers' Association, 1929), 105–6, and "Dominion Canal Statistics for the 1918 Navigation Season," *CRMW* (September 1919).

62 Sincennes-McNaughton were also offered an option to carry 80,000 tons of coal from Oswego, New York, to Montreal for Ogdensburg Coal & Towing. QUA, CSL, box 117, MTC minute book, 14 January 1919.

63 QUA, CSL, box 117, MTC minute book, 9 October 1917, 11 December 1917, and 18 February 1919.

64 The cost of the *Paipnooge* was originally split between the MTC17 and the Collingwood Shipbuilding Co. Collingwood's president, H.B. Smith, was a Network member and MTC17 shareholder. QUA, CSL, box 117, MTC minute book, 11 March 1919, and 13 May 1919. For Knox Brothers, Ltd., see LAC, RG 95, vol. 1584, Knox Brothers, Limited file.

65 QUA, CSL, box 117, MTC minute book, 13 May 1919, and 16 September 1918.

66 QUA, CSL, box 117, MTC minute book, 8 December 1919, 20 January 1920 and "1919 Directors' Report."

67 QUA, CSL, box 117, MTC minute book, 17 February 1920. The *Manola*'s bow section had been lost in a storm while the ship (in two pieces) was being towed to Montreal; see Eileen Reid Marcil, *Tall Ships to Tankers: The History of Davie Shipbuilders* (Toronto: McClelland & Stewart, 1997), 179.

68 Henderson was made vice-president tasked with special duties. QUA, CSL, box 117, MTC minute book, 24 June 1919. The closure of the MTC17's elevators is discussed in, QUA, CSL,

box 117, MTC minute book, 15 April 1919. For Tom Enderby's early career in Canada, see "The Enderby's [*sic*]," 17 January 2016, Coquitlam History, accessed 21 May 2020, http://coquitlamites.blogspot.com/2016/01/the-enderbys.html.

69 For CSL trans-Atlantic ambitions, see Salmon, "'Lying ... Partly Submerged.'"

70 The history of the British Empire Steel Corp. has yet to be written, but see David Frank, "The Cape Breton Coal Industry and Rise and Fall of the British Empire Steel Corporation," *Acadiensis* 7, no. 1 (1977): 3–34; and Tom Travers, *The State and Enterprise: Canadian Manufacturers and the Federal Government, 1917–1931* (Toronto: University of Toronto Press, 1979), 130–7.

71 QUA, CSL, box 117, MTC minute book, 20 April 1920.

72 QUA, CSL, box 117, MTC minute book, 22 June 1920, and MMK, CSL, minute book, 1996.39.7, 20 April 1920, 29 April 1920, and 26 June 1920.

73 These estimates, taken from Coverdale's report, are not definitive. The report claims thirty-eight MTC17 vessels were sold to CSL but only twenty-eight were actually transferred. See MMK, CSL, 996.39.7, minute books, vol. 13, "Finance Committee Minutes," 6 July 1921, and vol. 14, 21 November 1921, CSL 1996.39.46, Coverdale & Colpitts, "Preliminary Report," 10 March 1922, and QUA, CSL, box 117, Black, "Valuation Report," 1 July 1921.

74 Two older laker-sized hulls were shortened to canal length, a composite-hulled canal barge was converted to a powered canaller, and the rebuilding of the *Manola* as a deep sea freighter was completed. MMK, CSL, 1996.39.46, Coverdale & Colpitts, "Preliminary Report"; QUA, CSL, box 4, "Operations of Vessels," [1935]; and J. Moore, "The Boneyard Below the Bridge," *Freshwater: A Journal of the Marine Museum of the Great Lakes of Kingston*, 11, nos. 1–4 (1995): 3–28.

75 MMK, CSL, 1996.39.46, Coverdale & Colpitts, "Preliminary Report."

76 The estimated rate of return assumes that Wolvin paid shareholders the full par value of their stock. The Network's members' rate of return can be compared with those for the meatpacker, William Davies Co., which was controlled by Sir Joseph Flavelle. Flavelle was also chairman of the Imperial Munitions Board. See Michael Bliss, *A Canadian Millionaire: The Life and Times of Sir Joseph Flavelle, Bart., 1858–1939* (1978; repr., Toronto: University of Toronto Press, 1992), 356.

PART FIVE
CRISIS AND DECLINE

Figure V.15 Wm. Notman & Son, *Art Association Building, Phillips' Square, Montreal,* c. 1893. McCord Museum, VIEW-2543.1.

Figure V.16 Anonymous, *Dr. Noel Decarie's Office, Dental Services, Phillips Square, Montreal,* c. 1925. McCord Museum, MP-0000.587.60.

The Art Association, Phillips Square

The establishment of the Art Association of Montreal in 1860 was a demonstration of the city's increasing prosperity, whose burghers had time and money to develop their cultural aspirations. In 1877, following a significant bequeath by Benaiah Gibbs, a clothing merchant, local architects Hopkins and Wily designed a museum at the northeast corner of Phillips Square (Figure V.15). At the time, the area was primarily residential, a mix of terrace housing and villas. Gibbs himself had lived around the corner from the building, in a large house fronting on St. Catherine Street.

Expanded in 1893 by Taylor and Hogle, the building was abandoned in 1912 when the Art Association relocated to the Maxwell Brothers' neoclassical temple on Sherbrooke Street. The last incarnation of the Art Association building, bespattered by commercial signs, with its galleries carved up into shops and offices, speaks of the increasing commercialization of Phillips Square and St. Catherine Street after the First World War (Figure V.16).

CHAPTER ELEVEN

Crossing Imperial Boundaries and Constructing Intimate Linkages: Reading Soldiers' First World War Letters

Nicolas Kenny

October 1st, 1917. Talbot Mercer Papineau, resident of Montreal's Square Mile and a young Canadian officer stationed in Northern France, pens a letter to his mother, Caroline Rogers, then volunteering for the Red Cross Information Bureau in London. "I had a wonderful time opening parcels last night," he writes, thanking her for the socks, pencils, shaving cream, and snacks she had sent him. The chatty missive updates her about life – and its relative comforts – on the Western Front, provides news from his brother who is also in active service, mentions the weather and his walks with his dog through the trenches, over which the meeting of the full moon and the rising sun that morning had produced "a beautiful & unusual sight." "Nights are cold but the dogs help to keep me warm. I slept well last night. You need not worry. I am having an easy time of it," Papineau insists as he signs off, "very lovingly."[1]

October 2nd, 1917. Willie Firth, a young English naval reservist on a westbound train crossing Canada continues a letter begun the previous day for his girlfriend Mabel Stead back home in West Yorkshire. As in his other letters, Firth describes his daily routine and the scenery he contemplates from the window, repeating the affection he feels for the woman he has left behind. On the route between Calgary and Vancouver, he marvels at the snow-capped mountains and the wildlife he sees from the train. Above the clouds at three thousand feet of altitude, he comments, "it's nearest I have ever been to heaven." He wishes she could be there with him and promises to send the postcards he's already written. "Good afternoon kid & don't get down-hearted. I shan't be long away," Firth promises as he signs off, "with love."[2]

Two letters, written at virtually the same time, moving in different directions, but both towards the by-then failing heart of the British Empire; two minuscule fibres in the countless, interlaced threads making up the webs of contact and exchange, of power and authority, of class and gender, which, as historians Tony Ballantyne and Antoinette Burton have argued, weaved empires together.[3] Two letters written by young men of different social classes to female interlocutors with whom they shared bonds of love and intimacy; over the expanses of distance and time apart, their overarching purpose was to comfort, to reassure, to provide hope for happier times ahead. To the extent that empires are imagined not only as the products of spatial and institutional arrangements, but as networks of relationships, be they political or economic, coercive or affectionate, letters like these performed important functions, maintaining and solidifying the emotional bonds that linked people to one another as they moved through and across vast imperial reaches.

This chapter seeks to contribute to the present reassessment of Montreal's Square Mile society by exploring the intimacies underpinning the class, gender, and imperial dynamics of a period marked by turmoil and uncertainty, both politically and affectively. One of Canada's most exclusive urban districts, and undoubtedly its wealthiest as the adjective Golden sometimes affixed to the term Square Mile implies, this was a neighbourhood firmly, and visibly, implanted on the Montreal landscape. Its stately mansions, imposing churches, prestigious university, and elegant parks projected an aura of economic wealth, of social and cultural authority. This influence stretched into, and was built upon, the activities of its residents in the busy downtown financial district, through the smoky suburban manufacturing areas, and thanks to an ever-expanding rail and shipping infrastructure, across the nascent Dominion and to points around the globe. Historian Roderick Macleod has delved deeply into local-scale processes of planning, speculation, and the building of homes and cultural, educational, and religious institutions to demonstrate how successive generations of Square Mile residents methodically implanted the physical and social foundations of this power and influence on the slopes of Mount Royal throughout the nineteenth century.[4] At the same time, the community's very establishment, its economic fortunes, and self-perception as a bastion of Anglo-Protestant respectability and prestige also depended on broader imperial connections that far surpassed this immediate context. When Great Britain found itself at war in the summer of 1914, Montreal's anglophone elite rushed to duty at home and overseas. But by the time Papineau and others of his generation found themselves on the battlefields of Flanders and Northern France, the imperial framework on which was built the Square Mile's identity and hegemony was caving.

The First World War profoundly shook elite Montreal's sense of self as well as the institutions on which it was based.[5] This questioning, notes historian Brian Young, was tied to a larger "historical and societal context in the evolving forms of capitalist wealth, in the changing intellectual, cultural, and social institutions of urban society, in the shifting relations of ethnic power in Montreal, and in the diminishing authority of the Anglican Church."[6] This sense of fragility, I want to suggest, underlaid the intimate correspondence of one the Square Mile's most prominent wartime sons, and is made all the more manifest when set against the contemporaneous romantic letters of an unknown British serviceman writing from Canada. Though very different in tone and outlook, in the disparate temperaments and personal aspirations they express, and even in sheer volume, reading these sets of correspondence side by side reveals similar preoccupations, and shows how individual identities of class and masculinity were shaped by the crossing of material and social boundaries in various British imperial settings. As such, my sights are especially trained on the emotional tones and sentimental underpinnings of the letters of these two military men. Empire and war provoked intense, often traumatic emotional responses, to be sure. But these emotions were themselves equally constitutive of an empire reliant on the transnational movement in which these two men partook, their place in it defined through emotional linkages forged in a world that seemed on the brink of collapse.[7]

Papineau and Firth found meaning in and made sense of their wartime experience not just through their service and duties on the ground but also in the emotional bonds they maintained with loved ones across distances, as the day-to-day discoveries and longings they described in their letters make clear. Their expressions of joy and sadness, of homesickness and aspiration, speak to the ways in which intimate, affective experiences linked to social identity and a sense of place underlay vast empires. Reading Papineau's letters alongside Firth's exposes gendered conventions of emotional expression shared by empire makers of very different backgrounds, their mix of fragility and resolve in the familial setting a metaphor for the fraying imperial fabric enveloping them. Papineau's determined optimism and political ambitions foreshadowed the Canadian nationality around which Square Mile society would ultimately regroup, his death on the battlefield a reminder of the many false starts that such realignments entailed. Firth had no connection to Montreal, but the words of this anonymous, unknown, and otherwise unremarkable fellow soldier are a remarkable foil. Through this juxtaposition, we see in Papineau's letters how his Square Mile community shared in imperial subjectivities while attempting to navigate the ruptures that war represented.

Ships in the Night

Readers will likely be familiar with Talbot Mercer Papineau, who in the Canadian and British press famously debated his distant cousin Henri Bourassa over Canada's participation in the conflict. Raised by his mother on the family seigneurie at Montebello, the former home of his illustrious great-grandfather Louis-Joseph Papineau, he was educated in bastions of the Square Mile's elite: Montreal High School and McGill University. After having attended Oxford as a Rhodes Scholar, Papineau subsequently started a law practice in the Canada Life Building located in the heart of the city's business district. A supporter of Prime Minister Wilfrid Laurier, he aspired to a political career. He helped in the Liberal Party's 1911 election campaign and envisaged a run of his own at the next opportunity. Before the war, we find him living at 316 Sherbrooke Street West, kitty-corner to his alma mater on the eastern edge of the Square Mile.[8] When the conflict broke out Papineau was in Vancouver, speaking to the Canadian Club on the topic of nationalism in Quebec. It was from there that he sent a telegram to his friend Hamilton Gault, the Square Mile businessman and South African War veteran. In it Papineau volunteered for the Princess Patricia's Canadian Light Infantry, the regiment Gault had raised with his personal funds.[9]

Papineau was a prolific letter writer before and during the war, as confirmed by the reams of correspondence found in the archives, the trace of exchanges with friends, family members, and professional connections.[10] In an engrossing series of portraits of prominent Canadian personalities of the First World War, journalist Sandra Gwyn examines the extraordinary series of letters Papineau wrote to an artist named Beatrice Fox beginning in the summer of 1915. Though the two never met in person they were introduced by a mutual family friend who had suggested to Papineau, then on leave in London, that he might wish to communicate with a young woman from Philadelphia, a city he knew well as it was his mother's birthplace and the home of relatives to whom he paid frequent visits. Over the next two years, their correspondence gradually became more intimate and romantic, but in many ways tortured as well. Though Papineau's tone seems to have oscillated between coy, cold, and captivated, Gwyn also notes their growing affection and Papineau's sense of Fox as a "soulmate and safety valve" with whom he could share both his physical and emotional scars, surmising that they would likely have been married had he survived the war.[11] Less analysed is the voluminous collection of Papineau's letters to his mother, initiated at the outset of the war. I focus here especially on those he wrote from the front in the last year of his life, far from the material comforts of the Square Mile. This was for Papineau a period of turmoil and introspection during which he experienced the horrors of trench warfare, ruminated about his own actions and future, took a bold, if controversial, public political stand. In the words he put to paper, we see a Papineau deeply immersed in the fraternity of young men leaving behind the worlds they knew to participate in a clash of empires that sent them to far-flung places they otherwise would never have seen.

The last weeks of Papineau's life coincided with Willie Firth's journey half-way across the globe. For his part, Firth was of an infinitely more modest background. Born and raised in Low Moor, an industrial village on the southern outskirts of Bradford, England, built around a large iron works, Firth was employed as a weaving overlooker in a wool and worsted mill, an activity well-established in the region since the early eighteenth century.[12] He had joined the Royal Naval Reserves in April 1917 and from his service records we learn that he had spent time at HMS *Victory VI*, the Navy's training establishment at the Crystal Palace in London, then at HMS *Pembroke I*, the shore barracks in the southeastern town of Chatham.[13] The letters he wrote to Stead cover a long journey that autumn, as he travelled by train from Chatham to Liverpool, then on the White Star liner *Justicia* to Canada, alighting in Halifax and from there undertaking another train journey across the country to Victoria, where he was to take up service on the HMS *Lancaster*, a Royal Navy ship patrolling the West Coast. It is there that the small collection of letters ends.

On the surface at least, very little would seem to connect the enterprising and worldly socialite of Montreal's gentry, known to have something of a playboy character,[14] with an unassuming British villager of modest background and "cheerful disposition."[15] By pure serendipity alone might their paths have crossed in the imperial metropole, around which both their wartime experiences revolved. Or perhaps Firth happened to catch a glimpse of Papineau's diatribe in the papers the previous summer. We might almost discern minor similarities in their personal stylistic choices, their shared habit of wearing their hair short and brushed back and of adopting a gaze of steely determination likely attributable to their adherence to standards of fashion and military deportment of the day. Juxtaposing their letters, then, provides a number of outwardly different perspectives: working-class and bourgeois, metropolitan and colonial, in the trenches and at sea. Papineau's letters reveal the sentiments of a careerist with much at stake in the future of the nation and the empire, while those of Firth, some fifteen years younger, have what might be called a more innocent quality. They are the words of a young man uprooted from his daily life, along for the ride but manifestly in the hopes that the ride remains short.

TALBOT MERCER PAPINEAU

B.A., 1904; B.C.L., 1910

Born at Monte Bello, Que., December 25th, 1882. Appointed Lieutenant in the P.P.C.L.I., August 14th, 1914. Transferred to Headquarters Staff, Canadian Corps. Rejoined the P.P.C.L.I. Promoted to Acting-Major. Mentioned in despatches and awarded the Military Cross. Killed in action, at Passchendaele, October 30th, 1917.

Figure 11.1 Portrait of Talbot Papineau. From *McGill Honour Roll, 1914–1918* (Montreal: McGill University, c. 1926), p. 72. Canadiana, https://www.canadiana.ca/view/oocihm.9_89634/72. Public domain.

Figure 11.2 Portrait of Willie Firth. Imperial War Museum, 15359. Reproduced with permission.

What ties these sets of letters together, though, is the vivid picture they paint of the emotions with which such individuals navigated these exceptional times. Consciously playing the part or not, both were deeply embedded in empire formation. As white men hailing from the metropole and a settler Dominion, they were clearly on the side of power and authority, though Firth's working-class status and Papineau's pedigree and pretension to a political career at the highest level speak to the great disparities that underlie such characterizations. Papineau's ambitions and famous polemic aside, though, these were not the "ideologues" debating and intellectualizing the terms of imperial citizenship, such as those studied decades ago by Carl Berger in Canada, and more recently by Daniel Gorman in England.

While such studies recognize the "profound emotional attachment" underlying imperial identities,[16] and the extent to which they "constituted part of the mental infrastructure" of men and women at the time,[17] delving into these letters removes us from the high politics of imperialism and brings us to a more interior plane on which to interrogate the nature of these feelings and the ways in which emotions were themselves constitutive of shared identities. Firth's and Papineau's letters take us past the pride and patriotism of imperialism to show the sadness, yearnings, and insecurities its builders felt on the ground. In the words they scribbled to their loved ones, we see a transnational empire rooted in the warmth of home; in storm-tussled oceanic voyages and trench warfare, we see the fragility of youthful masculinity.

Imperial Intimacies

The intimacies on which empires were built and sustained has attracted extensive attention from scholars principally interested in the power dynamics shaping sexual and conjugal relationships between European settlers and Indigenous populations. Underlying such relationships was an intent to "refigure imperialism not merely as a territorial project but as an exercise in affect management with high stakes: an intimate business at all levels of power and hegemony."[18] My focus here is somewhat different as I interrogate not the intimacies operating between colonizer and colonized, but rather those at work within hegemonic groups. Nevertheless, anthropologist Ann Laura Stoler's suggestion that we pursue "connections between the broad-scale dynamics of rule and the intimate domain of implementation" remains useful in thinking of the ways the global movement generated by agents of empire during the First World War conditioned the interior feelings that shaped both their world view and their actions within their world.[19]

In order to shed light on the connections between the feelings expressed in the intimate sphere of the letter to a loved one and the conventions of class and gender that structed social relations, I draw on a growing body of work that approaches emotions not merely as individual responses to outside stimuli but also as collective experiences whose expression, performance, and meanings are contingent upon being shared with others. In describing "affective economies," for example, feminist theorist Sarah Ahmed shows how emotions are far from private matters, but instead "mediate the relationship between the psychic and the social, and between the individual and the collective."[20] Historians refer to collectives structured around shared understanding of emotion as emotional communities or regimes, groupings that often intersect with other social identities that might include gender, social class, racial, ethnic, or national background, age, political spheres, or any number of other categories. Whether conceived as communities to which one adheres, willingly or not, or regimes that govern attitudes and behaviours, these groupings coalesce around emotional norms, values and ideals held in common, and in which individuals find solace, or from which they are excluded.[21] Stoler suggests that unpacking the mechanisms of power and authority that propped up "macropolities" like the British Empire requires looking not at "abstract institutions" but to the "microsites of rule" where meanings were managed and social categories constructed.[22] Unfolding the brittle pages on which these military men wrote to the women in their lives reveals how they interiorized and wielded the emotional codes of their day while also laying bare the uncertainties, ambiguities, and fragility that were fissuring the foundations of the colossus with feet of clay which, by 1917, the empire was increasingly resembling.

Longing for Home

The letters of Papineau and Firth thus participated in sustaining emotional relationships, conventions, and communities that, during the Great War, spanned enormous distances and were continuously bruised by death and grieving. As Ballantyne and Burton show, intimate relations in colonial settings were the product of the far-reaching mobility inherent in empire. Indeed, they note, this "constant" movement "in and through the spaces of empire," multiplied the affective spheres in which imperial actors engaged, a mobility that can be understood as "a constitutive factor in the social life of sentiments" in such settings.[23] By the time they penned their letters, both Papineau and Firth had travelled over vast expanses, particularly by the standards of the early twentieth century when global mobility remained the limited purview of wealthy travellers or one-time migrants. They had crossed the Atlantic in opposite directions: Papineau moving back and forth between London and various points on the Western Front, and Firth covering North America from one end to the other and onto the Pacific Ocean.

Given the distance, the duration of their time away, and the uniquely challenging circumstances of war, their writing makes clear how this movement strained the pre-existing emotional bonds the two travellers had left behind. We see this repeatedly in their letters, where, in order to assuage the longing for home, the men seek to recreate its comforts and atmospheres on the page, itself imagined as a substitute for "an opportunity to sit down and chat with you."[24] Assigned to a night time watch on the ship deck, Firth tells Stead that his thoughts quickly wandered from the submarines he was meant to be looking out for, "I was thinking about you, being nice and snug in your little bed at home, dreaming sweet dreams, I daresay about me."[25]

While he often imagined Stead there with him, the two of them marvelling at the sights together, Firth more frequently tried to ease the loneliness and boredom by dwelling on thoughts of home. He pictures a Saturday afternoon, wondering how she will spend the evening, or describes seeing her "in the chapel, gazing in the old corner and trying to picture the missing face, which would like to be occupying it."[26] For his part, elements of Papineau's home life were less distant as he had the opportunity for occasional family visits with his mother in London as well as with his younger brother Wescott who was also stationed on the front. But through long stretches in battle, he too yearned for the family home, reminiscing of the lilacs and roses in bloom and happy moonlit evenings.[27] "I feel perfectly well but often tired," he wrote his mother in May 1917, "and it must be admitted rather sick of the war and anxious to be home with you at Montebello."[28] As we will see below, Papineau's viewing of home as a place of intimacy and emotional solace corresponded to the family's country estate, as opposed to the Square Mile itself where he resided in the context of his professional life.

The notion of home, of course, was itself a variegated idea. In the setting of empire, note Catherine Hall and Sonya Rose, home might refer as much to the imperial metropole as to the private family circle, and both men certainly understood it in reference to these sliding scales.[29] Firth becomes patriotically sentimental while gazing at the Welsh Mountains as his ship glided away from the "Dear Old land." In referencing his homeland, he repeatedly uses the endearing term "Old Blighty," popularized by South African and First World War soldiers as an affectionate and nostalgic moniker for England. As Firth visits several Canadian cities, his letters emphasize the differences of customs and habits with those to which he is accustomed. "You would laugh if you were to see the idea of getting [a] meal out here in the café," he exclaims, describing the long counters and "revolving piano stools" in Winnipeg's CPR diner.[30] Montreal in particular provided a dash of exoticism for the young visitor. Though he was there for less than a day, his walk through downtown seemed to rattle his small-town sensibilities. The French Canadians he encountered, and whom he describes as "a don't care sort of style people," amplified in his eyes the foreignness and decadence of the big city. "The temptation I have had today has been the toughest I have ever had to deal with," Firth writes his girlfriend, reassuring her of his fidelity as he described the "half-drunk" people offering the passing soldiers drinks and cigars in the street, which he dutifully declined.[31] As his westward movement progresses, he is most pleased with the reception of music and food the soldiers received in Regina, and the invitations to dinner in private homes extended in Victoria. While such heroes' welcomes kept him firmly grounded in the empire, his often mundane and day-to-day remarks highlighting the "different ways of doing things to what we have at home" underscored the emotional attachment to a home defined as a larger national entity.[32]

Worldlier and already familiar with various corners of Europe, Papineau's letters do not have the travelogue aspect that give Firth's correspondence its colour.[33] But his experience on the front nonetheless reinforced his sense of Canadian nationalism and attitudes towards home understood as a broader social and political framework. In contrast to Firth, for whom the trip across the empire appears as a once-in-a-lifetime event, the social networking and political calculations that were already part of Papineau's life in the Square Mile also shaped his perception of his wartime experience. During his time on the front, and on his visits to London, he remained closely connected with and preoccupied by the goings on in his Montreal world, seeking to maintain a position within it and preparing his path for the postwar period. In some respects, his feelings towards his home country were nonetheless tinged with bitterness. His letters to his mother evoke the Montreal "society" he had left behind but he also expressed disappointment in the lack of mail that arrived for him from his Square Mile circles. Towards those in Canada who would minimize the American intervention in the war he felt "very angry" and "indignant." Harkening to his maternal national origins, he insisted to Rogers that "I would rather be a good American than an Englishman any day!"[34]

But if there is one thing for which Papineau is still remembered, it is his passionate defence of Canada's involvement in the conflict in the form of an open letter to Henri Bourassa, founder of the Montreal daily *Le Devoir*, former Liberal Member of Parliament before a falling out with Laurier over the sending of troops to the South African War, and perhaps the most influential nationalist voice in French Canada at the time. Worlds apart in their upbringing, social and professional networks, and political stances, Bourassa and Papineau nonetheless shared a direct lineage with Louis-Joseph Papineau (he was grandfather to both Bourassa and Talbot's father), and both had lived on the former Patriote leader's Petite-Nation seigneurie at Montebello. It was, as Talbot Papineau explained, his time on the front lines that had inspired the emotional missive in which he lays out the full extent of his patriotic attachment to his home country. For him, Canada's taking up of arms in a shared imperial struggle was not contrary to the aspirations of national autonomy promoted by Bourassa, but a necessary step toward a more distinct identity and fuller political independence.[35]

The debate between Papineau and Bourassa has been extensively analyzed elsewhere, most recently by historian Geoff Keelan who argues that the officer's letter fostered a form of "cultural mobilization," that is to say the process by which the story of soldiers' experiences on the front lines entered into a shared national imaginary that inspired participation in the war effort and adherence to the underlying values through which the conflict was justified. Indeed, as Keelan points out, and as Bourassa himself remarked upon, though the letter was addressed to "My dear Cousin Henri," it was clearly destined to a broader national readership, intended to overcome deep divisions between French and English Canadians, rallying both groups around a "war culture [that] fell somewhere between imperialist and nationalist."[36] My objective here is not to revisit the two men's exchange in the context of the political tensions surrounding the war and the nation's future then tearing Canadians apart, but rather to stray briefly from Papineau's private correspondence with his mother to note how even in a very public forum such as the opinion columns of the daily press, emotional connections to a perceived idea of home continued to structure understanding of wartime imperial dynamics. In the war of words between Papineau and Bourassa, we see the fraying of a form of Canadian nationalism rooted in British imperialism to which Square Mile society had long adhered. Though far from the assemblies and gatherings he might have attended in Montreal, Papineau sought to keep a foot firmly at home by inserting himself in the national debate. Forced to navigate between the once unalloyed and now increasingly outmoded commitment to empire of Montreal's anglophone elite and its wholesale rejection by the French-Canadian intelligentsia, Papineau's search for a political middle way was fraught with personal emotion. As was Bourassa's scathing reply.

We need look no further than Papineau's opening lines to see how the context of war, and the conventions of early twentieth-century public discourse, broached political debate from a posture of emotional suffering. The letter-cum-manifesto begins agreeably enough with evocations of past conversations and a "pleasant friendship" developed within the family circle since "the time of my birth," but very quickly shifts to Papineau's "intense feeling and deep regret" towards Bourassa's "unhappy views," "unmoved" as he stubbornly remains by his countrymen's "beautiful but terrible … sacrifices" on the battlefield. At stake, Papineau insists, is nothing less than the "Soul of Canada," its pride and patriotism dependent on the country's willingness to fight its own "battles of freedom." Surely a nationalist like Bourassa would have "felt that in the agony of her losses in Belgium and France, Canada was suffering the birth pains of her national life." Having situated the discussion on this visceral level, Papineau proceeds to evoke his own emotional suffering at seeing "comrades suddenly struck down in death" in order to justify Canada's participation in an empire that is not a "political organism" but a "*spiritual* union."[37]

Laying claim to an ethnic and linguistic identity that surpasses the Square Mile world with which he was associated, Papineau framed his missive as an appeal to their shared French-Canadian background, taunting Bourassa for the "strife and enmity" he would provoke after the war, for the "disfavour and dishonour" he would bring "upon our race." In question, he insisted, was not only Canada's place in the British Empire, but also its "bond of blood relationship" with France, a bond he illustrated by evoking the villages he visited on the front alongside his correspondent's shared connection with Montebello. Hearing "the language I love so well" and seeing "types and faces that are like old friends" and "farm houses like those at home" reminds him of his "happy childhood days" at the manor. Accustomed to the social and professional worlds of the Square Mile and St. James Street, it might be noted, hearing French being spoken does not seem to remind him of Montreal. No doubt the reference to a small town rather than to the large metropolis was calculated to evoke more vivid images of an idealized home. These warm memories set the stage for a particularly vitriolic finale to the letter in which Papineau warns Bourassa of the "heavy day of reckoning" to come after the war. The "revengeful feelings" of those who served will be assuaged not by "physical violence" or other "illegal means … but by the invincible power of our moral influence."[38]

In a very explicit manner, Papineau's letter thus wields the intimacies linking individual to home and nation in order to incite patriotism and support for Canada's role in this imperial conflict. Bourassa, for his part, would have nothing of it. His response was caustic and no less personal. He declares Papineau, despite his name, "utterly unqualified to judge the feelings of the French Canadians." Why, given his professed attachment to the French language, should the letter have been written in English, Bourassa asks, noting that his cousin is "for the most part American," Protestant, more familiar with culture of France than of Quebec, and having inherited but "the most *denationalised* instincts of his French origin." Distancing himself from any personal connection, he denounces the false pretences under which Papineau uses "language bearing the touch of intimate relationship." The two had met but a handful of times, Bourassa specifies, never before his return from Oxford and on only one occasion did they discuss "matters of national concern." At that point, Papineau had positioned himself even more strongly than he against "any kind of imperial solidarity." Denouncing Papineau's inaccurate portrayals of his views, Bourassa reasserts his own "hat[red] with equal detestation" of all forms of imperialism. To him, Papineau had chosen to take "advantage of the emotion caused by war" to justify a slide towards ever-greater ties with the British Empire. His patriotism notwithstanding, it is precisely Papineau's "distance from home" that has "obliterated in his mind the fundamental realities of his native country." Indeed, Bourassa points out, recruitment for the war effort has largely proceeded "in inverse ratio of the enrootment in the soil and the traditional patriotism arising therefrom." Thus can be explained the greater propensity of recent British settlers to enlist relative to the Canadian born, of English Canadians relative to their more historically established francophone counterparts, and of city dwellers relative to rural inhabitants.[39] As such, it was Papineau's Square Mile pedigree that implicitly made him incapable, in Bourassa's eyes, of sharing in a common sense of home with French Canadians. Papineau made no mention of Bourassa's response in his letters to his mother that summer, beyond asking if she had seen it. He did, however, take manifest pride in reporting on the numerous congratulatory notes he had received from friends in Montreal and London.[40]

The tone of Papineau and Bourassa's respective open letters show how understandings of home, and of the ways in which one might be attached to it, were central in framing the most critical domestic political debate of the day. As historian Michael Roper reminds us in his analysis of the letters British soldiers wrote to their families, however, the idea of home carried for these men more personal meanings as well, "a short-hand for loved ones, bricks and mortar, a garden or a neighbourhood, perhaps a local landscape."[41] In one letter to his mother, Papineau becomes introspective when he learns he "may be sent home this winter for three months. Where *is* my home?" he muses. "I should like to see Montebello, a little of Montreal and visit New York and Philadelphia …"[42]

Indeed, for these soldiers, home was not necessarily a place at all, but an affective experience, located in familiar sights, sounds, and tastes that now seemed so distant. Food and music played a critical role in this emotional connection. The cup of tea offered by a ship steward brings Firth back to Mabel's house, and the apples and cake Papineau received on the front provide not just the comforts of home but also an opportunity to share such feelings with fellow soldiers. Hearing the "old songs of ours" played on the ship deck, Firth was overcome with homesickness. "It was very hard to hear those old hymns and to think we are parted, so far away. It upsets me a bit, but I lost myself in sleep … You will be able to understand my feelings," he wrote on another occasion.[43] In letters coincidentally written less than a month apart, both men evoked the rush of nostalgia they had felt upon suddenly hearing the hymn "Nearer, My God, to Thee," whose words and melody evoked for them both memories of home and the promise of soon being reunited. For Papineau, the piece translated into childhood memories of his mother playing music for the family. "I would gladly listen to you playing them again," he wrote. "No one ever played the piano so well as you … You must not get out of practice. You will play again for us at Montebello."[44]

Figure 11.3 Photograph of "Papineau Manor" showing Louis-Joseph Amédée, his son Louis-Joseph (right), Caroline Rogers and their three sons, Louis-Joseph (standing), Talbot (foreground), and Wescott. *South Side, Chateau de Montebello, Montebello, QC,* c. 1890. McCord Museum, MP-0000.962.2.

Figure 11.4 James Street, Low Moor. Mabel Stead's family home, where Firth's letters were addressed, was at number 57, visible behind number 59, centred in this photo taken in the 1970s. Low Moor Local History Group. Reproduced with permission.

Fragile Masculinities

Home, then, also appears as an emotional community of closeness and affection that provides a sense of grounding in a wartime empire marked by distance and violence. As scholars of masculinity in both Britain and Canada have shown, men of the period interiorized conceptions of manliness centred on ideals of strength, courage, and self-control. Empire, in this context, was an "object" of manly "desire," and its ultimate expression was war.[45] At the same time, the war itself began to reconfigure this gendering, as the onslaught of suffering and violence provoked the embrace of a softer masculinity associated with tenderness, domesticity, and empathy.[46] This was a "multi-dimensional" masculinity, historian Joanna Bourke observes, one in which "fortitude and tenderness" coexisted in men who retained the home as "the touchstone for all their actions."[47]

To the women with whom they corresponded, Firth and Papineau both affirmed themselves as a male protector and expressed this softness and search for domesticity. Though far away, both sought first to reassure, enjoining their interlocuters to remain courageous, to have faith in the men's speedy return, to take good care of themselves. "Keep cheerful," Papineau encouraged his mother in one typical letter, "We'll beat the old Boches yet."[48] Sensing her concern about his well-being, he insists she go out and socialize with friends as much as possible, his clumsy assurances that "there is no harm that can come of me for a month at least," presumably intended to help her take her mind of the dangers he would face on the battlefield.[49] One of hundreds of wartime volunteers working for the Canadian Red Cross Information Bureau in London, Caroline Rogers was herself a transnational agent of empire, deeply immersed in the emotional tensions of the war and the linkages between home and the front. Launched by Square Mile philanthropist Lady Julia Drummond in 1915, the Bureau coordinated support for injured Canadian soldiers located in London, on the front lines, or made prisoners of war, organizing hospital visits, liaising with families, sending care packages, and planning entertainment.[50]

There, notes Sandra Gwyn, Rogers was part of an "expatriate community of Square Mile Montrealers," upon whom the "furies of war had descended … with particular destructiveness."[51] Drummond herself had lost her son Guy, a friend of Papineau's, at Ypres, while others in this circle of elite Montrealers moved to the metropole in support of the imperial war effort mourned casualties in battle or in the sinking of the RMS *Lusitania*. The very purpose of the Bureau, noted its founder, was to succour the emotional bonds made fragile by the global conflict, "supply[ing] the personal touch so necessarily lacking in the awful business of war," bridging the distance between "our wounded soldiers in hospital" and "their next of kin across the sea."[52] As Iona Carr, volunteer and author of a retrospective on the organization's work explained, the Bureau strove to assuage the "anguish" and "dreaded consequences" felt by families separated by "that wide barrier of ocean."[53]

Wealthy members of Square Mile families doing this work had the means to bridge the distance separating Montreal from London. Drawn to the metropole in a time of imperial crisis, they temporarily reproduced abroad the social structures they had known at home, suggesting that the personal and professional networks, solidarities, and philanthropic work that had sustained this Anglo-Canadian bourgeoisie far surpassed the slopes of Mount Royal. The list of volunteers and visitors printed in Carr's retrospective attests to Square Milers' willingness and ability to collectively transport themselves to where they felt they could do most for the war effort: Allan, MacDonald, Molson, Stewart, Reford, to cite but some of the most prominent family names.

For military men of means, leaves spent in the metropole were therefore an opportunity to foster the social connections of both Montreal and London society even as they found comfort within a community reconfigured in relative proximity to the front. Papineau attended parties and partook in sports and leisure activities with the same friends he might have seen in Montreal or Montebello, and it was rumoured that he had an affair with Sarah Shaughnessy, widowed daughter-in-law of the Canadian railway magnate, Thomas Shaughnessy.[54] Letters from Papineau to Rogers sent in the days before one of his visits in November 1916 provides a sense of the social activity these breaks from the front entailed. "Will you arrange a dinner party and theatre for Saturday night then … and afterwards we could go to the Savoy and dance," he asks in a second consecutive letter. "Would suggest asking Beatrice and Martha Allan," he specifies before adding that he would like to "dine with Mr. Waldron on Sunday," that he has extended invitations to other friends on Monday, Tuesday, and Wednesday, keeping Thursday "free for the present in case of attractive invitations," and noting his intention to play squash and "have luncheon and tea party" every day.[55]

If this transplanted society offered respite from the sufferings of combat, the return to the battlefield meant taking up once more the prescriptions of masculine fortitude expected of soldiers in the Great War. Carr's portrait of the Bureau's work highlights the "guarded courage" perceptible in the letters received from the front, and displayed in those of both Papineau and Firth.[56] As for the words of comfort these men received, it is more difficult to assess how the emotional work they performed was expressed. In his letters to Rogers, Papineau often asks to be remembered to friends in London, makes frequent references to his correspondences with other Square Milers, either in Montreal or London (in particular with members of the Allan and Molson families), and often tells her of the lunches and card games shared with sons of prominent families also stationed on the front, including the architect Gordon Blackader, whose father was a well-known McGill physician; Charles Coristine, whose Westmount family owned a fur importing and manufacturing company; and Charles and Percival Molson of the famed brewing family. Even when it is not clear to whom Papineau might be referring, his use of first names or initials in designating certain individuals speaks to the familiarity he and his mother shared with members of these transplanted social circles. Recounting social interactions, passing on letters, sharing news and gossip, or grief when one of these men died in battle, were part of the everyday practices that maintained Square Mile sociability and affective bonds within wartime circumstances.

Rogers's letters to her son Talbot have not survived but clearly she also responded to the anxieties he expressed – about the war, his role within it, his exchange with Bourassa, and the life he might lead when it was over. On the basis of what Papineau wrote to his mother, Gwyn characterizes Rogers as "a hard-pressed single mother, undignified by widowhood, bringing up a quartet of young sons after being abandoned by a profligate husband, dependent upon a monthly allowance from her father in law," choosing for Talbot's sake to keep the Montebello estate rather than return to her native Philadelphia.[57] Given the emotional trials she would have experienced during the war, it seems reasonable to affirm that despite Talbot's enjoinments, and notwithstanding the protective stance he assumed, it was she who was, above all, a source of emotional fortitude for her son.

As for Mabel Stead, there is no indication that she would not have remained in Low Moor throughout the conflict. In what sometimes comes across as awkwardly expressed empathy, Firth's words of comfort were frequently grounded in the assumption that Stead shared the melancholy he felt across the distance separating them. "Don't get downhearted and dismayed," he writes, "I know it will be very hard for you, but keep your spirits up."[58] Since we have no trace of what Stead might have written to Firth, we cannot know whether she indeed missed him as much as he hoped she did. But in taking for granted that his romantic interest's longing was just as intense as his own, Firth was at once attempting to solidify the emotional bond between them while also expressing his expectations of her emotions. He seems to have delighted in playing the part of the valiant soldier, pined for by the waiting damsel as he courageously goes to war. At the very least, he appears to have been reinforcing his own protective masculinity by writing her into a position of emotional suffering that only his return could relieve.

Emphasizing the fun and adventure of their travels also served to portray the soldiers' youthful enthusiasm and confidence that everything was, and would continue to be, alright. Though he assured Mabel that he has dutifully resisted the temptations "ever on my path," Firth wanted her to know that he was both having a good time and staying true to what he "promised … in the days gone by."[59] Similarly wanting to alleviate his mother's concern for his safety, Papineau insisted upon a pleasant experience on the front, suggesting "[I am] enjoying myself enormously." "This is certainly 'the life,'" he wrote on a number of occasions, describing the excitement and camaraderie of his days in the trenches. If leaves in London were the opportunity to spend time together, his social obligations there also allowed him to express a carefree and debonair masculinity. He is sorry, he insists, writing that if "for the few days off I run with a lot of silly girls leaving you alone again. It nearly breaks my heart to think of it and yet we do look forward to our leaves here so much as a sort of 'take the lid off' occasion that I hate to be serious and slow and emotional. You won't understand I am afraid but so it is."[60]

In many of Papineau's letters, the emotional register varies from line to line. Wanting to make light of the tragedies of war, his references to bombardments and casualties, including the death of close friends, are often ensconced in the midst of otherwise chatty passages that describe the weather, his daily routine, or his giddy enthusiasm over the German helmets and shell casings he collects as souvenirs. In one instance he tells her of a celebrating a joint birthday with a friend on the front. "I carried a bottle of Champagne up with me. We had luncheon in a dug-out in which at the same hour the day before one man was killed and another wounded by a shell. There was a good deal of shelling, but to our left. It was very pleasant to visit the chaps in that way."[61] While this episode might strike us as foolish, morbid, or both, read in the context of the emotional regime in which Papineau was operating, the anecdote is revealing. As historian Mark Humphries shows, men suffering from the psychological traumas of trench warfare were routinely taxed by military officials as displaying weak and "flawed" feminine behaviour, committing "transgressions against dominant gender expectations."[62] Practices like collecting battlefield memorabilia (a hobby Canadian soldiers were evidently reputed to particularly enjoy) and mocking the conditions of war through macabre humour were some of the ways in which soldiers sought to cope with the extreme challenges of life and death in the trenches as well as affirming an idealized masculine detachment from emotional suffering, notes historian Tim Cook.[63] In their letters home, always vetted by censors, soldiers generally "reinforced rather than undermined idealistic notions." Lamenting their situation, explains historian Jeff Keshen, would only "project a weak and womanly disposition, as well as depress and worry their loved ones."[64] Though Papineau was undoubtedly being provocative in his tone, his nonchalance was meant to highlight his emotional fortitude, his toughness in the face of danger, and by extension to demonstrate to his mother that he was thriving and therefore that she needed not worry for him.

With the passage of time and as the distance from home in its many guises increased, the emotional resolve and buoyancy appears to fade in the letters of both men, and the need for comfort and reassurance becomes ever more apparent. Firth's letters take a more sentimental tone as his journey around the world wore on. "I never wished in all my time, more than I do now, for you to be in my company," he gushes from the mountain pass in the Rockies, the most emotional affirmation of his affection expressed to that point.[65] Papineau's emotional fragility was increasingly evident after he left a cushy clerical position producing communiqués, coordinating filmmakers, and writing historical accounts for the Canadian War Records Office under the aegis of Max Aitken, Montreal business magnate and British Member of Parliament and cabinet minister. He had assumed these duties a year and half earlier, following a two-month stint in hospital suffering from bronchitis but evidently "more hurt in mind than body" after his time in the trenches.[66] However, the privilege of his position relative to the men with whom he had taken up arms was increasingly niggling at him, and after an extended period of introspection he decided to reintegrate his battalion on the front lines. Political ambitions had much to do with his decision. As Gwyn notes, Papineau had missed a defining moment on the battlefield at Vimy. He was keenly aware that a heroic record of service would undoubtedly boost his electability in the next federal contest, a proposition that raised the ire of his commanding officer.[67]

In a letter to Caroline Rogers, though, Papineau emphasized the deeply felt sense of duty which seems to also have motivated him, sentiments other historians have chosen to foreground in analyzing his decision.[68] It is one of the longest letters in the collection. In it he begs his mother to accept a decision he knows will make her anxious. He expresses his willingness to give up his private car and writing room and return to the discomfort, fatigue, and "narrowness of existence" of life in the trenches in order to take an active part in supporting "the men in the field." "That is as I see it – as I feel it," he tells her, adding that it is "better to share in the making of history than in the writing of it."[69]

From that point on, Papineau's letters adopt a less exuberant and more reflective tone. While repeating he was "happy and proud" of his decision and that "there is nothing sad about things here," the emotional toll of the war becomes more apparent in his writing.[70] Still eager to report his "immense" enjoyment despite bombardments, the "narrow escapes," and the friends being killed, he now concedes that "this would be a great life if people didn't get hurt!"[71] Two months later, his enthusiasm gave way to resignation as he began to feel the war may never end:

"this life simply has become the normal existence."[72] Commenting on a novel she had sent him, Stephen McKenna's *Sonia*, Papineau wonders how his mother could have found it sad. But, he explains, "my emotions, I expect, are dulled or killed altogether."[73] He also tells her that he would prefer to "supress and control" his emotions until the war was over, when "we will find a fund of buried affection."[74] There is an obvious tension here between his claim of deadened emotion and the increasingly sentimental timbre of the letters. At the outset of the second battle of Passchendaele, he urged his mother once more to share in his feeling of satisfaction at having made the decision to return to battle. "Always know that if I do get killed I was completely happy and content ... Remember dearest, that if I can, my spirit will be with you to comfort you and my only unhappiness will be yours. I say this just in case, in order that you may know what my last thoughts were." Three days later, Talbot Papineau died going over the top.

Conclusion

As for Willie Firth, we know nothing of his time on the Pacific. Did the letters to Stead continue? If we can presume that they did, there is no indication of why they are not included with those of his journey to and through Canada. In February 1919, Firth telegrammed his family to announce he had arrived back in Liverpool, promising to be "home shortly."[75] Other documents reveal that he was demobilized in April of the same year, that he and Stead married in September 1921, and that at least one son was born in 1926.[76] At the outbreak of the Second World War, we find the family living in Bradford, he still working in the textile industry and she listed as performing "unpaid domestic duties."[77] Willie Firth died in 1974, followed by Mabel two years later.[78]

Firth's apparently otherwise unremarkable life as a family man in a working-class town offers a remarkably contrasting entry to the intimacies of empire from those expressed by Papineau, scion of an influential family, Square Mile mover and shaker whose death in battle has been remembered as a symbol "of all the golden promise cut down by the Great War."[79] Their respective letters offer fleeting glimpses into the way individuals defined their identities and understood their place in a world marked by profound uncertainty.[80] As historian Laura Ishiguro has shown in a study on letter writing in settler colonial families, even expressions of everyday banalities or attempts to downplay the experience of unusual circumstances – characteristics present in Papineau and Firth's missives – reinforced and normalized the power structures underlying imperial networks.[81] In the exceptionally traumatic context of war, both men sought through their epistolary practice to create a sense of rootedness, evoking both a political and familial home as a point of fixity in the vastness of empire. In laying bare everyday feelings, letters written to loved ones are especially useful for examining the terms in which this sense of place was anchored. These letters offer a window into the two men's inner turmoil at certain moments and are especially revealing of the performative stance of masculinity from which emanated this search for stability. Expressions of emotions cannot, to be sure, be taken as unfiltered markers of such emotions. To attempt as much would in any case miss the point, as the scholarly literature on the history of emotions has shown. Rather, these scribbled pages shed light on the emotional regimes at play in this extraordinary context. In writing to their girlfriends and mothers, men like Firth and Papineau were not revealing unvarnished feelings so much as drawing upon emotional codes and conventions that defined and reinforced the understandings and expectations underpinning these relationships. They reassured and sought reassurance. They displayed a masculinity that was as vulnerable as it was assertive. Above all, the love and longing they expressed offer the opportunity to reflect on the way large, polymorphous processes like empire were made and unmade by the bonds and strictures of emotional communities that spanned both time and distance.

And within these processes, what of Montreal's famed Square Mile in particular? As author Margaret Westley suggests in her portrait of the neighbourhood, the war "released forces of change" that profoundly challenged the community in its desire to regain a sense of normalcy. From liberated morals and whimsical styles, to changing gender roles and shifting demographic realities that diminished the weight of anglophone influence in the city, to deep political rifts over conscription and schisms within the Protestant church, Square Mile society emerged shaken from the conflict.[82] Also in question was English Canada's attachment to the British Empire itself. If the empire's appeal was already waning, noted Carl Berger, "the First World War killed it." With 60,000 compatriots fallen in battle, English Canadians adopted an increasingly inward focus to their nationalism.[83] Like the webs with which Ballantyne and Burton metaphorically assimilate them, empires, despite the structure of power and domination they create and perpetuate, are also "fragile and prone to crises where important threads [are] broken or structural nodes destroyed."[84] In his public and private correspondence through the war, Talbot Papineau contributed to these shifting cultural and political dynamics. Though his letter to Bourassa advocated a sustained imperial connection, his imperialism was clearly expressed as a form of Canadian nationalism. As a staunch Liberal, and from the disillusionment present in his last letters, we can speculate that Papineau's thinking would have continued to evolve towards a more pronounced nationalism had he had the chance to undertake his political career. But as we have seen, empires are constituted by far more than high politics and are built upon norms and values that condition social behaviour. The emotional uncertainties and fragility his letters display, confirmed by the comparison with Firth as being representative of a shifting masculinity, prefigure the social and cultural transformations brought upon the Square Mile. Understanding the nature of the spatial and symbolic imperial boundaries that men like Firth and Papineau criss-crossed throughout the war, then, also requires that we pay attention to the intimate linkages they constructed in their immediate communities and private lives.

NOTES

1 Bibliothèque et Archives nationales du Québec, P744, Fonds Talbot Mercer Papineau, Talbot Papineau [hereafter TP] to Caroline Rogers [hereafter CR], 1 October 1917.

2 Imperial War Museum, 15359, Private Papers of W. Firth, Willie Firth [hereafter WF] to Mabel Stead [hereafter MS], 2 October 1917.

3 Tony Ballantyne and Antoinette M. Burton, eds., *Bodies in Contact: Rethinking Colonial Encounters in World History* (Durham, NC: Duke University Press, 2005), 3.

4 Roderick Macleod, "Salubrious Settings and Fortunate Families: The Making of Montreal's Golden Square Mile, 1840–1895" (PhD diss., McGill University, 1997).

5 Elizabeth Kirkland, "Mothering Citizens: Elite Women in Montreal, 1890–1914" (PhD diss., McGill University, 2011), 308–15; Brian Young and Geoffrey James, *Respectable Burial: Montreal's Mount Royal Cemetery* (Montreal: McGill-Queen's University Press, 2003), 145.

6 Brian Young, *Patrician Families and the Making of Quebec: The Taschereaus and McCords* (Montreal: McGill-Queen's University Press, 2014), 260.

7 My examination of the emotional tenor of these letters in informed by the growing scholarly literature in the history of the emotions. Focusing on the exteriorizing of individual feelings as social discourse, this scholarship emphasizes how the expression of emotions is at once constitutive of social dynamics in ways that the discipline has long overlooked, and contingent on the social and cultural factors that codify what emotions signify and how they are shared in a particular context as well as how they operate as mechanism of inclusion and exclusion among social groups. For key historiographical examinations, see *The History of Emotions* (Manchester: Manchester University Press, 2018); *A History of Feelings* (London: Reaktion Books, 2019); Alain Corbin, Jean-Jacques Courtine, and Georges Vigarello, eds., *Histoire des émotions*, 3 vols. (Paris: Éditions du Seuil, 2016); Ute Frevert, *Emotions in History – Lost and Found* (Budapest: Central European University Press, 2011); Susan J. Matt and Peter N. Stearns, *Doing Emotions History* (Urbana-Champaign: University of Illinois Press, 2014); Jan Plamper, *The History of Emotions: An Introduction* (Oxford: Oxford University Press, 2012).

8 *Lovell's Montreal Directory for 1913–1914* (Montreal: John Lovell and Sons), 1760.

9 Sandra Gwyn, *Tapestry of War: A Private View of Canadians in the Great War* (Toronto: Harper Collins, 1992), 90, 98. In 2006 Papineau was featured in the CBC miniseries *The Great War*. Cast in the part was another aspiring political leader bearing a hallowed patronym: Justin Trudeau. On the memory of Talbot Papineau as "English Canada's perfect French Canadian," embodying

the "fanciful dream" of "an ideal Quebec participating in national endeavours and ultimately subservient to English Canada's vision of them," see Geoff Keelan, "The Forgotten Few: Quebec and the Memory of the First World War," in *The Great War: From Memory to History*, ed. Kellen Kurschinski et al. (Waterloo, ON: Wilfrid Laurier University Press, 2015), 249–50.

10 Significant collections of this correspondence are held in Library and Archives Canada, MG30-E52, R4911-0-8-E, Fonds Talbot Mercer Papineau.

11 Gwyn, *Tapestry of War*, 330. On Papineau in particular, see chaps. 5, 8, 12, 18, 22, and 23.

12 On the textile industry implantation in Bradford and throughout West Yorkshire, see Alan Fowler, "Great Britain: Textile Workers in the Lancashire Cotton and Yorkshire Wool Industries," in *The Ashgate Companion to the History of Textile Workers, 1650–2000*, ed. Lex Heerma van Voss et al. (Farnham: Ashgate, 2010), 231–52; David T. Jenkins and Kenneth G. Ponting, *The British Wool Textile Industry, 1770–1914* (Aldershot: Scolar Press, 1987), 3; Henry Rees, "Leeds and the Yorkshire Woollen Industry," *Economic Geography* 24, no. 1 (1948): 28.

13 Imperial War Museum, 15359, Private Papers of W Firth, RNVR Division Tyneside, NO. Z/11117.

14 Gwyn describes Papineau as a "clever, self-assured Montreal lawyer, brimming over with joie de vivre and clearly cut out for stardom," the city's most "sought-after" bachelor, thanks in part to his dashing looks and "legendary summer parties at Montebello." Gwyn, *Tapestry of War*, 90, 96.

15 This description of Firth's character, which predates his naval service, comes from a letter to Stead from her uncle, in which the latter also comments on the "ever happy" young man's abilities on the organ. West Yorkshire Archive Service, 38D84/1/2, Firth Family of Low Moor, Personal Papers, letter from Stead's uncle Tom, 8 February 1915.

16 Carl Berger, *The Sense of Power: Studies in the Ideas of Canadian Imperialism, 1867–1914* (Toronto: University of Toronto Press, 1970), 260.

17 Daniel Gorman, *Imperial Citizenship: Empire and the Question of Belonging* (Manchester: Manchester University Press, 2006), 2.

18 Tony Ballantyne and Antoinette Burton, eds., *Moving Subjects: Gender, Mobility, and Intimacy in an Age of Global Empire* (Urbana: University of Illinois Press, 2009), 10.

19 Ann Laura Stoler, *Haunted by Empire: Geographies of Intimacy in North American History* (Durham, NC: Duke University Press, 2006), 25.

20 Sarah Ahmed, "Affective Economies," *Social Text* 22, no. 2 (2004): 119.

21 William M. Reddy, *The Navigation of Feeling: A Framework for the History of Emotions* (Cambridge: Cambridge University Press, 2001); Barbara H. Rosenwein, *Emotional Communities in the Early Middle Ages* (Ithaca, NY: Cornell University Press, 2006). For discussions of the relative merits and weaknesses of Reddy's notion of emotional regimes and Rosenwein's conception of emotional communities, see Boddice, *History of Feelings*, chap. 3; Nicole Eustace et al., "AHR Conversation: The Historical Study of Emotions," *American Historical Review* 117, no. 5 (2012): 1487–531.

22 Stoler, *Haunted by Empire*, 42.

23 Ballantyne and Burton, *Moving Subjects*, 7–8, 10. As historian Elizabeth Vibert points out in the same volume, the "personal records of empire" such as the letters sent by these two men, allow us to trace not just the "intimacies of the domestic scene" but also the "larger relationship between colony and metropole." Elizabeth Vibert, "Writing Home: Sibling Intimacy and Mobility in a Scottish Colonial Memoir," in *Moving Subjects: Gender, Mobility, and Intimacy in an Age of Global Empire*, ed. Tony Ballantyne and Antoinette Burton (Urbana: University of Illinois Press, 2009), 69.

24 WF to MS, 21 September 1917.

25 WF to MS, 19 September 1917.
26 WF to MS, 22 and 23 September 1917.
27 TP to CR, 25 October 1916, 1 May and 15 August 1917.
28 TP to CR, 11 May 1917.
29 Catherine Hall and Sonya O. Rose, *At Home with the Empire: Metropolitan Culture and the Imperial World* (Cambridge: Cambridge University Press, 2006), 24–5.
30 WF to MS, 1 October 1917.
31 WF to MS, 28 September 1917.
32 WF to MS, 26 September 1917.
33 Analyses of Papineau note that little could "overawe" him (Gwyn, *Tapestry of War*, 94) and that he "moved easily between European trenches and the parlours of Paris and London." Geoff Keelan, "Canada's Cultural Mobilization during the First World War and a Case for Canadian War Culture," *Canadian Historical Review* 97, no. 3 (2016): 378.
34 TP to CR, 5 February 1916.
35 Papineau's letter to Henri Bourassa was published in *The Gazette, The Star*, and *The Herald* on 28 July 1916, and subsequently picked up by other papers, including *The Times* of London on 22 August. References here are to a later reprint in a pamphlet featuring some of Bourassa's English-language interventions relating to the war. Henri Bourassa, *Canadian Nationalism and the War* (Montreal: n.p., 1916), available at https://archive.org/details/canadiannational00bour.
36 Keelan, "Canada's Cultural Mobilization," 392. See also Geoff Keelan, *Duty to Dissent: Henri Bourassa and the First World War* (Vancouver: UBC Press, 2019).
37 Bourassa, *Canadian Nationalism*, 15–20, emphasis in original.
38 Bourassa, *Canadian Nationalism*, 22.
39 Bourassa published his response, in French, in *Le Devoir* on 5 August 1916. I cite here the English translation in Bourassa, *Canadian Nationalism*, 24–30, emphasis in original.
40 TP to CR, 15 and 18 August, 2 and 7 September 1916.
41 Michael Roper, *The Secret Battle: Emotional Survival in the Great War* (Manchester: Manchester University Press, 2009), 13.
42 TP to CR, 21 October 1917.
43 WF to MS, 24 September 1917.
44 WF to MS, 24 September 1917; TP to CR, 21 October 1917.
45 Mark Moss, *Manliness and Militarism: Educating Young Boys in Ontario for War* (Toronto: Oxford University Press, 2001), 15, 17, 22, 29; John Tosh, *Manliness and Masculinities in Nineteenth-Century Britain* (Harlow: Pearson, 2005), 199. See also George L. Mosse, *The Image of Man: The Creation of Modern Masculinity* (Oxford: Oxford University Press, 1999), 15.
46 Peter Gossage and Robert Rutherdale, eds., *Making Men, Making History: Canadian Masculinities across Time and Place* (Vancouver: UBC Press, 2018), 11; Roper, *Secret Battle*, 302–6. As historian George Mosse argues, the First World War both reinforced traditional militaristic ideals of the masculine warrior and gave rise, particularly among socialist thinkers, to a "gentler manhood that did not have to mimic the normative stereotype." Mosse, *Image of Man*, 107–8.
47 Joanna Bourke, *Dismembering the Male: Men's Bodies, Britain and the Great War* (London: Reaktion Books, 1996), 22.
48 TP to CR, 4 June 1916.
49 TP to CR, 26 June 1917.

50 Sarah Glassford, *Mobilizing Mercy: A History of the Canadian Red Cross* (Montreal: McGill-Queen's University Press, 2017), 102–3.
51 Gwyn, *Tapestry of War*, 205.
52 Julia Drummond, foreword to Iona K. Carr, *A Story of the Canadian Red Cross Information Bureau during the Great War* ([Montreal?] n.p., n.d.), 4.
53 Carr, *Story*, 8.
54 Gwyn, *Tapestry of War*, 384–5.
55 TP to CR, 15 November 1916.
56 Carr, *Story*, 50.
57 Gwyn, *Tapestry of War*, 207.
58 WF to MS, 24 September 1917.
59 WF to MS, 28 September 1917.
60 TP to CR, 14 November 1916.
61 TP to CR, 31 March 1916.
62 Mark Humphries, "War's Long Shadow: Masculinity, Medicine, and the Gendered Politics of Trauma, 1914–1939," *The Canadian Historical Review* 91, no. 3 (2010): 508.
63 Tim Cook, "'Tokens of Fritz': Canadian Soldiers and the Art of Souveneering in the Great War," *War & Society* 31, no. 3 (2012): 211–26; Tim Cook, "'I Will Meet the World with a Smile and a Joke': Canadian Soldiers' Humour in the Great War," *Canadian Military History* 22, no. 2 (2015): 48–62.
64 Jeffrey A. Keshen, *Propaganda and Censorship during Canada's Great War* (Edmonton: University of Alberta Press, 1996), 153.
65 WF to MS, 2 October 1917.
66 Quoted in Gwyn, *Tapestry of War*, 230.
67 Gwyn, *Tapestry of War*, 379–81. On the political calculus motivating Papineau's decision, see also Keelan, "Canada's Cultural Mobilization," 380.
68 Tim Cook, *At the Sharp End: 1914–1916* (Toronto: Viking Canada, 2007), 485; Desmond Morton and J.L. Granatstein, *Marching to Armageddon: Canadians and the Great War, 1914–1919* (Toronto: Lester and Orpen Dennys, 1989), 168, 179.
69 TP to CR, 22 May 1917.
70 TP to CR, 1 July, 24 August 1917.
71 TP to CR, 4, 10 July, 7 August 1917.
72 TP to CR, 16 September 1917.
73 TP to CR, 24 August 1917.
74 TP to CR, 17 October 1917.
75 West Yorkshire Archive Service, 38D84/1/2, Firth Family of Low Moor, Personal Papers, telegram, 13 February 1919.
76 Imperial War Museum, 15359, Private Papers of W Firth, RNVR Division Tyneside, NO. Z/11117; England and Wales Civil Registration Marriage Index, 1916–2005; England and Wales Civil Registration Death Index, 1916–2007. All registers consulted on www.ancestry.co.uk.
77 1939 England and Wales Register.
78 England and Wales Civil Registration Death Index, 1916–2007.
79 Gwyn, *Tapestry of War*, 400.
80 On this theme, see in particular Jane Errington, "Webs of Affection and Obligation: Glimpse into Families and Nineteenth Century Transatlantic Communities," *Journal of the Canadian Historical Association* 19, no. 1 (2009): 1–26.

81 Laura Ishiguro, *Nothing to Write Home About: British Family Correspondence and the Settler Colonial Everyday in British Columbia* (Vancouver: UBC Press, 2019).
82 Margaret W. Westley, *Remembrance of Grandeur: The Anglo-Protestant Elite of Montreal, 1900–1950* (Montreal: Libre Expression, 1990), 144.
83 Berger, *Sense of Power,* 264.
84 Ballantyne and Burton, *Bodies in Contact*, 3.

Figure V.17 Hon. George Drummond's house, Sherbrooke Street, Montreal, 1891.
McCord Museum, VIEW-2458.

A Consistent Material Palette

Mount Royal was never a volcanic crater, although it is composed largely of igneous rock, with deposits of limestone and shale. The mountain was an early source of building material. Aggressive quarrying of its limestone was one of the impetuses for the creation of the park in the 1870s. Montrealers were alarmed to see their mountain literally disappearing.

Trenton limestone deposits are found throughout the Island of Montreal, and limestone continued to be the building material of choice in the city until the very last decade of the nineteenth century. The native stone is tough and not easy to work, but it has unique properties. In January 1870, a local correspondent contributed an article on the stone to the *American Architect and Builder's Monthly*: "This stone possesses one great peculiarity over every other stone with which I am acquainted, viz: that it becomes whiter and brighter with age; this in a very light stone is a very great recommendation, for while dark stones are, most of them, improved with age and become mellower in tone, while building marbles and stone almost as pure in color when new, age only means dirt and stain."

Brick was, of course, also used for facing and backing, but a building of any significance was faced in stone. This situation was unquestioned until about 1885, when imported building stones began to appear, first in the financial district of the old city, and subsequently in the homes of the Square Milers who worked there.

There are a number of reasons for the decline in popularity of the local stone. An advanced transportation infrastructure of railway lines and steamship routes facilitated the importation of non-native stones. Foreign architects, chiefly from the United States, were coming to Montreal to execute commissions. They tended to specify materials, already familiar to them, that could be cheaply imported. There were also stylistic changes. Montreal limestone was notorious for its time-consuming, and therefore costly, ornamentation. Fin-de-siècle buildings with elaborately carved facades were much more practical to sculpt in the soft sandstones of Ohio, Vermont, New Brunswick, and Scotland. As well, by the last decades of the nineteenth century, buildings glowed with colour. It is no wonder that in an age that revelled in russets, deep greens, and rich browns, the pale soft grey of Montreal limestone was discarded in favour of the more interesting palette offered by other stones.

The house that Andrew T. Taylor (later Sir Andrew) designed for his uncle and aunt, Sir George and Lady Julia Drummond, must have been, with its grotesque "beastes" and richly textured red sandstone, an object of shocking opulence to passers-by strolling along Sherbrooke Street in the summer of 1889. Its sheer size and glowing colour commanded attention and admiration (Figure V.17).

As the new century was approaching, significant Square Mile houses were built in red brick. Edward Maxwell chose it for the Vincent Meredith house of 1896 and again for the John Thomas Davis house of 1908. Robert Findlay chose to use sandstone sparingly as accents within the red brick facades of the Herbert Molson house of 1912. Montreal grey stone was never again the material of choice.

CHAPTER TWELVE

The Death of the Golden Square Mile? Understanding the Transformation of an Urban District, 1945–1985

Harold Bérubé

On 7 September 1973, at the end of a long and controversial process, the City of Montreal issued a permit for the demolition of the Van Horne Mansion. In the following hours, workers started dismantling the interior of the building, designed by one of the fathers of "art nouveau," Édouard Colona. The next day, Saturday the 8th, the Victorian mansion was razed to the ground. The case of the Van Horne Mansion can be read as a shorthand version of the end of the Golden Square Mile: here, despite the vocal opposition of various groups, we have the demolition of a stately bourgeois mansion by greedy promoters, with the not-always-voluntary assistance of a short-sighted municipal administration and the complicity of a provincial government that did not consider the building to be part of Québécois heritage. Of course, by that point, the Square Mile was no longer in any sense an elite residential neighbourhood. Through a process that started in the interwar period but that accelerated significantly in the 1960s, a large percentage of the area had become a part of Montreal's central business district.

Most of the chapters in this book explore various facets of life in the Square Mile during its golden age, or discuss the considerable and complex economic and political reach of some of its residents, often major players in the deployment of capitalism within and beyond the borders of the British imperial system. My aim, in this chapter, is to offer some thoughts on the death of the Square Mile, or rather its decline as an elite residential neighbourhood and its transformation in the decades following the end of the Second World War. Cities are organisms in constant transformation, and this is doubly true of North American cities, unburdened by a medieval past. Neighbourhoods appear and disappear, sometimes gradually, sometimes

Figure 12.1 Wallis & Shepherd, *The Van Horne Mansion on Sherbrooke Street, Montreal*, c. 1900. McCord Museum, MP-0000.27.38.

suddenly. In Montreal, but also elsewhere in North America, historians working on such neighbourhood changes have been mostly interested in the dramatic cases of working-class districts created in the late nineteenth century and destroyed in the 1960s and 1970s in the name of urban renewal.[1] Sectors such as the Square Mile diverge from that model.[2] In fact, there are not many studies on the decline of the neighbourhood, and most have been focused on the destruction that followed that decline and the emergence of heritage conservation groups in Montreal.[3] Beyond that, more popular works on the district tend to offer relatively brief depictions of the "end of an era" represented by that decline, choosing instead to focus on a more glorious period.

To better understand the nature, mechanisms, and actors of the Square Mile's transformation as a neighbourhood in the decades following the Second World War, I first propose a critical examination of the narrative of the district's decline, emphasizing its limitations as an explanation for this urban transformation. I will

Figure 12.2 Wm. Notman & Son, *Interior Corridor in the Van Horne Mansion*, 1920. McCord Museum, VIEW-19337.

then explore some of the more plausible causes of this transformation, causes rooted in larger social, economic, and urban processes at work at the North American scale, but coloured by some of Montreal's distinct traits. Finally, I will offer my own analysis of the transformation of the district by focusing not on the prestigious mansions of its upper part, but on the often overlooked but still fairly affluent row houses of the lower part of the Square Mile. By setting aside the question of heritage conservation and offering a detailed analysis of real estate transactions for one central block in the lower part of the district, I will demonstrate that the Square Mile was, in many ways, a victim of the very forces that first allowed its growth and opulence in the nineteenth century.

Narrating the End of the Square Mile

In many ways, the Square Mile is an invented space. It never had any kind of formal existence as an administrative subdivision of Montreal's territory and started its existence as a small part of the much larger Saint-Antoine Ward. As a result, its precise boundaries vary, but it is generally described as the fairly small neighbourhood located between Dorchester Boulevard to the south (now René-Lévesque Boulevard), Pine Avenue to the north, University Street to the east (now Robert-Bourassa Boulevard), and Guy Street to the west. Although its development really took off in the 1850s and 1860s, the name "Square Mile" was only adopted in the early twentieth century, with the addition of the adjective "Golden" in the 1950s, an addition motivated by nostalgia, but also by the desire to sell real estate. During its heyday, it was more commonly called "New Town" or "Uptown."[4]

We do not have to search far outside of academia to find different voices recalling or narrating the death of the Square Mile. We may think, for example, of the opening pages of Stephen Leacock's *Arcadian Adventures with the Idle Rich* (1914) where the author – himself a resident of the district – paints a satirical portrait of its inhabitants that already suggests, if only through the name of the social club that is at the centre of many of the book's "adventures," a certain morbid quality:

> The Mausoleum Club stands on the quietest corner of the best residential street in the City. It is a Grecian building of white stone. About it are great elm trees with birds – the most expensive kind of birds – singing in the branches … Just below Plutoria Avenue, and parallel with it, the trees die out and the brick and stone of the City begin in earnest. Even from the Avenue you see the tops of the sky-scraping buildings in the big commercial streets, and can hear or almost hear the roar of the elevated railway, earning dividends. And beyond that again the City sinks lower, and is choked and crowded with the tangled streets and little houses of the slums. In fact, if you were to mount to the roof of the Mausoleum Club itself on Plutoria Avenue you could almost see the slums from there. But why should you? And on the other hand, if you never went up on the roof, but only dined inside among the palm trees, you would never know that the slums existed – which is much better.[5]

This quote, as well as the book in which it is found, emphasizes the disruptive economic activities and profound socio-economic inequalities that gave birth to the "best residential street in the City," an aspect generally underplayed in more romantic depictions of the Square Mile.

The reader will also find brief explorations of the district's decline in the coffee-table books written in the 1980s about the architecture of some of its most prestigious houses. In François Rémillard and Brian Merrett's 1986 book, *Demeures bourgeoises de Montréal*, the authors note that by the 1930s the Square Mile was no longer the preferred neighbourhood of Montreal's bourgeoisie. More modern suburbs such as Westmount and Outremont now played that role. And, after the 1930s, no new houses were built in the Square Mile, marking the beginning of its "déchéance" (decline).[6] By that point, the district was described as being essentially inhabited by the aging members of a few remaining bourgeois families. According to Rémillard, who offers a relatively nuanced analysis of the situation, this decline can be explained by the effects of the Great Depression and also by the expansion of Montreal's central business district and profound changes in the way of life of the elite in the course of the twentieth century. Still, the expansion of downtown was described as an "invasion" and the development of the railroad network within the boundaries of the Square Mile, beginning in the late nineteenth century, as something that happened "sournoisement" (surreptitiously) and that opened the district to "le bruit, la saleté et les odeurs" (noise, dirt, and smells).[7]

In a very similar book published in 1987 that makes good use of the Notman photographic archives, Donald MacKay mostly agrees, describing the interwar period as that of a "waning world" and explaining that, by the 1930s, the "appearance of tourist hotels and bawdy houses on Dorchester Boulevard and the invasion of commerce had chased the rich up the hill," marking the beginning of a long decline that would end in the 1950s.[8] He describes the Square Mile after the Second World War as "no longer a proud neighbourhood but an appendage to commercial Montreal, a place of apartment houses, hospitals, homes turned into offices, clubs, consulates, or McGill classrooms, with here and there an aged widow living out her life with memories of the richest, most powerful neighbourhood in Canadian history."[9] For MacKay, the decision of the City of Montreal to allow the construction of high-rise apartment blocks in the district in 1953 marked its entry into the world of modern developers.

It is important to note that both books were prepared and published barely a decade after the destruction of the Van Horne Mansion, at a time when it was not clear what fate had in store for what little was left of the Square Mile's golden age. In the writing, we can sense the authors' concern for the future of those vestiges. In fact, François Rémillard was a member of the "Save Montreal / Sauvons Montréal" coalition, created in the aftermath of the demolition to ensure that such an episode would not repeat itself. Through photography – contemporary in the case of Rémillard and Merrett, historical in the case of MacKay – they aimed to preserve and promote the district's architectural memory.

Margaret Westley tried to do something similar for the Square Mile's social and cultural memory in *Remembrance of Grandeur*.[10] Mostly based on the author's interviews with former residents of the district, the book paints a nostalgic portrait of the Square Mile's bourgeois society during the first half of the twentieth century. Although not entirely uncritical – it emphasizes, for example, the "splendid isolation" that characterized this highly privileged society within Montreal – the book, as its title suggests, focuses mainly on the lost grandeur of the district and its inhabitants. In Westley's telling, the First World War clearly marks the beginning of the end for the Anglo-Protestant elite living in the Square Mile, with the death of many of the "best and bravest of a generation" in that small community.[11] Still, she links the decline of this elite more closely to major economic and social changes of the twentieth century: the Great Depression of the 1930s, the rise of a mostly French-Canadian labour movement in Quebec, the ascent of Toronto as the new economic metropolis of Canada, and the relative complacency of Montreal's old economic elite. As to the Square Mile as a residential district, in "the mid-1950s, MacGregor Street was constructed through the Square Mile. A major traffic artery carried the noise and fumes of the vast postwar increase in automobile through the tranquil gardens of the huge mansions where children used to play. Yet there was hardly a complaint. The old families no longer occupied those mansions."[12] Indeed, Westley also underlines the fact that, by the 1920s, one could already find, beyond the borders of the Square Mile, younger and independent suburbs favoured by the sons and daughters of Montreal's Anglo-Protestant elite.[13]

A Changing Suburban Ideal and the Challenges of Persistence

In fact, another way of looking at the decline of the Square Mile as a residential district, to better understand the nature and mechanism of this process, is through the lens of suburban history. In this context, the new bourgeois suburbs taking shape outside Montreal's administrative boundaries at the turn of the twentieth century offer an interesting point of comparison. Why did the Square Mile die while they persisted? It is a multifaceted question, one that brings us to the heart of what the Square Mile was and was not as a residential district.

The Square Mile and the suburbs I am thinking about – places such as Westmount, Outremont, Notre-Dame-de-Grâce and, later on, the Town of Mount Royal – were born of the same impulse: the ambition to leave behind the dense and mixed urban core of the city to seek refuge in a home located within a predominantly residential neighbourhood on the periphery, closer to nature, but still within distance of the heart of the city, its businesses and institutions. They were conceived as relatively homogeneous neighbourhoods where the members of the elite could live among themselves.[14] But, as Montreal grew in numbers and territory, yesterday's periphery became today's central districts. It was not long before the pressure of urban development was felt, not only in the Square Mile but also in all of the early bourgeois suburbs of Montreal created in its wake.[15]

In the case of the Square Mile, it is a phenomenon that started early on. We may think of the arrival of the Windsor train station in the neighbourhood in 1889, but also of the increasing commercialization of St. Catherine Street in the 1890s, of the new and larger hotels and apartment buildings appearing on Sherbrooke Street and elsewhere in the 1900s, and of the beginning of the construction of the Sun Life Building in 1913.[16] Of course, as we have seen, other forces were at work to undermine other aspects – social and cultural – of the Square Mile's way of life, but we can still imagine a scenario where the district managed to maintain some of its material characteristics in the face of urban development, as Westmount did, for example.

This brings us to the notion of persistence, defined as the ability for a district to preserve, in the long term, its material and socio-economic characteristics. According to American urban historian Mary Corbin Sies, "a common pattern of four features in combination ensures the maintenance of the built environment and a high quality of residential amenities and local control over time. These features are 1) careful site selection; 2) comprehensive planning; 3) the creation of a defensive framework of property restrictions, local ordinances, and a variety of formal and informal boundary marking strategies; and 4) a consensus on the part of community members that maintenance of their residential environment is a paramount priority."[17] If we look at the Square Mile and compare it to its younger counterparts, the absence of this "defensive framework" stands out.

My own research on cases such as Westmount illustrates how such a framework functions and how it is lacking in the case of the Square Mile,[18] which was created as a neighbourhood within the boundaries of the City of Montreal at a time when its inhabitants were able to maintain a high degree of influence on its government. This influence is clearly illustrated by the activities of John Ostell, surveyor of the city, but also an important collaborator with many of the first promoters active in the Square Mile.[19] By contrast, Westmount, or the village of Côte-Saint-Antoine as it was then known, was incorporated as a distinct municipality later on, in 1879, at the initiative of the first suburban settlers of this rural sector and in reaction to the arrival of developers. Those early suburban settlers had direct control over this new local government and clearly their ambition was to use it to limit the activities of developers in the area by adopting what could be described as rudimentary urbanistic policies.[20]

In its early history, Westmount, as did other municipalities, adopted construction codes to fight two major plagues of the urban environment: fires and epidemics. The first code was adopted in 1892. As the years passed, most other municipalities –

including Montreal – did not go much further, but Westmount was at the avant-garde of more ambitious urbanistic measures. The construction code it adopted in 1909, for example, contained many new measures to preserve and protect the quality of the built environment in an era of intense speculation and development. But the most ground-breaking measure adopted by Westmount during this period was undeniably zoning. Almost unheard of elsewhere in the Province of Quebec before the Second World War, zoning was used more and more extensively in Westmount during the first third of the twentieth century. The first zoning measure, which was quite rudimentary, was adopted in 1897. But the 1909 by-law was much more ambitious and detailed, dividing the municipality into three zones with distinct sets of rules. This measure had a clear impact on Westmount's landscape, creating a more urbanized and diverse "Lower" Westmount, and a much more clearly residential and suburban "Upper" Westmount.[21] One last initiative linked to urbanism should be noted: the existence, early on, of an architectural commission. This commission, created in 1916, was composed of the mayor, four architects, and the manager and engineer of the city, and tasked with studying and approving the plans of all buildings constructed in the city.[22] This attention to the built environment and the use of so many different tools to protect it are central to the "defensive framework" described by Mary Corbin Sies.

Meanwhile, the Square Mile's inhabitants were ill-equipped to adopt similar measures. In the early twentieth century, they had to contend with an expanding municipal government, a complex and heterogeneous electorate, and elected officials who were becoming professional politicians, more interested in economic development and electioneering than in the preservation of a small and aging residential district.[23] The few measures adopted to preserve some of the neighbourhood's character, such as the 1931 by-law meant to preserve what was left of Sherbrooke Street's residential composition, came too little, too late.[24] And, as we have seen, in 1953, Montreal also opened the way for the construction of high-rise apartment buildings in the district. This absence of institutional defences contributed significantly to the gradual deterioration of the neighbourhood as an elite residential district. Of course, it is difficult to imagine a scenario where the Square Mile would have been able to sustain, unchanged, the pressures of urban development, but the example of Westmount certainly suggests that it could have adapted to these changes and preserved some of its original character with the right "defensive framework."

That is not, of course, what happened. Starting in the 1930s, but especially after the Second World War, an increasing number of houses from the upper, most prestigious, part of the Square Mile were demolished. The upkeep of these outmoded mansions had become too much for many of their owners, the neighbourhood was quickly changing, and the value of the properties – the land, not the houses – was increasing. While some of the houses were sold or given to institutions such as McGill University or the Royal Victoria Hospital, which incorporated them into their own facilities, most of them were simply demolished to make way for more modern additions to the district.

It was only with the planned demolition of the Van Horne Mansion that things changed ever so slightly. The house, built at the end of the nineteenth century for railroad tycoon William Cornelius Van Horne, was put up for sale in 1967, and it was not long before observers began worrying about its potential demolition. Still, it was only in 1973 that a buyer, developer David Azrieli, showed up, quickly proving that these fears were warranted since he planned to build a fourteen-storey apartment building on the site. Not long after the City of Montreal delivered a demolition permit, the Quebec government interrupted the process to evaluate the heritage potential of the house, but a few months later that process was halted. James McLellan was at the centre of the community-based campaign then organized to save the house and that led to the creation of a coalition of groups under the banner "Save Montreal / Sauvons Montréal."[25]

More demolitions occurred after the destruction of the Van Horne Mansion, but never without some sort of reaction from various community groups and actors within the municipal and provincial governments.[26] But, in a sense, it was quite late in the game, since few of the stately manors of the upper Square Mile were still standing at that time. However, at the very least, that is an incomplete picture of the situation. The Square Mile was never limited to a handful of spectacular bourgeois mansions inhabited by patrician families, and the history of its decline as a residential district cannot be limited to the story of their demolition.

A Closer Look at the Mechanisms of and Actors in the Square Mile's Redevelopment

Looking more closely at the evolution of the lower part of the Square Mile in the decades following the Second World War allows us to understand the transformation of the district differently, setting aside its heritage aspect to focus on its economic dimension. The 1950s and 1960s may have represented the end of an era for Montreal's Anglo-Protestant elite, but these decades also heralded in Montreal, as elsewhere in North America, a period of intense urban transformation involving the rise of mass suburbanization, the decline and destruction of working-class neighbourhoods, and the triumph of modernist architecture in expanding central business districts.

Figure 12.3 Harry Sutcliffe, *View towards the Northwest of Montreal, Including the Bell and Sun Life Buildings, Montreal,* c. 1935. McCord Museum, M2011.64.2.3.40.

When looking at the dynamic evolution of downtown Montreal during this period, one could be forgiven for not realizing that the city was quickly losing ground to its rival, Toronto, for the title of metropolis of Canada. In the first decades of the twentieth century, despite its national pre-eminence, Montreal seemed somewhat untouched by many of the transformations affecting similar North American cities, notably the proliferation of skyscrapers, the most striking manifestation of the hubris of North American cities during the Roaring Twenties (with the conspicuous exception of the Sun Life Building, the "largest building in the British Empire").[27] Various factors can explain this relative modesty. Among them, we note the economic elite were less prone than their American counterparts to flaunt the success of their businesses through the construction of costly but impressive flagship buildings, but also the fairly long-lived by-laws restricting building height during much of the first half of the twentieth century.[28] Things changed rapidly after the Second World War, especially in the 1960s. The old central business district, centred on St. James Street, was no longer well-adapted to the development of corporate

Figure 12.4 Place Ville-Marie in foreground with view of the IBM and Sun Life Buildings and the Queen Elizabeth Hotel, 1966. City of Montreal Archives, VM94-A0323–010.

capitalism during those decades of postwar prosperity. Nothing illustrated this shift better than the construction of Place Ville-Marie. As Don Nerbas demonstrated, the construction of this iconic skyscraper between 1958 and 1962, at the initiative of developer William Zeckendorf, was deeply tied to a narrative of urban and national modernization, and the building rapidly came to embody the values associated with a new capitalism distinct from the one on which the Square Mile was built in the nineteenth century.[29] The destruction of the building then occupied by the St. James Club to make way for the cruciform skyscraper certainly was a striking symbol of this transition. Its inauguration also marked the beginning of the transformation of what was then Dorchester Boulevard into the heart of a new central business district.[30] At the end of the 1960s, in his brief history of Montreal, historian John Irwin Cooper concludes that, by that time, "Montreal had lost much of its earlier individuality and had come to resemble other great American cities. The population, essentially nomadic, moved into, out of, and within the city. Having no roots, the Montreal population had no sense of the past and could learn nothing from the past."[31] Such a picture is a startling contrast to the tradition-bound Square Mile depicted by Margaret Westley in *Remembrance of Grandeur*.

A Different Kind of Urban Redevelopment

In this context, the Square Mile, and especially its lower part, was clearly in the way of the modernization of downtown Montreal. In this last section of this chapter, I propose an analysis of the transformations of the sector and of the main actors – owners, promoters, and developers – of its redevelopment in the postwar period by using a variety of sources. In doing so, I would like to tell an alternate story of urban redevelopment, one distinct from the demolitions observed in the upper part of the neighbourhood, but also distinct from the story of the demolition of working-class districts during the same period, one where the inhabitants (or at least the owners) of the transformed district were not so much victims but agents of the process. To do so, it is important to briefly revisit the Square Mile's past to better understand how the upper and lower portions of the district came to be so starkly differentiated and to emphasize that, despite obvious changes in the nature of the processes at work, there are echoes of this past in the redevelopment of the 1960s and 1970s.

In his thesis on the "making of Montreal's Golden Square Mile," Roderick MacLeod emphasizes, unsurprisingly, the Anglo-Protestant character of the district, but also – perhaps more significantly – the complicated history of its development, a story deeply tied to the rise of capitalist institutions in Montreal.[32] In short, in the second half of the nineteenth century, the Square Mile certainly was a *bourgeois utopia* for those residing there,[33] but it was also quite a business opportunity. Landowners and speculators such as John Redpath and Thomas Phillips lived there while also benefiting greatly from its development.[34] In fact, even in the second half of the nineteenth century, the Square Mile was not a homogeneous environment of stately bourgeois mansions with large well-tended gardens. Early in its development, the lower part of some of its largest estates were subdivided and gave way to denser blocks of terraced row houses.[35] Sherbrooke Street quickly became the boundary between those two different halves of the Square Mile, as clearly shown by maps of these subdivisions hand-drawn by geographer David Hanna in his 1980 article on the subject (see Figure 12.5). As he explains:

> The new landowners of the 1840s were generally businessmen whose wealth was derived from the economic opportunities available within the city. These men were the new elite of Montreal and like the fur traders wished to enjoy their wealth and display their status through the medium of prestigious estates located on the slope of Mount Royal. These same men, however, were not insensitive to the money-making opportunities of real estate dealings in a rapidly expanding local economy. Hence the estates became just one more link in their chains of lucrative investments in the city. They subdivided their properties, each implementing a conscious distinction between that part of the estate south of Sherbrooke Street where the flat lands was divided in small housing lots and that portion of the steep slope north of Sherbrooke Street where the land was retained for personal use or else divided into huge lots. This clear-cut differentiation set the stage for a high-density residential townscape on the plateau, and a low-density mansion townscape on the slope, the two basic components of the future neighbourhood.[36]

If we skip ahead and study aerial pictures taken in the mid-twentieth century, it is easy to see how that situation persisted, at least up to a point, and then to follow the relatively fast and drastic transformation that occurred in the lower part of the district in the 1960 and 1970s. In pictures taken in 1947, we can clearly see the persistent differences between the higher and lower parts of the district, despite the general densification of Sherbrooke Street.[37] Nonetheless, the whole sector is still fairly residential and distinct from the central business district in the south-east. In pictures taken a little over twenty years later, in 1969, things had visibly changed: we can observe clear manifestations of the encroachment of the central business district in the lower part of the Square Mile, with numerous new skyscrapers (including Place Ville-Marie), while the upper sector was feeling the effects of the expansion of the McGill campus.[38] The widening of Sherbrooke Street, in the

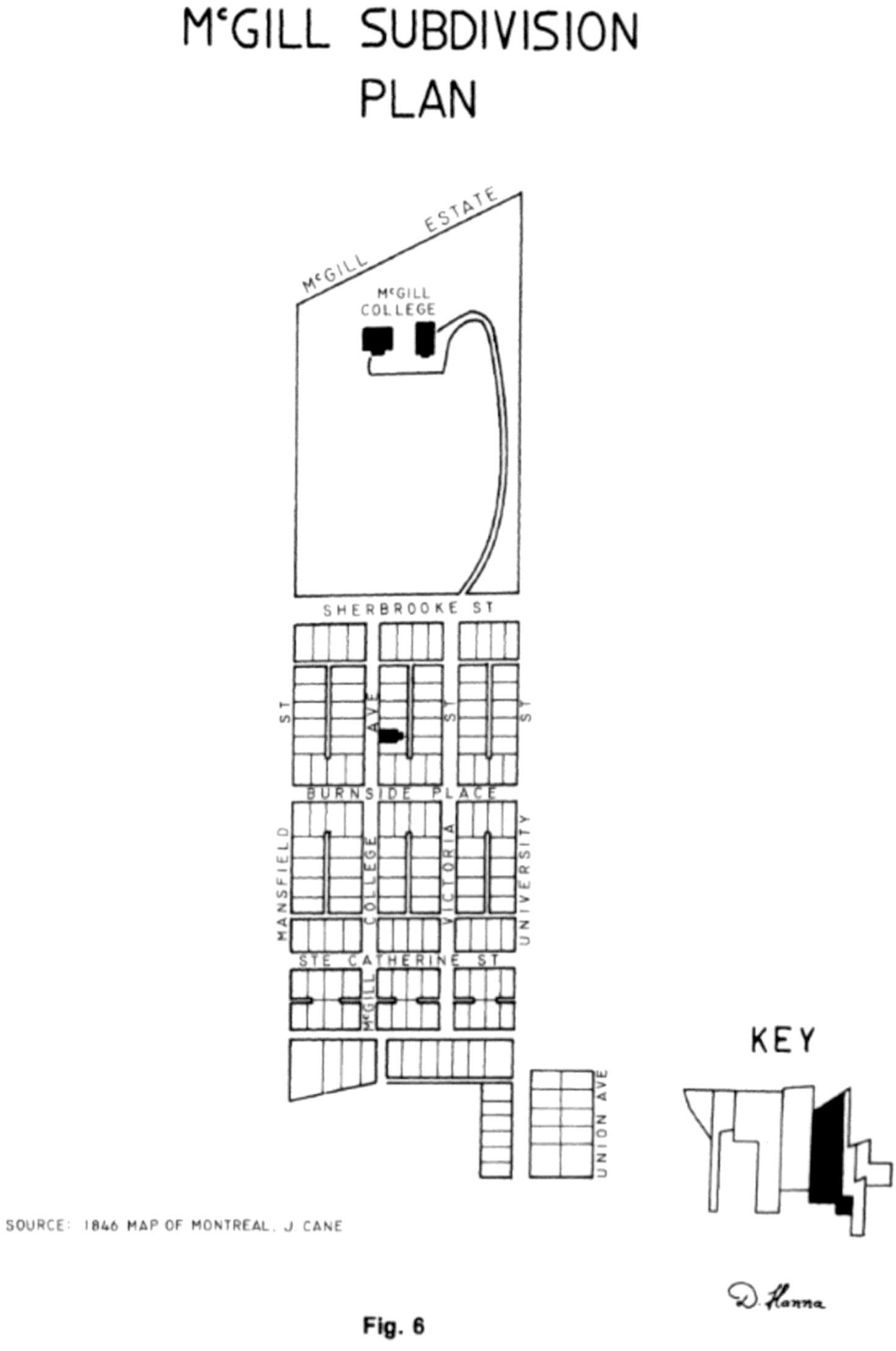

Figure 12.5 Map of the McGill subdivision plan of 1845, hand-drawn by David Hanna, taken from his article "Creation of an Early Victorian Suburb in Montreal" (1980). Image courtesy of the *Urban History Review / Revue d'histoire urbaine* and David Hanna.

Figure 12.6 Aerial views of the Island of Montreal, 1947–1949 (with elements added by the author). City of Montreal Archives, VM97-3.

Figure 12.7 Aerial view of the Island of Montreal, 1969 (with elements added by the author). City of Montreal Archives, VM97, S3, D09.

late 1950s, also played an important role in those transformations, transformations that would continue and lead to the demolition of the Van Horne Mansion.

If we look more closely, from an economic perspective, at what happened to the Square Mile between 1945 and 1985, we observe an upper-class variation on a relatively well-known narrative in North American urban history. To quote Howard P. Chudacoff and Judith E. Smith: "Attacking what they saw as a 'blight' and stimulating downtown investment became priorities for city officials, business leaders, and [national politicians], all of whom connected visible urban poverty, housing shortages, and downtown decline under the category of slum clearance."[39] In Montreal, as we have seen earlier, these efforts led to the draconian "renovation" of sectors such as the old Red Light District, the "Faubourg à m'lasse," and the neighbourhood of Goose Village / Victoriatown. Of course, even if the context is the same, the differences between those cases and the Square Mile were considerable. For one thing, the neighbourhood was anything but a blight and could not be considered "visible urban poverty." For another, the owners of those properties were not powerless and at the mercy of urban elites and experts as was the case, for example, of Victoriatown. Nonetheless, the sector was also becoming an obstacle to "progress" and the development of the central business district, and its residents were not immune to expropriations. In fact, from the perspective of affluent suburbanites relocating to newer sectors such as Westmount or the Town of Mount-Royal, the Square Mile would have appeared more and more as lost ground, a sector with no political autonomy to protect its character or integrity, and massive outdated mansions that cost a fortune to maintain. All of this being said, how did the inhabitants and owners of the sector handle the transformations, benefit from them, or resist them?

Visualizing Neighbourhood Changes in the Square Mile

I will use the case of the Sherbrooke-Burnside-McGill College-Victoria city block to explore the complicated answer to this question. The area located just south of the McGill campus, in the denser part of the Square Mile, was part of the university's estate before being subdivided and sold off in 1845 to help pay off the institution's substantial debts.[40] For this project, I used a combination of sources – the city's evaluation rolls, fire insurance plans, and documents found through the Registre foncier du Québec – to create a database detailing every transaction involving lots located on this city block between 1945 and 1985.[41] Thanks to these documents, I was able to paint a general portrait of the block, but also to follow more minutely the way it evolved as an urban space during the postwar period. In the early phases of the research project, seeing that it was difficult to translate the numerous individual transactions on these lots into a coherent picture, I explored different ways to solve the issue. Certainly, the aerial pictures collected by the City of Montreal were of some help to simply visualize what was going on with this city block, but I needed a more precise and complex tool to look at its evolution during the postwar period. The team of the Laboratoire d'histoire et de patrimoine de Montréal, especially Kim Petit and Laura Baretto, helped me create an interactive map of the block using the data recorded.[42] Without dwelling too much on the technical details of the process, I want to emphasize some of the difficulties we faced. One of the problems we had to solve was getting a clearer picture of the functions of the different lots that composed the block during the 1945–85 period, something we solved using the "registre de plans des propriétés de la Ville de Montréal."[43] Another problem we faced was significant inconsistencies in the sources regarding the exact measurements of the lots, as some of them were merged or subdivided over the years, leading sometimes to strange results when came the time to map them. Numerous minute corrections were needed to reduce those inconsistencies as much as possible. The result of these efforts is an online application where we can find details on the various transactions analyzed here; it is also a powerful visualizing tool to understand the transformation of the lower part of the Square Mile through various maps emphasizing either land use, type of owners, lot subdivisions and consolidations, and number of transactions per lot.[44]

I want to focus on two parallel movements that can be observed during the postwar period and that quite effectively summarize the drastic transformation of the sector during a relatively short period. The first and simpler one is the gradual consolidation of the various lots found on this city block. Whereas the subdivision of the block in 1945 was fairly similar to its original structure when it was first subdivided a century earlier, as of the 1960s, plans were made to merge them to make way for large urban renewal projects. These plans eventually took the form of two "super" lots now occupied by the 1981 McGill College and Place Mercantile buildings. The second and more complex movement we can observe through these maps is the evolution of the types of owners of these lots over the years (see Figure 12.9 to Figure 12.13). As we will see, as late as 1960, the city block was essentially in the hands of individual property owners, mostly members of the upper-middle class, with the notable exception of Strathcona Hall, on the northwest corner of the block, which is the property of McGill University. However, in five short years, a majority of these lots passed into the hands of corporations looking to transform them into more "modern" and lucrative properties in the context of the expansion of Montreal's central business district. Another five-year jump, to the year 1970, allows us to visualize two important developments: the failure of that corporate scheme, with

Figure 12.8 The Sherbrooke-Burnside-McGill College-Victoria block as it appears in the *Cadastre officiel de la Cité de Montréal. Quartier St-Antoine* (1998 [1869]), and the *Underwriter fire insurance plans* of 1915 and 1957. City of Montreal Archives.

Figure 12.9 Subdivision and type of owners of the Sherbrooke-Burnside-McGill College-Victoria block (1960). Image courtesy of the Laboratoire d'histoire et de patrimoine de Montréal (SCHEMA).

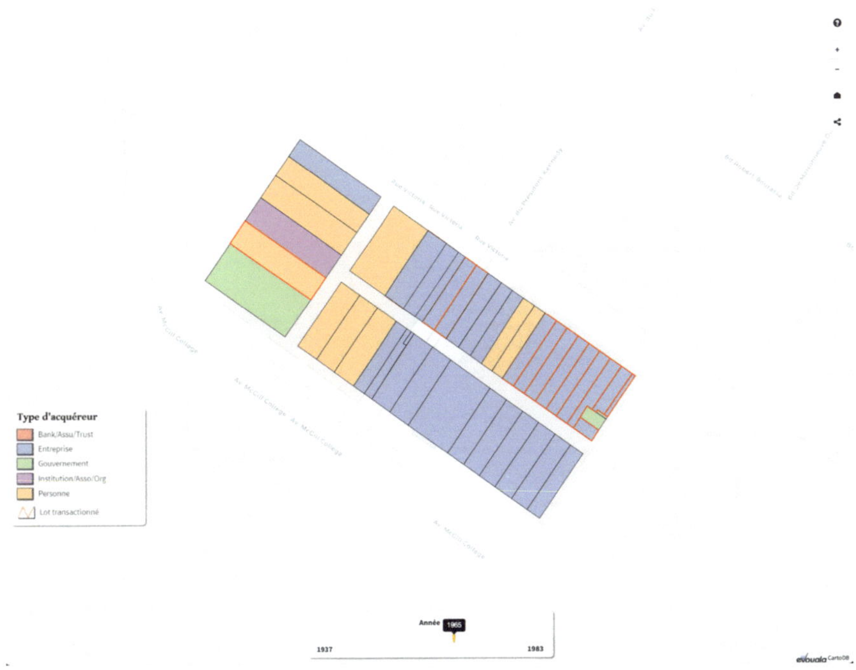

Figure 12.10 Subdivision and type of owners of the Sherbrooke-Burnside-McGill College-Victoria block (1965). Image courtesy of the Laboratoire d'histoire et de patrimoine de Montréal (SCHEMA).

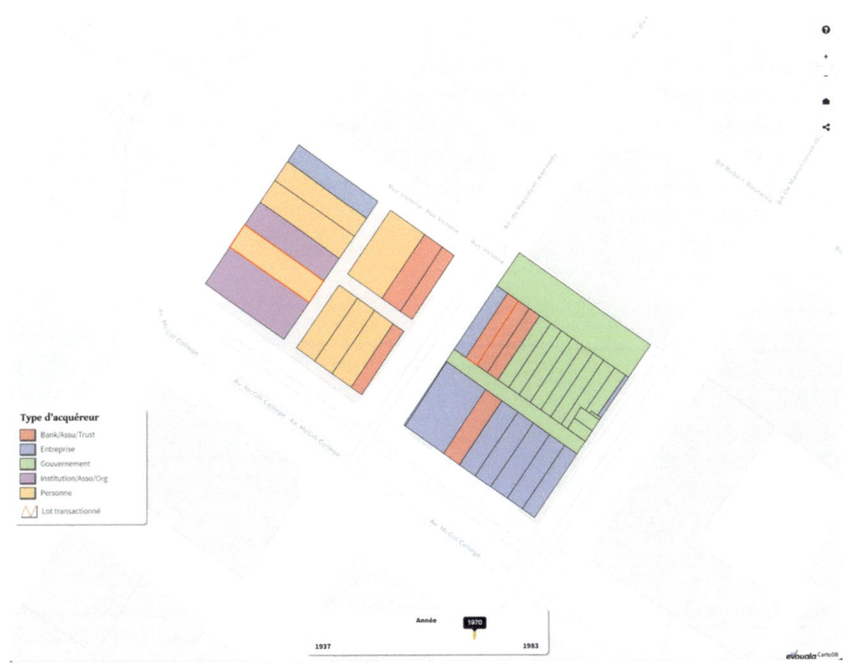

Figure 12.11 Subdivision and type of owners of the Sherbrooke-Burnside-McGill College-Victoria block (1970). Image courtesy of the Laboratoire d'histoire et de patrimoine de Montréal (SCHEMA).

Figure 12.12 Subdivision and type of owners of the Sherbrooke-Burnside-McGill College-Victoria block (1975). Image courtesy of the Laboratoire d'histoire et de patrimoine de Montréal (SCHEMA).

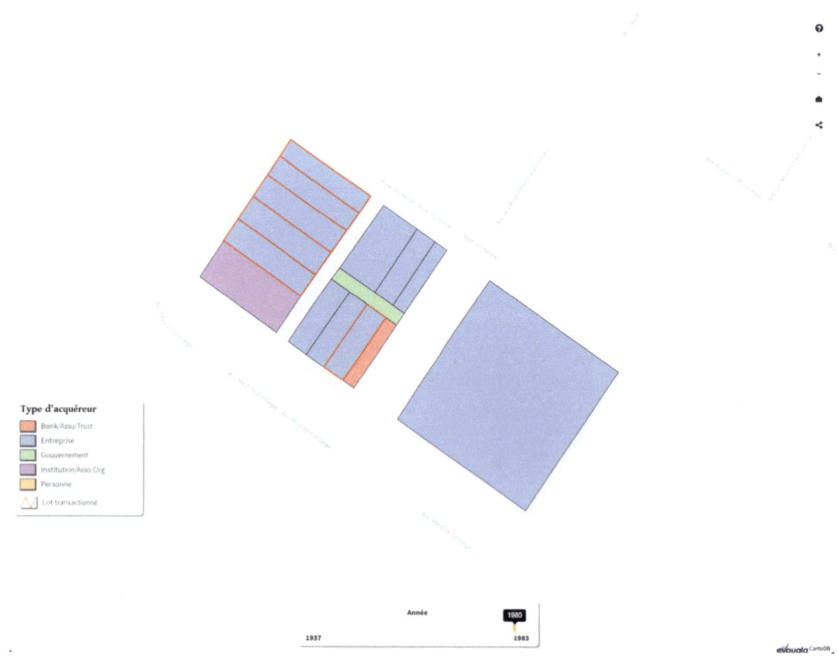

Figure 12.13 Subdivision and type of owners of the Sherbrooke-Burnside-McGill College-Victoria block (1980). Image courtesy of the Laboratoire d'histoire et de patrimoine de Montréal (SCHEMA).

many of these lots now in the hands of banks or the municipal government, and the expropriation of some of the properties to build President Kennedy Avenue. But, at the end of the decade, corporate actors once again took the lead in consolidating those properties and transforming them into an urban landscape that had very little to do with the Square Mile as it existed previously, even in its lower and denser part.

A closer look at some of these transactions allows us to better understand what was going on and who was involved in the "death" or rather the transformation of this part of the Square Mile. Looking at an insurance plan from 1915, we quickly realize that, at that time, the block was mostly residential, composed of a majority of row houses, along with one small apartment building, a few shops including a Chinese laundry, a synagogue, and McGill's YMCA (Strathcona Hall).[45] Observing the insurance plan of 1940, we see that twenty-five years later things had changed considerably. The majority of the row houses had been subdivided into apartments and students' rooms, clearly indicating that the original inhabitants of the lower Square Mile left for greener (suburban) pastures during the interwar period.[46] But if we look closely at the transactions recorded for the years 1945–50, they strongly suggest that most of the owners of these buildings were their former, aging occupants. During those five years, a little more than a third of the lots did not change hands, but widows and other successors sold a little more than another third of them. The balance (less than a third) was already in the hands of private corporations or non-profits such as the university.

In this context, the 1950s may be described as relatively stable years for this city block and, we may assume, for the rest of the lower Square Mile. Most of the transactions recorded in that decade suggest that the sector largely remained in the hands of individual owners. In some cases, the transactions took the form of exchanges within a single family, often for symbolic sums of money, as was the case for the Kaufman family and lots 1308–1 and 1308–2. In this instance, lawyer Benjamin Kauffman sold them to Anna Rosen, the widow of Isaac Kauffman (simply described as a gentleman), in 1944 for the sum of $1. Anna Rosen sold them back to Benjamin Kauffman, Dorothy Kauffman, and Elsie Kauffman ten years later for the same amount.[47] In most cases though, these transactions were exchanges between members of an affluent upper-middle class: merchants, engineers, managers, manufacturers, insurance brokers, notaries, and a few more "gentlemen."

The 1960s represent the beginning of significant changes that led to a major transformation of the lower Square Mile. The first clear sign that things were changing was a wave of expropriations between 1962 and 1964 in the southern part of the block, as the City of Montreal prepared for the creation of Boulevard de Maisonneuve, a new east-west thoroughfare that, in this sector, would take the place of

Burnside. The new boulevard included and replaced numerous streets along the way and was part of the city's larger strategy to cope with the increasing automobile traffic created by the development and expansion of the central business district. Another significant component of that strategy was, of course, the creation of the metro, and its Green Line was built along the new thoroughfare.[48] The owners of the expropriated lots had no choice but to accept the city's offer, although it was a lucrative transaction for all of them. For example, Jean Georges Richard (druggist) bought lot 1325 in 1950 for $105,000. Twelve years later, the city gave him $201,763 in compensation.[49]

In the meantime, two visibly linked private groups were at work in the sector and their presence truly marked the end of an era for the Sherbrooke-Burnside-McGill College-Victoria city block. Starting in 1957, the Intercontinental Development Corporation bought up a series of lots on the block and sold them all to McGill-Burnside Holdings Ltd. in 1961. The former owners of these lots and the corporation made a reasonable profit in the transactions. Between 1961 and 1964, the buildings on these lots were promptly demolished and, in 1964, transferred to a new entity: Mace Development Ltd. This corporation completed the consolidation of the block by buying almost all the lots still in individual hands. This time, the transactions were extremely profitable for those last few individual owners. For example, manufacturer Max Gruber bought lots 1318 and 1319 in 1958 for $95,000 and sold them six years later to Mace Development for an astounding $249,780.[50] By 1965, there was only one individual owner left on the block: notary A. Hyman Mettarlin, who bought lot 1316 in 1949 for $16,000. We will return to him later.

Behind the activities of Mace Development Ltd. was a major corporate actor involved in urban redevelopment in Montreal, but also elsewhere in Canada, notably in Toronto, in the postwar era: the T. Eaton Company Ltd.[51] Its ambitions for the entire sector were considerable. They clearly illustrate the continuation of the kind of urban modernization heralded by Place Ville-Marie. In fact, the project envisioned by Eaton for the sector was designed by I.M. Pei & Associates of New York and Vincent Ponte, both involved in the conception of the iconic building. The promoters of this new project presented it as "un des plus audacieux jamais entrepris sur le continent nord-américain" (one of the boldest ever undertaken on the North American continent), which most certainly was an exaggeration. Still, it was very ambitious. Involving the sector located between Sherbrooke Street, University Street, St. Catherine Street, and Mansfield Street, it promised to "renovate" about twenty acres of prime downtown property for a total investment of $125 million. Mace Development was essentially a creation of the Eaton Company and its British associate in this venture, First National Property Co., and was tasked with

CAHIER No 2 / PAGES 15-28 LA PRESSE RADIO TV / THEATRE / INFORMATIONS GENERALES

le carnet DE RAYMOND GUÉRIN

REGARDS SUR L'AUTEUR

Gigantesque projet de mise en valeur immobilière du secteur de l'avenue McGill College au coût de $125,000,000

- Projet canado-britannique
- Superficie de vingt acres
- Création d'un vaste boulevard
- Première phase: $30,000,000

Projet commercial de $125,000,000

Les plans généraux de mise en valeur du district central de Montréal situé entre les rues Sherbrooke, University, Sainte-Catherine et Mansfield, d'un coût de $125 millions, comprennent la création de passages pour piétons, de magasins et de restaurants et, ce, souterrains aussi bien qu'en surface.

Le conseil accepte le projet de contrat entre T. Eaton et Mace et la ville de Montréal

Un véritable boulevard

Le point principal du projet de Mace Development Ltd est la transformation de l'avenue McGill College en un spacieux boulevard d'une largeur de 115 pieds, soit presque le double de ce qui existe présentement, bordé d'arbres et divisé par une série de mails ombragés. Des tours jumelles de 34 étages seront situées en retrait de la nouvelle artère afin de former une plaza large de 220 pieds et de laisser la vue ouverte sur le Mont-Royal.

Un dédale de routes sous terre

Réseau de communications souterrain

Figure 12.14 Full-page report on the project piloted by Mace Development, *La Presse*, 30 June 1965, p. 21.

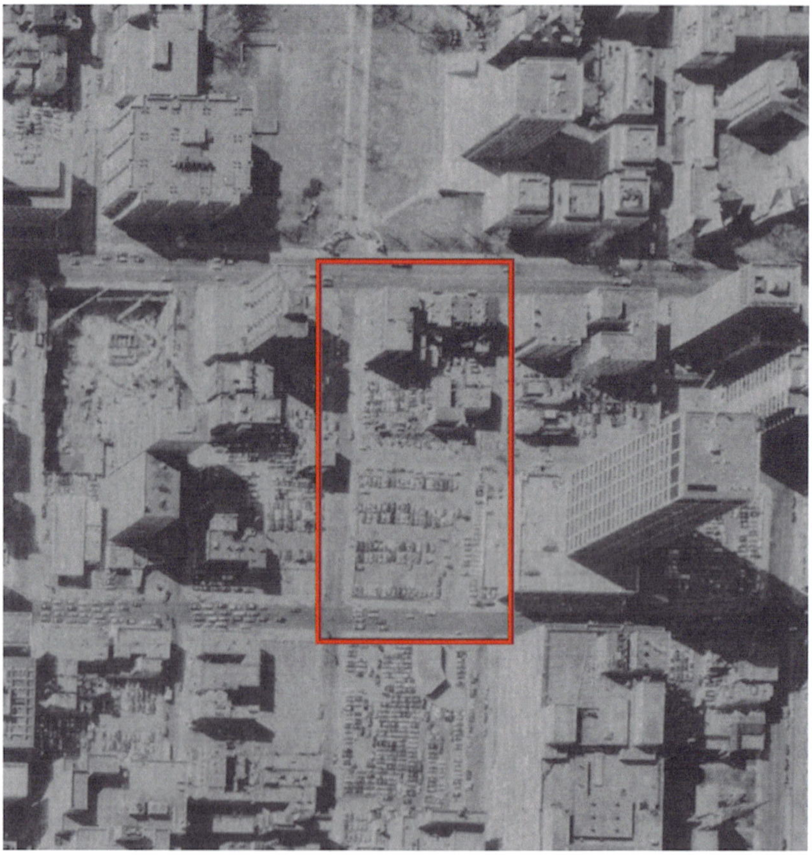

Figure 12.15 Aerial view of the Island of Montreal, 1973. City of Montreal Archives, D13 VM97-3.

buying the necessary lots and overseeing construction of the project. The plan, as presented in the metropolitan newspapers, was closely linked to the development of Montreal's metro and a complex deal was signed between its promoters and the City of Montreal to integrate McGill Station with the planned buildings and their numerous underground elements.[52] The first phase of the project was estimated at $30 million and was supposed to be completed in time for Expo 67. It included a new massive Eaton store and a 15-floor office tower in its first phase, and 34-floor twin towers during a possible second phase. Furthermore, it was to be structured around a widened McGill College Avenue (35 metres wide). In a report on the project in the pages of *La Presse*, lavish models and drawings of the project were reproduced and juxtaposed with a small picture of the "secteur à transformer" (sector to be transformed). The legend read: "Voici le secteur du centre-ville que les projets des compagnies Mace Development Ltd. et T. Eaton vont transformer au fur et à mesure de leur réalisation. Même si l'on constate que plusieurs immeubles sont déjà disparus du paysage. Il faut s'attendre à beaucoup d'autres travaux de démolition pour en arriver au boulevard de 115 pieds de largeur rêvé par les planificateurs" (Here is the sector of downtown that the plans of the Mace Development Ltd. and T. Eaton companies will gradually transform as they are implemented. We note, however, that several buildings have already disappeared from the landscape. We can expect a great deal of additional demolition to obtain the 115-foot wide boulevard the planners envision).[53]

But the dreams of the planners and promoters of the project and their allies at the City of Montreal quickly faded. Once again in the pages of *La Presse*, a journalist wrote in February 1968 that the project "est mort hier de sa belle mort, laissant derrière lui l'histoire de beaux rêves et celle d'une lente agonie" (died a natural death, leaving behind a story of beautiful dreams and one of a slow death).[54] The article emphasized that since its well-publicized launch three years earlier, the project had been more or less stagnant and recalled, as part of an explanation for the stagnation, the failure of a similar enterprise in Toronto.[55] The journalist went on to explain that Mace Development was now looking to sell the numerous lots acquired in this context and explained to readers that these properties were probably the most well-situated in Canada and that nowhere else in the country could such properties be as profitable to their seller.[56]

Still, in the 1970s, most of these properties remained vacant or became parking lots until the arrival of new corporate actors that completed the transformation initiated by Mace Development by consolidating the two parts of the block into "super" lots (now separated by President Kennedy Avenue). Two modernist towers would be built on these lots: in 1981, the 1981 McGill College building was inaugurated on the south side while, the following year, Place Mercantile was built on the north side. Two aspects of this final transformation of the city block are of particular interest in the context of this chapter and take us back to the tension between the properties of the Square Mile as heritage and business opportunities in a changing city: the fate of Strathcona Hall and the final transaction between an individual owner of the city block and a corporate actor.

Designed and built in 1904, using money given by Donald Alexander Smith, 1st Baron Strathcona, a wealthy member of Montreal's Anglo-Protestant elite and chancellor of McGill University between 1899 and 1914, Strathcona Hall was first used as the university's chapter of the YMCA. As the plans to construct Place Mercantile were set in motion, just a few years after the demolition of the Van Horne Mansion, "Save Montreal / Sauvons Montréal" sprang into action to try to save Strathcona Hall and some of its abandoned neighbours on Sherbrooke Street.[57] As

Figure 12.16 Strathcona Hall on Sherbrooke Street, c. 1910. McCord Museum, MP-0000.872.10.

Martin Drouin explains, by the early 1980s, the era of demolitions and reconstructions in Montreal had given way to an era of integrating old buildings into the construction of new ones. And, as *Le Devoir*'s journalist Alain Duhamel already noted in November 1980, the integration of the old into the new actually became a selling point used by promoters.[58] When McGill University agreed to sell the building to the promoters of Place Mercantile, the university made sure that the deed of sale included a clause to guarantee the conservation of the building. Despite this provision, the promoters partially demolished the building, invoking structural problems, forcing McGill to sue them and leading to the partial reconstruction of Strathcona Hall.[59] While the conservation of Montreal's built heritage has made some progress since the demolition of the Van Horne Mansion, the example of Strathcona Hall and its neighbours on Sherbrooke Street shows the limits of this integration that, then as in the following years, often took the form of facadism.[60]

As far as the question of the Square Mile and its properties as business opportunities, I would like to return, as a coda, to the interesting case of the last individual owner of a lot on the studied city block, notary A. Hyman Mettarlin. Owner of lot 1316 since 1949, when he bought it for the sum of $16,000, Mettarlin had a lot of leverage with the promoters of Place Mercantile, who needed that last lot to complete their consolidation of the block. The notary finally leased it in 1980 to the private corporation for a duration of fifty years for a sum starting at $10,000 a year and reaching $54,000 a year in 2030.[61] This is certainly a spectacular example of an individual landowner taking advantage of the transformation of this part of the Square Mile.

Conclusion

There are different ways of understanding and analyzing the Square Mile's decline in the postwar era. If we set aside the opulent mansions of the upper part of the Square Mile and their undeniable value in terms of heritage and look more globally at the neighbourhood, we are confronted with a district profoundly transformed by the forces of capitalism and urban redevelopment, embodied by the owners of those lots and the corporate promoters who bought, consolidated, and eventually transformed them into towering skyscrapers. As David Hanna explained regarding the first residents and promoters of the Square Mile, during the postwar period the owners of these lots of the lower part of the neighbourhood "were not insensitive to the money-making opportunities of real estate dealings in a rapidly expanding local economy."[62]

The very notion of a "death" of the Square Mile is problematic. Of course, it was no longer the Victorian *bourgeois utopia* described by authors such as Margaret Westley, but it never lost its residential aspect entirely, even though it became much more diverse and a lot denser. In the 1950s and 1960s, the Square Mile saw the construction of upscale apartment buildings. And their promoters certainly used the district's prestigious past as a marketing tool, adding "Golden" to the name of the district, a practice that still continues today.[63] So, in a way, the Square Mile did not die. It simply changed, as most urban districts do. And, even if we accept the idea of a demise of the Square Mile as it existed before the Second World War, we are forced to recognize that it died with the willing collaboration of many who lived there or were owners of lots in the district. Most of these individual actors generated significant profits in the process.

In his book *All That Is Solid Melts Into Air*, Marshall Berman explains: "The pathos of all bourgeois monuments is that their material strength and solidity actually count for nothing and carry no weight at all, that they are blown away like frail reeds by the very forces of capitalist development that they celebrate. Even the most beautiful and impressive bourgeois buildings and public works are disposable, capitalized for fast depreciation and planned to be obsolete, closer in their social functions to tents and encampments than to 'Egyptian pyramids, Roman aqueducts, Gothic cathedrals.'"[64] We can see this process at work in all North American cities during the twentieth century and the inhabitants of the Square Mile did not obstruct what they perceived as the forces of progress.

The Square Mile is not Victoriatown. Whereas this small working-class enclave disappeared entirely from Montreal's landscape and memory, the Square Mile survives through the mansions that are still standing north of Sherbrooke Street and through what I would call the romance of the Square Mile: the powerful imagery of the neighbourhood as the urban ghost of a more elegant – and Anglo-Protestant – past. It is a romance that is used (and abused) by the real estate industry as a way to sell condos and apartments. It also lives on in the way that the neighbourhood is often presented in popular history – notably through the beautiful photographs of the Wm. Notman & Son's collection.

The Square Mile houses were the victims of urban changes (rising land value, unsustainable housing, etc.) common to most cities on the continent. It is the way those changes occurred that is significant. In other, poorer, parts of the city, inhabitants were powerless in the face of often vast and ambitious plans of urban redevelopment, led by the municipal or provincial government, or both. Populations were displaced, communities shattered. In the Square Mile, although a certain way of life undeniably came to an end as the result of the district's transformations, a closer examination of the process suggests a much smoother and gradual transition. The owners of these buildings and properties played an active role in the district's transformation. They moved out of the district, leasing or selling their properties, including the last individual owners of the Van Horne Mansion. These actors were not interested in the heritage value of their houses, but in the economic value of their properties. In other words, the transition involved relatively empowered individual actors, belonging to the upper-middle class, who managed to profit from the arrival of corporations and holdings interested in transforming this former residential sector into a part of Montreal's central business district. Thus, in many ways, the Square Mile died as it was born, through the lucrative activities of landowners, developers, and promoters.

NOTES

The research project on which this chapter is based began years ago as a postdoctoral scholarship funded by the Fonds de recherche du Québec – Société et culture (FRQSC). Between then and now, I have been fortunate to count on the support of many. I would like to thank Alexandre Patenaude, who helped me assemble and organize the data on real estate transactions in the Square Mile; the Laboratoire d'histoire et de patrimoine de Montréal (LHPM); and in particular Kim Petit and Laura Baretto, who played a central role in helping me map and visualize the data. I would also like to thank the organizers of the very worthwhile "Crossing Boundaries & Constructing Linkages" conference, in particular Don Nerbas and Elizabeth Kirkland, who invited me to give the closing address with my thoughts on the decline of the Square Mile. I would finally like to thank Amélie Bourbeau, who agreed to read and comment on a preliminary version of this text.

1 In the case of Montreal, see, for example, Richard Morin, "Déclin, réaménagement et réanimation d'un quartier ancien de Montréal," *Urban History Review / Revue d'histoire urbaine* 17, no. 1 (1988): 29–39; Catherine Charlebois and Paul-André Linteau, *Quartiers disparus. Red Light, Faubourg à M'lasse, Goose Village* (Montreal: Éditions Cardinal, 2014); Steven High, "Little Burgundy: The Interwoven Histories of Race, Residence, and Work in Twentieth-Century Montreal," *Urban History Review / Revue d'histoire urbaine* 46, no. 1 (2017): 23–44.

2 Nicholas Lombardo's study of Jarvis Street in Toronto is a rare yet very interesting analysis of a similar case for an earlier period. Nicholas Lombardo, "White-Collar Workers and Neighbourhood Change: Jarvis Street in Toronto, 1880–1920," *Urban History Review / Revue d'histoire urbaine* 43, no. 1 (2014): 5–19.

3 For example, Martin Drouin uses the destruction of the Van Horne Mansion as the starting point of his study of the creation and evolution of the heritage movement in Montreal. Martin Drouin, *Le combat du patrimoine à Montréal (1973–2003)* (Montreal: Presses de l'Université du Québec, 2005), 33–58.

4 For simplicity's sake, I will refer to it as the "Square Mile" throughout the chapter. The best historical study of the creation of the Square Mile is Roderick McLeod, "Salubrious Settings and Fortunate Families: The Making of Montreal's Golden Square Mile, 1840–1895" (PhD diss., McGill University, 1997).

5 Stephen Leacock, *Arcadian Adventures with the Idle Rich* (1914; repr., Toronto: McClelland & Stewart, 1989), 7–8. For a deeper analysis of Leacock's views on Montreal, see Jean-Claude Robert, "Les identités montréalaises d'Ignace Bourget et Stephen Leacock (1865–1920)," in *Vivre en ville: Bruxelles et Montréal aux XIXe et XXe siècles*, ed. Serge Jaumain and Paul-André Linteau (Brusells: P.I.E. Peter Lang, 2006), 307–24.

6 François Rémillard and Brian Merrett, *Demeures bourgeoises de Montréal: Le Mille Carré Doré, 1850–1930* (Montreal: Éditions du Méridien, 1986), 47–9.

7 Rémillard and Merrett, *Demeures bourgeoises de Montréal*, 47–9.

8 Donald MacKay, *The Square Mile: Merchant Princes of Montreal* (Vancouver: Douglas & McIntyre, 1987), 8–9.

9 MacKay, *Square Mile*, 212.

10 Margaret W. Westley, *Remembrance of Grandeur: The Anglo-Protestant Elite of Montreal, 1900–1950* (Montreal: Libre Expression, 1990).

11 "The vast majority of these men [casualties from the 13th Battalion of the Royal Highlanders of Canada] were Montrealers from the Anglo-Protestant community. If we consider that most of the officers came from the 2,000 families of the upper class, we begin to understand why many feel that the decline of that group began with the loss of the best and bravest of a generation." Westley, *Remembrance of Grandeur*, 126.

12 Westley, *Remembrance of Grandeur*, 286.

13 Westley, *Remembrance of Grandeur*, 219.

14 An idea elegantly summed up as the "entre-soi bourgeois" by French sociologists Michel Pinçon and Monique Pinçon-Charlot, *Sociologie de la bourgeoisie* (Paris: La Découverte, 2003).

15 This vast decentralization process also affected the industrial sector and the working class, as demonstrated in Robert Lewis, *Manufacturing Montreal: The Making of an Industrial Landscape, 1850 to 1930* (Baltimore: Johns Hopkins University Press, 2000).

16 Robert, Rumilly, *Histoire de Montréal IV* (Montreal: Fides, 1974), 76–9; Jean-Claude Marsan, *Montréal en évolution* (Montreal: Fides, 1974), 324–5; Isabelle Gournay, "Manifestations du

gigantisme au centre-ville," in *Montréal métropole, 1880–1930*, ed. Isabelle Gournay and France Vanlaethem (Montreal: Boréal/CCA, 1998), 178; Isabelle Huppé, "Les premiers immeubles d'appartements de Montréal, 1880–1914: Un nouveau type d'habitation," *Urban History Review / Revue d'histoire urbaine* 39, no. 2 (2011): 40–55.

17 Mary Corbin Sies, "Paradise Retained: An Analysis of Persistence in Planned, Exclusive Suburbs, 1880–1980," *Planning Perspectives* 12, no. 2 (1997): 169.

18 Harold Bérubé, *Des sociétés distinctes: Gouverner les banlieues bourgeoises de Montréal, 1880–1939* (Montreal: McGill-Queen's University Press, 2014).

19 Ellen James, "Ostell, John," in *Dictionary of Canadian Biography*, vol. 12, University of Toronto/Université Laval, 2003–, accessed 7 July 2020, http://www.biographi.ca/en/bio/ostell_john_12E.html.

20 Arthur F. Bell, *The Charter of the City of Westmount* (Westmount: [City of Westmount], 1927), 1; Aline Gubbay, *A View of Their Own: The Story of Westmount* (Montreal: Price-Patterson, 1998), 37–9.

21 Bérubé, *Des sociétés distinctes*, 116–25. As Raphaël Fischler clearly showed, when it finally sprang into action on the zoning front, the City of Montreal used Westmount as its main source of inspiration. Raphaël Fischler, "Émergence du zonage à Montréal, 1840–1914," in *370 ans de gouvernance montréalaise*, ed. Harold Bérubé, Donald Fyson, and Léon Robichaud (Montreal: Éditions MultiMondes, 2014), 71–84.

22 City of Westmount Archives, *By-law concerning an architectural commission*, by-law 318 adopted 16 May 1916.

23 Michèle Dagenais, *Des pouvoirs et des hommes: L'administration municipale de Montréal, 1900–1950* (Montreal: McGill-Queen's University Press, 2000).

24 Archives of the City of Montreal, *No. 1132 By-law concerning the erection and occupancy of buildings on the north side of Sherbrooke street, between Durocher street and the City of Westmount, and on the south side of said Sherbrooke street, between City Councillors street and the City of Westmount, also the erection of buildings on said Sherbrooke street, between St- Denis street and the City of Westmount, amending By-law No. I 002 and repealing By-laws Nos. 446, 488, 601, 650, 715, 956 and 1047*, by-law 1132 adopted 24 July 1931.

25 Drouin, *Le combat du patrimoine à Montréal*, 33–58.

26 See, for example, the article in *La Presse* on the demolition of the Reford Mansion, entitled "Montréal veut démolir une autre belle maison bourgeoise." *La Presse*, 1 June 1989, A3.

27 On these transformations in the United States, see Robert M. Fogelson, *Downtown: Its Rise and Fall, 1880–1950* (New Haven, CT: Yale University Press, 2003).

28 Gournay, "Manifestations du gigantisme au centre-ville," 171–2.

29 Don Nerbas, "William Zeckendorf, Place Ville-Marie, and the Making of Modern Montreal," *Urban History Review / Revue d'histoire urbaine* 43, no. 2 (2015): 5–25. See also Paul-André Linteau, Sarah Marchand, and Jacques-André Chartrand, *Place Ville-Marie* (Montreal: Québec /Amérique, 2012).

30 Joanne A. Léveillée and Romain Paquette, "Une ville-région d'Amérique originale," *Bulletin de recherche* (Université de Sherbrooke, Département de géographie et de télédétection), no. 128 (1996): 17.

31 John Irwin Cooper, *Montreal: A Brief History* (Montreal: McGill-Queen's University Press, 1969), 185.

32 MacLeod, "Salubrious Settings," 79–119.

33 Robert Fishman, *Bourgeois Utopias: The Rise and Fall of Suburbia* (New York: Basic Books, 1987).

34 Gerald Tulchinsky, "Redpath, John," in *Dictionary of Canadian Biography*, vol. 9, University of Toronto/Université Laval, 2003–, accessed 13 July 2020, http://www.biographi.ca/en/bio/redpath_john_9E.html.

35 David Hanna, "Creation of an Early Victorian Suburb in Montreal," *Urban History Review / Revue d'histoire urbaine* 9, no. 2 (1980): 38–64.

36 Hanna, "Creation," 48.

37 City of Montreal Archives, Vues aériennes de l'île de Montréal, 1947–1949 (taken by the Canadian Pacific Air Lines Ltd, Aerial Survey Division), accessed 7 July 2020, http://donnees.ville.montreal.qc.ca/dataset/vues-aeriennes-archives.

38 City of Montreal Archives, Vues aériennes de l'île de Montréal, 1960–1992, accessed 7 July 2020, http://donnees.ville.montreal.qc.ca/dataset/vues-aeriennes-obliques-de-l-ile-de-montreal-1960-1992.

39 Howard P. Chudacoff and Judith E. Smith, *The Evolution of American Urban Society* (Upper Saddle River NJ: Prentice Hall, 2000), 273.

40 Hanna, "Creation," 48.

41 City of Montreal Archives, Série 02 – Rôle d'évaluation foncière, sous-séries 97–120, accessed 7 July 2020, https://archivesdemontreal.ica-atom.org/roles-devaluation-fonciere-1847–2003; Bibliothèque et Archives nationales du Québec, Liste des plans d'assurance incendie de Montréal, accessed 7 July 2020, https://www.banq.qc.ca/collections/cartes_plans/ressources_BAnQ/doc_cartographiques/doc_assurance/; Registre foncier du Québec en ligne, accessed 7 July 2020, https://www.registrefoncier.gouv.qc.ca/Sirf/.

42 That interactive map and the database can be consulted online on the SCHEMA platform. Laboratoire d'histoire et de patrimoine de Montréal, SCHEMA, Maps of the Square Mile, accessed 7 July 2020, https://schema.uqam.ca/application/run/2777.

43 City of Montreal Archives, Plan des propriétés de la Ville de Montréal, 1920–2000, accessed 7 July 2020, http://donnees.ville.montreal.qc.ca/dataset/registres-de-plans-des-proprietes-de-la-ville-de-montreal-1900-2000.

44 On the role of GIS in history, see the introduction and conclusion of Ian N. Gregory and Alistair Geddes, eds., *Toward Spatial Humanities: Historical GIS and Spatial History* (Bloomington: Indiana University Press, 2014).

45 Chas. E. Goad Co., *Insurance Plan of City of Montreal, Quebec, Canada, Volume II* (Montreal: Chas. E. Goad Co., 1915), 63.

46 Underwriters' Survey Bureau, *Insurance Plan of the City of Montreal, Volume II* (Toronto: The Bureau, 1940), 63.

47 Registre foncier du Québec, Deeds of sale regarding lots 1308–1 and 1308–2 (from the Bureau de la division d'enregistrement de Montréal).

48 Dale Gilbert, "Penser la mobilité, penser Montréal: La planification du tracé du réseau initial de métro, 1960–1966," *Revue d'histoire de l'Amérique française* 68, nos. 1–2 (2014): 68–9.

49 Registre foncier du Québec, Deeds of sale regarding lot 1325 (from the Bureau de la division d'enregistrement de Montréal).

50 Registre foncier du Québec, Deeds of sale regarding lots 1318–1319 (from the Bureau de la division d'enregistrement de Montréal).

51 On its involvement in Toronto, see Daniel Ross, "Remaking Downtown Toronto: Politics, Development, and Public Space in Yonge Street, 1950–1980" (PhD diss., York University, 2017), 202–96.

52 This deal was presented in *La Presse*, 26 June 1965, 3, 6. The project itself was the object of an elaborate series of articles in *La Presse*, 30 June 1965, 21.

53 *La Presse*, 30 June 1965, 21.

54 *La Presse*, 23 February 1968, 6.
55 The development and failure of this project is covered in detail in Ross, "Remaking Downtown Toronto."
56 *La Presse*, 23 February 1968, 6.
57 Claire Adamson, "Sherbrooke St. Houses Threatened Again," *S.O.S. Montréal* 3, no. 6 (1979): 6.
58 *Le Devoir*, 25 November 1980, 12.
59 Mélanie Belfour and Audrey Reifenstein, *Whatever Happened to McGill College Avenue?* (Montreal: Héritage Montréal, 1983).
60 Drouin, *Le combat du patrimoine à Montréal (1973–2003)* (Montreal: Presses de l'Université du Québec, 2005), 240–54.
61 Registre foncier du Québec, Deed of Emphyteutic Lease No. 4368 regarding lot 1316 (from the Bureau de la division d'enregistrement de Montréal).
62 Hanna, "Creation," 48.
63 As I was writing this chapter, in the summer of 2020, I was approached by a promoter who asked me to help him prepare a lavish coffee-table book celebrating that "golden" past and that could be given to those who bought units in his planned project!
64 Marshall Berman, *All That Is Solid Melts Into Air: The Experience of Modernity* (1982; repr., New York: Penguin Books, 1988), 99.

Figure V.18 Anonymous, *A.F. Gault House "Rokeby" before Demolition, Sherbrooke Street, Montreal,* 1924. McCord Museum, MP-0000.2081.102.

The 1920s: Beginning of the End

The ordered, cossetted world of the Square Mile was deeply affected by the First World War. Many households lost sons and heirs. By the 1920s, although there was still construction, the age of building the great mansions was over. After the war, wider employment opportunities put a strain on the retention and recruitment of domestic servants. Some of the households required a staff of thirty or so to function and they became difficult to maintain. Better transportation systems connected the suburbs of Westmount and Outremont to Montreal, making them more attractive to the new generation of Square Milers. As attitudes to overt ostentation changed, developers began to assemble properties to build "signature" apartment buildings, which could provide modern amenities to a wealthy, sophisticated clientele.

The idea of such a style of living was not foreign to the Square Mile. One of the first to be built was the Sherbrooke Residential Chambers, constructed about 1888 on the south side of Sherbrooke Street between Crescent and Bishop Streets, when the Montreal Lacrosse Grounds was subdivided into building lots. The Linton Apartments followed in 1904, built on the front lawn of "Mount View," the James Linton house. The New Sherbrooke Apartments was built in 1907, to the west of its namesake.

The early acceptance of the typology was noted as being unique to Montreal. An article in the *American Architect and Building News* in 1907 explained: "Montreal is the only Canadian city in which apartment houses are at all common. The great prevalence of French blood in its inhabitants, as well as the size and compactness of the city easily account for this."[1] The curious reference to the ethnic make-up of

Figure V.19 Anonymous, *Demolition of Gault and Stephens Houses, Sherbrooke Street, Montreal,* 1924. McCord Museum, MP-0000.2081.99.

Figure V.20 Associated Screen News Ltd., *The Chateau Apartments, Sherbrooke Street, Montreal, 1925–1926*. McCord Museum, MP-0000.2081.5.

Figure V.21 *Sherbrooke Street, Looking East from Du Musée, Montreal*, c. 1946. McCord Museum, MP-1987.15.5001.

the city no doubt was meant to indicate that Montrealers would be familiar with the Parisian model.

The construction of the Chateau Apartments in 1926 is illustrative of the changing landscape within the Square Mile. At the time that the Honourable Pamphile Du Tremblay (1879–1955) began the land assembly for his project, there were two substantial houses in place: the neo-Gothic residence of George Washington Stephens (c. 1870) and the neo-Gothic residence known as "Rokeby," which had been built for A.F. Gault in 1875 and designed by the celebrated local architect, John James Browne (Figure V.18).

Figure V.19 shows these two mansions under demolition in 1924. Two years later, the Chateau Apartments was ready for its first tenants (Figure V.20). The building was designed by the most prominent architectural firm in Canada during the interwar years, Ross and Macdonald. While the chateau style that they chose was associative to the castles of the French Renaissance, the construction technology was thoroughly modern – a steel frame clad in Tyndall limestone. The use of the highly fossilized Tyndall, imported from Manitoba, no doubt reflected its popularity after being used in the newly rebuilt Centre Block on Parliament Hill.

The demolitions that began in the 1920s accelerated after the Second World War, until the uniformity of the Square Mile was irreparably altered. The institutions that nurtured the residents were relocated or disappeared. Today, isolated mansions, largely still the property of McGill University, are dwarfed by high-rise apartment towers. There is still much to be admired, but it will require a concerted effort by both the Montreal community and the various governments to act if the Square Mile is to be saved for future generations.

NOTE

1 *American Architect and Building News* 91, no. 1619 (5 January 1907): 17–18.

Afterword

Brian Young

Montreal's Square Mile serves as an ideal case study in the meaning of Victorian civilization, in the construction of a late nineteenth-century Canadian identity, and in the complex intersections of race and gender within an elite Anglo-Protestant community. Readers will have been impressed by the jump start this collection gives to provocative interpretations, to research methodologies, and to the innovative use of archival sources. Authors neatly capture the Square Mile's contradictions: it remains somehow idyllic in nature, somehow vibrant as a community, and somehow marketable as landed property. Square Mile dreamers embraced Mount Royal for estates, parks, university, museums, and burial spaces; pragmatists, albeit often the same dreamers, envisaged it as real estate, asylum site, or simple physical obstacle for the transiting of automobile traffic. Max Hamon reminds us of the Square Mile's persistent place as a pan-Canadian cultural and social force. He moves the "overlap between intimacy and governance" and the persistence over time of "conservative family compacts" into the West, pushing back into the period of the Hudson's Bay Company's dominance and forward into the nineteenth-century industrial economy. Peter Gossage and Lisa Moore show how Annie Stevenson Anderson's pursuit of her husband, textile manufacturer David Morrice, for judicial separation of property became a case study in Quebec civil law of married women's rights. As a knowledgeable and privileged Square Miler, was she using the legal device of assignment to protect her property rights or was she in collusion with her husband to protect his wealth from creditors? For their part, Annmarie Adams and Julia Gersovitz pin the built Square Mile and its colonial and conservative architectural tradition squarely on specific architectural schools in Edinburgh and Glasgow.

This imperial connectivity spread broadly across economic and social roots. Jean-Philip Mathieu shows how the humble industrial nail, its use in Canadian building, and the development of new corporate rights around limited liability, brought the Scot Thomas Morland ownership of the Montreal Rolling Mills and residence on Bellevue Terrace.

As a cultural force, the Square Mile peaked with Queen Victoria. Several authors point to the early twentieth century as the onset of decline in the authority of Montreal's Anglo-Protestant elite; Stephen Salmon, for example, links it to the bleeding out of a Square Mile male generation on French and Belgian battlefields of the First World War. This diminishing, Nicolas Kenny suggests, was not just the physicality of steel or the Passchendaele agony of Andrew Hamilton Gault's Princess Patricia's Canadian Light Infantry. It was rather a complex matter of emotions and of "intimate relations across empire" in which "ideas of home" changed from actual place to "an affective experience." This broad hollowing out of what Sherry Olson calls the Square Mile's "human ecosystem" took multiple forms, including the environmental violence of modern technology. Harold Bérubé, for example, points to the ravage of neighbourhood by the automobile as two east-west thoroughfares, McGregor Street (now Avenue du Docteur-Penfield) in the 1950s and, a decade later, Boulevard de Maisonneuve ruptured Mount Royal's landscape and its natural north-south flow.

With its recurring themes of decadence, intolerance, racism, and violence, this work draws a sharp historiographical line in the sand from vestiges of City Beautiful or "feel good" business histories. Elizabeth Kirkland and Mary Anne Poutanen utilize a Redpath estate on Sherbrooke Street to construct a chilling narrative of murder and suicide in the foyer of a principal Square Mile family. Caught in this drama, Amy Redpath, the granddaughter of sugar baron John Redpath, used her third-generation wealth to contain media treatment of "private intimacies." In contrast to the shop floor relations of her grandfather's mill, Kirkland and Poutanen posit her domestic relations – financial, sexual, authoritarian – with two servants. The same Amy Redpath commandeered strategic university space, McGill's principal entrance on Sherbrooke Street, to mould public attitudes to education, time, and death through the Roddick Memorial Gates and Clock Tower. Canny, she would have understood Geoff Eley's wise remark that remembering is also about forgetting!

In a bold approach to understanding gender and the instrumentalization of landed property, Robert Sweeny takes a broad brush demonstrating the agency of "Landed Ladies" in what he calls "the wealthiest neighbourhood in the British Empire." His contribution, with that of Sherry Olson, serves as an introduction to the interdisciplinary research collective, "Montréal, l'avenir du passé." Twinning its formidable data base of land values and ownership with census returns, evaluation rolls, and leases, Sweeny shows that women owned one-third of landed property in the Square Mile. These Anglo-Protestant women used this ownership, he argues, in a more "polarized" fashion than their Irish-Catholic or French-Catholic peers in other parts of Montreal.

As a literary genre, writing an "afterword" is challenging. Reading these contributions lifted my mind's eye to the essence of the Square Mile, then and now, and to a flood of lived moments with many of the authors as colleagues, and former students, and as desk-mates in a dozen shared archives. Perhaps exaggerating – or perhaps not – Roderick MacLeod depicts the Square Mile as "a place of romance"; Harold Bérubé describes it as an "invented space." This symbolism and fluidity between history and memory is suggestive of how the Square Mile has been an encompassing membrane of my being in Montreal: a principal source for historical research and, simultaneously, the physical space of a *vécu*, what Robert Sweeny calls the "actually lived." My Square Mile prompts keywords like commutation and codification, elite family and contract, landscape artists and meteorological readings, Protestant university and Protestant burial, and the Notman photograph and staged croquet lawns. Square Mile institutions of university, church, orphanage, seminary, museum, stadium, park, bank, department store, and cemetery, have been critical markers in *my* reconstruction of the historical past and, concurrently, of my everyday work, consumption, and leisure. Historian and human merged!

I arrived at McGill University in 1976 and was introduced to its campus life that was located in the Square Mile's physical and cultural core. Over the next three decades, my office bounced through stages of the Square Mile's built environment: from the 1960s ten-storey concrete Stephen Leacock Social Sciences Building, to the terrace housing office space on McTavish Street; then up the Peel Street hill to the James Ross Mansion, converted institutionally into the law faculty's Chancellor Day Hall; and, finally, a sunset office in the Ferrier Building, originally the university's Percy Nobbs-designed power plant. For two years in the 1980s, I lived in the McGill Ghetto's greystone garrets: first on Aylmer Street and then on Lorne Avenue. Then, and for decades, my commuter walk took me along Square Mile sidewalks, west along Sherbrooke Street, past the Acadia Apartments facing the Ritz Carlton, the Montreal Museum of Fine Arts and, on the corner of Redpath Street, the Church of St. Andrew and St. Paul.

The Square Mile emerged only gradually onto my research radar. As a graduate student, I helped Gerald Tulchinsky research his biography of Mount Royal industrialist and real-estate developer John Redpath and then put my name to fellow

Square Milers John Young and Hugh Allan in the *Dictionary of Canadian Biography*. These works were in a business history biographical tradition, male entrepreneurial moments around markets and finance, sugar and ships, and factories and canals. Studying the Seminary of Montreal "as a business institution" in the 1980s, I spent summers doing archival research in its Grand Séminaire on Sherbrooke Street. Despite climbing the central stairs past its burial crypt, chapel, and classical and theological colleges, and past the tower of their "Indian" fort, their French garden, and Mount Royal views that were visible outside, I ignored this broad social and cultural history, concentrating on the priests' pockets, their notaries, and their management of peasant debt.

But already, innovative ways of analyzing hegemony in Montreal were pushing me up Mount Royal to new (at least for me) historical perspectives around family, gender, culture, and law. Alfred Chandler, Maurice Dobb, and Jean Bouvier ceded to reading Raymond Williams, Edward Thompson, Catherine Hall, and Robert Morris. As our research collective, the Montreal Business History Project morphed into the Montreal History Group, our notarial-archives research, around work and market phenomena like apprenticeship, gave way to judicial archives and *problématiques* on family relations, social institutions, and civil rights. This was a period when theses on English Montreal came in waves. David Hanna, Rhona Richman Kenneally, Mary Anne Poutanen, Peter Gossage, Donald Fyson, Cynthia Fish, Janice Harvey, Kathleen Lord, Roderick MacLeod, Kathryn Harvey, Jarrett Rudy, Elizabeth Kirkland, and others poked at its built environment, motherhood, diet, family violence, orphans, and female agency. The 1990s brought extended research in the rich McCord Museum archives, participation on the McCord's board of directors, and then the invitation to write a history of Protestant burials on Mount Royal. Community giants like the McConnells, Molsons, Prices, and Hagues peered out from nineteenth-century Notman photographs and Mount Royal Cemetery grave tablets and then, in real life, faced me in museum board meetings. Enveloped, my work honed tighter on comparative life narratives in the principal dynasties, on the Square Mile's material culture, and on the generational transmission of wealth and authority.

Rounding into the new century, the Montreal History Group, myself in tow, moved fully into a broad camp of studying the social and cultural muscles of wealth – Bourdieu's "social capital" – that is the exercise of differing forms of authority through phenomena that included smoking, promotion of the English peony, and seemingly benign institutions like the hunt club or school board. Alongside outsized manifestations of Anglo-Protestant capitalism like the Sun Life Building and, across the square, the Canadian Pacific Railway's Windsor Station, more subtle forms of

Victorian hegemony took significance: collecting Canadiana for a private museum of Canadian history, sponsoring and directing the brush of a landscape artist, or the building of a crematorium on Mount Royal as a wedge of Protestant burial science. Intimate sources like wills, commonplace books, and diaries assumed new meaning. In the 1820s, for example, fundamental legal principles around property rights in Quebec society were fought out when the family of James McGill contested his bequest to establish a university on his estate grounds. Or, the full meaning of class and gentility on the slopes of Mount Royal became clearer reading a diary entry, 8 July 1852, in which Anne Ross McCord and Marie-Angélique Desrivières, her friend for tea, watched immobilized from the gazebo of Temple Grove, as Montreal, east and below, burned in the "Great Fire." The Protestant Orphan Asylum, Christ Church Cathedral, the Crystal Palace, the Natural History Society, the McCord and Redpath museums, the Art Institute, and of course, McGill University, served to situate the Square Mile near the quick of what Catherine Hall would call the "logics" and "common sense" of Canadian life.

At the end, this collection stands out by its hammering at myths around a simplified "romance" of the Square Mile or the "good" Christian male philanthropy of a John Redpath. In its larger bite, it warns historians of the intellectual pitfalls of an unconsciously shared ethnic and colonial pride, of the blindness that may come from the overly simple osmosis of place, culture, and familiar memory, and of potential intellectual contamination emanating from tenure comfort in a university built on Square Mile wealth. It is Sherry Olson who speaks loudest here. Trapping the Square Mile's weight, its cultural insouciance, and its history, she damns its contradictions, its "bright side in go-ahead and ingenuity and [its] dark side in the ruthlessness of the growth machine." Written, one speculates, in pain from the experiences of the COVID-19 pandemic and the Trump presidency, and inserting the Square Mile into its larger historicity, she rages against "a unique concentration of corruption" that has spread across water, capital, body politics, and the "human soul."

Contributors

Annmarie Adams is an architectural historian specializing in the intersections of medicine, gender, and the built environment. She holds the Stevenson Chair in the Philosophy and History of Science at McGill University. Adams is jointly appointed in the School of Architecture and Department of Social Studies of Medicine (SSoM).

Dimitry Anastakis is the L.R. Wilson/R.J. Currie Chair in Canadian Business History at the University of Toronto. His work examines the intersection of business and politics in twentieth-century Canada, with a special focus on the automobile industry and its impact, and on the emergence of Canadian neoliberalism.

Harold Bérubé is full professor at the Université de Sherbrooke. His research interests focus on the political and cultural history of North American cities and their inhabitants, and he is co-editor of the *Urban History Review*. His current research project is on the role of the press in the urban ecosystem.

Julia Gersovitz, OC, is founding partner of EVOQ Architecture and fellow of the Royal Architectural Institute of Canada. She has received numerous awards for her architectural work, including being appointed as an Officer of the Order of Canada in 2018. Gersovitz is a Professor of Practice, School of Architecture, McGill University, and a professeure associée, Université de Montréal.

Peter Gossage is a professor of history at Concordia University. He is co-author with J.I. Little of *An Illustrated History of Quebec: Tradition and Modernity* (Oxford

University Press, 2012) and co-editor with Robert Rutherdale of *Making Men, Making History: Canadian Masculinities across Time and Place* (UBC Press, 2018).

Max Hamon is an assistant professor at the University of Northern British Columbia. He teaches and researches the history of Canada and colonial North America during the nineteenth century. His first book, *The Audacity of His Enterprise: Louis Riel and the Métis Nation That Canada Never Was (1840–1875)* (McGill-Queen's University Press, 2020), won multiple national awards. His current research concerns the history of the relationships between Indigenous nations and the Canadian state through the lens of policing.

Nicolas Kenny is a member of the History Department at Simon Fraser University. His research examines sensorial and emotional experiences of city life, particularly in Montreal and Brussels, and their role in the construction of urban dwellers' relationships to the urban landscape in the nineteenth and twentieth centuries.

Elizabeth Kirkland is a faculty member in the Department of History and Classics at Dawson College. Her current research explores the tragedy of young deaths in Montreal at the turn of the twentieth century and the experiences of young women and girls who migrated to Montreal to work as domestic workers from 1820 to 1920.

Roderick MacLeod has written extensively on Montreal's Anglo-Protestant community and its social, cultural, educational, and religious institutions. He is completing a study of the mountain as a "very conspicuous object" (to quote Newton Bosworth) of cultural hegemony, entitled "High Ground: Mount Royal and the Rise of Anglo-Protestant Montreal, 1816–1884."

Gregory P. Marchildon, OC, is a professor and research chair at the University of Toronto. He has written articles, book chapters, and books on twentieth-century Canadian history and contemporary public policy. He is a member of the Order of Canada and a fellow of the Canadian Academy of Health Sciences.

Jean-Philip Mathieu is a PhD candidate in the Department of History at McGill University. His research focuses on the corporation, class formation, industrialization, and the City of Montreal.

Lisa Moore is a PhD candidate in the Department of History at Concordia University. Her dissertation explores gender and juvenile justice in postwar

Quebec. She has worked as a research assistant for the SSHRC-funded project Familles, droit et justice au Québec, 1840–1920, and as a researcher for the Montreal Museum of Fine Arts.

Don Nerbas is an associate professor and St. Andrew's Society/McEuen Scholarship Foundation Chair in Canadian-Scottish Studies in the Department of History and Classical Studies at McGill University. He is the author of *Dominion of Capital: The Politics of Big Business and Crisis of the Canadian Bourgeoisie, 1914–1947* (University of Toronto Press, 2013).

Sherry Olson is a geographer at McGill University, a member of the Centre interuniversitaire d'Études québécoises, co-author with Patricia Thornton of *Peopling the North American City: Montreal, 1840–1900* (McGill-Queen's University Press, 2011), author of *Baltimore: The Building of an American City* (Johns Hopkins University Press, 1997), and contributor to the digital humanities projects EspaceCIEQ and MAP – Montréal l'avenir du passé.

Mary Anne Poutanen teaches interdisciplinary studies at McGill University and history at Concordia University. She is a member of the Montreal History Group and the Centre for Interdisciplinary Research on Montreal. The author of the award-winning book *Beyond Brutal Passions: Prostitution in Early Nineteenth-Century Montreal* (McGill-Queen's University Press, 2015), her current research focuses on hospitality in mid-nineteenth-century Montreal.

M. Stephen Salmon was Library and Archives Canada's business archivist from 1989 to 2012. His current research focuses on the business history of twentieth-century Canadian Great Lakes shipping. He is a founding director of the Canadian Business History Association.

Robert C.H. Sweeny lives in Montreal with Elizabeth-Anne Malischewski. He is a co-director of the historical GIS project Montréal l'avenir du passé (mun.ca/mapm), emeritus professor of history at Memorial University of Newfoundland, and professeur associé at UQAM. His book *Why Did We Choose to Industrialize?* (McGill-Queen's University Press, 2015) won the Governor General's History Award for Scholarly Research and was shortlisted for the François-Xavier Garneau Medal. He is currently working on a companion volume, *Gender, Property and National Identity.*

Brian Young is an emeritus professor in McGill's History Department and a member of the Montreal History Group. His publications involving anglophone elites include *Respectable Burial: Montreal's Mount Royal Cemetery* (McGill-Queen's University Press, 2013) and *Patrician Families and the Making of Quebec: The Taschereaus and the McCords* (McGill-Queen's University Press, 2014). He is co-editor of *Law, Life, and the Teaching of Legal History* (McGill-Queen's University Press, 2022), a collection of essays on the life of McGill University law professor Blaine Baker.

Index

Page numbers in *italics* refer to figures and tables.

Abbott, J.J.C., 4
Academy of Music, 44
Acadia apartments, 423
Adams, Annmarie, 6, 10–11, 200, 421
Ahmed, Sarah, 360
Aitken, Janet Gladys (Brodie), 258
Aitken, John William Maxwell (Max), 258
Aitken, Max (Lord Beaverbrook): 6, 10, 253–71; "creative destruction," 132, 253–4; family, 254–5, 258; industrial mergers, 70, 102, 258–9, 262–8; legacy, 269–70. *See also* Canada Cement; Canadian Car and Foundry; Commercial Trust Company; Montreal Engineering Company; Montreal Trust and Deposit Company; Steel Company of Canada (Stelco)
Alberta, 195, 267, 297, 317
Alexandra, Queen-empress, 280
Alexander Street, 29
Alice Graham Hallward House, 299–304
Allan, Andrew, *96*, 97
Allan, Beatrice, 369
Allan, Hugh: 424, *176*, 177–9; Allan family, influence of, 26, 318, 369–70; business interests of, 63–4, 117, 156, 318, 424; Ravenscrag mansion, *144*, 177–9, 217, 222–3; wealth, 62, 94, 98, 101, 177–9. *See also* Allan Shipping Line
Allan, Martha, 369
Allan Shipping Line, 63–4, 97–8, 177
Alymer, Henry, 220
American Architect and Builder's Monthly, 381
American Architect and Building News, 417
American Civil War, 63, 152
Ames, Herbert Brown: 20, 32, 226, 243; sociological survey of Montreal, 13n6, 219–20, 233, 244n2
Amherst, Nova Scotia, 265
Anderson, Annie Stevenson: 9, *152*, 421; Anderson v. Morrice, 147–8, 151, 158, 160–8; financial difficulties, 155–60; marriage, 151–3. *See also* community of property; Morrice, David
Anderson, James, 151
Anglican Church, 200, 227, 355
Anglo-Persian Oil Company, 114
Anglo-Protestant: 29, 44, 48–9, 394, 421, 423; decline, 388, 391, 410, 422; institutions, 407, 424
Angus, R.B., 66, 225
ante-nuptial agreement, 164
apartment buildings, 291, 389, 390, 403, 409, 417

Archer, F.B., *96*, 97
Archibald, Ian T., 287–90
Archibald, John Smith, 283, 287–9, 291, 293
architects, 77–9
architects, Scottish: "buddy system," 9–11, 282, 287, 289–307; education and professional networks, 291–3. *See also* Nobbs, Percy; Traquair, Ramsay; *and names of individual architects*
architecture, estates, 32–8, 40–5, 53, 179, 222, 395,
architecture, mansions: design, 279, 289; landscapes, 44–5, 385–91, 395; mythology and romance, 21–6, 29, 398; on mountains, 19, 32
architecture, schools in Canada, 295–7
architecture, styles: 8, 45, 54; American picturesque, 77; Beaux-Arts, 279, 305; Canadian, 282, 305; chateau, 420; classical, 79, 279, 302; colonial and conservative, 421; fin-de-siècle, 382; Greek revival, 77; Italianate, 54, 179; neo-classical, 179; neo-Gothic, 277, 313, 420; Palladian revival, 77; Richardsonian Romanesque, 79; Scottish arts-and-crafts, 79, 279, 281; Scottish baronial, 299, 304
architecture, terraces and row houses: 25, 66, 85, 145–5, 232, 351, 395, 423; environment, 31, 39, 40–4, 302; Prince of Wales Terrace, 96, 109–10, 116, *144*, 146
Architecture in Transition (Crossman), 305
Argentina, 332
Art Association of Montreal: 44, 60, 195, 227, *350*; board members and patrons of, 154, 165–6, 351
Article 1311, Civil Code of Lower Canada, 147, 163. *See also* Lower Canada Civil Code of 1866
atelier Maxwell, *285–6*, 291
atelier Pascal, 291
Athabasca district, 123
Atlantic Monthly, 294
Atwater, Albert William, 160, 162, 164, 167
Atwater Avenue, 222
Austen, Jane, 225
Australia, 291, 304, 332
automobile, 388, 404, 421–2
Aylmer Street, 152, 222, 423
Azrieli, David, 223, 391. *See also* Van Horne Mansion

Bagg, Abner, 58
Bagg, Stanley, 58
Bahamas, 63, 322
Ballantyne, Tony, 354, 361, 374
Banff, Alberta, 63
Bank of British North America, 62
Bank of Montreal: 77, 117, 131, 160, 262–3; design of, 77, 289–90; management of, 255–8, 266–8, 289–90
banks. *See* Bank of British North America; Bank of Montreal; Commercial Bank of Manitoba; Montreal Provident and Savings' Bank
Baptist, 220, 227
Baretto, Laura, 399
Barnett, D.F., 88
Baron Byng High School, 287
Barrio de Salamanca, Madrid, 23
Bauden, Henry, 44
Baumgarten, A., 66, 274n43
Beacon Hill, Boston, 23
Beaudouin, Mary, 228
Beaudouin, Melina, 228
Beaux-Arts Institute of Design (New York), 291
Beaux-Arts (Quebec City), 295
Beaver Hall Hill, 61, 220–3, 227–8, 236
Beckert, Sven, 82
Begg, John, 304
Belgium, 364
Bell, Peter Warren, 129–30
Bellevue Terrace, 226, 422
Berger, Carl, 311n72, 359, 374
Berman, Marshall, 409
Berton, Pierre, 4
Bérubé, Harold, 7, 11, 422–3
Bethune, John, 35
Biographical Dictionary of Architects in Canada, 283
Bird, Kym, 207
Birks, Henry, 225
Bischoff, Peter, 90, 105n38
Bishop's Palace, 226–7

Bishop Street, 417
Bissett, James, 129–30, *130*
Black, Henry, 330, 338
Blackader, Gordon, 370
Black Sea, 332
Bland, John, 279, 281–3, 298, 309n36. *See also* John Bland Canadian Architecture Collection
Bleury Street, 3, 153, 220, 242, 244n10
boarding houses, 228, 232
Bolivia, 270
Boston, 79, 291
Boulevard de Maisonneuve, 422
Bourassa, Henri, 356, 363–6, 370, 374, 377n35
bourgeoisie: 4–6; businesses, 82, 85, 87, 102; decline and transformation, 383, 387–91, 409; practices, 231, 239–40; social expectations, 173–4n63, 200, 209; spaces, 25, 220, 222–6, 229, 242–4, 394–5
Bourget, Ignace, 226
Bourke, Joanna, 368
Bouvier, Jean, 424
Bovey, Henry Taylor, 66, 70, 195
Boyer family, 242
Boyle, Margaret, 220
Bradbury, Bettina, 149
Bradford, England, 357, 373
Brazilian Traction, 270
Breland, Pascal, 124–5
Bremner, G.A., 282, 287
Britain: business environment of, 89–90; linkages to, 145; personal and familial networks, 86–7, 102, 268; war, 354–5, 368
British Army, 58
British Columbia, 197, 337
British Empire: personal and familial networks, 11, 124–5, 268; race and ethnicity, 35, 117; Square Mile linkages, 6, 87, 102, 127, 304
British Empire Steel Corporation, 338, 340
British Guiana, 255
British imperialism, 287, 311n72, 364
British North America, 62, 89, 90–1, 103, 133, 151
British Parliament, 90, 372
British ports, 58
brothels, 48, 387
Brown, Gerard Baldwin, 299, 305
Browne, John James, 77, 79, 153, 171n24, 420. *See also* architects, Scottish
Bryce, David, 299
Brydges, Charles John, 94, 97–8, 101. *See also* Grand Trunk Railway
Bulmer, Henry, 40–1
Burnside Place, 109, 112
Burton, Antoinette, 354, 361, 374
business directories, 8, 58, *61*
business networks, 8
Busy Man's Magazine (*Maclean's*), 265

Cacouna, Quebec, 63
Caesar, Julius, 271
Cahan, Charles, 254, 259, 261, 265–7
Caledonian Club, 293
California, 58, 202
Calvin family, 320–1
Cameron, Ewan, 179
Campbell, John McDermott, 95, 99
Canada: business networks, 90, 130; nationalism, 311n72, 374. *See also* Canadian Confederation; Canadian Dominion
Canada Car Company, 265
Canada Cement, 70, 262–8
Canada Coloured Cotton, 165
Canada Council for the Arts, 269
Canada East, 87
Canada Gazette, 91–2, 97
Canada Life Building, 356
Canada Lead Works, 95
Canada Rolling Stock Company, 114, 117
Canada Steamship Lines (CSL), 11, 315–16, 319–47
Canadian Bankers Association, 255
Canadian Bank of Commerce, 258
Canadian Car and Foundry, 70, 265–6
Canadian Centre for Architecture, 225
Canadian Cereal and Milling, 270
Canadian Club, 356
Canadian Confederation, 55, 91, *115*, 128, 133
Canadian Corps, 315
Canadian Cottons, 165

Canadian Dominion: business, impact on, 98, 316–17, 332; management of, 127, 137n44; territory, 120, 354
Canadian Expeditionary Force, 269, 316, 322
Canadian General Electric, 260
Canadian Great Lakes (company), 317–18, 330
Canadian History Makers, 165
Canadian Interlake Line Ltd., 325
Canadian Mounted Regiment, 195
Canadian Northern Railway, *68*
Canadian North West Steamship Co., 327–8, 330, 333, 335
Canadian Pacific Railway (CPR): infrastructure, 32, 225, 251, 362, 424; key figures, 4, 69–70, 114–17, 131, 154, 255; land, 32, 225, 247n45
Canadian Rubber, 64
Canadian Society for the Prevention of Cruelty to Animals, 165
Canadian Steel Foundries, 270
Canadian Towing and Wrecking Co., 332, 337
Canadian War Records Office, 372
Canadian Westinghouse, 260
Cane, James, 19, 37, *38*
Capper, Stewart Henbest, 297–9, 305
Careless, William, 293
Caribbean, 255, 260, 262, 322
Carleton House (Saskatchewan), 112
Carr, Iona, 369
Carruthers, James, 319, 344n40
Cartier, Jacques, 53
Cathcart Street, 37, 222, 231–2, 238
Catholic Cathedral (Cathedral of St. James), 48–9, 226–7
Catholic organizations: Grey Nuns, 228; Les petites soeurs des pauvres, 228; St. Patrick's Orphan Asylum, 228–9
Catholic parishes: 48–9, 226
Catholics, 46, 49, 277
Cayley, William, 88
Cayley-Galt (1858) tariffs, 88–9. *See also* Galt (1859) tariffs
Cedar Avenue, 223
Central Canada, 255
Central Powers, 316
Central Shipping (Chicago), 332, 345n51
Central Telegraph Company, 114
Centre Block, 420
Chambers, Lori, 164
Chandler, Alfred, 99, 424
Chateau Apartments, 420
Chateau Laurier, 291
Chislehurst, England, 184, 200, *201*, 202–3, *204*
Christ Church Cathedral, *48*, 227, 425
Christie, Nancy, 150
Christophe Colombe, 242
Chudacoff, Howard P., 398
churches: architecture, 48; relocation of, 42–3, 45
churches, Square Mile: American, 227; Christ Church Cathedral, 227; Crescent Street, 227; Dominion Square, 227; Erskine, 227; First, 227; Knox, 227; Olivet, 227; St. Andrew's, 227; St. Gabriel's, 227; St. James Street, 227; St. James the Apostle, 227; St. Paul's, 227; Stanley Street, 227
Churchill, Winston, 253
Church of St. Andrew and St. Paul, 315, 423
Church Street, 151
City Bank, 117
City Councillors Street, 29, 177
City Passenger Railway Company, 87, 117
Clark, Lawrence, 129
class: broad experiences, 6, 24–5, 82, 149, 191, 354–60; comparing experiences, 11, 13n6, 103, 211, 373; middle-class experiences, 19, 41–6, 96, 145, 173n61; upper-class experiences, 7, 398, 425; working-class experiences, 20, 233, 242–3, 287; 384, 391–2, 394, 410. *See also* bourgeoisie; working-class neighbourhoods
Clifton Suspension Bridge Company, 91
Clouston, Edward, 5, 131, 156–8, 255, 261–7
Clouston, James Stewart, 130
Cloverdale and Colpitts, 326
clubs, 4, 7, 43, 82, 153, 386–7, 424. *See also individual named clubs and societies*
Coleman, Maggie Shallow, 208
Collège de Montréal, 222, 227
Collingwood Shipbuilding, 322, 337, 346n64
Colona, Édouard, 383
Colorado, 195
Commercial Bank of Manitoba, 114, 126, 131
Commercial Trust Company, 258

community of property, 148–9, 160–2, 164, 167, 235–6. *See also* Anderson, Annie Stevenson; judicial separation of property; Lower Canada Civil Code of 1866; Morrice, David; séparation de biens; séparation de corps
Confederation of Manitoba, 120
Congregational College, 227
Connolly, William, 13n8, 116–17, 119, 132, 136n32
Conservatives, 164, 167
Construction (magazine), 283
Consulate General of Italy, 258
Convention of Forty, 128
Cook, Tim, 371
Cooper, Jane C., 202
Cooper, John Irwin, 394
Coristine, Charles, 370
Corporation Agencies, 267
Côte à Barron, 220, 244n7
Côte de la Visitation, 220
Côte-des-Neiges, 3, 19, 29, *46*, 152
Côte Saint-Antoine, 67, 72n22, 389. *See also* Westmount (suburb)
"cotton lords," 9, 154
cotton textile industry, 62–3, 155, 167
Couture, Joseph, 158
Coverdale, William, 326, 339
CPR. *See* Canadian Pacific Railway (CPR)
Craig Street Terminal, 287
Creighton, Donald, 3.
Crescent Street, 154, 227
Crescent Street Presbyterian Church, 154, 227
Crimean War, 87
Crockart, James Bisset, 287. *See also* architects, Scottish
Crossman, Kelly, 305
Crystal Palace (London), 357
Crystal Palace (Montreal), 44, 357, 425
CSL Network, 323–39. *See also* Montreal Transportation Company (MTC); Montreal Transportation Company (MTC17)
Cuba, 203, 270, 335
Cummings, Elizabeth, 297–8
Curry, Rhodes, 265
Custom of Paris, 148
D. Morrice & Co., 152
Darling, William, 81, 85, 100–1, 104n10
Davidoff, Leonore, 191
Davis, Mortimer B., 299, 302, *303*
Dawson, John William, 66, 70, 109, 289, 313, 327
Dawson, William Bell, 289
Deed Poll (1821), 129–30, 140n92
Deed Poll (1872), 129
Delorimier Downs Stadium, 293
Demerara Electric Company, 255
department stores, 57, 225, 270, 291, 423
dependency theory, 6
depression, economic, 88–9. *See also* Great Depression
Desrivières, Marie-Angélique, 425
developers: 12, 25, 410; historic, 33, 39–40, 145, 389, 423; modern, 25, 387, 391, 394, 417
Dictionary of Canadian Biography, 54, 272n9, 424
Dictionary of Scottish Architects, 283, 308n19
Diocesan Theological College, 227
Dobb, Maurice, 424
Doble, Arthur, 261–2, 267–9
Doggart, Arthur Robert, 291
domestic servants: 5, 45–8, 191, 229, 238, 243, 417; cooks, 208, 220, 234; geographic distribution of, 153, 242, 229–34, 243; housekeepers, 208, 234; housemaids, 199, 202–4, 207–8, 220, 234; housemen, 208; lady's maids, 234; tablemaids, 220
Dominion Car and Foundry Company, 265. *See also* Aitken, Max (Lord Beaverbrook)
Dominion Coal Co., 322–3
Dominion Cottons, 165. *See also* Gault, Andrew F.
Dominion Iron and Steel Co. (DISCO), 321
Dominion Securities Corporation, 255, 273n33, 274n51
Dominion Square, 40, 42, 48
Dominion Textile Company, 165. *See also* Gault, Andrew F.
Dominion Transport Company, 158
Dominion Wire Manufacturing Company of Montreal, 266
Donaldson Line, 63

Dorchester Street (now Boulevard René-Lévesque): boundaries of, 3, 19, 30, 220, 386; commercial use of, 387, 394; institutional use of, 43, 228, 277, 313; property value of, 222–3, 237; residential use of, 20, *52*, 54, 85, 229
Dougall, John, 66, 72n20
Dougall, Lily, 193, 212n21
Dow, William, 62
Downings, A.J., 77
Dr. Strong's Sanitarium, 198
Drouin, Martin, 408, 411n3
Drummond, Fairly, 298
Drummond, George Alexander: house of, 77, 79, 289, *290*, *380*, 382; Royal Montreal Golf Club and, 299; wealth of, 62, 66
Drummond, Guy, 368
Drummond, Julia Parker, 195, 368
Drummond, Maurice, 66
Drummond, Thomas J., 69, 73n28
Drummond Street, 225, 237, 255, 258, *259*
Duhamel, Alain, 408
Duluth, Minnesota, 325
Duluth Shipping, 332, 345n51
Du Musée Street, 273n31, *419*
Du Tremblay, Pamphile, 420
Dun, Wiman & Co., 85
Dyde, John, 97

Eaton's. *See* T. Eaton Company Ltd.
École des Beaux-Arts de Paris de Montréal, 291
École des Beaux-Arts de Paris, 79, *285–6*, 291–2
Edinburgh, Scotland: architecture, 299, *303*; as birthplace, 23, 37, 383–4, 287–9, 304, 305; professional networks, 297; training in, 292–3, 305, 308n23, 421. *See also* University of Edinburgh
education. *See individual named institutions*
Edward VII, King, 280
El Salvador, 270
Eley, Geoff, 422
Elliot, Florence, 289
Elliot, Mary, 289
Enderby, T.R., 337–8
English Canadians, 364–6, 374,
Erskine Presbyterian Church, 227, 313
Esquimaux Bay, 117
estates: 30–44, 53, 217, 222–5, 236–9, 318, 342n14; management and disbursal of, 126, 160, 198, 208, 269, 395. *See also* trusts; wills
ethnic networks, 8
ethnic power, 355
Europe, 45, 90
European settlement, 122–3, 129–31
evaluation roll, 10, 220, 241, 398, 423
Expo 67, 245n12, 406

factories: 64, 81, 83–5, 100, 424; individual factories, 87, 94, 130, 265; labour conditions of, 46; urban impact of, 55–7
Fair, John, 155, 158
Fairbanks Company, 260
Familles, droit et justice au Québec, 1840–1920 (FDJQ), 147–9, 162, 168–9n3
family: accumulation based on, 10, 164–5, 197–8, 236–40, 403; identity and, 119–20, 126–7, 363–6; intimacy and, 11, 111–12, 184–8, 356–62, 370; law and, 9, 136n32, 147–68, 170n12, 199, 422–5; loyalty v. corruption, 101, 125–6, 137n46; networks, 3–6, 113–33, 184, 193–5; obligations and, 9–10, 120, 195, 181–211
Faubourg à m'lasse, 245n12, 398
Fecteau, Jean-Marie, 92
Fenchurch Street, 127
Ferrier, James, 62, 70, 71n11, 423
Financial Panic of 1907, 260–2
Findlay, Robert, 79, 283, 299, 382. *See also* architects, Scottish
Findlayson, Roderick, 130
FIRE (finance, insurance, real estate) sector, 64–70
First National Property Co., 404–6
First World War: 66, 316, 362; impact on Square Mile, 19, 269–70, 351–6, 388, 417, 422; impact on views of Empire, 183, 360, 374; pre-war economic impact, 255, 262, 313
Firth, Willie: life, 353–60, *359*, 373; wartime letters, 11, 360–3, 366, 368–75
Fish, Cynthia, 424
Fish, Michael, 25
Fleet, Charles, 199
Fleming, Sandford, *115*, 266–7
Footner, William, 61, 72n22, 79

Forbes, John Collin, 280, 297
Ford, Charles Erskine, 97
Forest & Stream Club, 154
Forget, Louis Joseph, 239–40, 262–5
Forget, Rodolphe, 49, 258
Forres, Scotland, 114
Forrest, Thomas Morgan, 287. *See also* architects, Scottish
Forster, Ben, 88–9
Fort Garry, 120–1, 126, 128, 138n52
Fort William. *See* Thunder Bay, Ontario
Fox, Beatrice, 356, 369. *See also* Papineau, Talbot Mercer
France, 188, 315–16, 322, 353–4, 364–5
Fraser Institute, 44, 227–8
free traders, 88–9, 125, 129. *See also* Cayley-Galt (1858) tariffs; Galt (1859) tariffs
French Canadians, 37, 226, 295 362–6, 375–6n9
Frontenac Road, 242
Fullum Street, 242
Fur Trade Party, 130–1, 141n105
fur traders: 122–3, 133, 395; Deed Poll, impact of, 129; personal and family networks, 111–16, 132–3; Square Mile, links to, 5, 9, 32–5, 125, 131. *See also* Deed Poll; Fur Trade Party; Hudson's Bay Company (HBC); Smith, Donald (Lord Strathcona); Smith, Isabella Hardisty
Furness, Christopher, 323–4
Fyson, Donald, 147–8, 424

Galt, Alexander Tilloch, 88
Galt (1859) tariffs, 88–9. *See also* Cayley-Galt (1858) tariffs
gardeners, 44–6
Garden Island, Ontario, 320
gardens: 8, 57, 145, 366, 424; abroad, 203, 299; as status signifiers, 23, 27, 44–6, 49; transformation of, 388, 395
Gault, Andrew F., 154, 156–7, 165, *416*, *418*, 420
Gault, Andrew Hamilton, 356, 422
Gault family, 41, *42*
Gauvreau, Michael, 150
Gebhardt family, 195
Geddes, Patrick, 297
gender: 274, 424; class and, 354, 355, 360; empire and, 5, 24–5, 355, 368; family and, 5, 182–3, 191, 196–8; masculinity, 368, 371; property and, 10, 147–50, 165–8, 234–43; race and, 3, 5, 112, 421; spaces, 27, 43–5, 226, 231, 294
Georgetown, Quebec, 196
germ theory, 65
Gersovitz, Julia, 7, 25, 421
Gibraltar Cottage, 152
Gillies, Jessie, 220
Gladstone, William, 280
Glasgow, Scotland: as birthplace, 35, 287, *288*; training in, 289, 291–3, 421. *See also* University of Glasgow
Glasgow School of Arts, 291–2
Globe (Toronto), 154
Goose Village, 245n12, 398, 411n1. *See also* Victoriatown; working-class neighbourhoods
Gordon, George, 289
Gorman, Daniel, 359
Gorman, Joseph Browne Dick, 291 Gossage, Peter, 9, 112, 421, 424
Gould, Ira, 86
Gould Street, 151
Gould Street Presbyterian Church, 151, 154
Gournay, Isabelle, 282, 294
Government House, 102
Graham, Hugh, 66, 304
Graham, Jane, 85
Graham, Robert Walker, 304
Grahame, James, 131
Grain Growers' Guide, 68–70
grain trade: markets, 87, 317–19, 332, 337, 339; shipments, 321–2, 326–7, 332–5
Grand Séminaire, 222, 227, 424
Grand Trunk Railway, 63, 87, 94, 98, 242, 247n45
Grant, Cuthbert, 123–5, 138n58
Grant, Johnny, 124–5
Grant clan, 123–5
Great Britain: architecture, 155; government of, 89–90; personal linkages to, 86, 102, 268; war, 326, 364, 368
Great Depression, 7, 11, 256, 339, 387–9
Greater St. James Street, 221–2, 226
"Great Fire," 425

Great Lakes, 58, 317–18, 321–7, 330–5, 338–40
Great Lakes and St. Lawrence Transportation Co., 325
Great Unsolved Mysteries in Canadian History website, 183, 199
Great War: 4; economic opportunities, 11, 316, 319, 321, 324, 340; impact on people, 7, 339, 361, 369, 373
Great Western Insurance Company, 85
Greening, Frederick, 220, 226
Green Mountains, Vermont, 179
Greenshields, James, 44, 274n43, 316
Grey Nuns, 227–8, 229
Griffintown, 226
Gruber, Max, 404
Guelph, Ontario, 98
Gunnnel, Catherine, 208
Guysborough, Nova Scotia, 294
Guy Street: boundaries of, 3, 19, 29, 386; commercial use of, 226; institutional use of, 228–9, 231; property value of, 222, 233
Gwyn, Sandra, 356, 368, 370, 372

Haddington, Scotland, 283
Hagues family, 424
Haldane, William, 291. *See also* architects, Scottish
"Half-breed," 113, 119, 123, 126, 131, 134n6, 136n36. *See also* Metis; race
Halifax, Nova Scotia, 253–6, 258–61, 265, 269, 271–3, 357
Halifax Herald, 259
Halifax Shipyards, 338
Hall, Catherine, 362, 424–5
Hallward, Bernard M., 304
Hamilton, Ontario, 98, 260, 270, 323
Hamon, Max, 6, 9, 421
Hanna, David, 30–1, 40, 395, 409, 424
Hannan, John, 333
Hardisty, Joseph, 130
Hardisty, Margaret, 112, 119–20
Hardisty, Richard, 112, 114, 117, 120, 125, 128
hardware trade, 81–2, 85, 97, 99, 100–1. *See also* Montreal Rolling Mills; Moreland, Thomas
Hargrave, Joseph James, 131
Harrington, Anna, 201
Harris, Robert, 208
Harvey, Janice, 424
Harvey, Kathryn, 424
Haudenosaunee, 53–4
health care: ambulance services, 64; health spas, 195; live-in nurses, 228; Nurses Home, 228; private clinics, 228. *See also individual named hospitals*
Heaman, Elsbeth, 90, 133
Hele, John, 44
Henderson, Lawrence L., 322, 328, 337
Herbert Molson House, 382
heritage: activists, 25–6; conservation groups, 7, 384
Hervey Institute, 165, 227
Hill, Robert G., 283
Hillier, Bill, 58
Hinton, George, 85–6, 94, 99
Hochelaga (village), 53, 63
Hochelaga Ward, 221, 242
Holland, John Mansfield, 87, 89, 95
Holt family, 66, 69
Holt Renfrew, 291
Home Bank of Canada, 328, 330
Hopkins, Edward, 94, 96, 116
Hopkins, Edward Martin, 145
Hopkins, John W., 77, 79, 351
Hornyak, Joe, 208
Hornyak, Mary, 208
Hosmer, Charles R., 69, 274n43
hospitals. *See individual named hospitals*
Hôtel Dieu, 227
Howe, Joseph, 128, 137n42
Hoyle, Lydia, 40
Hudon, Victor, 154, 157
Hudson's Bay Company (HBC): community, 123–6, 139n72; HBC land claims, 127–31, 138n52; "HBC man," 9, 94, 112, 114–15, 121; linkages to Square Mile, 111–13, 115–17. *See also* Metis; Simpson, George; Smith, Donald (Lord Strathcona); Smith, Isabella Hardisty
Humphries, Mark, 371
Hutchison, A.C., 313
Hutchison, Wood and Miller, 313
Hutton, James, 85–6
Hyde, George, 290

Ibsen, Henrik, 195
Illinois, 87
Illsley, Hugh Percival, 289
immigrants, 55, 77, 79, 241
I.M. Pei & Associates of New York, 404
imperial: careers, 112, 126; identities and worldviews, 125, 360, 362–5, 368; landscapes, 8, 42–5, 304; networks, 87, 361, 369, 373, 422
imperial metropole, 5, 357, 362
Imperial Tobacco Company, 302. *See also* Davis, Mortimer B.
India, 220, 304
Indian tariff, 128–9
indigenous: kinship networks, 9, 111–14, 122–5, 133; land, 53, 135n22, 225; parentage, 5, 119, 132, 134n6. *See also* Metis; Smith, Isabella Hardisty
industrial age, 5, 117
Industrial Revolution, 39, 83, 318
industrial-settler capitalism, 133
infectious diseases, 64–5
Ingram, William John, 156
inheritance, 117, 119, 136n32, 147, 195, 236–8
Inland Lines Ltd., 323
Innis, Harold, 3–4
Insolvent Acts, 155
Intercontinental Development Corporation, 404
International Mercantile Marine, 316
International Milling Company, 270
International Power Company, 270
Interpretation Act (1849), 90–4
interwar period, 258, 269, 383, 387, 403
Inverness, Scotland, 283, 287, 289, 294
Investment Trust Company, 270
iron, 83, 98, 100–1, 265, 357. *See also* nail, industrial
Irving, Washington, 177
Isbister, A.K, 127
Ishiguro, Laura, 373
Izaak Walton Killam Hospital for Children, 269

Janes, W.D.B., 95
Jesuits' Collège Ste. Marie, 227
Jetté, Louis-Amable, 160
Jewish General Hospital, 302
Jews, 49, 227, 277, 287, 294, 302
John Bland Canadian Architecture Collection, 282–3, 298
joint-stock corporation, 82, 89–94, 97–8, 100, 102–3
Jones, Edward, 85–6, 94
Josephs family, 49, 62
Journal of the Royal Architectural Institute of Canada, 291, 298
J.P. Morgan, 287, 316
judicial separation of property: 9, 147–51, 160, 164–8, 421; marital collusion, 160–5; women's agency, 163. *See also* Anderson, Annie Stevenson; community of property; Lower Canada Civil Code of 1866; Morrice, David; séparation de biens; séparation de corps

Kauffman family, 403
Keelan, Geoff, 363–4
Kenneally, Rhona Richman, 424
Kennedy, Louisa Marion, 220, 240
Kenny, Nicolas, 6, 11, 183, 422
Keshen, Jeff, 371
Killam, Izaak Walton, 253, 269–70
Killam Trusts, 269
King, Edwin Henry, 94–5
King, Stuart, 304
King Edward VII, 280
King George, 114, 311n68
Kinghorn, George, 318–19
Kingman, Abner, 319
Kingston and Montreal Forwarding Company, 320
Kingston, Ontario, 318–19, 293, 337
Kinnear, Holly, 289, 293, 299, 304
Kirkland, Elizabeth, 9, 182, 422, 424
Kissell, Kinnicutt & Co., 326
Kohlberg, Jerome, 316
Kuznets cycles, 8, 55

Labelle, Abbé, 179
Laboratoire d'histoire et de patrimoine (SCHEMA), 399
Labrador, 114, 116–17
Lachine Canal, 39, 85, 99
Lafontaine Park, 242
Lagauchetière, 219

La Gauchetière Street, 29
Laird, Pamela Walker, 113
Lake and River Transportation Co., 327
Lake Commerce Ltd., 326
Lake Erie, 317, 333, 337
Lake of the Woods Milling Company, 316
Lake Ontario, 318, 333
Lake Superior, 128, 317
land: Indigenous land, 39, 63, 225; land sales, 115, 130, 408–9; landlords, 241–2; landscapes, 8, 12, 29, 42–6, 109, 179, 302; parks, 29–35, 42, 217–19, 354, 382, 420–23; speculation, 7, 30–41, 54, 226, 246, 395; urban land, 33, 45, 210, 390–1, 403–7, 422; value, 218, 221–9, 410
landowners, women, 40–1, 234–43, 423
Lanken, Peter, 25
La Presse, 406–7
La revue canadienne, 53
Latin America, 260
"Laurentian thesis" (Creighton), 3
Laurier, Wilfried, 69, 280, 263, 316–18, 323, 339
law. *See* Custom of Paris; Law of the Province of Quebec; Lower Canada Civil Code of 1866; Quebec Civil Code
Law of the Province of Quebec, 147–52, 162–8, 390, 421–5. *See also* Quebec Civil Code
Le Devoir (Montreal), 363, 408
Leacock, Stephen, 109, 386, 423
Leader (Newcastle, New Brunswick), 254
legal pluralism. *See* Anderson, Annie Stevenson; Custom of Paris; Lower Canada Civil Code of 1866; Morrice, David; Quebec Civil Code
Legislative Assembly, 88–94
Les petites soeurs des pauvres, 228
leveraged buyouts (LBOs), 316
Liberal Party, 129, 356, 363
limited liability corporations, 4–6, 60–4, 66–70, 89–94, 422
Lincoln Avenue, 222
Lincoln Memorial, 283
Linton Apartments, 417
List of Rights, 128
Liverpool, 98, 151, 357, 373
Lockhart, Elisabeth Fisher, 40
London: 10, 23, 29, 35, 27; business exchanges, 86, 120, 127–31, 262, 268–70, 321; education, 280; material exchanges, 112, 117, 357, 361–71; social and personal connections, 6, 58, 188, 203, 289, 256
London Assurance Company, 117
Longair, Sarah, 304
Lord, Kathleen, 424
Lord Acton, 70
Lord Beaverbrook. *See* Aitken, Max
Lord Mount Stephen. *See* Stephen, George
Lord Strathcona. *See* Smith, Donald (Lord Strathcona)
Lorimer, Robert, 281, 297
Lorne Avenue, 423
Lovell's Street Directory, 170n22, 223, 240
Lovett, Almon, 259, 261
Lower Canada, 38–9, 165. *See also* Upper Canada
Lower Canada Civil Code of 1866, 147–8, 150, 160
Lower Lachine Rapids, 87
Lyman House, *76*, 77
Lyman, Hannah, 40, 184

MacArthur, Duncan, 126
Macdonald, Alexander, 130
Macdonald, John A., 120, 125, 280
Macdonald, W.C., 63
Macdonald, William, 109, 298
Macdougall, Brenda, 125
Macdougall, William, 120
Mace Development Ltd., 404, 406–7
MacFarlane, Roderick, 132
MacGregor Street, 388
Mackay, A.B., 323
Mackay, Donald, 26, 387
MacKedie, John W., 158–60, 164
Mackenzie, J. Gordon, 94, *96*, 97
Mackenzie River, 123
Macleod, Roderick, 8, 116, 181, 354, 394, 423–4
MacTavish, Dugald, 116, 129
MacTavish, George, 129
MacTavish, John Henry, *115*, 126, 141
MacTavish, Simon, 33–5
MacTavish, William, 112

MacTavish Street, 116
Madeline Street, 290
Manchester, 151
Manitoba Act, 129
Manitoba Insurance Company, 114, 131
Manitoulin Island, 333
Mann, Eric, 299
Mansfield Street, 112, 290, 404
manuscript census, 10
Marchildon, Gregory P., 7, 10–11, 102, 131
Margaret, Miles, 141
maritime network, 323–6,
Maritime provinces, 333
Marks family, 327
Marler, Willam de Montmollin, 160–6
marriage: contract, 149, 203, 237; impact on familial and professional networks, 114, 120–3; law and, 40, 149, 235–42. *See also* Married Women's Property Acts; judicial separation of property
Married Women's Property Acts, 169
masculinity, 316, 355, 368–70, 374
masonic lodges, 58
Masonic Memorial Temple, 283
Masonic Temple, 287
Masson, Joseph, 236
Mathers, Isabella, 151
Mathews, T.H., 281
Mathieu, Jean-Philip, 8, 11, 422
Mathieu, Michel, 161
Maxwell, Edward, 79, 382
Mayerovitch, Harry, 282
Mayfair, London, 23
McConnell family, 424
McCord, Anne Ross, 425
McCord family, 167
McCord Museum, 424
McDonald, Donna, 116, 131
McDougall, John, 95, 157
McGill, James, 35, 109, 425. *See also* McGill University
McGill-Burnside Holdings Ltd., 404
McGill College Avenue, 21, 41, 228, 277, 399, 406–7
McGill Ghetto, 109, 423
McGill Station, 406
McGill University: 10, 12, 109, 114, 226–9; Chancellor Day Hall, 423; Ferrior Building, 423; financial gifts, 155, 208–10; McGill College, 35, 41–2, 407; McGill Faculty of Medicine and Health Sciences, 302; McGill Gymnasium, 228; McGill School of Architecture, 279, 295, 297, 299; McGill University Health Centre, 269; properties, 25–6, 145, 289, 304, 391, 407–8; Stephen Leacock Social Sciences Building, 423; students, 291, 296, 433
McGregor, James, 53–4
McGregor, Jessie, 228
McGregor Street (now Avenue du Docteur-Penfield), 422
McIntyre, Duncan, 4
McKay, Angus, 134
McKay, Elizabeth, 124
McKay, Joseph, 153, 171n25
McKay, Mrs. James, 126
McKay Institute for Protestant Deaf Mutes and the Blind, 166
McKenna, Stephen, 373
McKim, Mead & White, 79
McLaren, Thomas, 289–90
McLean, Malcolm, 316
McLennan, Bartlett, 315–22, 325, 339. *See also* Montreal Transportation Company (MTC)
McLennan, Hugh, 318
McLellan, James, 401
McLennan, John, 318
McLennan family, 11
McMaster William, 99, 276
McPhee, Janet, 183
McTavish, John Henry, 115
McTavish, Simon, 33–5. *See also* McGill, James
McTavish reservoir, 145
McTavish Street, *42*, *76*, *96*, *134*, 145, 423
Mechanics' Institute, 60, 77
Meighen, Robert, 225
Melbourne, 304
Members of Parliament, 81, 97, 114, 363, 372
Memphremagog, Quebec, 63
"Merchant Princes," 27
Merchants Bank of Canada, 156
Merchant's Exchange Building, 153

Merrett, Brian, 25
Metcalfe Street, 152, 289, *290*
Methodist Church, 62
Metis, 9, 112, 117, 119–29. *See also* "Half-breed"; Red River Resistance; Riel, Louis
Mettarlin, A. Hyman, 404, 408
Mexico Tramways, 270
Michigan, 87
Miller, Thomas F., 87
Miller Cartage Co., 330
Mills, Ada Maria, 172n44, 193
Mills, John Easton, 40
Minnett, Valerie, 200
Molly, Maureen, 123
Molson, Charles, 370
Molson, John, 97
Molson, Percival, 370
Molson, William Monkland, 97
Molson Bank Building, 153
Montreal: colonial hub, 5, 112, 362; culture and religion, 25, 277, 354; economic dominance of, 49, 152, 256, 392; geography, 21, 31–2, 217, 219; Indigenous land, 39, 63
Montreal Art Association, 195
Montreal City Passenger Railway Company, 87, 117
Montreal Cotton Company, 157
Montreal Daily Star, 63
Montreal Daily Witness, 74
Montreal Engineering Company, 258, 260–1
Montreal Fire Insurance Company, 62
Montreal Forum, 293
Montreal Foundling and Baby Hospital, 165
Montreal Freehold Investment Company, 165
Montreal Gazette, 23, 100–1
Montreal General Hospital, 64, 85, 102, 165, 208, 228
Montreal Herald, 153
Montreal History Group, x, 424
Montreal Homeopathic Association, 228
Montreal Horticultural Society, 44
Montreal Hunt Club, 154
Montreal Lacrosse Grounds, 417
"Montréal, l'avenir du passé," 220, 423
Montreal Maternity Hospital, 228
Montreal Museum of Fine Arts, 154, 423
Montreal Neurological Institute, 269
Montreal Provident and Savings' Bank, 60–2, 70, 71n11
Montreal Rolling Mills, 9, 81–2, 89, 98–103. *See also* Moreland, Thomas; nail, industrial
Montreal Saw Works, 99
Montreal Star, 67
Montreal Stock Exchange, 256, 258, 263
Montreal Technical School, 287
Montreal Transportation Company (MTC), 315–23. *See also* McLennan, Bartlett
Montreal Transportation Company (MTC17), 315–18, 330–9. *See also* CSL Network; Wolvin, Roy M.
Montreal Trust and Deposit Company, 258–61
Montreal Warehousing, 64
Montreal Women's Club, 295
Moore, Lisa, 9, 112, 421
Moose Factory, 130
Moose River, 131
Morden, W. Grant, 325, 327, 338
Moreland & Darling, 85
Moreland, Watson & Co., 87, 94, 98–9
Moreland, Thomas, 81–2, 85–7, 94–8, 100–3. *See also* Montreal Rolling Mills
Morgan, Henry, 225
Morgan, J.P., 287
Morrice, James Wilson, 154
Morrice, David, 9, 147–8, 151–62, 165–8. *See also* Anderson, Annie Stevenson
Morris, Robert, 424
Mortimer, Edward, 123, 148n54
Mortimer B. Davis House, 299, *303*
Mount Royal, 3, 19, 21–3, 354, 381. *See* also Mount Royal Park
Mount Royal Club, 66, 154, 268
Mount Royal Cemetery, 49, 191, 200, 424
Mount Royal Park, 29, 32–4, 217–18, 222
Mount Royal Terrace, 41
Mount View House, 417
Mrs. Simpson's Ladies School, 112
Mumbai, 304
Municipal Government of Montreal, 35–8, 403
Murray, Irena, 282
Muskoka, Ontario, 201
Mutual Steamship Co., 326

nail, industrial, 8, 64, 81–5, 87, 98–101, 422
National Policy, 154–5, 225, 232
National Trust Company, 258
Natural History Society, 44, 58, 227, 425
Naylor, R.T., 155
Neilson, Antoine Gordon, 294
Nelson, Scott Reynolds, 89
Nerbras, Don, 394
Nesbitt, A. Deane, 270
Nesbitt, Arthur J., 253, 256, 258, 260, 270–1
Nesbitt, James Aird, 270–1
Nesbitt, Thomson and Company, 270–1
New Brunswick, 261, 268
New City Gas Company, 62
New England, 83, 87
New France, 279, 295, 305
New Sherbrooke Apartments, 417
New South Wales, 58
"the New Town," 30–1. *See also* Hanna, David
New Town, Edinburgh, 23, 37
New York, 58, 208–13, 251
New York City, 260, 268, 287, 326, 366, 404
Newcastle (now Miramichi), New Brunswick, 254
Newfoundland, 205, 207
Newman, Peter C., 131
Nobbs, Francis John: 10–11, 79, 279–83, 290–1; buildings, 279, 297–8, 304–5; friendship with Ramsay Traquair, 281–2, 298–9; relationship with Scottish architects, 299–307. *See also* architects, Scottish; Traquair, Ramsay
Nobbs, Percy, 10–11, 79, 279–94, 297–99, *300–1*, 304–5, 309n36, 423
Nootens, Thierry, 147, 149–50, 163, 165
Norcoss, J.W., 325–8, 337
Norris, J.S., 323
North America, 323
North Atlantic, 226, 230, 333
North Shore Railway Company, 157
North West Company (NWC), 123–4
Northern Ontario, 130
Northwest, 112–7, 119–29, 131–32. *See also* Red River
Norway House, 123
Notman, William, 27, 181–2, 188, 191. *See also* Wm. Notman & Son
Notman, William McFarland, 181–2. *See also* Wm. Notman & Son
Notre-Dame-de-Grâce, 388
Notre-Dame-des-Neiges, 208
Notre Dame Hospital, 228
Nova Scotia, 6
Nova Scotia Steel & Co., 323
Nurses Home, 228

Ogdensburg Coal & Towing Co., 333
Ogilvie, A.W., 88
Ohio, 87, 382
Ohio Life Insurance and Trust Company, 87
Ohrstrom, George, 316
Old Architecture of Quebec, 297. *See also* Traquair, Ramsay
old city, 220–2, 227–8, 244n7. *See also* Square Mile
Old McGill (yearbook), 294
Olivier Street, 195
Olmsted, Frederick Law, 32–4, 217–18. *See also* Mount Royal Park
Olsen, Sherry, 8, 422, 425
Omner, Rosemary, 123, 141n108
Ontario, 58, 150, 165, 266, 333
Ontario Avenue (now rue du Musée), 72n20, 220
orchards, 8, 32, 35, 39, *52*, 53–4, 57
Ostell, John, 36–8, 60, 77, 79, 389
Oswego Navigation Co., 333, 335–7
Ottawa, 49, 94, 102, 128–30, 269, 291
Ottawa and Prescott Railway, 94
Outremont (suburb), 387–8, 417. *See also* Westmount (suburb)
Oxford University, 356, 365

Pacific, 6, 122, 361, 373
Panic of 1857, 85, 88–9
Papineau, Louis-Joseph, 358, 363
Papineau, Talbot Mercer: 6, 11, 354, *358*, *367*; open letter of, 363–6; political ambitions of, 355, 357, 259–60, 363; upbringing of, 356, *367*; wartime correspondence of, 11, 356–7, 361–2, 366–74. *See also* Bourassa, Henri; Fox, Beatrice
Papineau, Wescott, 362, *367*
Papineau Square, 63
Park Avenue, 3
Parliament Hill, 420

Parliament of Montreal Centre, 81, 97, 100
Passchendaele, 373, 422
Patten, Thomas, 21, *22*
Peck, Thomas, 100
Peel Street, 40, *96*, 97, 264f, 302–4, 423. *See also* Upper Peel Street
Penmans, 165
Pennsylvania, 333
Perry, Adele, 132, 134n8
Peterson, William, 299, 305
Peter W. Redpath and Jocelyn Clifford Redpath Memorial Fund, 208
Petit, Kim, 399
Philadelphia, 366
Phillips, Thomas, 35–9, 239, 395
Phillips Square, 222, *350*
Pickett, Steward T.A., 56–7
Piédalue, Gilles, 6, 68
Pillow, John, 81, 100
Pincher's Creek, Alberta, 195
Pine Avenue, 19, 223, 302, 386
Pitfield, Ward C., 269, 274n51
Piva, Michael, 88
Place d'Armes, 117, 222, 260, 290
Place Mercantile, 399, 407–8
Place Ville Marie, 40, 393f, 394–5, 404
Playfair, James, 323
Plimsoll, Ellen, 201
Plimsoll, George, 201
Plummer, James H., 156, 321
Pointe St. Anne, 242
Point St. Charles, 242, 290
Pointe à Callière, 229
Ponte, Vincient, 404
Port Arthur. *See* Thunder Bay, Ontario
Port Colborne, 333
Port Huron, 332
Portsmouth, Ontario, 320
Poutanen, Mary Anne, 9, 422, 424
Power Corporation of Canada, 270–1
Prairies, 6, 316
Prendeville, Marie-Adèle, 197
Presbyterian: colleges, 154; churches, 58, 151, 154–5, 245–5n54, *312*, 313; individuals, 138, 220, 254,
Presbyterian College of Montreal, 154, *156*, 227
Prescott Elevator Company, 94, 320, 337
President Kennedy Avenue, 403, 407
Price, Bruce, 251
Price, Katherine, 220
Prince of Wales, 85
Prince of Wales Terrace, *96*, 109, 116, *144*, 145–6
Prince Patricia's Canadian Light Infantry, 356, 422
Prince Rupert Place (originally Annonay Place), 145
property. *See* land
Protestant: churches, *48*, 61, 72n23, 138n60, 151, 154–5, 203, 227, 313, 423; colleges, 42; culture, 42, 48–9, 226; individuals, 148n60, 220, 313; institutions, 60, 165, 228–9. *See also* Anglo-Protestant
(Protestant) Church Home, 229
(Protestant) High School of Montreal, 61–2, 227, 356
Protestant House of Industry and Refuge, 165
Protestant Industrial Rooms, 229
Protestant Infant's Home, 229
Protestant Orphan Asylum, 165, 229
Province of Canada, 38, 82, 85, 89
Province of Quebec Association of Architects, *250*, 251, 390
public infrastructure, 58, 92, 177
public markets, 58
Puerto Rico, 270
Putney, England, 184, 212n9

Quebec: as a distinct society, 24; as a port, 27, 63, 325; law, 147–50; manufacturing centre, 154; marriage customs, 236, 240; religion, 226. *See also* Montreal; Quebec City; Quebec Civil Code; Square Mile
Quebec City, 27, 98, 168–9n3, 269, 295
Quebec Civil Code, 162–5 167–8, 240
Quebec Daily Mercury, 199
Queen Mary, 114
Queen's College, 227
Queen's University, 293
Queen Victoria, 422
Quiet Revolution, 49

race, 3–5, 251, 431. *See also* "Half-breed"; Metis
railroads: construction, 4, 92, 225, 251–3, 265, 316; financial troubles, 87–8, 316;

investments, 62–4, 69–70, 114, 255, 369, 391; linkages, 3, 98, 128, 305, 324, 381–2; management, 87, 94; nation-building, 4, 128, 133; relationship to Square Mile, 6, 32, 117, 131, 154–7, 268, 387, 425; street railway, 258–60, 270. *See also* Canadian Northern Railway; Canadian Pacific Railway (CPR); City Passenger Railway Company; Grand Trunk Railway; North Shore Railway Company; Ottawa and Prescott Railway
Ramsay Gardens, 299
Rankin, Colin, 129
Ravenscrag, *144*, 177–9, 217, 222–3
Raymond, Marie, 240
Raymond, Sophie, 236
Red Cross Information Bureau, 353, 368
Red River: 115–17, 119, 122–9, 138n52
Red River Resistance: 6, 120–8, 133, 261. *See also* Metis; Riel, Louis; Smith, Donald (Lord Strathcona)
Redlands, California, 202
Redpath, Alice Watson, 184, 195–7, 199, 202–3
Redpath, Elizabeth Grace (Betty), *184*, 195
Redpath, Emily, 195
Redpath, Grace, *184*, 200
Redpath, Harold, *184*, 195–7, 203, 212n14
Redpath, Helen, *184*, 201, 308n23
Redpath, Jane, *184*, 234
Redpath, Jocelyn Clifford "Cliff," 183, *184*, 188, 195–202, 205, 208–10, 212n15
Redpath, John: early years, 27–9; family, 66, 72n20, 183, *184*, 234, 308n23, 422; as landowner and developer, 35–40, 50, 239, 395, 423–5; status, 54, 62, 88
Redpath, John James "Jack," 171n24, 183–8, *184*, 191, 210, 222n9
Redpath, John Reginald "Reg," *184*, 189, 195, 202–3
Redpath, Maud, 193, 212n21
Redpath, Peter, 66, 94, 98, *184*
Redpath, Peter Whiteford, *184*, 187, 212n15, 195, 198–205, 208–210
Redpath Manor House, 200
Redpath Mansion Mystery, 183
Redpath Street, 151, 153f, 158, 423
Regina, Saskatchewan, 162, 362
Reiter, Eric H., 147
Rémillard, François, 25
Renaud, Anna, 162
rentier, 336, 239, 243
restoration projects, 17, 26
Reynolds, Scott, 89
Reynolds, Thomas, 94, 102
Rhind, James, 283. *See also* architects, Scottish
Rhind, John, 283. *See also* architects, Scottish
Richard, Jean Georges, 404
Richardson, H.H., 289
Riel, Louis, 120–1, 124, 126–8, 137n44, 137n46
Risher, Roswell Corse, 226
Ritz Carleton, 423
River and Lake Transportation, 330
Roads and Improvements Committee, 37
Roaring Twenties, 11, 392
Robertson, Farquhar, 319, 322
Robertson, John, 95, 99
Robertson & Masson, 236
Roddick, Amy Redpath: 9, 181, 183; early years, 183–91; family's health, 191, 195, 198–9, 202; later years, 203–8, 210; murder-suicide and aftermath, 199–202, 209–10; "outside world" image, 199–202, 205, 208–9, 422; surrogate head of household, 191–5, 197–9, 200–2, 240
Roddick, Emma, 193
Roddick, Thomas George, 193
Roddick Memorial Gates and Clock Tower, 432
Rogers, Caroline, 353, 368–70, 372–3. *See also* Papineau, Talbot Mercer
Rolland, J.B., 88
Rolls Royce, 278
Roper, Michael, 366
Rose, James, 86, 95, 98–9, 101
Rose, John, 86–7, 100–1, 187
Rose, Sonya, 372
Rosemount, 177, 345n46
Rosen, Anna, 403
Ross, Alexander, 123, 138n49
Ross, Bernard, 130
Ross, James, 137n46, 138n49, 225, 251, 423. *See also* Metis
Ross, William B., 254, 259
Ross & MacDonald, 301
Ross & MacFarlane, 301
Ross Line, 63

Rowand House, 126
Roxburgh, John, 291. *See also* architects, Scottish
Roxburghshire, Scotland, 151
Roy, Victor, 77, 79, 177–9
Royal Commision on Labour and Capital, 63–4, 70
Royal Engineers in Canada, 87, 97
Royal Infirmary, 299
Royal Institution for the Advancement of Learning (McGill College), 62
Royal Military College, 318
Royal Montreal Golf Club, 299
Royal Navy Reserves, 11, 357
Royal Securities Corporation, 10, 255–8, 260–1, 268–70
Royal Trust Company, 258, 261, 267, 342n14. *See also* Aitken, Max (Lord Beaverbrook)
Royal Victoria College, 193
Royal Victoria Hospital, 64, 114, 179, 199, 227, 299, *302*, 305, 391
Royal York Hotel, 291
Rudy, Jarrett, x, 424
Rupert's Land, 121, 129
Russia, 87

Saanich, British Columbia, 197
Sabbath Observatory, 62
Sacred Heart Convent, 227
Said, Edward, 114
Sainte-Agathe-des-Monts, 199
Saint-Gabriel, 63
Saint-Henri, 63
Saint John, New Brunswick, 254, 258, 279
Salmon, Stephen, 7, 21, 422
Saratoga, New York, 208
Sarnia, Ontario, 332
Saskatchewan, 112, 317
"Save Montreal / Savons Montréal," 387, 391, 407
Saxe, Charles Jewett, 283, 287
Schumpeter, Joseph, 253
"Scotch cousins," 121–3, 138n55
Scotland. *See* architects, Scottish.
Scottish Provincial Assurance Company, 117
Second World War, 289, 387, 391
Seminary of Montreal, 424
séparation de biens, 148–50, 164. *See also* judicial separation of property
séparation de corps, 149
Servante, Helen Elizabeth, 87
Servante, Henry, 87, 102
settler colonialism, 5–6, 114. *See also* land
Seventh Day Adventist Church, 313
sewer gas, 64
sexual assault, 48
Simpson, George, 114, 116, 125, 145
Shaar Hashomayim synagogue, *276*, 277
Shallow, Maggie, 208, 210
Shallow, Mary Rose, 199, 205, *206–7*
Shaughhnessy family, 66, 225, 369
Shaughnessy, Sarah, 369
Shaughnessy, Thomas, 225, 369
Shaughnessy Village, 222
Shennan, David, 287. *See also* architects, Scottish
Sherbrooke Residential Chambers, 417
Sherbrooke Street: 9, 191, 220, 422–4; affluence of, 229–37, 395; Amy Redpath's house, 181–2, *185–8*, 199, 202, 207–8; development of, 165, 226, 389–90, 404–8, 417; George Drummond's house, *380*, 382; institutional use of, 283, 351; mansions, 19, 44, 79, 153, 181n25, *188*, 199, 239, 410; prices, 222–3; terraces, 96–7, 116, *144*, 145–6. *See also* Sherbrooke Street West; Van Horne Mansion
Sherbrooke Street West, 256, 289, 356. *See also* Sherbrooke Street
shipping industry: 11, 316–18, 321–3, 326–8, 330–40; linkages to other industries, 85, 317, 333, 339; shipping magnates, 85, 94, 177; ships as commodities, 316, 318, 322–3. *See also* Allan Shipping Line; Canada Steamship Lines (CSL); CSL Network; McLennan, Bartlett; Montreal Transportation Company (MTC); Montreal Transportation Company (MTC17); Wolvin, Roy M.
Sholdice, Mark, 165
Sies, Mary Corbin, 389–90
Silver Heights, 126
Simpson, George, 114–16, 125, 129, 146
Simpson, Maria Louisa, 129
Sincennes-McNaughton Line Ltd., 336–7
Sir Thomas and Lady Roddick Library Fund, 208

skyscrapers, 392, 409
Smith, Donald Alexander (Baron Strathcona), 407
Smith, Donald (Lord Strathcona): 4–6, 9; Confederation of Manitoba negotiations, 120–7; early years, 114–16; HBC wintering parties' negotiations, 127–32; Square Mile, life in, 112–14, 117, 132. *See also* Red River Resistance; Smith, Isabella Hardisty
Smith, Edward, 123
Smith, Isabella Hardisty: *118*; correspondence of, 111, 119–20; early years, 117, 119; family and personal networks, 9, 111–12, 117; Indigenous heritage, 119, 122. *See also* Smith, Donald (Lord Strathcona)
Smith, James, 40
Smith, John Roxburgh, 291
Smith, Judith E., 398
Snell, Henry Saxon, 299, *302–3*
social networks, 6–9, 58, 132
Society Hill, Philadelphia, 23
South Africa, 66, 195
South African War, 114, 195, 356, 362–3
South Sea Company, 90, 103n4
Spasoff, Nichola, 297
Speir, William, 77, 79, 179
Square Mile, alternative names: "Golden Square Mile," 23–9; "High Ground," 32–3, 40, 45; "New Town," 30–2; "the city above the hill," 4, 14n6, 233
Square Mile: boundaries of, 4, 7, 19–20, 29–30, 37–8, 42, 59, 95–7, 109–10, 217–18, 220–3, 246n27, 384–8; myths about, 22–7, 29, 32–50; transformation and decline; 7, 19, 383–5, 387–8, 391–4, 409–10
St. Alexandre Street, 222, 226
St. Andrews, New Brunswick, 63
St. Andrew's Parish (Red River), 123
St. Andrew's Society, x, 58, 293
St. Ann Ward, 157–8
St. Anne's Parish, 226
St. Antoine Cemetery, 42, 49
St. Antoine Faubourg (later St. Antoine Ward), 29–30, 152, 157–8
St. Antoine Street, 32, 130St. Catherine Street: commercial use of, 19, 32, 225–6, 243, 290, 389, 404; institutional use of, *48*, 277; residential use of, 112, 177, 222, 229, 231, 239, 351
St. Denis Street, 226, 244n7
St. François-Xavier Street, 239–40, *257*
St. James Club, *43*, 154, 228, 394
St. James Street: commercial use of, 7, 226, 256–60, 265–270, 315, 365; decline of, 392; property value of, 221–2, 227
St. James Ward, Toronto, 151
St. Jean Baptiste Ward, 242
St. John the Evangelist Church, 200
St. Joseph Street, 158
St. Laurent Ward, 242
St. Lawrence and Chicago Steam Navigation Co. (SLCN), 327–8
St. Lawrence River, 152, 317, 320–1, 333, 338
St. Lawrence Ward, 29, 62
St. Louis Ward, 227
St. Marc Street, 283
St. Marie Ward, 242
St. Martins, Perthshire, Scotland, 151 St. Patrick's Literary Association, 117
St. Patrick's Orphan Asylum, 228–9
St. Patrick's Parish, 226
St. Paul's, Minnesota, 112, 125
St. Urbain Street, 287
Stairs, John F., 254–5
Standard Shipping, 325, 332
Stanely Street, 226–7, 277
Stanely Street Presbyterian, *312*, 313
"staples thesis" (Innis), 3–4
Starns, Henry, 88
Stavert, William E., 363, 267
Stead, Mabel, 353, 366–7, 370–3
Steel Company of Canada (Stelco), 70, 82, 102–3, 265–7. *See also* Aitken, Max (Lord Beaverbrook); Montreal Rolling Mills; Moreland, Thomas
Stephen, George (Lord Mount Stephen), 4, 64, 94, 114, 117, 225
Stephens, George Washington, 420
Stephens, Harrison, 43, 52f, 54, 62
Stern Metals, 316
Stillwater Coal Company, 157
stock market crash (1929), 270
Stoker, Bram, 258
Stoler, Ann Laura, 360–1

St-Onge, Nicole, 125
Strathcona Hall, 399, 403, 407–8
Strathcona House, 114
Strathspey Valley, Scotland, 123
strikes, 63–4, 66,
Stuart, John, 122–4
suburbs. *See* Notre-Dame-de-Grâce; Outremont (suburb); Square Mile; Town of Mount Royal; Westmount (suburb)
Sullivan, Alice M., 228, 232
Sulpician Seminary, 60
Summerhill Street, 229
summer resorts, 63, 196
Sun Life Building, 389, *392–3*, 424
Superior Court of the District of Montreal, 148, 151, 160–3, 167
Supreme Court of Alberta, 267
Supreme Court of Canada, 217
Sutherland, J., 102
Sweeny, Robert, 6, 10, 422–3
Sydney, Nova Scotia, 321
synagogues, 227, *276*, 277, 299, 403

T. Eaton Company Ltd., 291, 404, 406–7
Taché, Bishop Antonin-Alexandre, 126
Tadoussac, 114
Tait, Robert, 126
Tariff Reform and Industrial Association, 88
Tariff Reform Association, 88
tariffs. *See* Cayley-Galt (1858) tariffs; Galt (1859) tariffs
Taschereaus family, the, 167
Tasmania, Australia, 304
Taylor, Andrew T., 77–9, 289–90, 308n19, 351, 382
Taylor, Dunbar, 198
Taylor, James, 98
Taylor, Mary, 123
Temiskaming, 130
Temple Emmanuel, 227
Templeton, Francis Orr, 293
Texas, 58
textile industry: key figures, 9, 64, 147, 151–4, 158–68, 421; mills, 63–4, 154; textile crisis of 1883, 4, 155. *See also* Morrice, David
Theodore, David, 200
Thomas, Cyrus Pole, 77
Thomas, Peter, 270
Thomas, William Tutin, 77, 79, 313
Thompson, Edward, 424
Thomson, A.G., 319
Thoreau, Henry David, 31–2
Thunder Bay, Ontario, 319, 321, 327, 332, 337, 341n8
Toronto, 88, 254–8, 318, 388. *See also* Ontario
Toronto Dominion Bank, 222
Toronto Stock Exchange, 256, 258, 262, 318
Town of Mount Royal, 388, 398
Tramways Commission, 287
TransCanada pipeline, 271
transnational networks, 4–5, 113, 355, 360, 368
Traquair, Phoebe Anna (Moss), 297–8
Traquair, Ramsay: *280*, 281–3, 294, *295*; friendship with Percy Nobbs, 281–2, 298–9, *300–1*; influence on Montreal's architecture, 10–11, 279–93, 297; relationship with Scottish architects, 11, 279; views on women, Blacks, Jews, and Asians, 294–7. *See also* architects, Scottish; Nobbs, Percy
Traquair Sr., Ramsay Heatley, 297–8
trench warfare, 357, 360, 371
Trinidad Electric Company, 255
"triple alliance," 69. *See also* factories; railroads
Trois-Rivières, 147, 168n3
trust companies, 258–61, 270, 318–19
trusts, 4, 158, 236, 239, 269. *See also* estates; wills
Tulchinsky, Gerald, 423
Tupper Street, 222
Turnbull, John, 291, 293. *See also* architects, Scottish

underwriters, 265–6
Union Station, Toronto, 291
Union Street, 232
United Province of Canada, 38
United States: business, 90, 127, 258, 260, 316, 333; people, flow of, 195, 381
Université de Montréal, 295
University of Aberdeen, 114
University of Alberta, 297
University of Edinburgh, 291, 299
University of Glasgow, 304
University of Manitoba, 295

University of Toronto, 295
University Street (now Robert-Bourassa Boulevard), 19, 222, 227–8, 287, 386
Upper Canada, 165, 167
Upper Canada's Married Women's Property Act of 1859, 164–5
Upper East Side, New York, 23
Upper Lakes, 318–19, 333
Upper Peel Street, 251, 264. *See also* Peel Street
US Steel, 316
Utilities Securities Company, 261. *See also* Aitken, Max (Lord Beaverbrook)

Valentine, Hugh Allen Inglis, 290–1, 293. *See also* architects, Scottish
Vancouver, British Columbia, 293, 353, 356
Van Horne, William Cornelius: 69, 391; Canadian Pacific Railway and, 4, *115*, 225, 255; interest in art, 154, 171n29. *See also* Canadian Pacific Railway (CPR); Van Horne Mansion
Van Horne Mansion: 12, *384–5*, 410; community activism and, 25, 387, 391, 407–8; demolition of, 12, *26*, 223, 383, 387, 398
Van Kirk, Sylvia, 112,
Venezuela, 270
Vermont, 179, 382
Vickers Ltd., 323
Victor Hudson Cotton Mills Company, 154–5, 157
Victoria, British Columbia, 357, 362
Victoria Bridge, 152
Victoria College for Women, 227
Victorian civilization, 12, 421
Victorian hegemony, 425
Victoria Rifles, 183, 191
Victoria Skating Club, 87
Victoria Street, 238
Victoriatown, 245n12, 398, 410. *See also* Goose Village; working-class neighbourhoods
Victory of Frog Plain, 123
Vieux Montreal, 226
Ville-Marie Expressway, 32
Vimy, 372
Virginia, 322, 332
Wagg, Susan, 289
warehouses, 63, 158
Washington, DC, 129, 287
Waterman Steamship Co., 316
Watson, Charles, 81, 86–7, 95–102. *See also* Moreland, Watson & Co.
Welland Canal, 317–18
Wellington Street, 290
Welsh, James, 160
Welsh Mountains, 362
Wesleyan Methodist Theological College, 227
West Coast, 357
Western Canada, 154, 195, 225, 254
Western Canada Cement, 266–7
Western Front, 335, 353, 361
Western Hospital, 227–8
Westly, Margaret, 27, 374, 387–8, 394, 409
Westmount City Hall, 283, 304
Westmount (ship), 322, 330, 339, 345n46
Westmount (suburb): institutions, 283, 304, 313; residential, 270, 279, 387–90, 417; residents, 69, 370, 398. *See also* Côte-Saint-Antoine
West Virginia, 332
West Yorkshire, England, 353
Whalen, James, 327, 332, 343n33, 344n38. *See also* Canadian Towing and Wrecking Co.
wheat, 3, 6, 69–70, 87, 317–22
White, Richard, 113, 125
White Company, 260
Whitehead, William J., 156
White Star, 357
Wigtownshire, Scotland, 85, 104n10
Wiley family, 327
Williams, Raymond, 225, 424
Williams Manufacturing Company, 64
wills, 4, 165–6, 425. *See also* estates; trusts
Wilmington, Delaware, 294
Wilson-Smith, Richard, 259
Windsor Station, 251, 389, 424
Winnipeg, Manitoba, 125–7, 325, 332, 362
Winnipeg Board of Trade, 126
Winnipeg Opera House, 127
Wittet, George, 304
Wm. Notman & Son, 9, 27–31, 45, 181–2, 251, 387, 410, 423–4. *See also* Notman, William; Notman, William McFarland
Wolvin, Roy M., 6, 11, 315, 325, 338. *See* Canada Steamship Lines (CSL)
Wood, Grace, 184

Wood, John Wilson, 291, 313
working-class neighbourhoods: 20, 43, 287; destruction of, 384, 391, 394, 410; studies of, 13n6, 20, 233, 242–6. *See also* Goose Village; Victoriatown
Workman, Thomas, 81, 96 –7
Workman, William, 88, 97
Wright, James, 289–91

Yarmouth, Nova Scotia, 269
YMCA, 227, 403, 407
Young, Brian, 12, 167, 355
Young, John, 72n22, 424
Ypres, 368

Zeckendorf, William, 394
zoning, 65–7, 390, 412n21